HARVARD STUDIES IN BUSINESS HISTORY
II

EDITED BY N. S. B. GRAS

STRAUS PROFESSOR OF BUSINESS HISTORY
GRADUATE SCHOOL OF BUSINESS ADMINISTRATION
GEORGE F. BAKER FOUNDATION
HARVARD UNIVERSITY

LONDON : HUMPHREY MILFORD

OXFORD UNIVERSITY PRESS

JAY COOKE

PRIVATE BANKER

BY

HENRIETTA M. LARSON

ASSOCIATE IN RESEARCH IN BUSINESS HISTORY
GRADUATE SCHOOL OF BUSINESS ADMINISTRATION
HARVARD UNIVERSITY

Cambridge, Massachusetts

HARVARD UNIVERSITY PRESS

1936

PRINTED AT THE HARVARD UNIVERSITY PRESS
CAMBRIDGE, MASS., U. S. A.

CONTENTS

ILLUSTRATIONS

EDITOR'S INTRODUCTION

THIS book is the study of the rise, growth, and failure of a private banker. The author has insisted throughout in keeping in mind both the man and his work. She has found much to praise and not a little to blame. Commonly both the praise and blame are more implied than stated.

Probably most of us think of Jay Cooke as the financier of the Northern cause in the Civil War and as the sponsor of the issue of Northern Pacific securities that ended in disaster. These are both dramatic and important. There is a further significance, however, to the story of the life of Cooke: in its broad outline it is typical of the career of the investment banker of the time. Such a private banker, doing an investment business, bought securities for others, kept deposits to facilitate this work, bought and sold securities for the account of the firm, transferred credits, floated securities either singly or as a member of a syndicate, and acted as financial agent for corporations. He operated as a member of a group of co-partners rather than as a director or officer of a joint-stock corporation. He tried the experiment of having several houses, each a partnership, but with interlocking partners. He experienced difficulties in the control of partners, both the weak and the strong ones.

Jay Cooke was trained as an employee of the firm of Enoch W. Clark, of Philadelphia. After the failure of this firm he established his own business. Then, after a period of national operation and brilliant success (1861–73), Jay Cooke failed. But he did not fail in vain, for his experience went on through his descendants and continues there today in the firm of Chas. D. Barney & Co. Thus do we find a close parallel to the biological world: the individual dies but the group continues. This is the way of life and, we may add, of business. Like life, business is a procession of effort, often losing, often gaining, but always struggling and continuing.

There are two kinds of investment bankers. One is international and realistic. It is exemplified by J. P. Morgan & Co. It is cold and calculating. Emotion plays but little part; even patriotism is but one factor in life and not the most reliable. This type is careful of its friends and does not neglect its enemies. It is rarely understood in a democracy which does not think (or feel) in terms of income but in terms of speculative profits.

The second type of investment banker is exemplified by Jay Cooke. It is lacking in realism and tends to neglect caution. It can be enthused even with patriotic emotion. Preferring a cautious policy, it periodically adopts the contrary. Preferring to operate outside the realm of political influence, it will on occasion enter that realm in order to accomplish its purpose. This class is not admitted to the circle of the first class: it is suspected of not being orthodox and reliable. The time will come when its members will get into difficulty. When that time comes, the first class will hold out no helping hand. And so in 1873, Rothschild, Morgan, Drexel, and others watched the crash they had anticipated.

Nevertheless, the two groups were both made up of money middlemen. They were both active sponsors of the new financial capitalism. They were both part of what we may roughly call Wall Street; and as such they were similarly suspected and feared. The class to which Jay Cooke belonged may, however, count upon a feeling of sympathy which the Morgan type can never enjoy. Unsuccessful speculation is an American weakness that makes all its devotees akin.

As citizens, we decry the activity of financial capitalists. As historians, we record their activities without much analysis. As judges, we should recognize that the age of Jay Cooke (1857–73), the age of the elder Morgan (1873–1913), and the age of the First Security Company (1908–29) were but experimental. The bankers, both commercial and investment, were feeling their way toward a social service *via* the profit road, which, although marked with scars and disasters, constituted one of the most brilliant efforts in our material civilization. Just now we seek change through political control and the goal is not yet in sight.

The rôle played by Jay Cooke was in the drama of financial capitalism. In this drama the banker provides the funds — collects them, if you will. He is a money middleman who stands in between the owner of the capital and the final user. Beginning in the small way of making loans and discounts for short periods, he develops into the important position of providing large loans for longer periods and even working capital and long-time capital. Of course, it is in the provision of capital — the work of the investment banker — that Jay Cooke played his part.

There are two phases in the experience of financial capitalism that we need to consider, if we are to place Jay Cooke in his exact niche. In the first phase, the money middleman provides the capital, after considerable thought and care; but, once the loan has been made, he is passive in his relations to both the investing owner and the industrial user of the capital. This has been the normal type of financial capitalism at home and abroad. It may be called the *passive* type or phase.

In the second phase, which we may call *active*, the money middleman not only provides the capital but he follows up its use by some active participation in the affairs of the borrower. In other words, he has come to share in the responsibility for the use of the loan, whether by choice or necessity. Perhaps we shall find, when we have a longer perspective, that this phase began in Germany after 1870 and developed on Wall Street not long thereafter. We see it becoming effective in the work of the elder Morgan, 1873–1913. Jay Cooke felt the influence of the forces that call bankers into participation in industrial affairs when he embarked upon the task of financing the Northern Pacific Railroad. Had he succeeded in this work, he would have been one of the founders of the active phase of financial capitalism in America.

Into the realm of business we creep as young men to operate first as workers in the factory or office. Some of us move up to be managers, the heads of departments, perhaps, in which we have some influence upon the making of profits. A few reach the top as business administrators or policy-formulators. Jay Cooke climbed the ladder with great success. His rare ability in the popular sale of government bonds, however, proved to be his undoing. It gave him a sense of greatness which in normal times he really did not possess. He was not a great investment banker but an outstandingly successful propagandist for war bonds. His evangelical fervor enabled him to unite in holy, but temporary, matrimony the cause of patriotism and profit. The war over, the setting changed, he could not adjust himself to the new conditions of less business along normal lines. He failed as a policy-formulator. And then, when he undertook the financing of the Northern Pacific, holding up to his firm a fairly safe policy, he was unable to manage the execution successfully. His failure was dramatic and the repercussions widespread.

The author of this treatise on the work of Jay Cooke has rightly assumed that complete description is the only satisfactory explanation. Nevertheless, in the interest of economy, she has considerably reduced the story. In the midst of contemporary emphasis upon social theory and social forces we may prize a realistic unfolding of social evolution. The great actuality is the continuous stream of effort to get a living, paralleled only by the constant striving for human freedom. If we weave these together with the struggle to reproduce our kind, we have much of the broad pattern of human history. In the getting of a living, the earning of profits, we formulate policies for the organization and management of business. We establish controls and checks and balances. The whole is no stronger than the weakest link.

The life of Jay Cooke is a case in business history, rather long but pointed. The life of a business man like Jay Cooke is a segment of effort to direct and control, in which ability to form temporary patterns of thought and action plays a dominant rôle. Success lies in the effective organization, administration, and management of the business unit. Jay Cooke, the topmost financier of his day, exhibited some weakness in all three of these parts of business activity. Business men, like scholars and artists, are not simply good or bad, high grade or low grade; they have their points of strength and of weakness. In general, they are above the average in creative work, since they mold the clay of circumstance into the bowl of plenty, the cornucopia of modern society. At any rate, when we have studied business history, as Dr. Larson has done, we may judge, praise or blame, the work of business men. Our recent national pastime has been to judge without studying.

N. S. B. Gras

Boston, May 9, 1936

AUTHOR'S PREFACE

JAY COOKE left a collection of manuscripts which is remarkable both in its character and its size. Most important are the tens of thousands of letters which it contains. These record the relations of Jay Cooke and his firms with their customers or associates; and, since they consist largely of the correspondence between the banker and his partners and are concerned with the day-to-day business of the banking firms, they also provide the most intimate insight into the problems, policies, and conduct of Jay Cooke's business. The collection also contains numerous manuscript agreements and memoranda, which furnish important details on Jay Cooke's banking operations, and pamphlets, circulars, and posters, many of which are rare.

Unfortunately the account books of Jay Cooke's firms are not available for use. They were delivered to the trustees in the bankruptcy of Jay Cooke & Co., but they cannot now be found. The bankruptcy records contain helpful summary statements and reproductions of pages from the account books of Jay Cooke & Co. The original bankruptcy records are in the Philadelphia office of Chas. D. Barney & Co.

An extremely interesting part of the collection of Jay Cooke's papers is his Memoirs. These voluminous Memoirs, partly recorded in Jay Cooke's own hand and partly written from dictation by a granddaughter, Elizabeth Butler, were started on July 26, 1894, just before Jay Cooke's seventy-third birthday. The Memoirs contain a wealth of information and explanation on the banker's life and work, and they reveal much about the man himself. They have been very helpful, though it has been necessary to use them with care, since human memory is often unreliable.

The Jay Cooke Papers are in the library of the Historical Society of Pennsylvania and in the Baker Library at the Graduate School of Business Administration, Harvard University. In the former library are most of the correspondence before 1873, posters, circulars, clippings, and a miscellany of other material.

Baker Library has some correspondence before 1873, agreements and memoranda, pamphlets, voluminous correspondence after 1873, and Jay Cooke's Memoirs.

I have searched with little success for the business papers of Jay Cooke's partners and of the firms or individuals with whom he had business relations. The papers of Harris C. Fahnestock and of E. W. Clark & Co. and Fisk & Hatch have been destroyed. A representative of the Drexel estate in Philadelphia assured me that Anthony Drexel's papers had not been saved. The Northern Pacific Archives, however, in the offices of the road in St. Paul, Minnesota, proved rich in information.

I want to take this opportunity to pay my respects to Dr. Ellis Paxson Oberholtzer's *Jay Cooke, Financier of the Civil War.* Though with the exception of some earlier letters which I was unable to locate I have read the manuscript sources used by Dr. Oberholtzer, I have consulted his work from time to time with full appreciation of its value. I especially recommend this earlier study to my readers for further information on the personal life and the character and personality of Jay Cooke and for its generous reproduction of letters pertaining to war finance and the Northern Pacific. In view of the information given by Dr. Oberholtzer on Jay Cooke as a person, on his private life, and on the public aspects of his work, I have felt myself free to devote greater attention to his private business.

It is impossible to make as complete an acknowledgment as I should like of the help I have had in the preparation of this book. Miss Lillian Leuhrs and Miss Hellen Asher did some of the tedious work of searching New York and Philadelphia newspapers for information. Members of the Accounting Department of the Northern Pacific offices went to a great deal of trouble to assist me in getting material from the records of their road. Among the many business men who have been helpful, I am especially indebted to Mr. Herbert L. Clark, of Philadelphia, Mr. Harvey E. Fisk and Mr. Charles B. Harding, of New York, and Mr. Charles D. Barney, of Philadelphia. Since Mr. Barney was employed in the Philadelphia house of Jay Cooke and was his son-in-law, he could speak first-hand of the banker and his work. I have valued the opportunity to get the close and immediate contact with the subject which comes from personal conversation with one who actually knew the situation. I value it not only for the actual facts gained, but also for the suggestions it gave me and for the check on my own ideas and information.

It is a pleasure to acknowledge the help received from the officers and staffs of libraries. Mr. Julian P. Boyd, librarian, and Miss Mary M. Townsend and Miss Catherine H. Miller, of the Manuscript Division, of the Historical Society of Pennsylvania, have been extremely generous in their aid. I have also had every personal facility in the use of all materials in the Baker Library of Harvard University.

The help I have received at the Graduate School of Business Administration, Harvard University, has been varied in kind. This study has been made as a part of my work in the School, and I have been given clerical assistance whenever it has been needed. Miss Frances Carpenter has corrected the copy, has checked its contents, and has done most of the typing, besides taking a great deal of responsibility for proof reading. She has worked with rare patience and care, relieving me of much concern about a difficult part of the work. Professor Ralph M. Hower and Miss Elizabeth McClelland have read the manuscript, made corrections, and given many helpful suggestions. To Mr. Richmond Fletcher Bingham I am indebted for the map of Jay Cooke's railroad interests.

My deepest obligation is to Professor N. S. B. Gras. He has led me to see in business history both an interesting and an important field of historical study, and has guided me in attaining whatever insight I may have into the broader aspects of the development of our business system. Professor Gras suggested this study to me, and throughout every stage of its development he has given invaluable help.

H. M. L.

Boston, May 11, 1936

JAY COOKE
PRIVATE BANKER

I

A SON OF THE FRONTIER

JAY COOKE'S INHERITANCE

IN THE spring of 1817 Eleutheros and Martha Cooke set out from
eastern New York State to make a new home in the Illinois country. There was nothing remarkable about their going; it was
what Americans had been doing ever since the English had first
settled on this continent, always seeking the virgin land to the
west. Indeed, for several generations the Cookes had participated in the trek westward. The earliest one of the family to
settle in America was Henry Cooke, whose name first appears in
the town records of Salem, Massachusetts, in the late 1630's.[1]
Successive generations of his descendants helped tame the wilderness; they followed the frontier through Connecticut, southern
Massachusetts, and, after the Revolution, into New York.[2] The
War of 1812 for a time dammed the stream of general migration,
but peace broke the barrier, and thereafter for several years a
flood of settlers surged into the great interior. Martha and
Eleutheros Cooke were caught in that flood.

Of their journey to the New West we have only the barest
account.[3] They set out with a number of their neighbors, and like
many pioneer families they had a baby in arms. They crossed
most of New York State, a long if not a difficult journey through a
beautiful wooded and hilly country over which still roamed sub-
dued remnants of the great and proud Six Nations, to remind the
invader of how lately the region had been conquered by the White
Man. On the upper waters of the Allegheny the little party with
the help of Indians constructed a flatboat, and, aided further by
Indians, they guided their clumsy craft with poles and paddles
down the river, here quiet and there treacherous.[4]

Near Pittsburgh, they built a larger boat in which they floated down the Ohio, the great highway to the Mississippi country. The Ohio must have been alive at the time with craft carrying migratory Americans, immigrant Europeans, and profit-seeking traders, as well as pioneer farmers and woodsmen heading downstream to market, and our party very likely saw a steamboat on the way, for that amazing boat which could go upstream as well as down had then been on the Ohio for some six years.[5]

The Ohio River was like an arm of the settled coastal region reaching into the interior. Along the river were many settlements, scattered and crude in their newness. The most important was Cincinnati, a thriving town which was soon to boast of its branch of the Bank of the United States; Louisville no doubt already showed some promise of its future as the metropolis of Kentucky, but most of the settlements on or near the river were only small villages.

The Cookes chose to make their home at Madison, Indiana, just a short distance above Louisville. The next year, however, found them headed northward into unsettled country. A return trip to New York, *via* Lake Erie, had acquainted Eleutheros Cooke with the beautiful, rich country along the southern shore of the lake. So impressed was he with the promise of the region that on his return to Indiana he could not wait for spring but took his family by sleds some three hundred miles to their new home. That was in 1818.

We wonder today why families like the Cookes left settled communities for the wilderness. It is clear that they were not going for adventure. It is also certain that they had no illusions about finding such a Utopia as philosophers and literary romanticists dreamed of. They were too close to frontier experiences not to know something of the realities ahead of them. But that very knowledge urged them on. They knew that homes could be built in the new country and that communities would arise. To the pioneer there must have been something irresistibly attractive about the process of building, about the feeling that he was helping to make something grow; it gave a sense of importance to the individual. Ultimately, moreover, he would reap the fruits of his efforts in a better home and greater opportunities. But this all took faith and persistent optimism and something of the creative spirit.

Eleutheros and Martha Cooke made their first Ohio home in a new settlement a few miles south of the western end of Lake Erie. But in 1821 they moved up to a place on the lake shore, later to be named Sandusky. In that place their third child and second son was born on August 10, 1821, while the parents, in true frontier fashion, were living with another family awaiting the completion of their own house. No doubt with great hopes for the child's future, they gave him the name of an early American statesman, Jay.

It is tempting to find the key to an understanding of Jay Cooke in the spirit of the frontier; but it was not the spirit of the frontier, alone, that influenced him. It was the spirit of America, that giant who was just beginning to feel his great strength and whose strength was urged on by great hopes and expectations. It was, indeed, the spirit not only of America; in Europe, philosophers and poets, social reformers and statesmen, and, perhaps most strongly, inventors and business men, armed with a new mechanical technique and imbued with great ambitions, were beginning to catch the vision of a future which should be greater than the past. The cynical, critical eighteenth century was followed by the hopeful and expansive nineteenth. In business, which was to be Jay Cooke's field of activity, the nineteenth century was to witness such creativeness, such expansion, such overwhelming activity and growth, as had not been seen since the days of Good Queen Bess — which, in truth, went even far beyond the dreams of the most daring promoters of her time.

This spirit was intensely expressed in the pioneer on the American frontier. And why should it not have been? Nowhere has the world known such a wide expanse and richness of untouched resources, coupled with such freedom on the part of the individual to exploit them, as in nineteenth-century America. It was Jay Cooke's good fortune that he was born into such a place, for he had to a rare degree the combination of qualities which fitted him for leadership among a vigorous, expanding people. There are, it is true, certain intangibles in individuals which cannot be comprehended and even less explained — the great unknowns in personality. It is obvious, however, that environment, training, and the accumulation of experiences, especially in one's younger days, go far in the making of the individual. This was clearly true of Jay Cooke. The frontier boy was the father of the great banker.

Jay Cooke knew his home community almost from its beginning. He lived through that earliest stage in frontier settlement, so familiar to successive generations of Americans, when the Red Man was dispossessed by the White. The Cooke family's first home in Sandusky was built on a spot where the lodge of Ogontz, a Wyandotte chief, is said to have stood. The chief and his people had some time before been moved a little to the southwest of Sandusky. But they frequently returned just for a visit, for trade, or to receive goods promised them by the government. When old Ogontz returned to his former home, he found lodging in the Cooke barn and bounteous meals in the Cooke kitchen. Jay often rode on the chief's shoulder. Indians were, as a matter of fact, almost a part of the Cooke family's everyday existence. Jay remembered vividly in his later years how a prowling Indian was routed from the Cooke home at night; he recalled the drunken brawls of the Red Men, and the squaws ridiculously parading about in "plug" hats after receiving their allotments from the government.

The little village of Sandusky was only four years old when Jay Cooke was born.[6] For several years it was made up of but a few small houses and shops, huddled together close to the shore line of Lake Erie. The lake was, indeed, only a few rods from the Cooke house. Deep blue, green, or gray, according to the mood of the sky, it stretched far off until it was lost in the distant horizon. The lake was then still largely a highway for the Indian and the fur trader. It was only in 1818 that the first steamboat appeared on Lake Erie. On clear days one could have seen from Sandusky that intrepid forerunner of a new era, the pioneer steamboat, *Walk-in-the-Water*, puffing away between Buffalo, the outpost of the East, and Detroit, the gateway to the fur traders' and the Indians' West.

Along the irregular shore of Lake Erie, with its lovely island-studded bays and small peninsulas, was a stretch of forest a few miles deep. To the south and west lay a vast prairie, covered with waving grass and herds of deer and wolves, and innumerable flocks of wild turkey and prairie chicken. When the Cookes first came to Sandusky, the prairie was still the Indians', but here and there small settlements soon grew up and eventually spread out over the open country.

Though Jay Cooke was a child of the frontier, he was an heir of New England. His ancestry, as we have seen, was of New England itself, while his own father and mother were only once removed from it. They brought with them what was essentially a New England culture. Had the Cookes continued to live in southern Indiana, they would probably have become more of the South than of the North, for what could one family have done toward preserving its New England character in a community of a different descent? Jay Cooke's great opportunity, the Civil War, would then probably have come to him in a different guise. But Sandusky was of New England. It was located in Western Reserve, that large section of Ohio on the south shore of Lake Erie which, in the settlement of the individual States' claims to land on the basis of colonial grants, had been given to Connecticut. The village of Sandusky was in that part of the Reserve known as the "Firelands," which had been set apart especially for those people of Connecticut who had suffered loss at the hands of the British during the Revolution.[7] Naturally, the New Englanders transplanted much of the culture of the mother to the daughter soil. Though one hesitates to say that Jay Cooke received particular qualities from his New England inheritance and environment, it may have been more than a coincidence that a community which produced him, with his feeling of moral responsibility for himself and his fellow-men and with his independence and aggressiveness, should also in his generation have produced Oberlin College and leading abolitionists as well as outstanding leaders in other lines of social or political effort.

The Cooke family represented the best traditions of the middle class; Jay's ancestors, as far back as they are known, were apparently undistinguished but self-respecting and hard-working people. The founder of the Cooke family in America was a Puritan, and Martha Cooke's ancestors were Independents from Northern Ireland.[8] The first Cooke in America was a farmer and a butcher; he was a bold spirit, even daring to criticize the Salem town watch! [9] His son was a tanner and shoemaker. The latter's son was a farmer.[10] All of Jay Cooke's American forbears were small tradesmen or farmers; there was among them none of the colonial aristocracy of the pulpit or the counting-house. Jay's father was the first definitely to rise above the small-farmer or tradesman class.

Through successive generations of pioneering, Jay Cooke's forbears had lost contact with the land of their forefathers and had become truly American. Both of Jay's grandfathers were patriots in the Revolution. His Grandfather Carswell (pronounced Caswell), who made his home with the Cookes, loved to tell his grandchildren of his own war experiences. Jay probably learned his first lessons in patriotism from his grandfather's tales of the war in upper New York and his imprisonment in Montreal. Jay Cooke was thus by inheritance thoroughly American, both in mind and heart, a fact which came to have great significance in his later life.

FAMILY, HOME, AND BOYHOOD

Four children of Eleutheros and Martha Cooke survived childhood: Sarah, born in New York State in 1816; Pitt, born in Ohio in 1819; Jay, as we have seen, born in Sandusky in 1821; and Henry David, in 1825 (the father, possibly hoping that his sons would all become statesmen, wanted this son to be named Fox, but the mother's objections prevailed).[11] Jay was a middle child, enjoying none of the special privileges of the oldest nor the indulgences often accorded the youngest, but having the advantage of living in a group, of learning to co-operate in play and to share in responsibilities. As will be seen later, his sister, indirectly, and his brothers came to occupy an important place in his business life.

Jay Cooke's father was a striking person. He had a strong body and a keen mind. He was a lawyer, trained in northern New York, where he had read law under the noted Chancellor Kent.

He was shrewd and quick at seizing opportunities for advancement or profit. One visualizes him as a forceful, dramatic, and somewhat pompous individual. He was very fluent in speech, perhaps one should say verbose; he was known far and wide as an orator. At the same time, he was a person of stern discipline; in refraining from drinking, playing cards, or smoking, he showed notable restraint for a lawyer who rode the circuit on the frontier in those days. Like his generation he was sensitive in matters of honor, and while not a strict churchman he had strong regard for moral principles as he saw them.[12]

Eleutheros Cooke became one of the pillars of his frontier community. His law practice was extensive, at least geographically, but it left him time to be somewhat of a business man as well, and he became interested in real estate and transportation ventures for promoting his own community. True to his profession, he was also a politician. He served several terms in the Ohio Legislature and one term, 1831–33, in the national House, representing the Whigs of the Firelands, the same district which later sent John Sherman to Congress.[13]

One of the father's strong interests as a legislator was internal improvements, which was probably to have not a little effect upon the son. In the Ohio Assembly he worked for the building of a canal from Sandusky on Lake Erie to Cincinnati on the Ohio River. Other sections of the State, however, defeated this central route. Cooke, therefore, turned to the new railroad. He is said to have drawn up the charter granted by Ohio to the Mad River and Ohio Railroad, the first road built west of the Alleghanies.[14] So little were railroads then known — it is told — that some of the legislators thought they were a kind of "corduroy" road, a log road laid in marshy or swampy places. While in Congress, Cooke opposed President Jackson's Maysville veto; he was "saddened" by the "veto doctrine" which "threatens to blight and destroy, the brightest hopes of the West," while he had the greatest admiration for Henry Clay because of his stand on internal improvements. In a letter to an Ohio supporter, Representative Cooke commented thus on an effort of Clay on behalf of internal improvements: "He spoke today until he became nearly exhausted

— by the intensity, of intellectual exertion. . . . I have no time — I have no *power* — to comment upon this speech. It will be published . . . When I will send you one. But you can derive but a faint idea of its *powerful — thrilling — overwhelming* effect, from its cold perusal. He literally annihilated the opposition.'' [15]

The positive and energetic personality of Eleutheros Cooke stands forth clearly in the above letter. The father's oratorical ability descended to another son, as did also his talent for politics, but his forceful aggressiveness and his ability to write effectively were gifts which were inherited by Jay. Young Jay was, moreover, through his father's interests, nurtured in the hopes and plans for transportation development, that magic power which was so greatly to transform the West. It was no mere accident that he himself became a great railroad promoter.

Martha Carswell Cooke is to the historian a much less definite figure than her husband, though by no means a colorless one. She was distinctly a woman of her generation, an affectionate and devoted wife and mother, and a good home-maker. She was at the same time a woman of much spirit and considerable resources. She was a sincere churchwoman; in an older community she might have preferred the Episcopal church, but chance made her a frontier Methodist. Her religious nature impressed itself on her son Jay and undoubtedly accounts in no small measure for his loyalty to the faith. But Martha Cooke was not a solemn individual — one gathers that she was a very likable person, happy, optimistic, and of a sociable disposition, and somewhat of a contrast to her stern and ambitious husband.[16] Her children loved her devotedly, and after leaving home, through frequent visits and a regular exchange of letters, kept in touch with her. One wonders if it were not Martha Cooke who knit her family together into that close companionship and unity of interest which came to be such an important factor in Jay's business life.

The Cooke home was both a pleasant and a stimulating environment in which to be reared. It never knew poverty. It was happy, warmly affectionate, and somewhat idealistic in spirit. The father's work and interest gave it a breadth of contacts, some regard for intellectual matters, and a high position in the community which undoubtedly early impressed the children with a sense of their own importance and some feeling for leadership.

The frontier setting must have given the children a sense of change and improvement, some realization of the possibility of development. Every year brought additional families to the community, new institutions, and new business enterprises, while rumors of great improvements reached them from far and wide. The Cooke children were undoubtedly brought up very much like other frontier families. The frontier was no place for idleness; they early learned to become responsible for doing certain jobs at a definite time, an excellent training for business. But they also had time for play. The boys had their gangs, their debating societies, and whatever activities normally characterized the various stages of childhood and youth in frontier villages. There was much that was exciting and interesting in their existence, and much that gave play to whatever curiosity and self-reliance there was in them.

In his Memoirs Jay Cooke gives interesting glimpses into his boyhood. He tells, for instance, of an occasion, which even to the child was a significant one — the breaking of the ground at Sandusky for the Mad River and Ohio Railroad, the first railroad to be built west of the mountains. It was a festive event. Old "Tippecanoe" Harrison, the great hero of that region destined soon to become president of the United States, was there. Eleutheros Cooke was the orator of the occasion. What gems of oratory or lofty perorations to that great goddess, internal improvements, fell on the ears of the listening Sanduskians that day, or what visions they were shown of a great future, history does not record. But history does record that just such visions as Eleutheros Cooke probably revealed to them have since been more than realized. Music and cannon contributed to the solemnity of the celebration, and Jay himself was in the procession of boys marching in honor of the great event.[17] How much such an event influenced Jay in his later business undertakings, it is impossible to say, but it may have had a real effect on him.

The cars on the Mad River and Ohio were at first drawn by horses, but an engine was soon purchased. Jay Cooke remembered the first engine used. When a boy, he probably watched the assembling of the "Sandusky" in a shop in his own town from parts shipped from the East. And, wonder of wonders, it had a steam whistle![18] Jay thus early became acquainted with the infant railroad which was destined to become a giant in his day. Even as a boy he put his mechanical observations to use. He was skilful in making boats, and once he made a steamboat 16 inches long, with paddle wheels, smokestack, an old clock spring for an engine, and burning gum in the smokestack! His talent for business was even at this early age revealed, when he sold the boat to a colored boy for a dollar of precious pennies earned by shining boots.

The country around Sandusky, with its lake, islands, and bays, and its streams, forest, and prairie, was a paradise for a boy. Jay became a seasoned hunter and fisherman. By the age of eight he had learned how to handle the rod and gun. There was always plenty of game and fish — deer, wild turkey, prairie chicken, and squirrels in the woods and on the prairie, and an abundance of fish in the "cove." He remembered slipping out at four o'clock in the morning to hunt in the woods and on the prairie, or to take the canoe to the cove to fish, stopping in his mother's buttery for pumpkin pie and milk and filling his pockets with a goodly supply of doughnuts.[19] Thus was laid the foundation for the recreation which Cooke enjoyed in his busy later years, when, worn and weary, he sought a brook stream in the Pennsylvania mountains or his old haunts about Sandusky Bay.

Though Western Reserve came to be strongly abolitionist and Sandusky became a station on the underground railroad to Canada, not all the people living there were friends of the negroes. The Cooke family was always ready, however, to help the colored folks, Mother Cooke supplying food from her kitchen for many unfortunate fugitives. Jay's Philo Literati Debating Society had a debate on slavery. Their argument at once came to a practical test. Jay brought a Virginia mulatto, a nephew of the town barber, to the debating society. The society was divided on the colored question and a fight ensued; the friends of the negro race put the proslavery members to rout and barred the door. But the slave war did not end that night. When the village Fathers finally interfered to end it, the boys, having acquired a common enemy, were reconciled. To celebrate, they had a candy pull and rat hunt. The next morning found rats tied to the doors of the justice of the peace and of the other town Fathers who had threatened the boys.

Jay's first recollection of public worship was of a Methodist meeting held in a cooper shop in Sandusky. The seats were rough boards placed on kegs. The Methodists were pioneers in Sandusky, meeting in homes or other available places until 1828, when they built a low wooden church.[20] Jay's family attended this church, and there, as a sensitive and imaginative young boy, Jay probably learned, from some fiery frontier preacher, his first lessons on Sin and Salvation and the virtues of brotherhood and self-control. The subtleties of dogma and creed probably received no attention, being intellectual unrealities which had little place in frontier life.

The Cooke children's education was not neglected. Their father provided them with books and wrote them long, instructive letters when away from home. Many an evening mother and the children waited for the late post with its letter and bundle of books from father, which kept them up reading through much of the night. News, practical observations on events, poetry, romance, philosophy, history, and the marvels of science found an eager listener and reader in the boy Jay. Grandfather Carswell taught the children at home, hearing their lessons two hours or so of an evening. The Cooke children were also sent to the village schools — presumably private, since a public system was not organized under State law until 1838.[21]

Young Jay was a healthy lad with an abundance of energy. He was of medium size, light-haired, and blue-eyed. He was evidently a normal boy with perhaps somewhat more than the average boy's keenness of mind, thoughtfulness, self-reliance, and capacity to win friends. He attended school regularly until he was about fourteen and for short periods thereafter. Both of his brothers were sent away for further schooling, but Jay was not. At one time he certainly planned to go on, for when twelve years old he wrote his brother that he expected to be "digging up Kenyon hill of science next spring if god be willing." [22] Why the next spring did not find him at Kenyon College we do not know for certain, though it is probable that Jay's early experiences in business aroused in him an ambition which drove away thoughts of college.[23] His parents on one occasion at least urged him to go away to school rather than to accept an offer as a clerk, but Jay chose business. Then, as later, he was a person of action. Indeed, while Pitt and Henry were away at school, Jay stayed at home and worked; and, though younger than Pitt, he offered to send of his own earnings to his brothers. This concern for them may have been a self-conscious gesture in the boy, but it was later a fixed habit in the man.

THE BOY ENTERS BUSINESS

Jay showed an aptitude for business while still very young. At about the age of nine he was initiated into its mysteries, when he began to help, at noon or after school, in the store owned by his father and uncle and managed by the latter. He continued to do this for several years. At the age of ten he became an independent merchant; "capitalist," he would undoubtedly have called himself had he then known the term. With his own savings he bought a stock of toys and picture books, which he displayed in the window of the store and sold on his own account. When fourteen years old, he became a full-time merchant. Having got the notion that his father's finances were not in the best state, Jay — out of a feeling of responsibility, he later said — left school without consulting his parents and became a clerk in the store of Hubbard and Leiter, young men from New York who had established a dry goods, grocery, and hardware store in Sandusky. His salary was $250 a year. He stayed with this firm one year, during which time, in the leisure of winter days when there was little trade, he learned double-entry bookkeeping from one of the partners, and also chess. That the bookkeeping appealed to him more than the chess we may be certain, for purposive activity always had the strongest attraction for Jay.

In the summer of 1836 came his first great business adventure. A young merchant from St. Louis who was courting his cousin urged the lad to accompany him to St. Louis, offering a salary of $600 a year and promising to make a great merchant of him. The fifteen-year-old boy set out with his new employer. They crossed Ohio by stage to Cincinnati, a long and rough trip, and from thence went by river to Louisville. There, records Jay in his later years, he saw his first play, *Pizarro*; but he must have seen even more interesting things in that busy slave market and trading town. From Louisville they took a boat down the Ohio and up the Mississippi to St. Louis, which they reached about two weeks after leaving home. When they set foot on the west bank of the Mississippi, they were really at the gateway to a different country, the country of the Chouteaus and the American Fur Company, which stretched over endless plains, inhabited by the Indian, fur trader, and trapper, and reached into the almost uncharted mountains far to the west.

St. Louis was then, according to Jay Cooke, a place of about 7,500 souls.[24] It was a rough, frontier river town, and it was a lively place. It was an important fur market, and a wholesaling center, and it had a branch of the Bank of the United States of Pennsylvania, the successor of the second Bank of the United States. St. Louis was the most important trading place in that central region; indeed, it was the entrepôt for the fur trade and the Indian trade of the whole Upper Mississippi and its tributaries. Steamboats, by then a familiar sight on western waters, busily carried the frontier trade from up the rivers to St. Louis and down to the older city, New Orleans.

Jay stayed in St. Louis only a year, but it was a year filled with new experiences.[25] He was enthusiastic over the beauty of the surrounding country, writing home about the "undulating and glorious prairies of Illinois," on which he went hunting, returning "with undiminished admiration for the works of creation and also with plenty of game!" He met strange people who spoke a language unfamiliar to him and whose manners and customs were different from those of New England-like Sandusky in Western Reserve. The people of St. Louis were not altogether to his liking.

He wrote home that "the population of the city consists of part French (almost savages) Spaniards, Italians, Mexicans, Polish (all noblemen!!!) Indians, a set of gambling Southerners, and a few skinflint Yankees. There is but few respectable persons in St. Louis. . . . The Mexicans look as if they had just emigrated from his Satanic majesty's dominions and by far the most unoffending are the poor, the injured, Indians." Yet, that Jay tried to adjust himself to the new scene may be gathered from the fact that he attended dancing school, where he learned to waltz and talk French! "Picture to yourself," he wrote Pitt, his imagination running riot, "your brother Jay in a spacious ball-room with a beautiful French brunette by his side . . . dressed in a fine brown coat . . . with white silk vest, black cassimere pants, white silk stockings, fine pumps, white handkerchief and gloves, hair dressed and all erect, talking Parley Voo with the beautiful creatures."

While he wrote home of such things, his letters show that he was also interested in more serious matters. "My thoughts are or ought to be those of my father," he wrote to his brother, "for have I not been directed by him to the paths of integrity and honor and have not his opinions and views been instilled into my youthful heart? Has he not in his counsels pointed out the vices and snares which you know youth otherwise seldom escapes from and has he not implanted in my heart a love and veneration for my country which can never be effaced? Yes, he may rest easy, for though I do not honor to his name I will *not* disgrace it." These letters reveal in the boy something of the growing self-consciousness of youth as well as the energy, the enthusiasm for living, and the feeling for moral considerations which became such marked qualities in the man.

The business of Jay's employers seemed promising in the spring of 1837. There were prospects that merchants from the surrounding country and caravans headed westward would give them considerable trade. Indeed, they apparently expected to find enough business to become very shortly a wholesaling concern. But the panic ruined them, and soon young Jay was on his way homeward. Besides his rich experience and a great store of new ideas and information, he brought home with him about $200, furs and Indian blankets for presents, and something of the manner of the southern gentleman and the feeling of the capitalist, both of which made trouble for him with the boys of Sandusky. Such a nuisance did the cocky merchant make of himself that the old justice of the peace finally told Jay's father that, if his son were complained of again for walloping the neighbor boys, the constable would have to get on the job.

Jay's next business venture took him to Philadelphia. After attending Adams Academy in Sandusky, where he edited and wrote in his own hand the monthly school paper during the winter of 1838, he left for the Quaker City in the spring to work for the Washington Packet & Transportation Company, whose president was William G. Moorhead, the husband of Jay's sister.

Philadelphia at the time ranked second in importance in the United States as a commercial and financial center. Indeed, at one time it had been the leading city on the seaboard. The location in the Quaker City of such important financial institutions as the first Bank of the United States, Girard's Banking House, and the second Bank of the United States bears witness to the important position Philadelphia had occupied in American finance. The energetic aggressions of its neighbor to the north had come seriously to threaten Philadelphia's leadership, which was further weakened by the expiration of the national charter of the second Bank of the United States. Even thereafter, however, Philadelphia continued to be an important banking center, and it carried on an extensive commerce, both foreign and domestic. Its strongest fields of business were the West and the Southwest, and it was still in the 1830's an active competitor of New York for the business of the great inland empire.

Jay's coming to Philadelphia brought him, a real frontier boy, into the heart of the most developed section of the United States. It was a long distance from Sandusky, where news of the outside world came only by slow and expensive post, where life was rough, simple, and close to nature, and where the active life was the ideal, to the sophisticated city of culture and wealth, such as Philadelphia was at the time. Jay soon succeeded, however, in making himself quite at home. But that is a story which will be left to later chapters.

In Philadelphia, Jay came into contact with one of the wildest speculative booms this country has ever known. The panic of 1837 had wrought havoc in business, but flouting its warnings the country had rushed almost into a frenzy over internal improvements, especially in some of the Middle Atlantic States and the New West and South. There banks were established and securities were optimistically sold to support a veritable orgy of spending for the improvement of transportation. Magnificent canal systems were projected and railroads planned far beyond the immediate capacity of communities to support. Nicholas Biddle was in some respects the arch-promoter, and the immediate hinterland of Philadelphia was one of the busiest scenes of speculative activity.

The Washington Packet & Transportation Company, which brought Jay Cooke to Philadelphia, was one of the enterprises which had then sprung up. It had been started by Pennsylvania Democrats, including Senator Porter and several members of the Canal Commission. A large part of the money needed for its establishment had been borrowed from the Bank of the United States of Pennsylvania, then recently chartered by Pennsylvania. Jay Cooke said in his later years that he "always suspected that this money furnished by the Bank was in some way as a recognition of the gratitude the Bank felt for its new charter." [26] This gave the young clerk a striking illustration of the use of the government for private gain.

The company carried passengers and freight between Philadelphia and Pittsburgh, a distance of about four hundred miles by the devious route then used. The trip consisted of alternate journeys by rail and water: by rail from Philadelphia to Columbia on the Susquehanna River, then by river and State canals along the course of the winding Susquehanna and Juniata rivers, through beautiful forest-clad hills, next on the Alleghany Portage Railroad over the Alleghany Mountains, and finally by canal and river to Pittsburgh. From there travelers could get steamboats going daily to points on the Ohio, Mississippi, and Missouri, or they could go by stage to Erie and Cleveland on Lake Erie.[27]

Jay's duties with the packet company were varied. He kept books, solicited trade, handled publicity for the company, and served as general assistant. It was a strenuous job; he even came to blows with the boys of a rival concern.[28] Through this work Jay gained his first introduction to the press. He handled the advertising of the line in various Pennsylvania papers. Advertising was then still in its infancy, little realizing the power it was later to hold, while the advertising agency had not been born. Young Cooke's notices in *Poulson's American and Daily Advertiser* show, however, that he had the modern view of the function of advertising. While the advertisements of other packet companies were merely trite announcements, as was usual then, those of the Washington Packet & Transportation Company were sales talks which very effectively emphasized the comfort and speed of the line and gave information about time schedules and rates. We shall later see how this first connection with the press developed into a close alliance, which in no small measure accounts for Jay Cooke's great success as an investment banker, and perhaps for his failure as well. Advertising was destined to develop into a colossal servant of trade; it was to broaden the market for a given product or a given concern, but in doing so it also broadened the area of competition and heightened its effects. Of its tremendous possibilities, however, Jay Cooke perhaps little dreamed when composing the notices for his transportation line.

Jay's advertisements give an interesting picture of the means of travel at the time, by what were claimed to be expeditious and comfortable carriers, from Philadelphia to the inland water system. The cars, noted the advertisements, left the depot on Broad Street daily at ten o'clock. Passengers taking this line arrived in Pittsburgh at least half a day earlier than by any other line leaving the same hour. The cars were eight-wheeled, "which insure safety, and were built with a view to comfort and convenience." The boats, which were new, were "finished and furnished equal to any in the State," and were "commanded by careful and experienced captains, who pledge themselves to render a passage as pleasant and expeditious as possible." [29] Realizing that "expedition in the delivery of merchandize is particularly desirable at this season of the year," the Washington Packet & Transportation Company advertised in the summer that for an extra charge it would deliver freight at Pittsburgh *six days* after leaving Philadelphia.[30] To us who today drive between Philadelphia and Pittsburgh in about as many hours, this seems slow. How great an improvement it was in its time, however, could be realized only by those who just a few years before had traveled that long, rough road when the horse and the rocky, treacherous river were man's only aids in making the trip.

Bankruptcies were epidemic in the late 'thirties, and again Jay lost his position because of the failure of his firm. Late in the summer of 1838 the company failed, participating in the collapse of the whole speculative movement of which it had been a part. In the fall Jay returned home a second time jobless, but as before he carried with him concrete evidence of his industry. Strangely enough, he had not been much impressed by the teachings of the Sage of the Quaker City, for he spent most of what he had saved in Philadelphia in buying a fine new suit of clothes.[31] Jay Cooke never learned to be thrifty.

As before, however, Jay was not long without a job. While in Philadelphia he had earned his board by working evenings at the Congress Hall Hotel, keeping books and, at times, tending the bar. The hotel was located on the corner of Chestnut and Third streets, the center of what was then Philadelphia's financial section. Here Jay had often been observed by Enoch W. Clark, a stock and exchange broker on Third Street, and in the spring of 1839 Clark, through the proprietor of the hotel, offered him a position as clerk in his brokerage house. The offer was accepted, and on April 3, 1839, young Jay again arrived in Philadelphia, this time to begin his career as a banker. He was then almost eighteen years of age, and he had robust health, strong ambition, and, for one so young, a considerable stock of experience.[32]

JAY COOKE'S BANKING INHERITANCE

A BUSINESS man's career is obviously the result of many factors. One cannot say such was the man and therefore such was his career; but, rather, such were the man, his cultural inheritance, and the institutions and conditions within which he worked, and through the mysterious interaction of these elements was fashioned his career. We are now about to see Jay Cooke become a part of that great stream of institutional life called business. To understand what lay before him, it is necessary to know something of the conditions under which he was to work. It is especially important to have some understanding of the course of development of banking in the United States before and during his time.

DEVELOPMENT OF SPECIALIZED BANKING IN THE UNITED STATES

The firm of Enoch W. Clark, which Jay Cooke entered as a clerk in 1839, was a part of a stream of banking development which had a long and important past. To understand this properly, it is necessary to keep in mind one of the great changes which had then for some time been coming in American business. Specialized business units were taking the place of the non-specialized mercantile firms which had for generations carried on an extremely varied business and supplied most of the business needs of their communities. At the time of the Revolution, the big business man was the foreign merchant. He was not only the trader, both wholesale and retail, but also the shipper, insurer, banker, and even manufacturer. There were, it is true, butchers and bakers and candlestick-makers; even the broker was making his appearance in certain kinds of business. But the dominant individual, the man of wealth and influence, was the merchant. He continued to dominate American business for over a generation after Independence; note Stephen Girard of Philadelphia, John Jacob Astor of New York, and Thomas Handasyd Perkins of Boston. A new order was in the making in America, however, an order in which specialization in function was to be the outstanding characteristic of business units.

Those merchants had, among other functions, supplied banking services to their communities. Thus American experience had duplicated that of medieval Europe, where for centuries the merchants and the money-changers had been the bankers of their business world. Even before America had been discovered, however, specialized banking had appeared in the Old World, the Bank of St. George, of Genoa, being the first of a line of banking development which brought forth such notable institutions as the Bank of Amsterdam, the Bank of Sweden, and the Bank of England. The English colonies in America, both because of their youth and their political dependence on a mercantilist mother country, had not acquired specialized banking; but before independence from Great Britain had become a legal certainty banking had begun to separate from the business of the merchant.

When the merchants of Philadelphia, Boston, and New York finally found themselves free to establish banks, which they needed so badly, they soon set up in their respective communities a specialized, incorporated bank, modeled in a general way after the English pattern. The banks thus established were the Bank of North America, in Philadelphia; the Massachusetts Bank, in Boston; and the Bank of New York. Those banks were organized by men of business experience to meet existing commercial needs; that is, to furnish means for foreign and domestic exchange, issue notes, and carry on a general loan and deposit business. In 1791 was established the first Bank of the United States; run on sound principles, this institution not only helped to meet the banking needs of the country but also served indirectly as a regulating force on banking in general. Following the establishment of those earliest banks there was a fairly conservative development of chartered banks until about the time of the War of 1812.[1]

In the meantime, the antibank element in the electorate had become sufficiently strong to prevent the recharter of the Bank of the United States in 1811. From then on, the history of banks in the United States has been the story of competition between the conservative creditor interests, which have stood for sound banking, and the debtor interests, which have looked upon banks as established primarily for the purpose of granting extensive credit and which have had little regard for the safety of deposits or the value of notes issued. This condition in banking was a logical result of the fact that the settlement and economic development of the United States were almost continually advancing faster than the available capital was able to finance. A robust, ambitious people with visions of a frontier blossoming into rich communities was not to be restrained by any great regard for the interests of the stockholders or depositors, or by consideration for the note issues of banks. This situation was to have a strong bearing on the career of Jay Cooke.

A powerful, sound national bank might have been able to restrain the more extreme tendencies in banking, with the result that there would have been a higher degree of regularity and dependability in banking throughout the country. But the destruction of the first Bank of the United States in 1811 left banking to local interests and to the wisdom or folly of State regulation. Except during the amazing interlude of the few successful years of the second Bank of the United States, from about 1823 to 1831, this condition was widely prevalent. Generally speaking, the strength of banks varied in direct proportion to their nearness to strong centers of capital and business, though even within the leading cities institutions reflected differences in those who managed them. The absence of uniformity and dependability in banking made the strong well-managed banks largely restrict their business to the institutions and individuals with whom they were closely acquainted. The result was that there were many needs of business which the chartered banks failed to meet, particularly in payments between distant places and the transfer of funds in general.

Chartered banks, however, by no means had a monopoly on

banking. Nonspecialized mercantile banking continued to exist in the United States, as it did in Europe, long after chartered banks had appeared. As business increased, such banking began to separate from other business and to form specialized private banks. The disappearance of the Bank of the United States in 1811 was the immediate occasion for the establishment of the first important private bank in the United States, Stephen Girard's Bank, of Philadelphia.

The new bank was patterned after English institutions and was encouraged and aided by a somewhat similar concern in England. Prior to its establishment, Alexander Baring, the great English merchant-banker, had written at length to Girard of the possibilities, advantages, and functions of a private bank. Private concerns had a special advantage in foreign exchange, which required decision and could not be managed by a board; business could not be transacted confidentially with twenty-four directors; incorporated banks were limited by the necessity of regularity in their business and the fact that they were exposed to the jealousy and observation of their neighbors — thus ran Baring's argument. The English banker offered generous credit to Girard's Bank, establishing a precedent which other American private bankers were later to follow.[2]

Girard's Bank was intended to be primarily a commercial bank, particularly for financing foreign trade, but the War of 1812 turned it to the investment business.[3] When the secretary of the Treasury early in 1813 offered a loan of $16,000,000 to be sold to the public in sums of $100 or multiples thereof, Girard's Bank was appointed one of the subscription agencies. It is interesting to note that Girard had an advertisement placed "in six of our public Papers until the 13th instant inclusive,"[4] a striking contrast with Jay Cooke's extensive advertising of Civil War bonds. The loan failed to sell. Perhaps Girard's advertising was not persuasive enough, but more probably the country was not ready for a popular loan. Since the war had seriously cut trade, there was a large amount of idle funds in Girard's Bank. Accordingly Girard, together with David Parish, bid for $8,000,000 of the loan, which

with John Jacob Astor's bid took all that remained of the $16,-
000,000 offered.[5]

The work of Girard and his bank in selling this war loan has
special meaning in a study of the life of Jay Cooke, who was to do
notable work in financing the Civil War. Though separated by
only a generation in time, the efforts of Girard and Cooke were far
apart in method. The American merchant-banker, who participated in the financing of the War of 1812, really had less in common with Jay Cooke than with the Fuggers,[6] merchant-bankers of
Augsburg who helped finance Charles V, Emperor of the Holy
Roman Empire, or with Jacques Coeur,[7] the French merchant
prince who assisted the king of France in the delivery of Nor-
mandy from the English.

Girard's Bank was the first of a group of private banks which
was to play a significant part in American business, a group which
included such important houses as Brown Brothers and Prime,
Ward & King. These banks, and others like them growing primarily out of foreign trade, were very similar to English private
banks, and, like Girard's, were largely engaged in foreign banking.
Like Girard's Bank, also, they entered into the investment business, coming to serve, particularly, as a bridge for carrying capital
from Europe to America. J. P. Morgan & Co. of today is a direct
descendant of this early type of institution.

These private banks are mentioned only as background for Jay
Cooke, not because of any institutional connection. They were
rooted in America's foreign trade, and, though strong, were few
in number compared with another type which was more nearly
indigenous in that it grew almost entirely out of American experience and conditions. That was the stock and exchange
brokerage house. It had neither the capital nor the wide business
experience of the mercantile banking houses. Moreover, its beginnings were usually small; it grew with the growth of domestic
business; and it looked inland and participated in the opening of
the West and in the business which resulted therefrom.

One must beware of being too positive in speaking of those institutional beginnings of which so little is known and which seem

to have taken such varied forms as almost to defy classification and generalization. But it is clear that, about the time of the War of 1812, stock and exchange brokers began to assume some importance on what we may call the periphery of banking activity. In the inflation of banking which came during and after the War of 1812, with the resulting chaos in bank notes and exchange and increase in investments offered to the investor, the brokerage house rose to a position of considerable importance. Eventually it became an important figure in domestic exchange and investments, just as Girard and his successors continued to be for a long time in foreign financial relations.

The growth of a group of bankers primarily domestic in their work was a part of an extremely significant development in American business. The dominant business men of the past generation had their basis in foreign trade. They were busy carrying on an international trade, with London as its center. They were more at home in Calcutta or Canton than in Cincinnati, while Chicago had not yet come into being. Their successors, however, faced inland. They used the wealth their fathers had accumulated (and all that could be borrowed abroad) in building factories, digging canals, and constructing railroads, and in outfitting settlers in the West. This transfer of capital and business enterprise, which largely took place in the second quarter of the century, and the accompanying development of the interior of the United States, is one of the most significant accomplishments of business in the nineteenth century. It was this development which, coupled with an inadequate and unsatisfactory system of chartered banks, made possible the rapid growth of the type of banking of which E. W. Clark & Co. was a part.

S. & M. ALLEN AND THE TRAINING OF ENOCH CLARK

E. W. Clark & Co., so important in the life of Jay Cooke, was in reality an offshoot of one of the pioneers of this native development, S. & M. Allen & Co. The Allen concern was the training school of Enoch W. Clark, and it illustrates strikingly the early stages of that stream of banking development of which Jay Cooke became a part. The later work of Clark and Cooke can be under-stood better if viewed with the perspective gained from some knowledge of the experience of this, their business ancestor.

The origin of the Allen business was in a general way similar to that of innumerable other enterprises of the time. In 1808 Solomon Allen, the son of a propertyless missionary preacher on the frontier in New York State, began to sell lottery tickets to add to his income as a printer.[8] After a few years he left printing in order to give all his time to the "Lottery, Exchange & Broking Business" of "S. Allen's Lottery & Exchange Office in Albany." This developed into a varied business: Allen sold lottery tickets for a number of projects, among them Harvard College and the Washington Monument; he dealt in bank notes from all parts of the country, promissory notes, "Eastern and Southern Bills," bank shares, and shares in "first rate Privateers;" and, in addition, he sold a variety of goods, such as writing paper and legal blanks, "Ladies Elegant Thread cases," "American Gun-Powder," and, both retail and wholesale, Rogers' "Patent Vegetable Pulmonic Detergent" for coughs, consumption, and asthma!

Allen continued for some time to deal in his strange conglomeration of goods, but Albany soon proved too small for him. In 1815, therefore, he and his brother Moses formed a partnership to conduct a lottery and exchange business in New York. Allen's Truly Lucky Office was launched on the wave of inflation which flooded the country with the closing of the first Bank of the United States and the War of 1812, bringing much unsound currency and a strong speculative spirit.

The business established in New York required connections in other places. The Allens soon, therefore, extended their enterprise, as was then customary among lottery and exchange houses, by organizing branch partnerships throughout the country. These partnerships consisted of the Allens and one or two resident partners in each branch house. By 1828 there were Allen houses in Philadelphia, Baltimore, Washington (D. C.), Pittsburgh, Richmond, Fayetteville (North Carolina), Savannah, Albany, Providence, Portland, Boston, Mobile, and New Orleans.

In 1818, the very year when Jay Cooke's parents settled in

Ohio and three years before Jay Cooke was born, a young kins-man of the Allens became a clerk in their Philadelphia house.[9] Enoch W. Clark, born in Easthampton, Massachusetts, in 1802, the son of a flourmill and sawmill owner, had, like many another ambitious son of New England of his generation, left home to seek a fortune in business. He served for about seven years in the Allen house in Philadelphia, and in the middle 'twenties he was sent to Providence to become resident partner and manager of a new Allen office at that place.

An important part of the work of the Allens until 1823, and of most of their offices till 1827, was that of selling lottery tickets. Lotteries had come to be looked upon as a legitimate means of financing private as well as semi-public and charitable under-takings, and the work of selling lottery tickets had become a busi-ness of considerable proportions.[10] For several years Solomon Allen managed the sale of the Union Canal lottery in Pennsyl-vania, guaranteeing to sell certain amounts of the different issues of tickets. In this work may be seen the beginning in America of the underwriting of enterprises requiring considerable capital. The Allen houses were so-called lottery brokers, but they both bought and sold on commission and took outright large amounts of tickets of different lotteries which they sold at their own risk, both retail and wholesale. Thus they were early slipping over into what was in a real sense investment banking.

The Allens continued to sell lotteries until late in the 'twenties; the New York house dropped this line of business in 1823 and the Philadelphia house in 1827, while several of the branches which had been dealing in lotteries were discontinued. Why the Allens left this business at a time when lotteries were still popular is not clear, but they were probably sufficiently astute business men to see that the future was with stocks and not with lotteries. It was evident that the rapid increase of corporations engaged in bank-ing, insurance, and transportation, during the 'twenties, made necessary more agencies for the disposal of stocks. The New York Stock Exchange, formally organized in 1817, was then enjoying a growing business.[11]

The Allens' stock business developed gradually. The New York house was the leader in the development of this interest, and in 1823 it relinquished lottery dealing to "attend to the purchase and sale of Stock & Exchange both foreign and domestic." It dealt mainly in bank shares, both on commission and for itself.

The shift of the Allens from the lottery to the stock business and the closing of a number of their branches illustrate a business problem which will be seen again and again in the story which is before us. Business is highly dynamic; it expands and contracts, and the very things with which it is concerned also change. Only that entrepreneur is successful who can adjust himself to the constant change in business. It is not merely a question of being prepared to take on new business but also of being prepared to drop the old and even to deflate one's organization. Jay Cooke, as we shall see, faced that very problem about forty years later; but his adjustment was not so successful as that of the Allens gave promise of being in the late 'twenties.

An important interest of the Allens throughout the whole life of their firm was dealing in domestic currency and exchange. They did practically no foreign business, presumably because they did not have such contacts as would enable them to compete with houses rooted in foreign trade and well entrenched in foreign exchange. But they were at home in domestic exchange; with their branch houses they had the set-up for doing this type of business, which the individual chartered banks were hardly fitted and certainly not equipped to do. From the beginning of the New York firm throughout the life of the Allen houses, they dealt in the various types of specie, bank notes from almost every State, and United States Treasury notes. The bank-note business was very complicated, for it was no easy matter to recognize counterfeits and value correctly the hundreds of bank notes in circulation; the value of the notes depended on the strength of the issuing banks, which varied all the way from the leading institutions of Boston, Philadelphia, or New York, whose notes were as good as gold, to frontier banks which had little if any assets. There was, also, the additional difficulty of securing regular and safe transportation for notes and bills at a time when there was no regular and responsible way of shipping by post or express.

The branch partnerships also provided the necessary organization for carrying on a considerable and widespread business in promissory notes, drafts, or bills of exchange, which had their origin largely in domestic trade. It is not clear to what extent the Allens were merely brokers or how far they were working on their own account. Their offering of credit on any particular place depended on the amount of funds available on that place, and, as their business grew, they came to offer drafts in sums to suit purchasers. Their exchange business by no means, however, expanded with definite regularity; it was probably retarded in its development by the activity of the Bank of the United States in inland exchange from 1823 to 1833,[12] which may, indeed, be the explanation of the dissolution of many of the Allen partnerships in the late 'twenties.

The Providence office, of which Enoch Clark was manager, was one of the Allen houses which were closed in 1828. On the dissolution of this firm, Enoch Clark and his younger brother, Joseph W., joined in a partnership to continue the same business in Providence. This enterprise proved unprofitable and lasted only about five years. With the astonishing facility which only a young and small concern can exercise, they changed to the produce commission business. This shift in their interest was in line with the development of local opportunities, for dealing in produce was then increasing rapidly under the stimulus of the growing industry of Providence and its environs. The Clarks dealt in "prime New-Orleans Cotton," butter, flour, hams, sperm candles, linseed oil, whale oil, tobacco, coffee, mackerel, Malaga wines, and the like. Late in 1832 they began to advertise that they wished to purchase cotton yarn, but this interest seems not to have developed further. They were running into hard times. The many mortalities in the produce commission business in Providence at the time, as shown by newspaper announcements of dissolutions, indicate that business difficulties were then common. In the spring of 1833 the partnership was dissolved.[13]

Enoch Clark again joined the Allens, this time to do business in

Boston. In June, 1833, he became resident partner and manager of S. & M. Allen & Co., which was established to conduct a "Stock, Foreign, and Domestic Exchange Business," on State Street. The Allens had by that time grown to be one of the outstanding stock and exchange concerns of the country, having offices in New York, Philadelphia, Charleston, New Orleans, and Cincinnati. The new Boston house dealt in exchange, principally on Philadelphia and New York but also on London. This venture ended in the summer of 1834, a turn of events probably due to the Allens' difficulties in the early part of 1834.

Again Enoch and Joseph Clark formed a partnership. They announced themselves as successors of S. & M. Allen & Co. and established their office in the Allen place of business. Though they carried on the same type of business as the Allen concern, their trade in stocks was apparently insignificant. In the spring of 1835, when there was a great increase in trading in securities, they advertised definite numbers of certain shares either as wanted or for sale. These were all shares of local enterprises, principally banks, then the most common stock on the market. Like Enoch Clark's former undertakings, however, this concern was also short-lived. In 1836 the older brother returned to Philadelphia, while the younger stayed on in Boston, carrying on an exchange and stock business alone for a time and thereafter through a succession of partnerships.

In the meantime the Allens in Philadelphia and New York had been going more heavily into stocks, following the boom in the organization of corporations, assisted by a considerable importation of British capital, which threw millions of new stocks on the market. They advertised in newspapers that they would "buy and sell the various Stocks in the market, on Commission" and that they dealt in "all kinds of city and Western and Southern Bank Stock, also Pennsylvania 5 per cents, Rail Road, Canal, Insurance and other Stocks." The broadening of the Allens' work in stocks reflects a clear trend toward the development of a nation-wide trade in securities.

Early in 1834 the Allens ran into trouble. The panic following the deflation of the Bank of the United States, which began in

1833, caught them with heavy loans and many securities. They were saved from suspension by the action of leading New York business men who examined the condition of the New York and other Allen houses and counseled patience on the part of their creditors, saying that on a conservative valuation the Allens' assets exceeded their liabilities by half a million.[14] The heaviest liability was a loan of $3,500,000 which the Allens had contracted to sell for the State of Pennsylvania.[15]

It was the stock business which finally proved to be their undoing. The wave of promotions which flooded the market with new stocks in 1835–36 loaded the Allens, as so many others, with a heavy burden of securities. Failing to dispose of these to meet their obligations during the panic of April and May, 1837, they had to suspend payments,[16] and before the end of October all their partnerships were dissolved.[17] The total liabilities of the partners and partnerships were well above $1,000,000, and their creditors included many of the largest American banking houses of the time, principally private banks engaged in a considerable stock business. Their assets were mainly securities of such concerns as the New Orleans Canal and Banking Co., the Boston and New York Illinois Land Co., the Georgia State Bank, the Bank of Louisiana, and other companies generally based on the speculative hopes of the New West and South.[18] Thus the history of one firm records a story of financial frustration which was to repeat itself many times in the United States and in which Jay Cooke was on one occasion to play an important part.

Establishment of E. W. Clark & Co.

Shortly before the panic broke, Enoch Clark returned to Philadelphia. He was then about thirty-five years old and he had been in business for over eighteen years, a period of continual moving from place to place and shifting from business to business, with nothing tangible except debt at the end! But Enoch Clark had acquired something intangible of great importance: he had worked in three different cities, which represented differing con-

ENOCH W. CLARK

ditions and traditions; he had lived through several business cycles and observed the recurring succession of inflation, panic, depression, and recovery; he had become familiar with the business of trading in domestic stocks, currency, and exchange; and he had acquired a wide acquaintance among business men.

One may wonder why Clark did not again join the Allens. Aside from other possible explanations, there is the patent one that it must already have been evident to him that the Allens, and business in general, were headed for trouble. If trouble came, an unencumbered pigmy would have greater strength than a shackled giant, and so it turned out to be.

In February, 1837, Clark and his brother-in-law, Edward Dodge, joined in establishing a stock and exchange house in Philadelphia.[19] They started with a capital of $15,000, of which Clark supplied two-thirds and Dodge one-third, profits to be shared in the same proportion.[20] The capital for this enterprise was borrowed from a friend of Enoch Clark and the father of Dodge, who lived in Providence, Rhode Island.[21] E. W. Clark & Co. was a pigmy, indeed, but since it was new it was relatively unencumbered, while many of its neighbors, even those who escaped insolvency, were severely crippled by debts.

The Clark firm proposed to "purchase Eastern, Western, Southern, and most kinds of Bank Notes, at the lowest rate of discount," and buy and sell "Spanish, American and English Gold," and also "Stocks of all kinds" on commission; and to sell drafts on "New York, Baltimore, Washington City and Boston in sums to suit," and buy drafts "on the principal cities of the United States." It is true that exchange suffered in the business depression following the panic and that there was not much chance for a retail trade in stocks for some time thereafter. But since much of the banking structure — jerry-built in the wild middle 'thirties after the fate of the second Bank of the United States had been sealed — was destroyed [22] and currency was thrown into such great confusion, there was plenty of work for the dealer in currency and exchange. It was apparently this situation which enabled E. W. Clark & Co. so rapidly to establish itself in the domestic exchange business. By the time Jay Cooke entered its employ in the fall of 1839, it was regarded as one of the leading stock and exchange houses in Philadelphia.

The institution is, in the final analysis, the men who constitute it. This observation applies especially to a firm like E. W. Clark & Co., which had no capital and no important connections nor even any considerable prestige. The most important factor in Enoch Clark's firm was Clark himself. It was of great importance to Jay Cooke that he came to work with him and to learn about banking from so able a man and one who was so well acquainted with the business life of his time.

More is known of the work of E. W. Clark & Co. than of the man who gave the firm his name. Like most business men, who are notably remiss in leaving records of themselves, Enoch W. Clark must be seen by the historian chiefly through his work, about which we have some information. We might, it is true, describe his eight descendants who today are partners in E. W. Clark & Co., investment bankers of Philadelphia, and from their characteristics construct a composite picture which could be imagined to be like Enoch Clark. His portrait, which looks down upon those same eight descendants from the walls of their banking house, is that of a large portly man, who enjoyed the material things of life, was good-natured, and at the same time had both strength of will and keenness of mind. Seeing him through the eyes of young Jay himself, as he saw Clark when first with the firm, we get a picture of a very genial and at the same time an admirable person, a successful banker, and a solid man of business. Clark was such a man that the tradition of his high qualities as a banker still lives in Philadelphia today.

JAY COOKE ABOUT THE TIME HE ENTERED E. W. CLARK & CO.

A BROKER'S CLERK

YOUNG JAY was happy to return to Philadelphia and he was enthusiastic over the prospects which the new work offered him. A month after entering upon his duties with the Clarks he wrote his brother, "I have got on the right side of fortune in Philadelphia and if prudence, punctuality, and good behavior, as far as in my power, can keep me there, I shall remain *statu quo*, as you say, forevermore." "This business is always good and those who follow it always in time become rich," he wrote in his unrestrained optimism, and "I am not afraid but that I shall be able to help myself." [1]

Enthusiasm, optimism, and self-confidence were strong in young Jay. He had a buoyant temperament which, joined with a pleasing manner, an attractive appearance, and a way of inspiring confidence, helps explain that magnetic quality in him which had so much to do with his business success. He was of medium height, slender, and somewhat awkward.[2] He had a fair complexion, blue eyes, light hair, and a "radiant countenance, . . . [a] winsome and intelligent expression resting upon that unusual face." [3] From his letters, one may judge that he had a quick, inquisitive, and retentive, though not especially critical, mind, combined with perseverance, ambition, and a strong sense of loyalty to his employers.

A rich store of information has come down to us about Jay Cooke's earlier years in business. One source is, of course, Jay Cooke's Memoirs which, though colored by the retrospection of old age, give much that is of value. Another and even more useful source for the early years consists of the letters which the youthful business man wrote home. Those letters, which were for a long time carefully saved by the Cooke family, have been lost, but not before they had in part been recorded in print. For preserving much of the contents of those letters we are indebted to Mr. Ellis Paxson Oberholtzer, who quoted generously from them in his *Jay Cooke: Financier of the Civil War.*

Jay Cooke Learns about Banking

The Clark brokerage establishment occupied the first floor of an old residence on Third Street, close to Girard's Bank.[4] The equipment of the firm must have been as simple as its home was unpretentious, for those mechanical aids today so essential to a bank of any size had not yet been invented. The typewriter and calculator, the stock ticker and telegraph, and even the safety vault were of the future; a letter-press, however, may have been in the office as a promise of what was to come. As for hundreds of years, the pen and the account book constituted the main articles of equipment, and, therefore, to write a clear hand, to be able to figure with accuracy and speed, and to do simple bookkeeping, were the essential qualities of a broker's clerk. Jay could do all three.

Jay Cooke's Memoirs contain some interesting information about business in his early years with the Clarks. Banks opened at nine in the morning, were open all Saturday, and, besides Sunday, were closed only on Christmas Day, New Year's, and the Fourth of July. Brokers had longer hours; they had to be at their offices at eight in the morning and they often remained until eight or nine at night. The brokers and private bankers, who were not then clearly distinguished from each other, were, it seems, carrying on a much more active commercial business than the chartered banks. Through their hands flowed the exchanges of the country, both foreign and domestic; most of the out-of-town drafts were obtained through them; the largest portion of collections on drafts, notes, and out-of-town bills receivable were made by them; they sent home for redemption "the vast quantity of currency," that is, bank notes; and they dealt in gold and specie.

It seems curious to us that merchants and others did most of their borrowing in those days through brokers. According to Jay Cooke this was a profitable business, for he remembered periods

when business paper was discounted through brokers at 9 to 18
per cent per annum. He does not tell us exactly what the services
were which the brokers performed in this connection, but at least
through the early 'forties they worked principally as go-betweens
for the borrowers and lenders, though for an increasing part of the
business they assumed the risk by loaning to the borrower out of
their own resources or what they themselves had borrowed from
merchants or bankers.

The exchange business was notably lucrative. It is axiomatic
that the possibility of securing high profits is enhanced by in-
stability and uncertainty in business. In times of suspension of
specie payments, said Jay Cooke, exchanges were "thrown into
utter confusion," the premium on gold and silver rose to 15 and
20 per cent, and discounts on currency constantly fluctuated between 1 and 20 per cent. In the late 'thirties and early 'forties
suspension of specie payments was chronic in the United States
and bank currency was in a thoroughly demoralized state. "It
was a grand time," according to Jay Cooke, "for brokerage &
private banking."

The Clark firm carried on a varied business in those years, judging by their advertisements in the *North American and Daily
Advertiser* in 1840 and thereafter. They dealt in specie and bank
notes; they posted in their office and, beginning early in 1840,[5]
printed in the above paper a daily list of fraudulent and broken
banks and of counterfeit and altered notes; they redeemed notes
for banks on specific agreement;[6] and they handled commercial
bills. The extent of their business in drafts is suggested by the
fact that from 1840 to 1842 they advertised that they would collect on drafts and furnish drafts payable in fifteen cities in the
South.[7]

Jay Cooke's Memoirs explain how the Clark firm, which started
with so little capital, financed its business. When his employers
came to Philadelphia, said Cooke, they had little capital, but
"rich merchants who had more money than they required in their
own business, lent it to them and, what was more, lent them their
names as references." Wherever one may turn in the business
history of America of that period, one finds that the merchant was

the capitalist who financed most enterprises. The profits of the Clark firm soon built up a larger capital, but that was not enough. When more was needed for the daily business it was borrowed. In a day's work they might overdraw their account with the bank some $80,000 or $100,000, which was then covered by securing advances directly from banks or through other brokers, but "not always without difficulty." [8]

Though the firm was small and its equipment simple, it had one great advantage for Jay: it gave him an opportunity to show what he could do. In such a concern as the Clark house, it was to be expected that the young clerk would have varied duties and would be given responsibilities if found equal to them. Among other things, he at first served as messenger and delivery boy, going to banks on business for the Clarks. An important part of his work soon came to be to serve as teller, which he did expeditiously and accurately: "there was no counting over; one count was sufficient; and it was all so easily and gracefully done," in the words of one who had often observed him. After Jay Cooke had been with the firm about a year, he wrote his brothers that he was writing many letters each day — "some days 15 or 20 letters to all parts of the United States, and more than both of my bosses do" — and frequently when the partners left early in the day, he had to settle with the banks for heavy overdrafts.[9] Before he had been with E. W. Clark & Co. two years, he was given the power of attorney to sign for the firm.[10] His employers thus early discovered that the young teller had both ability and a high sense of responsibility.

Jay Cooke's Memoirs recount incidents or experiences from his early years with the Clark firm which give us considerable insight into his work and observations. One such experience had to do with a "beef speculator" (a cattle trader) who did business with the Clarks. When this "speculator" found it impossible to borrow cash from the Bank of the United States of Pennsylvania, he might give that bank his notes for four months and take in payment its twelve-months post notes in denominations of one, five, and ten thousand. He frequently brought to the Clarks from one to two hundred thousand of those post notes, stowed away in his tall beaver hat. "We would cash them," said Jay, "at from 10%

to 12 from their face value & marketed them generally in Boston through the old firm of Gilbert & Sons," from which the Clark firm realized from 3 to 4 per cent. But that was not all that they made from the transaction; they paid the "beef speculator" in Virginia, Ohio, and western Pennsylvania bank notes, which he used in paying for cattle in those States, but they paid him the notes at par, while they had bought them at a discount.

Through the relations of the Clark firm with the Bank of the United States of Pennsylvania, the successor of the second Bank of the United States, Jay saw something of the working of that unique institution. At the beginning of his clerkship he visited the bank daily to exchange its checks, which the Clark firm had collected, for its thousand dollar notes. These notes were clipped in two and sent to New York, by different routes for the sake of safety, to meet drafts which the Clarks drew daily on that city. After the first suspension of the bank, in 1839, the Clarks purchased its five dollar notes in different markets throughout the country and presented them for redemption, a profitable business since it was not generally known that the bank could not, under its charter, suspend specie payment on that denomination. The Clarks made another profit out of those same notes by purchasing gold and silver for the bank to use in redeeming them; at one time in about two weeks, says Jay Cooke, they purchased around half a million dollars in coin, "carting it up to the bank late at night, so as not to attract attention."

Jay must have heard a good deal about the operations of the Bank of the United States of Pennsylvania. This bank, which had an agency in London and a number of branches in the United States, principally in the South and West,[11] was engaged in financing trade, notably the cotton trade until 1839, and in marketing securities. In the course of its business, it extended credit to southern and western banks and merchants which it obtained from other large banks in eastern cities and in London on the basis of its own credit or securities issued by States or banks, many of which the Bank of the United States guaranteed.[12]

The brilliant but unsound operations of the Bank of the United States of Pennsylvania undoubtedly got much attention from the other bankers of Philadelphia. There was at first something to be admired in the positively daring way in which Biddle supported the credit of the United States and southern and western development, but one can well imagine that the conservative banking heads of Philadelphia shook with suspicion of such business. The resignation of Biddle from the presidency of the bank in 1839, together with the break in American credit in England in the same year and the inglorious closing of the bank in 1841, justified their suspicions.

Jay Cooke should have derived from the fate of this bank some notion as to what happens to an institution which so ambitiously overreaches itself in extending credit to essentially speculative enterprises. But owing to his youth and enthusiasm, what might have been a good lesson may have failed altogether to register on his consciousness. In some respects his experience was later to duplicate that of Nicholas Biddle.

The final closing of the Bank of the United States of Pennsylvania in 1841 had a special significance to banking in the United States. After the disappearance of the second Bank of the United States, this had been the only chartered bank which had the organization to enable it to become a national institution; the other chartered banks of the time were all individual banks or branch systems limited by the boundaries of a State. Branches were not absolutely essential to an interstate business, which could be conducted through correspondents, but it is reasonable to believe that at a time when communication between distant parts of the country was a matter of weeks, trustworthy branch offices would have been extremely useful. Properly run, Biddle's bank should have made for greater stability, but to manage such a bank, when communication was so slow and when there was such a diversity of economic conditions existing throughout the United States, would have been a herculean task. Biddle might have been able to do this if his bank had not inherited from the second Bank of the United States a very heavy load of securities and if he had worked in an upward rather than a violent downward swing of the business cycle. Had he succeeded, the banking history of the United States might have been different.

It was not only the Bank of the United States that was having trouble. The years during which Jay Cooke served as clerk in the Clark concern, that is, from 1839 to 1843, were a period of depression in America. General business conditions were then not unlike those existing in the depression years of the early 1930's. For about two years after the panic of 1837, many business men had refused to admit that thorough deflation had to come. Disregarding the warnings of the panic, they had continued their promotion activities. There had been an attempt, under the leadership of Nicholas Biddle, to save American business by securing loans in England and pegging the price of cotton, our most important commodity for the settlement of foreign balances. These measures were designed to ease the credit situation and to prevent that widespread liquidation which would otherwise have been inevitable. But there was a limit to the credit that could be secured in England; and there was also a limit to the extent to which cotton could be held for higher prices when the English cotton price was rapidly falling. The limit was reached in 1839 and the result was serious for American business.

Then began a period of severe depression and deflation which lasted for several years. Bankruptcy was epidemic. Credit dried up. Prices fell drastically. Not the least serious was the fall in confidence which came with the widespread repudiation on the part of certain States of their obligations and those of banks which they had sponsored.[13] American credit in Europe fell to a very low point from which it was not to recover until after the Civil War.

Though times were bad and many banks suspended and closed, the Clark business flourished. Within certain limits, the more difficulties banks had the more profitable was the work of the exchange dealers and brokers. In November, 1839, Jay proudly wrote home that his employers were doing an annual business of a million "and giving a clear profit of $40,000 or $50,000 a year." Frequently they would "pocket $500 a day." In January, 1840, he wrote, significantly changing to the first person, "we do a tremendous business." They bought and sold at commissions of from one-eighth to one-quarter of one per cent, thus making a goodly sum on their business of $50,000 a day. The young clerk calculated that if they made one per cent a day on a large amount, as they often did, they increased their capital by three and one-half times a year; at a quarter of one per cent a day, about their average rate of gain, they nearly doubled their capital in a year. "We keep money all over the United States," wrote Jay. "Every mail which leaves the city for the south, west, north and east bears rich packages, the proofs of our enterprise." In December, 1840, he reported that "we are doing a very heavy business at present. We have over $180,000 on hand in Mobile and Alabama funds, all of which when disposed of will pay a smashing profit." [14]

This business did not, however, come without effort to the Clark firm. Indeed, the competition among brokers must have been very considerable. There were old firms in Philadelphia and several young ones like the Clarks. One of the newer concerns, that of Francis Drexel, later became very important to Jay Cooke and his business. Drexel was an Austrian portrait painter, educated in Switzerland and Italy, who had emigrated to America because of the Napoleonic upheaval in Europe and had married a daughter of one of Philadelphia's most respectable families. He had spent many years as an artist in South America, where he had won the friendship of the great revolutionary leader, Bolivar. After considerable roaming about he had returned to the Quaker City, where he opened a stock and exchange house in 1838.[15] As will be seen later, it is an interesting coincidence that in the very year Jay Cooke joined the Clarks, Anthony J. Drexel, aged thirteen, entered his father's office. The difference in the background of the two boys is significant. One came from a cosmopolitan home which had its immediate roots in the culture of Europe; the other came from the Middle West, from a family that had for generations been busy building America, paying the price in the narrowness of its culture, a price which most Americans have had to pay, but at the same time striking deep roots into the country. The two boys were to develop into prominent bankers whose careers clearly reflected their different origins.

The Clerk Becomes a Financial Reporter

Banking was far from occupying all of Jay Cooke's time and interest in those early years. For a short time after joining the Clarks, he continued to earn his board and room by keeping the books at the Congress Hall Hotel, and he was not a little flattered that as "paymaster-general of Mr. Sturdivant's forces" he was treated with deference by the "nigs" and given "the best of everything." An extra job of an entirely different nature was that of writing a "money article" for the *Daily Chronicle*, of Philadelphia, which he began in the spring of 1840 and continued for about a year.[16] The material he used for those articles was collected in the course of the day from the correspondence of the Clarks, his own daily experience, and from any other sources from which he could get information about the market, banking conditions, or general business. This work was invaluable to the young clerk; it forced him to study carefully the course of business and to form judgments about financial matters, and it gave him an acquaintance with newspaper men. Jay's money articles were well written and comprehensive, and they showed an astonishingly mature insight into money and banking. Exchanges, discounts, lists of counterfeits, the value of the currency of certain banks, trade and business practices, prices of staple commodities, sales of stocks, even causes of panics and the effect on business of the crossing of the Atlantic by the steamship *Great Western* — an endless variety of matters was touched upon. On September 28, 1840, the young financial writer commented significantly in the *Daily Chronicle* on the condition of the banks: "Anyone who has kept an eye over the movements and operations of banks and bankers for a few years past, can plainly discern the causes which have led to all our financial revolutions. The suspension of specie payments in 1837, and the general crash that immediately followed were but the effect of wild speculations and imaginary prosperity."

Jay Cooke's writing of a money article for the *Daily Chronicle* has not a little historical significance: it marked a definite step in the development of the means for supplying printed information to business men. Our informative government reports, statistical and other business services, and trade or financial journals were then all of the future. The merchant had for some time been served after a fashion by the *Prices Current* of important marketing centers like Philadelphia and New Orleans or the commercial news of such papers as New York's *Commercial Advertiser* and the *Boston Daily Advertiser*. But the rise of specialized business units, separate from mercantile concerns, had not yet received much recognition from the press, and the banker would have searched in vain for information of particular value to his affairs.

The appearance of a special financial article was in a real sense a harbinger of a new era. Jay Cooke was not the first financial reporter in the United States, for the aggressive Bennett's *New York Herald* had begun to carry such an article on June 15, 1835, and the *New York Daily Express* only a short time thereafter; but as a financial reporter Jay Cooke was helping to break new ground. How far the development has come in our day may be seen from the fact that what was then done as an odd job by a boy of nineteen is now the work of highly trained men who enjoy national reputations and have powerful corporations behind them. There is a great difference between Jay Cooke's column in the *Chronicle* of 1840 and Alexander Noyes's articles in the *New York Times* of 1935, or between the early money article of the *Chronicle* and the *Wall Street Journal* of today. That difference speaks eloquently of the complicated nature of our present business set-up. The fact that the *Herald* and the *Chronicle* carried financial articles indicates, however, that they were beginning a hundred years ago to sense the need not only of supplementing further the information which the business man, in an increasingly complex situation, was able to gain through his own contacts, but also of giving special attention to the field of banking and finance. We look upon this today as another illustration of the drive toward specialization that characterized American business in the second quarter of the past century.

THE CLERK'S LEISURE TIME

Something of the personality and character of the young clerk and the influences molding him can be inferred from his interests and activities outside of work. Then, as later, Jay was intensely interested in life about him. He was quite conscious of the business and moral value of proper acquaintances — "I have a number of valuable ones who may be of service to me hereafter," he wrote to his brother. He was of a sociable turn though he apparently did not attach himself closely to any group. He enjoyed being invited to the homes of his employers but, as he wrote his brother, he missed the jolly dancing parties at home, missed taking "the soft hand of your fair partner in yours, to steal soft looks from her orbs of soul."

Jay liked Philadelphia. When first there, he took long walks about the city, observing the people, viewing the parks and gardens, and seeing the Chinese museum, where, he wrote home on one occasion, "I learned more of the Chinese nation . . . than I ever knew before." Or he saw a play. One Christmas Day evening he went to the Chestnut Street Theater, "where we . . . shook our sides until eleven o'clock." The *Lion King* made quite an impression on him — "It is one of the most thrilling and beautiful pieces I ever saw," he wrote home. No wonder, for it had such exciting scenes as that in which the tiger darted upon the sleeping captain of the banditti! And also "songs, dances, battles, and the usual quantity of love!" Of course, he had to round out the evening with "ice cream, fruits, etc., very fine!" Once he took a drive up the beautiful Schuylkill, writing home that "there are some of those palaces and castles which kings might own and be proud of. . . . Oh, this is indeed a delightful city and the more I see of it the more I like it." Thus the young "tired business man" sought, as he said, "to refresh my business faculties."

After Jay had been in the city a year, he became too busy or too absorbed in other things to give much time to such amusements, even though he was given free theater tickets because of his writing for the *Daily Chronicle*. That work took much time, but when he did have leisure, he spent it at home practicing on the flute or reading the life of Cromwell, *Graham's Magazine*, Scott's and Burns's works, the *Popish Church*, or other books which he had purchased. He planned "to buy some of the most useful classical works." Thus we see young Jay groping for culture. But his search for knowledge and beauty through books was never to go very far; he was neither studious nor contemplative by nature, and the responsibilities and demands of his work and later his family left him little time for such things. As so often happens to the business man, study was left behind with his youth.

Sunday always found Jay at church, in which he had a real and sincere interest. His home training had ingrained in him a strong sense of moral values; these were, it is true, the orthodox, conventional values, but they were important in influencing the young man. The church he attended was a Methodist Episcopal church down town in Philadelphia whose pastor is said to have been an eloquent preacher and a forceful leader.[17] One may well wonder how far Jay's association with the church, its members, and its pastor, helped mold him in his impressionable years and develop in him certain habits and virtues which came to have an influence on his business life.

Young Jay Cooke disproves the old belief that it is the thrifty boy who becomes rich, for he was not inclined to be saving. He liked to have money in his pocket in order to spend it. He wrote to his brother, no doubt expecting to impress Pitt with his own affluence, "I seldom trust myself when I go out for a tramp in the evening with less than one or two dollars and never have a cent in my pocket when I return." In the fall of 1840 he wrote home, "As for my money affairs . . . I am a little extravagant and am about square so far, but shall be more saving in future. I am obliged to dress well, and in the city $300 don't go far." Besides his salary of $300, or a little more, for the first year, the young clerk was then earning his board and room at the Congress Hall Hotel and enjoying the privilege of free admittance to the theater by virtue of his writing for the *Chronicle*.[18] A more thrifty youth could have saved something, no doubt.

Though Jay spent freely, he nevertheless appreciated the value of money. He wisely philosophized that "money is chiefly the object for which all men contend," but it was not as an end in itself that he was interested in money, for "I look upon riches but as naught more than the means whereby one can display his social and generous spirit." Wealth, not for its own sake but for what it can buy and do; perhaps therein lies one clue to an understanding of Jay Cooke's motive for engaging in business as well as his failure to accumulate a large capital. He had no fear of not getting on with the earning of money. He wrote his brother Pitt, who was studying to become a lawyer, "As you lawyers never expect to be worth much, I shall have the pleasure some time of helping you out of trouble perhaps. Castles in the air. Heigh ho!" To gain possession of those castles he expected to go into business for himself when twenty-one.

PARTNER IN E. W. CLARK & CO., 1843–1857

GRADUALLY the country recovered from the depression following the panic of 1837, and the United States, like Europe, entered another period of prosperity which ended in 1857. 'Thirty-seven and the bad years immediately following were almost forgotten. The romantic spirit was again at work. A new energy and enthusiasm and new ambitions, fanned by the successful outcome of the Mexican War and by Manifest Destiny and bursting into flame under the heat of the discovery of gold in California and the rise in prices which came in the late 'forties and early 'fifties, drove the people to attempt greater things. Indeed, the United States had never before known such a plethora of plans and activity as then made its appearance.

The textile industry was growing in New England, consuming more and more cotton (as were the English mills at the same time), increasing their production and making high profits which enriched the Boston capitalists, and creating a class of wage earners whose food was drawn from widening agricultural areas. The iron industry, responding to the call of the factory, the railroad, and the farm, took on a new life. The southern cotton planter was moving on toward the limits of his empire in the Southwest; the pioneer of the North was bringing under cultivation much of the upper valley of the Mississippi, even to the falls of St. Anthony; settlement was slowly threading its way into the Oregon Country; while the adventurous 'forty-niners and their followers were feverishly sending California's gold eastward to furnish capital for a great economic expansion.

Both cause and effect of this great scattering of people and economic and business development were the improvements in transportation then being made. The building of wagon roads, especially plank roads, was getting much attention. Canal building reached its height in the 'forties but thereafter went into a decline. Railroads, at first projected to supplement waterways, came to be looked upon as the highways of the future and the means whereby one ambitious rival city could outdistance another in competition for the trade of the great hinterland. In the United States, as in Europe at the time, railroads became one of the great objects of investment and construction activity.

Conditions Favorable to Private Banking 1843–1857

The tremendous economic growth which the United States experienced at this time brought a great increase in the demand for banking service. In this development American experience paralleled that of Europe, but the situation in the United States was different in that whole new regions were opened up or settled: California, the Oregon Country, the Upper Mississippi Valley. This meant extensive land transactions, the building of wagon roads, canals, and railroads, and the financing of settlers in their first years, all of which required capital from the outside. In the older sections, also, capital in larger and larger amounts was needed to build railroads, factories, and commercial buildings.

There was also an increasing trade to finance. The growth in trade, especially after the depression began to lift, was beyond the actual increase in population or cultivated acreage. American economic development in the nineteenth century was peculiarly three dimensional: there was at one and the same time the horizontal spreading out over virgin lands and the vertical development of business methods and organization in both old and new communities. A widening market area and a changing technique were bringing about greater specialization in all lines of business. The old order was giving way to the new: the place of merchants like Astor, Girard, and Perkins was being taken by the Vanderbilts, Brown Brothers, and the Lawrences, specialists in transportation, banking, and marketing. Every man was going to market for more and more things as the years passed, while goods in the domestic trade were being sent longer and longer distances and in greater and greater amounts.

It was inevitable under those circumstances that many new financial agents and institutions should be established, but, unfortunately, the foundation on which they were built was none too good. In spite of much agitation, no national system of banking had been provided to take the place of the second Bank of the United States and there was no adequate national circulating medium. The Bank of the United States of Pennsylvania, which had given some promise of becoming the great national bank, had, as already noted, gone down in 1841. Banking was, therefore, in those years left to the wisdom or folly, the integrity or dishonesty, of State-chartered banks and private bankers and brokers. Individualism and localism dominated American banking as they were to do for generations to come; irregularity in banking flourished, and a great diversity of standards continued to be the rule. This was not altogether strange — it was to be expected that under the circumstances the growth of the nation's banking system would continue to be more or less unsound — but the problems it brought were very real.

The older sections of the country were more fortunate than the rest in respect to banking. Strong incorporated banks continued to develop in the eastern cities. This was no doubt in a measure the result of improvements in State regulation, but the strength of banking in the East rested in the final analysis on long experience and the necessity for protecting large accumulations of capital by following conservative banking practices.

But it was not so everywhere. In general, State banking was weaker in proportion to its distance from the larger centers of business, or in proportion to the strength of debtor as opposed to creditor interests. There were exceptions, of course, places where tradition and aggressive, conservative leadership left their mark. In general, however, the newer West was weak in chartered banking. In the Mississippi Valley, experiments with State-chartered banks were not very satisfactory. In most of the lower valley, banking was left prostrate by the events of 1837 to 1841, and recovery was slow. The settled portions of the upper valley tried incorporated banks, both State and privately owned, but rarely with success. After some experimenting, Missouri in 1837 established a State-owned bank,[1] which became one of the few sound western banks of that time but which made inadequate provision for the banking needs of the State. Illinois also experimented with State-owned banks, but without success. Its second State bank, chartered in 1835, went down under the weight of a speculative mania involving it in the promotion of internal improvements. In June, 1842, it suspended operations and soon thereafter went into liquidation. John Marshall's Bank of Illinois, of Shawneetown on the Ohio River, at one time a flourishing institution serving even young Chicago, suspended operations in 1842 and went into liquidation. The Bank of Cairo, the last of Illinois' early chartered banks, went bankrupt in 1843.[2] In Wisconsin Territory the banking situation was similar: the Mineral Point Bank and the Bank of Wisconsin, at Green Bay, were closed in 1841, and the Wisconsin Fire and Marine Insurance Company, which carried on banking though not authorized to do so, had its charter revoked in 1846.[3] The charter of the one bank in Iowa Territory was withdrawn in 1845.[4]

From the time of the closing of those western banks there were, with the exception of the State Bank of Missouri, no incorporated banks in the Upper Mississippi Valley until the introduction of free banking systems,[5] for which provisions were made in Illinois in 1851, in Wisconsin in 1853, and in the other western States only after the panic of 1857.[6] The banks organized under the free system in the West were for a time not satisfactory, so that they really did not meet the banking needs of the section.

A very serious evil in State banking was the fact that the object of many banks, especially in the West or away from centers of commerce, capital, and experience in finance, was not the furnishing of needed banking services but the issuing of notes, a paper panacea for the ills coming from the shortage of capital and the inadequacy of the circulating medium. This, as has already been seen, was by no means a new development at the time; it was a marked aggravation of an evil which had existed for three decades. It was the old American story of trying to do banking without capital. It gave the new regions capital of a kind, but a kind that was almost worse than useless. Aside from other considerations, the chaotic condition of the currency which resulted created a serious problem in itself.

The situation was decidedly favorable to private banking. The rapid expansion of business, when chartered banking was so inadequate or unreliable and the currency so chaotic, meant more work for the broker and the private banker. The latter had been the banker of the frontier and continued to be so, moving with the advance of settlement into new regions, often combining banking with mercantile or real estate business. Where incorporated banking fell into disrepute or proved unsuccessful in more or less settled places, as for instance in the upper Mississippi country in the 'forties and 'fifties, the private banker found an especially lucrative business. But even in leading business centers the private banker continued to flourish side by side with the chartered bank, doing very largely the exchange business of the time. In 1843 *Hunt's Merchants' Magazine* stated that the discredit attached to banking associations and the excellent facilities of private banks for making collections had led to a great increase in the business of private banking houses of good standing, and that "mercantile banking is concentrating in the hands of private houses of known integrity, wealth, and business habits, because of the superior facility they afford over associations of irresponsible men, doing business in palaces at enormous expense." [7] Which all sounds like Baring's comments to Girard thirty years earlier! [8] Private banks also had the advantage over chartered banks of being very much less subject to regulation and interference; and they could be established with little capital.

The extent of private banking in the United States in those years may be suggested by the fact that in June, 1854, the American *Bankers' Magazine* listed 240 private bankers, exchange dealers, and brokers in New York City, and 369 private bankers in the principal towns and cities of the United States outside of New York. There were 20 private bankers in Philadelphia, 10 in Boston, 23 in Cincinnati, 15 in St. Louis, 11 in Chicago, 16 in New Orleans, and 16 in San Francisco. [9] Among those concerns we find names which, only slightly changed if at all, have lived down to our own day, such as Brown Brothers, of New York; Lee &

Higginson, of Boston; Drexel & Co., of Philadelphia; Riggs & Co., of Washington; and E. W. Clark & Co.

The private banks varied greatly in form and function. The partnership was the most common type of organization. Most banks were single concerns, but chain and branch banking, that is, interlocking units, were not uncommon. These varied from the small western group bound together by one or more common partners or a chain of banks linked by partners who were members of two or more banks of the group — such as the Iowa chain in which Hoyt Sherman was a partner — to the branch or group systems in the larger cities, among which the Clarks, Riggses, Drexels, and Browns were outstanding. Younger partners were sent out to head the outlying branches just as had been done ever since business ventures were first sent to distant places hundreds of years ago. The business of the private banks varied more than their form; it ranged from the nonspecialized frontier merchant, who furnished some banking services, or from the investment broker, who was in reality only a rudimentary banker, to the full-time banker, who did all kinds of banking and frequently emphasized one aspect of it, as for instance the western real estate banker and the domestic or foreign exchange banker in the eastern cities.

THE EXPANSION OF THE CLARK ORGANIZATION

By 1842 the Clark firm had laid a foundation in capital, reputation, and business contacts which made it ready to take advantage of the opportunities the times so richly offered. In the 'forties and 'fifties Philadelphia was one of the three leading financial centers in the United States; though the Quaker City had lost the second Bank of the United States, it was still regarded as a leader in banking, for it had a large banking capital and its banks were essentially sound institutions. On such a financial foundation, Philadelphia had built an extensive foreign trade and, aided by an improving transportation system, also a strong domestic business, especially in the new South and West where it hardly recognized a superior. The fact that Philadelphia occupied such an important position with respect to American business was one of the factors accounting for the success of E. W. Clark & Co.

Growing opportunities made necessary a larger organization. The expansion of the Clark firm took the form of a group of partnerships somewhat similar to those of S. & M. Allen, with whom Enoch Clark had so long been associated, and not unlike the branches of the Bank of the United States. The advantages of a group or branch system, in the then existing circumstances, are obvious. The Clarks became bankers on a truly national scale.

The first branch to be added to the original Clark firm of Philadelphia was E. W. Clark & Brothers, of St. Louis. This house was established in November, 1842, by the two Philadelphia partners and Enoch Clark's two brothers of Joseph W. Clark & Co., of Boston, each having a one-fourth interest.[10] St. Louis was then a promising place for a new banking house, for it was the most important commercial center in the newer West and, since its branch of the second Bank of the United States had been closed and local joint-stock banking was in an undeveloped state, it offered a considerable opportunity for private banking.[11] Luther C. Clark of Boston was the resident partner and manager of the St. Louis house until 1847, when he was succeeded by a brother-in-law of Edward Dodge.[12]

In 1844 a New Orleans house, E. W. Clark, Brothers & Farnum, was formed by E. W. Clark & Brothers, of St. Louis, and George W. Farnum, of Philadelphia, the latter becoming the resident partner and furnishing one-half of the capital of $50,000.[13] This house was soon closed. Probably it could not successfully compete with other established firms in that section, for instance, the Riggses, of Washington, who were strong in the newer South; or the closing of the house may have been due to the fact that the Clarks saw the greater possibilities of the region north of St. Louis and chose to grow with that section. As the Lower Mississippi Valley had been in the 'thirties, the upper valley became in the 'forties and 'fifties the focusing point of western commercial development and speculative interests.

The establishment of a Clark house in New York in August, 1845, came as a logical consequence of the growth of the Clark business and its extension over a wider area. New York City had by that time become the central point for business in the United States. Indeed, it had been very important for some time, but Philadelphia and Boston had earlier maintained a relatively independent position. The course of development, however, gave New York the leadership, as is seen in the concentration there of both foreign and domestic exchange, bank deposits, and the investment business, which was well under way by the 'forties.[14] A New York house had, therefore, become almost a necessity for the Clarks. Edward Dodge and, later, Luther C. Clark became the resident partners in New York,[15] and they opened their office at 60 Wall Street in the heart of New York's financial district. E. W. Clark, Dodge & Co. started with a capital of $50,000, the Philadelphia house subscribing two-fifths, and the Boston, St. Louis, and New Orleans houses each one-fifth.[16]

The next Clark office to be established was E. W. Clark, Brothers & Co., of Burlington, Iowa, which was an outgrowth of the St. Louis house.[17] Burlington was in those days one of the most important trading places above St. Louis on the Mississippi; its trade reached into Iowa, which had no chartered banks at the time, and it commanded much of the business of the upper Mississippi.

One house of the Clark group which is interesting out of proportion to its significance was Clark's Exchange Bank of Springfield, Illinois, which was started in 1852. This was the Clarks' only chartered bank and was probably organized for the purpose of securing a legal note-issuing bank for the group.[18] The capital was nominally $100,000 at first and later half a million, but the law of 1851 did not require the actual paying in of the capital subscribed.[19] Conditions seemed favorable to this concern; it was one of the first banks chartered in Illinois after the enactment of the free banking law of 1851, and its local incorporator, N. H. Ridgely, had been chief clerk of the St. Louis branch of the Bank of the United States and cashier of the principal office of the State Bank of Illinois from 1835 until 1848, after which he had served as the trustee of the bank.[20]

Jay Cooke's position with the Clarks grew in importance with the expansion of their organization and business. In January, 1843, then twenty-one years of age, he became a partner in the Philadelphia house, E. W. Clark & Co.[21] He was given a one-eighth share in the profits of the firm, this share being taken from Enoch Clark's two-thirds. In view of the fact that young Cooke made no contribution of capital, his membership in the firm was clearly in recognition of his ability. As new houses were organized, new partners were taken in to serve as resident managers of the individual houses. By virtue of his membership in the Philadelphia firm, the leading house in the group, Jay Cooke, either as an individual or through the joint interest of E. W. Clark & Co., also acquired an interest in the other houses, that is, in all the Clark houses except that at Boston, which like the Philadelphia house remained independent.

Thus, it is seen, Jay Cooke became an integral part of a large organization which established itself in American business at several strategic points. The Clarks were in a position to connect the commerce and wealth of three leading centers, that is, Boston, Philadelphia, and New York, with widespread trade and investment opportunities, particularly in the newer West. The advantages of their branch system were very real in view of the condition of banking, currency, and domestic exchange in the United States.

THE CLARKS' COMMERCIAL BANKING

In the existing records of the Clark houses little is revealed of the personalities and activities of the members of the firms or of others connected with them. This is not unusual, for business records are almost always singularly impersonal. From Jay Cooke's Memoirs and other sources, however, something can be gleaned about the young banker's life, particularly outside of business. In 1844, after an ardent courtship by post, Jay Cooke and Dorothea Elizabeth Allen were married. They took a suite at the Congress Hall Hotel, where they lived for several years. Jay, Jr., was born in 1845 and seven other children by 1857, three of whom died in infancy.[22] So the young banker came to be a man of family. His affectionate nature found a focusing point in a home which both gave him much and required much of him; and his youthful enthusiasm for business became merged into a more mature attitude based on a realization of greater needs and heavier responsibilities.

Marriage brought a change in Jay Cooke's church affiliation which may have been of some significance to his business. The Cookes joined an Episcopal church. This change in Jay Cooke's church membership clearly came neither from any ulterior motive nor from any consideration of dogma or creed but just as a matter of convenience, as so often happens. Membership in this denomination, however, became an important factor in the banker's life; it gave him contacts with certain men who were of consequence in business, and it was within his church group that he made his closest friends and won some of his most devoted supporters.

Unfortunately, we know little about Jay Cooke's work as an individual in his early years as a partner in the Clark houses. We can visualize it in part, however, from a picture which can be drawn of the business of the Clarks. Even if full information were available on Cooke's work at this stage, there would be some justification for subordinating it to the activities of the Clarks; up to a certain point in his career, the Clark business was important to him principally as a training school and as a means whereby he became acquainted with business men — the work of the Clark firms was the background out of which he later emerged as a leader in American banking. With this in mind, we shall turn from Jay Cooke himself to the work of the Clarks.

Throughout the 'forties and 'fifties the work of the Clarks was principally in domestic exchange; only the Boston Clarks dealt at all in foreign exchange. After the middle 'forties, the Clark houses became one of the largest domestic exchange organizations in the country.[23] Each of their offices became the clearing house for their business in the whole section in which it was located: the Boston house took care of a part of the New England and Canadian business of the other Clark houses; New York covered some of the New England and Canadian business and New York State;

Philadelphia, the middle region; and St. Louis, the West. A very extensive system of correspondents, extending to most points in the Union, supplemented the Clark group. Riggs & Co., merchant-bankers of Washington, were among the most important of these. The Clarks at times sent out traveling agents to make collections, but this was evidently done only for special cases or in times of depression.[24]

The exchange business of the Clarks from 1842 to 1857 consisted of the usual purchase and sale of all kinds of funds on all sections of the United States and Canada. As before, a large part of their work continued to be dealing in bank notes; these they bought and sold or sent home for redemption. They became expert in this line of business. The Boston and St. Louis houses periodically issued bank-note guides for determining the value of bank notes.[25] Two numbers of the *Clark's New England Bank Note List* are in the Harvard College Library; each is a pamphlet sixteen pages in length which names the various note issues of the banks in every State and gives their current value.[26] *Clark's Moneytype*, a pamphlet containing descriptions and many facsimiles of the currency listed, is said to have been the only guide to "wild-cat currency" published in St. Louis.[27] The Clarks also did a considerable business in the handling of business paper used in the transfer of funds. They sold drafts "in sums to suit purchasers" and handled drafts, acceptances, and certificates of deposit on banks from all sections of the country. Personal checks had not yet come to figure in this part of their business. The Clarks also did a great deal of collecting on drafts and promissory notes. Indeed, they advertised regularly that they made collections on all accessible points in the United States and Canada "on the best terms, and with despatch." When they ran short of funds on a city or a section, they would advertise that funds on such places were wanted; and the reverse if they had a supply on hand.

Something of the way in which their work in domestic exchange was carried on in those days may be seen from the relations of the Philadelphia and New York Clarks with Corcoran & Riggs, of Washington, from 1845 to 1847.[28] Those two Clark houses and the Riggses made collections on personal notes and drafts for each other and took bank notes on their region, charging according to a more or less established scale. Corcoran & Riggs and the Philadelphia Clarks carried accounts for each other and drew on each other; Treasury notes were often used to balance their accounts. The relations of the New York Clarks and the Riggses were different in that they merely acted as agents for each other, their accounts being regularly balanced in New York through deposits in or drafts on the Bank of America.[29]

The two letters below illustrate the way in which the Clarks' exchange business was conducted, in this instance with their correspondents in Washington, D. C.[30]

New York 23ᵈ Feby 1846

MESSRS CORCORAN & RIGGS

GENT

Your favours of 20ᵗʰ & 21ˢᵗ recd with enclosure, Incy dfts on Bk of Amᵃ $734²⁶ & 304⁴¹ Also Banknotes &c as follows

Par	85		
Eastern	211	@ 15 −	31
State	718	@ 5/8-4.49	
Canada	5	@ 3 −	15
Corning cert.	19.80	−	37
Auburn "	49.05	−	63
Genesee "	28	−	37
O. Lee & Co. cert.	49	−	63
Chautaque cert.	19	−	37
Cleveland "	98.10	−2	
	1,281.95	9.32	
	9.32		

$1,272.63 deposited to your cr in Bank of America

Herein for returns

Lewis W I Holmes on Sylvanus Holmes
due 25/28 Feb. ⎫
Accepted ⎰ $731

Yours &c

E W Clark Dodge & Co.

pr J D Maxwell

This letter is especially interesting in that it shows what varied forms the transfer of funds took. The drafts on the Bank of America, of New York, could be cashed by the New York Clarks at their full value. "Par" bank notes were presumably notes of New York City banks which were worth their face value. "Eastern" bank notes were, it is likely, issues of New England banks; I am assuming this from the fact that the New York Clarks handled New England funds and that the exchange charge was only 15 cents on $100. "State" bank notes were apparently notes on banks in New York State outside of the city; they were charged five-eighths of a cent on $1.00. The certificates of deposit were on banks or bankers in New York State. Enclosed in the letter was an acceptance which Corcoran and Riggs were to collect for the Clarks.

The letter below shows another way of balancing accounts. Incidentally, it also reveals a practice of Enoch Clark's firms which had not a little to do with establishing the credit and reputation of his houses.

Phila Nov 3/46

MESSRS CORCORAN & RIGGS

  Gents

    We sent per last mail 1 Coln [collection] We drew today 1000$ favor of Judge G . . . Mallery — & enclose to pay the same,

Treasury notes $950
Bk Potomac 50
———
Yr dt $1000

We are told that Treasury notes are *Cash* in Washington — we send all ours to NY where we use them at par. — but as we drew the above & could not find district funds today we send them to "Head quarters" as we dont like to draw so much without funds.

Yours Truly
E W CLARK & CO

Very little conclusive evidence has been found to indicate to what extent the Clarks carried on their exchange business on commission and how far they actually dealt in exchange on their own account. Their practice varied from time to time and from place to place, but the general trend was clearly in the direction of dealing more and more for themselves. At first they were doing almost exclusively a commission business, handling bank notes and commercial paper as middlemen between merchants, banks, and others, and this they continued to do to some extent.[31] Jay Cooke's Memoirs indicate, however, that by 1840 they were already buying and selling bank notes on their own account. By 1846 they were buying bills of exchange for themselves,[32] which apparently developed into a considerable business; their later advertisements indicate that they were purchasing time as well as sight bills. Promissory notes were apparently not discounted but only handled on commission down to 1857.

The exchange business of the Clarks was, except for its size, typical of the times, and, like many exchange dealers, the brokers were imperceptibly becoming bankers. The Clarks at first generally called themselves brokers, though sometimes they were referred to as bankers, but about the middle 'forties they began to call themselves bankers and their houses, banking houses; by the early 'fifties they were commonly referred to as bankers.[33] If we use as a criterion contemporary ideas of what really constituted a bank, it is difficult to say when they really became bankers, for contemporary ideas were so varied.[34] The function of such a concern was rarely clear cut; the mixture of the broker and banker characterized the large number of business units like the Clark group, and it is difficult to say where one ended and the other began, though it is undoubtedly correct to say that most brokers were doing some banking and private bankers some commission business. One thing is certain, that the Clarks were throughout this period growing more and more in the direction of banking. This was, of course, in general true of so-called exchange brokers. There is no reason to think that the Clarks' designation of themselves as banking houses was not by the middle 'forties justified.

The issue of notes was generally considered a fundamental function of banks at the time. While private (unchartered) banks were generally forbidden by law to issue notes, the Clarks, like

many others, found a way of circumventing the law. They did
this through the issue of their own drafts, which circulated somewhat like bank notes — such drafts had come into common use at
the time when the branches of the second Bank of the United
States issued drafts.[35] The Clark drafts were elaborately en-
graved on bank-note paper in various denominations, usually one,
two, and five dollars. One Clark house drew the draft on another
Clark house, payable at sight to a specific individual or order, and
possibly a third Clark house put it into circulation. A common
draft was signed by E. W. Clark & Co., of Philadelphia, drawn on
E. W. Clark, Brothers & Co. of Burlington, and issued by E. W.
Clark & Brothers of St. Louis. Owing to the high credit of the
Clarks and the dearth of specie and reliable bank currency and to
the fact that Burlington was somewhat off the main lines of trade,
such Clark drafts, issued in large amounts, circulated freely
throughout parts of the West.[36] It has been said that the Clark
drafts and the currency of George Smith of Milwaukee and
Chicago constituted at one time a large portion of the currency of
parts of Illinois and its neighbors to the north and west.[37] Their
general acceptance was due to the soundness of the men behind
them — one would have to search long to find a better banker
than George Smith, the Scottish banker who became such a power
in the West, and Enoch W. Clark was of the same calibre. The
issue of such drafts was very profitable, for little capital was
needed to keep a large amount in circulation, and they often remained in circulation a considerable time before they were presented for payment.

Both law and public opinion were, however, against the issue of
circulating paper by individuals or concerns which were not under
some public regulation. The trend was toward the elimination of
private paper in favor of notes issued by banks under State regulation. It was no doubt because of this trend that Clark's Exchange Bank of Springfield (Illinois) was established; the time
had come when it was desirable — both because of law and
opinion — to secure a regular means of issuing bank notes. The
Illinois free banking law of 1851 provided that banks established
under this law could issue notes on certain bonds deposited with

the State for security.[38] The Clark's Exchange Bank began with the issue of $250,000 in circulating notes, depositing Illinois and Missouri State bonds with the State treasurer; [39] by October, 1858, the amount issued totaled $352,271, of which $347,571 had been returned for payment.[40] The circulation of the Springfield bank is said not to have been profitable, for the reason that the notes were so soon returned in payment of taxes; collectors throughout the State found it convenient to bring the Clark notes to Springfield, the capital of the State, and to present them for redemption in order to get the gold needed for paying taxes.[41]

Concerning the deposit and discount business of the Clarks, little direct evidence has survived. From the very beginning they must have carried deposits for and made advances to their customers in the exchange business, especially for their correspondents. This type of business increased as their work grew and they accumulated a larger working capital and greater prestige. A local deposit and discount business no doubt came to the St. Louis Clarks because of inadequate local banking facilities, and by the 'fifties they were, like other private bankers, advertising that they paid interest on deposits.[42] That the deposit business of the Clark houses became considerable is seen from the fact that at the beginning of 1854 the Philadelphia house alone had deposits of almost a million dollars.[43] Their discounting was, probably even more than their deposit business, dependent on their other interests. Certainly it was closely connected with their exchange and commercial banking in general. As will be indicated later, it also went hand in hand with their investment dealing.

E. W. CLARK & CO. IN THE INVESTMENT BUSINESS

THE CLARKS were primarily exchange dealers or commercial bankers from 1837 to 1857, but they also carried on a considerable investment business. This particular combination of work was characteristic of exchange brokers and private bankers at the time. It was that very breadth of interest which made the Clarks and other similar concerns peculiarly well fitted to carry on banking in a rapidly changing business environment. As the investment business developed in the United States, the Clarks came to deal more and more in securities or other long-time investments.

There were interesting developments in the types of securities issued at this time. When E. W. Clark & Co. was first established, the securities on the market were principally government bonds and common stocks of banks, insurance, manufacturing, and transportation concerns, that is, canals and railroads. In the late 'thirties began the multiplication of kinds of securities which reached such a high point in later decades. Two new types appeared which were to become of vast importance: bonds of private enterprises, particularly for financing transportation projects, grew rapidly in importance after about 1839; and stocks with prior dividend rights came to be used in the 'forties as a device for bringing new capital into a concern that was not paying adequate dividends on its existing stock to attract investors.[1]

Trade in securities in the United States had not yet to any considerable extent become a specialized business. It is true that stock brokers had appeared early in the federal period to serve the brisk trade in the bonds of the new United States which had followed upon the introduction of the Hamiltonian System. Out of this business had come in 1792 an informal agreement of brokers which crystallized into the New York Stock and Exchange Board in 1817 and which was followed by similar developments in Philadelphia and Boston. By the time of the organization of the New York exchange a considerable business in stocks had developed, owing to the growth of corporations for carrying on banking, insurance, manufacturing, and transportation; and the late 'twenties and the 'thirties brought a great increase in the securities business. Much of the trading in stocks, however, never reached the broker nor the exchange; it was handled by the merchant, as a part of his trading operation or as an adjunct thereto, by the private exchange banker, or, to a lesser degree, by some chartered banks.

The sale of the original issue of securities was even slower to develop specialization than trade in securities already on the market; it was long carried on by a very diversified and even a hit-or-miss system. Not until the pressure of Civil War needs brought a new organization under the leadership of Jay Cooke did anything like our present-day system for marketing new issues appear in the United States. For his leadership in that crisis, Jay Cooke was prepared by his work with the Clarks.

MARKETING NEW SECURITIES IN THE EARLY 'FORTIES

To understand the Clarks' early work in investments, it is necessary to get a general view of the marketing of new securities in their day. By the 1840's various channels had developed for selling new issues, that is, for collecting capital for new enterprises. A community having sufficient capital to do so, naturally financed some of its own projects. In New England, for instance, banks, insurance companies, textile mills, and in some measure transportation projects sold stocks and bonds locally. This was largely a direct transaction between the promoters and the investors; indeed, the investors were often the promoters. Many textile mills were started by a few individuals, who themselves subscribed for the shares and interested other friends, business associates, or banks in them. William Sturgis, of Boston, who invested for himself, for his firm, and for John P. Cushing, all of whom had accumulated considerable capital in the China trade, is an example of a capitalist who bought local shares around Boston, largely without the use of a middleman.[2]

Investments seeking more than a narrowly local and personal market were forced to rely more or less on middlemen. This was especially true of the West, that region which had great schemes but little capital. The securities sold in the larger market were, primarily, federal and State bonds, the issues of canals and railroads, and also shares of banks and insurance companies. In settled communities some of these, for instance shares of banks and transportation projects, were partly sold directly to local capitalists or banks, who often took them not because of the value of the investment but to aid local enterprise; but transportation projects, like State bonds, reached out through agents to banks, capitalists, brokers, or private bankers in some large business center, generally that with which they had the closest relations. The brokers or private bankers distributed the shares or bonds within their community or to capitalists with whom they were in touch or agencies like themselves in other places. In this way something like a national system of security marketing without any one dominating center was provided. The same Boston Sturgis who was referred to in the preceding paragraph bought stocks and bonds in New York through Prime, Ward & King, thus entering into a larger domestic, though not a centralized, market.

In the late 'twenties and the 'thirties, promotion of new enterprises had gained considerable support from foreign capital. The British and Dutch investors, weary of government loans and encouraged by the high rates offered by American securities, had developed a strong interest in investments in the United States.[3] They had purchased stock of the second Bank of the United States, State bonds, Erie Canal stock, and other transportation securities. Close relations had been built up between American merchant-bankers and foreign bankers who purchased American securities to hold or to distribute among foreign investors.[4] Outstanding among those foreign bankers were the Barings of London, the Hopes of Amsterdam, and the Hottinguers of Paris, who all had one or more American agents or correspondents, and the international Rothschilds who in 1837 had sent their own agent, August Belmont, to New York.[5]

The Bank of the United States of Pennsylvania had for a time given promise of developing a new channel of relationship between American investments and foreign investors in its attempt to use its credit to secure credit from foreign bankers with which to finance new American enterprises based on State credit.[6] A succession of unfortunate events, that is, the panic of 1837, the bursting of Biddle's bubble, and the repudiation of their debts by a number of States, even by rich Pennsylvania, practically destroyed foreign interest in American investments.[7] At the same time a severe depression settled upon Western Europe. So completely did the European market for American securities disappear that an agent of the federal government who went abroad in 1842 to sell a loan reported that his mission was hopeless.[8]

Practically the same thing happened to the market at home. The breaking of the investors' confidence by failures and repudiation, coupled with a continuous fall in prices of goods, real estate, and securities, and fear of what legislation would be enacted, drove out of the market whatever liquid capital had remained. Even in the worst of the depression, money was said to be plentiful in New York City. Notwithstanding this plenteousness of money, reported *Hunt's Merchants' Magazine* in 1842, operations in stocks had been limited, speculation having ceased almost altogether. Bank stocks were no longer a desirable investment, and State bonds had not been in demand, except New York's, while Pennsylvania bonds were nominally forty cents on the dollar in the market.[9]

E. W. CLARK & CO. ENTERS THE INVESTMENT BUSINESS

E. W. Clark & Co. was established to do a stock and exchange business. No evidence exists, however, of its stock business in the early 'forties except advertisements in the *North American and Daily Advertiser*, of Philadelphia, announcing that the Clarks bought and sold State and city bonds on commission. Undoubtedly they shared in the general stagnation in the investment market. In the meantime, as has been seen, their business in domestic exchange grew by leaps and bounds, and the growth of the Clark organization and prestige gave them a strong foothold in both eastern and western business.

Benefiting from the general increase in speculative activity and interest in securities, the Clarks by the middle 'forties were giving considerable attention to the stock business. By 1846 the Philadelphia house was furnishing the daily stock market reports for the *North American and Daily Advertiser*, which it continued to do throughout the 'fifties. The opening of the Clark house in New York gave them a foothold in what was already the most important market for securities in the country. Both the Philadelphia and the New York houses at this time advertised their stock business quite extensively, and both houses bought and sold on the stock board daily on commission.[10]

The first bonds of any importance sold by the Clarks of Philadelphia, recalled by Jay Cooke in his Memoirs, were those issued by Texas before its annexation by the United States. Many of the officials of the United States, said he, purchased of these securities, no doubt fully aware of the fact that their value would be enhanced by annexation; and he believed that on the question of the annexation of Texas "the opposition from the North was undoubtedly overcome through the cohesive power of public plunder."

In the meantime the Clarks were placing themselves in a position which enabled them to profit from the war which was later to come with Mexico, in the bringing on of which Texas had its part. In 1845, we find E. W. Clark & Co. writing thus to its Washington correspondents, Corcoran & Riggs:[11]

Our object in writing now, is to ascertain if something cannot be done to our mutual advantage in placing funds to the credit of the Govt in St. Louis at this time or thro the Spring & Summer. We understand that the Govt are Constantly placing large sums in St Louis & that they make their remittances in cks upon the eastern cities.

We presume you can manage to get hold of these operations & if so we have no doubt they would prove profitable. Please make the necessary inquiries and let us know.

The war with Mexico gave the Clarks — as wars had given so many bankers at other times — their first great opportunity in the business of selling government securities. They participated with Corcoran & Riggs, of Washington, in selling two war loans.[12] The Washington firm bid for the whole issue of $18,000,000 of Treasury notes in 1847 and was awarded about $14,000,000 on its bid of one-eighth of one per cent above par, the Clarks being the principal participants with the Riggses in this bid. Of the 1848 loan, one of almost $16,000,000, the Clark house of St. Louis was awarded close to a million and Corcoran & Riggs almost $15,000,000, in which the Clarks also shared.[13]

The nature of the participation of Jay Cooke's firms in these loans was not unlike Girard's part in the loans of the War of 1812. The Clarks bid for a certain amount at a certain price and took upon themselves the responsibility of meeting the bid. In the case of the bid of E. W. Clark & Brothers they acted independently; in the other bids the Clarks, Barings, and others were associated with Corcoran & Riggs.[14] The association was merely in purchasing, however, and there is no indication that there was joint responsibility for selling or joint management of the sale of the securities.

In contrast with Jay Cooke's later management of the sale of Civil War loans, it is interesting to note the way in which these bonds were sold. Because of the long waiting of capitalists and bankers for reliable investments after the lean years of the early 'forties, there was no difficulty in finding a market and the bonds were disposed of directly to banks and individual customers of the purchasing houses.[15] This explains why the loan did not seek the small investors, as the Civil War loans were later forced to do.

The bonds were sold at a sufficient premium above what the bankers paid the government to make the undertaking worth while. One gathers from Jay Cooke's Memoirs, however, that that was only a small part of the gain made from the transaction;

the Clark houses were able so to manage their handling of the loan that they also made a considerable profit from the transfer of the funds.

Legal technicalities and the miserable state of domestic exchange gave the Clarks an excellent opportunity. The secretary of the Treasury advertised that the money received from the sale of the loan could be deposited in any of the subtreasuries of the United States.[16] The St. Louis Clarks sold exchange on Philadelphia and New York at a 2 to $3\frac{1}{2}$ per cent premium, drawn against funds held by their eastern houses derived from the sale of government bonds; they deposited the funds collected from the exchange operation to the account of the government in the St. Louis subtreasury. Since it took the mails ten to fifteen days to carry the drafts to the eastern city, the Clarks in the East had the use of the money in the meantime. Thus in addition to the profit on selling the loan, they made a handsome gain in the form of the exchange charge and interest.

The result of the operation left the government's money in St. Louis, but it was needed in the East. How could it be transferred without transgressing the Independent Treasury Act, which provided for the deposit of federal funds in subtreasuries of the United States which had no facilities for the transfer of funds? E. W. Clark & Co. and Corcoran & Riggs arranged with the secretary of the Treasury a way of transferring the money to the East which the bankers so designed as to enable themselves to make further profit from the loan. Under this plan, the Clarks drew up a bond, had it certified by the United States judge in Philadelphia, by the collector of the port, or the director of the mint, testifying to the fact that they were good for the amount stated. This bond was then mailed to Washington and in return the Clarks received a subtreasury draft on some southern or western point, stating that at a given time, generally in four months, the sum stated, that is, $200,000 or $500,000 or so at a time, was to be deposited in the United States subtreasury at New York or Philadelphia. Now, said Jay Cooke, when it is considered that at certain seasons of the year 60-day bills on good northern houses given in the South in payment for southern produce could be purchased in southern cities at 3 to 4 per cent discount and were promptly disposed of at 6 to 8 per cent per annum discount, when it took only a few days to get returns on these, it is seen how favorable the subtreasury system was to the Clarks. By using the money safely, they netted 5 to 7 per cent on each transaction without the slightest risk. Secretary Walker tried to get around this by stipulating in the next call for bids for government loans that the money had to be deposited in the subtreasury nearest the home of the bidder. "But lo!" says Jay Cooke in his Memoirs, "when the bids were opened one share was allotted to the firm of E. W. Clark & Bros of St Louis Mo," in which city was located one of the subtreasuries. As a result they were able to profit in this loan, also, from exchange operations between the East and the West.

This episode shows that the American practice of taking every advantage possible of the government in matters of finance has a long ancestry. We could hardly expect the Clarks to have had any enthusiasm for the issues at stake in the war with Mexico, but we might have expected them, nevertheless, to show some restraint in taking advantage of the government. To the bankers this was, however, like any other business transaction, and in an age of strong individualism and an undeveloped code of business ethics it could have only one result. In the last analysis it was one of the costs of a rapidly developing country, which had turned thumbs down on the second Bank of the United States, a bank which had gone far to provide a splendid system for conducting domestic exchange.

Through war finance the Clarks secured a working capital and some experience in the marketing of investments. This is the old, old story of what wars do to business; serving a government's wartime needs has laid the basis for many a fortune and many a reputation.

In the years 1848 to 1857 the Clarks did a considerable investment business. This development in their work was the result of two things: (1) the increase in the prestige and capital of the Clarks, and (2) the tremendous increase in investment opportunities and in the demand for investments. The latter was of great significance. In those years, particularly around 1850, there was something of a revival of the European demand for American securities and an increase in the granting of mercantile credit by the British,[17] both of which affected the American investment market. Europe was still, however, wary of American investments, and she was, moreover, largely occupied at home with the construction of railroads and the establishment of banks.[18] Within the United States there appeared a veritable mania for buying securities and land. In the late 'forties there was a considerable expansion in bank credit. The discovery of gold in California, and a few years later in Australia, led to the pouring of the precious metal into Europe and America, which dramatically speeded up business. News of Sutter's gold reached the East in the summer of 1848. By 1849 the California fever was raging and the influx of gold was already having its effect on prices and speculation.[19] In 1849 the commodity price level, which since the low point of 1843 had risen several times only to fall again, turned definitely upward. About the same time there was a marked acceleration in the rise of railroad stock prices, which had been going up slightly for several years.[20] The result of all this was such an interest in speculative investments as the country had never before known.

There were in the late 'forties and 'fifties several popular fields for investment in the United States. One was industry in the East, which was taking considerable capital but was largely financed locally, especially in New England, and with little recourse to middlemen. Another was railroads; the great era of railroad construction was just getting under way, and railroad securities, or State and municipal bonds for aiding railway construction, were becoming increasingly important on the market. The third inviting investment field was western lands. The Clarks dealt in all three of these, in railroads, municipal and State bonds, and lands.

SELLING MUNICIPAL, STATE, AND RAILROAD SECURITIES

In the selling of municipal and railroad loans the Clarks reached out through the press to a wider market. Their first striking effort of this kind was their handling of the bonds of the city of St. Louis, Missouri. From early in 1850 throughout 1851 those bonds were advertised almost daily, various amounts being offered at different rates of interest for different issues.[21] The type of appeal used is illustrated by an advertisement which appeared in the *North American and United States Gazette*, of Philadelphia, through the last half of 1851:

$50,000 Saint Louis Bonds — The subscribers offer to those who are seeking good & safe investments, the six per cent twenty year bonds of the city of Saint Louis, payable principal and semi-annual interest, at Phoenix Bank, of New York. We consider them as safe an investment as Government or State Loans, & they can be had at a price which will yield a much greater income.

The city of Saint Louis is in a most flourishing condition, & always meets her engagements promptly. The revenues of the city for the present year will exceed half a million of dollars, & by the special clause in the city charter the interest on the bonded debt must be paid first before appropriations are made for other objects. The debt of the city will not exceed one and a half millions of dollars at the end of the year, & her means, in her corporate capacity, as assessed by the Auditor, consisting of wharves, stores, water works, lands etc. exceed two & one quarter millions of dollars.

Full particulars will be furnished, & documents, showing the present position of the city's finances, can be examined by calling at our office.

June 13–1851   E. W. Clark & Co. 25 S. Third st.

This was a time when municipal and State bonds were much in evidence in the investment market. Besides the St. Louis bonds, the Clarks also sold bonds of the States of Illinois and Missouri and of the municipalities of Quincy (Illinois) and Keokuk and Burlington (Iowa),[22] which were issued mostly in aid of projected railroads and were sold on commission.

E. W. Clark & Co. also gave considerable aid to railroads in Philadelphia's immediate hinterland. From 1854 to 1857 it sold large amounts of bonds for Allegheny County to aid in the building of the bridge over the Allegheny River by the Pittsburgh & Connellsville Railroad, which is now a part of the Pennsylvania.[23]

According to Jay Cooke's Memoirs, E. W. Clark & Co. also sold bonds for the Pennsylvania, which by the end of 1854 provided a through line from Philadelphia to Pittsburgh; [24] for the Pittsburgh, Fort Wayne, and Chicago, a consolidation of roads which by 1858 reached from Pittsburgh to Chicago and later became a part of the Pennsylvania Railroad; [25] the Philadelphia and Reading, a road going into the coal region northwest of Philadelphia; [26] the Chartiers Valley in southwestern Pennsylvania; [27] and for the Northern Central, a line from Baltimore to Harrisburg (Pennsylvania) and northward.[28] For those roads the Clarks sold bonds on commission, but for one local road they assumed greater responsibility; E. W. Clark & Co. served as the bank of the Sunbury & Erie, sold its bonds on commission, and also purchased Philadelphia city bonds issued in its aid to the extent of $117,000.[29] This connection illustrates the prevailing tendency for the young railroads to ally themselves with a certain bank or banker.

The Clarks also participated in financing two roads outside of Pennsylvania. One was the Vermont Central, of which we shall hear more later. The other was a Missouri road, presumably the Atlantic & Pacific, aided by the issue of Missouri State bonds and bonds of the city and county of St. Louis.[30] In the spring of 1856 the St. Louis Clarks sold $1,700,000 of "Pacific Railroad" bonds, $750,000 in New York and the rest in the West, mostly to Illinois banks; they held $150,000 of these for the Grayville (Illinois) Bank, which was closely associated with the Clark group, and $250,000 they took for themselves at an average cost of 90 per cent. From these transactions they made a good net profit.[31]

In their work as investment middlemen, the Clarks in those later years advanced far beyond their early position as mere stock brokers. They continued to deal mostly on commission but they also became risk bearers. They subscribed for considerable amounts of the Mexican War loans and from time to time they, themselves, invested a considerable capital of their own in new bond issues. They also entered the business of serving as bankers for railroads. They were well on the way to become investment bankers.

THE CLARKS AND JAY COOKE INVEST
IN WESTERN LANDS

Like eastern bankers and capitalists in general, Jay Cooke and the Clarks participated in the western land business. A strong speculative movement in land arose in the United States in the late 'forties and raged until it was stopped by the panic of 1857. Settlers, land dealers, promoters, politicians, and eastern capitalists were again, as so often before, charmed by the Lorelei — but not always a fatal Lorelei — of the West. Large amounts of soldiers' land warrants — a bonus granted to veterans by various acts of Congress [32] — were put on the market by soldiers who received claims to 160 acres but did not wish to go to the West.[33] Bankers and capitalists, as individuals or in companies, purchased warrants, either to hold them for a rise or to secure title to land and thus gain from a rise in land prices. In 1848 E. W. Clark, Dodge & Co., of New York, in 1849 J. W. Clark & Co., of Boston, and in 1850 E. W. Clark & Co., of Philadelphia, began to advertise that they bought and sold land warrants at highest prices.[34]

By means of land warrants and direct purchase of land, the Clarks acquired considerable land both as individuals and firms. One profitable tract, obtained by Enoch Clark in settlement of a debt, was in the heart of Chicago.[35] In the 'fifties a great deal of land was also held in and about Galena, Illinois,[36] some on joint account for E. W. Clark & Co., of Philadelphia, and E. W. Clark & Brothers, of St. Louis.[37]

One particular land venture is especially interesting. A number of the Clark partners, including Jay Cooke, entered into a joint-account venture with Anthony J. Drexel and other Pennsylvania business men for the purchase of western lands mainly through warrants. Pitt Cooke, Jay's older brother who had for some time been engaged in the real estate business in Sandusky, was hired to select the lands and make the necessary business and legal transactions. He spent most of 1855 to 1857 in the West, where with the assistance of Rice Harper of Sandusky and W. J. Barney, a real estate dealer of Dubuque, Iowa, he selected tens of thousands of acres at a time. He worked mainly in and around Fort Dodge and Decorah, Iowa, though he also bought some land on individual accounts in Wisconsin, Minnesota, and Missouri.[38] It was no easy matter to select the best land on those endless prairies, but it was even more difficult to secure title to them. At one time in 1856 Pitt Cooke got 3,280 acres when "400 or 500 thousand acres of warrants [were] in hands of greedy land agents, Settlers Speculators & Every One else" and all were trying to get a slice of the 47,000 acres available. Wrote Pitt to Jay on one occasion, "I got every one of my Entries just as I wanted them while 100s did not [get] an acre, but keep this quiet. It was all done by paying something for it." [39] After the land was obtained, there was the further task of securing the location of county seats and railroads in places advantageous to one's land.[40] But so promising were the prospects that Pitt Cooke and his brother-in-law, William Moorhead, played with the idea of forming a colonization company to sell land to prospective emigrants in Germany.[41]

The joint-account lands were divided in 1856 but Pitt Cooke continued to buy on individual accounts.[42] Some of the lands could have been sold at a good profit before the panic of 1857.[43] Jay Cooke, however, kept a lot of his purchases. How extensive his land holdings were may be suggested by the fact that in 1860 he paid taxes on 4,742 acres of Iowa's rich land, 996 acres in southern Minnesota, 1,520 in Wisconsin, and 480 in Missouri.[44]

Thus Jay Cooke acquired a direct interest in the upper Mississippi country which probably influenced his later activities. Pitt Cooke's enthusiasm for the prairie region no doubt also increased his interest in the West. Who could resist the intriguing lure of the land where Pitt Cooke saw "the rolling, beautifully undulating prairie, rich in soil in bright flowers, & luxurious grass waving in the mild western breeze," and where "every little way a laughing pebble bottomed brook comes dancing down between the rolling swells of the prairies & ever & anon in the distance groves of timber dot the magnificent view?"[45] That was virgin Iowa as Pitt Cooke saw it.

Another West was also beckoning to Jay Cooke and the Clarks in the 'fifties: rich, romantic California, the grave of many hopes but also the land of fortune. It would have been strange if they could have stayed entirely out of that mecca of the gold seeker. In the early 'fifties miners, merchants, and capital were pouring into the San Francisco country. Gold was pouring out. Francis Drexel of Philadelphia, that cosmopolite who was equally at home in many countries and who, perhaps from his extensive experience in foreign business, early saw the importance of the new gold, set up a branch house in San Francisco. The Clarks did not go so far; at first they merely received on consignment shipments of gold dust and nuggets, but later they dealt in gold through an agent in San Francisco,[46] a business which they never developed far. The Clarks' main western interest was in the Upper Mississippi Valley.

Profit and Loss in the 'Fifties

The Clarks shared in the world-wide boom of the early 'fifties. When capital was rushing headlong into new enterprises and trade was growing by leaps and bounds, they were not slow to take advantage of new opportunities for gain. In the five years, 1849–53, the Philadelphia house made net profits of $487,000. In 1853 they made handsome profits, the Philadelphia house netting $170,500 [47] while the four main houses are said to have made a total of half a million.[48] In the same year E. W. Clark & Co., of Philadelphia, celebrated its success by moving into a new four-story brick building.[49]

But as the Clarks participated in the boom, so were they also to participate in the reaction. In July, 1854, money became tight and a panic threatened. This was a logical consequence of the speculative mania for investment in lands, railroads and ships, manufacturing, and even mining which had raged for some time, based on an undue expansion of bank credits and heavy importations of capital. The immediate cause of the difficulty was the discovery of such frauds in the issue of certain stocks as the country had never before seen: the Schuyler frauds in the New York & New Haven, the Kyle frauds in the Harlem, and the Crane frauds in the Vermont Central.[50] The collapse of faith in business morals is always serious; in this case it aroused suspicion of securities of

all kinds, particularly of railroads, and precipitated a panic.
Many business houses fell, and gloom spread over the whole
country. Eleutheros Cooke, fearing the worst, wrote to his son
Jay that if things went wrong they could resort to "sheep culture
in Tennessee." [51]

The weakest point in the Clark system was the Boston house.
Joseph Clark was apparently more of the speculator than were
Enoch Clark and the partners in the other houses,[52] which may
explain the strained feelings between Joseph and Enoch Clark.[53]
The situation reveals the weakness of a business organization in
which responsibility is shared without a corresponding sharing of
control. The Philadelphia and New York houses had to help the
Boston firm; the New Yorkers felt bitter that the Bostonians should
have gotten in so deeply and hoped it would be a lesson to them.[54]

According to a letter of Jay Cooke, the Philadelphia house
prospered in spite of difficulties and was in a sound condition at
the time of the panic: [55]

We use our money at $1\frac{1}{2}$ to 3 per cent. per month from day to day
and frequently it pays 1/8 to 1/4 a day. We have done a noble business
since 1st of January; profits up to 1st July $135,000. This storm has
not resulted in any direct loss — but some of our big customers we
have to let off and extend for and help out, or else break them and kill
the goose that lays the golden egg. We have about 400,000 in this
shape, all abundantly secured, we think, and paying good interest, and
then about 400,000 cash funds and 200,000, or thereabouts, in paper
and short loans, besides lots of bank stock, Morris Canal prefd., and
bonds and other investments. Our bills payable and demand loans are
lower than usual and but little of it at all likely to be called in; and if it
is called in, we have such securities as Philadelphia City 6s, pledged
with the parties upon which we can get loans readily elsewhere.

In this letter Jay Cooke, the banker, comes clearly into view.
We see something of his spirit and of his business principles and
motives. He regarded the experience of 1854 as a serious warning
and advised that his firm liquefy its assets and give more attention to safety than to high profits:

We must all feel grateful that we have escaped in this terrific storm;
it has been the hardest I have ever known and I have felt very anxious

and have an unusual strain on my mind. . . . We must all snug up, work out of debt and then our minds will be relieved of a vast burden. We can all make money as fast as it is good for us by a regular legitimate business; in fact, I for one don't care to be worth more than I now am, although I think it would be folly to leave the business, and especially such a business as ours, and where all is so pleasant.

It is interesting to see how closely Jay Cooke's ideas on the situation corresponded to those of Enoch Clark. The senior partner, who was then in Europe, sent his advice home: "I hope you are acting on safe principle. Keep snug and do not try to do a large business. You can make money enough by being moderate and carrying easy sail." [56] To keep snug and carry easy sail was undoubtedly a safe principle but one may wonder whether any leadership could have kept so scattered an organization with so many partners to a conservative policy at a time when speculative profits were so high.

By the middle 'fifties Jay Cooke had become the leading member of the Philadelphia Clark house. Enoch Clark, who had for years been the dominant figure in the group, was forced by illness to withdraw from active participation in the work of the firm though he remained a partner until his death in 1856.[57] Two of his sons had by then become partners, Edward W. in 1849 [58] and Clarence H. in 1854,[59] but they were still too young to assume leadership in the larger firm matters. As senior member of the Philadelphia partnership, Jay Cooke came to be the most important figure in the whole Clark group. His leadership was based not only on seniority but was granted to a considerable measure because of personality and ability. From the letters exchanged by the partners it appears that they liked Jay Cooke and regarded his opinions highly. It fell upon him to try to co-ordinate the business of the different Clark houses, which was no easy task. When the houses had been doing a commission business, co-ordination had not been so vital, but it was a different matter when the Clarks entered upon the type of business where the commitments of one house could tie up the capital of all the houses. It was difficult if not impossible to bring about co-operation in such a loose organization as the Clark system

of chain or branch banks and to reconcile the necessarily conflicting interests and diverse ambitions of the various houses.
Needless to say, these were not always reconciled, which was
one reason for the difficulties of the Clarks in 1857. Herein we
see an adumbration of the situation in which Jay Cooke & Co.
played a dominant rôle in 1873.

In the years 1855 to 1857 the Clarks again rode the crest of
business revival and boom. They made high profits but they were
enjoying an ill-founded prosperity and were not unaware of the
danger.[60] When the storm finally broke in the fall of 1857, they,
like many other firms, were gravely involved. They had notes
and drafts outstanding; they carried extensive demand deposits
on which interest was paid,[61] as was already customary among
private banks; they used call loans in financing their business
from day to day; and they, like the Allens under similar conditions
in 1837, had invested heavily on their own account in securities
which would be of little help in the event of a panic.

The panic came in September, 1857, and the Clarks found
themselves in a tight place. Their situation is described in a letter sent by Edward Clark from New York to Jay Cooke in Philadelphia: "They are having the same sort of fun here as we had in
Phil\a last week. Money is *not tight* — it is *not to be had at all.* No
money, no confidence & value to anything. A week more of such
times and the Bks will fail — our position is precarious only because the money market [is] in this State." [62] The St. Louis house
was in great trouble. The panic struck the West with extreme
severity. The head of the house wrote: "Many, if not all who
have money on deposit with us are in great need. . . . We have a
large indebtedness, cash & maturing, to meet, and I dont know
how it is to be done: in fact I *am not equal* to *this* occasion, and I
cannot keep up *courage.*" [63] A close observer of the business of the
Clarks revealed a serious weakness of the firm: "It has all along
seemed to me utterly impossible for your house, in all its branches,
extended as I have known it to be on securities constantly diminishing in value and on which no money could be raised, to sustain
itself amidst the almost universal crash of banks and financial and
commercial houses." [64]

Jay Cooke probably did not have a clear memory of the financial aspects of the panic of 1837, but a tight money market, heavy indebtedness, and securities which could not be turned were the things the Clarks, like most other financial houses at the time, had to face in the panic of 1857 as their fathers had done in 1837. The general American situation was in some respects similar to that prevailing in 1837; there had been in both instances undue expansion of credit, by an unstable banking system, for investments in projects which could not be productive for a long time. There were, however, some elements in the later situation which were not so evident in the earlier panic: the American money market was affected by a boom in England and on the Continent, taking the form, particularly, of the establishment of banks and the building of railroads, which called home capital invested in America; moreover, the situation in the United States was complicated by the fact that, while the money market of the country had come to be concentrated in New York, the banks of that city had not kept their reserves sufficiently liquid to meet unusual demands.[65] Many of the banks in New York paid interest on deposits, which practice forced them to let their money out on call for stock market operations; when large demands were suddenly made by their depositors and they called their loans, the stock market was thrown into a panic and loans could not be collected, that is, the reserves were unavailable. Then followed a tight money market and suspensions. In the fall of 1857 there was a general suspension of banks throughout the country;[66] only some places in the South were provident or fortunate enough to be able to withstand suspension and escape devastating deflation.

The Clark houses were unable to hold up under the strain. The immediate cause of their suspension was the Boston house.[67] J. W. Clark & Co. had contracted to sell a large issue of bonds for the State of Missouri and in the course of the negotiations it had borrowed heavily with the bonds as security. When the loans were called, the firm could not respond and was forced to suspend.[68] On October 3, the Boston house and E. W. Clark, Dodge & Co., of New York, suspended, and on October 5, E. W. Clark &

Brothers, of St. Louis.[69] The Philadelphia partnership was dissolved on October 13 with a view to reorganization.[70]

The Clark system of banks was permanently broken. For this the panic cannot altogether be blamed, for it is quite possible that the fundamental reason for their dissolution was the difficulty of managing a group of houses so loosely strung together. As long as the business of such a group was primarily done on commission it was not so difficult to handle; but, when it involved loans or investments which tied up capital, the problem of control came to be extremely important. One house might well absorb the capital of all, while the others were powerless to prevent it. The problem was not unlike that with which Nicholas Biddle had unsuccessfully struggled. It is the story, old in the history of banking in the United States, of the dominance of the local as opposed to the general interests.

The Clark system of banks was never restored. The business of the Burlington branch was transferred to St. Louis,[71] and the Clarks withdrew from the Springfield bank, which was reorganized by N. H. Ridgely.[72] The failure of the Boston, New York, and St. Louis firms brought heavy losses to their partners — something of the extent of their business may be seen from the fact that the New York Clark house had liabilities of over half a million.[73] These three firms were all reorganized by the local partners, and the chain or branch feature of the Clark organization disappeared.

Jay Cooke did not join in the reorganization of E. W. Clark & Co. The occasion for his retiring from the banking firm with which he had so long been associated was the panic, but it is probable that he would in any event have taken the step eventually. The settlement of the estate of Enoch W. Clark would necessarily have brought a reorganization. And though a strong personal friendship and regard existed between Cooke and his partners — tangible evidence of which was the fact that Jay Cooke had charge of the settlement of the estate of Enoch W. Clark, which Pitt Cooke regarded as an honored position given by one who was "your friend as far as man can be friend" [74] — it is reasonable to suppose that so able a man as Jay Cooke had proved himself to be and one with so commanding a personality would not long be satisfied short of occupying a dominant position where he would have almost complete independence. Leaving the Clark firm was the first step in that direction, and by 1857 he was ready for that step from the point of view both of banking experience and of capital.

THE BANKER TURNS TO TRANSPORTATION
1858–1860

IN 1858 to 1860 Jay Cooke did what so many business men and companies, by necessity or from choice, do after a severe business disturbance. They lie low for a while, conserving their resources as best they may and looking for new work if definitely out of the old; when something in the way of stability has returned and business is really going forward, they take up their work again, often strengthened by what their enforced rest has brought them in the way of readjustment or of conservation of their resources. Jay Cooke could have had no intention to retire from business, which had proved so rich and satisfying for him, while still in his thirties. But there was no point in establishing a new bank before he had settled his old firm affairs and while business was still seriously disturbed. As a consequence, he remained for three years on what he called "free foot." The freedom of those years, he said in his Memoirs, gave him much needed rest and recreation. But he was not idle. In that time he entered upon a kind of work which was to have an important bearing on his later career as the most daring railroad financier in the United States. The short interlude of three years was to be in the way of preparation for the strenuous years that were to come.

READJUSTMENT AFTER THE PANIC

Panics have a way of juggling persons and property. Like wars they upset the traditional pattern of business principles and practices and bring about a general levelling of the business structure, out of which eventually rise new business ideas, new institutions, and often a new leadership. The panic of 1857 left its mark. The business organization, largely jerry-built in the boom of the late 'forties and the 'fifties, was severely damaged and many financial and mercantile firms disappeared; railroads and canals were crippled by the fall in traffic and the deflation of the speculative movement behind them; the newer West, the Mecca of the home-seeker and the land speculator, was left almost prostrate.

The panic not only helped break Jay Cooke's relationship with the Clarks but it also destroyed much of his property. The assets of the St. Louis and Philadelphia Clark houses shrank consider-ably in the liquidation, but the big loss came from the failure of the New York house. Cooke's conduct in the settlement of the obligations of his firms was commendable. His brother Pitt criticized him severely for being so magnanimous in turning his property over to the partnership and reminded him of one of his partners who had deeded some property to his wife; [1] his father likewise reprimanded him, urging that many Scripture passages say the curse of heaven is on the man who neglects his family.[2] This generosity reveals a quality in Jay Cooke's character which no doubt had much to do with his business success. But after all had been settled, Jay Cooke still had what he later called a "fair fortune." [3]

During the half year following the suspension of the Clark houses, Jay Cooke was busy helping to settle their affairs and also acting as chief executor of the estate of Enoch W. Clark. This work gave him time to take stock of the business possibilities about him. There was, immediately after suspension, some talk of his returning to Sandusky, but it is doubtful that he ever seri-ously contemplated leaving Philadelphia, though he might well have wished himself back in quiet Sandusky on Lake Erie. He was obviously too deeply rooted in Philadelphia and its environs to leave. One of his strongest business assets was his wide ac-quaintance with bankers in Philadelphia and its hinterland. Other considerations also bound Jay Cooke to the Quaker City, par-ticularly his friends and his church associations. He had become active in the Sunday school movement, which was then receiving much support from business and professional men; besides his work in his own church, he sent magic lanterns and books to help the less fortunate Sunday schools throughout Pennsylvania.

While panics take away, they also give. Jay Cooke was one of those fortunate individuals who can wrest profits out of a depression. As the smoke cleared after the panic, new opportunities rose out of the ruins. The result was that from 1858 until the end of 1860 he undertook to reorganize and rebuild transportation concerns which had all but been destroyed by the panic. Transportation was not wholly a new field to him, for the Clarks had bought and sold the stocks of many projects. But they were bankers of the passive kind who furnished the capital and then considered their work done. In this they were typical of their time, for bankers in the United States before 1857 were not often concerned in the promotion and management of the enterprises they financed. There had been instances of banker participation in the management of business concerns—note the Baltimore & Ohio in which Brown Brothers had been active; but the rule was for banking houses to be go-betweens for the capitalist and the enterprise seeking capital. The banker as promoter and manager was still of the future.

The passive position of the banker at this time in the United States makes an interesting contrast with the active participation of European financial institutions in the development, particularly, of transportation. On the Continent a movement had gotten strong headway for mobilizing and creating credit for promoting industry and transportation. The Brothers Pereire, led by St. Simonian teachings to vision a great society built on engineering and business, in 1852 founded a remarkable credit institution, the *Crédit Mobilier Français*. This concern, organized as a joint-stock company, was designed to promote new enterprises. It invested its own means and its deposits in securities or in organizing subsidiary companies, and it made short-time loans. It also negotiated the sale of new issues and served as a bank of issue. In the first year of its existence, the *Crédit Mobilier* managed the sale of the French Crimean War loan of 250,000,000 francs and marketed the bonds of the South, East, and Grand Central railroad companies and of the *Crédit Foncier*, besides granting extensive loans. It became active in the promotion of companies, not only in France but also in Austria, Russia, and other countries, particularly in the field of transportation. Its operations continued to be extensive for several years and its profits high.[4]

In Germany a number of similar institutions sprang up. We shall note only the *Bank für Handel und Industrie*, or the *Darmstädter Bank* as it was popularly called, which was founded in 1853. Like other similar institutions at the time, this bank was patterned after the *Crédit Mobilier*. The *Darmstädter Bank* effectively cultivated the public loan business and took an important part in the promotion of German industry and transportation. It invested its own or its depositors' means, formed syndicates, or otherwise aided in floating new security issues. It founded a number of concerns in the ownership and management of which it continued to participate.[5]

The *Crédit Mobilier* idea was slow to gain support in London, where the banking tradition made the banker the passive agent in the movement of capital.[6] Individual bankers became promoters, it is true, but not as representatives of their banks; the great mercantile or private banking houses invested in company securities, but on the whole they left promotion to others.

In the 'fifties American practice was following English tradition, in its own small way of course. America knew neither the syndicate nor the banker-promoter of the Continent. But the time was to come when Continental methods were to invade the United States. Jay Cooke was to play a leading rôle in introducing the active banker into American business.

Jay Cooke's work in transportation in the 'fifties provided a necessary prologue to his later work. It gave him experience in railroad promotion and construction and insight into railroad finance. Equally important for the purposes of this story is the picture which it gives of the problems of financing railroad construction in the 'fifties, which forms an excellent background against which to see later problems and developments.

An Introduction to Railroad Construction and Finance

The old observation, that a man is molded by his associations, has nowhere greater significance than in business. In the 'fifties, when business was still eminently personal, a business man to a considerable extent built his success on personal contacts and friendships. It was through his brother-in-law, William Moorhead, that Jay Cooke came into close contact with transportation in Pennsylvania. It is recalled that he had come to Philadelphia in 1838 to work for the Washington Packet & Transportation Company with which his brother-in-law was connected. After the failure of this concern, Moorhead had for a time been consul at Valparaiso and had been engaged in the business of supplying California with flour in the booming gold days, a venture which had netted good profits; but most of his time had been spent in furthering transportation projects in Pennsylvania.[7]

There were two Moorhead brothers active in business in Pennsylvania besides Cooke's brother-in-law. J. K. Moorhead, trained to be a tanner, had since 1827, when he became contractor for construction on the Susquehanna Division of the Pennsylvania Canal, participated in the building and management of canals, telegraph companies, and railroads in his State. He was also a power in politics, holding several public offices before he was sent to Congress by the new Republican Party in the late 'fifties.[8] J. B. Moorhead had his hands in two of Pennsylvania's most important interests, that is, transportation and iron manufacture. It was he who later brought Jay Cooke into the iron business.

The Moorheads had been canal men but, as the railroad grew in importance, they forsook the old work for the new. They became the construction engineers and in a very real sense the promoters of the Sunbury & Erie Railroad, which is today a part of the Philadelphia & Erie.

The Sunbury & Erie, chartered by Pennsylvania in 1837 to help Philadelphia compete with New York for the trade of the great inland empire,[9] had been projected to run from the upper point of navigation on the Susquehanna River to a new port on Lake Erie.[10] But its hopes had at first been blasted by the depression following the panic of 1837, and until the early 'fifties very little progress had been made. Spurred on by New York's railroads to Buffalo and Dunkirk on Lake Erie,[11] the legislature of Pennsylvania in 1852 authorized municipal corporations within the State to subscribe to the stock of the company and otherwise aided the Sunbury & Erie to resume construction. A contract was made with William and J. B. Moorhead for building the road.[12] Since the stocks and bonds were not sold in sufficient amounts, the Moorheads had to take securities as pay for their work; [13] they sold the securities, exchanged them for materials, or used them as collateral for loans. In 1854 the road was in desperate need of funds. Many banks refused it aid,[14] but the Girard Bank, Drexel & Co., and E. W. Clark & Co. came to its assistance.[15] The city of Philadelphia [16] granted the road a loan in the form of an issue of $2,000,000 in 6 per cent bonds,[17] and other municipalities helped in the same way.[18]

The method of selling the Philadelphia loan was characteristic of the time. A Philadelphian was appointed to sell a portion of the bonds, for which he was to receive a traveling allowance and one-half of one per cent commission.[19] He was instructed not to sell below 90 and commission in Philadelphia and 95 in Europe. Failing to obtain this, he was to attempt to borrow $200,000 or $300,000 at not over 6 per cent, for from one to five years, pledging bonds at 80 or 85 as collateral.[20] E. W. Clark & Co. took $117,000 of these bonds,[21] but on the whole the loan went very slowly.[22]

Construction was carried forward a few miles in 1854 and 1855,[23] but the road continued to have financial difficulties. In 1855 it tried to sell $6,000,000 in mortgage bonds but failed.[24] In 1858 the State of Pennsylvania came to the rescue. The Sunbury & Erie was authorized to issue $7,000,000 in 5 per cent bonds, giving as security a mortgage on the road's property and franchises; [25] with half of the bond issue it should purchase from the State a part of its canal system.[26] With this aid the road made considerable progress,[27] and it finally reached Lake Erie in 1864.[28]

In 1858 Jay Cooke became connected with Sunbury & Erie finance. He secured loans for the road on its notes and he sold the road's bonds, presumably to pay off the notes.[29] And through his contact with the Sunbury & Erie he was brought into the reorganization of Pennsylvania's canals and gained a foothold in transportation finance and management.

Reorganization of Pennsylvania Transportation

Pennsylvania's proud system of internal improvements — built at a time when canals were looked upon as a major means for bringing trade to a city or a community — was sold in 1857 and 1858 because it had become a liability for the State. In 1857 the Pennsylvania Railroad purchased the great State works extending from Philadelphia to Pittsburgh.[30] In 1858, the remainder of the public works was sold to the Sunbury & Erie Railroad for $3,500,000 in bonds.[31]

At this point Jay Cooke entered into the affair. The Sunbury & Erie proposed to sell the canals so as to secure the means for finishing its construction. Companies were, therefore, organized to buy the canals from the Sunbury & Erie; the North Branch, the West Branch, and the Delaware Division were all purchased by concerns in which Jay Cooke was interested and with whose financing he was in some way connected.[32]

Cooke was closely associated with the company which purchased the Delaware Division. This canal extended along the Delaware River for 60 miles northwestward from Bristol to Easton, Pennsylvania, connecting with the canal of the Lehigh Coal & Navigation Company and the Delaware & Raritan Canal, and at its southern terminus joining the tidewaters of the Delaware River.[33] The canal carried, principally, anthracite coal and some lumber and whiskey. The Delaware Division Canal is said to have been the most profitable of the public works of Pennsylvania; the highwater mark of its profits was in 1855, but thereafter a decline set in, owing to growing railway competition.[34]

Jay Cooke was active in both the organization and management of the Delaware Division Company which purchased the Delaware Division Canal. There were eleven incorporators of the company subscribing to a total of 24,000 shares.[35] Jay Cooke took 1,000, J. B. Moorhead 2,000 shares, and E. W. Clark & Co. 9,000. Among the other subscribers were President Fell of the Lehigh Valley Railroad, President Marsh of the Morris Canal & Banking Company, and Samuel Hepburn, an iron man of Carlisle, Pennsylvania.[36] Here was a typical instance of banker, capitalist, and industrialist uniting in one project.

The Delaware Division Company was a promotion scheme. It purchased the canal from the Sunbury & Erie at a private sale for $1,775,000.[37] Payment to the railroad is said to have been made in the form of $1,200,000 in 6 per cent bonds secured by a first mortgage and the balance in cash, stock, and notes with collateral security.[38] Jay Cooke, who was for a time president of the Delaware Division Company, said that "we . . . issued stocks & bonds, refunded the State the price agreed upon & then retired with good round profits." [39] How those "good round profits" were made was suggested by a contemporary railroad journal, which said that those who managed the deal with the Sunbury & Erie received $25,000 in commission, that the stockholders received two full shares for one paid for, and that by paying good dividends they created a market and sold their shares at a profit.[40] The financial statements of the company for 1860–61 show that good dividends were paid and that a considerable amount of the stock was watered.[41]

Both the Sunbury & Erie and the Delaware Division Company illustrate a development in transportation finance which was to have great significance in the future. Stocks had been the common medium for financing new concerns, but those companies were financed largely from the sale of bonds. The time was near at hand when stocks would represent merely the promoters' bonus while the necessary capital would be derived from the sale of bonds.

Jay Cooke's work with the canal companies was chiefly to organize new companies to take over the State canals, and his profits were the profits of promotion. His work with railroads at the time was of a different nature. His first direct experience in railroad construction was gained in the reorganizing and rebuilding of an abandoned road owned jointly by Pennsylvania and Maryland.[42] This road ran from Chambersburg, Pennsylvania, to Hagerstown, Maryland, a distance of 22 miles.[43] It was of interest to Philadelphia capitalists because it provided a link between the Philadelphia & Reading and the Baltimore & Ohio railroads and as such might attract to Philadelphia trade then going to Baltimore. In 1858 the road was sold [44] to two Pennsylvanians [45] and the Franklin Railroad Company was formed for rebuilding it.

Jay Cooke and E. W. Clark & Co. undertook to finance the project by selling its bonds, in payment for which service they were given a considerable portion of stock.[46] They sold most of the bonds through the banks along the road, especially at Hagerstown, Greencastle, and Chambersburg. The bonds were none too popular in the communities concerned,[47] but Jay Cooke's unusual sales ability brought the desired results.

The financial management of the Franklin Railroad during its construction was also in the hands of Jay Cooke, and he had charge of the purchase of rails and other materials for the road.[48] In his Memoirs he refers with considerable pride to the fact that the Franklin Railroad was very superior in construction while built at a very low cost, averaging about $10,000 a mile.[49] On its completion in 1860,[50] the road was leased to the Cumberland Valley Railroad, which guaranteed its mortgage bonds,[51] and it later became a part of the Pennsylvania system.

There is no evidence which indicates that Jay Cooke made much money from the Franklin,[52] but he gained some experience in railroad building and he made contacts with iron manufacturers and bankers, all of which was later to be very useful to him. Perhaps most important was the fact that he became acquainted with Harris C. Fahnestock, a young teller in the Bank of Harrisburg who was treasurer of the Franklin Railroad. Fahnestock later became Jay Cooke's partner and worked brilliantly for Jay Cooke & Co., in the Washington office during the Civil War and later as head of the New York house.

Cooke's next venture in Pennsylvania railroads had to do with the Ironton, a short road owning a mining property, which was tributary to the Lehigh Valley Railroad in the vicinity of Bethlehem.[53] His work for this road consisted wholly of helping to finance construction. He and E. W. Clark & Co. sold the bonds of the road, secured temporary loans for its lessee, and took a large portion of the stock at a low cost, which entitled them to choose three out of five of the road's directors.[54]

Other transportation projects in Pennsylvania appealed to Jay Cooke for aid, one of which was the Chartiers Valley Railroad in western Pennsylvania, of which J. K. Moorhead was president.[55] Cooke was asked to organize a company to lease and finish the Chartiers in return for preferred stock and mortgage bonds,[56] but he did not accept the offer. This episode was important to him chiefly because it brought him into contact with W. Milnor Roberts, a construction engineer who was later to play an important part in Cooke's work for the Northern Pacific.

While assisting in the reorganization of companies and in the building of roads, Jay Cooke dealt for himself and others in a variety of transportation stocks and bonds, some outside of Pennsylvania. He purchased considerable amounts of the bonds of the canal companies with which he was concerned.[57] He was also associated with William Moorhead in dealing in the securities of the Schuylkill Navigation Company.[58] In 1858–60 he was interested in the Southern Pacific, a short railroad in Texas,[59] and in 1859 he purchased bonds of the Steubenville & Indiana Railroad.[60] Thus with the broadening of railroad building, his investments also broadened.

Very little information has been uncovered with regard to Jay Cooke's method of handling his relations with these various projects. His banking business in Philadelphia was done largely with E. W. Clark & Co., in whose office he maintained a desk for a few years after he had left the firm. He had some capital of his own, but he also borrowed from the Farmers' and Mechanics' Bank and from Drexel & Co., giving bonds as security. While financing the Franklin in 1859–60, he borrowed heavily of the Bank of Harrisburg and the Bank of Chambersburg, of which his friends Weir and Messersmith were cashiers. His loans from these banks, in sums up to $30,000,[61] were both time and call loans and were secured by his notes and collateral. Cooke received the loans mainly in the form of "marked" notes, issued to him by the banks; when these notes, which might circulate a considerable time, returned to the bank of issue, they were again sent to him for reissue or were retired, in which case the bank drew on Cooke through a Philadelphia bank for the principal and interest on the loan.

JAY COOKE MEETS NEW ENGLAND RAILROAD INTERESTS

One other railroad was of significance to Jay Cooke in those years because it brought him into contact with a group of railroad men who were later to bring him into the Northern Pacific. This road was the Vermont Central, built from Windsor on the Connecticut River to Burlington on Lake Champlain [62] to form a link in a chain of roads projected to connect Boston with Montreal on the St. Lawrence and Ogdensburg on Lake Ontario.[63] Closely connected with the Central was another link in the same chain, the Vermont and Canada, which extended from near Burlington to the foot of Lake Champlain; [64] two men prominent in the Central, John Smith and Lawrence Brainard of St. Albans, were incorporators and directors of the Vermont and Canada,[65] and the older road leased the younger.[66]

The history of the Vermont Central in its early decades is the story of almost constant litigation between various groups interested in the road, one side alleging that the other was illegally profiting at the expense of the road. It is unnecessary, even were it possible, to recount the unsavory history of the Vermont Central. Let it suffice to say that, beginning in 1852, there was a long struggle between various groups to control the road; the struggle involved both the Vermont Central and the Vermont and Canada, turned bondholders against stockholders, and centered, particularly, around the trustees of the first-mortgage bondholders of the Central.[67]

Those who suffered loss from the irregularities in the road's management exhausted all legal possibilities for protecting their equity in the concern.[68] Among them were E. W. Clark & Co. and Jay Cooke. The Clarks had secured bonds of the Vermont Central from Joseph W. Clark & Co., which had assisted in financing the road.[69] The Philadelphia Clarks had sold bonds in Philadelphia and had themselves retained some bonds, which were among the "traps" inherited by Cooke from the old Clark firm in 1857. As a member of the firm in 1856 and 1857 and later as a representative of his own and others' holdings in the Vermont Central, Jay Cooke took an active part in the Vermont Central fight until 1861.

In 1856 an attempt at redress failed because the necessary assent of all concerned could not be obtained.[70] A "war fund" was collected for supporting further action,[71] but it was alleged that Smith and Brainard, trustees and also owners of a factory which manufactured cars for the Vermont Central, used $5,000 of the road's money for opposing the move, charging the amount to the road's expense.[72]

Jay Cooke next led a movement for buying up mortgage bonds in order to bring about foreclosure;[73] and in 1860, representing the Philadelphia interests in the Vermont Central but principally on joint account with Anthony J. Drexel,[74] he bought large amounts of first-mortgage bonds at about $18 and second-mortgage bonds at $1.75 and $2.00 a hundred.[75] Cooke and his confederates in Philadelphia and Boston, however, failed to break the power of the Vermont "gang," and after 1860 Jay Cooke was too much involved in government finance to have time to participate in the Vermont Central fight. But the Vermonters did not forget him.

The story of Jay Cooke's early work in transportation has been told not for its intrinsic importance but because of what Cooke gained from it. The work he did in 1858–60 helped in some measure to replace the capital he had lost in the panic. Moreover, it may have been because of his observations of such examples of ineffective financing as in the case of the Sunbury & Erie that Jay Cooke came so strongly to emphasize energy and centralized control in selling the loans with which he later came to be connected. Most significant, however, is the fact that in those years he gained a foothold in the transportation business and an acquaintance with the organization, construction, and operation of transportation concerns and with men of prominence in the transportation world. He became acquainted with such men as Samuel M. Felton and Isaac Hinckley of the Philadelphia, Wilmington & Baltimore, J. Edgar Thomson and Thomas H. Scott of the Pennsylvania, Geo. W. Cass of the Pittsburgh, Fort Wayne & Chicago, W. Milnor Roberts, construction engineer of a number of roads, and the "solid men" of Boston and New England, including the Smith-Brainard group of the Vermont Central.

JAY COOKE & CO. AND EARLY CIVIL WAR
FINANCE, 1861–1862

WE HAVE now come to the beginning of the most important part of our story, that which deals principally with Jay Cooke's activities as an investment banker. So far, we have seen him accumulating knowledge of finance and acquiring that self-confidence which success gives. We have also observed banking in the United States developing into a more effective system though still very chaotic. Banking, like our economic organization in general, had for some time been changing in the direction of greater specialization and large scale activity, with its center in New York. The Civil War accelerated that development. The war necessitated the speeding up and the enlargement of our financial machinery in order to carry the heavy burdens of war finance. The result was a great change in both commercial and investment banking. The outstanding individual figure in that development was Jay Cooke, who worked through his banking firm, Jay Cooke & Co.

JAY COOKE ESTABLISHES HIS BANKING HOUSE

Jay Cooke & Co. was established in Philadelphia on January 1, 1861. The organization of this firm was the result of no sudden impulse. It had been talked about in 1856,[1] and it was probably with a view to establishing his own bank that Jay Cooke had retired from the Clark firms. The lingering effects of the panic of 1857 had made it unwise to start a new banking house for some time after the panic, especially when Cooke could find profitable employment for himself and his capital in transportation finance. But in the fall of 1860 he and his brother-in-law, William Moorhead, began to consider seriously the establishment of a bank in Philadelphia. Business by then seemed well recovered from the panic, and in the normal course of events the outlook for the future should have been favorable. But the situation was complicated by the strained feeling between the North and the South, which had been intensified by the election of Lincoln in November, 1860, and had found concrete expression in the adoption of the ordinance of secession by South Carolina in December. These developments had been accompanied by a severe disturbance in business.

The prospective partners were quite aware of the seriousness of the national situation. Jay Cooke's brother, a newspaper man who had entry to the inner circle in Washington, warned them that the Union was endangered and that he feared the United States was "entering upon a long period of disaster, politically and financially. . . . All of you," he counselled his brother Jay, "yourself, WMG. [Moorhead], and the Clarks, get your money matters in as snug a condition as possible — keep taking sail, and dont be tempted by a few days of brighter promise, to go into any new operations, but persevere in 'hauling in,' until you are beyond the reach of casualty." [2]

The brother's advice did not deter Jay Cooke. Had he foreseen the conflict which was to come, he might have remembered that wars had in the past brought lucrative work to those bankers who had been in a position to profit from war finance. Indeed, his memory of the Clarks' profits from Mexican War finance must still have been very vivid. But most important in influencing Jay Cooke, who usually took the long-time point of view, was his indomitable faith in his country, whose energy and resources, in his opinion, made inevitable a great future for American business.

Jay Cooke & Co. was a partnership. The two partners, Cooke and William Moorhead, had a two-thirds and one-third interest, respectively, in its profits. Jay Cooke became the manager, while Moorhead furnished capital and whatever business his prestige and influence could bring.[3] The partnership had no definitely stated capital. Cooke said years later that he considered himself worth $150,000 at the time of the organization of his firm; this consisted of a mortgage for $15,000, real estate in Baltimore estimated at $35,000, the Cooke residence valued at $12,000, western land valued at $25,000, first-mortgage and second-mortgage bonds and stock in the Vermont Central to the amount of $40,000, and stocks and bonds, cash, and the remainder of his interest in E. W. Clark & Co. totaling $23,000. Moorhead stated that "about the first of the year 1860 I regarded myself as being worth about $500,000, the greater part of which was in first-class interest-paying bonds. . . . My income was then over $20,000 a year." [4] A relatively small amount of the assets of the partners was in any sense liquid. Moorhead is said to have estimated the actual cash capital on the opening of the firm as "perhaps the small sum of five or ten thousand dollars," [5] which was an astonishingly small capital for a firm that was shortly to do so large a business.

In view of the fact that Jay Cooke & Co. started with a relatively small capital and was almost a one-man concern, it was to be expected that it should be organized as a partnership and not as a corporation. To be sure, incorporation was necessary for banks that issued circulating notes, but other lines of banking could be carried on without a charter. The private bank was then a common institution in the United States; in June, 1861, the *Bankers' Magazine* [6] listed 31 such firms in Philadelphia alone. Many of them were relatively insignificant, but some had come to hold a respectable and even an important place in Philadelphia banking. The situation was substantially the same in other cities.

The office of Jay Cooke & Co. occupied the front part of the first floor of a brown stone building at 114 South Third Street.[7] It was close to the old Clark place of business and the "first door above the Girard Bank," as the cards of the firm modestly announced.[8] Jay Cooke & Co. had a number of distinguished neighbors. The Girard Bank, in whose shadow it was started, was not only one of the oldest but also one of the largest incorporated banks in the city, its capital being $1,250,000. Around the corner on Chestnut Street was the Farmers' and Mechanics' Bank with a capital of $2,000,000; and also on Chestnut Street the Philadelphia Bank, capitalized at $1,800,000, and the Bank of North America, the oldest chartered bank in the country, with a substantial capital of $1,000,000 and approaching fourscore years in age. In 1861, the total capitalization of the incorporated banks of Philadelphia was $12,201,660.[9]

There is no way of estimating the capital or relative importance of Philadelphia's private banks. The most influential had come to be Drexel & Co., which had by the 1850's acquired considerable strength in domestic exchange and in railroad securities. It had a strong ally in New York in Read, Drexel & Co. By 1861 the Philadelphia Drexel house was under the direction of Anthony J. Drexel, the son of its founder.

Compared with many of its neighbors on Third and Chestnut streets, Jay Cooke & Co. must on first thought have appeared rather insignificant at the beginning of its career. The strength of such a firm cannot, however, be measured by its capital or its age alone, but also by the quality of the men who direct it. Both Cooke and Moorhead were men of long and successful experience in business and wide contacts in finance and transportation.

Jay Cooke & Co. was designed to deal in bank notes, bills of exchange, and stock, to discount paper, and to receive deposits. It is interesting to note that private banking was then still largely unspecialized in function. There were a few firms, however, which had gone far in the direction of specialization, such as Brown Brothers & Co., with houses in Boston, New York, Philadelphia, Baltimore, Liverpool, and London, who were leaders in foreign exchange, and Drexel & Co., of Philadelphia, and Read, Drexel & Co., of New York, who were coming to be known for their investment business.

Specialization was increasing, and it is probable that, had the Civil War not come, Jay Cooke & Co. would very soon have developed into an outstanding dealer in railroad securities, since the stage was set for a period of great activity in railroad building. In view of Jay Cooke's later career this is worth remembering. But the war upset the normal functioning of the American economic system and concentrated effort on the struggle between the two sections. This meant decreased activity in some lines and an increase in others and considerable readjustment in the work of individuals and firms. The circumstances of the time turned Jay Cooke & Co. to government finance. The power and prestige of the firm were built up through war finance, and, in order to sell government securities, Jay Cooke practically revolutionized the methods of marketing investments in the United States. The Civil War was in a very real way a turning point in the history of our investment banking, a development in which Jay Cooke was the leader.

THE WAR TURNS JAY COOKE TO GOVERNMENT FINANCE

Political developments came rapidly in the early months after the establishment of Jay Cooke & Co. in that fateful winter of 1861. Event followed quickly upon event until secession became a reality and war virtually began with the firing on Fort Sumter in April. There had been somewhat of a recovery in business after the adjustment to the shock of the late fall, but this did not prove lasting. Imports fell, trade slackened, and business paper available for discount decreased; and though there was an abundance of money, speculation on the stock market was held in check by the weakness of the Treasury and uncertainty about federal finance.[10]

The condition of the United States Treasury had been none too good for some time, and in the winter and spring of 1861 increased expenditures and reduced income — notably from the fall in imports — made the situation worse. The Treasury had to resort to loans. The public debt rose from $66,000,000 to $90,000,000 in the first half of the year.[11]

The methods used by the Secretary of the Treasury, Salmon P. Chase, in floating these early loans were very different from those later adopted by Jay Cooke. The loans were marketed through competitive bids as the Mexican War loans had been. That is, the government was its own broker. In February, 1861, a 6 per cent, 20-year loan of $8,000,000 was offered. One hundred and fifty-six individuals and banks, mostly from New York, Boston, and Philadelphia and wholly from the East, bid for $14,461,-250 at from 75 to 96. Bids were accepted for 90.10 to 96, which placed the whole loan. The heaviest purchasers were Ketchum,

Son & Co. and Read, Drexel & Co., both of New York, who took $2,749,000 and $1,345,000, respectively, at 90.10. Neither Jay Cooke nor the Philadelphia Clarks bid for this loan. Another $8,000,000 was offered in March. Bids were received from 176 bidders at 85 to 100. All the bids below 94 were rejected, and, as a result, bonds for only $3,099,000 were sold. Of this amount, New York's Bank of Commerce was allotted $2,500,000, a total of $2,825,000 being taken by New York City; four Philadelphia bidders received $35,000 of the bonds; and $153,000 went to six Boston subscribers. The New York and Philadelphia Drexels were refused $3,300,000 for which they had bid 93.17.[12] This loan left a very bad feeling in financial circles. Many bankers thought that Secretary Chase was not justified in rejecting all the bids below 94,[13] and then, as later, many prominent bankers held that it would have been better if he had sold the bonds for what the market offered. Here was the beginning of a policy which ultimately brought a break between the Secretary and the bankers and which prepared the way for Jay Cooke.

The Treasury's activities were watched closely by Jay Cooke in the spring of 1861. The banker soon saw that there were possibilities for his firm in government finance. He had a distinct advantage over others in that he had a means of approach to the Treasury through his brother, Henry D. Cooke, who was a political friend of Secretary Chase. Henry Cooke became such an important factor in the work of Jay Cooke & Co. that it is well to digress at this point to consider what sort of a man he was.

Henry D. Cooke had greater talent for politics than had his brothers, Pitt or Jay. He was an impressive looking person, engaging in manner; he had exceptional powers of expression, both in writing and in speaking; and he had that sensitiveness to personality which gives great power over individuals. From his youth, his training seems to have been directed toward a political career. He had been sent to Allegheny College and Transylvania University [14] and prepared for law. While he was at college, his father wrote him not to study too hard, to exercise all he could in order to preserve his health, and to "know that all my best hopes are centered in you." What those hopes were, is suggested by the

advice of the father to the son that he should study German, since
knowledge of the language would have great weight with the German
people if he went into politics, and that the secret of good
public speaking was much and careful preparation.[15]

After completing his education, Henry Cooke accompanied
William Moorhead when the latter went to Chile as United States
consul.[16] Henry went on to San Francisco where he engaged in
trade, but before long he returned home heavily in debt.[17] He
thereupon found employment with the *Sandusky Register*, which
with the help of his father and brothers [18] he purchased in 1856.[19]
He became very much interested in politics and moved to the
capital of Ohio, where he became owner and editor of the *Ohio
State Journal*, an important political organ of the State.[20] This
newspaper venture was financially unsuccessful and caused
Henry's father and brothers much concern. It is not a little revealing
that, in the opinion of his brother Pitt, "Harry" was so
anxious to get into politics that he would stay if it cost him six
times what his newspapers were worth.[21] Debts never worried
Henry, and he was always willing to accept financial help from
others.

Henry Cooke eventually got into politics but probably not in
the way he had expected. His newspaper was the leading Republican
paper in Ohio and it became the organ of Salmon P. Chase,
one-time Abolitionist governor and later senator from Ohio, who
was appointed Secretary of the Treasury by Lincoln. The *Ohio
State Journal* also supported John Sherman, representative to
Congress from the "Firelands," who was appointed senator to
succeed Chase in 1861. Henry Cooke and Rush Sloane, a relative
of the Cooke family who lived in Sandusky, had been the managers
of Sherman's campaign for representative, and Jay Cooke
had contributed to campaign expenses.[22] These political connections
and experiences of Henry Cooke were to have a very significant
bearing on the history of Jay Cooke & Co.

The Cookes saw opportunity for themselves in the appointment
of Chase as Secretary of the Treasury. "I see Chase is in the
Treasy," wrote Jay to Henry on March 1, 1861, "& now what is
to be done — cant you sell out the papers & open a Banking house

in Washⁿ. & be something respectable — or at least can't you inaugurate something whereby we can all *safely* make some Cash?" Eleutheros Cooke at this time urged his sons to take advantage of their relations with Chase. "By the way," he wrote Jay on March 25, 1861, "I took up my pen principally to say, that H. D.'s plan in getting Chase into the Cabinet & Sherman into the Senate is accomplished, and that now is the time for making money, by honest contracts out of the govt. In perfecting loans — & various other agencies — the door is open to make up all your losses. If H. D. don't avail himself of the hard earned favor of the Admⁿ, he deserves poverty."

Jay Cooke and his brother went directly after anything they wanted from the government. For instance, immediately after Chase's entry into the Treasury, Jay Cooke urged Henry to get a government contract for a certain engraver, with the understanding that they should receive a 15 per cent commission on the contract: "You must quietly give Chase to understand that you wish him to give it to Carpenter & that it is for your interest that he should & you *need* some little favor at this time." [23] The Cookes also tried to get the work of making transfers of money for the Treasury, expecting to profit from the fact that they would be given from 30 to 120 days to make transfers. [24] Jay Cooke & Co. was badly in need of something in the way of working capital at this time, and experience with the Mexican War loans had taught its active partner how government funds could meet that need. The Cookes kept close contact with Chase, but the Secretary did not give favors without being certain that they were merited; he was too honest and he was too fearful of criticism to act otherwise. Before receiving any significant amount of work from the Treasury, therefore, Jay Cooke & Co. had to demonstrate what it could do.

Jay Cooke's first participation in Treasury loans was in the sale of Treasury notes in April. The notes, convertible into 6 per cent bonds and offered at par or above, brought from 100 to 100.27. Again, New York's Bank of Commerce was allotted $2,500,000; a few Boston capitalists were given over a million; and Read, Drexel & Co., $185,000. The only other large subscriber whose bid was accepted was Jay Cooke & Co., and it was granted the respectable amount of $200,000.[25] This was a good beginning for a banking house less than four months old.

Jay Cooke participated in a small way in other federal loans in April. Chase offered another issue of Treasury notes and close to $9,000,000 of a 6 per cent 20-year loan, no minimum being stipulated.[26] Henry Cooke urged Jay to get up a party to take at least a million in bonds.[27] In this instance, Jay Cooke & Co. entered into an agreement with the Drexels to secure bids for the loan, but they were able to bid for only $159,000 in bonds, at 85 to 88. The attitude of the bankers and capitalists of Philadelphia is indicated by the fact that they took a total of only about $187,000. Subscriptions were received by the Treasury for only $7,441,000 at from 60 to 93, which shows how rapidly the credit of the government was falling. Bids were accepted for $7,310,000 at 85 and above. By far the larger proportion of this loan went to New York City: the American Exchange Bank took $825,000; the Bank of Commerce, $550,000; and Ketchum, Son & Co., $1,875,-000. Of the $1,684,000 in Treasury notes sold at par at the same time, Drexel & Co. and Jay Cooke & Co. took $141,000 for four banks and one individual in Philadelphia.[28]

Jay Cooke was disappointed at the weak showing made by his city in the sale of these bonds and notes; but he held, characteristically enough, that small as the bid was it was just so much more than would have been offered had he not taken an interest in it. [29] He instructed his brother to tell Chase how he had worked against the current, not losing an opportunity to make it known that he had accomplished something to his credit.

While Jay Cooke was working on this latest loan, Henry wrote him about their progress with the Treasury: "We are just beginning to get 'inside the ring,' and there are several 'good things' in prospect, which a little management and patience will bring out all right." [30] Pitt Cooke, in the meantime, had come to believe that his brother might play an important rôle as a financial patriot: "'Morris of Philadelphia' was the back bone of the Revolution. He was their only financier that could always do *something* for the cause in the Sinews of war & now Cooke of Phil[a] must not

forget his financial Patriotism. His mantle has fallen on the right Shoulders." [31] It is significant that, at the very beginning of the Civil War, Jay Cooke was made aware of the possibility of his playing an important part in the impending struggle. Pitt, not so practical and, indeed, rather ineffectual as a business man, had sensed the potentialities of the situation and had the imagination which would enable him to visualize his brother in such a rôle.

Jay Cooke had carefully observed the sale of the loans in the winter and spring of 1861. He had become convinced that the old way would not serve the coming needs. Chase had sold to bankers and capitalists, and they, being responsible and conservative investors, bought with an eye to security and profits. Already their bids had become much lower than at first, and Chase was not a little impatient with them for bidding so low. Jay Cooke soon realized that the securities of the government would not sell high in great amounts purely as investments. The bankers advised Chase to sell at the market, that is, for whatever the loans would bring. Cooke could understand the position of the bankers, but his deep sensitiveness to the importance of the irrational in people's make-up led him further. He visualized the great possibilities of the emotional appeal, the appeal to the patriotism of the people, as an incentive toward purchasing the loans. This led directly to the idea of a wide participation by the general public in government loans.

It is significant that Jay Cooke did not consider the possibility of syndicating government loans at this time, that is, using the device whereby strong banks jointly undertook to distribute a loan, maintaining its price by "rigging" the market. Indeed, the modern syndicate was apparently not at the time used either in America or in England, though it had made its appearance on the Continent. Jay Cooke did not suggest the use of the syndicate, but he did suggest something that was almost as revolutionary, that is, a popular loan.

An opportunity to try out the patriotic appeal in the selling of war bonds came in the early summer of 1861. Pennsylvania, still distrusted because of the repudiation of its bonds in the early 'forties, had decided to raise a three-million loan for the military

defence of the State.[32] This loan, says Jay Cooke in his Memoirs, was to have been offered for the best price obtainable, which it was said might be as low as 75. Here was an opportunity to try Cooke's scheme for a patriotic appeal. Accordingly, he pleaded with the officers of the State and convinced them that they should try to sell the loan at par on patriotic principles.[33] This was a new departure, and one can well imagine that the conservative banking fraternity of Chestnut and Third streets was sceptical of the outcome.

Jay Cooke & Co. and Drexel & Co. were appointed general agents for the sale of this loan. Henry D. Moore, then treasurer of the Keystone State, has left a statement explaining how Jay Cooke came to be associated with Pennsylvania finance. At Cooke's request, Moore, who had not previously met Cooke but knew him by reputation, called on him at his office on Third Street. The banker then expressed the desire that Moore make his bank a State depository. Jay Cooke, writes Moore, said that "he had no doubt he could put me in the way of some business transactions that would make me some money." Moore engaged Cooke and Drexel to sell the loan, placing it principally in the charge of Jay Cooke.[34]

Jay Cooke went aggressively at the job of selling the loan, and here we get our first view of his strength as a salesman. The methods he employed were novel but were suited to the situation. Advertisements were inserted in newspapers, and circulars were scattered throughout the State. Strong appeal was made to the people's patriotism; but, since Cooke was wise enough to know that the patriotic motive would not affect all who had money to invest, the financial return of the loan was also stressed. Drexel & Co. and Jay Cooke & Co., said one handbill,

respectfully appeal to the patriotism and State pride of Pennsylvania in this hour of trial, that they come forward and manifest their love of the old Commonwealth by a prompt and cordial response to her call.

But independent of any motives of patriotism, there are considerations of self-interest which may be considered in reference to this Loan. It is a six per cent Loan free from any taxation.

Agents were sent throughout the State to see bankers and others. State Treasurer Moore and Cashier Weir of the Bank of Harrisburg, a friend of Cooke and a man of unusual wit and resourcefulness, visited Pittsburgh and the western part of Pennsylvania with a view to urging bankers to take the loan. Fahnestock, the young and aggressive banker who had been treasurer of the Franklin Railroad, interviewed bankers in the counties in the neighborhood of Harrisburg. Jay Cooke himself worked in Philadelphia.[35] As was to be expected, bankers quite generally protested that the loan was not worth taking at par, but Jay Cooke matched their financial scepticism with his patriotic fervor.

The loan was oversubscribed. It was taken by banks, large and small, by railroads, insurance companies, and by individuals in amounts as low as $50. Even conservative Mercer subscribed for $300,000 for his Farmers' and Mechanics' Bank,[36] no doubt expecting to sell on the strength of the demand which publicity had built up for the loan.

The Pennsylvania loan was a godsend to Jay Cooke & Co. It gave the bank something which it needed badly: writing about this loan some years later to Cooke and Moorhead, the Treasurer of Pennsylvania stated that he gave "to your House *all* the financial benefit of it by large deposits accruing from this loan, notwithstanding I was cautioned by Mr. Drexel not to deposit money with your House, for the reason that you had no Cash Capital and that I would run great risk if I did it." [37] These deposits gave Jay Cooke & Co. its first considerable working capital since the deposits were only gradually drawn by the State.[38]

The success of the Pennsylvania loan was a personal victory for Jay Cooke. It proved the efficacy of his method of aggressively pushing the sale of bonds by interviews and widespread advertising and by appealing to the patriotism of large and small investors. More than that, the loan made Jay Cooke known to bankers and citizens of Pennsylvania. Nor was that all; the State Treasurer, according to his own words, "wrote to Mr. Chase and gave him a history of the negotiation of our loan at par, and expressed to him my earnest belief that if he would give you the negotiation of the government loan, you would be as successful with it as you were with our state loan." [39] Jay Cooke did not miss the opportunity to advertise his success. With the expressed purpose of strengthening the cause of the North, he sent the names of the loan subscribers to newspapers throughout the country, to Jefferson Davis, President of the Confederacy, to Secretary Chase, and to *The Times* (London).[40]

JAY COOKE DRAWS CLOSER TO THE TREASURY

By the summer of 1861 the war was on in earnest. It gave promise of being a long, hard struggle. The Cookes continued, therefore, to lay plans for active work for the government, and they watched every opportunity. Jay Cooke had by then won the personal friendship and the financial hearing of the Secretary of the Treasury, and Henry was close to many men in power in Washington. In view of later developments, it is interesting to know that Henry Cooke urged Chase not to resort to a European loan until all efforts at home had failed.[41]

Things were developing rapidly for the Cookes, and by July they were laying specific plans for strong participation in selling the loans of the government. "I have talked with Sherman who is on the Finance Committee in the Senate," wrote Henry, "about our plan of agencies, commissions &c, and he will help us as far as in his power. He will be the leading spirit of the Committee, and his aid will be invaluable." [42] What these plans were, was revealed by a letter of Jay Cooke to Secretary Chase in which he wrote that Drexel & Co. were willing to join them in opening "a first class Banking Establishment in Wash^n *at once* trusting to our energy capital & credit for success, as well as those natural advantages that would legitimately & honestly flow towards us from your personal friendship & the fact that our firm was ardently & fully with the Administration." They proposed to make Treasury operations their main business and felt that they could be of great help to Chase. "We would refer to Drexel & Co.," said Cooke, "as the heaviest house in Philad^a with correspondents all over this land & doing also a heavy business in Germany. Mr. Reed their

New York partner . . . has probably transacted more business in Gov. Loans & Treasy notes than any other New York firm & is the particular frd of Mr. Cisco [head of the United States subtreasury at New York] and stands very high as a business man." For raising the hundreds of millions which would be needed, Cooke suggested that Chase arrange to pay a commission of one-fourth of one per cent on sales and engage the Cooke-Drexel combination to manage the sale of the loans. They would save the government large sums "besides *insuring* prompt success." If Chase felt disposed, continued Cooke, to "give us the management of the Loans, to be issued by the Government during the War allowing us a fair commission on them subject . . . entirely to your supervision & advice we are ready to throw ourselves into the matter heartily & at once." [43]

This letter was not sent directly to Chase. As came to be Jay Cooke's practice in his correspondence with public officials, he sent the letter to Henry Cooke with instructions to read it to Chase and get his reply. All he wanted, he said, was the assurance that Chase would give them the management of the loans, since "Tony Drexel" was unwilling to join them in a Washington house "without some definite understanding." [44] This was characteristic of Drexel, who always tried to eliminate the unknown from his business.

One is almost awed by Jay Cooke's nerve. What would John Stevens of the National Bank of Commerce, of New York, have thought, if a Philadelphia "broker," with negligible capital and a small organization, had been commissioned to sell hundreds of millions of government bonds? It is true that Cooke expected an alliance with the Drexels, a house to be reckoned with; and jointly they could command a capital of two to three million. [45] But nobody in the United States knew how to sell hundreds of millions of bonds. Such a thing had never before been done. And there was no organization for disposing of such amounts through one house, if at all. Aside from the financial aspects of the matter, there were also political considerations. Could the Secretary and the Administration have stood the criticism which the appointment of a special agent at the time would have aroused?

We do not know what Chase said in answer to Jay Cooke's proposal; it is probable that he made no definite promises, for the Drexel-Cooke Washington project was dropped. It is not so difficult to understand Drexel's reluctance to form an alliance with Jay Cooke; he was too cautious a banker to risk his banking houses in the uncertain business of selling government loans. It is noteworthy that, from July, 1861, throughout the war, Jay Cooke and Anthony J. Drexel went different ways.

According to Jay Cooke's Memoirs, he had an active hand in two efforts to aid the Treasury in the summer and fall of 1861. He states that he helped to get the subscription to a 60-day loan offered the United States by Philadelphia banks after the Union disaster at Bull Run in July. The fact that the statement heading the subscription list is in Jay Cooke's hand bears witness to his participation in securing this subscription.[46]

Jay Cooke also said that he was consulted by Secretary Chase on the first $50,000,000 loan to the Treasury by the Associated Banks of Boston, New York, and Philadelphia, in the summer and fall of 1861, and that he was present at a number of the meetings of bank officers in regard to this loan.[47] Since he was not connected with a clearing-house bank, he could not participate directly in the negotiations between the bankers and Secretary Chase.[48]

More important than the actual part played by Jay Cooke in these efforts to help the government at this crucial time was the change which came in Chase's loan policy. The method used earlier of selling loans on competitive bids might have disposed of some bonds both in Europe and at home at a little below par in the fall of 1861.[49] But the Secretary chafed at the idea of submitting the United States to the indignity of selling its bonds at less than their face value. He, therefore, sought the aid of the clearing-house banks of the three large eastern cities; and these banks, acting in three separate associations, promised to loan $150,000,000 to the government throughout the fall of 1861,[50] with the understanding that the loan should be paid from the proceeds of the sale of Treasury notes.[51]

In carrying out the terms of the agreement, Chase, unfortunately, came to odds with the banks. When the Associated Banks first made their agreement with him, they had little business and were in an unusually liquid condition, having specie reserves of $63,200,000.[52] With such a reserve, they might continue to help the government indefinitely, if all went well.

But all did not go well. The first problem was to sell the Treasury notes. Some method had to be devised for distributing the notes over a wider market in order to relieve the strain on the banks of Boston, New York, and Philadelphia. Since there was no national system to which the Secretary could appeal, he named 148 agents, mostly presidents of banks, to sell the notes in their respective communities throughout the loyal North. They were allowed a small sum for advertising and a commission of one-fifth of one per cent of sales on the first $100,000 sold and one-eighth of one per cent on whatever was sold above that sum.[53]

Jay Cooke was appointed to cover the city of Philadelphia and its environs, including New Jersey.[54] He carried on a vigorous selling campaign, advertising in newspapers and carefully explaining the notes to prospective buyers. Although the Treasury had allowed him $150 for advertising, on his settlement with the Treasury he submitted vouchers for over $3,000 spent in advertising, which was almost half of his total commissions for selling notes.[55] The success of Cooke at this time went far to demonstrate to Chase the value of unified direction of sales under an energetic agent.

But the notes sold were far short of the needs of the Treasury. The Associated Banks, therefore, had to take over the sale in order to replenish their own dwindling reserves,[56] which fact showed how dangerous it was for them to become too heavily involved in the obligations of the government.

The banks also ran into another difficulty. They had expected the government to draw on them, but Chase insisted that they should deposit the loan in the Treasury in the form of coin paid on instalments. Thus he turned his back on the highly developed system of bank credit which is an essential part of modern banking and exchange. Payment in specie was in accordance with an old subtreasury rule, which Chase insisted on observing even though the rule had been modified. But even this requirement was for a time met by the banks without serious difficulty, for the rapid disbursements of the government returned the coin to circulation and eventually to the banks.[57] The Secretary's inability to understand the problems of the banks and his apparent unwillingness to adjust his demands to what was expedient from the point of view of sound finance did much to break the bankers' loyalty to the Treasury at this time.

Two unfortunate occurrences complicated matters for the Treasury in 1861. One was the Trent affair, which brought a threat of war with England, a circumstance which for the time being made it impossible to sell the securities of the federal government in England and which made the outlook at home very dark. The other event was the failure of Secretary Chase to recommend in his December report heavy taxation to meet the rapidly mounting deficit of the government,[58] which the bankers were convinced was necessary for saving the credit of the country.

The efforts of the banks to aid the government were paralyzed by these events. A heavy fall in the market price of government bonds made it impossible to sell Treasury notes with which to replenish the banks' reserves; and the lack of confidence which rapidly spread throughout the country drove money into hoarding and stopped the regular flow to the Associated Banks. The banks thought that suspension of specie payments was inevitable, and they voted to suspend at the end of December, 1861. The banks throughout the country and the government immediately followed their example.[59] In this manner came an event, the results of which were to be of utmost importance both to the government and to business in the United States until specie payment was resumed in 1879.

The efforts of the Associated Banks to help the government thus ended most unfortunately. Much of the blame for suspension was placed upon Chase, but W. C. Mitchell holds, in his *History of the Greenbacks*, that the trouble came rather from the weakness of the system of bank loans:[60]

Suspension was inevitable whenever anything occurred to check the redeposit in the banks of money paid out by the treasury, or to prevent the banks from replenishing their reserves by selling the securities received from the government. A severe blow to the national credit would inevitably produce such effects. It so happened that the publication of the disappointing treasury report and the Trent affair were the first occurrences of this nature momentous enough to arouse general uneasiness. . . . To assume that the banks could have continued indefinitely to carry their double burden — supplying both government and public with loans — is to assume that no serious reverse would have befallen the national credit. . . .

For the banks to finance the war was henceforth impossible.

While the Treasury and the banks were muddling through their difficulties in the fall of 1861, Jay Cooke had continued to make plans for the establishment of a Washington house. Though the Secretary had made him no definite promise of business, the project at least had his approval.[61] In February, 1862, Jay Cooke & Co. opened its doors for business at 452 Fifteenth Street.[62] The new Washington house was a partnership organized separately from the Philadelphia firm. In addition to Jay Cooke and William Moorhead, the firm included two men who came to be of great importance in the business of the group, Henry Cooke and Harris C. Fahnestock.

Henry Cooke was obviously chosen as partner because of his acquaintance with politics and politicians and with newspapers and publicity methods. He had had no business experience, except his unsuccessful trading enterprise in California and his unprofitable venture in Ohio newspapers, and he had no capital to contribute to the firm.[63] But he had excellent qualifications as a lobbyist.

Fahnestock's contributions to the partnership were of a far different nature. His experience had been somewhat like that of Jay Cooke. As a young boy he had worked in his father's store in Harrisburg, Pennsylvania, and, in 1851, at the age of 16 he had entered the Harrisburg Bank of his uncle, J. W. Weir.[64] Jay Cooke first became acquainted with Fahnestock through his friendship with Weir and through relations with the Harrisburg Bank. We have already seen that Fahnestock was associated with Cooke in managing the rebuilding of the Franklin Railroad and that he had later impressed Cooke with his success in helping to sell the Pennsylvania $3,000,000 loan.

The place which these two men came to occupy in the firm is indicated by Jay Cooke in his Memoirs: "As my brother knew little of financial matters I looked round to find one I could rely upon & whom I believed to be fully capable of managing the office whilst my brothers qualities were such as just suited the position for we had to deal with Congress, the Cabinet & President & other public men. I found such a partner in my young friend at Harrisburg Mr H. C. Fahnestock."

The Washington house gave Jay Cooke & Co. two things: (1) a more nearly complete organization for carrying on business for the government; and (2) a medium through which closer relations could be maintained with the Treasury and with politics in the nation's capital. Henry Cooke came to know all the officers of the government and the newspaper men worth knowing, and through him his brother kept track of what was happening in Washington and made his own wishes known to the government. Henry Cooke became the specialist of Jay Cooke & Co. on public relations.

As time passed, Jay Cooke's relations with the Secretary became closer and closer. A second time, in March, 1862, he was appointed agent for selling Treasury notes.[65] From time to time he got various jobs to do for the government; he was commissioned to protect the government's certificates of indebtedness from depreciation, to purchase gold for the Treasury, and to buy exchange on England,[66] and more and more he came to be an unofficial adviser to the Secretary. He was consciously using every opportunity to strengthen himself and his firms with the Treasury. "*We* must all study," wrote Jay to Henry, "by our watchful care of the interests confided to us to justify this confidence and to show him that the Treasury is a gainer by our confidential connection with it. . . . I want the Governor [Chase] to trust to our good management, integrity & skill & pledge myself that he will have no cause to regret his confidence."[67]

In those early days as later, the Cookes had one difficulty with the Treasury. They found that it was hard to get adequate remuneration for their work. On being commissioned to buy gold in March, 1862, Jay Cooke was rightly puzzled over how they should be paid by the Treasury. "We can do the work but must be careful not to work for *honor* alone," wrote Jay to Henry. Jay Cooke went into the problem at length:

I can easily understand how we can purchase & deliver Gold &c but do not understand how we are to get *paid* for it. Your letter does not say that we can sell the 7 3/10 at any *discount,* How is this? Of course we cannot sell any except at market rate the same as we deal in the Gold — We purchased today by tel° at New York a large amount at 1 per cent disc't & have bought nearly 300,000 *here* & *there* within a few days at 3/4 to 1 dis'. & we are selling to all who come at 1/2 disc't & some parties are calling at 5/8 & 3/4 — you must see the Govⁿ & get the matter in shape, at present there is no chance of selling at better than present market rates — further as our commission is so small (not *half* enough for it should be a 1/4 per cent as we have frequently to divide the comⁿ with others) we can illy afford to lay out of our money which a purchase of Gold *before* we are in funds would involve.

Jay Cooke suggested that they be given $250,000 of 7.3 per cent Treasury notes to be sold at the market price on a one-eighth of one per cent commission. The money received from the sale of the notes was to be retained by the Cookes, interest being paid to the government, and this was to constitute a fund with which to buy gold "without *loss* of *interest* or inconvenience of advancing." While selling the notes, they could "be picking up the Gold buyer 5 & 10 days" on one-fourth of one per cent commission.[68]

In the meantime much was happening which was making the future very dark for the United States Treasury. The year 1862 proved to be very difficult. The suspension of specie payments at the end of 1861 brought serious problems. The Trent affair with its international complications together with military delays and reverses, which brought frightful losses of men and ever mounting expenditures, all made it hard for the government to secure money by the sale of its loans. The London *Economist* in October, 1862, concurred with Gladstone in saying that the independence of the southern States was "as certain as any future event could be." [69] At home much criticism arose of the military and financial policies of the government, the opposition becoming especially strong in the border States. Speculation in gold, centered in New York, gave eloquent evidence of uncertainty as to the outcome of the struggle.

The situation was getting worse for the Treasury. In the absence of a strong tax program, it was clear that the government would have to seek new means for meeting the rapidly mounting costs of the war. There is good reason to believe that a considerable amount of government securities could have been sold at somewhat lower prices than the Treasury was willing to grant.[70] A number of the country's most prominent bankers, including Coe, Vermilye, and Gallatin, of New York, Haven and Bates, of Boston, and Mercer, Rogers, and Patterson, of Philadelphia, urged increased taxation and the sale of long-time bonds at their market value,[71] but to no avail.

Both Congress and Secretary Chase, who believed that selling bonds below par would dishonor the credit of the government, chose irredeemable paper currency.[72] In making this choice, the government broke with many influential bankers. Not a great amount of greenbacks was issued immediately, however — only $222,932,111 by December, 1862.[73] While the greenbacks did not aid in meeting the emergency of the winter of 1862, when the act providing for them was passed,[74] they helped to make possible the sale of bonds. The eventual depreciation of the currency in reality made possible the sale of bonds below par in terms of gold while the fiction of sale at par was nominally maintained. In the meantime, Chase resorted to various short-time shifts to meet the emergency brought by an almost empty Treasury.[75]

Provision had also been made for a large issue of long-time bonds. The second great step taken in 1862 for financing the war was to provide for the sale of $500,000,000 of government bonds.[76] These were six per cent bonds, callable in five and maturing in twenty years, hence known as the five-twenties. They were at first convertible into legal tender, a provision which was intended to aid in their sale. It was stipulated that they could be sold at their market value. The five-twenties were meant to serve the double purpose of making the legal tender paper money more acceptable because of its convertibility into five-twenty bonds and of furnishing the government with funds.

Secretary Chase offered the new five-twenties at par, but he had little success in selling them. As the months passed he came to understand why the loan went so slowly. He explained to Jay Cooke that [77]

very few subscribe for large amounts of a loan except with a view to profits from resales and it is too plain for comment that where the government is always in the market offering her bonds at par for her own notes, subscribers to these bonds in large amounts cannot expect to make profits if they take them at par. . . . All the information I can collect leads me to think that no higher rate than 97 50–100 [97.5] or at most 98 could be obtained for the bonds in this way and there is some reason to fear that not even those rates could be obtained. On fifty millions the best rate suggested would involve a loss to the country of two per cent, or one million dollars. I do not like to incur this loss if it can be avoided.

The issue of enough legal tenders would eventually have lowered the value of the currency to a point where the bonds could have been floated at par. That could not have been done rapidly enough, however, to meet the then pressing needs of the government without a severe disturbance of prices and business. What, then, should Chase have done? He probably did not seriously consider sale in Europe in 1862, for he had earlier concluded that such a negotiation would be both expensive and uncertain.[78] August Belmont, the American representative of the Rothschilds, who knew European finance as no other American banker knew it, had been asked by Chase in 1861 to investigate the possibility of selling loans in Europe. In the late autumn of 1861, he had reported emphatically to Chase that he did not see the remotest chance of negotiating any portion of the loan in England or on the Continent. "Any direct or indirect attempt on the part of our Government to do so would be worse than useless," in the opinion of Belmont, "and you will have to look for all your wants to our home markets." [79]

The five-twenties might have been sold if offered at their market price, which had been authorized by the act providing for the bonds. But Chase preferred to maintain the fiction of selling them at par. He found a strange legal justification for doing so; he held that only if the bonds were offered below market value could any one buy with the expectation of selling at the market value at a profit.[80]

In the absence of machinery for providing a market for bonds by price control, the only course remaining was a vigorous selling campaign. High pressure salesmanship might spread the bonds widely among smaller investors. This was exactly what Jay Cooke had been advocating for nearly a year. He had demonstrated his ability to sell bonds; he had two banking houses ready to serve the government; and he had won the confidence of the Secretary. In October, 1862, Secretary Chase appointed Jay Cooke his special agent for selling the great five-twenty loan.[81]

THE SALE OF THE FIVE–TWENTIES AND THE ESTABLISHMENT OF THE NATIONAL BANKING SYSTEM

THE SALE of the five-twenties stands as a notable achievement in the history of American finance. It helped provide the "sinews of war," so necessary to the successful prosecution of the civil struggle on the part of the North; but beyond that, it had a very special significance, seen in its larger perspective. The sale of the five-twenties was an important step in the evolution of business institutions and practices in the United States; it was the beginning of a development which in a large measure laid the foundations of the American system of security distribution.

The market for American securities had before the Civil War been found largely among bankers and capitalists in America and Europe, and it had not to any considerable extent depended on the small investor. His capital generally went more directly into farming or some other undertaking without the aid of bankers. Two features of the pre-Civil War system of selling securities are of considerable importance in this connection: (1) the banker was to a high degree a passive agent in the collection of investment capital, and (2) secondary or retail distribution was not well developed. Before the coming of the panic of 1857, changes were already under way which undoubtedly would have led in time to the establishment of specialized institutions for a wide marketing of securities in this country. Such a system, however, could reach a high development only with the coming of adequate business to support large scale dealing, with the appearance of a potential market as the result of widespread savings and a desire to buy stocks and bonds, and with the building of the business structure and technique necessary for selling securities. All these came about through war finance. The financial leader in the development was Jay Cooke, and it was the five-twenties which gave him the first great opportunity to develop his methods.

JAY COOKE'S ORGANIZATION FOR SELLING THE FIVE-TWENTIES

The terms on which Jay Cooke sold the five-twenties were as follows. He was expected to sell a million a day though he did not guarantee to sell any particular amount. He did not have exclusive control of the sales; the United States Treasury and designated depositories were also authorized to receive subscriptions. Jay Cooke was given full responsibility for the acts of subagents, whose appointment and management were in his hands, and he had complete charge of advertising the loan, collecting proceeds of bond sales, and distributing the bonds to purchasers. He was allowed a commission of half of one per cent on the first $10,000,000 sold, and three-eighths of one per cent on the remainder, out of which all expenses and commissions to subagents were to be paid. He had to give bond to cover his responsibility for the funds handled.[1]

The basic idea underlying Jay Cooke's handling of the loan was that it should be spread widely among the people, reaching many investors, small and large. He saw several advantages in a democratic distribution of the loan: (1) Small investors would be more susceptible than large investors to the appeal of patriotism. (2) The small investors would not be so likely to resell their bonds at once and thus throw them on the market where they would interfere with new issues, a principle in security distribution which has since been widely accepted. (3) By spreading the bonds widely and selling them gradually, as would necessarily be done when selling to many buyers, it would be possible to avoid seriously upsetting the financial mechanism of the country. And (4) Jay Cooke saw in the democratizing of the loan a means of binding the loyalty of many people to the cause of the North. The soundness of such a loan policy at the time is obvious.

It would be interesting to know how far this method of handling the loan was devised by Jay Cooke out of necessity and how far he had derived it from the experience of others. It is true that the speculative mania in England and France around 1720 had cut deeply into the classes of small means, but the bursting of the speculative bubbles had all but destroyed the stock business in those countries. Investment in State "stocks" had thereafter for a time been left to capitalists as had also shares in business enterprises. In the nineteenth century, the market in Europe had widened again, reaching a high point in the state finance of Napoleon III. Jay Cooke was familiar with the policy of the French ruler, who for financial as well as political reasons looked to the small investor to finance the French in the Crimean War and to meet the later needs of his empire.[2] A scrapbook sent to Secretary Chase by Jay Cooke contained clippings which referred to the selling of the French loans in 1854–55, when the government offices of the French Departments "were besieged by crowds of peasant subscribers," and which told about the loan of 1859 when $100,000,000 had been raised by France in one day.[3]

To sell the loan as Jay Cooke proposed was no easy matter. It involved two stupendous tasks: (1) to educate the small investor in the buying of bonds and to convince him of the value of the securities, and (2) to create an organization for the distribution of the bonds. The latter task involved a fundamental change in the country's method of bond distribution.

The success of the five-twenty sales organization lay first and foremost in the personality and character of Jay Cooke. He was eminently qualified for this work. He had a wide acquaintance among bankers, and he knew banking and exchange. Jay Cooke, moreover, was thoroughly convinced of the rightness of the cause of the North. His patriotism was very real and his loyalty to the Union was deep, while his opposition to slavery was that of one who had been reared in a strong Abolitionist community. Though Cooke loved the Union and Liberty, one must not conclude that his motives in supporting the government were purely altruistic: according to his own words he was after profits as well. Pure patriotism, it is true, might well have influenced him to enlist in the army, though men of forty who had families did not generally enlist. It must be recognized, however, that money is as necessary as men in modern warfare, and that Jay Cooke with his talent for finance was probably worth a small army of soldiers.

But that is neither here nor there. The motive is not so important as the fact that Jay Cooke had the qualities which make for leadership in such a cause. A more coldly rational person would probably have failed in the job, for it required something of the spirit of the crusader. When Jay Cooke found a work he believed in, he threw all his energies into it. He was a person of great physical and emotional power as well as considerable mental strength. He was also a thorough optimist; it is true that his optimism was not always soundly based, nor were his enthusiasms sufficiently checked by reason, but there can be no doubt but that his positive outlook was a source of strength. That outlook was based on great self-confidence and a never wavering faith in the justice of God and in his own rightness with God. It may be a question how far a man's religion affects his conduct but it is clear that Jay Cooke derived immeasurable power from the security, the absence of paralyzing doubt, and the confidence which his faith gave him.

Jay Cooke also had an unusual capacity for winning supporters. His integrity, his kind and sympathetic nature, his enthusiasm, and his optimism were attractive qualities. He was not, however, without opponents; some men honestly disagreed with him, many differed because of opposing interests, and still others were jealous of his successes. He disliked having enemies but he was not a compromiser. He attacked his opponents with directness and strength, but it was characteristic that he did not bear resentment. Moreover, he never brooked half-hearted support on the part of those who were working with him. The least evidence of a flagging interest or of Copperheadism among his men brought a firm reprimand. Jay Cooke was very much of an autocrat; but he was a benevolent autocrat. He gave credit where credit was due and also those tangible rewards which go far toward making men work. On the whole, his power as a leader lay in his positive ways of winning supporters and in his capacity for arousing loyalties, inspiring them with enthusiasm, and transforming them into action.

Jay Cooke had been appointed agent for the sale of the five-twenties in October, 1862, but it was the work of several months to develop an adequate selling organization. With the help of his

JAY COOKE, THE WAR FINANCIER

own organization, his banker friends, and other bankers moved by loyalty to the North or by commissions, he gradually built up his system. It was this system which made it possible for him to reach the small investor and thus sell a popular loan.

The keystone of the whole system was Jay Cooke himself. He made the plans, selected the leading men, determined policies, directed advertising, and kept in close touch with the subagents. And, when his time allowed, he saw investors, large and small, personally. Indeed, he was so much in evidence that to the common man he became the personification of the loan, just as Lincoln came to symbolize the Union and freedom for the slave, and Grant, victory.

The center of operations was Jay Cooke & Co., of Philadelphia. Since it had the burden of managing the sale of the loan, its personnel had to be expanded greatly; it soon came to have about thirty clerks,[4] which was a considerable size for a bank less than two years old. The Washington house served as a liaison branch with the government. Henry Cooke got the earliest word from Chase on his plans and on the condition of the Treasury, and, when Jay could not do so himself, he carried to the Secretary the recommendations and ideas of his Philadelphia brother. He also got the latest news from the War Department and rumors floating about Washington; and he had close contacts with reporters. What Mrs. Stanton quoted her husband as having said, what the editor of the *Star* thought, or how the War Department interpreted a situation — all was grist for Henry Cooke's mill. Long letters were written daily by Henry to Jay Cooke, and by means of code telegrams he sent military news which had an important financial bearing and which might reach Jay Cooke before the public heard of the event.[5]

Jay Cooke & Co. was ably assisted in selling the loan by certain key men, who were both retail and wholesale distributors. In the East a number of those men were given some responsibility for setting up and managing the selling organization in their areas.[6] The Cooke banks managed sales in the region around Washington and Philadelphia. In New York Jay Cooke's leading associates were Fisk & Hatch, and Livermore, Clews & Co., with Vermilye & Co. and Clark, Dodge & Co. giving active aid. Fisk & Hatch had been organized in 1862 by a former paying teller of the Bank of the Commonwealth and a former cashier of the Bank of Jersey City.[7] Livermore, Clews & Co. was also a young house, but Henry Clews, one of its partners who was recognized as a shrewd observer of the stock market, had been active in taking government loans in New York at the beginning of the war.[8] The head of Vermilye & Co., then recently established, was well known in New York. Clark, Dodge & Co. needs no introduction here; they dealt mainly in securities over the counter. In Boston Jay Cooke had excellent support from Spencer, Vila & Co., and in Baltimore from John Wills.

These bankers proved to be men of considerable ability, but most of them had neither great prestige nor capital. Jay Cooke's alliance with private bankers was to be expected, especially since chartered banks had come to disagree so strongly with some of the policies of Chase. We do not know, however, whether it was from choice or necessity that Jay Cooke failed to enlist the active aid of such important private bankers as Read, Drexel & Co. and Ketchum, Son & Co. in New York. It may be noted that this was the beginning of a cleavage which was later to have an important bearing on Jay Cooke's banking career.

In the West, where leadership in banking was less highly developed, Jay Cooke kept a closer personal hold. He did this particularly through traveling agents, who were paid salaries and expenses. They were young men, carefully selected for the qualities which fitted them for work in the particular locality to which they were assigned. Jay Cooke gave them full information about their work, aroused their enthusiasm, and sent them out, not forgetting to write encouraging letters to them from time to time.

One of the earliest traveling agents was Robert Clarkson, who was sent out from the Philadelphia house of Jay Cooke & Co. in December, 1862, to organize the bankers in the larger cities in the West.[9] He visited the more important centers in Ohio, Indiana, and Illinois, and also Milwaukee, Wisconsin, where he called on the bankers and arranged with them for the sale of bonds. Clarkson reported fully to Jay Cooke about what he accomplished and also about political conditions in the places he visited. Later, traveling agents likewise arranged agencies, in small places as well as large, encouraged subagents, and reported to Jay Cooke the political and financial pulse of the western country. By the fall of 1863 there were several active agents in the field; one in Pennsylvania, two in Ohio, one in Indiana, in Illinois, and in Michigan, two in Wisconsin, and one covering Missouri, Iowa, and Minnesota.[10]

Everywhere were subagents, large and small. These were mostly bankers; but, where there were no bankers, insurance men, real-estate dealers, or leaders in the community were brought into the ranks. Apparently, anyone who chose might become a subagent. There were in all some 2,500 agents selling five-twenties in the loyal States and Territories. They sold bonds, advertised the loan, and sought out potential buyers. The bankers made advances to bond buyers, thus indirectly lending their own credit to the government, which greatly facilitated the selling of the loan.[11] The banks aided further by taking payment in various forms other than the legal tender required by the government.

To work with so scattered and varied a body of subagents, under very unstable business conditions, was a management problem of the first magnitude. In these days of the Federal Reserve System, it is difficult to imagine a time when there was not a single co-ordinating agency in the whole banking system of the United States. Without the railroad and the telegraph system, Jay Cooke could not have organized the country so effectively. As the Civil War was the first American war in which these new means of transportation and communication were of great military importance, it was likewise the very earliest in which they aided in mobilizing capital with which to finance the war. The railroad system had by then reached all important points east of the Mississippi; and telegraph lines connected all settled parts of the country, even reaching California in 1861, while consolidations, especially under the Western Union, were greatly improving the effectiveness of the system.[12]

Jay Cooke used the telegraph as no American business man had ever before used it. It kept him in constant touch with the leading loan agents throughout the country, bringing him daily, even hourly, reports on sales, so that he knew at any time the exact condition of the loan. By means of the wires, also, Jay Cooke received instant intelligence of events which had a bearing on the sale of government bonds. He kept his eye on military progress in the field, political events in Washington, and the stock and money markets in New York — three strategic points in determining the success or failure of a loan. The Cooke banks had private wires to facilitate the sending of messages between Washington and New York; one concern guaranteed an answer in five minutes.[13]

In his plans for selling government bonds Jay Cooke made no provision for sales abroad. He held that he could appeal more effectively to patriotism if the bonds were sold only at home, and he thought it was not to the interest of the United States to be in debt abroad.[14] An exception was made late in 1863. William Evans of London, who had come to the United States with a letter of introduction to Jay Cooke from John Bright,[15] arranged to represent Jay Cooke in London. Evans sold $30,000 of five-twenties, one-third of which was taken by John Bright, the staunch friend of the North.[16] This one exception shows how exclusively Jay Cooke's early efforts were limited to the United States. Secretary Chase sent Robert J. Walker to England on a fruitless mission to try to place some bonds, but Jay Cooke had nothing to do with that effort.[17]

Jay Cooke thus built up an astounding system for selling bonds. Nothing like it had ever been seen in the United States. But an organization was not enough; people had to be persuaded to purchase the bonds. The banker saw from the very first that a favorable opinion had to be developed in support of the bonds, and to accomplish this he turned to the press.

CREATING A FAVORABLE PUBLIC OPINION

In his use of the press Jay Cooke showed his gift for doing the practical thing even though there was little precedent for it. When asked years later where he got his ideas about advertising, he recalled how he had been impressed with the advertising of Dr. Jayne, a pharmacist, and of John Wanamaker, who had opened his Oak Hall Clothing Bazaar in Philadelphia in February, 1861.[18] To us it is obvious, however, that Cooke's ability to utilize the press had a broader foundation, that it lay deep in his own personality and experience. He had an uncanny understanding of human nature, and from his earliest years in business he had come to see the possibilities of using the press to direct people's thoughts and actions.

Fortunately, recent developments in newspaper printing [19] and in the organization of the press had made possible the utilization of newspapers for advertising on a large scale. The cheapening of printing helped bring a great increase in periodicals in the 1860's,[20] and the consolidation in the collection and distribution of news and advertising made it easier to promote government loans on a national scale. The young Associated Press [21] made the dissemination of publicity easier, and advertising agencies, which stood between the advertiser and the publisher, such as S. M. Pettingill & Co. and Peaslee & Co. (really L. F. Shattuck, a friend of Secretary Chase), proved very helpful, though none had as yet become organized on a national scale.[22]

Cooke employed rare strategy in his handling of the press. He paid newspapers generously for carrying advertisements of the loan, binding them to the cause, as he said, "by kind and liberal treatment." [23] The newspapers which enjoyed the benefits of Jay Cooke's advertising were expected to carry publicity without compensation, which proved a most effective force in molding northern opinion and in establishing the prestige of Jay Cooke and the government loans.[24]

The crowning feature of Jay Cooke's system was the way in which he used the press to create public opinion favorable to the government loans. Never before in the history of the United States had so much been done in emergencies to secure financial support for the government. Stephen Girard had done well when in 1813 he had placed advertisements in six papers to run daily for about two weeks;[25] the Mexican War loans had been given only the most casual notice in the newspapers. But not so with the five-twenties; they stared every reader in the face within northern territory, and argued him into buying bonds.

General advertising agencies were not employed in the earlier part of the five-twenty campaign. The writing and distribution of material for the press was under the management of Sexton, a clerk in the Philadelphia house of Jay Cooke. Toward the end of 1863, however, S. M. Pettingill & Co., of New York, was engaged to help advertise and publicize the loan.[26] Much of the advertising and publicity was handled by the leading loan agents and the subagents, many of whom tirelessly fired up their local press, used their influence to keep editors loyal, and distributed printed matter on the loan. Much of the publicity was introduced through Philadelphia newspapers, like the *Inquirer*, *City Item*, *Press*, and *Bulletin*, and was copied elsewhere, voluntarily or under pressure. So extensive did the advertising become that there was hardly a newspaper in the country, not too disloyal, that did not carry five-twenty advertisements or publicity of some kind.[27]

Five-twenty printed propaganda assumed various forms. There were the 25 × 40 inch posters in heavy capital letters, bearing a likeness of the symbolic eagle, which told the busy person where he could get five-twenties,[28] or the circular giving more complete information for him who had time to read. Hundreds of thousands of miscellaneous posters and handbills were printed and spread far and wide. The material in newspapers ranged from the short notice of an agent stating that he had bonds to sell to the long advertisement or article treating of any variety of things which closely or remotely touched upon the loan. The articles and advertisements were simple and readable, striking in form, and appealing in argument.

Jay Cooke's five-twenty publicity was in a real sense educational. There were many people in the United States who knew little or nothing about bonds, and it was necessary to give them the most elementary information. Jay Cooke prepared and broadcast through newspapers, circulars, and broadsides, an article entitled, "The Best Way to put Out Money on Interest." [29] This article contained the famous letter from the "Berks County Farmer," which was so characteristic of Cooke's methods. This letter and its reply, both of which were fictitious, followed the simple question and answer method which Jay Cooke used so effectively. Having a few thousand to invest and feeling that government loans were safe and good and "that it is my duty and interest, at this time, to put my money into them," the farmer asked for information about the bonds. "Do you take country money, or only Legal Tender Notes, or will a check on Philadelphia, or New York, answer for subscriptions? . . . As I cannot come to Philadelphia how am I to get the Bonds? . . . What sizes are the bonds? . . . Will I have to pay the same tax on them as I now pay on my Railroad or other Bonds? . . . Will Secretary Chase get enough from Custom House duties and Internal Revenue, Income Taxes, &c., &c., to make it certain that he can pay the Interest punctually?" And so on. Jay Cooke "cheerfully" answered the letter, simply, clearly, and in great detail, subtly playing up the strength of the government and closing with "I am very truly, your Friend, Jay Cooke."

Several themes ran through five-twenty advertising and publicity. Nationalism and patriotism were dominant, for Jay Cooke knew the effectiveness of an emotional appeal. Readers were reminded that Chase had saved the country from the indignity of turning to European bankers.[30] After Hooker's repulse in May, 1863, it was said that the loyalty of the people of the United States was not only the loyalty of success, for the people were still buying bonds;[31] and after Chancellorsville, that military reverses "make no change in the popular faith which remains unshaken and true to the immortal destiny of the Republic." [32]

The most stirring patriotic appeal was one which was scattered far and wide in newspapers and on broadsides. This appeal illustrates so strikingly Jay Cooke's own feeling and thinking and his energetic expression that it was very clearly inspired, if not actually written, by him:

TO FARMERS, MECHANICS AND CAPITALISTS!

You have a solemn duty to perform to your government and to posterity!

Our gallant army and navy must be supported by every man and woman who has any means, large or small, at their control. The United States Government, to which we owe our prosperity as a nation, security of person and property of every sort, calls on each individual to rally to its support — *not* with donations or gifts — though who could withhold them — BUT WITH SUBSCRIPTIONS TO HER LOANS, based on the best security in the world, the untold and scarcely yet tried resources of this mighty Continent, which *were* developing rapidly when the rebellion broke out, and to maintain which, AS A PRICELESS HERITAGE TO POSTERITY, this defence against rebellion is made.

There is no miscalculation, and can be no failure — the cost has been counted, and the burthen will be light to us, and gladly borne by posterity. What our Revolutionary Fathers are to us, WE will be to coming generations, if we fail not in our plain and simple duty!

The owner of every foot of ground, of every house and workshop, owes a debt of service in the field, or of his means in this noble work!

Talk not of Taxes! they *secure* the Loans. Take the Loans! and the Taxes will fall more lightly — and they supply the ready, *present* and *required* means to strike the death blow at rebellion and the foul disturbers of the Nation's peace!

Talk not of Rulers! They are the ministers of GOD! who rules the world and the destiny of this mighty Nation! Our first duty is to God — our next to our country — fail not of either!

Your nearest patriotic Bank or Banker will supply this loan, on which so much depends!

It was not only a matter of patriotism but also of justice. The loan, according to one of Jay Cooke's spokesmen, was founded on "the justice of our cause, and, we firmly believe, the protection of Divine Providence." [33] Its success afforded "the most unmistakable and overwhelming proof of the unabating zeal for the right, the sterling integrity . . . of the American people." [34]

Jay Cooke knew that especially with the larger investors the loan would have to stand on its appeal to people's business sense. And so it was explained that "these Bonds are, in effect, a *First Mortgage* upon all Railroads, Canals, Bank Stock, and Securities, and the immense products of all Manufacturers, &c., &c., in the country." They were the safest investment that could be made in the United States: "Full and ample provisions made for the payment of the interest and liquidation of the principal, by Custom Duties, Excise Stamps, and Internal Revenue, serves to make the Bonds the Best, Most Available and Most Popular Investments in the Market." The ability of the government to pay the interest and principal was stressed more than any other financial aspect of the matter. The country's unlimited resources were continually referred to as conclusive evidence of its strength. When England could pay her enormous debts, what could not the United States do? For the benefit of those who were inclined to hoard gold — and they were many — Jay Cooke stated that $1,000 in gold invested in five-twenties would in five years be worth $2,000.[35] Prudence and self-interest, it was said, dictated that there should be no time lost in subscribing.[36]

Thus it was shown that the path of duty and right, as well as the road to riches, led to the subscription office. Here was the happy coincidence of an opportunity to serve both self and country. Was not this the secret of the strength of Jay Cooke's appeal? Indeed, has it not been the secret of many great accomplishments in the past? Have not great leaders often won followers by resting a selfish effort on an exalted emotionalism? The ability to do this was what particularly distinguished Jay Cooke from those conservative bankers whom he so strongly criticized for their lack of patriotism.

But there were people who could not be reached by appeal to their investment sense or their patriotism. They might be influenced, however, by the example of others. Accordingly, across the pages of newspapers were paraded the various types of people buying bonds. There was the tottering old lady who brought money in her handkerchief —"She is shown into the back room and given a seat." "Next comes a hale old farmer from Berks county, with his $5,000. He has heard of the loan; some of his neighbors have invested; he has read Mr. Cooke's letter, and he has concluded to put his money where he is not only sure of his interest, but he is aiding the Government." [37] A portly gentleman, "one of the 'solid men' of Philadelphia — at whom you can scarcely look without having visions of plethoric pocket-books and heavy balances in bank," took bonds for $25,000.[38] The un-named "War Democrat" won immortal fame by making a present of $660 to the government! [39]

The description of the progress of the great five-twenty drama made interesting reading. One article entitled, "A Day in Jay Cooke's Office," described a thrilling scene:[40] the rush of orders, the hurrying about of messenger boys, the nursery maid who bought a bond for $50, the letters received stacked in quires, the telegraph messengers, and people in a never-ending procession. "In the midst of all this may be seen the agent of the Government, receiving visitors, answering questions, giving directions," and footing up deposits for the day in the Treasury of $1,150,000!

A regular feature was the daily announcement of sales. The amount sold each day was reported in newspapers the country over, as were also sales by sections, States, and cities. The number of subscribers in a day was often noted, and certain places were complimented on their zeal.

Thus Jay Cooke, in the judgment of one newspaper,[41]

occupied every avenue of intelligence, appealed to the patriotism of loyal men everywhere, and by reasoning, entreating, education, and explaining — by showing to the people the great good that would come from sustaining the government — the folly and the shame that any other course of action would exhibit — by taking advantage of the patriotic feeling we see in the great reaction now sweeping over the North — he succeeded in popularizing the great five-twenty loan, and now finds the people so anxious to convert their currency into bonds that it is only with difficulty he can meet the sudden and increasing demand.

Conditions Affecting the Sale of Five-Twenties

There were many unstable factors at work determining the standing of government securities in the market which had to be reckoned with from day to day. Favorable or unfavorable, they had a profound effect on the sale of the five-twenties, and Jay Cooke fought unceasingly to control their effects.

The strongest among the influences working against the loan were the recurring military reverses of the North, the seeming lack of energy and decisiveness in the conduct of the war in the East, and the great loss of men. Criticism of the military policy of the government grew, and the Copperheads became more and more aggressive in their attacks. Senator John Sherman wrote with much feeling to Jay Cooke about his observations throughout the country in July, 1863:[42] "I have now been in several cities of the Union and I regret to say that the opposition to the Admin. is deep seated and will surely break out in mobs & riots. Perhaps it cannot be avoided. It is an incident of Civil War and is undoubtedly encouraged by a party press. But the authorities at W. ought to understand that they now are to meet new dangers and that they must seek a more hearty & reliable support from some quarters than they have had."

The security and gold markets in New York made immediate and sensitive response to the various influences touching the credit of the government. The gold exchange had been established shortly after the depreciation of legal tenders had set in; and dealing in gold, a necessity for the merchant and importer after the currency no longer commanded its face value in gold, soon attracted speculators. There were professional speculators in New York; but outside of New York the heaviest orders came from Washington and from Baltimore and Louisville, the gateways to the war zone. A contemporary observer in Washington reports that "members of both Houses, and of all political creeds, resident bankers, the lobby agents, clerks, and secretaries, haunted the War Department for the latest news from the seat of war. The daily registry of the Gold Room [in New York] was a quicker messenger of successes or defeats than the tardier telegrams of the Associated Press." [43] Indeed, men in all walks of life throughout the country, who could put up the necessary ten per cent margin, participated in the mania.

Since the reverses of the North were many in 1863, the gold market was largely bullish. A high premium on gold meant that currency was relatively cheaper. It might appear that the depreciated currency would, therefore, have hastened the buying of gold bonds, but it must be remembered that purchases depended not only on price but also on confidence in the government.

As far as gold was concerned the problem was to keep the price from going too high. Jay Cooke like many others believed that the price of gold was in part artificially raised by speculators; in this he was clearly wrong as far as the long-time trend was concerned but in a measure right with respect to violent short-time fluctuations.[44] Jay Cooke regarded the gold speculator as a rebel [45] and used all the force of his publicity to discredit him. There is no evidence which definitely proves, however, that Cooke entered the market to force down the price of gold during his five-twenty campaign.

Recognizing that the solution lay essentially in the people's attitude toward the government, Jay Cooke did all he could to create a favorable public opinion and to prevent the idea of defeat from getting too strong a hold. The Cookes did not hesitate to express their feelings about military matters to those in power, and on one occasion Jay Cooke even pleaded with President Lincoln to remove General McClellan from his command. The banker firmly believed that the slowness of the sale of five-twenties was largely due to "Macs" dilatory policy, and the subsequent removal of McClellan led him to think that he had been the immediate cause of the change in the command of the army.[46]

The five-twenties not only had to overcome a lack of confidence in the government but they also had to face competition in the money market.[47] Since the legal tenders bore no interest, inland banks shipped them to New York or other eastern depositories where interest was paid on demand deposits, thus securing an income without the risk involved in holding government securities. This meant that the funds for buying government bonds were drained from the country and poured into New York, where they earned their keep by working as call loans, which meant speculation on the gold and stock exchanges.

Jay Cooke's opposition to legal tenders made itself heard in connection with the discussions preceding the adoption of the third legal tender act. In his report of December, 1862, Secretary Chase had made known that the Treasury had unpaid obligations of $276,912,517.66.[48] But instead of recommending heavy taxation, he had proposed further loans and the establishment of a banking system to provide a uniform currency. On the question of a further issue of greenbacks, he had been uncertain.

With the soldiers clamoring for their pay and complaints coming from far and wide, it was not strange that many congressmen were in a greenback mood. When the question came up early in January, 1863, Jay Cooke opposed a further issue of greenbacks because he believed that it would merely increase speculation. He recommended the use of three-year interest-bearing notes in the belief that they would be held by banks for income and would not immediately be sent to eastern banks. If used in making payments to soldiers and for quartermasters' supplies, these notes would be issued gradually and scattered widely.

Jay Cooke explained in his Memoirs how he urged his plan upon the House Committee on Ways and Means. On being questioned whether he really believed in the plan, he made a reply which reveals his personality and the working of his mind: "I felt that in answering I was stating a great truth & making a vastily important announcement & said, raising myself to my full heighth & pointing towards Heaven. In the Name of my God I believe every word will be fulfilled that I have promised if this bill is enacted into a law." Then he explained his theory to the congressmen. He likened the United States Treasury to the ocean and the paymasters to clouds dropping rain in the form of interest-bearing notes over the land; the rain later, through exchange for gold-bearing bonds, was collected into streams which flowed back to the ocean. If non-interest-bearing notes were used, however, and were disbursed in large quantities at a time, they would "produce evil through floods [inflation of prices and speculation] or by stagnating in immence morases & swamps (the cities of NY & other Eastern cities) there to create miazm fever & nightmare & every imaginable & permanent evil."

But the supporters of greenbacks were too powerful, and the Committee on Ways and Means proposed a further issue of non-interest-bearing legal tender.[49] Jay Cooke again urged Chase that "the plans of the Committee are absolutely ruinous and will prolong and extend, an hundred fold perhaps, the evils of the present hour." Henry Cooke also took up the fight; he wrote an article for the *Washington Chronicle* [50] in which he pointed out that the issue of $300,000,000 more greenbacks would bring a proportionate decline in currency as compared with gold. He urged the adoption of the proposal of Representative Stevens, which virtually embodied Jay Cooke's plan; he pointed out especially that, by virtue of bearing interest, those notes would be retained for income and would not have an inflationary effect on prices and, consequently, on the cost of carrying on the war.

The bill, as finally passed, authorized the Secretary of the Treasury to borrow up to $900,000,000. [51] This could be done in three forms: (1) The Secretary could sell, on such terms as he deemed most advisable, ten-forty bonds bearing interest of 6 per cent in coin. (2) Non-interest-bearing legal tender notes to the amount of $180,000,000 could be issued at his discretion. And (3) three-year Treasury notes bearing 6 per cent interest in lawful money could be issued to the extent of $400,000,000, to be sold on the best terms available or paid to such creditors as were willing to accept them at par.

This act seemed like a victory for Jay Cooke. Though it provided for a further issue of greenbacks, it was only half the amount originally considered. And the proposed Treasury notes bore an interest rate approximately 3.65 per cent in coin, as Cooke had suggested. But, as Jay Cooke explains in his Memoirs, the principles of the act were completely frustrated by Chase's method of administration. Instead of scattering the notes through payments to soldiers and for supplies, Chase disposed of them to the banks in New York and other large cities. Cooke's recommendation about interest was practically nullified by attaching interest coupons maturing every six months. In the opinion of Jay Cooke, "at the end of each six months the debt would become nothing more than an ordinary green back for the time being & the mischief arising from the 50 mil[lion] immediate inflation of the currency would be productive of evil & the funded character of the issue & much of the enducement to fund into long gold bearing bonds would be done away with."

The additional issue of greenbacks did not work exactly as Jay

Cooke had prophesied. Currency continued to depreciate, it is true, and the gold bonds became cheaper in terms of currency. But there is some reason to believe that the credit of the government was at the same time actually strengthened by the fact that internal taxation was beginning to bring in money. In the fiscal year ending June 30, 1863, new internal taxes were collected to the amount of $37,640,787.95;[52] the next three months brought in half again as much; and October and November duplicated the receipts of the summer quarter. Small as these sums were, they indicated nevertheless that the government had made a beginning toward paying for the war out of taxation. The will to tax and the ability to be taxed were thus both brought to the support of the public credit.

JAY COOKE HELPS ESTABLISH THE NATIONAL BANKING SYSTEM

No discussion of the five-twenty campaign is complete that overlooks the close connection between the sale of the government bonds and a very important change in our banking system. The establishment of the new system went hand in hand with the five-twenty campaign and Jay Cooke was in no small measure responsible for the inauguration of the system. By a strange turn of events, the exchange broker, who had for twenty years profited from the chaotic conditions of currency and banking in the United States, participated in setting up new banks which were to go far toward destroying the very basis of his earlier profits.

Cooke was in no sense responsible for the origin of the movement for the establishment of a national banking system.[53] On the contrary, he at first opposed it. While he was convinced that such a system would be of great value in effecting regularity and uniformity in currency and banking, he thought it would be hazardous under the uncertainty of war conditions to make the attack on State banks which would inevitably result from establishing national banking associations. He knew from his correspondence with bankers that many of them would resent any move toward the establishment of a system which might encroach on their own independent and profitable preserves.

Secretary Chase was determined, however, to establish a national system of note-issuing banks. Early in January, 1863, the measure providing for the national banking system was introduced in Congress. Though the bill had some strong friends, among them John Sherman, William Fessenden, Thaddeus Stevens, and Samuel Hooper, it met persistent opposition and was far short of the necessary number of votes. Chase, therefore, turned to the Cookes and convinced them that they should come to his aid.

The Cookes went to work with all the means they could command. They requested the newspapers which carried five-twenty advertisements to publish editorials and articles in support of the proposed system. Many articles were written by Jay Cooke or his brother Henry. As the former says in his Memoirs, he likened a community without a good bank "to a country glowering under the dark shadow of hills, the valleys being occupied by stagnant morasses & marshes in wh. the will of the whisp danced at night & the gloomy croak of the frog was heard, the snakes & lizards were the enumerous inhabitants. Myasthmatic mists rose even to the summits of the hills & every condition was gloomy & sad." But, if the "civilizing & energizing influence" of national banks appeared, the scene would change: "the marshes & morasses being drained would become fertile fields, the springs & rivulets chocked & hindered as they had been by morass & marsh would now flow laughingly down & be gathered into pure resevoirs, furnishing supplies of water for fountains & resevoirs & for manufacturing purposes."

Again we have an illustration of the power of the press. For about six weeks in the months of January and February, newspapers far and wide set forth the evils of existing State banking with its heavy toll on trade due to a chaotic currency and urged the benefits to be derived from a national system. The master stroke of the Cookes in this connection was to have clippings from his home newspaper placed on the desk of each senator and representative in Congress.[54]

Jay Cooke & Co. did not depend on newspaper publicity alone. They also dispatched letters to bankers and others and mailed

A Mural in the First National Bank of Philadelphia Commemorating the Signing of the First Charter Granted under the National Banking Act

Secretary Chase is seated at the table with Jay Cooke and Kate Chase at the left and a soldier, Hugh McCulloch, Comptroller of the Currency, and Clarence H. Clark, President of the First National Bank of Philadelphia, at the right

thousands of copies of the bank bill. Jay Cooke and his five-twenty organization also personally interviewed many people, explaining and urging the value of the proposed system.

The bill passed. Secretary Chase wrote to the banker expressing deep gratitude for his aid: "Your services in behalf of the Uniform Currency bill are fully appreciated by me: except that appreciation the consciousness of usefulness to your country must be your sole reward." [55]

The passing of the bill was but a beginning. The real test of the measure was still to come. Hugh McCulloch was made Comptroller of the Currency and it became his task to administer the act. McCulloch was a Maine-born Indianan who had done notable work with the State Bank of Indiana.[56] McCulloch's task was a big one, especially to induce banks which had profited from the old system to organize under a national charter. He was fortunate in having the support of the Cookes, who saw in the new banks a market for five-twenties.

Jay Cooke aided in several ways in the establishment of the national system. Most important was his pamphlet entitled, *How to Organize a National Bank under Secretary Chase's Bill*, which was issued in the summer of 1863. This publication was an extremely useful handbook for those who contemplated organizing under the new system; it explained all the steps in organizing a bank, gave samples of legal forms required and even of by-laws of a national bank, and it answered the many questions that would be asked about legal and other aspects of national banks.

Jay Cooke himself was largely responsible for the organization of three institutions. One was the First National Bank of Philadelphia, which received charter number one [57] and was opened for business on July 11, 1863.[58] Among the 73 incorporators of this bank were Jay Cooke, C. H. Clark, and Anthony J. Drexel. This was largely a Cooke-Clark bank. The three largest shareholders were E. W. Clark & Co., Jay Cooke, and William Moorhead, in the order given, who held almost half of the stock of the bank;[59] the Clark and Cooke groups each had two directors on the board, and C. H. Clark was president.[60] No other large private bank was represented on the board of this bank.

The First National of Philadelphia became very useful to Jay Cooke in the selling of government securities. It started with a capital of $150,000, which was increased to $500,000 in November, 1863, and $1,000,000 in January, 1864.[61] With this capital the bank was able to buy extensively of government bonds. By December, 1863, it had purchased $650,000 of five-twenties, of which $500,000 were deposited with the Treasury to secure circulation and $100,000 to secure deposits.[62]

In October, 1864, the directors of the First National Bank of Philadelphia created a loan department which was to have custody of and manage the investments of the bank in federal or other government securities.[63] This illustrates how war finance, which was providing large issues of securities for which there was a continuous market, was drawing the commercial banks into the investment business. In the case of some banks — as for instance the First National of New York — dealing in governments was to lay the foundation for a larger business in securities.

Another bank which owed its origin directly to Jay Cooke was the First National Bank of Washington, D. C., which started with a capital of $500,000,[64] all but $15,000 of which was subscribed by members of the two Cooke banking houses.[65] This bank was housed on the second floor of the new building in which Jay Cooke & Co., of Washington, occupied the first floor, and it was to all intents and purposes a part of the Jay Cooke group.

The larger banking interests of New York City were slow to welcome the new system. John Thompson, publisher of *Thompson's Bank Note Detector*, was instrumental in organizing the First National Bank. In October, 1863, this bank had the modest capital of $200,000, one-half of which was invested in bonds to secure circulation; the Second National was organized with a capital of $300,000, and the Third, with a capital of $500,000.[66]

Before any of these New York banks were organized, Secretary Chase and Comptroller McCulloch had encouraged a movement for establishing in New York a national bank with a capital of at least $5,000,000.[67] The national system had been making slow progress, and they felt that a large bank in New York would help establish the prestige of national banks the country over. The larger banks and capitalists of the city, however, were not interested in the project; the Bank of Commerce, the American Exchange Bank, and the Metropolitan Bank were openly hostile. For the time being the project was dropped.

Some time later Chase and McCulloch called on Jay Cooke to aid in establishing such a bank. Cooke gives in his Memoirs an explanation of how he responded. He first canvassed Philadelphia for subscriptions on a Monday morning, securing over half a million, and then he went to New York. There on three successive days he met with the committee chosen some months before to secure subscriptions to the proposed bank; he helped them plan a campaign, which consisted of personal calls on important bankers and capitalists, and he filled them with enthusiasm for the project. He also enlisted his five-twenty men, and he, himself, saw a number of capitalists from whom he secured subscriptions, including $100,000 each from Daniel Drew and Hoyt, Sprague & Co. By Thursday night the five-million goal had been reached. Thereupon, wrote Jay Cooke in his Memoirs, with a dramatic flourish colored no doubt by the retrospective imagination of an old man,

I immediately telegraphed the Sec. of the Treasury that the 4th Nat bank was established . . . within the three days, & calling in the money editors of all the prin dailies . . . gave them list of the completed subscriptions. This list with the circum attending the estab of this 4th Bank with 5 mill. capital was duly put next morning in all the papers & that night at the Union League Club under the auspices of Mr. Hutton a supper was furnished the committee with many invited guests includ Hon. Wm M Everts & some other subscribers. I received many hearty congrat. & about midnight left for Phila.

The Fourth National Bank was opened for business on March 1, 1864.[68]

According to Cooke's Memoirs, this was not the end of his jousting in New York for the honor of the national system. When the large State-chartered banks of that city showed that they were not inclined to turn national, he let it be known that he contemplated bringing about the organization of a national bank with a capital of $50,000,000. Banks throughout the country would be

invited to become stockholders, and they and the national
Treasury would be encouraged to keep their New York deposits
with this bank.

Cooke believed he had considerable influence in bringing the
large New York banks into the national system. As a matter of
fact, however, there was no strong movement in that direction till
after the adoption in 1865 of a measure for taxing the issues of
State-chartered banks.[69] Whatever Cooke's influence was, one
cannot help wondering whether his aggressiveness in the matter
was to his own best interests. Did it, perhaps, arouse some feeling, some enmity, against himself? After all, he was an outsider.
Were such instances, in a measure, responsible for some of the
opposition to his position with the Treasury and for his failure to
build up a strong institutional following among New York bankers and capitalists?

The West was, on the whole, more friendly to the national
banking system than was the East. Jay Cooke's organization did
much both to encourage and actually to help establish national
banks in that section. Some of his subagents and traveling agents
became active propagandists for the system, especially the
latter, who in the fall of 1863 devoted themselves largely to the
cause of national banks. They went to the cities or to backwoods
communities; they conferred with bankers and merchants, met
arguments against the new system, and answered questions about
procedure in organizing a bank.[70] Their methods are illustrated
by a letter from a traveling agent to Jay Cooke:[71]

I left Detroit Friday Oct. 16 at 8 A.M. — spread circulars through
the cars — arrived at Pontiac 9½ o'clock — visited the two banking
houses, and opened to them the advantages of the National System.
Found both well disposed but short of capital — urged that they
should promote the sale of 5–20's among their friends and customers
— getting them to join their investments for the establishment of
National Banks. Having made satisfactory progress with the bankers,
I called on the Post Master and other officials and prominent men to
enlist them in the cause — distributed circulars freely, and at 1½ o'c.
P.M. started in a hired conveyance for Romeo, 24 miles off the R. R. . . .
I had learned of a few wealthy men of the place who had intended form-

ing a bank, and procured some 5–20's but had now given up the project. I thought it might be revived. I found Romeo to be a lively place in a rich region of well to do farmers. I called on all the prominent merchants, lawyers &c and went out 3 miles to see Dr. Gray who has $20,000 of 5–20s. I enlarged with all these gentlemen on the subject . . . and finally showed them that if they did not establish a bank themselves, to be managed and enjoyed by themselves — so inviting a field would surely be occupied by others.

Thus Jay Cooke helped to destroy what had been the very basis for much of his own earlier banking career. Nothing that had ever happened in American banking did so much to change the private banks as did the establishment of the national system; it took away much of the private banks' work by making domestic exchange simpler and less risky, and its attractiveness induced many to take out a national charter. Many private banks remained, but they came more and more to be of two distinct types; the unspecialized bank which continued to serve the frontier, and the bank developing in the direction of specialization, as a mortgage concern in the West or as a note broker or a dealer in foreign exchange or investments in the larger centers of business.

As had been anticipated, the national banks in time aided the Treasury, but they were not immediately very useful in taking government bonds. By November, 1863, they had on deposit with the United States Treasury less than $4,000,000 in bonds for securing circulation; by the same time in 1864, however, they had taken $81,000,000; and by 1865, $277,000,000.[72] As we shall see later, they were helpful in retailing bonds, but not so helpful as the Secretary had expected. This was due both to their immaturity and to the lack of centralization in the national system.

THE PROGRESS OF THE LOAN

The five-twenties sold slowly for a long time. It took months to organize the selling and publicizing, and in the dark winter of 1862–63, when the finances of the North were at their worst and the Confederate States secured a loan in Europe,[73] the low credit of the United States was distinctly unfavorable to the selling of its loans. By spring, however, Jay Cooke's organization was ready for intensive work and five-twenty advertising and publicity launched a heavy attack which was backed by the improving credit of the government.

The sale of five-twenties began to pick up in March, 1863. Jay Cooke's success then became so marked that it encouraged confidence in the government and thereby helped raise the value of the greenbacks relatively to gold.[74] On a day late in April bonds were sold to the unprecedented amount of almost $2,500,000; on May 1 about $5,000,000 were sold to some 5,000 subscribers.[75] The largest total subscription for cities generally came from New York, with Philadelphia and Boston next in turn; of the western States, Ohio was the leader, while the States beyond the Mississippi trailed along with their few thousand.

In spite of difficulties in May and June, sales continued to be surprisingly high. Serious military reverses threatened confidence again, but through the press Jay Cooke kept up a persistent fight against the idea of defeat. So heavy were sales that the Treasury was unable to furnish bonds fast enough to meet orders, which was serious for the subscription agents since it gave subscribers an opportunity to change their minds.[76] At one time Jay Cooke found, through a conference with subagents in New York, that "all the agents [are] almost disposed to back out & quit the business — the delay of Bonds is ruinous & they say it is getting to be intolerable." [77] But the loan continued to sell well. At the end of the fiscal year, June 30, 1863, it was reported that five-twenties to the amount of $175,037,259.44 had been sold, all but a few million since February.[78]

As June passed, uncertainty about the fate of the five-twenty loan complicated matters for Jay Cooke. The right to convert legal tenders into five-twenties was to expire on July 1, and Secretary Chase had the power to discontinue selling the loan at that time.[79] The Secretary did not make known until shortly before that time whether he would continue the sale of the loan or retain Jay Cooke as agent. This uncertainty made it risky for Jay Cooke either to curtail his selling campaign or to continue maintaining an expensive organization which might find itself without work.

Chase hesitated because of widespread criticism of his employment of Cooke. The success of the Philadelphia banker spoke eloquently, however, and many bankers wrote to the Secretary urging that he continue employing Jay Cooke as fiscal agent. Joshua Hanna, of Pittsburgh, the outstanding banker of western Pennsylvania, who was a friend of Chase though at times critical of Jay Cooke, urged the Secretary to retain his special agent. After a careful examination of the details of the Cooke machinery he had been "much surprised to find the expense of it so great and I run no risk of successful contradiction when I say no man can within three months get up as efficient a plan at less cost and that neither he or any one else can continue it under 1/8 per ct." Hanna said that many people's nerves were weak on government securities "and nothing less than the whole strength of the present agency can prevent a decline & consequently suspension of sales by the government." [80] The rumor that Chase contemplated a change brought the comment from the *New York Herald* (which was often critical of Jay Cooke) that this would "deprive the government of the aid of about the most zealous and worst paid servants it has," and that it was doubtful that people would continue to buy just because they had started to.[81] Chase decided to retain Cooke as agent, and the sale of five-twenties was continued without the convertibility feature. This instance illustrates one difficulty with which Jay Cooke had to deal; fearful of criticism, Chase often kept him uncertain as to his relations with the Treasury. A man with less patience or less willingness to assume risks would probably not have continued to work under such conditions.

Jay Cooke's aggressive selling continued to dispose of large amounts of bonds. Victories at Gettysburg, Vicksburg, and Chattanooga were powerful allies, which even draft riots in New York and losses at Chickamauga could not overcome. On a certain day in October bonds were sold for $15,000,000.[82]

The heavy sales brought their own problems, and these show how complicated was the task of managing the sale of the five-twenties. The Cooke organization continued to be hampered by the slowness of the Treasury in furnishing bonds; at the end of

November, unfilled orders for bonds amounted to $33,000,000.[83] Great difficulty was also met in transferring the proceeds of sales to the place and form in which payments had to be made to the government. The existing system of currency and domestic exchange complicated matters seriously, and the cost of exchange was necessarily a matter of considerable concern. In smaller towns or in places where exchange on a depository city was unfavorable, the cost of transmitting money was likely to consume commissions from sales.[84] Indeed, the sale of bonds in the West had by the summer of 1863 so affected the exchange market that eastern funds were in many places scarce. Agents could not afford to sell bonds for one-eighth of one per cent when one-fourth of one per cent was paid for transferring the proceeds.

The form in which payments were made to Jay Cooke placed a considerable risk on him. He had to take commercial paper, drafts, checks, and certificates drawn on remote States or villages and make collections on his own responsibility. There was also danger of loss from counterfeits, closed banks, or other irregularities. Such losses Jay Cooke had to bear.[85] When it is remembered that there were some 2,500 agents selling the loan who were not bonded and were under practically no government regulations and had no unity of institutional control, it is evident that there was considerable risk.

The most serious problem, when sales were large, was that of securing the proper means for making payments to the government. Jay Cooke was required to make payments to specified government depositories, the New York Subtreasury or the Treasury at Washington, and in the form of "lawful money of the United States." When in the fall of 1863 the sales became so large, it not only became difficult to secure the necessary legal tender, but there was also the danger of causing a stringency in the money market by too rapid an absorption of the greenbacks. A letter of Henry to Jay Cooke of October 3, 1863, clearly sets forth the problem:

W G [Moorhead] went yesterday to Washn to see if we couldn't arrange with the Sec'y to take mint certificates in N.Y. & Boston &c in payt for bonds — and also certified B'k checks — as it is an absolute impossibility to get legal tenders enough to pay for Sub^{ns}. The sales since he left have been $21,500,000–$6,600,000 yesterday, and $15,100,000 today — We deposited [in government depository] today here $2,600,000 and in N.Y. Boston &c $5,000,000 — in all 7,600,000. And Monday will deposit as much more — So as not to swell our balance at the Treasy too much. We have not yet encroached on your mint certificates at the bank (F & M) — but will have to do so Monday — We made McIntyre take $1,700,000, certified checks today, which he carries till Monday, when we will arrange for him to hold them and let the Banks pay the l. t's. [legal tenders] in instalments so as to prevent too great a stringency in the money market — for want of legal tender — Should he decline, we can put in the Mint certifs — and relieve the banks — Our deposits would have been much larger today, but for the *impossibility* of abstracting from the circulation of the 3 cities named more than 7 or 8 millions in a day without creating a panic.

At times it was nearly impossible to get legal tender. On November 21, Jay Cooke noted that "today we got in nearly $700,-000 in Cks on Bks & N York dfts by mail & not *one dollar* of legal tender." At that time Jay Cooke & Co. had almost $17,000,000 in various banks in the large eastern cities waiting for legal tender with which to make deposits.[86] The Cookes maintained that there was no advantage in holding large balances for the government since they had to pay interest from the time a bond was ordered up to the time of delivery to the Treasury.[87] Indeed, this situation would force the use of the funds in order to earn interest, which was not a small job in itself, though at times it must have been very profitable. Secretary Chase was much concerned over the Cookes' large balances, because of the criticism which was thereby aroused of his employment of a special agent.[88]

Early in 1864 total sales of five-twenties approached the limit provided for the loan, that is, $500,000,000. It was then rumored that Chase contemplated extending the loan beyond the original limit. Jay Cooke protested strongly; he felt that, since this would be contrary to the original understanding and since he had told bond buyers that the loan would close at $500,000,000,[89] it would be violating the honor of the government and jeopardizing his own reputation. It was finally decided to close the loan at the original point. The last day on which five-twenty subscriptions were accepted was January 21, 1864.[90]

JAY COOKE'S GAINS FROM SELLING FIVE-TWENTIES

There was a widespread opinion among politicians and others that Jay Cooke had been paid too liberally by the government for selling the loan. The Secretary's report on the cost of the loan showed that it had been remarkably low. According to the records of the United States Treasury, on the first $10,000,000 sold one-fourth of one per cent was spent on advertising, traveling agents, freight, postage, and other expenses; and Jay Cooke and the subagents each received one-eighth of one per cent. For the remainder of the loan, one-eighth of one per cent went as commission to the agents, one-eighth to expenses, and the remainder to the general agent for his commissions and the expenses for which he was responsible.[91]

Five-twenty sales totaled $510,776,450.[92] For the amount over $500,000,000 and for the subscriptions received by the Treasury or subtreasuries of the United States, Cooke received no commission or allowance, although those sales were in part due to his campaign. To those who bought directly from the Treasury for resale, the one-eighth of one per cent subagency fee was allowed; the commission thus allowed totaled $122,190.34 on the $148,823,-500 sold in this way.[93]

Jay Cooke was credited with the sale of $361,952,950.[94] The whole cost of selling this amount, including commissions and all expenses from the time the bonds left the Treasury until the money was deposited in a depository, was $1,350,013.15.[95] The sum of $435,700.31 "was paid to the general agent [Jay Cooke] as compensation for responsibility, for services, and for expenses chargeable upon the one-eighth allowed to him." [96] Jay Cooke wrote to Chase that after allowing for expenses — freight on bonds, advertising, etc. — and bonds lost, some of which he hoped to recover, his net commission was $220,054.49, or one-sixteenth of one per cent.[97]

It is doubtful that any other banker would have taken the risks involved in distributing the five-twenties at so low a remuneration. Besides the risk of loss from deliberate dishonesty or from accident, there was the risk of having to make contracts, at times, in advance of a definite agreement with Chase. We have already noted the uncertainty about continuing the loan beyond July 1, 1863. Another uncertainty arose in the matter of commissions. Jay Cooke's original understanding concerning commissions was that one-half of one per cent would be allowed on the first $10,-000,000 and one-quarter or more, as determined later, on the remainder.[98] After the first $10,000,000 had been sold, Cooke made definite arrangements for continuing the sales campaign, allowing one-fourth of one per cent, the whole amount guaranteed to him, for commissions and expenses of agents.[99] In June, Chase agreed to allow three-tenths of one per cent, with the understanding that he would ask more of Congress if necessary.[100] Finally in October the commission was set at three-eighths of one per cent.[101] This nominally left one-eighth of one per cent to Jay Cooke.

So low was Jay Cooke's own share of the commissions that in October, 1863, he wrote to Chase offering to sell loans without compensation for his labor if the government would assume the risk and pay actual expenses.[102] He commented thus on his work as agent:

I have constantly risked my whole fortune & that of many friends whose bonds you hold in the Treasury to the extent of nearly $18\frac{1}{2}$ millions as security . . . have made expenditures of money prior to any sales of Bonds — have increased three fold the expenses of my different offices & have struggled through the year with a weight of care & anxiety upon me that had I foreseen the extent of I should have shrunk from with dismay.

When it is considered that Jay Cooke and his two houses, whose personnel had been greatly increased in order to handle the loan, spent almost a year and a half in selling the five-twenties, one can readily agree with Secretary Chase that this was very economical financing, particularly in view of the lavish expenditures in other departments of the government. In the words of Joshua Hanna, the loan agents had all worked for a small commission — the New York agents were actually not making over one-tenth of one per cent — and yet there was not a more loyal and efficient group to be obtained for the work.[103] The Secretary held that he was "clearly of opinion that the services rendered by the general agent and the sub-agents could not have been as successfully performed, nor, indeed, performed at all by the Treasury Department itself." [104]

The money compensation for selling the loan, however, can obviously not be measured in terms of commissions only. The Cooke banking houses no doubt profited in an indirect way from their connection with the Treasury. From Jay Cooke's close association with the Treasury, it followed as a matter of course that his firm had an advantage in the market. Once in a while the correspondence of the Cooke partners reveals something of their trading for themselves in government securities. "The day has passed off very quietly," wrote a clerk in the Philadelphia house in January, 1863,[105] "our transactions netting about $500 — having bought & sold [Treasury] cert[ificate]s & gold, and Treasury notes." Only three days earlier Henry Cooke had written as follows from Washington: "I hope you took advantage of the recent hoist in govts and cleared out at a handsome advance — all your 5^{208} 81.^{8} and certifs — as I suggested several days ago . . . to me it seemed clear that the time to sell had come." [106] Jay Cooke & Co. had their orders for the New York market executed by Fisk & Hatch, Colgate & Hoffman, Tallmadge & Manley, or other bankers and brokers in New York. It must be remembered in this relation that the only two partners who were at all qualified to trade in securities were young Fahnestock and Jay Cooke, himself, and the latter was so engrossed in the sale of loans that he could not have had much time for operations on the market. Theirs was primarily a selling not a trading organization.

It is impossible to check the total profits of Jay Cooke's houses against gains from selling five-twenties for the actual period in which they were selling the bonds, that is, from early October, 1862 (though little was sold in the first months), to January, 1864.

In the three years 1862–64, however, the profits of the two houses totaled $1,264,813.87.[107] For the period of December 15, 1862, to June 2, 1864, a division of profits was made by the Philadelphia house, giving $300,000 to Jay Cooke, $150,000 to Moorhead, and $50,000 to O. P. J. (Old Patriarch Jacob), the charity account. Deducting the $220,054.49 net commission on five-twenties and allowing for the difference in the length of the periods compared, it is clear that the profits from trading were not great. It is certain that some of these profits directly or indirectly resulted from the Cookes' relations with the Treasury. It must be remembered, however, that other bankers were also making large gains at the time; in reality it was a time when a high rate of return was the rule.

The most striking gain to Jay Cooke and his firms from their management of the sale of the loan was the increase in their prestige. Jay Cooke's name came to be known far and wide — possibly of American business men only Stephen Girard and John Jacob Astor had been so widely known among the American people. Jay Cooke won a firm position with the press of the country; his five-twenty agents were loud in their praise; [108] and his notable success in selling five-twenties together with the great business of his firms made him outstanding among American private bankers.[109] But even success had its price, as will be seen later.

In the five-twenty campaign appeared the shadow of a figure that was later to dominate in American investment banking. There had been aggressive bankers before in the United States — men like Nicholas Biddle, who had vigorously promoted various enterprises — but they had not developed far. In the sale of the five-twenties Jay Cooke started a series of changes which were to revolutionize American investment banking and help bring the full development of the active financial capitalist.

JAY COOKE AND LATER WAR FINANCE
1863–1865

THE closing of the 6 per cent loan, that is, the five-twenties, ended for a year Jay Cooke's work as agent of the government for the sale of its securities. The banker, thereupon, turned his attention to other affairs, and his firms were free to participate more actively in the expanding business of the time. But Jay Cooke's relations with the Treasury remained close, and he was called on from time to time to do special tasks for the government. Early in 1865 he was again commissioned to manage the sale of a great war loan which came to be known as the "seven-thirties."

JAY COOKE AVOIDS WAR-TIME SPECULATION

As usually happens in time of war, the Civil War brought a strong rise in prices and an active speculative spirit into American business. Many new transportation projects and new ventures in coal, iron, and oil were started. Promoters were busily organizing new enterprises to capture accumulating war profits, and investors were eager to secure for themselves the benefits of rising prices. The speculative influence was again at work. While some of this activity did not have a substantial foundation, a great deal of it was justified by a growing population working with an increasing capital and an improving technique.

Had Jay Cooke not gone so heavily into government finance but followed, instead, the interests which he himself had pursued from 1857 through 1860 and William Moorhead for a much longer time, he could probably have secured a strong position in Pennsylvania's transportation, industry, and mining, which were then on the threshold of a great development. Occupied as he was with war finance, he refused participation in a number of copper, iron, and coal enterprises.[1] His partners, especially Moorhead, entered into several ventures,[2] and Jay Cooke joined his partners

THE BANKING HOUSE OF JAY COOKE & CO. AND THE FIRST NATIONAL BANK
WASHINGTON, D. C.

in investing in a few mining and transportation concerns. One was the Preston Coal & Improvement Company, located in the Schuylkill anthracite field in Pennsylvania and organized in 1864, of which Jay Cooke and William Moorhead were original incorporators.[3] They also invested heavily in the Sterling Iron & Railway Co. in Orange County, New York.[4] Only in the promotion of one enterprise was Jay Cooke, himself, closely concerned while engaged in war finance; that was the Warren & Franklin Railroad, which Jay Cooke, J. Edgar Thomson, Thomas A. Scott, William G. Moorhead, and other Pennsylvanians were building in the newly developed oil region of the northwestern part of their State.[5] These ventures kept the Cookes in touch with Pennsylvania industry.

Throughout the whole period of the war, Jay Cooke was generally opposed to going into new enterprises. One investment of his partners, a venture in oil, brought the first test of his headship of the two firms. Petroleum, which had recently been discovered in western Pennsylvania, promised to become the great bonanza of the time; so rapidly did the business in oil stocks grow that in the fall of 1864 the Petroleum Board was formed in New York.[6] Moorhead and Fahnestock were enthusiastic about oil and entered into several oil companies, even encouraging clerks in the Washington house to invest. Jay Cooke protested strongly, and, when Fahnestock held that there was nothing improper in their actions, he took a firm position on the rights and obligations of partners: "If I am not to know what ventures my junior partners propose to make, what means they propose to withdraw from the firm or borrow outside (which is the same thing), or in other words what departures are proposed from the strict and legitimate course of business, why I wish to know it. It is my right as I understand the ordinary nature of such a partnership as ours." [7]

Jay Cooke also objected to his partners' trafficking in supplies for the government or in vouchers, or making investments which meant taking advantage of the war needs of the government. His brother Henry, whose conscience was none too tender in such matters, became involved in speculations in quartermasters' vouchers and certificates in Cincinnati.[8] Jay Cooke ordered the business to stop, and his houses henceforth stayed out of such operations.[9]

One thing is clear from the banker's investments at this time: he strongly opposed what he considered speculation. He particularly objected to trading on margin and to short selling, but he also opposed investments in questionable projects which, if successful, promised high returns. To Jay Cooke that was gambling, and gambling was to him in the same category as card playing, intemperance, and dishonoring the Sabbath. Moreover, it was dangerous to his business, and he was first and foremost a banker.

JAY COOKE ATTACKS GOLD SPECULATION

Though Jay Cooke did not himself speculate, he had not a little influence on speculation in New York. There, on Wall Street, the speculative spirit of war time found its most dramatic expression. That erstwhile king of stock gamblers, Jacob Little, had by then passed from the New York scene; but Vanderbilt and Drew were at their height, and many younger men, such as Morse, Jerome, Keep, Tobin, and Gould, helped to make up that motley group which, through Harlem and Rock Island corners and all the devious ways and means of the Street, under the uncertain conditions of war-time business, made and lost fortunes. New York at this time became conspicuous for its newly rich and for its ostentatious wealth. And Wall Street was synonymous with speculation.

Wall Street's interest and activity really revolved around gold, and it was in connection with gold that Jay Cooke came in closest touch with speculation in New York. There were regular actors in the gold drama and their stage was the Gold Room in New York. There, gold bulls and bears met in person or in the form of orders from all over the country. A contemporary has left a colorful picture of the Gold Room which helps to explain the attacks of Jay Cooke and others on gold gambling:[10]

In the days of the war an unexpected victory converted the gold arena into a den of wild beasts. The bulls fought against the inevitable decline with the ferocity of gladiators. . . . Men leaped upon chairs, waved their hands, or clenched their fists; shrieked, shouted; the bulls whistled "Dixie," and the bears sung "John Brown;" the crowd swayed feverishly from door to door, and, as the fury mounted to white heat, and the tide of gold fluctuated up and down in rapid sequence, brokers seemed animated with the impulses of demons, hand-to-hand combats took place, and bystanders, peering through the smoke and dust, could liken the wild turmoil only to the revels of maniacs.

Here was concrete evidence that much of the fluctuation in the price of gold was the work of speculators. Some blame should undoubtedly rest on them; only those who are innocent of the ways of business believe that business is altogether the result of the working out of large impersonal economic forces. Short-time factors are always open to a certain amount of control, to manipulation. The mistake of the business man often is that under the pressure of the present he does not see beyond the short-time elements. He occasionally makes the mistake of disregarding altogether the working of larger economic forces, placing responsibility or blame on individuals. It is easy to conclude that the problem is one of balancing properly the impersonal and personal, the long-time and short-time elements; but to find the proper balance is not so simple.

Jay Cooke was realist enough to know that cliques could manipulate prices; but he apparently did not see the limits of their influence. The method he recommended for attacking the problem was to meet the speculator on the market. Jay Cooke had interfered little, if at all, to break gold speculation in 1863. He and his press attacked gold gamblers, however, and continued to urge the people to invest their means in bonds, thus helping the Union, and not in gold, which, he said, gave aid to the South.

Chase, doubting his own legal authority, was reluctant to allow the Philadelphian to use government funds for fighting gold speculation. A legal basis for interference by the Treasury was, however, provided early in 1864, when Congress passed a joint resolution which authorized the Treasury to pay interest on the public debt in advance and to sell gold.[11] This measure had the strong support of Jay Cooke and his Washington brother.[12]

The result was a most dramatic attack on the Gold Room, an event which ranks with Black Friday of 1869 as one of the two great gold panics of the greenback period. On this occasion the Philadelphia banker led the attack.

In April, 1864, gold was high and greenbacks were low, but Chase was reluctant to use the power given him by the "gold bill." He tried the device of selling gold certificates to be used for paying import duties, thus relieving the market of some of the demand for gold. But the price of gold continued to rise,[13] and fear settled upon business. Cooke urged the sale of gold for greenbacks in order to raise the value of the latter in terms of the former.[14] He figured that by using $6,000,000 to $7,000,000 of gold from the Subtreasury in New York he could buy all of the $12,000,000 to $18,000,000 of greenbacks in New York. In this belief he was not alone. The flimsiest of Washington politicians and the most solid business men of New York and other cities urged Chase to take action. Telegrams came to the Secretary from all over the country.[15] Chase finally went to New York to see what could be done. The story continues in Jay Cooke's Memoirs:

One morning Mr Chase arrived in New York & at a time when I was also there. The "gold bugs" hearing of his arrival rushed the price of gold up to 288 [evidently should be 188] and about noon Mr Chase sent for me to come to the subTreasury — & asked me all about my plans & although very nervous & doubtful as to the propriety of lessening his gold supply a single dollar yet the crisis was so grave that he could see no other way than to give me authority to carry out my plans.

Jay Cooke planned the campaign confidentially with Crawford, of Clark, Dodge & Co., "who could keep so vast a secret even from his own partners & had the discretion & wisdom to carry out my instructions to the very letter." Indeed, the banker insisted on secrecy in these gold dealings to such an extent that even his own partners did not know what he was doing. Fahnestock wanted to know what Cooke was up to, for then "without detriment to the public service we could load or unload as might be best."[16]

The difference in the attitude of these two partners on the question of profiting from a secret knowledge of the affairs of the government shows in clear relief the honesty of Jay Cooke in his relations with government finance.

The next morning the sale of gold began. It was sold gradually, so as not to create suspicion, and payment was required in greenbacks or in checks that could be cashed for greenbacks. "That first day we sold 2,700,000 — & the next morning before any one had reached Wall St I carted the 2,700,000 from the subTreasy to Clark Dodge & Co office & stowed it away under thier remotest & secret counters from whence it was with as little show as possible delivered rather late in the day." By the time $2,500,000 had been sold, prices fell to 170.[17] When an additional $1,250,000 had been sold the next morning, the price dropped rapidly and a great panic prevailed. Word had gotten around that the Treasury was selling gold. Cooke stopped selling when gold reached 160, in order to avoid a still vaster panic,[18] though shortage of gold in the Treasury would eventually have put an end to the sale of gold.

But already havoc had been created on Wall Street. The stringency in the money market resulting from the purchase of greenbacks by the government in exchange for gold[19] brought a general drop in the stock market, and several operators were ruined. Anthony W. Morse, one of the most sensational speculators of the war period, was carried under by the fall in Fort Wayne Railroad stock, from which fact this particular panic is known in Wall Street as the Morse Panic.[20] This event probably did not strengthen the Philadelphia banker with the Wall Street fraternity.

Jay Cooke wanted to continue dangling the sword of Treasury sales over the speculators, but Chase hesitated to use Treasury funds for this purpose without stronger authority than he then had, and he even doubted the efficacy of gold sales as a means to control the price of gold.[21] But Jay Cooke continued to believe that the Treasury should interfere. One day, in a moment of strong feeling against the "gold bugs," Cooke wrote to the Secretary, lamenting that Chase should relinquish his grasp on the speculators when he was so near to accomplishing his purpose.

"It seems to me," he wrote in a somewhat self-righteous tone, "that I am the only one unselfish enough to desire the government to get the entire upper hand, even if it does hurt our own pockets. I know that you are true and faithful and unselfish, but I could name many here whose actions are entirely the other way." [22] This impetuous note was followed by a calmer one the next day, but it revealed clearly its writer's estimate of the patriotism of New York business men: "I wrote fully — perhaps too warmly last night — Still I wrote under the impression that *noone* here heartily loved their country better than their pockets." [23] About a month later Chase was again forced to call on Cooke to check the advance in gold. [24]

The sale of gold by the government had no permanent effect, however, on the gold market. Speculation continued to rage in New York and the price of gold again resumed its upward course. [25] Chase then tried another device, that of meeting the export demand for gold by selling exchange upon London at a rate below the prevailing market rate, [26] but this also proved ineffective. In the meantime, another scheme had been brewing. It was based on the principle that, if the gold market could not be controlled, it should be destroyed.

The "act to prohibit certain sales of gold and foreign exchange" was passed in June, 1864. It forbade trading in gold "futures" and all those practices which are the special tools of operators on the market, and it also placed limitations on dealing in foreign exchange. Aimed at a central market was the provision which forbade any transactions in gold "at any other place than the ordinary place of business of either the seller or purchaser." [27]

The gold act went into effect at once. The Gold Room was closed. But the price of gold continued its upward flight. [28] Foreign exchanges were thrown into a hopeless confusion. In New York arose strong criticism of the act; a special meeting of the Chamber of Commerce sent a committee to protest to Chase. [29] On July 2, the act was repealed. [30] Thus ended the first attempt of the federal government to interfere with trading on an organized exchange.

Other more fundamental factors were driving the gold price

upward.[31] The inflation of the currency, both by the issue of legal tender and State bank currency, had its effect, as the hesitation of Congress in voting taxes also had. A pall of fear had fallen upon business in the winter and early spring. But in the later spring and summer of 1864 another factor was at work driving downward the credit of the government and upward the value of gold relatively to currency.

The military situation was bad. Grant was hammering away at Lee in the Wilderness, suffering heavy losses and making little apparent gain. In May occurred the battle of Spottsylvania, which was indecisive; in June, Cold Harbor, where the Union men were literally mowed down, and the attack on Petersburg, which Grant stormed with a terrific loss. After that, Grant settled down to a long siege which lasted until the spring of 1865. In the first part of July, Early led his Confederates within sight of the dome of the Capitol at Washington. The city was in a panic. Only Early's hesitation in attacking is said to have saved the capital. In the meantime Pennsylvania was invaded and terror spread when Chambersburg was reduced to ashes.

There was some relief in the autumn when dashing Phil Sheridan dramatically turned defeat into victory down in the Shenandoah Valley and made it improbable that another invasion of the North would come from that region. Sherman, who had with devastating results been defeated at Kenesaw Mountain in June, pushed on southward to Atlanta, which he entered in September. On August 5 Farragut took Mobile Bay, the last important port of the Confederacy.

Though there had been some gains for the North, they were few in number and a high price was paid for them. Despair was widespread, as was criticism of the government because of the terrific loss of men. On August 2, 1864, Jay Cooke wrote a letter to his brother Henry, who was then in Europe, giving a gloomy view of things: [32]

You will hear the news of our sad reverses before Petersburg; also of the raid into Pennsylvania and the burning of Chambersburg. Grant has lost prestige and people begin to doubt even his success. Sherman before Atlanta we have our fears about, not from any knowledge of any particular danger just now but on general principles. He is far from his base and in an enemy's country. We fear for his communications. The presence of the enemy in the Shenandoah valley and all along the Potomac is disheartening. The rebs are gathering a harvest sufficient to feed the army at Richmond a year and our forces under Sigel, Hunter, Crook, etc., are entirely inefficient — get whipped and driven across the Potomac as fast as they show themselves, whilst Pennsylvania and Maryland are entirely unprotected and we here in Philadelphia really think seriously of sending our valuables into some "vast wilderness" — not a fortification, breastwork or rifle pit, nor a regiment or battery between this city and the 40,000 rebs of Shenandoah valley.

The Treasury Fails to Sell Bonds without Jay Cooke's Aid

In the meantime the condition of the Treasury had become serious. Its loans had been selling slowly and expenses had continued to be terrific. In a similar emergency in 1862 the Secretary of the Treasury had turned to Jay Cooke. Great as his success in selling the five-twenties had been, however, he had not in 1864 been entrusted with the loans because of the severe criticism of Chase for employing the banker as loan agent of the Treasury.

The criticism came from various sources. It was to be expected that the choice of one banker to have complete charge of the five-twenty campaign would not be acceptable to everybody, for it meant a great opportunity for one man. Some bankers were opposed to giving so much power to a man who headed only a small private bank; speculators on the New York markets saw in him one of their worst enemies; and many were antagonized by Jay Cooke's positive and aggressive patriotism. New York was most critical of him and certain of its newspapers became openly hostile, such as the *World*, the irascible Bennett's *Herald*, and the conservative *Journal of Commerce*. Even in his home city there was a group of bankers who were piqued by his success. And the belief spread throughout the country that Cooke was growing fabulously rich from his work for the government.

Criticism of Chase for the employment of the Philadelphia

banker led to the introduction of a resolution in the House of Representatives requesting a report on the services rendered the government by Jay Cooke & Co. and on the cost of those services,[33] and a similar attack was launched in the Senate.[34] Complete and convincing replies were made, which not only defended Jay Cooke but even showed conclusively that he had received remarkably little remuneration for his work.[35]

Though Jay Cooke had clearly served the Treasury well and at a low cost, Secretary Chase did not employ him to sell the next loan, the "ten-forties." The reason which he gave was that "I have not forgotten the calumnies for which my employment of a general agent was made the occasion and I confess it was principally with a view of avoiding these calumnies that I abandoned the general agency system." [36]

The ten-forties sold with disappointing slowness. From the time they were placed on the market in March until the end of June, only $73,000,000 were sold, mostly to the new national banks as a basis for currency issue.[37] This was a very great disappointment to Chase and it resulted in a most difficult situation for the Treasury.

There were three important reasons for the failure of the ten-forty campaign. First, owing to the unsatisfactory military situation in the spring of 1864, the country was in a discouraged state of mind. Second, Secretary Chase unfortunately set the interest rate at 5 per cent, and that at a time when the outlook for the North was none too bright and when the market was so weak that financiers urged him not to risk so low a rate.[38] And third, the loan was not sold effectively; Chase tried to apply Jay Cooke's methods in selling the ten-forties, that is, he advertised widely and employed many agents,[39] relying on the aid of national banks, but he could not infuse the energy into the system which Jay Cooke had been able to give it.[40]

Failing to secure sufficient funds from the sale of the ten-forties, Secretary Chase was forced to resort to his earlier expedient of short-term loans.[41] Even this left a considerable deficit at the end of the fiscal year, June 30, 1864; the cash balance in the Treasury was then $18,842,558.71, unpaid requisitions totaled

$71,814,000 (principally for the army), outstanding certificates of indebtedness amounted to $161,796,000, while the daily expenditures were over $2,000,000. [42]

At this point occurred the resignation of Chase. The feeling between the head of the Treasury and President Lincoln, which had long been strained, reached its breaking point over the appointment of an assistant treasurer in New York. The resignation of Chase was unfortunate for Jay Cooke and his firms; they had won his confidence and had proved themselves worthy of it. Though the Secretary, influenced by the "calumnies" which his reliance on the banker had aroused against himself, had not given Cooke the management of the ten-forties, still in other matters his dependence on the Philadelphia banker had increased. The Cookes might well have come to see in Secretary Chase a guarantee of a close relationship between themselves and the Treasury in the future. [43]

The choice of a successor to Chase was of vital importance to Jay Cooke & Co. Jay Cooke and his partners hoped that John Sherman of the Senate Finance Committee would be appointed; he was a close friend of the Cookes and in agreement with them on many matters of government finance. But to their disappointment Senator Fessenden was given the place. Jay Cooke was soon to see the bearing of Fessenden's administration on the standing of his house with the Treasury. A letter to Chase gives his interpretation of the new Secretary's lack of friendliness: "Although Cisco and those New Yorkers have told Fessenden that they don't consider me a financier, but only a good advertiser of patent medicines, yet I say it boldly I could take the financial branch of the Treasury and in two months (if I had my own way) put gold to 150 and advance 1881s to 120, 5–20s to 115 and get all the money the Treasury needed on 10–40 five per cents at par." [44] While Jay Cooke was complaining of the New Yorkers, Morris Ketchum of New York, a private banker who had designs on the Treasury's business for the prestige it would give him, [45] wrote to Fessenden, defending himself against the friends of Chase, who, he claimed, were trying to weaken his standing with the Treasury. [46]

Fessenden frankly explained to Cooke that he could not think of engaging in negotiations with his firms as there had been so much criticism of his close relations with the Treasury.[47] The new Secretary, however, consulted the banker on Treasury policies, and early in his administration asked him to write out his recommendations. Cooke recommended the sale of three-year notes, bearing interest at the rate of 7.3 per cent in currency, and also other measures for raising the market value of certificates of indebtedness and for meeting arrears in payments to soldiers. He made one suggestion which throws not a little light on his own character: "If you will pardon me, I would suggest that God's favor be invoked upon our efforts to maintain the financial credit of our nation by a strict observance of His Holy Day and that hereafter the awful scandal of Christian people working all day on the Sabbath in the Treasury Department be done away with entirely." [48]

We cannot stop to consider all the measures employed by Fessenden for financing the government in the summer and fall of 1864; [49] two will suffice to indicate the methods used and the results attained. Late in July, $200,000,000 of three-year notes, bearing interest of 7.3 per cent in currency, were offered. They were sold mainly through national banks and were advertised after the manner of the five-twenties, but the loan went slowly and as the autumn passed it became evident that the sales would be far behind the government's needs even though the credit of the government was improving considerably. To meet the growing deficit, an issue of $40,000,000 in five-twenties was also offered. Fessenden was impressed with the manner in which Jay Cooke took $10,000,000 of the loan, which he disposed of by enlisting the aid of his leading five-twenty men in New York and by purchasing bonds on the New York market to support the price.[50] Convinced of the strength of Jay Cooke, Secretary Fessenden negotiated with him for the sale of the $25,000,000 which remained of this loan.[51]

The Secretary tried in this connection to bring together Morris Ketchum and Jay Cooke. Late in the fall of 1864 the Secretary proposed that the two bankers co-operate in selling the five-twenties on one-fourth of one per cent commission and that they undertake to sell the new seven-thirty bonds at three-fourths of one per cent commission on the first $50,000,000 and five-eighths on the remainder.[52] Cooke consented to a joint operation, but it did not materialize. The Philadelphian claimed that while he was trying to raise the price of government bonds, the New Yorker was depressing the market in order to get better terms from the government;[53] and he finally wrote to the Secretary that he could not enter upon the proposed combination: "To please you I tried my best to work with Mr. K., but could not. I wouldn't do it for all the world. I wish to say nothing disrespectful or harsh of him, only that in my opinion any connection [with him] would so clog my movements, and chill my spirits, and lower my self-respect that my efforts to do a great work for you would be nearly a failure. He has his ways and I have mine."[54] In the meantime, Ketchum had declined to take the proposition on Fessenden's terms.[55]

It might appear on first thought that Jay Cooke was short-sighted in his attitude toward Ketchum, whose house was regarded as strong and whose connections were good. Ketchum and his son were close friends of J. S. Morgan of London and his son, J. Pierpont, of Dabney, Morgan & Co., of New York. The fathers had been in partnership in banking in New York before J. S. Morgan had joined George Peabody in London, and during the war the Ketchums had co-operated with young Morgan in two profitable deals. Their taking advantage of northern military adversity in the fall of 1863 to make a profitable operation in gold must have seemed like treason to Jay Cooke. The Ketchums were successful in profit making, but Cooke distrusted them. As it proved, he was fortunate in not being associated with them, for in August, 1865, young Ketchum was caught in what was said to be the "most astounding and extensive fraud ever known in this country." He had forged gold checks on a number of prominent firms to the amount of over $2,500,000. Ketchum, Son & Co. was dissolved and young Ketchum went to prison.[56]

December of 1864 passed and January gave no promise of improvement for the Treasury.[57] The Secretary finally commissioned the Philadelphia banker to head the proposed loan campaign for selling the three-year notes bearing 7.3 per cent interest on terms which the latter would accept. Fessenden appointed Cooke just before giving up the headship of the Treasury to Hugh McCulloch, thus relieving his successor of responsibility for the act, which he himself could defend on the floor of the Senate.[58] Again necessity had driven the Treasury to seek Jay Cooke's aid.

JAY COOKE ORGANIZES FOR SELLING THE SEVEN-THIRTIES

The terms of Cooke's appointment as general subscription agent for the sale of the seven-thirties were, briefly, as follows: It was expected, though not stipulated, that $2,000,000 a day would be realized from the sale of seven-thirties under the agent's management. Cooke was to receive a commission of three-fourths of one per cent on the first $50,000,000 and five-eighths on the second, the rate of commission to be fixed later for sales beyond $100,000,000. As in the case of the five-twenties, all expenses for advertising, clerical force, subagents' commissions and so on were to be paid by the general agent. The Treasury simply undertook to deliver the notes on the lines of any railroad by express at its own cost; and no notes would be delivered until the payment therefor had been made to the Treasury and the certificates of deposit received at the Treasury. As protection for the Treasury, it was stipulated that, should the Secretary think it proper to suspend Jay Cooke's appointment at any time, he could do so with some compensation under certain conditions for legitimate expenses incurred.[59]

The terms were clearly designed to give every protection to the Treasury, and Jay Cooke was outraged at them. "Some passages of this letter," he wrote to his brother, referring to the Secretary's statement of the terms, "are more fit for the instructions to a fool or a dishonest agent than one deserving confidence & tried & trusted heretofore to millions. . . . If my services — my character — my Bonds are not entitling me to confidence of the debt as of old & if I am to be cut short any moment by himself or his successor I am not disposed to work my life blood out under such depressing circumstances." [60]

It was the good fortune of Jay Cooke that the loan campaign was carried on under Hugh McCulloch, who assumed the head-ship of the Treasury early in March, 1865. McCulloch under-stood finance as had neither Chase nor Fessenden. He had had a long experience as an outstanding banker, and it was he who, as Comptroller of the Currency, had organized the national banking system. In that work he had had close contact with Jay Cooke, and both men respected and trusted each other.

It is not necessary to examine in detail the seven-thirty cam-paign; it was conducted in essentials like the five-twenty cam-paign, with the differences that naturally grew out of the earlier experience. On the very day he was informed of his appointment, that is, January 28, 1865, the loan agent dispatched circular let-ters to banks and bankers which gave detailed instructions on all matters concerning which agents should be informed.[61] To the leading agents personal letters were written. The traveling agents were sent out at once, after Jay Cooke had spent two hours "in-structing them & 'firing up their hearts.'"[62] Everywhere the response of Jay Cooke's organization was immediate and en-thusiastic.

It is tempting to linger over the selling of this loan. It is in-teresting to follow Jay Cooke's twenty-four, more or less, travel-ing salesmen who as before drummed the seven-thirties over much of the country.[63] Traveling agents covered Kentucky, Tennessee, and New Orleans and went into South Carolina and Georgia; in-deed, the moment a southern community came under the control of the North, the ubiquitous seven-thirty agent was there to sell seven-thirties.[64] Pitt Cooke and two other men were sent to the Far West, to convince the Californians that greenbacks were as good as gold; they were ably assisted by Wells, Fargo & Co., the main subscription agent on the Coast.[65]

Like most men who worked for Jay Cooke, the traveling agents were fairly well paid but they had to work hard. Ten dollars a day was the usual allowance for expenses, while salaries are known to have been as low as $50.00 a month and as high as $333.33.[66]

The Working Men's Savings Bank!

NIGHT OFFICES
FOR SUBSCRIBING to the 7-30 LOAN

Where Working Men and Women who haven't time by Day, can go in the EVENING, and invest their earnings, where they will be forever safe---where Cities, Counties and States can't tax them --and where they will draw the BIGGEST INTEREST!

OFFICES OPEN EVERY EVENING. AT

LOT BETTS, 1331 Avenue **B**, Yorkville.
JO POE, corner Sixth Avenue and Forty-ninth Street
C. G. PARSONS. JR. 60 Bleecker Street.
FRANK SEEGUR, 104 Avenue **C**.
JAMES R. YOUNG. 765 Broadway.
CRANE & FASSIT corner Broadway and Canal Sts.
BOWEN & BUTTRICK. cor. Fulton & Clinton st. Brooklyn.

WARD & BOCKHAVEN, 313 Broad Street, Newark.
EDM STEPHENSON, 338 Third Avenue, at 5th National Bank
SECOND NATIONAL BANK. Jersey City.
W HARLAN PAGE No. 1 Court Street, cor Montague, Brooklyn
JOHN SEELEY, 733 Broadway.
S W WOOLSEY, 136 Grand Street, Williamsburg
HENRY OLTMANS, 100 Graham Street, Williamsburg.

CHAS McCARTEE Post Office Greenpoint, L I

Fetch on your little sums of $50 & $100. MAKE THE U S GOVERNMENT YOUR SAVINGS BANK

A VICTORY LOAN POSTER, 1865

Those men traveled for months, by train or boat or horse; they went into the backwoods and into communities where northerners were not welcome. They wrote voluminous reports back to Jay Cooke; one agent sent him a 36-page report which is like a sociological and economic survey of southern Illinois.[67] In some places those agents found little support, as in the case of one, covering Maryland, who was pleased to find in a certain town ten loyal men, though the postmaster was the only one who was at all likely to aid and even he "had given up the idea." [68] There probably was never a more enthusiastic and persistent group of bond salesmen than Jay Cooke's traveling agents.

A new feature in the seven-thirty campaign was the night agency. At the end of March, 1865, the Philadelphian instructed his Washington brother to establish 30 to 40 night subscription offices in Georgetown and Washington, at the end of the counter in the corner drug or grocery store, with a card in the window and some one to distribute circulars, talk up and sell seven-thirties to workmen and soldiers, and to serve "lunch occasionally to the brawny fisted subscribers." [69] In June night agencies were opened in New York — in the suburbs, the factory districts, and along the docks.[70] These agencies were advertised as "The Workingmen's Savings Bank." Some of them were conducted by the proprietor of a drug or grocery store; others were set up as special loan agencies. In some, doughnuts and coffee were served. Indeed, according to Wilkeson's descriptions of them, night agencies were not unlike workingmen's clubs. There met the mechanic, the peddler, the clerk, the sailor, and saloonkeeper; even boys and women; Moor, Chinese, Irish, German, and native American. And there "rude finance [was] discussed with homely sense between workman and workman, political prejudice cured or silenced by a witty word tossed over the shoulder, question after question answered across the counter and the whole matter and genius of the 7:30 understood and appreciated." [71]

Nor were the soldiers neglected. Agents were commissioned to follow the army to sell notes to the boys as they were paid; and arrangements were made to send the notes to a designated person in case a soldier was killed. When the war was over, Jay Cooke's agents were sent to demobilization points to sell seven-thirty notes to the soldiers when they received their last payment.[72]

As in the five-twenty loan, the most important part of the sales organization was the "army of banks, bankers, brokers" and others serving as agents of Jay Cooke. In March, 1865, they were said to number between four thousand and five thousand.[73] Again, most important among the agents were those in larger centers who acted as wholesalers in their region. The most important wholesale distributors were such concerns as the leading five-twenty agents in New York and Preston, Willard & Kean of Chicago. But not all the wholesale distributors were in large cities. Bankers in such towns as Shawneetown and Belleville, Illinois, leaders in their sections of the State, had subagents in several little towns.[74] Some of the wholesale distributors were directly under Cooke and some were under other agents. There was nothing inflexible about Jay Cooke's system; it was adapted to the needs of different times and places. As in the earlier loan, the duties of the more important agents were to arrange for advertising, print and distribute circulars, send out traveling agents, arrange for subagencies — whatever was necessary to distribute the seven-thirties.[75]

As before, Jay Cooke was the manager of the campaign, and his Philadelphia house was the center of operations. His ingenuity and aggressiveness in promoting the sale of the seven-thirties and his ability to fill the many agents and subagents with enthusiasm over the loan bear witness to his capacity as an organizer and to his dynamic personality. Something of the spirit of Jay Cooke was caught by Sam Wilkeson in a portrait which he drew of him at work in his Philadelphia office: [76]

He is a large man who gives you instantly the impression of not having done growing — of having a great deal of youth straggling behind his manhood, and that has not yet marched up, but is going to come in soon, and camp right down on the table at which he is writing. You don't see 7–30s in him at your first look, nor 10–40s, nor 5–20s, nor any finance, nor any statesmanship, nor any power. But you do see and you linger over the sweetness and tenderness of his mouth, the boyish freshness of his face, the boyish weight and disorder of his brown hair, the childlike brightness of eyes behind whose laughter you see thinking going on, the superabounding suppleness and quickness of full-muscled boyhood in a large man's motions. Certainly that man shall quit banking soon and play leap frog. You are sure of it. . . .

A new telegraph boy rushes in. . . . He throws down his despatches. . . . [Jay Cooke reads] "Keokuk, Ia.; $20,000. That's well off to sundown. Good! Lowell, Mass.; $17,000. Good also! That's from the factory girls. McConnellsville, Ohio; $20,500, nearly all in fifties and hundreds. Lafayette, Ind.; $10,300. Augusta, Me., Louisville, Ky., Des Moines, Iowa, $20,600. Won't somebody just tell me where will be the Repudiation of the National Debt that is diffused East and West and North and South? . . . It is the depositing by the People of their money, and their faith, and their affections, in the perpetuity of their government, and in the boundless resources of their country, and in its power and its glory — it is this that makes these telegrams bewitching and important."

JAY COOKE BINDS THE PRESS TO THE CAUSE

We may admire Jay Cooke's organization, but we are thoroughly amazed at his use of the press to advertise and publicize the loan. Indeed, effective as five-twenty publicity was, it was amateurish compared with the use of the press in the seven-thirty campaign. Again by appeals to patriotism and to self-interest and by spreading the idea that everybody was buying seven-thirties, by educating and by arguing the value of the loan, seven-thirty publicity became a factor of immeasurable importance in turning the people of the United States to investing in government bonds.

In the seven-thirty loan Jay Cooke had the advantage of starting with a press that was friendly, no doubt remembering the green pastures of five-twenty days. The examination of dozens of important newspapers in the larger cities in the East has failed to uncover an adverse comment on Jay Cooke's appointment as general seven-thirty agent; on the contrary the newspapers were all unanimous in their commendation of Cooke. The *Constitu-*

tional Union spoke of him as "our modern *Midas*" who, if he did not with his magic touch turn greenbacks into gold, at least brought them nearer a gold valuation. "The 7:30 Loan," continued the paper, "which was comparatively in an expiring condition, has been galvanized into healthy and active life by this wonderful agency.... Last week more than Ten Millions of Dollars was subscribed."[77] The *Boston Daily Advertiser* referred to the sale of the five-twenty loan as "the most remarkable instance of a national subscription in our annals, and we believe without precedent in those of any other nation."[78] The press, generally, was in a mood to support Jay Cooke.

At the head of the advertising and publicizing of the seven-thirties was Samuel Wilkeson. Wilkeson, a writer for Greeley's *Tribune*, was a nervous person, erratic, very positive, and not always well reasoned, but he had a vivid imagination and unusual powers of description and narration. His fluent and dramatic pen was well suited to publicizing government loans. Wilkeson's chief assistant was John Russell Young, another journalist.

The publicity and advertising were, again, as in the five-twenty campaign, distributed through various channels. There was the same "firing up" of strategic editors,[79] the same bringing of the influence of subagents to bear on their local press,[80] and the same scattering by Jay Cooke & Co. of thousands of letters, circulars, and posters. Peaslee & Co., a New York advertising agency headed by L. F. Shattuck, took over a great deal of the work of actually distributing material and regularly sent to hundreds of editors copy for news and editorial articles and instructed them how to interpret events and statements on finance by prominent men.[81] The Associated Press, which had not yet become a national institution, was again daily supplied with information on the largest single western subscription, the number of subscriptions by $50 subscribers, the total subscribed, and so on.[82]

Newspapers all over the parts of the country controlled by the federal government carried seven-thirty publicity and advertising.[83] There was no mining village in the western mountains too remote or southern village too recently conquered by the northern armies for their newspapers to carry advertisements of the loan. Moreover, foreign-language papers, trade papers, and religious journals all participated. It is not without amusement that one notes that a Democratic or Copperhead newspaper carried side by side a fierce attack on the finances of the government and Jay Cooke's conspicuous advertisement explaining how safe and profitable an investment the seven-thirty notes were!

Pamphlets, broadsides, handbills, circulars, and posters were mailed to individuals, left for distribution with bankers, postmasters, and shopkeepers, and nailed up on posts and walls.[84] There was the famous "Questions and Answers," somewhat like the "Farmer's Letter" of the five-twenties. There was, also, the very popular "Facts and Figures." Among the many forms in which this appeal was printed was the following: A large sheet $13\frac{1}{2} \times 19\frac{1}{2}$ inches in size bore at its top a symbolic picture of Liberty, and below it the Facts and Figures, which consisted of a series of short articles and notes, somewhat statistical, on the nation's ability to pay the war debt, how buying gold made one a rebel, gold gamblers, why the United States could carry a bigger war debt than England, why government bonds were better than other stocks and bonds, and the number of subscribers, with the stirring comment, "What a parade in History will this volunteer army of small takers of their Government's War Loan make, marching steadily up in reserve and support of the armies of Freedom bloodily fighting and dying in the field." On the reverse side of the large sheets were the words of popular songs of the war: "Will None O'Yez Hould Me," "We are Coming Father Abraham," "The Sword, Flag, and Plow," "Johnnie is Gone for a Soldier," "The Volunteer's Wife to her Husband," "Hail Columbia," "John Brown's Soul," "The Star Spangled Banner," "It is Great for our Country to Die," and others. "Facts and Figures" was very popular. It was distributed generously, and various parts were from time to time printed in newspapers.

Two pamphlets were published which were long, factual or theoretical defenses of the credit of the government and of its debts.[85] One, entitled *How the National Debt Can Be Paid*, was written by William Elder of the Treasury Department. It was a carefully compiled statistical analysis of the "Wealth, Resources and Power of the People of the United States," as well as a comparative survey of the past debt experience of the United States and England. This pamphlet was scattered at home and abroad, where it was translated into French and German. Late in May it was copied extensively by newspapers throughout the United States.

The other pamphlet, *How our National Debt May Be a National Blessing*, created a veritable tempest of discussion. Wilkeson, to whom Jay Cooke suggested a line of argument in defense of the debt, in his unrestrained ignorance of economic theory said our debt was "just so much capital added to our wealth." This pamphlet was ridiculed in the press,[86] satirized in doggerel,[87] and corrected by the economist,[88] for it was decidedly not of the prevailing classical school, and newspapers widely held that Jay Cooke was a good bond salesman but no economic theorist. This controversial publication did not express altogether a unique idea, for the idea of a national debt was not without advocates in Europe at the time.[89] Jay Cooke was not a good economist, but he understood something of the working of public opinion, and his object was to stop "the most doleful prognosticating as to the crushing debt — the awful mortgage upon us & our children" [90] at a time when serious talk of repudiation of the national debt was interfering with the sale of seven-thirties.

On the whole, there was in Jay Cooke's publicity sound reasoning and accuracy. The emotional appeal was strong, for only thus could many investors be reached, but there was enough of the rational and the informative to save it from becoming ballyhoo and pure propaganda, as such appeals often are. It was, moreover, characteristic of Jay Cooke that there was a complete absence of rancorous references to the South. Jay Cooke always made a positive appeal; his cause and his efforts stood by their own strength, not on the weakness of others. Here was an effective and creditable use of that Fourth Estate which has come to hold such a strong place in modern affairs. Jay Cooke, indeed, made "a well administered system of appeals to the pecuniary patriotism of America." [91]

The Loan Sells with Great Success

The sale of seven-thirties went remarkably well from the time Jay Cooke became general subscription agent in January, 1865. Even a Confederate newspaper commented in February that "under the auspices of an eccentrick financier named Jaye Cooke . . . these bonds are commanding a rapid sale, and are pronounced a splendid success." [92] On March 3, a bill was passed authorizing the issue of $600,000,000 more of seven-thirty notes. [93] John Bright, that good English friend of the North, "seemed much tickled with the quiet way in which you talk of so monstrous an issue," wrote a Londoner to Jay Cooke, referring to a letter from the banker. [94]

There were difficulties, as with the five-twenties. Certain agents made trouble by granting a discount on sales out of their own commissions. [95] On several occasions Jay Cooke had to enter the market in New York in order to support the price of seven-thirties; [96] in March he asked Secretary McCulloch "to let me have control of 10 *millions* with which from time to time to manage the market — probably not a million would be used." [97] There were other difficulties, but they were more or less similar to those appearing in the five-twenty campaign.

In the spring of 1865 events were working to the advantage of the North. On April 9 Lee surrendered and the long, hard struggle came to an end, but money was still needed in large amounts to pay the army and to transport the men home. [98] It was not a question then of whether or not the seven-thirty notes could be sold, but whether enough could be sold at par, when there was much talk of repudiation of the debt, to meet the needs of the government. The daily sales went far beyond expectations. A characteristic comment scattered about the country in newspapers in May contained the following: "The great success of the 7:30 loan must always be looked upon as one of the most powerful evidences of the strength of the United States Government and its strong hold upon the confidence and affections of the people. On Saturday, May 13th, the subscriptions were over thirty million dollars, and for the week ending on that day over ninety-eight million dollars, and in the three months that the loan has been in charge of Mr. JAY COOKE, over five hundred million dollars." Between the surrender of the Confederates on April 9 and the end of July, $530,000,000 of seven-thirties were sold.[99] With that the loan was closed,[100] the total sales having been $830,000,000. "No loan ever offered in the United States, notwithstanding the large amount of government securities previously taken by the people," said Secretary McCulloch in his report of 1865, "was so promptly subscribed for as this." [101]

Not only was the sale of so large an amount in so short a time unprecedented, but the wide distribution of the seven-thirties was also a new thing. "These notes," said the Secretary, "were distributed in every part of the northern and some parts of the southern States." [102] And apparently they were taken by all classes of people. Thus wrote an agent from Vermont: "Farmers who live in little cabins, wear homespun clothes, and ride to church and town in two-horse wagons without springs, have in many instances several thousand dollars loaned to the Government." An agent in Iowa reported that "there is hardly a farmer but has more or less in his possession." [103] "In the rural hamlets of the country the old farmers, who had been in the habit of hoarding their money in old chests or keeping it on deposit in village banks," said a newspaper, "were educated by Jay Cooke & Co., to know that it was infinitely better to put their savings on interest, and that the best investment they could make was in government securities." [104]

Thus ended the sale of the great seven-thirty loan. In essentials it had been carried on very much as had the five-twenty campaign, but the later effort worked with a finesse and sureness that was not achieved in the earlier one. In the victory loan of the Civil War, Jay Cooke reached the climax of his career.

With these loans, security distribution in America entered its modern phase. The old system of selling small issues through bankers who reached only a relatively small number of investors had proved inadequate. In its place came large-scale, high-pressure selling through an aggressive sales force which reached into

the savings of even the laborer and the farmer and which was supported by a measure of control of the price of government securities on the New York market. The era of the baby bond, the
door-to-door salesman, and "pegging" of the market was in its
beginning.

JAY COOKE AND HIS FIRMS AT THE CLOSE OF THE WAR

JAY COOKE, who had in 1861 so modestly opened his banking house "first door north of Girard's Bank," was at the close of the war the best known American banker both at home and abroad. Now that it has been seen how he rose to that position, it is time to stop for a view of the man himself and of the organization which he had constructed; and to see, further, how that organization was reshaped to meet peace-time conditions. This is the interesting story of a business firm reaching out for new work after the old had vanished.

THE ASSETS OF JAY COOKE AND HIS FIRMS

The strength of the banker and his firms at the close of the war lay principally in the prestige of Jay Cooke himself. No American business man had before that time been so widely known. His name had become a household word in America; he was thus a forerunner of Rockefeller, Ford, and Morgan, who in our own day represent the thorough entrenchment in popular interest of our industrial and financial leaders. Given wide publicity by the press, the Philadelphian had caught the popular fancy: he had helped save the Union; he was a successful man, a good churchman, a generous giver, and a man of integrity; he had broad sympathies and a likable nature; and he had not a little of the dramatic in his personality, a quality which has a wide appeal.

First and foremost, however, the reputation of Jay Cooke rested on his success as a banker. There was a sound basis for his success. He had had the wisdom and good fortune to support the side that won; the strong position of the government loans after the war reflected great credit on the man who had sponsored those loans when they were not regarded highly in the market. Moreover, his success in selling the bonds under adverse conditions had shown that he was a man of great power and resourcefulness. No bank or banker in the United States had ever established such close contacts with the banks of the country as had Jay Cooke and his two houses. With the inland banker, especially, he was in an extremely strong position. It was to be expected that the leadership he had established in war time would also be effective in peace-time business.

The capital of the Cooke firms at the close of the war was by no means so large as their reputation as bankers might suggest. Indeed, Jay Cooke & Co. had no actual firm capital outside of its current profit and loss account. It was understood, however, that the partners' private holdings were subject to the needs of the business and that their uninvested funds should be kept on deposit to serve as capital. We have no measure of the partners' private resources. The only members of the firm who had any considerable fortunes were the two original partners, whose property, generously estimated at $150,000 and $500,000 in 1861, had been increased during the war. The largest increases probably came from the firm dividends.

From the time of its establishment in January, 1861, to the end of the year 1865, the Philadelphia house had made a total net profit of $1,137,302.57. This had all been divided at various times: one-tenth to the "Old Patriarch Jacob," which was the firm's charity account; and, of the remainder, two-thirds to Jay Cooke and one-third to William Moorhead. The Washington house had in the same period divided $720,000, presumably one-tenth to the charity account and the rest among the four partners.[1] In other words, the two houses had by the beginning of 1866 disbursed among the partners profits totaling $1,681,572.31. Since the partners drew no salaries, this included their whole income from their banking business. It is worth noting that these dividends were far short of the amount which the political critics of Jay Cooke claimed he had made from his handling of the war loans.

By no means all of the Cookes' profits were plowed back into the business. The partners had spent considerable portions of their incomes. Henry Cooke had paid some of the debts which he had contracted in California, and he spent freely in maintaining his home and in travel, drawing on the firm for that which his income did not cover. Jay Cooke, on the other hand, had contributed heavily to the assets of his firms; he estimated that for his own expenses he had drawn an average of $15,000 a year for the four years up to 1866, which must be regarded as a modest sum. Moorhead also left his income from dividends with the firms. At best the total amount of the partners' assets could not have been far above $2,000,000 at the close of the war.[2] Some of this was in the form of deposits with the Cooke firms, but by far the larger portion was invested in homes, western lands, stocks in iron mining concerns, and in other securities.

Jay Cooke Has Faith in the Future

Jay Cooke and his partners were optimistic about the future. It is true that the ending of the war soon brought a conclusion to their floating of war loans, but they expected to secure a large share of the work of refunding the government loans and transferring the ownership of bonds, which would surely come sooner or later. On such business the Cookes staked their greatest hopes of immediate work.

There were certain elements in the situation which also presaged strong activity in business and gave promise of work for the banker. The coming of peace between the North and the South saw not only the preservation of the unity of that large diversified economic area which is the United States but also the elimination of slavery, which had been for over a generation a disturbing element in American political and economic affairs. The extension of settlement together with industrial development, which had been given a strong impetus by war demands and war prosperity, also promised an unprecedented advance. Favorable to business, though not yet clearly discernible then, was the fact that the war had established what appeared to be a strong coalition between eastern business and western agriculture in which business held a dominant position. Very significant, moreover, was the changed attitude of Europe; war prosperity and the freeing of the slaves made America seem more attractive to prospective immigrants, while the success of the North made the money bags of London and the Rhine cities look with interest toward the United States. All this meant more work for the banker.

The horizon was not altogether cloudless, it is true. A marked fall in prices and a slump in business — the primary post-war depression — had followed upon the close of the war; the question was whether that development was merely temporary or the beginning of a period of depression. There was the further problem of political, economic, and social reconstruction in the South and of the restoration of that section to its place in the national government. There was uncertainty as to the future value of our currency and the course of prices. And no one could foresee clearly what policies the government would adopt with respect to the refunding of the loans and other matters of importance to business.

Though quite aware that there were uncertainties, Jay Cooke and his partners were optimistic. There was no denying that they were the strongest "government" house in the country, which fact should give them much work in the immediate future. But more important than anything else, in Jay Cooke's view, were the tremendous resources of the United States. The endless primeval forests and prairies and the rich mines, the productive powers of which were beyond calculation, waited only for capital and labor to turn them into profits. It is important to remember that faith in the resources of the United States was a fundamental element in Jay Cooke's business creed.

JAY COOKE & CO. PREPARES FOR NEW WORK

Jay Cooke believed that not only the distant but even the immediate future of his firms was promising. So strong was his belief that a profitable business was before them that in 1866 he and his partners took steps to prepare themselves for heavier work. They improved their banking office, extended their organization, and admitted several new partners to their firms.

Shortly after the seven-thirty campaign had closed, the Cookes set about providing larger and more suitable quarters for the

parent house in Philadelphia. Throughout the rushing business of
war finance, this office had consisted of a modest half of the first
floor of the building in which it was located. The Cookes now
leased the whole of the first floor, and they rebuilt and refurnished
it at a cost of $60,000.[3]

The result, said the *Philadelphia Inquirer*, was "undoubtedly
the most magnificent and costly establishment of the kind in the
United States." [4] The building was 52 feet wide and 80 feet deep.
The details of the interior are interesting. The ceiling was supported by six fluted pillars and was "beautifully finished in fresco
of tasteful design." The floor outside of the counters was laid
with squares of marble, and inside of the counters with rich Brussels carpeting. The counters and furniture were of solid walnut.
The room was lighted with gas; the chandeliers were said to be
beautiful but simple. Dominating the interior was a massive safe
placed in the center of the back of the room: [5]

This safe is perfectly fire and burglar proof. It consists of a sort of
vault, composed of an inner and outer wall of considerable thickness,
lined on the inside with strips of steel, securely riveted to the ceiling, as
well as the four walls. This vault is entered by an outer and an inner
door of remarkably substantial make, and which are furnished with
combination locks. Within this safe or vault is placed a large iron safe
of the newest and most approved patent.

Surmounting the top front of the safe was a large American eagle
of bronze on a pedestal on which appeared the name of Jay Cooke
& Co. surrounded by gold stars!

The northern side of the building was occupied by the "banking
department;" the southern, by the "government department,"
which handled government bonds and other securities. A special
place, set off from the rest by a railing, was provided for women.
In the rear of the government department was the office of Jay
Cooke. "This private office is quite spacious in extent and very
handsomely furnished with walnut chairs, sofas, &c, all of which
are covered with copper-colored leather. A rich carpet covers the
floor, and the room is lighted by a handsome chandelier." From
Cooke's office a narrow passageway led to a private consultation

THE PHILADELPHIA OFFICE OF JAY COOKE & CO., 1866

room. This room was also richly carpeted and contained chairs and sofas covered with damask velvet.

The place was thoroughly modern as judged by the most advanced standards of the time. It contained "well appointed wash rooms," and it was heated by a furnace in the basement. The basement also contained a "well appointed culinary establishment and a handsomely furnished dining-room, where all of Messrs. Cooke & Co's clerks and other employees daily take their dinner, free of expense to themselves."

The building, said the *Inquirer*, "certainly indicates that the affairs of the firm are in the most prosperous condition, and presage a still more brilliant future." With the wisdom of hindsight, we now see that this was the beginning of a series of extravagant expenditures by the Cookes which tied up capital badly needed in their business.

Of far greater significance in the advancement of the business of Jay Cooke's firms was the addition of a New York house. It is clear that the Cooke organization built up during the war was not suited to the needs of post-war business. The Washington and Philadelphia houses provided a nearly ideal combination for managing the original flotation of government securities. The Washington firm served as a necessary link between the Treasury and the general agent of the government for the sale of its loans, while the actual sale of the bonds had undoubtedly been managed as well from Philadelphia as it could have been handled from any other place. With the end of the war, however, the focal point of the Cookes' investment dealing shifted to New York, which had become the central market for trading in securities. New York had also become the unquestioned leader in commercial finance and the greatest reservoir of capital in the country; Philadelphia was no longer in the race with her neighbor to the North. Jay Cooke & Co., therefore, had to have a New York house in order to secure deposits of inland banks and to have the advantage of being in direct touch with the heart of the investment business. A New York house would give them a base in the center of America's private financial operations just as the Washington house had given them in public finance.

The establishment of a New York house came under consideration soon after the end of the war. In the fall of 1865 Jay Cooke cast about for openings and considered uniting with Robinson and Ogden, a young bond brokerage firm which was soon to go bankrupt.[6] Late in the fall of 1865, however, it was decided to establish a new partnership in New York. Jay Cooke & Co., of New York, was organized early in January, 1866,[7] and on March 1 opened its doors at 1 Nassau Street, on the northwest corner of Wall and Nassau. The new house proposed with "patientia, labor et perseverantia" to succeed — "Deo Volente," the partners piously added.[8] One wonders what the other New York banking houses thought of this invasion of their territory. Now that they had entered their territory, the Cookes could certainly no longer expect to secure much co-operation from Fisk & Hatch, Clark, Dodge & Co., and Vermilye & Co., hitherto their associates in New York.

Jay Cooke expected at the time soon to extend the Cooke organization to London.[9] Such a move would have been somewhat unusual earlier, since the American bankers' practice of sending temporary representatives to Europe had only in rare instances, such as the Browns, developed into the establishment of branches of American banks in London or other foreign centers of capital before the war. Two Americans, it is true, had risen to a high place in London banking: the Bostonians, Joshua Bates of Barings and George Peabody, who had established Peabody & Co. in London in 1835.[10] Though these men had a special interest in America, their houses were essentially English and were, like other European concerns, represented in America by their agents only, especially by T. W. Ward of Boston and Duncan, Sherman & Co. of New York. Peabody had retired in 1863 and Bates had died in 1864.[11] The disappearance of these men from business, together with the weakening of Anglo-American financial relations during the war, severed some of the personal ties which had bound America to European finance.

While some connections were broken off, others were established. Indeed, two American firms which were to become the strongest financial connections between America and Europe had their inception in the war years. J. & W. Seligman was started in New York during the war and opened branches in Frankfort and London.[12] J. Pierpont Morgan & Co. was established in 1863 in New York by the son of Junius S. Morgan; the latter, a Boston merchant who had become a partner in Peabody & Co., had in 1863 organized J. S. Morgan & Co. in London to succeed the old Peabody firm.[13] The establishment in New York of these two houses with strong European connections was the beginning of a movement which was soon to assume large proportions.

Banking relations with Europe were to receive a powerful impetus from the business which developed between Europe and the United States in the late 'sixties. Commercial finance, the tourist trade (it was estimated that the Paris exposition would bring $200,000,000 to Europe from America [14]), and the possibilities of selling American securities in Europe made American bankers, then feeling severe competition at home, look across the ocean. Jay Cooke saw in Europe a potential market for government refunding loans. But how could bonds be sold in Europe, which had during the war become so cool on the question of American investments? "The only successful plan," concluded Cooke, "will be a popularization there after the American plan & in this American agencies of foreign houses are of no account whatever. . . . We [if concerned] should have to open a house to go to work there." [15] Jay Cooke's plan to establish a London house secured the blessing of the Secretary of the Treasury, but its realization depended on the passing of the bill which was to provide for the floating of a large refunding loan.[16]

Frank Evans, the son of a London iron merchant and bank director, seems to have been considered the most likely candidate for the position of resident partner of the proposed London house in 1866.[17] The Evanses had since war times been friends of the Cookes, and they had been Jay Cooke's agents in London for selling five-twenties and, later, Philadelphia and Erie bonds.[18] They did not have any considerable financial standing or resources; but according to Bagehot, the editor of the *Economist*, wealthy men were not then establishing private banks in London.[19]

The plans for a London house did not for the time being materialize because of the failure of the Cookes to secure the government business for which they had hoped. Not until Jay Cooke and his firms entered the railroad business was the London project again entertained and finally realized.

Jay Cooke's Partners in 1866

The expansion of the Cooke organization brought several changes in the membership of the firms. In 1866 the number of partners was doubled, four additional members being admitted to the three houses; two were admitted to the Philadelphia house, only, while the other two became members of the three houses. The membership of the Washington house rose from four to six; Philadelphia, also taking on Henry Cooke and Fahnestock, grew from two to eight; and New York started with six partners.[20]

The increase in the number of partners did not mean a proportionate change in the distribution of the profits of the firm. No formal partnership agreement was drawn up, but the responsibilities and rights of the individuals were understood among themselves. Judging by the proposed division of profits for the New York house [21] and the actual distribution for the Philadelphia firm in 1866,[22] the individual partners' shares in profits were approximately as follows: Jay Cooke received about 30 per cent; Henry Cooke, Moorhead, and Fahnestock around 15 per cent each, or half of Jay Cooke's portion; Pitt Cooke received about 7 per cent; while each of the three remaining partners received about 5 per cent of the total. Salaries were not paid to the partners.

In the long run a business enterprise can be no stronger than the men who constitute it. Since Jay Cooke's firms did not have a large capital, it was especially important that they rate high in men and management. A brief consideration of Jay Cooke's partners will give some basis for judgment as to the strength of his organization.

Harris C. Fahnestock became the resident head of the New York house. As far as the technical aspects of Jay Cooke & Co.'s banking were concerned, a better man could hardly have been secured for the place. Though only about thirty years of age, he had had a broad banking experience, especially in railroad and government finance, the latter gained as a partner in the Washington house of Jay Cooke throughout the war. He was given special charge of the New York firm's business in government securities. Fahnestock had certain qualities which make for survival in an intensely competitive system: he was keen, quick, and independent in thought and action; he had great capacity for adjusting himself in a thoroughly dynamic situation, being a realist with unusual insight into a present situation and the factors which would be effective in the near future; he was an excellent judge of men; though possessing a high measure of the conventional virtues, he was by no means sentimental in matters of business. Fahnestock did not have such a warm appealing personality as Jay Cooke; he did not care for popularity, though he believed in standing well with men of importance in banking.

Edward Dodge, also a resident partner in New York, was a much older man. He had been Enoch W. Clark's original partner in Philadelphia and had helped establish Clark, Dodge & Co. in New York. Dodge was invited to join the Cookes because of his familiarity with business on Wall Street. His special work was to have charge of loans, which required a close knowledge of the whims of the money and the stock and bond markets. The Cookes felt flattered that he won admission to the New York Stock Exchange without a single blackball, and they expected much of him as a partner.[23]

The third resident partner in New York was also new to the firm — Pitt Cooke, Jay's older brother. He had tried to enter West Point but had failed to pass the physical examination. Though he had studied law, he had engaged in the real-estate and produce commission business, with his home and headquarters at Sandusky.[24] It was he who in the 'fifties had selected the lands in the West for Jay Cooke and other Philadelphia buyers, and during the war he had dealt in quartermaster's supplies.[25] Pitt Cooke had been only moderately successful in business,[26] and he was qualified for banking neither by experience nor temperament. He was of a sensitive and introspective nature, deeply affectionate and kind;[27] but he also had the weaknesses which frequently go with those qualities. His health was poor. Unlike his brother, he was not a strong churchman, though he was not without faith in God. In his business relations he showed much good judgment, but he lacked energy and decision.

Henry D. Cooke was the resident head of the Washington house. Never can there have been a bank executive who was much less of a banker than Henry Cooke! He was an assiduous lobbyist, a profession in which he was adept. He proved to be a spendthrift, a "good fellow," easily influenced, lacking in business judgment, with an exaggerated opinion of his own importance, and inclined to tie up the business of the firm in speculative enterprises and loans to politicians.[28] His work as a lobbyist was of great value to the Cookes during the war, but he was not useful to any other part of the business.

It is significant to note that one of Jay Cooke's weaknesses as a business man was his concern for his brothers. This concern grew not out of an ambition to establish a Cooke family banking dynasty but out of a desire to take care of brothers who had been unable to provide well for themselves. There was much of a clannish character in the Cooke family. Jay Cooke had come to be looked upon as the pillar of the family, and family loyalty laid upon him the task of helping the others. In return, they gave him their gratitude and worship, which was reward enough for the banker who desired nothing more strongly than to be highly esteemed.

Two new members were added to Jay Cooke & Co. of Philadelphia. They were John W. Sexton and George C. Thomas. Sexton, who had come to the Cookes from a local dry-goods concern, had for some time been a clerk in the Philadelphia house. He was put in charge of the banking department, but he never came to occupy an important place with the Cookes. More important was Thomas, who was put in charge of the government department in the Philadelphia bank and was next to Jay Cooke in command of the house. Thomas brought practically no capital to the firm — he had saved about $3,000 from his earnings as a clerk — but he had had some business experience. For six years he had worked in the dry-goods establishment of his father in Philadelphia, just down the next street from Jay Cooke's office, and for three years he had served as a clerk in the office of Jay Cooke & Co.[29] Thomas was a young man of unusual business talents; he was ambitious and energetic; and he had excellent judgment in matters of business and a character and personality which made him trusted and liked.

William Moorhead was definitely associated with none of the houses though a partner in all, but he was not without influence. After retiring from the presidency of the Philadelphia & Erie Railroad in 1864, he gave some attention to banking. There was not, however, a close understanding between him and Jay Cooke. The two might have been mutually helpful to each other, but Moorhead was conservative and came to be suspicious of the enthusiasm of his brother-in-law, while Jay Cooke considered him much too cautious. In his fears over federal finance during the war — fears which in Jay Cooke's opinion approached Copperheadism — Moorhead had obstructed rather than aided Jay Cooke, with the result that the latter no longer had full confidence in his partner. Moorhead's position in the firm was, therefore, rather anomalous.

Among all the partners of Jay Cooke there were only two men whom one could really call bankers. They were Fahnestock and Thomas. Fortunately for their firms they were first-class men. The others had no special talent for the business and, with the exception of Moorhead, slavishly followed the leadership of Jay Cooke.

THE MANAGEMENT OF JAY COOKE & CO.

The addition of the New York house and the doubling of the membership of the Cooke firms increased greatly the problem of administration within the organization. It was no longer possible for Jay Cooke to manage the details of the business as closely as he had done during the war. A sort of compromise system resulted, whereby each house had a measure of local autonomy but was subject at the same time to any supervision which the leading partner might give.

One partner came to be recognized as the resident head of each house: Fahnestock in New York, Henry Cooke in Washington, and Jay Cooke in Philadelphia, with Thomas serving in his absence.[30] The exact influence these heads had over their individual houses depended on the individual and the situation.

Within the New York and Philadelphia houses, the work was somewhat departmentalized. It has already been noted that Fahnestock headed the most important department, that which handled the business in government securities in New York, and Dodge was head of the banking department. In Philadelphia, Sexton was put in charge of the banking department, and Thomas had charge of the government department.

The dominating and co-ordinating figure in this diversity of partners and firms was Jay Cooke, himself. He was called the Tycoon by his partners,[31] a name which was well chosen, for in those years he ruled his partners with a strong hand. The partners never as a group considered the affairs of the firm, even its general policies. Jay Cooke consulted them, especially the leading partners, but he seems to have made the final decision in larger matters of policy; details were necessarily left to individual houses in which one partner usually dominated. Jay Cooke was informed daily, or more often, of the work and condition of each house. He also visited the New York and Washington houses frequently.

The banker's supervision of his partners extended even to the latters' private business and conduct. In view of the fact that the capital of their houses consisted only of the private holdings of the partners, he was insistent that they should keep free of speculative projects and maintain their investments in a fairly liquid condition. He did not hesitate to speak firmly to Henry about his reckless spending; even Pitt was reprimanded for spending too freely and not paying his debts.[32] Many a letter in the Jay Cooke Papers reveals the stern judge rather than the kind brother.

The extent to which the Tycoon ruled his associates is illustrated by an incident in which Huntington, the cashier of the First National Bank of Washington, was involved. Huntington was far from satisfactory to Jay Cooke and received severe reprimands. Cooke accused him of speculating, and on one occasion in 1866 the unfortunate cashier committed the offence of driving a four-in-hand with his wife and another couple in Central Park in New York on a Sabbath afternoon, a real indiscretion in those days when the command to keep the Sabbath Day holy was still strictly interpreted. Jay Cooke heard of this and firmly and "in great sorrow" wrote Huntington. Such an act, wrote he, "if known on Change in NY or elsewhere amongst financial People would create remark & bring great discredit to the Bank under yr Charge & the fds with whom you are so confidentially associated." "Credit," noted Cooke, "is a tender plant. Nothing so affects it as such a stupid display as a four-in-hand." Yet not only because of credit — "God sees, if man does not." Such actions as this, warned Cooke, would *destroy your position with us*. . . . I pray and beseech you to think." [33] While we may be amused at this incident, translated into terms which we can understand it merely reveals what is as true today as it was at that time, that the business man who deviates from accepted practice is under suspicion in business. Jay Cooke understood that a reputation for character was necessary for a lasting success in banking.

But if he was exacting and stern, at times to the point of unreasonableness, Jay Cooke was also very considerate of his associates. He was the benevolent, paternalistic despot. With everyone, from his partners down through his staff, he was generous and understanding to a fault. He had the gift of seeing people as individuals, and he had a sensitive regard for their feelings. He entertained them in his home and was interested in their personal difficulties and good fortune. In contrast with the business executive who always places his business above his men, or even the one who carefully balances the individual and the business considerations, with Jay Cooke the personal consideration dominated. He had infinite patience with the weaknesses of his partners and assistants. As a result, his organization contained some weak men. But it was at the same time characterized by a remarkable loyalty to its leader.

The problems in the administration of such an organization were serious. To act wisely in determining the larger policies for the future was in those uncertain post-war times extremely difficult. There was, also, ever present the problem of co-ordinating the work of the many partners and the three houses of Jay Cooke & Co. and the First National Bank of Washington in a system in which one partner or one house might endanger the whole. In the final analysis, the future of the group depended largely on Jay Cooke; rarely does one find a case where a business enterprise is so much a one-man concern. For that reason it is well to get a good view of this very interesting banker, of his character and personality and also of his activities outside of business which throw light on the man, himself, and have a direct bearing on his work.

JAY COOKE, THE MAN

By the time with which we are now concerned, Jay Cooke had become a "man of property," with all that the term implies. Aside from his business, he was a pillar of society, one of those who support its established institutions both by his manner of living and by his means. He had acquired a philosophy and made a place for himself which were of deepest significance to his business.

Jay Cooke had a strong sense of social responsibility. He accepted without question the democratic philosophy of the brotherhood of man and its corollary that man is his brother's keeper. This philosophy, coupled with a desire for the approval of his fellow-men, made him liberal in giving of his time and means in helping those who were in need. Judging by the letters in the Jay Cooke Papers which contain requests for aid, there was some truth in his brother's statement that Jay was "bled by *Every body*, by the world, the church, & the *Old Scratch*." [34] This trait worried his family, particularly Pitt. His generosity was even carried into his business; each of his firms had a charity account known as the Old Patriarch Jacob, and every year the Old Patriarch got a tenth of the total dividend for the year. The fund was dispensed by Jay Cooke, his partners, or members of the staff who were assigned to look into requests for help.

The banker not only gave money; he also gave of his time and interest. His Sunday school boys sought his advice; a father thanked him for giving his son an artificial limb, and pathetically asked if he knew where the son was.[35] "As I lay awake last evening," wrote a banker friend to Jay Cooke, "unable to fall asleep my mind dwelt a good deal on the present glorious awakening of the millions of immortal souls to the consideration of their eternal interests & I felt as if I should like to hear from you in one of your cheering letters such as you used to write & stir me up to more zeal & more earnestness." [36]

Jay Cooke's aid did not all go into personal charities; he also supported institutions, charitable, cultural, social, or political. He was a member of the Christian Commission and an enthusiastic supporter of the American Sunday School Union and the Y. M. C. A. He was a member of the Academy of Natural Sciences and of the Historical Society of Pennsylvania. Like many other conservative business men, he also belonged to the Union League and the Home Labor League (a protective tariff organization).[37] At one time he gave $30,000 to Kenyon College, and, from time to time, smaller gifts to Princeton, Dartmouth, and other schools, and to the Academy of Natural Sciences.[38]

But the institution to which Jay Cooke gave the most was the Church. St. Paul's Episcopal Church, built on Old York Road near his home, was with good reason called the "five-twenty" church,[39] for Jay Cooke practically built and supported it. To the thank-offering collected at the coming of peace between the North and South he contributed almost $50,000.[40] He gave liberally, moreover, to needy preachers (the vacations they spent at his summer home were famous),[41] to earnest divinity students,[42] frontier churches, John Wanamaker's Sunday school building,[43] and missionary organizations. He sent books and magic lanterns to Sunday schools which could not afford such things. The books given us, wrote a southerner, "have been distributed in *ten* different states to poor and destitute Sabbath Schools, thus carrying life and salvation to the perishing; in hundreds of neighborhoods your name is now known and cherished as a household word. Yes you are loved and spoken of throughout the South as 'The big warm hearted Banker.'" [44] He endowed a chair in an Episcopal divinity school in Philadelphia and gave generously to other theological schools, including St. John's in Cambridge, Massachusetts. It is said that Jay Cooke once proposed to Phillips Brooks, the famous Boston preacher, that he undertake to lead a campaign, to be financed by Cooke himself, to evangelize the United States,[45] an incident which is very revealing of the character of the banker.

One element which was a real force in Jay Cooke's life was his strong Christian faith. As has already been seen, his Christian philosophy and his beliefs were simple in nature and were impatient of denominational differences.[46] His was the age of sentimental expressions of faith, it is true, and his was also a generation to whom membership in a church was a part of the conventional order of things. Jay Cooke had not known Darwin and Huxley and Spencer; it is doubtful that in his frontier nurture he had ever even heard of William Ellery Channing. His conception of God was that of an all powerful and benevolent Father. The duties of a Christian were to worship Him, to keep His commandments, and to treat one's fellow-men as brothers.[47]

The Church was a very important institution to Jay Cooke. Attendance at worship on the Sabbath was as much a part of the day as was business on other days. He taught Sunday school in church on Sunday mornings and conducted a Bible class in his home Sunday evenings. He was very active in the American Sunday School Union and in other similar church organizations. In his home family prayers came at eight every morning. Guests were expected to be present at prayers and to go to church with their host.[48] Before St. Paul's was built near Ogontz, the family drove the long distance into the city for worship. Loyalty, order, and discipline characterized the banker's relations with his church.

Jay Cooke adhered with remarkable closeness to the model pattern of the Christian gentleman. Even his severest critics never found the least occasion to criticize his private life. His business records — the tens of thousands of letters between the partners — reveal the same regard for what he thought to be the right. It appears certain that, where there was in business an obvious application of a moral rule, Jay Cooke took the ethical stand to be right with himself and with God. He objected to the running of trains on Sunday, even though this objection might mean financial loss.[49] His moral code, like the code of the Church, was, however, constructed to fit simple, personal relationships.

In complex business situations, which were not clearly measured by accepted precepts or on which no definite ethical standard had been developed, Jay Cooke was apparently not clearly conscious of the moral issue if there were one. It was one thing not to steal from your neighbor; it was quite another to urge that neighbor to invest his savings in a railroad none too certain to succeed. We must remember, however, that the business code of that time, as well as of recent times, did not place upon the dealer in bonds responsibility for what he sold; he should not, of course, misrepresent actual facts regarding the business of a firm whose bonds he sold, but, where judgment was involved, the old common law doctrine of *caveat emptor* still held. This fact has often been overlooked in estimating the work of our investment bankers. One cannot entirely defend the system as it was in Jay Cooke's time or in more recent years, but one can at least understand why it existed and see how difficult it would have been for individuals or firms to oppose it or to act contrary to general practice.

There was one aspect of Jay Cooke's religious life which was of greatest significance to his business. His reputation for integrity undoubtedly had great practical value, but the heart of it all was the fact that he believed firmly in the goodness of God and his own rightness with Him. This did much to build up his self-confidence, to liberate his energies,[50] and to make him buoyantly optimistic. "God is good to us — let us be *true to each other* & to *Him* & all will be well in the future"— such was his philosophy.[51] He seems to have believed sincerely that God had chosen him, as He had chosen Abraham Lincoln, to be an instrument to save the Union.[52] Such a belief may be dangerous to a business man in that it lessens self-criticism; dangerous or not, it has a tremendous significance. In fact, it cannot be too strongly emphasized as a power in Jay Cooke's life.

One quality which one might expect to find in Jay Cooke was conspicuous in its absence: although he had a quick and incisive mind, he did not have a cultivated intellect. He was not a student, nor was he of a contemplative nature. Books, other than religious, held little interest for him. He did not like to travel, even refusing to go to Europe when it seemed to his interest to do so. It was rarely that he went far off the beaten track between Sandusky, Washington, Philadelphia, and New York. His friendships, moreover, sprang out of his sociable nature and the needs of his business rather than from a desire for the stimulus of new ideas.

Jay Cooke was an interesting contrast with the international banker. Compare Cooke, for instance, with his contemporary, J. Pierpont Morgan. Young Morgan was cosmopolitan; he had been born in New England, brought up in England, and educated in Germany. He had traveled and read widely and was the heir to a deep culture. Morgan was the cultivated individual, with contacts and an outlook that were more international than national.

Indeed, there was little of urbanity, of intellectual curiosity, or sophistication about Jay Cooke. He was in many respects just an ordinary person. But he had more than the usual energy, enthusiasm and attractiveness of personality, a great capacity for winning the co-operation of those who worked with him and for organizing them into effective action; he also had great self-confidence, rooted in a strong faith and a happy adjustment to life, considerable ability, and a reputation for integrity. One might well say that he was essentially a typical American, a man of great energy, great enthusiasms, and kindness of heart, narrow in his interests and outlook, but utterly lacking in that astuteness and sophistication which belong to a more cultivated type.

The most concrete expression of the personality of Jay Cooke and the source of much of his strength is found in his home. The Cooke family, with its four children, was very happy, and their home was a place of cheer, good will, and hospitality. A few years before the war, they moved out from Philadelphia to the Chelten Hills northwest of the city. There they lived comfortably and unostentatiously for several years. During the war, Cooke acquired an estate in the Pennsylvania mountains, South Mountain, to which he went for hunting and fishing, and a small island, Gibraltar, in the bay off Sandusky. On this island, with its large, comfortable house, the Cooke family spent a few weeks in early summer and fall.

Gibraltar was a lovely spot. The Jay Cooke Papers contain many letters which give us intimate glimpses into the life of the place: the graciousness of the hostess, the fawns in the woods, the pet cat, Tibbie, who "was always ready to welcome" Jay Cooke, and Bernardo, the St. Bernard, who to his master's very deep regret had to be "destroyed" because he had bitten a visitor.[53] During the season when it was open, the place was filled with guests, including many famous men.[54] "This is a very busy place," wrote Jay Cooke from Gibraltar in the summer of 1866, "we eat read sing roam — sail, row troll & still fishing to our hearts content." [55]

The lake surrounding Gibraltar was a paradise for the fisherman. Jay Cooke had a passion for fishing. He knew the fish, their ways and habitat, and he fished on just the same grand scale and with just the same feeling of satisfaction with which he conducted his business.[56] In his Memoirs is an interesting chapter on fish and fishing in which he recounts with great pride the story of his miraculous draught when, after others had given up in despair, he caught enough fish to feed a multitude of three hundred editors and statesmen for three days!

An expression of the banker's enhanced prestige was his new home, Ogontz, completed in 1866. As soon as the war was over, he had started to build this mansion on a beautiful location among the rolling hills, trees, and brooks of the Chelten Hills. It took more than a year to build the house and the cost was over a million dollars. The mansion contained a conservatory, a library, an amusement room, a music room — some fifty rooms in all, it is said. There was an Italian garden, and a beautiful natural park all around the mansion. Ogontz was one of the most costly homes in America at the time and one of the best known.[57]

Ogontz was in many ways an expression of the personality of its owner. It was spacious, comfortable, and hospitable, and it had been furnished almost without regard to cost. The materials of which it had been built, the labor which went into it, and its furnishings were almost wholly American;[58] as with so many of his time, a narrow nationalism dominated Jay Cooke's interests.

Like so many other successful business men, Jay Cooke became interested in art. His interest was not that of a person with a cultivated appreciation, but rather the interest of one who had reasonably good taste, respect for the beautiful, and a feeling that a man of wealth should surround himself with artistic things. It is not without amusement that we read that after Jay Cooke had, early in 1867, bought two paintings, for each of which he paid $5,000, it was rumored that he was going in for art collecting. This brought a new kind of client to Jay Cooke & Co. (according to Fahnestock's facetious reference to the affair in a letter to Jay Cooke) ranging from the artists, themselves, to "petroleum aristocrats" and "shoddy millionaires" with pictures to sell, "fleeing the wrath to come out of contraction and reconstruction." [59]

Money, said Jay Cooke in his first year as a "banker" in Philadelphia, was desirable only as a means to exercise one's social and generous spirit. In Ogontz he had full scope for such impulses, and he gave them free rein in the seven years he lived there. Relatives, friends, partners, business associates, numberless prominent public officials, American Indians, the members of the Japanese embassy in Washington, all enjoyed the hospitality of his home. Tales of his entertainments are interesting. Signor Blitz and other sleight-of-hand artists, Japanese jugglers and acrobats, amateur plays, billiards and other games were there for the amusement of guests. Ogontz was in every way an expression of its owner's joy in living.

The Christmas of 1866 — the first which the Cooke family spent at Ogontz — was an especially happy time. The partners and their families were fêted there during the holidays. Perhaps

The Drawing Room at Ogontz, Jay Cooke's Mansion

that very Christmas, members of the household played, as they often did at Christmas time, *The Cricket on the Hearth*. There was in the household, we may be sure, the same simple good will that lived in Dickens' Christmas stories. Poor Old Scrooge probably would not have found many who agreed with him in that place, for no one could long remain under Jay Cooke's roof without catching something of its good cheer and happiness.

On that very Christmas Eve, Fahnestock — the most independent of the partners — penned a letter to his host and senior partner which indicates that all was well with Jay Cooke & Co.: [60]

I often regret and do on Christmas evening that I lack the happy faculty of speech when my heart is fullest of grateful and pleasurable emotions. Never were partners so happily associated as we all, and especially at this season, on which five years ago our preliminary arrangements (for the Wash^n House) were made, do I revert with pleasure and thankfulness to our successes, due first to a good Providence and second to you, with the Cooperation of WMG and Harry and this year of Pitt and the Commodore and Sexton and *George* all *glorious* good fellows. So happy a combination of business and social relations falls to the lot of few men. Be assured that I love you and all the rest of them and it will be my greatest pride if in the future you are as well satisfied with me as in the past.

We can picture the host on this Christmas Eve, a man of forty-five years, a little over medium height, well built though not heavy, with a genial face, bright and kindly eyes, full whiskers and heavy hair which was light brown and just turning gray; a man of excellent health, much energy, and great self-confidence, and yet rather quiet, enjoying the happiness of those about him. His social and generous spirit must then have been satisfied. He had realized his great ambition.

JAY COOKE AND POST-WAR FINANCIAL POLITICS
1865–1869

MOST of the efforts of Jay Cooke and his partners in the years immediately following the war were concerned with government finance. This took two forms: the attempt to influence government policy and the actual work of the Cooke firms in buying and selling government loans.

At the close of the war the United States faced the difficult problem of rebuilding the financial structure of the government, which had been hastily put up during the war. An inflated monetary and price system had resulted from the war; what should be done about the resumption of specie payments and the depreciated greenbacks? A revolutionary change had come in the American banking system; would it stand the test of peace and reconstruction? Heavy import duties and internal taxes had been laid during the war; could they be reduced without injuring the national credit? A stupendous debt had been piled up, a debt so large that it made the conservative London *Economist* wonder and admire;[1] could the obligations soon maturing be paid, and could the funded debt be refunded at a lower interest rate?

On the various questions of government financial policy in those years, Jay Cooke took somewhat of a middle position. He agreed with Hugh McCulloch, the Secretary of the Treasury, that everything possible should be done to maintain the credit of the United States, but, as to the methods for meeting the financial problems of the government, he took a realistic position which made him more liberal than the Secretary. Like McCulloch, however, he was uncompromising in his opposition to the radicals, whose interest in the debtor, then as today, frequently made them lose sight of the problems of government credit.

Admitting Jay Cooke's patriotism and interest in social well being, it is reasonable to proceed on the assumption that his position on questions of government finance was in a large measure an expression of the needs of his business. His whole financial prestige was based on the policy of the government, since he had in selling the war loans maintained that the loans could and would be paid in full. But more than that, every one of the financial questions carried over from the war had a bearing on the immediate work of his banking houses. This situation threw Jay Cooke into the maelstrom of politics.

JAY COOKE'S STANDING WITH THE GOVERNMENT

It was of first importance to Jay Cooke and his firms that they stand well with the Treasury. He himself never sought any official position with the Treasury. There was some talk of his being appointed secretary by Grant,[2] but such an appointment would obviously not have been to the advantage of his business.[3] For a number of years the banker succeeded, however, in being on good terms with the Treasury. He was a close friend of Hugh McCulloch, who was Secretary of the Treasury from 1865 to 1869 and with whom the Cookes had worked, enthusiastically and successfully, in establishing the national banking system and in selling seven-thirties. McCulloch was a banker of extensive experience and a public officer of the highest type; he was a person of conservative judgment and of great integrity.

It was to be expected that McCulloch, as head of the Treasury in those difficult times, would seek the advice of bankers and others experienced in government finance. Since no one surpassed Jay Cooke in this field, the Secretary looked to him for help. McCulloch sought Jay Cooke's advice and enlisted his aid in meeting criticism of the Treasury's policies.[4] The banker differed with the Secretary at times, and then he did not hesitate to make his difference known to him; but generally Cooke agreed with McCulloch, and he always used his great influence over the press in supporting him.[5] There was a close mutual dependence between the Secretary and the banker.

There was also a close friendship between the Cookes and W. E. Chandler, who was for some time assistant secretary under

McCulloch.[6] On the other hand, Van Dyke, the assistant treasurer in New York, caused the Cookes much trouble; he was not tractable, said Fahnestock, and "requires constant vigilance & ingenuity to cope with his numerous vagaries."[7]

The Cookes were fearful that McCulloch might be forced to resign, especially that Johnson might remove him in 1867,[8] but he remained in office until the expiration of President Johnson's term. They were then much concerned over his successor. Their choice was Governor Dennison, of Ohio, who would have been very friendly toward the Cookes.[9] Jay Cooke was fearful that a New Yorker would be appointed.[10] He tried to arrange a conference with President Grant to talk the matter over with him, but failed.[11] The appointment of Boutwell to the Treasury was, however, fairly satisfactory to the Cookes. They thought that he was friendly toward them and that he had no alliances.[12]

For the Philadelphia banker to retain his standing in government finance, it was necessary that Congress pass certain bills and that sentiment be favorable to the employment of his house by the Treasury. The Cookes had a strategic hold in the Senate through their friendship with John Sherman. They frequently consulted him on financial legislation, and, though the bankers and the senator were not always one, on the whole they were in close agreement. Among the faithful friends of the Cookes in the Senate were also Cattell of Pennsylvania and Schenck of Ohio.

Jay Cooke and his partners had various means by which to keep in touch with Congress and to bring pressure to bear in their own favor. There was first and foremost the Washington brother, the official contact man and lobbyist for the Cookes. It is difficult to estimate the value of Henry Cooke to the group. Like the Rothschilds, he tried to stay close to men in power. He seems to have known everybody worth knowing; he entertained lavishly at his home; his office was almost like a political club. Needy congressmen sought loans at his banks — Jay Cooke & Co. and the First National — and President Grant enjoyed many a cheering glass at his home. Jay Cooke also had other contacts with the capital city. In 1867 and 1868 he was kept informed of the action of

Congress by letter and by wire in code from "Star," a newspaper man.[13]

The political influence of the Cookes was greatly strengthened by their hold on the press. Jay Cooke and his partners were, above all, realistic in handling editors; they gave many small favors to newspaper men, such as presents of wine, grapes, or fish, or they helped their families when traveling, but another consideration was more important. As Pitt Cooke said, "Its only a question of *price* you will pay whether these Editors will lie *for* you or against you." [14] When necessary, the Cookes did not hesitate to pay a good price in the form of options on securities.[15] Through friendship or pressure, they were able to keep pretty well in line with their wishes a number of strategic papers, such as the *Philadelphia Inquirer* and the *New York Times* and *Tribune*.

Strong as the Cookes were, there were many influences and interests working against them. The rapid growth of investment banking houses brought serious competition. The brokers and stock and gold speculators, who wanted to be able to manipulate the gold market and generally favored expansion of the currency, recognized in Jay Cooke's position with the Treasury and in his power in the money and gold markets an obstacle to their activities.[16] His somewhat ostentatious way of living, moreover, aroused criticism; it gave the demagogue an effective illustration of how the banker had waxed rich off Civil War finance, when what he had done, said one critic, could have been done by any good $5,000-a-year man.[17]

Opposition to Jay Cooke became very outspoken in the press. There were several strong editors who were consistently opposed to whatever was done or proposed by him and his partners. Among them were the Bennetts of the *New York Herald* and Childs of Philadelphia's *Public Ledger & Daily Transcript*. The Bennetts were fierce opponents of what the Cookes stood for. One wonders if the banker had criticized the elder Bennett for his attitude toward the government during the Civil War. Childs was at first somewhat less direct and positive in his attacks, but he was, nevertheless, persistent; he was a man of influence, being connected with the Associated Press, which was concerned with the dissemination of news both by telegraph and ocean cable.[18] Both Childs and Bennett were of a type which could neither understand nor be understood by Jay Cooke. The editors were intellectually and socially too sophisticated to comprehend his simple idealism, while he, very likely, could not appreciate their position because he understood neither their personalities nor their experiences.

More important, perhaps, than business or personal considerations was the situation in the government. The division within Congress on the Reconstruction question and the lack of agreement between the executive branch and Congress practically paralyzed action on financial questions in the early post-war years. At first the Cookes had hoped that an open break between the President and Congress could be prevented, but the President's veto of the Civil Rights Bill destroyed any such hopes.[19] Though holding no brief for the "unregenerate" South and heartily favoring opposition to what they considered the President's lenient Reconstruction policy,[20] Jay Cooke and his partners did not go the whole length of the radicals on Reconstruction and were positively opposed to their financial policies.

At the time of the State elections of 1867, the Cookes hoped that wiser counsels would prevail in Congress and that there would be less of impeachment and negro suffrage and more of tax reduction and definite financial policy.[21] But there was no increase of wisdom in finance. The big struggle came in the election of 1868. Though Jay Cooke disapproved of the stand taken by the Republican nominating convention in 1868, he believed that Grant, the presidential nominee, was sound on financial questions. The banker subscribed liberally to the Republican national committee, which gift was acknowledged by Chairman Chandler with the request that he be given further discretion in aiding, on Cooke's private account, Schenck, Logan, Bingham, and certain candidates in other States — "It would be a good investment for you." [22] The "political" account of the Washington and Philadelphia houses for the year was $17,825.[23] By such means the Cookes helped to stem the tide of financial radicalism which almost overwhelmed Congress in the late 'sixties.

The Currency: Resumption but not Contraction

Jay Cooke's interest in post-war financial politics touched upon most of the financial issues before the government. Some, like internal taxation and the tariff, were of no direct concern to his business. Many were so closely related to his work that they can be considered only in relation thereto. Two large issues, the currency question and the payment of the war debts, took so much of the interest and energy of the Cookes over such a long period of time that they must be considered separately.

On currency questions Jay Cooke took decidedly a middle position. He considered the issue of greenbacks defensible under war conditions, but after the war he favored the exchange of greenbacks for national bank notes.[24] He held that bank notes were very much better, because they were based on the wealth of the stockholders of the banks as well as on the securities of the United States. The greatest benefit to be derived from the national system, in his opinion, was its uniform currency.[25] He worked hard to frustrate the movement for substituting greenbacks for bank currency, refuting the argument that the banks were recipients of special favors for which they did not pay the government.

Jay Cooke was neither a contractionist nor an inflationist in the early post-war years. Though he did not publicly attack Secretary McCulloch's contraction policy, he did not approve of it for the reason that he thought there was not enough money to handle the growing business of the country.[26] In only one instance in those first post-war years, however, did he definitely support an increase in currency: he favored increasing the bank note circulation above the legal maximum of $300,000,000 in order to supply southern banks without taking so much away from the North.[27] He was vehement in his attack on easy money schemes, then so widely championed, and he saw in demands for inflation the hand of the New York stock speculators.[28] They wanted an easy money market and the spur of inflation in order to raise the price of their stocks, while he thought it necessary to keep inflation down and the credit of the government up in order to make the bonds desirable.

The whole money question was tied up with that of resumption of specie payments. Immediately after the war, Jay Cooke, like McCulloch, Chase, Horace Greeley, and many other prominent men, favored early resumption.[29] Indeed, McCulloch was even accused of following Cooke's wishes in this connection.[30] Cooke strongly supported McCulloch's bill before Congress in the winter of 1866 which was a preliminary move to resumption, but his stand was based on a plan for refunding the government loans which "would release capital from its present lethargic condition"[31] and bring it to the United States from Europe. A recent study of the greenbacks suggests that with proper preparation resumption would have been possible at that time, especially if such a plan as Cooke advocated had been adopted for importing capital.[32]

By 1867, however, Jay Cooke had changed his position on resumption. This appears to have been due fundamentally to the less favorable condition of business and the failure to strengthen the Treasury by vigorous refunding of the war debts, but the immediate reason was that Jay Cooke & Co. was then helping the Treasury to meet its short-time obligations by selling five-twenties. "As to getting back to specie payments," wrote Jay Cooke to his brother, "the least said about that the better as it is the premium on gold that enables us to sell the 5–20^s. If purchasers of 5–20's supposed that we will get back to specie payments within a year or two they would not touch them at present prices."[33] The remoteness of resumption made Fahnestock burst into song, not without an element of rejoicing:[34]

> "Oh the vanished days of gold,
> The vanished halcyon days of specie
> Bullions dead and coin is fled,
> On paper winglets to Hel-vetia!"

McCulloch again urged a return to specie payments in 1868 and President Grant seemed to be leaning in that direction in 1869, but the Cookes still opposed resumption and tried to prevent the President from proposing an immediate return to specie.[35] Fahnestock held that there was not enough specie in the United States to make resumption possible: "In the monthly return to Comptroller is a printed item 'Specie & other lawful Money' opposite this line a bank will fill in $156,312.50 and it looks very good on paper. But rummage in the vaults of the bank and you will find in detail specie 312.50 other lawful money 156,000." As for the specie hoarded in the common man's stocking, "ascertain the contents of that Stocking and you will find that his Coin and Greenbacks consisted largely of the latter and that the Coin embraced chiefly his smooth quarters and pistareens which he couldnt pass before suspension, an occasional Counterfeit Mexican dollar, specimen dimes half dimes and three cent pieces & an old 'pocket piece' half soveriegn." The New York partners had counted their coins, said Fahnestock, "and the 'demnition total' is Garland has a Canadian 5 cent piece and old Pitt has a Japanese coin, lozenge shaped, valued at $3. *We* shout therefore resume immediately." [36]

This was exactly the position of Jay Cooke in the autumn of 1869. "It is plain then," he said, "that if we resume — it must be on a basis of *confidence* and not *ability* to pay on demand. If the Government can possess itself of specie enough to inspire Confidence it can resume — but the Treasury must be strong — stronger than the cliques and opposing influences of trade — or confidence will be lost and suspension follow." [37]

He took a strong position against those who proposed the contraction of the currency in order to raise the money of the country to the specie level and even advocated a moderate expansion of the currency to keep pace "with the new habits and enlarged area of Country." [38]

Why should this Grand and Glorious Country be stunted and dwarfed. — its activities chilled and its very life blood curdled by these miserable 'hard coin' theories — The musty theories of a by gone age —. These men who are urging on premature resumption know nothing of the vast & growing west which would grow thrice as fast if it was not cramped for the means necessary to build RailRoads and improve farms and convey the produce to market. They know nothing of the wants of the Great Empire of the South — Capable of producing six (6) millions of Bales of Cotton next year, if the land owners could get aid. Let the President cast off all advice that tends to choke the *South & West* and recommence a policy that will keep the wheels of industry and trade and Commerce actively moving and the whole country will Applaud him.

Though he was against contraction, the Philadelphia banker favored planned resumption to take effect in the near future. In the early fall of 1869 he recommended that Congress announce at once that resumption should take place January 1, 1872, and then take steps to prepare for the event. He proposed the retirement of greenbacks to the extent of $100,000,000 and the issue of an equal amount of national bank notes in order to relieve the government of a part of its load. The Treasury should in the next two years accumulate $100,000,000 in coin by selling three-year compound interest notes for gold, even selling a gold loan in Europe if necessary. The national banks should, he recommended, accumulate a specie reserve of at least $60,000,000; this could be built up by the Treasury by withholding from the banks gold interest due on bonds deposited to secure circulation. In answer to the familiar argument that resumption would bring about a lowering of prices, the banker maintained that this would not necessarily happen; he believed that European demand and competition at home would neutralize such a tendency and that a sliding tariff would help make the adjustment more smoothly.[39]

Thus, throughout the years immediately following the war, Jay Cooke stood for resumption based on orderly preparation and recognition of the condition and needs of business. He used all his influence to effect such a solution of the difficulty, but his work was futile. Not until 1879 did resumption of gold payments become a reality. Had it come sooner and in an orderly way, there would very likely have been a healthier condition in business and, possibly, better times for Jay Cooke & Co. in the uncertain years of the late 'sixties and early 'seventies.

Jay Cooke Favors Refunding the National Debt

Throughout those years Jay Cooke continually emphasized the close relationship between the currency question and the national debt. Indeed, he held that to refund the debt was the most important financial task before the government and that a proper management of funding would help solve other financial questions.

The first debt question which had to be met was that of "repudiation." Even before the war had ended, there had been rumblings of the approaching storm over the proposal that the principal of the five-twenty bonds be paid in currency. The debtor movement which gained such a strong hold in Congress after the war raised the question to a serious issue. This was to Jay Cooke an attack both on the credit of the United States and on his own prestige, for in selling the bonds he had on his own authority and initiative advertised that they would be paid in gold. To follow any other course, he held, would be ruinous to both the national credit and his own houses.

The banker, therefore, used all the influence he could command to oppose the movement for redeeming the five-twenties in currency. The "monstrous doctrine," as he called it,[40] gained great headway in 1867; it became so strong that even Senator Sherman was won over to the position that the government had a right to redeem the five-twenties in currency.[41] Jay Cooke made a strong appeal to the press and the public through the *Philadelphia Inquirer.*[42] He urged that the government was legally responsible for payment in gold, and he struck at the argument of the demagogue by saying the bonds were not held by a privileged class but by the people at large. In a strong letter to Senator Sherman he urged that when the act of an agent has stood unchallenged by the principal for years, the act becomes legally binding.[43]

The issue was fought out in the election of 1868. "If the Repub^n party is to turn *repudiators I will desert them,*" wrote Jay Cooke to Henry in the summer of 1868.[44] "This whole matter must be at *once understood before I give any money*. The scoundrels deserve hanging for the irreparable injury they are doing to this glorious nation." To the satisfaction of the Cookes, Grant

was elected and in his inaugural address took a strong position on
the question. The issue was settled when on March 18, 1869, a
measure was adopted by Congress pledging the payment of the
obligations of the United States in gold unless otherwise stipulated in the law providing for the issue of a specific obligation.[45]
Cooke considered this action a very great victory for himself and
he later took satisfaction in the fact that every promise he had
made to the bond buyer was fulfilled.[46]

Of all the issues before Congress in those years, none was directly of such great importance to the Cookes as that of managing
the debt. They expected to do much of the refunding for the
Treasury; and they had good reasons for that expectation; in
addition to the fact that they felt that their work during the war
had made them better qualified than any other house for assisting
the Treasury in its operations, there was more or less of an understanding with McCulloch.[47] It was, indeed, in anticipation of this
work that the Cookes extended their organization in 1866.

To take care of the obligations due and to refund the longer-
term loans promised to be a stupendous job. On October 31,
1865, the debt of the United States totaled $2,808,549,437.55.
Somewhat less than half consisted of interest-bearing obligations
maturing not later than October, 1868; $454,218,038.20 were in
greenbacks and fractional currency; and the remainder, or more
than a billion, was due at various times between 1871 and 1904.[48]
To meet the obligations soon maturing was a problem of first
magnitude, but it was also very important to reduce the interest
on the long-time obligations.

The Civil War loans had been scattered widely among all
classes in the United States, but a considerable amount had
trickled across to Europe, mostly to Germany.[49] Late in the war
the Seligmans had been busily buying government securities in
New York to sell in London and Frankfort, and the Rothschilds
had also been buying, presumably through August Belmont.
Frankfort had become the head market on the Continent for the
securities of the United States.[50] The *Commercial and Financial
Chronicle* estimated that the amount of federal securities in
Europe in the spring of 1866 was not less than $200,000,000.[51]

Jay Cooke anticipated that a large portion of the funds for paying the obligations soon due and for refunding would come from Europe. Indeed, as early as the fall of 1865 he and McCulloch had considered plans for refunding the bonds which had crossed the ocean, and it was with a view to this business that Jay Cooke had made preparations for opening a London house. Cooke was right in thinking that Europe promised to be a good field for funding operations. Toward the close of the Civil War, England's attitude toward American government securities had changed. The interest of the Jewish bankers of Hamburg, Cologne, and Frankfort was, like that of London, considerably brightened by the conservative position taken by McCulloch in his report of 1866 and by the manner in which the Treasury proceeded to handle the debt after the war closed.[52] Moreover, certain developments in European finance encouraged the growing interest of European capital in American investments in 1866 and thereafter. There was somewhat of a depression in the stock markets, especially in England, which had just gone through an orgy of speculation in railroad securities and was reaping the reward. The failure of the great house of Overend, Gurney & Co. in 1866 was a dramatic event in a severe panic which broke the finance companies and the mania for railroad investments.[53] The British and Continental investor thereupon turned to government bonds as a safer investment.

The first funding measure was introduced in Congress in January, 1866. It proposed to give the secretary almost unlimited discretion in funding the loan, even to the point of exchanging new bonds for greenbacks and setting the rate at which the bonds should be sold.

The Cookes aided in securing the passage of this bill though they were not wholly in sympathy with it. They objected to its contraction feature, but their objection was overcome by the fact that the bill actually made possible an immense amount of refunding. Again the Cookes went the rounds of important editors and newspapers. "If big papers favor it, it will pass," was their creed.[54] The Cookes brought the usual pressure to bear on members of Congress, especially upon Sherman, who objected both to the contraction feature and to the immense power given to the secretary.[55] The Cookes could not, however, touch some things which stood in the way of the measure. The disagreement between Congress and the President was a serious obstacle to most legislation.[56] McCulloch was also differing with the radical reconstructionists, and they were striking back at him.[57] The Cookes astutely refrained from giving the appearance of sharing in the controversy: "We, of course, attend to our business quietly — and don't mean to be drawn into any quarrel, if we can help it." [58]

In the opposition to the bill they saw the hand of New York. Henry Clews was against it. "Jno A Stewart read me quite a lecture also on it," wrote Jay Cooke. "I suppose he & Cisco & Vermilye & all those who are not particularly consulted have talked it up & with others are the source of opposition in the house." Henry Cooke was convinced that the gold ring and stock speculators in New York were doing their best to defeat the measure.[59]

When the contraction feature of the bill was amended so as to limit the rate of withdrawal of greenbacks, the measure became law in April.[60] Though it gave almost unlimited discretion to Secretary McCulloch, it did not satisfy Jay Cooke. The Secretary, cautious financier that he was, believed in tackling the problem piecemeal; his idea was to sell new securities at an interest rate that would insure success and with a view toward meeting immediate needs. Jay Cooke, on the other hand, favored a daring plan for a refunding loan to be sold at a low rate of interest and with all the vigor of the great five-twenty and seven-thirty loans.

In a memorandum to McCulloch,[61] the banker proposed a long-term loan bearing 5 per cent interest, both the principal and interest payable in coin. The proceeds from this loan should be used in funding not only that part of the indebtedness which had to be taken up immediately but also a considerable portion of the outstanding seven-thirties due in 1867 and even the old five-twenties. Such a loan, held Cooke, could be sold if it were exempt from all taxes, if the savings in interest were made into a sinking fund for the extinction of the debt, and if one per cent were allowed for a vigorous "popularizing" of the new issue.

A 5 per cent loan, in the Philadelphian's opinion, would not only decrease the interest burden on the government; the lowering of the interest rate on government securities would also aid business. He urged that a high rate on governments had a bad effect on the money markets and the business of the country; it compelled producing and commercial interests in the United States to pay high interest, which increased the difficulty of competing with the products of other countries where capital was cheaper.

As soon as the first refunding measure was passed, the Cookes began to work for a consolidated 5 per cent loan. On April 23, 1866, Jay Cooke wrote to his Washington brother: [62]

I am very glad to hear that there is still some prospect of McCulloch taking hold of the 5 per cent loan. With Sherman's assistance in the Senate & such assistance as we can give in the House, in the form in which it is now suggested there can be no possible difficulty in putting it through. Tell McCulloch that I can if necessary get the signatures of all the leading parties in N York to the absolute feasibility, propriety & necessity of such a plan to reduce the rate of interest. I cannot think of anything that would be hailed with greater applause by all the commercial interests of the country than such a reduction.

The Cookes were influential in getting John Sherman to sponsor a new funding bill which followed Jay Cooke's recommendations.[63] It proposed a consolidated loan to bear not over 5 per cent interest, to run for thirty years and to be tax free; the interest thus saved should be put into a sinking fund for the redemption of the loan; and a maximum of 2 per cent was to be allowed for negotiating the loan.[64] Provision should be made for the sale of the new loan in Europe as well as at home.

Never had the Cookes worked harder for a measure nor spent more freely. "We must take the risk of all the expense," wrote Jay to Henry Cooke, "but the work must be done in order that the backbone of Congress may be stiffened, . . . *In this matter we must not fail.* I would consider it equal to a defeat for Vestryman or Squire if we were licked in this matter. It won't do. Sherman has done nobly & I hope he will talk more enthusiastically in the matter & take it for granted that there will be no opposition. Thats the way we generally manage things." [65] Fessenden and Sherman in the Senate, Hooper and Morrill in the House, as well as President Johnson and Secretary McCulloch opposed the tax exemption clause. Some opposed the provision for sale in Europe; others, the amount allowed for selling the loan.[66] "Nearly all the old fossils there," wrote Henry Cooke, referring none too reverently to certain New York bankers, "are remonstrating violently against it. . . . They are writing to Fessenden and other members of the Committee of the Senate & House — Hooper is receiving piles of letters against me." [67] The New Yorkers had three objections to the bill: (1) such a loan could not be negotiated, (2) the clause exempting the new issue from taxation would be unpopular with the opposition, and (3) the allowance of 2 per cent for distributing the issue was too high.[68]

This instance gives a striking illustration of the way in which the Cooke press machine worked. No stone was left unturned to prepare the way for the bill. Jay Cooke, himself, saw important editors in Washington, Philadelphia, and New York, and he supervised the drawing up of articles on the loan.[69] Henry managed the Washington editors — "Shall have to carry some lots of 10/40s for a few parties who want to operate in anticipation of an advance, in case of the passage of the new law. This personal interest stimulates their zeal, and makes them cheerful workers." [70] Fahnestock looked after the New York press. The thoroughness of his method is revealed in a letter to the head partner: [71]

I have been drilling several of the press gang the past week or more. Norvell [*Times*] you know goes his whole length. Young in the Tribune came out strongly this A.M. (a little unpractised in financial writing) and Clark only objects to the 4th sec. Hennessey [*Times*] you know all about.

Stone of Jour[*nal of Commerce*] came in cranky and unapproachable. Pitt saw him and will report to you at length.

Jackson of Express was sour but Pitt brought him to me and *had it out* and closed with a thirty day option upon 100 m [thousand] 5/20 6–S @ 102!!

Melliss [*World*] is to come in this P.M. Cornwallis talks all right.

Will in this way go all through the list and see that they all come into line, doing meanwhile whatever's needful

Shattuck [of Peaslee & Co., advertising agency] is writing up a circular letter to his newspapers all over the country which I will revise before it goes out. Will manage it so that they will take up the subject & *ride it* hard. Write your ideas daily and will talk it into them and do all we can for the good cause.

The results were all that could be wished. Most of the New York and Philadelphia dailies came out strongly for the loan.[72] New York's leading financial journal, the *Commercial and Financial Chronicle* supported it.[73] The publicity continued for some time. Circulars were sent to hundreds of editors throughout the country by Peaslee & Co.,[74] and a hundred thousand copies of Senator Sherman's speech in favor of the bill were scattered over the country.[75]

But the cause was a losing one. "I soon found," commented Sherman later on his own efforts in support of the measure, "that it was idle to press the funding bill upon Congress, when it was so much occupied with reconstruction and with Andrew Johnson."[76] The Cookes were disgusted with Congress. "I shall be heartily glad when Congress adjourns," confided Henry to Jay. "It has 'worn out its welcome.'"[77] Jay Cooke did not seem to realize, however, that he was partly to blame for urging the adoption of so extreme a measure.

When Congress assembled in the fall of 1866, there was some prospect that things would go more smoothly. It soon became evident, however, that the radicals were out for revenge against southern opposition to their Reconstruction measures.[78] Nevertheless, another funding measure was proposed to Congress.

While the Cookes were working on this bill, which again looked forward to a European loan, a banking group was getting together with a view to aiding in the sale of the new securities. Jay

Cooke was approached by a number of New York bankers and brokers who wished to participate in placing such a loan. They agreed to spend $10,000 in helping to secure the passage of the bill, with the understanding that, if Jay Cooke were appointed agent to handle the loan, he would assign to them the European negotiation, Cooke receiving one-fifth of the profits of the venture.[79] The members of the New York group were J. Pierpont Morgan, who represented J. S. Morgan & Co., of London; H. R. Baltzer, who represented Bischoffsheim & Goldschmidt, a Jewish London house with roots in Germany; Arthur Kimber, New York representative of another German firm in London; and Ernest H. Biedermann and Louis Marx, New York brokers with German connections. These men, in Fahnestock's judgment, were doing the largest American business in Europe; it may be that the Cookes agreed to divide with them in order to forestall direct negotiation with the Treasury.[80]

But nothing came of the matter,[81] presumably because the loan did not materialize. A month later a group, apparently made up of the same men, proposed a joint-account venture for disposing of half a billion of bonds in Europe. At this time the Cookes did not encourage this overture since they feared it would bring entangling alliances, and they wanted to be free some day to establish their own foreign house.[82] This they actually considered doing late in 1868, when Fahnestock and Henry Cooke went to Europe to look over the prospects and Clarence H. Clark was urged to become the resident partner in London. On this trip Fahnestock visited London, Paris, Frankfort, Berlin, and Amsterdam to see the leading American bond houses "with a view both to general business and the funding of the 6% bonds." [83]

The establishment of a foreign house did not then materialize because the refunding legislation on which it depended was not passed. The mills of Congress ground financial grist slowly in those days, and the years 1867, 1868, and 1869 came and passed without the adoption of further funding measures.

Jay Cooke and his partners were far from successful in influencing post-war financial politics. They were greatly disappointed over the failure to provide for the refunding of the whole debt. Their political influence in the years 1865 to 1869 undoubtedly helped to break down certain dangerous financial prejudices and to support such measures as strengthened the credit of the Union, but this was done at a high cost in energy, money, and prestige. The writing on the wall should have been plain: their position with Congress was not strong. That they did not see the warning was unfortunate for Jay Cooke and his banking houses.

XII

DEALING IN GOVERNMENT SECURITIES
1865–1869

JAY COOKE's firms were the largest dealers in government securities in the United States from the war years through 1869. Though that was their chief interest,[1] their work was of a radically different nature from what it had been during the war. The center of their operations shifted to New York, and their business became more closely integrated with general banking than it had been before. But, unfortunately for Jay Cooke's firms, it was both a highly competitive and a temporary kind of business.

COMPETITION INCREASES IN INVESTMENT BANKING

David A. Wells, a keen observer of business, in 1869 pointed to an extremely important development which had then recently occurred in the United States. Large numbers of the people, said Wells, under the influence and example of high profits realized in trading during the period of monetary expansion, had abandoned the pursuits directly productive of wealth and sought employment in commerce, trading, and speculation. "As a consequence we everywhere find large additions to the population of our commercial cities, [and] an increase in the number and cost of buildings devoted to banking, brokerage, insurance, commission business, and agencies of all kinds." [2]

It is impossible to understand the work of Jay Cooke and his firms in the late 'sixties and early 'seventies without continually keeping in mind that investment banking had developed greatly during the war. It had emerged from the war as a more or less specialized institution with a technique of its own. Moreover, under the stimulus of an increasing trade and of the needs of war finance, particularly, many new banking houses had been estab-

WALL STREET ABOUT 1870

Jay Cooke & Co. occupied the building marked EXPRESS on the
corner of Wall and Nassau Streets

lished which were largely interested in the investment business. The system had become both specialized and somewhat over-extended.

A few of the outstanding houses illustrate the development. The Drexels came out of the war much stronger than they had gone in. Under the stimulus of the government loan business, three of Jay Cooke's own five-twenty agents in New York had grown so strong as to become his rivals there; they were Fisk & Hatch, Henry Clews & Co., and Vermilye & Co. In 1863 Levi P. Morton entered banking in New York. Morton was closely connected with Junius S. Morgan of London; the two men had been partners in a Boston mercantile firm, and a son-in-law of Morgan became Morton's partner in his New York banking house and later in its London branch.[3] Another concern which appeared under the stimulus of war business was J. Pierpont Morgan & Co., established in New York by the young son of the above-named Junius S. Morgan, of London.[4]

At the same time another group was entrenching itself strongly in New York banking. They were the "Dutchmen," who had connections with strong Jewish bankers, principally in Frankfort. They were not all recent arrivals, for Belmont (who like the Rothschilds, whom he represented, originally came from Frank-fort) and Speyer had come to the United States back in the 'thirties.[5] Both public and private finance during the war and post-war conditions gave a strong impetus to the migration to this country of German-Jewish capital. Among the individuals aiding the transfer of that capital the Seligmans and Jacob Schiff came to be very important.

J. & W. Seligman & Co., as we have noted before, was estab-lished in New York during the war. This firm had grown out of a mercantile business, at first scattered in various places in the United States and in 1857 joining to form a firm in New York for importing clothing. Early in the war the Seligmans did an ex-tensive business supplying the army with clothing. In 1862 the clothing firm became a banking house, and in the same year a branch was opened in Frankfort and two years later in London. Through the Frankfort house, particularly, the Seligmans sold a considerable amount of United States government securities during the war; they were probably the leading American house in the sale of United States securities in Europe in their first years. By the end of the war, they had laid a good foundation for an extensive American-European business.[6]

Jacob Schiff came to America in 1865, and in 1866 he became a partner in a new firm of brokers, Budge, Schiff & Co. This firm also had strong German connections and established another bond between German capital and American investment opportunity. This concern was destined to last only a few years, and Schiff was in the 1870's to join the young firm, Kuhn, Loeb & Co.[7]

The development of investment banking houses would not have been so important to Jay Cooke if there had been a commensurate increase in business, but the close of the war put a check to much of the business out of which those houses had sprung. Until new work could be found to take the place of the old, it was clear that there would be strong competition in investment banking; it was not to be expected that those bankers would let lucrative business fall to Jay Cooke without a protest. The Drexels and Jay Cooke's powerful five-twenty agents were equipped to do the type of work which Jay Cooke expected to specialize in, while the houses with European connections had an advantage in the transatlantic business in United States securities.

THE COOKES' WORK FOR THE TREASURY

It was a severe blow to Jay Cooke's banking houses that a consolidated refunding bill was not passed. Under the loan act of April 12, 1866, the determination of the loan policy of the government was left wholly with McCulloch. His policy was not to recommend any drastic refunding with a view to lowering the interest rate; it was rather to meet only immediate obligations through the use of the funds which he was able to accumulate in the Treasury and through the sale of new securities.

The extent of the loan transactions of the Treasury in the early post-war years is shown by the following table: [8]

PUBLIC LOAN TRANSACTIONS OF THE UNITED STATES TREASURY
1865–1869

	Purchase	Sale
October 1, 1865–June 30, 1866	$620,321,725.61	$712,851,553.05
July 1, 1866–June 30, 1867	746,350,525.94	640,426,910.29
July 1, 1867–June 30, 1868	692,549,685.88	625,111,433.20
July 1, 1868–June 30, 1869	253,222,718.31	238,678,081.06
	$2,312,444,655.74	$2,217,067,977.60

The correspondence of the Cooke partners indicates that they took a considerable part in these transactions. They helped sell new five-twenties and were especially active in the conversion of the seven-thirties, purchasing on the market and selling to the Treasury.[9] They were also given specific assignments from time to time which they performed on commission,[10] making their sales and purchases for the government over the counter, with out-of-town banks, and through brokers. The purchase of obligations not yet mature was done secretly for the obvious reason that the government probably would otherwise have had to pay a higher price for them.[11]

The Cookes from time to time also helped uphold the market for government securities. The technique for supporting the bonds in the market was relatively simple. When United States loans sagged to a point which would interfere with further sales or injure the credit of the government, the Treasury secretly stepped in and purchased its own securities, frequently through Jay Cooke. To do this properly the Cookes insisted that they should have exclusive oversight of government operations so that transactions by others would not neutralize their efforts.[12] When conversions were to be made, it was necessary to maintain the prices so that securities would be offered for conversion and it was important not to sell new securities or purchase old ones too fast.[13] The transactions were greatly complicated by the fact that the money market was extremely unstable during those years. The currency was subject to severe fluctuations owing in a measure to the manipulations of speculators who attempted to corner currency. Fluctuations in gold also had a disturbing effect, though with one or two exceptions the movements were less severe than during the war period.[14]

Jay Cooke had a very practical view of the function of the government with respect to the currency and gold markets. When a stringent market interfered with the selling of government securities and upset business in general, he attributed the stringency to an inelastic currency unable to adjust itself to seasonal changes in business and to the manipulations of speculators. His remedy lay in the Treasury. Jay Cooke was no adherent of laissez-faire principles; he was a realist and, undeterred by theoretical considerations, would use whatever reasonable means were available to accomplish an end. He conceived of the money in the Treasury as a sort of reserve to be used for stabilizing the money market and thus protecting government credit as well as business in general. It is the legitimate province of the government, he wrote McCulloch on the occasion of a tight market in 1868, to protect commerce when there is a panic, especially when the panic is brought about by improper actions.[15] In this instance he recommended that the Secretary should not draw on government deposits in banks and should purchase bonds in exchange for greenbacks so as to increase the currency in circulation and relieve the money market. He was not convinced by his New York brother's comment that the trouble was due to overtrading and that relieving the market then would simply aid the speculators in stocks and produce.[16] After the gold panic of 1869, he commented on the function of the government in a way which illustrates his ideas: [17] "All that can be done [by the Treasury] should be daily & hourly & *watchfully* done to relieve the market from Panic & to restore confidence & then to *Keep* things in place by the strong hand of Government." He went so far on this occasion as to suggest that the Treasury should stabilize gold at a definite point from time to time, say between 133 1/3 and 145 in terms of currency.[18]

While McCulloch and Boutwell did not go so far as Jay Cooke had urged them to, they were quite aggressive in their relations with the bond, currency, and gold markets. Outstanding examples of Treasury action were the sale of gold at the time of the

Overend, Gurney & Co. panic in England in 1866,[19] the threat of the Secretary to sell greenbacks to break the tight money market occasioned by the locking up of currency by speculators in the fall of 1868,[20] and interference at the time of the gold panic in 1869. But there were many other instances when the Treasury interfered, usually with the object of protecting government securities. These transactions were made largely through Myers, a gold broker, and the Cookes. Nine-tenths of such sales, said Jay Cooke in 1869, were made through his firm; [21] the desirability of secrecy moved the Treasury to give this business largely to one agent.[22]

Much opposition arose to the Secretary's activities in the bond and money markets. Indeed, he was blamed for everything untoward that happened. "When gold and government bonds go up," said the *Inquirer* on September 23, 1867, "and money goes begging on the street, the fault is Mr. McCulloch's; when gold falls and the rates for money advance, the Secretary of the Treasury is to blame. If speculative stocks are high it is Mr. McCulloch who is fostering a reckless spirit of speculation; if they are dull and on a decline, it is Mr. McCulloch who is crippling business and destroying confidence."

Criticism of the Treasury's policy led to attempts on the part of Congress to curb the powers of the secretary, especially to forbid secret sales of gold and to limit the employment of a special agent. In the winter of 1867 a committee investigated the sale of bonds and gold by the Treasury but found nothing specifically wrong in the transactions.[23] It was widely held, however, that such sales should be announced publicly in advance.[24] In 1868 came Logan's attack in the House, calling on the Secretary for information on favoritism in the sale of government bonds and gold.[25] Such an investigation, said the *New York Herald* on March 19, 1868, will reveal "how Jay Cooke and others have become enormously rich by doing that which the department itself should have done." In the winter of 1869 occurred a significant episode centering around Senator Conkling's bill prohibiting secret sales of gold.

Jay Cooke interpreted this bill as a direct attack on himself and his banking houses. The Philadelphia *Ledger* had pointed out that many who had advance information about sales were able to take advantage of the market beforehand in addition to making millions in commission.[26] In his characteristic way Cooke brought the matter to Anthony Drexel. He sent the *Ledger* article to "Toney," stating that it was "but one of a series of wicked and malicious misrepresentations of facts & I cannot think it is true as some think that they are instigated by my old friends." [27] Drexel denied that he had had anything to do with the article, as did also the editor of the *Ledger*.[28] This incident is worthy of note, not because the Drexels were alone in opposing Jay Cooke but because it is a clear expression of the banker's feeling that they were beginning to stand in his way.

The Cookes fought the bill in Congress. Wrote Jay Cooke to Henry: "You know how to pull & who to pull — it ought to be made fully known to Fessenden who knows the foolishness & falsity of this whole scheme & to Sherman Cattell &c. Kill it — & all similar schemes." [29] Henry Cooke fought hard to line up the strategic men against the bill. Having heard in the course of his lobbying that Drexel was also seeing congressmen, he made a revealing comment: "I have not much fear of these fellows — They make a noise, but don't know where to take hold — nor what ropes to pull — like landsmen in a gale of wind at sea. If it were not for their salt-water allies — Hooper, Conkling &c, I could snap my fingers at the whole crew." [30]

The bill did not pass. But Secretary Boutwell, who in March, 1869, succeeded McCulloch, followed a policy which accomplished much of what Congress had been unable to bring to pass; no doubt in part as a concession to public opinion, Boutwell discontinued secret sales of gold.[31] The effect on the business of Jay Cooke & Co. we shall see later.

While the position of Jay Cooke was being weakened by such attacks, other large government houses — particularly Fisk & Hatch, Henry Clews & Co., Vermilye & Co., and the "Dutchmen" — were using their influence to secure as much of the government's work as possible.[32] McCulloch had continued to rely heavily on the Cookes in spite of criticism, but by the fall of 1868 the short-term obligations had been converted into long-time bonds.[33] Only the greenbacks and the long-time debt remained.

Some financing had to be done to carry government expenses and pay interest on the bonds at a time when the income of the government was actually decreasing,[34] but this was small as compared with earlier operations.

When nearing the end of the funding of short-term obligations, the Cookes had reason to believe that the Treasury might proceed to refund the old 6 per cent five-twenties. In his report for 1868 Secretary McCulloch, with a view to converting the five-twenties, proposed the issue of half a billion of 5 per cent bonds, principal and interest payable in coin, to run for thirty years.[35]

As early as the preceding June, Henry Cooke had written to his Philadelphia brother that the Secretary had in mind such a conversion and would give the work exclusively to the Cookes.[36] Fahnestock and Henry Cooke, thereupon, went to Europe, among other things to look over the prospects for conversions;[37] by about this time, according to the *Commercial and Financial Chronicle*, approximately $700,000,000 of our bonds were held in Europe.[38] Unfortunately for the Cookes, nothing came of the proposed operation.

The year 1869 was singularly barren as far as business for the Treasury was concerned. There were no important new loans to be floated, and old ones could be bought only as the Treasury's resources permitted. The change in the administration in March put the Cookes more than ever on a purely competitive basis; they knew that their position with the Treasury was not so strong as it had been.[39] It was true, as one partner regretfully stated, that the Cookes were "at length free from Entangling alliances with Govt patronage."[40] Except for one dramatic episode of which we shall hear later, the days of their importance in the affairs of the Treasury were over.

THE LOAN BUSINESS OF JAY COOKE'S FIRMS EXPANDS

The work of the Cookes as agent for the United States Treasury constituted only a part of their transactions during the years from 1865 to 1869. In 1867, they co-operated with the Drexels and the Clarks of Philadelphia in selling a loan of $23,000,000 for the State of Pennsylvania.[41] They also engaged in floating some small railroad bond issues. The major part of their income, however, seems to have been derived from their commercial banking and from the purchase and sale of government securities on their own account. It is impossible to give the whole story of their banking activities as no detailed accounts are available. From the correspondence of the partners, however, a fair picture of their banking can be reconstructed. The central interest in that picture is the deposit and loan business of the Cookes.

It was desirable for the Cookes to have a considerable cash capital but they never had sufficient cash to meet their needs. "It takes 2 or 3 millions to trade with here & that is hardly enough to keep a good Stock in trade," according to one of the New York Cooke partners in 1866.[42] This amount the Cookes were far from having; as stated earlier, the total wealth of the partners was probably not far above $2,000,000 at the end of the war, and of that the larger portion was in fixed investments and homes. In 1868, Fahnestock urged that a house of their standing ought to have a large cash capital. Even Vermilye, he said, had a cash capital of $1,000,000.[43]

This lack of capital existed in spite of the fact that some of the large profits of the firm had been plowed back into the business. Dodge and Fahnestock of New York and Jay Cooke and Moorhead of Philadelphia kept their otherwise unemployed funds on deposit in the various houses on interest and left their bonds with the firms to be used as collateral.[44]

More important than the Cookes' resources were the funds of the government on deposit in their banks. These consisted of the funds collected in the course of their transactions for the Treasury and of actual government deposits in their First National Bank of Washington. The proceeds from government transactions were frequently and regularly turned over to the Treasury, but even so it took some time to make the transfers. These deposits were valued highly by the Cookes and were largely the reason why they worked so hard to secure government business.[45] The First National Bank of Washington was important to the Cookes because it was a government depository.[46] Huntington, the cashier, stood well with the Treasury. The *Reports of the Comptroller of Currency* give the deposits of the Treasury in this bank as $4,611,900.49 for a specific date in 1865, $783,390.13 in 1866, $884,597.12 in 1867, $301,779.44 in 1868, and $95,535.95 in 1869.[47] From 1866 to 1868 the bank also held considerable deposits for disbursing officers of the United States.[48] The actual deposits were no doubt at times higher than the above figures indicate, for until 1869 the date of the report to the comptroller was known in advance, and the Cookes prepared their balances with a view to making a favorable report.[49] Since no interest was paid to the government on these deposits, they meant a clear gain.

Government deposits in the First National Bank became smaller in 1868 and were so small in 1869 as to be of little use to the Cookes. From 1866 through 1868 bills were introduced in Congress for placing restrictions on such deposits.[50] The failure in 1866 of the Metropolitan National Bank in Washington, which carried heavy government deposits, elicited much criticism of the depository system and gave the critics of Jay Cooke an opportunity to point out that the First National of Washington enjoyed similar favors at a like risk to the government.[51] In 1868 an antidepository measure was the occasion of another struggle in Congress. The measure was introduced by Samuel Randall, a Pennsylvania congressman, and was supported by the Philadelphia *Ledger*. The latter claimed that the First National of Washington had held government deposits ranging from $913,911 "to the handsome amount of $6,155,801." [52] There was much truth in the *Ledger's* statement that the antidepository bill failed because of the influence of the man managing the First National of Washington.[53]

The fundamental reason for the decline in deposits, however, was the actual decrease in the government's loan business. The Cookes foresaw that the lessening of their work for the Treasury, together with the pressure of public opinion, would weaken their deposit business. "The beginning of the end of the depository system has come," said Fahnestock in 1868. "Hunt[ingto]n deps are down to 900th. . . . I dont believe they can *ever* increase, and on the contrary we must look for the entire discontinuance & withdrawal of them before long. . . . if the depository business be closed *entirely*, we should have to carry among us 900[th], which is easy enough now that money is a drug, but wont be after awhile." [54]

Most of the resources of the First National of Washington were invested in government loans and in advances to the other Cooke banks, particularly to the Washington house.[55] The national bank also carried on a relatively large accommodation loan business,[56] more than the Cookes approved of, and some regular commercial banking.[57] Sometimes its loans and investments were so heavy that it had to draw on the other Cooke houses.[58] But on the whole it was a valuable source of funds for the Cooke banking business.[59]

The most stable deposits in the Cooke banks were private deposits. Though the Cookes did not go heavily into commercial banking, they nevertheless held considerable deposits for individuals and banks, especially for national banks. Such deposits in the Washington house of Jay Cooke & Co. were not large— there were few people in Washington who had money. The deposits held by the Philadelphia house were large but mainly local; this house frequently held considerable balances for other local banks, especially the First National (of which Jay Cooke was a director) and the Central National, and for the New York banks with whom it had business.[60] The New York house, because of its location in the commercial center of the whole country, had deposits of many banks of the great northern inland.[61] In fact, it became a matter of distinction for inland banks to have funds with Jay Cooke & Co. Like many other earlier banks, it paid interest on demand deposits, which fact encouraged the hinterland banks to send their reserve funds eastward, thus securing both income and liquidity.

Though the Cookes were not primarily lenders of money or credit, their loan business was an important part of their work. Since they paid interest on demand deposits, they had to employ those funds at a profit at all times. The three Cooke firms handled this matter differently, owing to the men who headed the banks and to the differences in the business environment of the houses. On the whole, however, they did very little in the way of lending on commercial paper.

Jay Cooke & Co. of Washington and the First National Bank of that city, as already noted, had considerable out on accommodation loans,[62] granting many loans in order to secure the good will of politicians.[63] For this they were severely criticized by the Philadelphians and New Yorkers, who felt that they should have the use of the surplus funds of their Washington houses.

The Philadelphia house generally had large balances with other banks.[64] It carefully avoided accommodation loans and it apparently was not interested in the discounting of commercial paper. But it lent considerable amounts to reliable corporations, especially to good railroads such as the Pennsylvania.[65] Its policy was to loan mostly on call with governments as security.[66] Jay Cooke was on the whole thoroughly conservative and continually had in view the necessity of keeping their assets "snug." He frequently admonished both Washington and New York to keep safe; and, when a tight money market was threatened, he ordered them to call in all their loans.[67]

The New York house did by far the largest lending on call. Sometimes it had several million out on such loans.[68] Of all the Cooke firms, it had the most rigid loan policy. The New Yorkers looked on time loans as poison; almost all their loans were on call.[69] The reason is obvious: "Mr Dodge likes to have money on Call because when F[ahnestock] wants to buy [securities], he can get it at once, & then when F Sells he has a place to put his money — These loans on Call are therefore very handy where we are buying one day largely & selling next as largely." [70] Jay Cooke and Fahnestock urged accepting only government securities on loans (or, if an exception were made, strong railroad bonds), as they were "Cash in an instant in any market . . . [and] there are no 'friends' here in a tight money market." [71] Fahnestock, especially, stood for a high degree of liquidity and security. Dodge, who as head of the banking department had charge of the loans, was not so strict. He was sanguine by nature and he was after profits.[72] He was, therefore, likely to take stocks as security, which was a continual source of irritation to his partners.[73] They objected to taking "bubbles inflated by reckless adventurers, on the Street," when they "can as well have Governments for all the money we don't use." [74] Eventually, Dodge's propensities were curbed and stock loans were terminated.[75]

An important part of the loan business of the Cooke houses was their advances to each other. All the Cooke banks loaned to each other, sometimes even lending securities to be used as collateral; [76] and they deposited collateral when it was understood that the loan should run any length of time. Interest was charged as from other banks, not always without disagreement over the rate.[77] Oftentimes they drew heavily on each other without warning, making the house drawn upon scurry to meet the draft.[78] Usually, the Cooke houses seem to have been more lenient toward each other, so that there was a considerable advantage in being one of the group.[79]

The system whereby one house could draw on another was not altogether satisfactory, however, for the weaker house was likely to lean on the stronger. Jay Cooke & Co. of Washington was almost a constant problem for the other two houses, especially after its government business reached such a low point in 1868.[80] Though the government deposits of Jay Cooke & Co. and the First National of Washington became small and their individual deposits negligible, Henry Cooke wanted to do a big business. This was a chronic problem in early group banking systems. Jay Cooke had met it when with the Clarks, and he could not have been altogether unaware that the branches of the second Bank of the United States had drained away the capital of the mother bank. He recognized the problem but he was unable to solve it.

In those early post-war years the Philadelphia and New York houses were in closest co-operation in the use of their funds. The rule was for the former to keep good balances with the latter, which was in reality the outlet for surplus funds.[81] This situation was due to the superior loan market in New York and was evidence of the growing dependence of Philadelphia on New York in financial matters.

The Cookes were also frequent borrowers from others. Aside

from their own houses they had no one on whom they had any particular claim in borrowing; that is, they had no financial allies. Indeed, the interlocking of interests of financial concerns, which later came to be so important an element in the money and investment market in New York, had apparently not yet developed very far. The Cookes felt the need of such support; they reached out for it in their connection with the First National Bank of Philadelphia and in sponsoring the organization of the National Life Insurance Company of the United States of America.[82] But those institutions did not help them materially. For loans they, therefore, had to depend mainly on borrowing from other banks, mostly on call. Philadelphia borrowed considerably,[83] but the New York house was the heaviest borrower. The New Yorkers' loans were mostly secured by government paper,[84] to some extent by their customers' collateral; [85] they secured some loans on stock security, apparently from banks whose officers were their special friends.[86]

The banking departments of the leading Cooke houses worked hand in glove with the investment interests of the Cooke banks. Sometimes they dealt almost exclusively in short-time credit, loaning out their resources and even at times borrowing to lend again at a higher rate. In this way they employed their means when the returns from such lending were more certain or profitable than from investments. But their chief interest was the investment business; when it was good, they put most of their energies into it.

TRADING IN GOVERNMENTS

Besides their transactions with the Treasury, the Cooke houses did a varied business in investment securities in those years. None of them speculated in stocks, as a rule, though they made some purchases to hold; Mariposa and Atlantic Mail, purchased by Dodge, were long to remind them of how evanescent stock values could be. The New York and Philadelphia houses, like other banks of this type, did a small stock commission business, chiefly for inland banks, charging $12\frac{1}{2}$ cents a share.[87] Jay Cooke was opposed to stock speculation on margin and did not encourage such dealing on account with them; in this he was following the usual practice of private bankers such as the Clarks and Fisk & Hatch.[88] Dodge of the New York house, however, favored stock dealing and made advances on customers' purchases.[89] Their commission trading in government securities for individuals and banks was considerable; they purchased a great deal for national banks for securing circulation, charging a commission of $2.50 a thousand.[90]

The most important work of Jay Cooke's banking houses in the early post-war years was their dealing on their own account in government bonds. The two Washington firms, Jay Cooke & Co. and the First National Bank, did not carry on much local trade; they generally kept a considerable proportion of their resources invested in government securities,[91] but their dealings were principally confined to the Treasury and to the other Cooke banks. The Philadelphia and New York houses dealt with the Treasury, with local brokers and bankers, with individuals over the counter, and with out-of-town bankers.[92] They were more in the nature of wholesale jobbers than commission dealers or retailers. The Philadelphians seem to have purchased principally in anticipation of immediate orders from the Treasury, banks, or individuals, or to sell to New York.[93] The purchases of the Philadelphia house were also much smaller than those of the New York house; their correspondence reveals no instance of their holding as much as a million.

There were good reasons why the Philadelphia house did not go so extensively into trading for a rise as New York. First of all, Jay Cooke was not a trader. Furthermore, Philadelphia could not so closely follow the market as New York. The ticker telegraph for reporting prices from New York did not come into wide use until the late 'sixties, so that the Cooke banks outside of New York had to get market reports by telegraph. As Fahnestock said to Jay Cooke in 1866,[94] "I cannot telegraph often enough to keep you out of scrapes such as are mentioned in yr letter of yestdy. The changes are so numerous, so sudden, so impossible to anticipate, that they can only be FELT when they come." Very

HARRIS C. FAHNESTOCK

important, also, was the fact that New York had a more highly developed call loan market than Philadelphia.

The New Yorkers were the traders in the group. They did not let the grass grow under their feet, as they accused the "rural" Philadelphians of doing. Fahnestock had charge of the "government" department, and he proved to be a masterly trader; he bought not only to meet immediate demands but also to profit from short-time fluctuations or to hold for a longer-time rise. Indeed, that became an important part of the work of his house.

It was a difficult time, however, in which to speculate. The money market was highly nervous.[95] It was working with an inelastic bank currency and depreciated greenbacks, nervously fluctuating in value in terms of gold, subject to manipulations by speculators and contraction or expansion by the government, and sensitive to endless rumors on the Street. What will gold do in view of Bismarck and Napoleon and shipments to Europe, asked Fahnestock. The answer, he said, could "be condensed into a prediction that gold will go down, unless . . . it goes *up!*"[96] Other things were also upsetting the bond market, such as the Overend, Gurney & Co. panic in England in 1866, wars and rumors of wars on the Continent, and corners in New York.[97] Matters were especially complicated by the prolonged failure of Congress to declare itself for a definite policy on resumption of specie payments and on government securities and by the failure to secure political order throughout the country. As Wall Street so often has been in our history, Jay Cooke and his partners were thoroughly exasperated with the government. "Those vagabond congressmen will keep the market uneasy all winter with their wild schemes and it wont do to have much stock on hand," said a Cooke partner in 1866.[98] Later they were especially concerned over impeachment: "The effect *abroad* is so pernicious that you cannot too strongly urge that the Judiciary Com speedily report adversely to impeachment. They have not a *ghost* of a case and to settle that is infinitely better for the finances than to have it worrying along and disturbing everybodys confidence."[99] At the time of adjournment in the spring of 1867, Jay Cooke expressed his feeling that it would be well if Congress would go fishing for six or eight months.[100]

It is clear, however, that for a time the Cookes had a great advantage in their close association with the Treasury. Moreover, their excellent lobbying machine in Washington kept them well posted on political matters. A typical letter of Jay Cooke to his Washington brother shows how broad was the information sought:[101]

Give us promptly and in advance all the information you can about the feeling of the President & Congress and, anything relating to the Secys movement. There seems to be an impression gaining ground here that the meeting of Congress and the measures that will be at once foreshadowed will create a disturbance in the money market and some expect a heavy advance in gold but I don't think that such results can be anticipated. Is there anything in the aspect of affairs to justify a large advance in gold and could not the Sec'y check it, as it is well known that he would like to realize upon some of his if it could be done without depressing the money market. Have a talk with him about these things and report to me what the prospect is.

One must not suppose, however, that the Cookes were the only bankers using such tactics. It was the common practice for the large investment bankers to court the government. Indeed, the New York Cookes were not altogether satisfied with the work of their Washington associates. The problem was to be more clever than the others. The only safe way was to know more than others knew, to keep well informed night and day — "Its the only way to work & be sure of success. Its old Rothschilds way."[102] But that became increasingly difficult, especially after the coming in of President Grant and Secretary Boutwell, who were not especially attached to the Cookes and who had many other acquaintances among bankers.

The correspondence of the partners gives some insight into the trading of the New York house in government securities. In the first year of peace, that is, through 1866, the New Yorkers carried on a large and lucrative trade in bonds. Much of their buying in 1866 and 1867 was in anticipation of Treasury needs; but they also sold a great deal to banks which sold American securities abroad. They were unusually "long" in the market; their correspondence does not reveal a single instance when they sold short in 1866, though they were often low on bonds. A letter of Fahnestock's illustrates their position in those years: [103]

As nearly as I can carry in memory (Statement not made up yet this Evg) we have [the following government securities on hand:]

62^s	– 450 to 500*th*	to which add 2 1/4 Millions Compounds
64	– 150*th*	bot up for a big trade with Treasy
65	– 200	which we had first put in working
10 40 –		shape and had been turning nicely
81 –		the past four days.
7–30–2300		

3150–

The extent of their trading is suggested by the following random selections from letters: turned $800,000 government today; bought $600,000 and sold $500,000 at advance of 1/4 to 3/4; bought $350,000 and sold $700,000 at advances of 1/8 to 1/4; business today of $2,000,000; hold $2,500,000 seven-thirties; $2,000,000 to $3,000,000 trade today. [104]

The year 1867 began with lowering prices and general uneasiness. [105] Throughout the year the market was more uncertain than in 1866. At times the New Yorkers were short on some bonds and long on others; their daily turnover was sometimes large, but frequently there was little trading. [106] Their biggest business in this year was probably that of meeting the demands of the Treasury.

The year 1868 was unsatisfactory. Both in the spring and the fall there were long periods when the Cookes' trading was at a minimum. The Treasury was buying less. Political conditions and a tight money market made Fahnestock curtail buying. [107] Unfortunately, he was in Europe during the difficult times in October and November. [108] At the end of the year the New Yorkers were in a pinch and were appealing to the Philadelphia and Washington houses for aid. [109]

The situation became even worse in 1869. It was made all the more difficult by a growing difference between Jay Cooke and

Fahnestock over the New Yorker's trading. Strange as it may well seem, in view of his later venture in Northern Pacific, Jay Cooke was not a speculator. His Philadelphia house loaned more money and borrowed less and depended more largely on the commission business than did Jay Cooke & Co. of New York. There were two good reasons for this. Besides being more of a broker and banker than a trader in investments, Jay Cooke took a bearish attitude towards business in 1867 to 1869 and he thought security prices were headed downward. He, therefore, believed in keeping their resources liquid and safe. Much of the time he favored a quick turnover of their government securities, and he almost always urged that only a small stock of bonds be held. Fahnestock, on the other hand, was fundamentally a trader, though he recognized the dangers in speculating.[110] Moreover, he had a more optimistic view of the current market than did Jay Cooke, and he sometimes chafed at Cooke's bearish recommendations and did not always heed them.[111]

The differences between the two leading partners reached a climax in 1869 owing to the uncertainty of the market throughout much of the year. Jay Cooke had been a bear on governments almost ever since the war, but in 1869 he became more strongly convinced than ever that those securities were heading for a drop and he urged Fahnestock to go short or curtail buying. On his urging,[112] Fahnestock went short a million in certain governments in January at a loss of $10,000, a loss which was more than covered by going long on other bonds. February told the same story, and also March. Fahnestock at this point protested against Jay Cooke's policy:[113]

Since the high pressure war times (our first season in N. Y.) I have not taken large risks, and in our present movement I have kept our stock [of governments] within 3 mill — but of course only for a short turn. As I remarked, there are times when I go short because it pays, but at this time the state of the market is such that precisely the reverse is the case, and bonds will all *certainly* be *higher*. Please remember that my government dept has made nearly all the money that has been made in N. Y. and the bulk of it by *having stock* [bonds] *on* a rising market. . . . And do you know that you have *never once* advised me to buy governments since I have been there, always contending that they were too high and must tumble and therefore recommending me to sell out.

Yet, the New York partner recognized that the business in governments was "simply speculative" and that they might, "like any of the gold room people, be right or wrong." [114]

Against Jay Cooke's wishes Fahnestock carried $1,000,000 to $2,500,000 in April at a gross profit of $64,000. In May they carried $3,000,000 at a paper profit of $75,000; in June they likewise carried bonds at an apparent loss of $37,000; while July brought a paper profit of $131,000. From that time on there was a steady shrinkage in values, but Fahnestock believed that influences at home and abroad would "overrule the possible vagaries of politicians which may after a while cause temporary trouble *but cannot prevail.*" [115]

Though Cooke protested strongly, Fahnestock persisted in going long on bonds for some time. They were, he said in the summer of 1869, the heaviest government dealers in New York. [116] "You are pleased," he wrote Jay Cooke, "when we control the market and are the leading house in all the government purchases, . . . and yet you want us to take no risks — that is to keep our bonds down to a sum which, while it would be ample in Phila or Boston, would oblige us to *relinquish* our leading position, take rank with the *smallest* dealers and would absolutely render it IMPOSSIBLE to make any considerable amt of money." [117] "We cant sell the Government millions *unless we have them,*" held Fahnestock. "We *cant make money* unless we are willing to run risks. The brokerage part of the business is a bagatelle — any thirty second man can do it." In the past year even expenses could not have been made out of the commission business. [118]

The autumn, however, found Fahnestock less sure of his position. He recognized at the end of the summer that the days of rapid trading in bonds were gone; and he believed the trade, thereafter, would be close and at a comparatively small profit on each transaction. [119] It was the gold panic of Black Friday, September 24, that finally broke his courage. The panic left the

Cooke partners a chastened lot, none more than Fahnestock. The gold mess had taught him a lesson, he wrote to Jay Cooke: "We have got to find a different way to make money from the way in which *all our New York* money has been made." [120]

Unfortunately, there are no records from which to get conclusive information about the relative income of the three houses from the various lines of business in those years. In the three and a half years of the New York house, said Fahnestock, $1,638,000 had been made in government securities (both commission and speculative dealing), while the other business totaled $493,000. Almost one-half of the last figure resulted from Treasury gold commissions; the stock profits were $240,000, against which $52,500 in losses had already been charged off, while $290,000 were tied up in two bad stocks, Mariposa and Atlantic Mail.[121] Only $71,389.58 had been made until November, in 1869.[122] It was clear that, at least for the time being, the business of trading in governments was almost dead.

XIII

JAY COOKE'S OTHER BUSINESS INTERESTS
1865–1869

HAD the Civil War not turned Jay Cooke to government finance, he would undoubtedly in the years 1865–69 have become an important figure in the financing of private business undertakings. Even with his extensive activity in public finance, however, he still gave some attention to other lines of business and maintained contact with them. This was very significant; it came to be the basis on which he built a whole new business when his work in government finance became too small to occupy his organization fully.

During the war and early post-war years the United States experienced a great economic development, an acceleration of the change that had for several decades been transforming American business. New coal mines were opened in the East, and the exploitation of silver and other treasures began to take on large proportions in the western mountains. Textile mills, shoe factories, packing plants, and iron establishments — spurred on by new processes, new tariffs, and the war demands — in their rapid growth marked the spread of greater industrial specialization. The westward movement of agriculture, which had been retarded by the panic of 1857, proceeded at an accelerating pace, scattering land-hungry people over the rich lands beyond the Mississippi.

Accompanying these developments, the extension of transportation facilities reached dramatic proportions after the war. Railroads were then no longer built as feeders of canals or as local enterprises. They were organized to connect important centers, built to join the Atlantic and the Pacific, and even regarded as links in a chain of carriers connecting that ancient, still dreaming Orient with the hustle and bustle of the New World.[1]

The rôle of the banker in all this was strategic; his work was to supply the capital for supporting the men and purchasing the materials needed for the building of a great economic structure. Jay Cooke was continually besieged by people with ideas, inventions, or projects, for the exploitation of which they wanted financial aid. Some of them he regarded as altogether too chimerical; others he peremptorily dismissed because they did not interest him or because he was too busy to consider them; but a few appeared to him as sufficiently promising to win his help.

Many Projects Seek Jay Cooke's Aid

Jay Cooke refused to consider projects which were altogether new to him or fields which had not already become recognized as profitable. For instance, the inventor of a match and match box (the matches held between leaves of sandpaper were ignited on withdrawal [2]), who wanted a capitalist to unite with him in manufacture, sought his aid in vain.[3] The inventor of a "steam wagon," which could pull a 20-ton load in cars over the prairie roads of Minnesota, wanted Jay Cooke to finance the cost of improving the gears, which were so imperfect that they became overheated after going only two and a half miles.[4] An early prophet of air-conditioning, working on the theory that knowledge is more effective than prayer in warding off disease, wrote Jay Cooke that he had a scheme for drawing off vitiated air whereby he could supply Jay Cooke's new house and, he believed, his office and carriage with "the same kind of air you had at Lake Superior." The banker told the man to use common sense![5] Gold and silver mining projects were dismissed with the blunt statement that Cooke did not want any such property.[6]

Among the other ventures which Cooke refused to help launch were various telegraph and cable companies.[7] Further, a certain Antoine de Gagorza urged on Jay Cooke a scheme for a canal through New Granada. He claimed to have in his possession surveys of a long-lost route between the Atlantic and the Pacific, in the search for which England, France, and the United States had spent millions. He maintained that he could furnish the permission of Colombia for the building of such a canal which

Secretary Seward had failed to get by treaty.[8] Such was the procession of new projects which continually sought the banker's aid and sought it in vain.

A FINANCIAL ALLIANCE WITH LIFE INSURANCE

It was characteristic of Jay Cooke that he was unwilling to enter upon an untried field of business, but one that had proved itself he looked on favorably. This was not altogether a good policy, for on two occasions, at least, it meant that he entered upon work which was being overdone or from which the cream of profits had for the time being been skimmed. An illustration of this is insurance. Life insurance, which had profited greatly from war prosperity, grew rapidly in the early post-war years. The extent of its growth is shown by the fact that the life insurance written in the United States increased from $200,000,000 in 1860 to $2,000,000,000 in 1870.[9]

Jay Cooke conceived the idea of organizing a life insurance company to be controlled by himself and his close associates. His purpose was, he said, "to lay out anchors for the obtaining of money," that is, for Jay Cooke & Co. to draw on when necessary.[10] A plan for a grand organization was drawn up; it was patterned after the New York Mutual except that the profits should go to the stockholders.[11] The participating or mutual type of insurance had come to prevail in the United States, but after the war the stock company had made a dramatic appearance when the Universal was projected in New York[12] and the Travelers of Hartford took on life insurance on the nonparticipating plan.[13]

In January, 1868, Jay Cooke's project asked for a national charter from Congress.[14] This was a notable innovation, for there were then no insurance companies incorporated under the national government, federal charters having been granted only to the first and the second Bank of the United States and a few railroads. This insurance project based its request for a federal charter on the grounds that its head office was to be in the District of Columbia. Jay Cooke believed that a federal charter would not only give the concern distinction but that it would also give it the great advantage of being free from State requirements as to reserves.[15]

The request for a charter met strong opposition in Congress. No convincing reason could be given for granting a federal charter to an insurance project. The mutual companies in self-defense strongly opposed it,[16] and there was much criticism on general principles of the nonparticipating type of life insurance.[17] The Cooke lobbying machine, however, functioned well. The bill was passed and, much to the relief of its sponsors, was signed by President Johnson.[18]

The National Life Insurance Company of the United States of America was organized at once. The Cooke partners and the Clarks took most of the stock, some being scattered in strategic places to the advantage of the company.[19] Of the twelve directors, five were Cooke partners and two were Clarks. This preponderance of banker control of an insurance company was unusual and could probably not have been duplicated in the United States at the time.[20] It was a forerunner, in a sense, of that close integration of insurance and financial institutions which was later to become so important in the United States. The two important figures in the control of the concern were Clarence H. Clark, who was president, and Jay Cooke, who was chairman of the financial and executive committee. The actual insurance business was in the hands of a secretary and actuary who had had considerable life insurance experience.[21] A significant feature of the company's organization was the number of former or actual officers of the federal government connected with the concern [22] — an expression of Jay Cooke's feeling for staying close to the government.

An extensive selling organization was set up. Local business men were requested to apply and national banks were invited to become agents. Above the local agents were regional general agents. The most important center was, of course, New York. Jay Cooke & Co. was the general agent there, but it turned the work over to Orvis & Whitman, who served as a specialized agency.[23] Jay Cooke & Co., of Washington, had charge of its community and the South, from which business the Washington house was thereafter expected to get most of its work.[24] The whole United States was thus at once parcelled out to general agents, and the establishment of agencies in Canada, Cuba, and London was considered.[25] The central office was in Philadelphia, the home of the president of the company.

The National Life Insurance Company of the United States of America was introduced to the country through extensive advertising and publicity. The security of the company arising from its large capital, the low cost of the insurance it offered as compared with the mutuals, and the particular advantages derived from the fact that it was not subject to State laws, were stressed in favor of the National Life.[26] It offered "in their purity all the best and most liberal forms of insurance," including the ordinary life, reduction of premium policy, endowment, and children's endowment; and it featured a special income-producing policy.[27]

The success which Jay Cooke had anticipated for the concern was never realized. Much trouble arose: agitation was soon started for the repeal of the company's charter; there was some difficulty between the Clarks and the Cookes over the appointment of agents and the division of the territory; the New York office did not function satisfactorily; and the general agents throughout the country were disappointed with the results, some of the more important ones resigning, among them Wells, Fargo & Co. on the Pacific Coast.[28]

The truth of the matter is that the company failed to write as much insurance as had been expected from so large an organization.[29] The project had been unfortunately timed, having been started when there was overexpansion in life insurance and a general slowing up of business; and it probably suffered from the fact that the men behind it were primarily interested in banking. Nevertheless, by the end of the first two years the total receipts, including the capital of one million, were $2,237,603.[29]. The total disbursements for the two years were $769,341.78, including expenses of $637,095.80; and the net assets at the end of the period were $1,468,261.51.[30] This was not a bad start, but it did not satisfy Jay Cooke, who thought the returns not worth the trouble and who regretted that he and his partners had tied up half a million in the concern.[31] Having in the meantime become active in railroad finance, the banker took no further hand in promoting the enterprise.

This company is important to our story only because it illustrates how Jay Cooke and his associates were reaching out for financial power and profit. It has a legal significance, however, which gives it a general meaning beyond its relationship to their business. It is the only insurance company that was ever chartered by the federal government. It continued to function under its national charter, but it soon lost the advantages of such incorporation since the transaction of business within any State came to be conditioned on the meeting of its insurance regulations. Some time after the Supreme Court had in 1901 handed down its decision in New York Life *vs.* Craven, which held that life insurance was not an object of federal regulation, the company took out an Illinois charter. It had by then become middle western in its business as well as in its organization. In the early 1930's, it succumbed to the depression.

COAL AND IRON PROVE UNPROFITABLE

One of the big fields of development in Pennsylvania during and immediately after the war was the iron and coal business, and it would seem that Jay Cooke and his partners should have been in a position to profit by that development. They ventured in iron and coal, it is true, but their unfortunate experiences explain why they did not enter heavily into local mining and manufacturing.

The Cookes' experience with coal was most discouraging. Though their Preston Coal & Improvement Company was located in the rich Schuylkill anthracite field, it was a continual source of trouble. The books of this concern had been opened at the office of Jay Cooke & Co., in Philadelphia, and shortly after the company had been started the Cookes had been forced to buy back a large portion of the stock and bonds because purchasers were dissatisfied with the returns.[32] To develop the concern, moreover, took more money than had been anticipated, and

Preston had its share of the labor difficulties then so common in the anthracite fields.[33] The crux of the whole problem seems to have been that prices were falling more rapidly than costs.[34] Preston continued to share in the difficulties of the industry, and even a dividend out of capital failed to raise its standing.[35] The Cookes hoped to sell it in order to secure much-needed funds for their banking business, but several years passed before they were able to dispose of the property.[36] On the whole, this connection brought only discredit to Jay Cooke & Co.[37]

Their Champlain iron-works were just as troublesome. Much capital and expert management were necessary to get them into good order, but the Cookes could supply neither.[38] The mines, located in northeastern New York, were also far from a market. To relieve his partners and J. K. Moorhead, Jay Cooke in 1867 bought their Champlain holdings in exchange for shares of Preston, South Mountain Iron Co., Sterling Iron Co., shares and bonds of the Warren & Franklin Railroad, and shares of the Erie Land Co.[39] Some idea of what was happening to the iron-works may be obtained from the fact that in 1866, when business was not yet so bad, the Cookes had tried to sell the Champlain works for $470,000 while in 1867 they were willing to sell at $225,000.[40] In 1868, the manager of the concern wrote to Jay Cooke that the iron in the mine was good iron, the forges were in good order but were closed, and the machinery was put away![41] Their experience with other iron-works was no better.

The reasons for the bankers' failure in iron and coal are fairly clear. It was a difficult time in the industry: prices were falling rapidly while costs were staying high. To make money — or even to survive — required the most expert and careful management. Had the times been good, or had the Cookes been skilled managers in those lines, they would very likely have made something out of the coal and iron concerns in which they were involved. Andrew Carnegie was at the time making a success of his iron-works,[42] but he knew the iron game and he was a wizard at management. The Cookes were bankers, and they were evidently unable even to secure good hired managers. The result was that Preston and Champlain and other similar enterprises became decidedly burdensome to them,[43] and all seem to have turned out unfortunately.[44] They absorbed much capital without any returns at a time when the Cooke firms needed every cent they could muster.[45] It is not strange that the burden of Jay Cooke's advice to his partners was to get their money out of coal and iron and put it into their banking.

RE–ENTRY INTO TRANSPORTATION FINANCE

Jay Cooke was neither an iron nor a coal man by experience or interest; indeed, it was only the promise of high profits during the war which had brought him into iron and coal at all. But in transportation he was at home. He had come to have close contacts with canal and railroad finance and construction before the war turned him almost exclusively into government finance. Throughout the war years and down to 1869, he and his partners had relatively little to do with railroads but enough to provide an interest to which their emphasis could be shifted when government finance failed them.

Railroad building did not reach its greatest post-war importance in investment finance until about 1869.[46] In the earlier post-war years, government securities dominated the investment market, and in concentrating on governments the Cookes were, like most other strong investment houses, doing the most profitable and the safest thing. "We cannot afford to build R R's & neglect our manipulations of Govt Securities. They are good enough," said Pitt Cooke in 1866, clearly voicing the opinion of his partners.[47] On being asked to help finance the Northern Pacific in 1866, Jay Cooke wrote his partners that he would not consider the offer. His reasons reveal how cautious a banker he really was:[48]

What Wm G. & myself fear is becoming identified with any of those great projects, in such a way, as to inevitably draw us into advances. Our true future is to Keep out of entanglements & to undertake nothing or be connected with nothing that will require any advances. We will always have plenty of opportunities offered us to negotiate after concerns are fairly organized & plenty of opportunities to use our

money and our time; So dont let us get into any of these entanglements except those that grow out of our connection with the Gov't &
for the Govt.

Jay Cooke felt that there was no possibility of doing much in
railroad finance as long as government securities were bearing so
high a rate of interest. But as the trading in government securities decreased, dealing in railroad securities increased and a like
change came in the work of the Cookes. In other words, the shift
in the work of the Cooke firms followed the changes in the investment market.

The banker seems not to have considered going heavily into
eastern railroads. Indeed, he and his partners took practically no
part in extending the eastern lines and reorganizing them into
larger systems. During the war they had acquired some interest
in certain Pennsylvania railroads,[49] and in 1867 Jay Cooke & Co.
co-operated with E. W. Clark & Co. and Drexel & Co. in selling
a loan for the Lehigh Coal & Navigation Co.[50] One may wonder
why Jay Cooke did not do more in the transportation field in
which he had made so strong a beginning in the late 1850's. There
was much railroad activity around Philadelphia which required
financing in the late 1860's; the Pennsylvania was extending its
holdings as were also the four great anthracite railroads,[51] and the
Chesapeake & Ohio was just coming into being.

The main reason why Jay Cooke & Co. did not actively participate in financing eastern railroads was probably that the most
successful roads had made contacts with other bankers at a time
when Jay Cooke was busy with government finance — the Drexels, for instance, had become the bankers of the Pennsylvania. It
is also possible that none of those projects gave sufficient promise
to interest Jay Cooke, and they failed to appeal to his imagination. In 1869, we do know, he refused the offer of financing the
Chesapeake & Ohio,[52] at the very time that he associated himself
with a western railroad. It may be that he deliberately chose
western in preference to eastern railroad finance. There can be no
question but that the vast possibilities of the West appealed to
him much more than did rebuilding or reorganizing in the East.

Jay Cooke's re-entry into railroad finance was modest at first. His firms bought and sold shares for customers on commission, of course, and they bought some on their own account. But they refused to take on large railroad projects. They entered into only a few smaller ventures. In 1866 they attempted to sell bonds of the Philadelphia & Erie and in 1868–69 of the Port Huron & Lake Michigan through the Evanses in London. A few bonds were sold early in 1866 before the stringency appeared in the money market and before the Overend, Gurney & Co. panic broke, but nothing was accomplished by the later effort. The English people, said their London agent, had been fleeced so much that they were wary of the bonds of a road not yet built.[53]

In 1866–68, the Cookes were offered participation in the sale of small amounts of securities of other railroads in the older parts of the country,[54] but the West was beckoning. In January, 1865, and February, 1866, they were asked to sell the bonds of the Northern Pacific, but they did not seriously consider those requests.[55] At that very time, Durant was negotiating with them for the Union Pacific, for which they and E. W. Clark & Co. had already sold some bonds. Fahnestock thought this a promising job, the best of the Pacific roads, but he held that no advances should be made to the road if they undertook to sell its bonds.[56] Jay Cooke examined the condition and the prospects of the road, with the result that his firms undertook to sell some bonds for the branch from Leavenworth on the Missouri River to Lawrence, Kansas.[57]

It was apparently their work for the Union Pacific which in 1866 called to the Cookes' attention the North Missouri Railroad, which was projected to connect St. Louis with the great Pacific railroads at Kansas City and Leavenworth, Kansas.[58] On receiving a satisfactory report from W. Milnor Roberts, an engineer whom they had engaged to examine the project,[59] the Cookes agreed to negotiate the sale of $3,000,000 of 7 per cent, 30-year bonds. Jay Cooke & Co. was to receive 5 per cent on par for the negotiation and carry all expenses.[60]

The sale of these bonds was not very successful. They were offered at 85 and were advertised widely as a safe and profitable investment, but the common experience of the bankers who were selling them was that people preferred Uncle Sam's securities.[61] After some six months only about a million had been sold, which was not enough to keep up with construction.[62] In March, 1867, the Cookes offered to split their commission with brokers and other parties in New York to whom they offered the bonds, but the bonds did not go.[63]

In July, 1867, Jay Cooke & Co., E. W. Clark & Co., and Drexel & Co. purchased outright $600,000 of the bonds, which they offered at 85.[64] It was still difficult to sell in competition with government securities and with the bonds of the great Pacific railroads guaranteed by the government.[65] When bonds were sold, however, the profits were good. The Cooke-Clark-Drexel combination ventured further to the extent of a million,[66] but, owing to the difficulty met in selling the bonds and to changes in the road's organization, the Cookes soon discontinued helping the North Missouri.[67]

Jay Cooke's experience with the North Missouri probably deterred him from tying up soon again with any other projects. When the question of financing the Northern Pacific was revived in the fall of 1868, he held that since it took so long to sell a million of bonds for a "live" road like the North Missouri, "there is no chance for a project away up in the snows of Minnesota." [68]

The Union Pacific had in the meantime continued courting Jay Cooke. In September, 1866, he refused an invitation to go on a trip to view the road from Omaha to an important junction at the hundredth meridian.[69] If he had gone, would he have become so enthusiastic over the Minnesota region when he later visited the upper Mississippi–Lake Superior country? In November the Cookes were intensely interested in the rumor that Chief Justice Chase would accept the presidency, first of the Union Pacific road and later of the Central, which "would be a great thing for us — then we could popularize his loans!" [70]

In the spring of 1867 Jay Cooke's firms were asked to become special agents for selling around $100,000,000 in bonds of the Union Pacific, but they refused. Durant, the general manager, insisted that the road needed a "live" house to take over the exclusive financing of both the railroad's mortgage bonds and the

bonds guaranteed by the United States government; he agreed
that the road would never ask for an advance of its agents of
over a million, well secured by bonds.   Jay Cooke and William
Moorhead were offered membership on the road's board.   Pitt
Cooke and Fahnestock strongly favored entering into this
project.   Pitt urged that the Union Pacific held great promise
for them: "Its the Great Enterprise of the day   Its figures
are large.   In acting as their loan agents we can at all times be
amply secured." [71]

The outcome of the negotiation is given in a letter of Pitt to his
Philadelphia brother, which shows that governments still stood in
the way:[72]

I Said to Durant that you Could not accept a position in the management of the road, & at present could not undertake the negotiation of
Bonds & Advances. That we deferred these matters to the head of the
house in Phil[a] & that your feeling was that while Government continued to pay as high as 6% in Gold for money it would be almost impossible to negotiate RR Bds That you favored a 5% Govt Bond which
would induce Capital to interest itself in the Great Enterprises of the
Country

Was this a tide in the affairs of Jay Cooke which, taken at its
flood, would have led to success? As we see it now, the answer is
affirmative. John J. Cisco, who had been United States treasurer
in New York during the war, took the job; and his new firm, John
J. Cisco & Son, won both profits and prestige from financing the
great Union Pacific.[73] At the same time, Fisk & Hatch sold the
bonds of the Central Pacific.[74] Until the completion of those roads
which in 1869 joined the Missouri, a branch of the Mississippi, and
the Pacific, these two firms had much profitable work. It would
be interesting to know what Jay Cooke thought about the matter
as he watched the steady progress of the two roads and the success of Cisco and Fisk & Hatch. It may not be without significance that only a few days after the completion of the
first transcontinental railroad by the union of those roads on
May 10, 1869,[75] Jay Cooke made his preliminary contract with
the Northern Pacific.

Jay Cooke Enters the Upper Mississippi Country

Various influences had been encouraging Jay Cooke's interest in the upper Mississippi region. One was his faith in the value of the land in those newer States. In the 1850's he had bought land in Iowa, Wisconsin, and Minnesota, much of which he continued to hold. In 1866–67 he purchased more land, this time in Minnesota's pine forests.[76] This land was bought with agricultural land scrip on joint account for Jay Cooke and William Moorhead, the venture running three years from October 1, 1866.[77] When the account was closed at the end of the three years, 44,334.09 acres of land had been purchased at a total cost of $37,143.70. In the final settlement Cooke and Moorhead each received 19,000 acres, the remainder going to Banning, real-estate dealer of St. Paul, as compensation for his services.[78] This was all rich pine land lying in Cloquet and St. Louis counties, that is, around Duluth, Minnesota. At the same time Cooke and Moorhead also purchased certain lands on the St. Louis River containing promising water-power sites.[79]

Jay Cooke's interest in the upper Mississippi country was strengthened in the summer of 1868 by his trip to Duluth. His party went from Detroit to Duluth by boat, stopping at various points on the way. Jay Cooke studied the western point of Lake Superior with care, employing Indians and half breeds to paddle him about in their large canoes,[80] and he was impressed with the possibility of developing a harbor there. Duluth was then a village of but six or seven frame houses, a land office, and a schoolhouse. But Jay Cooke's imagination was fired —"I felt sure that vast cities would grow up at Duluth & Superior." He had seen a vision of a great land with marvelous possibilities, and he was tempted. Small wonder that the beautiful lake, with its magnificent natural harbor, flanked by almost endless stretches of lovely pine, beyond which were prairies rich with potential treasure, touched an imagination like his!

After the banker's return to Philadelphia, temptation came to him in the form of the Lake Superior & Mississippi Railroad Co. Though he had known of the road for some time,[81] not until he had visited Duluth did he take a serious interest in it. The Lake Superior & Mississippi was then largely controlled by Philadelphia iron and railroad interests, and prominent in its promotion was the same William Banning of St. Paul who had helped select Minnesota lands for Cooke and Moorhead. Thirty miles had already been built,[82] and the railroad had a magnificent grant of pine lands. It was projected to connect the two bodies of water whose names it bore and to be the first road to penetrate the dense pine forests between St. Paul and Duluth, Minnesota. It was expected that those same forests would yield much freight and that the monopoly control over Minnesota transportation held by Chicago and Milwaukee interests would drive considerable wheat and other freight to the Lake Superior & Mississippi.[83] The road would thus deliver much heavy traffic to be carried eastward on the water lanes of the Great Lakes.

In the autumn of 1868 the Cookes and Clarks bought on joint account a small block of the road's bonds together with some bonds of its subsidiary, a land company.[84] When they decided to try to sell the bonds in Europe, Jay Cooke's partners urged him to go across to negotiate, but he would not go — it is said that he had a fear of the ocean. Fahnestock finally made the trip, accompanied by Henry Cooke (who liked nothing better than to roam about the Continent) and J. Hinckley Clark.[85]

The trip proved disappointing and revealing to the American bankers. English, German, and Dutch capitalists refused to take the bonds of the road.[86] The reasons were well summed up in a letter sent to Jay Cooke by Fahnestock while he was in London:[87]

At this writing we have no prospect of placing the bonds. There is no limit to money here, but recent experiences in American Railway securities have not had time to be forgotten, and longer time must elapse before *new* Enterprises can find favor. There is we find a wide spread feeling of uncertainty—apprehension that Napoleon & Bismarck have not yet settled accounts, and that a great war must come before affairs can rest upon a permanent basis. Be this as it may it is the *feeling* and guides people in their business matters. . . . The greatest misfortune is that the bonds have already been hawked all around. The second is that here people are accustomed to building roads chiefly upon *paid up stock* and using bonds only as auxiliaries. They dont like to put money especially into a mortgage that is secured by *prospective* property.

Fahnestock's letter gave an excellent analysis of the European, especially the English, attitude toward American railroad investments. The banker learned much from this trip. It is a pity that Jay Cooke, himself, did not observe investment finance through the eyes of Europe; had he done so, he would undoubtedly have had a clearer understanding of those larger European influences which had such an important bearing on American business in the years immediately following.

Undeterred by Europe's attitude, the Cookes and Clarks proceeded to sell the Lake Superior & Mississippi bonds in America. They made an agreement with the road to sell its 7 per cent gold bonds to the amount of something over $2,500,000, retaining whatever they could make above 85 cents (later 90) on the dollar and receiving a generous stock bonus.[88] William Moorhead and J. Hinckley Clark became directors of the road. The Lake Superior & Mississippi was a promising road and the commissions were liberal — it looked like a good thing.[89]

The two banking groups divided the territory: Jay Cooke & Co. managed advertising and selling in New York and E. W. Clark & Co. in Boston, the two co-operating in the Philadelphia area. They agreed to sell at 95, a commission of $2\frac{1}{2}$ per cent being allowed to other agents.[90]

A vigorous advertising campaign was inaugurated. Pamphlets, maps, and "Questions and Answers" were distributed.[91] Jay Cooke urged his New York house "to get your editors to puff" the bonds,[92] and Wilkeson and Painter were engaged to write up the road.[93] The fluent pen of Sargent, a Duluth real-estate promoter, wrote for the *Times*.[94] The newspaper men were "lubricated" by options on the bonds. "Three fourths of them are not worth a Cent in the way of influence, and in fact the only men I would care to give option of a few at $92\frac{1}{2}$ are Norvell [of the *Times*], the Post and the Tribune. Perhaps a word from the Herald would do no harm and the World too, but you have not money to spare and I hate to waste them on the unscrupulous ~~devils~~ Bohemians." [95] Cooke was informed two days later that the financial writers of the *Times* and *Post* were given an option on $20,000 each. "Two others, avaricious dogs," wrote Fahnestock, "have spoken kindly of the loan and will be passing round their hats soon!" [96]

The bonds went fast. Washington, as usual, accomplished nothing to speak of;[97] Wilkeson found the Pennsylvania Germans slow;[98] but New York bought in large lots.[99] Budge, Schiff and Co., "a young & enterprising house," wanted half a million.[100] Within a month after sales began, Jay Cooke and his partners were in high spirits over their success.[101] They sold $2,077,000; the Clarks, $521,000.[102] "This loan," came word from the New York Cookes, "is spoken of as the most successful negotiation in the Street." [103] It left Jay Cooke and his partners enthusiastic over the Northwest, an enthusiasm for a time fanned by the good profits they made from buying and selling Lake Superiors on the market.[104]

In the meantime, the Cookes had become more closely interested in Minnesota real estate. They had secured an interest in the Western Land Association, a subsidiary of the Lake Superior & Mississippi, which owned rich pine lands and town sites along the line of the road.[105] Jay Cooke and William Moorhead also entered extensively into Duluth real estate on joint account, purchasing lots and building houses.[106] The manager of this venture was George B. Sargent, who was later to add a colorful, though discordant, note to the affairs of Jay Cooke & Co. Sargent was of the old bankrupt house of Cook, Sargent & Co. of Davenport, Iowa, private bankers. He had come to Iowa in 1836 and had for 30 years been active in the land business in that region. He had brought immigrants to the State. He had been government land surveyor in Illinois, Missouri, and Minnesota, and in the late 1860's he settled in Duluth as private banker, real-estate dealer, and general promoter.[107]

Thus, at the very time that their work in government securities was slipping, Jay Cooke and his partners became interested in the development of the Northwest. At the same time, also, they tasted the sweets of a successful railroad promotion. They were on their way to something very different from government bonds and small mines and railroads. They were soon to meet a crisis in the affairs of their firms, and then they were to stake their future on the great northwestern section of the United States.

ENTERING NORTHERN PACIFIC FINANCE

IN THE spring of 1869 the Northern Pacific promoters again offered Jay Cooke the work of financing their road. When they had in 1865, 1866, and 1867 approached him, he had shown no interest in their project, but now it was different; the promoters were not only heard but even welcomed. The decrease in the business in government securities had brought this change in Jay Cooke's policy. In 1869 it was estimated that approximately $1,000,000,000, or about two-fifths of the American debt, was in Europe,[1] having gone principally to London and Frankfort. The American investors, whom the Cookes were equipped to serve, had been selling their government bonds and were going more and more into railroads. It was possible that Jay Cooke's firms would have something to do with refunding the government debt, but there was no certainty as to when that would be undertaken or how much work it would bring the Cookes.

RETRENCHMENT OR NEW WORK

With their business in government securities in such a state, the Cookes were forced to take serious stock of their affairs. One thing that was agreed upon was that certain leaks in the firms had to be patched. The New York partners urged that something be done about the Washington house;[2] even Henry Cooke admitted that there was little business for it to do.[3] Henry Cooke had always been the cause of much worry to his partners because of his extravagance, debts, and commitments to risky enterprises. At that very time he was living in a house which cost $75,000 and was building another for upwards of $100,000.[4] Besides, he had personal notes and overdrafts with Jay Cooke & Co. and the First National in Washington to the amount of $416,000, quite inadequately covered by unsalable securities.[5] The brothers had entreated Henry to reform,[6] and he promised to cut expenses, not to invest further, and to sell out all he could, besides turning his residence over to William Moorhead in trust for the firm.[7] But in the next year and a half his debt to the firm increased over $30,000.[8] The only apparent result of this attempt at reform was a growing ill-feeling between the Washington and New York houses. Things came to such a pass that the former gave its New York business to other firms, thus paying out money in commissions which should have been retained by the Cookes.[9]

There is no reason to believe that the Cookes considered a general curtailment of their organization to fit their decreased business at this time. Such action would have meant a loss of prestige, and prestige was their greatest stock-in-trade. Jay Cooke and his partners did not foresee any long-time lack of business. Though conditions were somewhat uncertain for the time being, they, like business men and business commentators in general, were optimistic for the long run.

Here was a first-class question of policy, and the Cookes chose not to retrench but to look for other work. A London house was again considered. The foreign commercial business was developing rapidly, and such houses as the Mortons and Drexels were profiting thereby. Fahnestock seems especially to have favored the entry of the firm into this work. He felt that if they had a London house they could compete for the foreign business, but without it they could only sit by and watch the "dutchmen" reap the harvest.[10]

Fahnestock was more strongly conscious of the need of a foreign connection than Jay Cooke. This was in part a result of a growing difference of opinion between the two partners as to the kind of work their houses should do. The Philadelphian had virtually become a bond broker, while the New Yorker was tending more and more toward certain aspects of commercial banking. The difference in their attitudes toward a foreign connection was also a reflection of a difference in their conception of the importance of Europe to American business. Jay Cooke was a westerner; he had been reared on the frontier. Most of his business career had been spent in Philadelphia, which essentially looked inland. He had never been to Europe. In his lifetime he had seen a tremendous development going on in the West, much of which had come about without the aid of foreign capital. Moreover, one of the biggest financial enterprises of the century, the American Civil War, had been financed by American money. The Philadelphian was a strong nationalist in the sense that he felt that the United States could and should be as independent of Europe as possible, in business as well as in government.

Fahnestock, on the other hand, was a New Yorker in his business outlook. His office was near the Battery where the ships from across the seas continually paraded by. He was familiar with the interests and attitudes of European bankers through his business acquaintances who represented them in New York. Moreover, on his trips to Europe Fahnestock had gained a feeling for the financial power of England and the Continent and for the way business was carried on with America. He seems to have realized more clearly than did Cooke the necessity of being in a position to tap European capital and the opportunities offered by the European-American commercial business.

In the meantime, the railroad movement had once more become conspicuous in the United States. It manifested itself in several ways: in the replacing of old roadbeds and equipment, in the reorganization of smaller railroads into larger systems, and in the building of new railways. By 1869 the construction of new lines had gained considerable momentum: in 1866, 1,742 miles had been built; in 1867, 2,499; in 1868, 2,979; and in 1869, 4,999 miles.[11] Speculators, promoters, and politicians were again seeing in western railroad extension a great opportunity, and the high interest rates offered by railroad bonds were attractive to investors. The awakened interest in transportation found expression in the spring of 1869 in a strong speculative movement in railway stocks and bonds.[12]

Bankers were fully aware of the opportunities offered by railroad finance. But there were important differences in the position taken by various banks in the railroad business. Some private bankers were principally concerned with serving the needs of established railroads, that is, providing short-time loans for operating or long-time loans for replacing equipment, rebuilding or extending lines, or for combining them into larger systems. Such loans were not very extensive — rarely above $5,000,000 — and the margin of profit was also not large; but at the same time, in working with established railroads having considerable earnings, the risks were small and the work was fairly constant. A railroad generally depended on a particular bank for much of its business, so that Brown Brothers came to be recognized as leading bankers for the Baltimore & Ohio and Drexels for the Pennsylvania.

It is extremely significant that the government's business had occupied Jay Cooke just at the time when certain bankers had been gaining a strong position with eastern roads. This was also true of other bankers heavily engaged in government finance. When their government business began to dwindle and they looked to railroads for work, they were outsiders. It became necessary for them, therefore, to seek new roads. Henry Clews joined the Rock Island.[13] As noted before, the Ciscos took charge of the sale of the bonds of the Union Pacific, and Fisk & Hatch did the same work for the Central Pacific, selling over $80,000,000 of bonds.[14]

Jay Cooke and his partners had been slower to enter into railroad finance than the other government bankers. Though they had made small excursions into the railroad field, not until the spring of 1869 did they seriously contemplate going heavily into railroads. It is probable that Jay Cooke and his partners were then influenced by certain developments in transportation which had come to be conspicuous in that year.

Imitation is a fundamental factor in business; it sometimes helps explain movements and events for which there is scarcely any other adequate explanation. Its influence is seen clearly again and again in American history; extensive canal building, the rapid spread of the corporation, and the later mania for mergers are in part explained by the strong power of example. Certain events played on Jay Cooke's imagination in 1869: the completion of the first transcontinental railroad must have struck him with great force; not so dramatic but nevertheless important was the fact that in the same year the Pennsylvania

System gained control through to Chicago while the consolidation of the New York Central and Hudson River railroads and the Lake Shore & Michigan practically gave Vanderbilt a continuous line to the same western terminal.[15] Railroading on a large scale was in the air.

This must have impressed Jay Cooke strongly, especially since he had failed to seize earlier opportunities in railroad finance such as the Union Pacific had offered him. Unfortunately, it is difficult to recapture lost business opportunities; time is a most important consideration, and timing may determine the success or failure of a project. At this strategic point the Northern Pacific again knocked at the door of Jay Cooke & Co. Was he going to accept its offer this time?

THE NORTHERN PACIFIC TURNS TO JAY COOKE FOR AID

When the Northern Pacific again sought Jay Cooke's aid in 1869, it was still only a promotion organization, the result of over a generation of discussions, surveys, and proposals for a railway extending westward from the Great Lakes to the Pacific.[16] In 1864 some New England men had secured for a proposed Northern Pacific Railroad Company a federal charter and an immense land grant and had organized a company and made plans for financing the road by selling stock.[17] Having failed to sell stock, the promoters had appealed to business men and capitalists of Boston and New England, proposing a continuous rail line from Boston to the Pacific with the view to securing for Boston a superior connection with the Northwest trade and the Orient.[18] This dream of Boston business men for an overland connection might be looked upon as a substitute for their old-time trade around the Horn.

The idea of furthering the regional independence of Boston and New England won the endorsement of several business men of the section who entered into the project. J. Gregory Smith, prominent in Vermont politics and in Vermont Central Railroad affairs, became president of the company and for several years he occupied a dominant position in its affairs. Smith visualized the

Northern Pacific as the larger part of a transcontinental railroad, the central portion of which should be supplied mainly by Sir Hugh Allan's projected Canadian Pacific [19] and the eastern, by Smith's own Vermont Central and other New England roads.[20]

It soon became evident that, even with a pretentious plan, the Northern Pacific would not appeal to investors. The region the road proposed to traverse was little known to investing interests and it had been only barely touched by settlement. The Union and Central Pacific railroads had also gone through much unsettled country, but they had had the advantage of government aid.[21] Following the example of those roads and claiming that the proposed railroad would be of great use in transporting troops to the Indian country and in helping to settle the Northwest, the Northern Pacific Company asked for a government guarantee of interest on its bonds for 20 years. But the bill that might have given effect to this failed to pass Congress.[22]

It soon became clear to President Smith that the enterprise was too exclusively a "downeast" affair to appeal widely to either capitalists or politicians. A plan was, therefore, devised for bringing in wider interests; the proprietorship of the road was divided into 12 equal portions, each to cost $8,500 and furnish one director.[23] Prominent business men from various parts of the country, most of whom were important in railroad affairs, were induced to subscribe: Smith and Canfield of Vermont; Wm. B. Ogden, prominent Chicagoan and president of the Chicago & Northwestern; Wm. G. Fargo, D. N. and A. H. Barney, and B. P. Cheney, who had strong express interests; Geo. W. Cass, president of the Pittsburgh, Fort Wayne, & Chicago; and J. Edgar Thomson, president of the Pennsylvania.[24] The Northern Pacific again prayed Congress for aid, fortified with its imposing array of names, a prominent engineer's favorable report on the territory through which the road was to run, favorable communications from prominent army officers, including U. S. Grant, and an alliance with a proposed Southern Pacific road.[25] The majority of the Senate Committee on Pacific Railroads reported in favor of government assistance to both a southern and a northern road.[26] But Congress, already influenced by the antirailroad sentiment arising in different parts of the country, was no longer in a generous mood toward railroads.

Blocked in their attempt to get federal aid, the Northern Pacific promoters determined as a last resort to seek loans for financing construction. They secured from Congress in March, 1869, the authority to issue bonds secured by a mortgage on the railroad and telegraph line.[27] It was obvious that under the circumstances only the most vigorous loan campaign would have any effect. The Northern Pacific had a good reason for turning to Jay Cooke.

Although the enterprise was only a promotion organization without any means, Jay Cooke was ready to give it a hearing, and after some investigation he drew up the terms on which he would consider assuming the work of financing the construction of the road. On May 16, 1869, a week after the completion of the first transcontinental road, he signed a preliminary agreement[28] with the Northern Pacific which should become effective if, after having made thorough surveys and investigations, Cooke was satisfied that the project was a feasible one. He was then to have charge of the sale of $100,000,000 of 7.3 per cent bonds and to serve as banker for the road.

THE ENGINEER AND THE REPORTER SURVEY THE ROUTE

Jay Cooke proceeded at once to have surveys made of the proposed route. The promoters of the road wanted immediate action and Pitt Cooke urged that they wait for no long preliminaries, holding that an exploring party would add no information that could not easily be gained otherwise and that money was more readily available then than it would be a year later.[29] As it proved, the New York brother was right, but the Philadelphian would not proceed without a preliminary investigation. Two exploring parties were, therefore, sent out, one to cover the western coastal and mountain section and the other to examine the eastern portion.

The western party was a mixed group. Its leading members were W. Milnor Roberts,[30] an engineer of broad experience and

excellent judgment, a clergyman named Claxton, and Samuel
Wilkeson, a facile journalist who had been associated with Jay
Cooke off and on since war days. This party explored the region
bordering on Puget Sound, the Columbia River, and Lake Pend
d'Oreille, and the country of the Yellowstone.

The party surveying the eastern portion set out more like a
luxurious camping party than a group proposing to survey
through hostile Sioux territory. At the Red River, however, the
ministers and their wives and other sightseers turned back while
Engineer Edwin F. Johnson, C. Carleton Coffin of the *Boston
Journal*, former Governor Marshall of Minnesota, and Philip
Holmes, of Jay Cooke's New York house, proceeded westward
over the Great Plains with military escort.[31]

The reports to Jay Cooke were extremely favorable. He received profuse letters from Claxton, the clergyman, from Wilkeson and "Carleton," the journalists, as well as from others of the
party. Wilkeson's enthusiasm was extreme. He was impressed
with the beauty of the country, and it was to him a land of rare
treasure. "Our enterprise is an inexhaustible gold mine — There
is no mistake about it," he wrote to Cooke. There was gold to be
panned out of the rivers, salmon to be pitchforked out of the
streams —"you are dead sure of 40, 50, 60 bushels of wheat way
up to the tops" of the mountains, and the water power gave
promise of future Lowells and Manchesters! [32]

More important were the conclusions of Roberts, who was a
strong contrast to the clergyman and the reporters. He was very
cautious.[33] He inspected the settlements already established
along the proposed route. He gave a great deal of attention to
the resources of the region; much of the land, he reported, could
not be cultivated while some could be used if irrigated, but there
were many valleys with the richest soil and immense stretches of
the finest forest. Most of all, he carefully searched the passes for
the most economical grades and made notes on the various factors determining costs in railroad building.

After his return to the East, Roberts made a report based on
his own investigations and the surveys of others. He concluded
"that the Northern Pacific Railroad route, with the land grant

secured to the Company by the Government, possesses great intrinsic value, and will be, as a whole, a remarkably favorable line in all important respects; a line which, if judiciously located, honestly constructed, and properly administered, will pay within a few years a fair dividend on its cost." He estimated the total cost of construction and equipment, including interest on the bonds during construction, to be $85,277,000.[34]

The surveying parties had been made up with a strong eye to their publicity value. As usual with Jay Cooke, the politician, the press, and the pulpit were enlisted in the cause. As the surveying proceeded, a barrage of publicity for the Northern Pacific was scattered throughout the country. The journalists of the surveying parties wrote long communications to their respective newspapers, which were copied far and wide and eventually were published in pamphlet or book. Thus the newspaper reader the country over was familiarized with the beauty and the promise of the "Seat of Empire," as the northwestern region was called.[35]

There is no doubt but that those reporters were sincerely impressed with the country traversed. They had a meritorious task to perform, that of breaking down the erroneous ideas about the Northwest so prevalent throughout the country. But in their enthusiasm their extravagance of expression sometimes went too far. Note a paragraph from Wilkeson's description of the Puget Sound country:[36]

Oh!! what timber. On the Atlantic slope, where it was my misfortune to be born, and where for fifty-two years I have been cheated by circumstances out of a sight of the real America, there are no woods. East of the Rocky Mountains trees are brush. They may do for brooms; pieces of ships are got out of them, and splinters for houses. But the utmost throe of the Atlantic-slope soil and climate could not in ages produce a continuous plank which would reach from stem to stern of a thousand-ton clipper-ship. Puget Sound, anywhere and everywhere, will give you for the cutting, if you are equal to such a crime with an axe, trees that will lie straight on the ground, and cover two hundred and fifty feet of length and measure twenty-five feet around above two men's heights from the ground. . . . They are monarchs, to whom all worshipful men inevitably lift their hats.

This was too extreme to be taken seriously, and it helped transform the Seat of Empire into Jay Cooke's "Banana Country."

Two significant results sprang from these surveys. First, Jay Cooke was thereby convinced beyond doubt of the feasibility of the Northern Pacific project, a conviction based on the sound observations of Roberts and colored by the glowing descriptions of Wilkeson, Claxton, and "Carleton." Secondly, the publicity growing out of the surveys did not have an altogether favorable effect. It undoubtedly served to interest many people in the Northern Pacific country. But, while it might appeal to the small investor, it antagonized bankers and capitalists. The larger investor and financier has always tended to be wary of extensive publicity. Jay Cooke's wide use of the press partly explains his failure to win the support of strong bankers and capitalists.

SEEKING A EUROPEAN ASSOCIATE IN FINANCING THE NORTHERN PACIFIC

While the surveyors proceeded with their explorations and the whole country was being educated to an appreciation of the untold wealth and beauty of that western country, which needed but a railroad to make it blossom with happy settlements and civilization, the attitude of the financial world toward the Northern Pacific was being tested.

Jay Cooke's first thought was of Europe. Since the building of the Erie Canal, no great American transportation concern had been established without European help. The Cookes now had prospects of a big project to offer European capitalists. On first thought it would appear that Europe ought to have been interested. "This summer," held Fahnestock, "Europe must take R R bonds. They cannot get govts." [37] American government bonds had, it is true, been salted away for safe-keeping, but Fahnestock overlooked the fact that Europe did not need to rely on the United States to take its idle capital. The governments and railroads of other countries offered opportunities which might well displace the American borrower in the European loan markets.

William Moorhead, the inactive partner of the firms, was sent to Europe to find someone to co-operate in handling the Northern Pacific loan. There is a great deal to be said for the view that Cooke himself should have gone, both because of his power of persuasion and the wisdom of his observing the situation in Europe at first hand. Moorhead had some excellent qualifications for negotiating with European bankers; he would be sympathetic with the conservatism of the great European bankers and could meet them in the restrained manner which they respected. Unfortunately, however, he was uncertain about the feasibility of the project, and he did not have the confidence of Jay Cooke, who had always considered Moorhead overcautious.[38]

Moorhead found the situation discouraging when he reached London in July, 1869. England had not yet recovered from the failures of 1866 which had grown out of inflated railroad finance. Furthermore, American railroads were without much standing in England. Certain roads were fostering the feeling that American railroads were not sound, and it was becoming apparent to capitalists that the great Union and Central Pacific roads would not be profitable for years.[39] The alleged misrepresentation in Paris of the bonds of a southwestern railroad by General Frémont had injured American railroads considerably.[40] A further difficulty was the fact that the bankers of Europe knew little about America.[41]

The plan of the Cookes was first to seek an alliance with the Rothschilds in their campaign for selling $100,000,000 of Northern Pacific bonds. This was unfortunate for two reasons. First, it was unprecedented to offer an American railroad loan to the amount of $100,000,000 in Europe; a $5,000,000 loan was not uncommon and even a larger one might have been accepted, but anyone who proposed to sell a loan for $100,000,000 would be regarded with suspicion, to say the least. Secondly, it was a mistake to offer the loan to the Rothschilds. They were unusually conservative and unlikely to embark on such a project, and they were not interested in American railroads, nor in any American enterprises for that matter. There were other smaller London investment houses which were interested in such loans and would presumably have been more favorably disposed toward the Northern Pacific.[42]

Moorhead failed to interest the Rothschilds in his initial encounters,[43] and it was not long until he concluded that there was little chance for help in Europe. He, therefore, wrote an emphatic letter home in which he urged his partners not to enter upon Northern Pacific financing. He regarded the company in "the light of speculators — men who have nothing to lose but everything to gain, in getting the road built, with the money of others." He urged the Cookes not to undertake the project unless they could associate with themselves a strong house which would furnish half the means. The Rothschilds, he felt certain, would not take hold. If they refused, Barings would not participate, and then Morgan would not. There remained only the Germans.[44]

Both Cooke and Fahnestock considered the Rothschilds' aid indispensable and they were determined not to give up so easily. "Their acceptance," said Fahnestock, "would *insure* our success and make it *Easy*, and moreover would insure us a life long connection with the greatest house in the world and give us a controlling position in all the large negotiations offering. . . . It will accomplish for us all the advantages of a foreign house without its disadvantages." He held that it was impossible to place bonds rapidly in America and that Europe was the great market for them. But since Europe was flooded with bonds, it would be necessary for the Northern Pacifics to be backed by a great house. Jay Cooke should go across to see the Baron Rothschild, urged Fahnestock, for he could better than any one else "influence those old money bags & make them understand what America is and what is the capacity of the West." [45]

Jay Cooke instructed Moorhead to propose to the Rothschilds that they and the Cookes should undertake to sell $5,000,000 each, promising them participation in the refunding of the national debt and "perhaps the transfer of government deposits from Baring to Rothschilds." [46] Armed with the reports of the surveys and the assurance that Northern Pacific affairs were progressing successfully, Moorhead again approached the Rothschilds. They replied

that they would be interested if the United States would guarantee the bonds, and that they would be even more interested in
co-operating in a government negotiation![47]

The letter reporting Moorhead's failure with the Rothschilds
speaks eloquently of the poor prospects of the Northern Pacific
bonds in the London market:[48]

> I spent a long time yesterday with them. The Baron, and his Sons.
> . . . The old gentleman said they never engaged in anything that re-
> quired risk, or trouble, in the management. This he regarded involved
> both. The amt too he said was very large. And there was no road
> built — no considerable amt of cash capital paid in — he said it would
> be impossible to sell the bonds. They could not offer them. He dis-
> cussed evry point. I argued the value of the lands — refered to the
> Ill[inois] Central bonds, which were based on land &c &c, but with-
> out the least avail. He is determined and no power in America, or
> England, can change his mind.

This statement of Rothschild's position shows clearly that he
and his house were in the passive phase of investment banking.
Unlike the Germans, who were soon to reach out for world con-
quest, and the American bankers on Wall Street, who before
long were forced to try to make American business honest and
efficient, Rothschild assumed that his policy should be to make
strict inquiry into his client's position and then, if he made the
loan, to keep his hands off. On the whole this has been the
dominant attitude of English and French bankers to the present
time. Jay Cooke was a leader in helping to change the attitude of
American bankers on this matter.

Moorhead was no more hopeful about securing the aid of other
European bankers. He did not believe that anything could be
done "through any other banking house of Capital, or position, in
Europe." The English and the Germans required finished roads
to induce them to purchase or agree to sell large amounts of
bonds. Individual speculators might be induced to go in on such
a proposition, but "they are not to be found among successful
bankers, nor among those possessing large capitals." In other
words, the European bankers would look upon the Northern

Pacific bonds as being equivalent to stock and, as such, fit for speculators rather than conservative investors.

Again Moorhead warned Jay Cooke not to attempt too much alone. "You may say this is a golden opportunity for your making a fortune," wrote Moorhead, but he was convinced Jay Cooke & Co. could not secure the means with which to build the road rapidly westward. By no means should support be taken from such men as Chief Justice Chase or other friends who would look to Cooke for results. Men of wealth should be sought out, advised Moorhead, men who had "a capital of 20 or $30,000,000 to invest & thus give character to it, before they rely upon the sale of bonds abroad. . . . If you can get Stone [of the New York Central] of Cleveland, you have one good man whose judgment is A no 1. If you could secure Com Vanderbilt and a few other Rail Road Capitalists, who could put in a few millions of dollars, & who would give some attention to the management, you would make a strong point." While this advice of Moorhead was obviously very businesslike, still under the circumstances it was impracticable.

DEPRESSION IN THE HOME MARKET IN THE FALL OF 1869

In the meantime Jay Cooke had been making plans for introducing Northern Pacifics at home. He conceived the idea of forming a pool to purchase a portion of the bonds [49] in order to supply funds with which to build a section of the road and thus secure a concrete basis for further sale of bonds. The project aroused a considerable interest among politicians,[50] but there is no reason to think that there was any real enthusiasm for it among capitalists.[51] Before the matter could be put strongly before them, however, an event occurred which for a time diverted attention from such new enterprises.

In September, 1869, the financial drama enacted on Wall Street reached a tense point. It has been noted from time to time how uncertain the money, stock, and bond markets were in those early years after the war. Business was nervous and jumpy. Nobody could foretell what the government would do about money, whether it would return to the gold standard or inflate further; nobody could know when the government would buy or sell gold or greenbacks. The result was that business men did not know what to do, whether they should buy or sell their commodities, stocks, bonds, and so on, or expand or contract their business. In this atmosphere of uncertainty, speculation flourished. The late 1860's are notorious for pools and corners in Wall Street, for corruption in business and government, and for the sudden acquisition or loss of wealth. In such an atmosphere was hatched the gold conspiracy which ended so disastrously in the American Black Friday of September 24, 1869.

We need not stop for the details of the conspiracy. On September 24 came the crisis. Unheard-of things happened on Wall Street. At the beginning of the day the gold clique held calls for well above $100,000,000. The conspirators, most of whose gold had been acquired below 144, continued to push the metal up rapidly, expecting to force the bears to cover at around 160.[52] But to do this took money; the conspirators had prepared for this by an arrangement with Gould's Tenth National Bank to certify their checks but they were forestalled by bank examiners who unexpectedly appeared on the scene. The price was pushed up until the short interests are said to have stood at $250,000,000. The price reached $162\frac{1}{2}$.[53] There were then not over $15,000,000 in gold and gold certificates in New York with which to meet those contracts. The short interests were frantic. Among them were some 250 prominent firms in New York, many of whom were leading bankers and merchants who had entered the gold market to cover legitimate business. Jay Cooke & Co. of New York was among the shorts because of the speculations of Dodge.[54]

The only hope for the shorts was to get the Treasury to sell gold. Under similar circumstances during and after the war, the Treasury had interfered, but, because of widespread criticism of the policy of the previous administration, President Grant and Secretary Boutwell had persistently sought to divorce the Treasury from Wall Street, and in this instance they had been subtly encouraged to maintain their hands-off policy by the gold clique. The President's suspicions were finally aroused,[55] however, and the short interests and others convinced him and the Secretary that nothing but interference by the Treasury could avert widespread ruin.

The Cookes were among those who hammered away at the government. Jay Cooke and Fahnestock, whose house was heavily loaded with governments and short on gold,[56] instructed Henry Cooke in Washington to urge the President and the Secretary to increase the purchase of bonds and the sale of gold. On the day before the panic broke, Henry Cooke reported to his Philadelphia brother that Boutwell had ordered the "advance payment of the Nov. Coupons at our suggestion — and I think he will also take this further step." In the evening he added that he was hopeful of success: "Something will be done — I think it will be in the form of instructions to Butterfield [assistant treasurer in New York] to advertise to buy *tomorrow more* bonds [paying in gold]." [57]

At noon of September 24 the price of gold broke in New York, falling in fifteen minutes like a gigantic shuttlecock from 160 to 133. Something had happened behind the scenes. The sale of gold by a group of bankers and merchants, under the leadership of James Brown, of Brown Brothers & Co., had weakened the market. Then had come the news that the government would sell.[58]

Henry Cooke claimed that it was he who had induced the Secretary to put a stop to the gold raid. It is clear enough that he had a hand in the affair, but it is also evident that President Grant's suspicion had been aroused several days before the final step was taken and that business men far and wide implored the Treasury to act.[59]

Saturday found the Street in ruins. The firms which were not known to have failed were suspected of weakness. Monday was no better. Firms failed right and left. The money market tightened. How bad conditions were may be seen from the fact that 5 per cent a day was charged for carrying Vanderbilt railroad stocks. Money rates rose to staggering heights, and the fall of stock prices struck Wall Street with terror. Lockwood & Co., with a capital of $5,000,000 and a fine record over 25 years, was unable to hold up under its load of Pacific Mail, Lake Shore, and Chicago & Northwestern stocks. The whole Street was in a mess and it was difficult to clear up. Jay Cooke & Co. offered their offices to a committee of the gold board which succeeded in straightening out some of the accounts.[60]

The Cookes urged Boutwell to continue selling in order to ease the market. But Boutwell, reported Henry Cooke on Saturday, viewed the ruins and regretted what he had done: "He appears to be astounded at the suddenness and terribleness of the result of his action upon the gold brokers and operators — and has been made the victim of a terrible pressure all last evening and this morning to reconsider. We have stood by him, and encouraged him and he will hold fast. . . . I take care that he sees all the newspapers say in approval of his course." [61] Henry Cooke, in constant communication with his two leading partners, continued to urge Boutwell to maintain his policy of relieving the gold and money markets.[62]

Jay Cooke made a very significant proposal at this time. He suggested that the Treasury undertake to stabilize gold by announcing from time to time the point at which it would hold the metal by means of purchases or sales on the market. A little gold would accomplish this, held the banker, while the effect on gambling would be strong.[63] The idea was not put into effect; it was too much to ask of a government committed to a laissez-faire policy in financial matters as was the administration of President Grant. It is quite probable, however, that, if wisely handled, this plan for stabilization might have had a salutary effect at the time.

The Cookes were grateful that they had lived through the panic. They felt that their prestige was enhanced thereby when such strong houses as Lockwoods had failed.[64] But they had lost enough. "I have been writing up our side of the Gold muddle," wrote Pitt to Jay, "until I can demonstrate that black is white (in all Cases except Jim Fiske & the devil) Have settled with all our correspdts now I believe — with most of them easily — with one or two a little reluctantly." [65] The New York house suffered a loss on gold which was at first estimated at $28,201 — the loss on Dodge's gold account for the whole year was $76,954.04.[66]

The gold fiasco left Jay Cooke & Co. a thoroughly chastened group of partners, none more than Fahnestock. The gold mess had taught him a lesson: "We have got to find a different way to make money from the way in which *all our New York* money has been made." [67] Pitt Cooke was grateful that they had been preserved in the crisis and he recommended the cutting of expenses, thinking it more important to be snug than to make money.[68] Jay Cooke also recommended drastic action to put their houses in order. From his Gibraltar fishing haunts on Lake Erie, he instructed the Philadelphia house to get rid of its $430,000 of governments, to push Oil Creek, Warren & Franklin, and Lake Superior bonds, and to "get in every dollar you can & loan only on what is instant cash." [69]

Jay Cooke was at this time seriously disturbed over the political situation which, he feared, promised nothing good for the currency and government bonds. "Considering the wicked want of honesty in high places & in all political circles," he believed that the future of the debt was very uncertain. "Why my faith in the great majority of *Republican* leaders is so weak that I feel sure that if they thought more votes could be secured by adopting an 'outheroding' policy a la Pendleton only ahead of his in atrocity— they would do it — So few are bondholders So few are honest — that the cry of plenty of greenbacks & easy times may at any moment be seized on by them." If it were not for Grant, Cooke would "not hold govts at par as things now stand." [70]

It is difficult to unravel the tangled skein of Cooke affairs in the fall of 1869. In accordance with their policy of making their assets more liquid, they tried to sell their Lake Superior & Mississippi bonds, of which the New York house held $100,000 and Philadelphia $40,000.[71] It became perfectly clear to the Cooke partners that in New York, as in Europe, there was too much competition from "many other good bonds offering all around us." [72] More bonds were offered than could have been absorbed at the prices demanded.

At the same time Jay Cooke had some experience in the difficulty of managing a railroad. The Lake Superior & Mississippi was meeting intense competition at various places. A projected rival railroad, the St. Croix & Superior, showed signs of reviving in the fall of 1869,[73] and the Mississippi terminal of the Lake Superior & Mississippi was threatened by the railroad interests of Milwaukee and Chicago. To counteract this in a measure, it was proposed that control be secured of the St. Paul & Sioux City, going southwest from Minneapolis, which was important in the wheat trade.[74] To assist further in securing wheat for the St. Paul-Duluth road, a grain-elevator concern, the Union Improvement and Elevator Company, was organized. The Cookes took a considerable interest in the company, though very reluctantly as it meant tying up money without any immediate prospects of gain.[75] Jay Cooke was thus learning that there were many interests to be conciliated or fought in building and managing a railroad in the new Northwest.

Again there were echoes of the government business. The Micawber of the firm, Henry Cooke, reported that Boutwell had said he would depend on them in refunding five-twenties: "I am sure we can *control* the whole business — if the Rothschilds will second our efforts." [76] The Rothschilds — always the Rothschilds! Moorhead was certain the great international house would co-operate with the Cookes in the refunding of United States five-twenties. Bleichroeders, the Rothschilds' agent in Berlin, proposed co-operation with Jay Cooke & Co., Young Stern of Stern Brothers, of London, was likewise interested, and Belmont was talking with the Cookes about business matters. "Our great business some day must be over the water and we must some time commence even in a small way to build it up." [77] The same refrain from Fahnestock!

It was not a happy prospect that lay ahead of Jay Cooke and his partners in the autumn of 1869. In the depressed condition of business it was obvious that they could hope for little profitable trading in government bonds, and there was no immediate prospect of refunding. Jay Cooke & Co. had either to retrench or find new work. Considering the condition of business at the time, selling bonds on commission might be dull but at least it would not be risky. Perhaps the Northern Pacific was the way out.

Jay Cooke Agrees to Finance the Northern Pacific

Much as he needed work, Jay Cooke did not regard the new project in the autumn with the confidence he had had in the summer. In October he was ready to "try to do it here in America — I will buckle on my armor . . . & see what can be done," [78] but as time passed his caution increased. He continued to study the reports of the surveyors and also voluminous reports, surveys, maps, and other information on the route available in Washington.[79]

His partners strengthened his doubts. Moorhead warned him to beware of his enthusiasm and urged that to undertake the project without a government guarantee of the bonds was "a fearful risk & one a Banking House ought not to take." He even disapproved of Cooke's plans to form a pool to take $5,000,000, because "it would be only a drop in the tub" and "those subscribing would look to you for relief." Moorhead would refuse to go into the scheme, for it meant ruin — "Let us follow the legitimate banking business." [80]

Fahnestock had also come to think that the task was impossible. A bonded debt of $58,000 a mile seemed large, he said, in comparison with the Union and Central Pacific's debt of $16,000 to $32,000 a mile. Even with a government guarantee, the bonds of the former were selling at 85. He admitted that the lands of the Northern Pacific were good ultimate security, "but American acres are like the sands upon the seashore." The unprofitable period before the road could operate was another problem. The market, moreover, was flooded with railroad bonds: "Today in this market are offered 18 new R R bonds. . . . Our advices from the Continent are that not only are dozens of new American RRs offering, but Russia, Turkey and every other Country is projecting new ones & marketing the securities." Without government concessions and an associate in Europe, the job should not be undertaken.[81]

Henry Cooke's belief in the possibility of securing government aid encouraged Jay Cooke to hold on to the project. The Washington brother, who needed badly to mend his own finances, was positive that government aid could be secured,[82] and he undertook to lead a campaign to that end. He found President Grant unwilling to increase the public burden when people were grumbling about expenses, but he would "say nothing against our project of aid from the Gov't." [83] The Cooke partners recognized that the situation required co-operation with the proposed southern route; they were ready to make common cause with General Frémont,[84] who was promoting a road along the thirty-second parallel from eastern Texas to San Diego.[85]

At this point James G. Blaine, the Speaker of the House of Representatives, offered Jay Cooke support. In the summer of 1869 the Speaker had undertaken to sell, in return for a sizable commission, the bonds of the Little Rock & Fort Smith Railroad in Arkansas which had been acquired by some Boston capitalists.[86] Since the Fort Smith was a possible link in a Southern Pacific road, Blaine approached the Cookes, advising them not to undertake financing the Northern Pacific without federal aid.[87] Jay Cooke consented to a conference with Blaine but he could not be tempted to buy Fort Smith bonds.[88]

The Speaker later wrote the financier a letter offering better terms.[89] Blaine offered Jay Cooke Fort Smith stocks and bonds at what was represented as a great bargain. But this was no mere investment; it was an opportunity to acquire power! Blaine reminded the financier that Napoleon lost because he neglected the *Quatre Bras*:

What I now offer you is the *Quatre Bras* of the Southern continental Rail Road. That secured the field of Waterloo is yours — *Yours without a Struggle!* That neglected, the enemy may carry off the prize. Your House can be and ought to be the leading Rail Road power of the world — and the sceptre is without your grasp. The field which I thus open to you is second only, *if indeed second*, to that great northern enterprise which you are so carefully considering. *By controlling both you double the profits of each* and you prevent the collisions and strifes which unjudicious rivalry would surely engender. And to have control of two Continental lines of Railway is an object, allow me to say, worthy of the highest ambition of any man!

The Speaker of the House of Representatives made another offer, the intent of which cannot be mistaken:

I may say without Egotism, that my position will enable me to render you services of vital importance & value — services for which I cannot desire or accept profit or gain to myself. I am willing however and ready to do all for you in my power at any time you may desire. . . . *I am willing to serve you where I am absolutely debarred from any participation in profits. Are you not willing to aid me when you can do so with profit to yourself at the same time.* Just how your subscription to the enterprise will aid me I need not explain — *Sufficient that it is so.*

Jay Cooke did not consider the offer.[90] He felt that the only thing to be gained was Blaine's support, which could be obtained in another way without the proposed payment of $91,500 for what would probably be worthless stocks and bonds. Moreover, Cooke did not want to be identified with congressional railroad cliques.[91] One suspects that the heavy loan to Blaine by the Washington house of Jay Cooke was granted to secure the Speaker's good will.[92] In view of the later disclosure of the Speaker's railroad affairs, it is evident that Jay Cooke was wise in refusing to enter into the scheme.

It soon became evident that there was no immediate prospect of government aid for the Northern Pacific, certainly not unless the Southern Pacific group should take the initiative. If they did so, the Northern Pacific would join them in working for legislation for both projects.[93]

As the autumn passed, the Northern Pacific promoters became restive.[94] The Black Friday panic had given Jay Cooke occasion for postponing his final decision, which was put off again and again throughout the autumn.[95] In November the president of the road strongly urged him to come to a decision, for the Northern Pacific had to act soon to forestall the action of other railroads which might deprive the enterprise of much valuable land in Minnesota.[96] Smith urged the point that Jay Cooke had become so fully identified with them and had become so essential a part of them in the public mind that they could not conceive of his not going on with the enterprise. Moreover, he said, "It is an enterprise worthy of your energies & in its civil and more especially in its great religious relations." Smith knew that an appeal to Cooke on behalf of the Christianization of the Northwest would have its effect.

By December Jay Cooke's partners had recovered somewhat from the shock of the panic, but they were still uncertain as to what they should do about the Northern Pacific. Fahnestock was impressed by the fact that Fisk & Hatch was taking over the financing of the Chesapeake & Ohio, which the Cookes had refused in the summer — "these railroads are the big plum now," [97] he said, and yet he agreed that there was much in the opposition of the old English fogies. Pitt Cooke, who had at first been very enthusiastic,[98] took a positive stand against the Northern Pacific. He warned that they should not get themselves "tied to the project in such a way that all the rest *can lay down on us*, as they surely will do as soon as they get us committed publicly & pecuniarily." [99] Moorhead continued his gloomy prognostications.[100] Of Jay Cooke's partners only Henry Cooke continued to be really optimistic.[101]

By this time, Jay Cooke was apparently no more enthusiastic about the Northern Pacific than were his New York partners.[102] Since there was no immediate prospect of government aid, he shrank from undertaking a project of such magnitude. He, therefore, proposed a modification of the original plan, that is, to abandon for the time being the construction of the whole road and to build only as far as the Red River, deferring a request for government aid until that line was built. He was encouraged by President Smith's assurance that they had no disposition to build faster than could be done prudently and economically and that they would curtail or stop work at any time when conditions made it advisable.

It was this assurance of President Smith that finally made Jay Cooke decide in favor of the Northern Pacific. In his decision he was joined by his partners, even by Moorhead, who gave hearty support to the modified plan.[103] Jay Cooke requested a number of changes in the preliminary agreement,[104] and the final contract was signed under the date of January 1, 1870.

It is important to note the main features of the contract.[105] Bonds, ranging from $100 to $10,000, should be issued by the company to the amount of $100,000,000 for 30 years at 7.3 per cent, principal and interest both payable in gold. These were to be secured by a first mortgage on the road and all its land and other property. Jay Cooke & Co. became the sole agent of the Northern Pacific for the sale of its bonds which, sold at par, should be credited to the company at the rate of 88 per cent of the face value plus accrued interest, both in lawful money of the United States. The cost of advertising and popularizing the loan should be borne by the railroad.

Jay Cooke & Co. was also to be general financial agent of the company and custodian of all its funds. The proceeds of all bond sales should be deposited with it until needed for disbursement on account of construction and equipment or to meet other legitimate expenditures of the road. The financial agent was given the right to purchase iron, rolling stock, and other things needed by the road, provided such purchases had the approval of the executive committee of the Northern Pacific. Jay Cooke & Co. bound itself to make advances to the company for construction and equipment to the amount of $500,000.

The contract gave Jay Cooke & Co. a strong position in the proprietorship of the Northern Pacific. It stipulated that the 12 original shares should be increased to 24, one-half going to Jay Cooke & Co. This portion the Cookes were to secure on the same condition as the 12 original shares had been obtained; but the relatively small amount resulting therefrom they were to retain as a fund for advertising. The 24 shares were to be entitled to about 80 per cent of the stock of $100,000,000, a small percentage to be turned over immediately as fully paid-up stock and the remainder as sections of the road were completed and put into operation; the remaining 20 per cent should be delivered to Jay Cooke & Co. as fully paid-up, at the rate of $200 of stock for each $1,000 in bonds sold. In other words, the Cookes by this contract received a potential claim on about three-fifths of the stock of the Northern Pacific. It is significant to note, however, that the bankers' control was not proportional to their ownership. They were allowed to select two out of thirteen directors and two of the eight members of the executive committee, and, if they disposed of any of their stock, they were to retain power of attorney over it.

A significant provision which had not been in the preliminary agreement was added to the contract. It was stipulated that a land company should be organized to own and improve town sites. One-half of its 24 shares should go to the bankers.

The final contract bound Jay Cooke & Co. to provide, within 30 days, $5,000,000 for financing construction of the road from a point on the Lake Superior & Mississippi Railroad, near Duluth, to the Red River. Beyond that, it made no definite time stipulation concerning the provision of funds or the construction of the road except that construction should proceed "with due and proper regard . . . to the success of the party of the second part in . . . the negotiation and sale of the securities of the Company."

Though in the literal meaning of the contract, Jay Cooke & Co. assumed little risk as financial agents for the Northern Pacific — they did not guarantee the sale of bonds beyond $5,000,000 and they bound themselves to advance only $500,000 — the potential profits were considerable. The Cookes expected to make a commission of 12 cents on every dollar of bonds sold without having to bear the cost of popularizing the loan. The funds of the road deposited with them would cost them little and might add considerably to their working capital. Furthermore, if the project were successful, the Northern Pacific account would probably remain with Jay Cooke & Co. in the future. The purchase of iron and equipment also promised earnings, that is, from commissions and credit granted by the seller and commission on bonds used in payment. If the project were successful, the Cooke firm might profit considerably from its stock in the Northern Pacific and its subsidiary land company. The bankers had no feeling of assurance, however, that the undertaking would be very profitable.

The promise of work for the Northern Pacific shed some light on an otherwise gloomy prospect at the beginning of 1870.[106] The year 1869 had brought worry, dissension among the partners, but little in the way of profits. The Washington house had nothing to divide. The New York house had nothing, for it had paid its heavy tribute to the falling market for government bonds and to the gold panic. The New Yorkers had had to put into effect a drastic cut in their expenses.[107] Only the Philadelphia house, sticking to its floating of new securities and its commission business, had something to distribute among the partners, a total of $150,000.[108] Would the business of the Northern Pacific be the way out of the difficulties of Jay Cooke & Co.? As it appeared to Jay Cooke, the Northern Pacific might prove profitable, but in any event such work appeared much less risky than a jobbing business in government securities in such uncertain times.

THE NORTHERN PACIFIC UNDER WAY
1870

Two thousand miles of railway to be built through a wilderness! The Northern Pacific was projected to begin at the westernmost point of Lake Superior, where were Duluth, speculative offspring of the Lake Superior & Mississippi Railroad, and, across the bay, Superior City, object of the waning hopes of many a town-lot gambler. In the wide stretch of territory between Lake Superior and the Missouri River there were no white settlements or villages, save military posts, Indian agencies, and trading stations; it was still the land of the Indian, consisting only of dense pine forests, almost untouched by the axe, and prairies not yet familiar with the plow. The rough land between the Missouri and the mountains was buffalo hunting ground, the paradise of the Indian. At the falls of the Missouri were Fort Benton and a small village. In the mountains of Montana, which had only recently been dignified by territorial organization, were a few self-sustaining mining settlements; in Idaho, likewise, a few mining villages; then nothing until one reached Walla Walla in Washington Territory. Near the coast were the thriving city of Portland on the Oregon side of the Columbia River and small villages on the Sound fostered by the great forests at their back. In all, two thousand miles of country inhabited mostly by the Indians!

The region was not altogether without trade. From the Hudson Bay and Pembina districts, freight came up the Red River and was carried to St. Paul by the creaking Red River carts. On the Missouri as far as Fort Benton went steamboats which carried supplies up the river, and buffalo hides, beef cattle, and precious metals down. Branches of the Columbia River gave to the Idaho settlements an outlet down the Columbia, by water and short railroads, or a connection with the Central Pacific country.

Even though there was little trade, the resources were there, the richness of giant pine, black soil, silver, and gold, and streams and forests filled with wild life. That this country would sometime be opened up to the use of man was as certain as anything could be. The question was whether a road could be built and sustained until the country had been settled. When would that be? The whole problem was obviously one of timing. Indeed, one of the most important as well as one of the most difficult aspects of promotion and investment is timing. It is not so hard to judge the direction of change — it was clear around 1870 that the West would eventually be settled and that railroads would be needed; but to judge the rate at which the change would come was quite another matter.

The Northern Pacific was the biggest single business enterprise that had up to that time been undertaken in the United States. The Erie Canal had been a marvel in its day, and as an engineering feat the Union Pacific and the Central Pacific railroads, which connected a branch of the Father of Waters with the great western ocean, were comparable with the Northern Pacific. As business enterprises, however, those differed vastly from the Northern Pacific. The Erie Canal had, with the aid of the great State of New York, been built to serve existing needs. The completed Pacific railroads, which had accomplished through two organizations what the projected Northern Pacific planned to do in one, had leaned heavily on the strong arm of the federal government and had a significant financial and sectional backing, the Central Pacific being based on the developed needs and capital of California. But the Northern Pacific started to build single-handed through a tremendous sweep of unoccupied territory.

The Philadelphia banker had good reason to think that he could do the unusual thing. His houses had a much greater prestige than those which had financed the Union and Central Pacific roads. Moreover, Jay Cooke had the success of his Civil War financing to give him the assurance that he could do great things. Indeed, there was in his mind much similarity between financing the war and financing the building of the great northwestern railroad. Both had national significance; appeals could be made for both on the basis of patriotism and social good. It was worthy of a great people to save the Union; it was similarly worthy of a great people to bring to the use of man a wilderness which could be made to provide happy homes for millions and produce wealth for the whole nation.

The Land Grant, the Hope of the Northern Pacific

The foundation of Jay Cooke's hopes for the Northern Pacific was its lands. Bond sales would have to bear the immediate burden of construction, and a government guarantee of interest or other tangible aid would give invaluable support. But the fundamentals were land sales and traffic. To understand the importance of the lands in Jay Cooke's Northern Pacific plans is essential to an understanding of the whole negotiation.

Jay Cooke had a vision of the Northwest, peopled and rich. To occupy it would take time, it is true, but things had been moving fast in the United States since the war. It was not impossible that, with proper management, millions of people could in a few years be moved onto the rich prairies. If they knew its promise, they would come. Hence publicity and organization to bring them. Jay Cooke was a master at both. He had commanded capital during the war. Why not organize people now?

The settlement of the road's lands would accomplish two objects: (1) it would provide a means of redeeming large amounts of bonds at once and build up a sinking fund for paying off the bonds at their maturity; and (2) it would provide traffic, that essential to a railroad's success.

Pioneer that he in reality was, Jay Cooke looked upon land as the most substantial wealth. It was the Illinois Central, which had had a long and successful experience in selling its land grant, which encouraged him to have faith in lands as a support for railroads. A circular issued by Jay Cooke & Co. under the date of April 24, 1871, illustrates the banker's position on this question:

If the land grant of the Illinois Central has enabled the road to pay a large dividend annually, and to maintain its stock upon the market at $140 per share, what will a land grant of much better quality and six times as great per mile, enable the Northern Pacific Railroad to pay to its stockholders? . . . It is calculated that the sale of 287,000 acres of land annually, at only $4 per acre, and the investment of the proceeds in Northern Pacific bonds, as a Sinking Fund, compounded semi-annually, will pay off the whole debt of the Northern Pacific Railroad Company before maturity.

Jay Cooke had taken measures to assure that the income from lands should be used to redeem the bonds. His contract with the road stipulated that all proceeds from the sale of lands should be deposited with the trustees of the bondholders to be invested in first-mortgage bonds at not over 10 per cent above the face value of the bonds and accrued interest. Bonds could also be used in payment for lands at the same rate. It was stipulated that a minimum of $2.50 an acre should be charged for the land. In order to make certain that proceeds from land sales should be used to redeem bonds, Jay Cooke arranged that he himself and J. Edgar Thomson, president of the Pennsylvania Railroad, should act as trustees of the bondholders.[1]

The banker realized that strong efforts would be necessary to sell and colonize the lands. There was no question but that the Fertile Belt, as the publicity of the Northern Pacific named the territory, would sometime be settled, for the tide of immigration was already flowing into accessible places; but Jay Cooke believed that immigration and settlement would have to be stimulated with every means possible if it should come soon enough to help the road. He, therefore, from the very first urged that the road set up an organization for selling and colonizing its lands. A circular issued by his firm on October 20, 1869, and the pamphlet entitled *The Northern Pacific Railroad: Its Route, Resources, Progress and Business* give the essentials of his plans.

Jay Cooke suggested that land offices should be established by the Northern Pacific in various places in the United States and in Europe, especially in Germany, Holland, and the Scandinavian countries. Able men should be placed at the head of these offices, and they should secure the help of the press, local bankers, and foreign ministers and consuls. As soon as the construction of a

25-mile section of the road had been completed, the land thereupon acquired from the government should be minutely surveyed and plotted. The distinctive feature of each quarter-section should be fully recorded, "showing woods, streams, lakes, prairies, hillocks, etc." From this information the land buyer or settler could select his farm and even the site of his buildings. The railroad should aid him by extending liberal credit on the lands purchased. But that was not all; the land offices should have models of small houses to cost from $200 to $1,000, which the railroad would have "built, in the lumber country around our Road in Minnesota, by Machinery and from the same pattern, all ready to put up, and can be erected in a day, the Railroad conveying them to the land selected." The prospective settler could select his house and have it put up before he arrived.

The Northern Pacific should also see that the immigrant's or settler's journey to his new home was economical, safe, and pleasant. To prevent the discomforts, indignities, and even dangers which were the common lot of the immigrants, an agent of the company should accompany groups of immigrants; he should see that they were properly cared for on board ship and he should also protect them from "sharpers" and look after their comfort after landing. Let one such group arrive and see their beautiful new land, and they would by their letters to those back home induce many more to come! It was a sound idea and one that should in time have worked well.

An interesting feature of Jay Cooke's plans was his recognition of the value of transplanting communities: "We will seek to gather together into localities such as Westfield, Northampton, Lowell &c. communities of emigrants, taking some from every class of the community, & sending them in a body, to establish a town or village of their own. . . . The same idea of transferring communities will be extended to Great Britain & all parts of Europe." Such communities should, however, be superior: "We want good Presbyterian & Congregational communities. They are highly intellectual. You cannot often find institutions like Oberlin. . . . I wish we had a dozen Oberlins along the line of our road." [2] All this shows that Cooke had in view the building of permanent settlements of high quality.

Jay Cooke's plans with regard to the lands of the Northern Pacific reveal both his strength and his weakness. He had a remarkable facility at making plans for doing great things, and for doing them in a way which was from a social point of view, and hence from the long-time business point of view, most commendable. But he did not hedge his purposes or plans with power; though he staked the success of the enterprise on the sale and settlement of lands, he himself could act only in an advisory capacity in setting up or directing the organization which was to handle the matter so vital to the success of the Northern Pacific and hence to his financing of the enterprise.

The Northern Pacific Pool is Formed

The general direction of Jay Cooke's strategy in Northern Pacific financing was well thought out. The first move was to secure the means with which to finance the building of the road from Lake Superior to the Red River, that is, to the western boundary of Minnesota. On the strength of the success of this first effort should be based two other moves: a campaign would be launched for selling bonds abroad and at home and an appeal made for government aid. Eventually the stimulation of immigration was expected to settle the lands, providing funds from land sales with which to repurchase bonds and in time furnishing traffic for the road.[3]

As soon as the final agreement with the Northern Pacific had been made, Jay Cooke proceeded to carry out his first plan by organizing a pool to furnish the means with which to build to the Red River. The terms of the pool agreement were made very attractive. The subscribers were to purchase at par $5,000,000 of Northern Pacific bonds, bearing 7.3 per cent interest in gold, and, in addition, 12 out of the 24 interests in the company, that is, the half allotted to Jay Cooke & Co., for which $600,000 should be paid. The pool subscription was broken up into 12 shares costing $466,667 each, which could be subdivided into smaller parts. Payments were to be instalments spread over about 15 months. The stock was to be allotted as sections of the road were completed, the pool finally receiving $41,000,500, or almost half of the total stock. It was stipulated that the subscribers should leave their stock proxies with Jay Cooke & Co. and that they should not dispose of any of the bonds for which they subscribed, except with the consent of Jay Cooke & Co., at least until such sales should cease to interfere with the plans of the company for financing the construction and equipment of the whole line of the road.[4]

As a further inducement it was designed "to organize a private Land Company for the purchase and sale of desirable town sites, and other valuable lands" from which large profits were anticipated. Interest in this concern was to be divided in the same proportion as subscriptions to the pool. Jay Cooke looked upon the land company as one of the best features of the whole scheme [5] and he recommended it very strongly to pool subscribers.

The pool campaign opened early in January, 1870. The object was not only to sell the pool bonds but also to get prominent men to invest. Fahnestock urged Jay Cooke to "get Tom Scott," the vice-president of the Pennsylvania Railroad — "The endorsement of a large R. R. man goes a great way." He reported that if the interest of Joy of the Michigan Central could be won, Weld and Thayer of Boston would invest; they were men with clean hands as they were not concerned in Crédit Mobilier. Erastus Corning would doubtless take hold. Belmont would be valuable because he was a Democrat. There were hopes of interesting President Garrett of the Baltimore & Ohio. And so on. Wilkeson urged upon Jay Cooke that "Henry Ward Beecher will, I think, *if sweetened to the highest extent you sweeten your Philadelphia* friends, sell out $10,000 Pacific Mail, and invest in our Bonds. He intimated as much to me just now. Next to Horace Greeley he is the most important man in America to get." [6]

Jay Cooke managed the drive for pool subscriptions with his usual enthusiasm. He visited Washington, Baltimore, and New York, and talked with many prominent men. His energy and drive again brought success of a kind; by January 24 the entire

A TYPICAL LETTER OF JAY COOKE

pool had been taken.[7] But among the subscribers were none of the prominent railroad men or financiers whom the Cookes had hoped to enlist.

Though the pool campaign was made to appear in the best light by Jay Cooke, there is no question but that it proved extremely disappointing. Fahnestock was so impressed with the difficulty of forming the pool that he wrote a strong warning to his senior partner. He objected to making advances for pool subscribers: "In case of failure of Congressional aid it might prove a long winded investment and we ought to be careful to limit the investment to amounts which people can afford to have tied up." [8]

Again Fahnestock cautioned Jay Cooke concerning the whole project.[9] "I cant for the life of me get up *your* enthusiasm in the Northn Pacif, chiefly I suppose for the reason that at every step here I am confronted by the experience of others who have bonds to sell and *cannot place them.* By the experience of the foreign houses who know the number and relative cheapness of bonds now offering in Europe." Bonds of the Central Pacific were then selling in New York at 94, Union Pacifics at 84, Missouri Pacifics at 88 to 90 — "all earning money and not dependent upon Congressional favor for their actual construction." Kansas Pacific gold sevens were selling in Frankfort at 63, which was equal to 77 in currency in New York. These bonds did not have so much land behind them as the Northern Pacific, but they had "*more road* and govt aid besides in hard subsidy." Though people had faith in Jay Cooke's ability, held Fahnestock, they were fearful that the thing might break down. They argued that lands could not build the road in half a dozen years, which was a long time to wait for earnings and to pay interest.

Fahnestock warned that they should face the thing squarely. "I dont like the fact that capitalists of the larger sort do not take to the scheme and the heaviest takers are among parties reached by personal influence." This was a trenchant judgment that Jay Cooke should not have disregarded. With a prophetic note of warning the New Yorker stated that while he was as anxious as Cooke "to make all the profits that are to be made out of the money passing through our hands," he believed "that people who invest in this enterprise will most of them do it upon Jay Cooke's *recommendation* and reputation, and if the investment should *not* be profitable the reputation of the house would suffer correspondingly." [10]

But, nevertheless, plans went ahead for the road. As soon as it became evident that the pool would supply some means, engineers were put to work to make surveys preliminary to construction. On February 15 came the enthusiastic message from the chief engineer of the Northern Pacific in Minnesota: "Ground broke on the Northern Pacific Railroad to-day One hundred men at work. Hurrah for the great enterprise! Shall push the work vigorously." [11] Jay Cooke thus came to be harnessed to the job. It was up to him to furnish the money. By that time the banker had become an aggressive promoter of the Northern Pacific.

MORTGAGING THE LAND GRANT

The pool had subscribed to mortgage bonds, but as the charter and amendments then stood only the railroad and its telegraph line could be used as security for a mortgage. [12] Since there was neither railway nor telegraph line, that was no basis for a bond issue and it was imperative to provide further security for the bonds. The only possibility was the land grant, but to mortgage the land grant required further legislation. Hence the Northern Pacific again turned to Congress. On February 8, 1870, a joint resolution was introduced in the Senate by Ramsey of Minnesota. [13] The resolution proposed that the Northern Pacific be authorized to issue bonds secured by a mortgage on all the property and rights of the company including its land grant. It also provided for a change in the route in Washington Territory as suggested by Engineer Roberts, which actually meant an increase in the land granted.

The Cookes knew that this particular request would meet strong opposition. They did not, therefore, enter upon the struggle unprepared. Long negotiations were carried on with some of the promoters of the Southern Pacific. [14] Ex-Governor Marshall of Minnesota was allotted a liberal salary and a share in the pool, to be carried by the Cookes, with the idea that he should aid the Northern Pacific cause;[15] Marshall did not then hold public office but his political experience and contacts gave him not a little influence. Ignatius Donnelly, that free lance of Minnesota politics, the author of the *Great Cryptogram*, who had a remarkable mind and had had considerable experience in Congress but who possessed more enemies than friends, was hired to lobby for the Cooke interests in Washington.[16] Congressman Wilson of Minnesota was allotted a share in the pool with the idea that he should serve as a checkmate to Oakes Ames of Massachusetts.[17] Speaker Blaine, who was interested in the Southern Pacific because of his Fort Smith connections, received a substantial loan from the Washington house of the Cookes.[18] W. E. Chandler, a politician then on free foot, was retained as Northern Pacific attorney in Washington.[19] Throughout the course of the bill, the Cookes and the Northern Pacific lobby patched weak places, and the press was, as usual, remembered.[20]

When the resolution came up for discussion in the Senate, a powerful minority used every parliamentary device to kill or maim the bill. It was clear that the Union Pacific was fighting it hard.[21] But its most vocal senatorial enemies came from Ohio, Illinois, Iowa, Kansas, and California; Ramsey of Minnesota was none too enthusiastic — he was friendly toward a rival project in his own State. The mortgaging of the land grant was not seriously questioned. The attack was on further concessions to the road on the grounds that the Northern Pacific's grant was already twice as large per mile as that of any other road and that railroad corporations were using their lands and power in a way which was detrimental to the interests of bona fide settlers.[22] Here was clear evidence of that hostility to railroads which shortly broke out in the Granger Movement. But it is likely that the resolution would have passed if the provisions extending the land grant area had been withdrawn or if the supporters of the measure had acceded to limiting the price of the land to $2.50 an acre.[23]

Several amendments were proposed. Thurman of Ohio would

limit the sale of all the land grant, except for town lots, depots, and so on, to actual settlers in lots of 160 acres or less at a maximum price of $1.25 an acre, and he would require the road to carry government troops and supplies without charge. Cameron of Pennsylvania, who had been reminded by Jay Cooke of the faithful support the Cookes had given him, proposed an amendment limiting the iron used in building the Northern Pacific to that produced in the United States. "In the State of Pennsylvania?" queried Pomeroy of Kansas. "In Kansas if you like," replied suave Cameron of the iron State! [24]

Some of those amendments were dangerous to the Northern Pacific. To put severe limitations on the sale of lands would destroy the possibility of profits from the lands and thus doom the project. Government troops and supplies were, moreover, expected to furnish much of the income of the road in the Missouri River region. Jay Cooke was disgusted; it was all wrong, he said, that, when capitalists were ready to raise money, politicians should throw obstacles in the way of what was just and right. [25] To counteract the opposition he instructed his brother to make any pledges necessary to aid in the passage of other bills, as for instance the Southern Pacific Railroad bill. [26] On April 20 enough supporters were secured in the Senate to pass the Northern Pacific resolution, with Cameron's iron amendment, 40 to 11. [27]

In the meantime the press had taken up the fight. A conspicuous figure in the contest was, again, the Philadelphia *Ledger*. On April 19 and 25 this newspaper attacked the Northern Pacific in long editorials which were widely quoted both in the United States and Europe. "Public attention all over the country," it said, "is being aroused to the huge robberies of the public domain," four western railroads having been granted nearly as much land as the States of Ohio, Indiana, Illinois, Wisconsin, and Michigan contained. The Northern Pacific, the greatest beneficiary of the government, was crying for more. The *Ledger*, suggesting that a commission of 12 per cent, or $600,000 on $5,000,000, indicated a most extraordinary risk, described the Northern Pacific as a get-rich-quick scheme of a ring of operators who had control of the project but had put comparatively little, if any, money into it.

The *Ledger* made a gloomy prognostication about the financial conditions which would follow upon the present orgy of investments:

There is scarcely a doubt that the next financial crisis in this country will come through the wild and extravagant expenditures of money on railroads, many of which projects are not only in advance of any existing business from which they can derive the least traffic, but it is openly confessed that the roads are expected to make the business on which they hope to live. Not only is this so, but there are numerous competing lines of this character, rendering it physically and morally impossible that an adequate trade can grow up to their capacity and maintenance in the next fifty years.

Looking backward, it is clear that the *Ledger* was, on the whole, right with respect both to the Northern Pacific and the dangers inherent in too extensive railroad building. Since the Cookes were committed to the enterprise, however, they could not overlook this criticism. Take the *Ledger* article to Grant and show him what kind of a friend he has, Jay Cooke wrote his Washington brother. As early as February he had tried to spike Anthony Drexel's friendship with President Grant when he had suggested to his Washington brother, remembering Grant's hatred of former President Johnson, that he should let fall on the ear of Grant that "Tony was the only man who met Andy Johnson at the Broad St. Depot & walked arm in arm with him to the carriage." [28] The Cookes met those attacks with increased publicity in newspapers. The Philadelphia *Evening Bulletin* and *Press* were looked after. The editor of the *Washington Chronicle* was reserved an interest in the Northern Pacific pool with instructions to follow the *Bulletin*.[29] The press of the country was expected to copy these prominent papers.

Though the Northern Pacific bill had passed the Senate, the Cookes anticipated a stiff fight in the House. "We are taking measures to have the House thoroughly canvassed," wrote Henry to Jay. "There are three men in the House whom I deem it very important to make our *active* friends, Gen. Butler, Logan and Schenck. The latter we have already. Butler & Logan *you* must see." Make Butler a retainer as counsel in the interest of the road, ordered Jay Cooke. And thereby hangs a tale! It was pure oversight that Ben Butler had not already been attended to. One of the Cooke lobbyists, W. E. Chandler, informed Jay Cooke that Butler had a right to expect the banker to communicate with him on the subject. A certain congressman told the truth when he informed the House of Representatives that the Northern Pacific men had been warned that loud voices would be raised against them if they did not take proper steps. Chandler had told Butler that he, himself, was for the bill because he was a friend of Jay Cooke. "So am I Mr. Cooke's friend," came the classic reply, "but I do not always go on the principle of 'Love me — love my dog.' Besides Jay has said nothing to me of this." Butler was in the meantime promptly attended to.[30]

The Northern Pacific mortgage campaign in Congress calls forth some pertinent questions and reflections. We have here what seems like political bribery, and it is by no means an isolated instance. Yet it is impossible to characterize it as outright bribery. In the voluminous correspondence of Jay Cooke and his partners, there is no clear evidence of direct purchase of votes or influence. Jay Cooke & Co. carried an option on bonds for a congressman whose favor was desired, granted him a loan, or retained him as counsel or to give speeches on the Northern Pacific. It also contributed to election funds and maintained an active lobby in Washington. Though this might be said not to transgress directly any rule of political morality, it is undeniable that there was the intention to secure political favors.

It is pertinent to ask why Jay Cooke and his associates resorted to such measures. It has become almost traditional in America to place the blame for such practices on business. To say that business alone is responsible, however, only partially allocates the blame. It is true that there were many business men who, like Drew or Gould or Fisk, traded on the weaknesses of the politician, and there were many more who were not neglectful of opportunities for obtaining favors from the government. At the same time it cannot be denied that Jay Cooke and his contemporaries often became the victims of the politician who daringly collected his toll. That was the time when the degradation of American democracy had first reached its depths. Universal suffrage — enjoyed by people of diverse origin and varying political ideals and by people who had discovered that in this land of rich resources and great opportunities the political means could secure for them what their economic means were inadequate to obtain — had brought into the seat of government a sorry lot of men. There were some fine characters among them, men who were really great public servants, but there were so many of the other kind that one American historian has called this the time of the nadir of national disgrace.

Given such a system, should Jay Cooke have refused to attempt to influence public officers? By so doing he would inevitably have eliminated himself from some business which was both profitable to him and useful to society. By the same token, all business men in similar situations would have done the same, which action would have put an immense check on productive activity. It is a question whether bribery was not a function of American "democracy" and one of the recognized means of securing action in a rapidly developing country where the political constitution and philosophy were high above the cultural and moral level of the people. Undoubtedly Jay Cooke did not reason very far in this matter. He saw in the hungry politician a force which would work against him if he did not pay, and being a man of action he chose to pay the price.

In the House as in the Senate the northern tier of central States was for the bill and their immediate neighbors to the south, against. On May 5 there was tense filibustering — "I wouldnt pass through another such day of anxiety and suspense for a dozen Pacific Railroads," said Henry Cooke.[31] Donnelly saw in the opposition the hands of the Central and the Union Pacific, who would not even hesitate to use corruption, he said, to defeat the Northern Pacific. "If they have defaulted in paying interest a resolution might be put through . . . to place the road in the hands of government officers. If this was rushed through the

House and sent to Senate it would bring them to their knees." [32]
In the jungle of business, beast was ready to devour beast!

On May 10 and 11 there was filibustering again. The Northern
Pacific supporters felt that they were being held up by an unreasonable minority, while the opposition maintained that they
were only asking for an opportunity to get a consideration of the
bill and its amendments.[33] The supporters of the Northern Pacific
had refused to compromise on amendments and were to all
appearances attempting to force the bill through the House.[34]
Twenty-four new amendments were offered, some of which were
ludicrous — one stipulated that only Americans could buy the
stock of the road and that all American citizens should ride on
Northern Pacific trains free of charge; another, that the road pay
7 per cent of its gross earnings to the States and territories
through which it passed!

The bill went back to the committee. The Cookes continued
to bring influence to bear on some important men in the House.
Governor Geary canvassed his Pennsylvania delegation, and
President Grant made it known that he thought the bill ought to
pass.[35] (Had the Cookes promised to support the President's
favorite project, the annexation of San Domingo?[36]) Jay Cooke,
restive over the delay in bringing the bill up for vote, was daily
informed by Wilkeson of the progress of the prodigal: May 20,
kill the fatted calf; May 23, keep the fatted calf in clover; and
then dolefully on May 24, turn the fatted calf back into the
pasture![37]

On May 25 the bill was reported for passing without amendment. The battle raged, but on the next day the resolution was
passed without amendment.[38] Much to the relief of Jay Cooke,
it was signed by the President, though against strong opposition
in the Cabinet and criticism in the press.[39] Of the 85 negative
votes, 56 were contributed by New York, Pennsylvania, Ohio,
Indiana, Illinois, and Wisconsin. In the opinion of Ignatius
Donnelly the bill was carried by the support of the other Pacific
railways;[40] Oakes Ames voted for the measure, but whether it
was a promise or a threat which had made the Bostonian change
his mind is not known.

The way was clear for the issue of Northern Pacific bonds, and the road had a more magnificent land grant even than before — one which no other road could equal. But in a real sense this was not a victory. The long struggle in Congress had delayed construction of the Northern Pacific, and the weakness of the road had been broadcast at home and abroad. It was clear, moreover, that the enterprise would not be granted further favors by Congress.

The Northern Pacific Again Fails in Europe, 1870

While the Northern Pacific political campaign was being waged in Washington, its financial campaign was extended to Europe. Though the Cookes had failed with the Rothschilds, there were in London, Frankfort, and Paris, and in other financial centers such as Amsterdam, Brussels, and Vienna, many bankers who commanded rich money bags and who were willing to pour out their treasure for a consideration.

Those bankers were, however, far from friendly to many enterprises that came their way. European capital had been badly scorched by the finance companies and railroad mania that had swept over Europe in the 'fifties and 'sixties. The panic of 1866 had made bankers and capitalists think; it had left them extremely cautious and for a time they dared take little but government bonds. By 1870 their interest in governments had developed into another mania; money was poured into the coffers of governments, stable or unstable, sound or unsound, and undeveloped countries like Turkey, Russia, India, Egypt, Honduras, Paraguay, Argentine, and Peru threw a magic spell over European capital.[41]

At the same time American railroad securities were in considerable disrepute abroad. The speculation and fraud in Erie shares and Atlantic & Great Western bonds and debentures had stimulated antipathy to all American securities, especially those of railroads. "The New York speculators will find," said the London *Bankers' Magazine* early in 1870, "that they cannot with impunity trifle with the interests of English investors without permanently damaging the market for their securities." [42]

One aspect of the European situation was in the Northern Pacific's favor. The depression of 1866 had lifted and capital was more buoyant though there was not yet a clearly defined upward trend. The improvements in the market were spasmodic rather than continuous, and the outbreak of the Franco-Prussian War created a serious panic in July of 1870 and initiated a strike of capital which continued to weaken the markets throughout the remainder of the year.[43]

Unfortunately, the European negotiation was entrusted to George B. Sargent of Duluth. Jay Cooke could not be spared. Moorhead had failed once. Fahnestock might have gone, but he was never very enthusiastic over the Northern Pacific. One may well ask why Sargent was chosen for the mission. He was very personable; he had the gift of speech, and he had tremendous enthusiasm for the Northern Pacific — in Jay Cooke's mind a very important thing. But he was not convincing; he was pompous, and he depended on extravagant living and conspicuous dinners for impressing his prospects. Indeed, Sargent was a typical western real-estate promoter.

The European negotiation was opened in New York in connection with Budge, Schiff & Co., a three-year-old house in which Jacob Schiff and Henry Budge were partners.[44] The house was without much means or prestige; Schiff had joined it almost penniless in 1867 at the age of 19, but Budge had banking connections in Frankfort, from whence the partners had come. Budge, Schiff & Co. secured from the Cookes a definite offer of a European agency. The plan was that they should associate with themselves Moritz Budge, of Frankfort, and Robert Thode & Co., of Berlin, for selling Northern Pacifics in Germany and Holland. Budge, Schiff & Co. took a share in the pool. They were to sell the bonds at par in currency, receiving an allowance for publicity and advertising and a commission of 10 per cent in stock and 6 per cent in cash.[45]

The association of Jay Cooke & Co. with this young house is very significant. The Cookes were not very enthusiastic over it. Jay Cooke thought that there was an advantage in the fact that Budge and Schiff were young and anxious to succeed, but Fahnestock was worried by the fact that they had everything to gain and nothing to lose.[46] Fahnestock had tried to win Bleichroeders, Rothschilds' agents in Berlin, through their New York representative.[47] Because of Moorhead's failure with the Rothschilds, the New York partner was sceptical of making any strong European connection and believed that Budge, Schiff & Co. was the best they could do.

In March, Sargent and Henry Budge sailed for Europe.[48] After a brief negotiation, the broker secured the promise of co-operation from Moritz Budge and Robert Thode and signed a final agreement with Jay Cooke & Co. The German bankers agreed to sell $50,000,000 in Northern Pacific bonds through agents whom they proposed to secure throughout western Europe. An extra commission of 1 per cent in cash and 3 per cent in stock was to be allowed if $20,000,000 were sold before January 1, 1871. As a pledge of their good faith, the associates deposited half a million in gold with Jay Cooke & Co. Unless renewed, the contract was to expire on January 1, 1871.[49]

The plan was to popularize the bonds and sell them in small amounts to a large number of investors. This required extensive publicity. The German agents were allowed $100,000 for this purpose,[50] and Henry Budge and Sargent co-operated with them in working up a favorable opinion. The latter visited the larger cities of Germany and Holland, establishing himself wherever he went in a conspicuous style.[51] Some 30 newspapers in Frankfort, Berlin, Hamburg and other places were won to the support of the Northern Pacific. Even the *Neue Frankfurter Zeitung*, the most influential newspaper in South Germany and a consistent critic of American enterprises, was won over.[52]

But the press is like a two-edged sword, and there arose a tremendous counter-publicity. In England and on the Continent circulars condemning the road were sent to bankers,[53] and newspapers carried articles to discredit it.

The climax of the attack was the action of the Berlin *Bourse* in cautioning investors against purchasing American first-mortgage railroad bonds.[54] In an open letter to the *Bourse*, dated July 16, 1870, Jay Cooke did his best to dispel the opposition. He urged that during his thirty years in railroad finance he had never fostered an enterprise which had failed to pay its bonds and interest punctually. After explaining at length the great possibilities of his road, he invited the *Bourse* to send a committee, at his expense, to America to investigate the project. This letter was printed and distributed widely as a pamphlet.

The Cookes recognized in the anti-Northern Pacific propaganda the hand of the Philadelphia *Ledger*. The evidence for this seems fairly substantial; most conclusive is the fact that the Drexel paper in the spring of 1870 made severe attacks on the Northern Pacific, which were copied far and wide and which the *Ledger* was said to have mailed to bankers in Europe and America.[55] The strong criticism of the Northern Pacific by *The Times* of London was thought to have been due to the friendship of the financial editor of *The Times* and the editor of the *Ledger*.[56]

It is impossible to know how far these attacks injured the cause of the Northern Pacific in Europe. Moorhead believed that they had little effect one way or the other — people in Europe depended upon facts, not propaganda, he said;[57] but anyone who is familiar with the loans which were taken by Europe in 1870 doubts that European investors were especially discriminating. It is doubtful whether there was at the time much interest in American railroads, but criticism of Jay Cooke's project might well have prevented the building up of a favorable opinion.

The German market was none too promising, and it became evident that it would be necessary to issue bonds in England at the same time. Sargent, therefore, proceeded to London. There he found strong feeling against American railway securities.[58] Moreover, no road was offering so large an issue as the Northern Pacific. In March, Turners, of New York and London, offered $5,000,000 of first-mortgage bonds of the Indianapolis, Bloomington and Western, an Indiana and Illinois road then almost completed; and in April, J. S. Morgan offered $4,000,000 in gold 7 per cent first-mortgage bonds of the Illinois and St. Louis Bridge Co.[59] Both these projects would serve needs already existing.

Early in May, Sargent confidently reported to Jay Cooke that the General Credit and Discount Company would undertake to sell their bonds. To have won this house would have been an answer to the Cookes' prayer — a strong house would have assured success. But they found all kinds of objections: among other things, they did not like to work under the German bankers who had the general agency for Europe; they wanted to wait for the favorable vote of Congress on the Northern Pacific mortgage bill; and they were frightened by the attack of the *Ledger*. Sargent tried to soothe them with a sumptuous dinner on the Fourth of July, about which he wrote to Jay Cooke.[60]

I send you a bill of fare and list of guests to a dinner I gave McDonald & Lord Borthwick Sampson [of *The Times*] & others. It was a *grand success* and when I say so you know what it means. I had the American flag floating from my apartments at Alexandria Hotel and which looks out on *Hyde Park* — and a Band of music playing alternately American & English airs during the whole dinner — There never was a dinner went off with better feeling — Old Macdonald of Genl Credit sung a National Scottish song with *great* credit to himself altho it was too late in the evening to be criticized much.

One must not judge Sargent's method too harshly; there was precedent for it in London in connection with government loans.[61]

Two days later the General Credit and Discount Company decided not to undertake to sell Northern Pacifics unless three trustees could be appointed in England to hold the funds, subject to the certificate from time to time of some English engineer sent to report. Sargent would not consider the suggestion. And yet the negotiation was not entirely closed, he said, before the Franco-Prussian War broke out.[62] With his usual facility at finding excuses and a great feeling for the dramatic, he blamed the war for stopping the negotiation.

The first effect of the war was panic and paralysis in the securities trade; there was fear the conflict might become general.[63] A reaction soon set in; when it became apparent that the war would last longer than had at first been anticipated, the market settled down and a strike of capital followed. It was ruinous under war conditions to try to place Northern Pacifics. Budge called off negotiations in Germany.[64] The loan agent was, however, instructed to remain in Europe.[65]

Sargent had become impressed with the necessity of breaking with the Budge, Schiff associates. They were difficult to deal with and had proved a real handicap in London; in view of the war there was less chance than ever that anything could be accomplished in Germany. Hence it was urged that the war be used as a pretext for breaking the contract with them. It appears from the Jay Cooke correspondence that there was an opportunity to break the contract shortly after the war began, as both Robert Thode and Henry Budge requested the return of their deposit of half a million — the panic in Germany resulting from the war had put them in a difficult place. Jay Cooke, however, refused to give up the deposit; it is quite possible that Jay Cooke & Co. found it difficult to part with half a million in gold at that time. The Cookes could have had no illusions about the usefulness of their European associates, for the tone of the Germans' letters showed that little co-operation could be expected.[66]

The next episode in the wanderings of Sargent and his Northern Pacific cause promised to be significant. Through the Budges, Sargent had been introduced to Bischoffsheim & Goldschmidt, of London. The Bischoffsheims were one of those Jewish banking families with good connections in most of the financial centers of Europe. Like so many, they had started in Frankfort. They had in time become interested in the *Société Générale de Belgique* in Brussels, in the *Banque des Dépôts de Pays-Bas* at Amsterdam with branches in Antwerp, Brussels, and Genoa, and in the *Société Générale pour favoriser l'Industrie et la Commerce de France* in Paris. Henri Bischoffsheim had become a partner with Goldschmidt in London in 1850. The Bischoffsheim family was further strengthened by its relatives, the Bambergers, who were in the *Deutsche Bank* in Berlin, in the *Banque de Paris*, and the *Banque de Paris et des Pays-Bas*.[67] The panic of 1866 had helped put the Bischoffsheims, like other Jewish houses, in good standing.

Henri Bischoffsheim had become a partner with Goldschmidt in London in 1850, and Bischoffsheim & Goldschmidt had come to take a prominent place in railroad finance. They had been in Italian railroads; they are said later to have thrown Jay Gould out of the Erie and reorganized McHenry's Atlantic & Great Western; in 1870 they went heavily into loans to Honduras for financing railway construction; and they were in Egyptian finance.[68] Here was a firm that seemed to command money and that was not too conservative.[69] "The house is *rich* is in good credit very influential and *bold*" — thus Sargent characterized them.[70]

The whole autumn of 1870 was spent in an unsuccessful negotiation with this London house. There was a prolonged bargaining, on the one hand, with Bischoffsheim & Goldschmidt, which continued to press for better terms;[71] and a prolonged bickering, on the other, with the Budge associates who, knowing that they stood in the way of a successful contract with the London house, asked impossible terms.[72] At the end of the year Sargent cabled: "Bischoffsheim delayed go ahead with loan America." [73]

This discouraging note with which the year closed was representative of the whole year for Jay Cooke & Co. Its pool campaign had been only moderately successful; it had failed to bring strong supporters to the Northern Pacific, and many who subscribed did so because of their faith in Jay Cooke. It had also been a most discouraging year as far as Congress was concerned; the mortgage bill of the Northern Pacific had only with difficulty been passed, and several other measures which were supported by Jay Cooke and his interests failed — surely the Cookes must have seen that their standing with Congress was none too good. And, what was most discouraging, there was apparently little promise of aid from Europe. Small wonder that Jay Cooke wrote at the end of the year, "I would not again undertake such a job for all the money in the world." [74]

REORGANIZATION AND EXPANSION OF JAY COOKE'S
BANKING BUSINESS, 1870–1871

THE beginning of the campaign for financing the building of the Northern Pacific had been none too hopeful. One may well ask why the Cookes did not retreat, or call a halt, when Congress and the bond market showed such determined resistance. One reason was that Jay Cooke did not know how to beat a retreat — he thought he could beat a charge which would bring into line even the most lethargic money bags. In this failure to curtail there was nothing unusual. American business men have often held with irrational tenacity to the idea that it is dangerous to draw in their activities, even in difficult times. It has been characteristic of them that they have known almost nothing about curtailing — they have been headlong expansionists, and that was especially true after the Civil War when the spirit of enterprise was very high. Another important consideration for Jay Cooke was the fact that one price of leadership is continued success; a confession of failure, while it may actually indicate strength, is often regarded as a sign of weakness and leads to loss of prestige.

Though Jay Cooke would not give up the project which he had so vigorously undertaken, he saw clearly that to push the sale of Northern Pacific bonds was not enough. Like most American bankers then dealing chiefly in investments, the Cookes needed business and needed it badly. The Washington house had not declared a dividend since 1867; the New York house had divided nothing in 1869 or 1870; only the Philadelphia house had had something to divide in 1870, the snug sum of $444,000, but even that was largely offset by obligations assumed for the Northern Pacific. At that time, Jay Cooke & Co. was carrying a heavy burden of deposits; it was paying 5 per cent compounded monthly and one-half of 1 per cent government tax on its correspondents' accounts or demand deposits.[1] Obviously something had to be done.

Consolidation of Jay Cooke & Co.

Jay Cooke and Fahnestock agreed that they had to have a thorough reconsideration of their none-too-efficient organization. As was usual when times were difficult for Jay Cooke & Co., the Washington house again came under fire. Fahnestock and Moorhead had long considered that house the weak link in their chain of firms, and all the old arguments against it still existed. By the fall of 1870, the New Yorker threatened to resign if the Washington house were not discontinued; he said he could make more money, with infinitely less care and labor, outside of the firm than he could possibly make from any business Jay Cooke & Co. was likely to do. Fahnestock looked at the Washington house as a banker, but its primary function was to serve as lobbying headquarters. The president of the Northern Pacific urged the retention of the house as a means of maintaining good relations with the administration, while McCulloch held that closing Jay Cooke & Co. of Washington would be looked upon as the abandonment of the field of government finance.[2]

As a compromise, Fahnestock suggested that the current business of the house be turned over to the First National Bank of Washington, while the office of Jay Cooke & Co. be maintained against future opportunities, but Henry Cooke held out for closing the First National and retaining Jay Cooke & Co.[3] Since he himself was clearly under fire, he proposed to sell his investments, collect some of the political loans, and go to Europe for a year on an allowance from the firm.[4] Jay Cooke decided in favor of the Washington house,[5] and, through his appointment as governor of the District of Columbia in 1871, Henry Cooke became more strongly attached than ever to the capital city.[6]

There was no valid excuse for Jay Cooke & Co., of Washington, as a bank. Since the First National could obviously have carried its banking business, why should it continue to drain the energies of the whole organization? If lobbying headquarters were needed, Henry Cooke could have retained his office. It may even be questioned whether it was wise to maintain a permanent office for this purpose, for the presence of the Cookes in Washington gave evidence to those who opposed them because of their persistent efforts to influence the government.

The Cooke partners were more successful in bringing about a reorganization of their partnerships than in discontinuing an inefficient house. Jay Cooke's organization had always been a disjointed affair; there were four firms, including the First National of Washington, held together mainly by the leading partners; and there had been no clear unity of policy or of practice in administering the business. The system was obviously weak. To strengthen it, a reorganization was arranged which became effective January 2, 1871. For the first time in the history of Jay Cooke's houses, articles of partnership were drawn up and signed by the partners.[7]

Both the structure and the membership of the group were changed. The three partnerships were merged into one. This did not, however, bring any significant reform in administration or management and the three different houses continued to function as they had always done. More significant were changes in the membership of Jay Cooke & Co. Sexton of Philadelphia and Dodge of New York were dropped, the latter much against his will.[8] Sexton was considered both harmless and useless. Dodge was in bad standing with Fahnestock and Cooke because he had handled his banking department in a way which they considered too speculative; it was he who had tied up $300,000 for the New York house in Mariposa and Atlantic Mail.[9] Moorhead wished to withdraw but finally consented to remain on condition that he be released later.[10] Jay Cooke, Jr., and James Garland were admitted to partnership. The latter had been a teacher in a business college in Philadelphia and had for some time been a clerk in the New York house, where he had come to be recognized as a first-rate broker; he was put in charge of the bond department in New York.[11] The shares of the different partners in the profits of the firm were as follows: Jay Cooke, Sr., 30 per cent; Fahnestock and Moorhead, 19 each; H. D. Cooke, 10; Pitt Cooke, 7; Thomas and Garland, 6; and Jay Cooke, Jr., 3. Those shares represented their whole income from the firm as the partners received no salaries. The Old Patriarch Jacob was still retained as a silent and noncontributing partner, receiving 10 per cent of the profits before division.[12]

The most significant feature of the new partnership rules was the fact that they were designed to build up a capital for Jay Cooke & Co. Hitherto the partners' share in the distribution of the firms' profits had been left on deposit or, more generally, had been invested in such a way as to be unavailable for the use of the business. At the time of the formation of the new partnership, the firm held undivided profits and deposits for the partners of less than $2,000,000, some of which was invested in bonds difficult to sell without loss. The total assets of the partners and the firms were estimated on January 1, 1871, to be $6,000,000, but a very large proportion was in real estate and securities for which there was not a good market.[13]

The new agreement attacked the problem of capital in two ways. First, it attempted to prevent the dissipation of the partners' assets: it forbade the partners to engage in hazardous or speculative business or, without the knowledge of the other partners, to make any investments outside of the business of the firm; and it also forbade them to assume any liability for others by means of endorsing or becoming guarantor in any way outside of the business of the co-partnership without first obtaining the written consent of all the members of the firm. Second, the agreement attempted to build up and protect the working capital of the firm: the partners were made liable for losses in proportion to their interest in profits, and it was agreed that, for three years, a total of not over $100,000 of the profits should be withdrawn annually, to be distributed in proportion to each partner's interest.

A substantial capital was needed at this time more than ever before. Several banking houses in New York had acquired great financial strength, either through the building up of a capital of their own or through acquiring support from Europe, and without a considerable capital the Cookes would be severely handicapped in competition with those richer bankers. As long as all went well, the Cookes could count on considerable bankers' deposits which could be used as a working capital. But the money and securities markets, as well as business in general, were then in a highly nervous condition. Jay Cooke realized that business was tightening up. It was to insure against losses on securities from a fall in prices and a shrinkage of trade and against possible stringencies and panics, that a larger capital was necessary.

EXPANSION INTO FOREIGN BANKING

To set the house in order was a good thing, but it was not enough. Jay Cooke & Co. had to have more work. As a result, a most important step was taken: Jay Cooke's banking house, following the example of several other American bankers, entered into the field of foreign banking.

This step grew out of the work and interests of Fahnestock and the New York house. While the emphasis of Jay Cooke and the Philadelphia house had continued to be on the distribution of new securities on commission, the New Yorkers had for some time been developing a greater interest in certain aspects of commercial banking, that is, in the holding and transfer of funds. The New York house had early taken the lead over Philadelphia as an inland bankers' bank, a development which was in line with the growing concentration of banking and trade in New York. Although the New York house had acquired an extensive correspondence throughout the North and the East, its work had not been profitable since the war business had subsided. Indeed, Fahnestock's house had been especially unfortunate in recent years. In the three years when it had been riding high on the business in government securities, it had distributed among the partners over $1,000,000.[14] But in 1869 there had been nothing to divide, and 1870 similarly proved a dry year, as it evidently did in general for the "Street."[15] Fahnestock, therefore, had come to see that the business of his house had to be increased.[16]

The domestic business could be extended by a more intensive cultivation of old fields and the opening of new, particularly with a view to getting foreign commercial accounts. In the fall of 1870, a representative of the New York house had been sent "through the Eastern States and Canada to follow up the programs of genteel solicitation." The recovery of the South opened up a new field, though one that had to be cultivated with care; Fahnestock was definitely interested in the southern business, but Jay Cooke urged staying north of the Mason and Dixon line.[17]

It was the foreign business, however, which Fahnestock was especially interested in developing. As a basis for this work his banking house already had a considerable business in connection with the importation of English iron on commission for American railroads. Some of this business had grown out of the Cookes' dealings in railroad bonds, or had even been the reason for their dealing in some bonds in that they sold bonds for a road to pay for the iron it ordered through Jay Cooke & Co. For some time before February, 1871, the New York house of Jay Cooke had imported iron on order on joint account with Vibbard, Foote & Co., a New York firm dealing in railroad iron. In 1870 the share of Fahnestock's house in the profits on this business footed around $90,000. Payment for the iron imported had been made by Jay Cooke & Co. through the Browns and Morgans at a charge of 1 per cent upon four months' acceptances. Altogether, the iron importing business provided considerable work in London which the Cookes could themselves do if they had a London house.[18]

Jay Cooke & Co. had up to that time conducted all its large foreign transactions in government or other securities through the agencies or branches of European banks in New York; all its remittances for interior correspondents had been in exchange drawn by other houses; and sterling and other foreign drafts received had been sold to dealers in such papers.[19] But by the spring of 1870 Fahnestock had come to believe that the time was ripe for entering the foreign business. Foreign exchange, he held, was very profitable, if handled properly, and perfectly controllable in both volume and risk. It was especially profitable when large government transactions were to be made, such as the transfer of the money for the purchase of Alaska.[20]

Fahnestock first tried to enter the exchange business through establishing an account with some foreign house. This method had two advantages: no gold capital would be required and the business could be developed gradually as opportunities presented themselves. Only first-class connections, such as Rothschilds or Barings, and the most favorable terms would, in the opinion of Fahnestock, enable them to compete successfully with Brown Brothers.

Fahnestock approached representatives of both the Rothschilds and the Barings in New York. August Belmont assured him that the Rothschilds would not be interested.[21] The New York agents of the Barings were more encouraging; Fahnestock had explained to the Wards that his house would like credit with the Barings, particularly for the importation of railroad iron. Insurance policies and shipping documents would be delivered in London in exchange for the acceptance of four to six months' bills. Those documents were to be sent to Jay Cooke & Co. in New York, who would place the London bankers in funds before the maturity of the bills.[22] This, according to the Wards, differed from the ordinary commercial credits in that the documents were delivered before the maturity of the bills.[23]

On submitting Fahnestock's inquiry to the Barings, the Wards gave a high estimate of Jay Cooke & Co., which is significant because it would under the circumstances represent a conservative judgment of Jay Cooke's firm:[24]

Jay Cooke & Co. are a very respectable house and would very generally be allowed a capital of several million dollars and would be classed in the first rank of the new houses here, and probably not so much, or more, involved in new R R. enterprises than many others, and in regard to their enterprises they stand in a position to make money out of them if any one does . . . the house in all respects standing well and being clear of Treasury relations, which formerly tied it up to a particular line of business.

Encouraged by the Wards, Fahnestock wrote to the Barings, but nothing came of the matter.[25]

It was probably the failure to secure satisfactory foreign connections which again turned the attention of the Cookes to the possibility of establishing a London house. It was becoming evident by then that American bankers were coming to depend more and more on their own houses in London rather than on correspondents. We have noted earlier that several branches of American houses had been opened in England and on the Continent during and immediately after the Civil War. In 1869–70 a number of New York houses had established branches in London. In the fall of 1869, Morton, Bliss & Co., of New York, and Sir John Rose organized Morton, Rose & Co. in London. In the spring of 1870 Turner Brothers, of New York, opened on Threadneedle Street; Bowles Brothers established a London branch; and Henry Clews became a partner in the new London house of Clews, Habicht & Co.[26] If the Cookes were to compete with those houses, they would have to have an aggressive base in London from which to work.

In the early summer of 1870 Jay Cooke and his partners again considered establishing a London house. The problem of securing a satisfactory resident manager was met by enlisting Hugh McCulloch, for whom both Jay Cooke and Fahnestock had the highest regard, to head the concern.[27] The choice of McCulloch was in some respects very fortunate, for he had distinguished himself as banker, as Comptroller of the Currency, and as Secretary of the Treasury. McCulloch had a great deal of prestige though he had not had experience in foreign banking.

Before the end of 1870 arrangements had been completed for the London house. Two resident partners were secured besides McCulloch: one was Frank Evans, a friend of Jay Cooke's family and a native of London engaged in the American commission business;[28] the other was J. H. Puleston, a partner in Puleston, Raymond & Co., of New York, who had a close familiarity with American securities and was, in the opinion of Fahnestock, both in his social qualifications and his business experience well suited to the position.[29] The firm was named Jay Cooke, McCulloch & Co. Articles of co-partnership were drawn up which were essentially similar to the rules governing Jay Cooke & Co. There were ten partners in all in the new house: the three residing in London and all the American partners except Garland. Of the profits, 32½ per cent was apportioned to the London partners, 58¾ per cent to the American partners in proportion to their interest in Jay Cooke & Co., and 8¾ per cent to Garland and Moorhead's son, who were at first chosen to be partners but were dropped because only ten members were allowed in a partnership under English law.[30]

Commodious and dignified quarters for Jay Cooke, McCulloch & Co. were leased at 41 Lombard Street in the City of London. McCulloch established himself in Hyde Park in a style fitting to his own reputation and to the prestige of the firm, and he found London business men both congenial and friendly to his house.[31] It remained to be seen what could be accomplished by combining "English oak & American ideas." [32]

The London house was to conduct an exchange business, issue commercial and travelers' credits, loan money on government and other bonds, cash coupons for United States, State, and railroad bonds, purchase railroad iron as ordered by Jay Cooke & Co., and negotiate the sale of railroad and other securities. In fact, in the words of Jay Cooke it should do "everything in the way of business transactions between the two countries. We ought to do the largest business that is done between America & Europe, within a reasonable time of the opening." [33] It was hoped that, as soon as the London house had established itself properly and had acquired correspondents and connections on the Continent, it would also secure the London business of the United States government. This business, which had long been in the hands of the Barings, was extremely valuable, for the government kept with its London agent large deposits from which disbursements were made for the Navy and the State departments both in Europe and Asia.

To secure the government accounts in London was no easy matter. First of all, there was no good reason why the business should be taken from the Barings. If a change were to be made, however, there were other bankers as hungry for the business as were the Cookes. Their most formidable rival was Morton, Rose & Co. Morton was a close friend of President Grant and entertained him at Newport, where the Mortons were prominent socially.[34] Morton's London partner was Sir John Rose, who had helped draw up the Treaty of Washington which finally settled the explosive *Alabama* affair.[35] Moreover, the Cookes had no particular standing with the Navy; Jay Cooke's Washington house had once refused to discount a personal note of the Secretary of the Navy! [36]

The Cookes set out, nevertheless, to get the Navy account, expecting that the account of the State Department would go to the Mortons. Senator Cattell of New Jersey was engaged to aid them in return for a generous commission on the account.[37] In the course of the negotiations, President Grant said that "he could never forget McCulloch's conduct during his imbroglio with Johnson, and it went greatly against the grain to give him recognition under his administration at London." Various means were used to influence the President: Mrs. Henry Cooke had "incidentally, a good talk with Mrs. G. [Grant] about Navy account," and General Porter, the President's secretary, promised to use his influence with Grant.[38]

President Grant had too many friends for his own peace of mind or for the good of the Cookes. He finally resorted to a compromise, offering Morton, Rose & Co. the State Department account and dividing the Navy account between Clews, Habicht & Co. and Jay Cooke, McCulloch & Co. This made the Cookes indignant, for they had little respect for Henry Clews. The matter was settled, however, by the Mortons' refusal of the account because they feared offending the Barings, which made it possible to give the State Department account to Clews, Habicht & Co., of London, leaving the Navy to the Cookes.[39]

The assignment of the Navy account to Jay Cooke & Co. was strongly opposed by Editor Childs and others among Jay Cooke's enemies. On hearing rumors of the canceling of the appointment, Jay Cooke sent word to Grant that his organization could do twenty times more for his re-election than those other parties, and that those who were attacking Jay Cooke were Copperheads "and were the most intimate friends of Johnson about the time he [Grant] complains of McCulloch." [40]

Again the Cookes had won — to have lost would have been a death blow to their London house, said Jay Cooke.[41] How important the account was is shown by the fact that from May 24 to November 3, 1871, Jay Cooke, McCulloch & Co. received government deposits of $3,000,000.[42] The handling of a deposit of $1,000,000, about which we have information, suggests what value the account had to their business. The government in this case furnished Jay Cooke & Co. a draft for $1,000,000 to be deposited in London. The sum was remitted in the form of 60-day bills to Jay Cooke, McCulloch & Co.; from that time until the maturity of the 60-day bills in London, Jay Cooke & Co. had the use of the money, and it either covered the London bills just before maturity or became indebted to the London house. At the end of the 60 days, Jay Cooke, McCulloch & Co. began to pay the government 4 per cent on the deposit. Since disbursements were gradual, this meant that it gave the London house a considerable working capital at a low rate; moreover, a commission of 1 per cent was charged on all drafts against the deposits.[43] The Navy account helped to provide the Cooke firms with a working capital, and, in addition, it was expected that the prestige gained from the account would also bring to Jay Cooke, McCulloch & Co. the business of American merchant ships.[44]

In one respect the Navy account was not altogether a boon for the Cookes. Unquestionably the affair put them in a bad light with the Barings and probably with other bankers in London, who must as a matter of course have looked on Jay Cooke, McCulloch & Co. as an interloper. So far as the business of Jay Cooke, McCulloch & Co. was independent of the other bankers of London, this did not matter; but, if the London house of Jay Cooke should need to borrow or should want help in disposing of bonds, then it would be too bad not to have the good will of the other bankers.

Entry into foreign exchange made connections in other European financial centers almost imperative. Travelers' credits were at the time drawn on Paris in large amounts by Americans. This business yielded the customary commission of $1\frac{1}{2}$ per cent besides exchange and other pickings. Fahnestock suggested opening an account with Harjes, the Paris house of the Drexels; he saw in this a chance to make an ally rather than an enemy of the bankers.

Jay Cooke did not favor this plan [45]— it may be that he was concerned about the Drexels' growing strength abroad. Shortly after Jay Cooke, McCulloch & Co. had been established, the Drexels had formed a connection with J. S. Morgan of London, who had for some time been their London correspondent, and on July 1, 1871, the Drexel house of New York was merged with that of J. S. Morgan's son to form Drexel, Morgan & Co.[46] "The combination of these two conspicuous banking firms with the branch houses and connections named," said the *Commercial and Financial Chronicle*, "must place the new firm among the few leading banking houses of the world." [47] Such a combination might well have put fear into the Cookes! The union of the Drexels, who were strong in America, and the Morgans, whose long career in London had just been crowned with the successful selling of the French indemnity loan, made a power to be conjured with in finance.

Fahnestock looked toward making foreign exchange, including the extension of commercial credits, the most important feature of his house. A man of excellent experience with Dennistouns in London was hired to assist French, a leading clerk in the New York house, in managing the business.[48] Jay Cooke took little active part in this work; recognizing his partner's knowledge of that line of business, he left its management completely to him.[49] On the strength of the foreign business Fahnestock expected not only to make the New York house self-sustaining but also to support the London house and carry a part of the weight of the Washington house.[50]

Working Toward a Safer Business

While working toward a better organization and reaching out for new work, Jay Cooke and his partners tried to discontinue some of their more risky business and develop safer methods. In other words, they were looking toward strength by cutting down on the dissipation of their energies and by increasing their effectiveness.

They discontinued some lines of business and refused to take on others. After 1869 they did not speculate in gold [51] but bought the metal only on order or as needed in their own business. And in 1871 the New York house disposed "of that heavy load *The Stock Desk*;" they had lost considerable amounts on stocks and it did not look well on the Street for such a house to borrow on stocks to support its customers' margins.[52] Jay Cooke, moreover, refused to participate in mining ventures because there was "an element of risk about them & many contingencies which the ignorant & poor & the public at large should not be invited to participate in." He also advised his partners to have nothing to do with Mexican finance: "I have long studied this Mexican question," he said, "but the whole difficulty lies in the character of the people of Mexico & of its rulers. They are more unstable & unreliable than the Apaches or Crow Indians. In fact, they have no commercial or financial character whatever." [53]

In the investment field, Jay Cooke maintained that they should deal only in United States government and railroad securities. About the former there was no longer any question; they were accepted by the most conservative investors. Next to governments, first-mortgage railroad bonds in promising roads were, in the opinion of the banker, the soundest investments.[54] That high-grade railroad bonds were good is seen from the fact that the yield of a group of such bonds for the year 1870 was 6.408 per cent.[55]

Most significant because of its great possibilities was the adoption by Jay Cooke & Co. of a new device in floating new issues of securities. This device, which we know today as the underwriting syndicate, was to go far toward revolutionizing corporation finance and investment banking in the United States. The underwriting syndicate was first used by Jay Cooke in 1870, and he is generally credited with introducing it in the United States. That he introduced the term "syndicate" in connection with the refunding of a portion of the federal debt in 1871 is certain, and he was apparently the first in the United States to use group underwriting on a large scale.

It is by no means certain when group action of this kind originated. Elements of modern syndicate practice can be found in the transactions of mercantile banking groups in medieval Genoa, Florence, and South Germany, which made loans to municipalities, princes, and even emperors. The study of the work of the Bardi and Peruzzi, the Bank of St. George of Genoa, the Frescobaldi, the Fuggers, Welsers, and other bankers of medieval Europe would throw much light on the history of group financing and might even reveal something very much like the modern syndicate. In the early nineteenth century the purchase of government bonds on joint account by groups of merchants or bankers had become well established in both Europe and America. Further study may reveal that those efforts employed all the features of the modern underwriting syndicate. American instances of joint-account handling of security issues are the purchases by Girard, Parish, and Astor of a federal loan in the War of 1812, and the participation of the Clarks and Corcoran & Riggs in financing the war with Mexico. Those groups were formed for joint purchases, which in a real sense meant both underwriting and selling though presumably not as a group but as individual firms. The developments in France and Germany led to specialized group underwriting in the 1850's, two decades before that type of syndicate came to be widely used in America and England.

In the late 'sixties Jay Cooke & Co. and E. W. Clark & Co. made a definite advance toward the modern underwriting syndicate in their purchase of bonds of the Lake Superior & Mississippi Railroad, which they advertised and sold on joint account through joint management. The next step in the development of the underwriting syndicate was to separate the function of underwriting from purchase or sale; that is, for a group to guarantee the sale of a specified amount of an issue and provide a central organization for disposing of the bonds if necessary, with the understanding that if the bonds were not sold the syndicate members would be responsible to the extent of their underwriting.

Jay Cooke first employed the underwriting syndicate in the sale of a $2,000,000 bond issue of the Pennsylvania Railroad in 1870. His banking house organized a group of eight business concerns which underwrote the sale of this issue.[56] The actual selling was entrusted to five of the eight underwriters under the management of Jay Cooke & Co., thus separating underwriting from purchase and sale. Because it is an early example of such a business form, the syndicate agreement is reproduced below:[57]

Messrs Jay Cooke & Co.   March 18th, 1870
    Gentn.
        We the undersigned have bought on Joint a/c with you, of the Pennsylvania R. R. Co Two Million (2,000,000) Dollars of their General Mortgage Bonds @ 90 flat. — With the agreement on the part of the Penna R. R. Co that they will not offer any more General Mortgage Bonds for sale until these are disposed of, and that they will then give us the option of taking any Bonds which they may wish to sell, if we desire to do so.
    The 2,000,000 Bonds are divided between us as follows:

Fidelity Trust Co.	250,000
S & W Welsh	250,000
Stuart & Bro	100,000
Jay Cooke & Co	280,000
E W Clark & Co	280,000
Drexel & Co	280,000
C & H. Borie	280,000
W H Newbold Son & A	280,000

We the undersigned each agree to take of Messrs Jay Cooke & Co $50,000 Bonds (March 18th) — and pay for them — as bonds in excess are sold each party to send & pay for same with interest at 6 % from March 18. Whether bonds are sold or not, parties having an interest of $280,000, and the others in the same proportion shall pay for the Bonds as follows — April 15th $50,000. May 1st $50,000. May 15th $50,000. June 1st 80,000. with interest at 6 % from March 18th — it being agreed that each party shall have the right to pay more rapidly if they so elect. Jay Cooke Co; E W Clark & Co; Drexel & Co; C & H Borie; W H Newbold Son & Aertsen; will offer the bonds for sale at 92½ and accrued interest will allow ¼ % commission to other brokers. The parties hereto to bear the expense of advertising in proportion to the amount of the Bonds they have subscribed for, no Bonds to be sold except through the parties named above.
    It is understood that all sales are for general account and profits to

be divided proportionately to the amounts for which the several parties
are responsible

Signed   E W Clark & Co
W H Newbold son & Aertsen
Samuel & Wm Welsh
C & H Borie
Drexel & Co
Stuart & Brother
N B Brown Pt

A NOTABLE VENTURE IN GROUP FINANCING

In the ebb and flow of Cooke affairs one thing always remained
in the minds of the partners: that their strength lay in the government business and that nothing bore as great promise for them
as the refunding of the Civil War loan. Had McCulloch, the
Secretary of the Treasury, and Sherman, the senatorial leader in
finance, had their way, the loan would have been refunded shortly
after the war was over, but government finance shared the fate of
other affairs of state in those turbulent post-war years.

The question of refunding again came up in Congress in 1870.
Jay Cooke put all his strength behind the refunding bill, but the
opposition was powerful. It was very significant that the Philadelphia *Ledger* should attack the bill. A careful scrutiny of the
measure before Congress, said the *Ledger*,[58]

will suggest enough to excite the apprehensions of all who understand
the subject and are concerned for the public welfare. . . . Any one
familiar with these transactions knows that there are enormous incidental profits growing out of such operations, as with the control of
fluctuating money, foreign exchange, gold and United States bond markets, values may be raised or depressed at pleasure, the new bonds
sold, and the proceeds of sale in money held for use and profits to the
agents, before transmission to the Treasury, and for the purpose of
affecting market values. The country would thus be constantly in
peril of perturbations and excitements destructive to all legitimate
trade, and these reacting on the public revenues would impair national
credit, and prevent the accomplishment of the object proposed by the
bill.

When the *Ledger* opposed the Northern Pacific, it was on solid ground; its concern about the social good was justifiable when it stood out against the freezing of capital in enterprises which would not soon be productive. But in view of Jay Cooke's earlier handling of the loan transactions of the government, its opposition to the refunding bill in 1870 was both unreasonable and unfair. When the government had been in great need of funds during the Civil War and the Drexels and other bankers had cautiously refrained from becoming heavily involved in government loans, Jay Cooke had done a really significant patriotic service at great risk in return for an almost negligible commission. After the war, there was no patriotic appeal for Jay Cooke in refunding; inevitably he would be motivated by a desire for profits. But the very fact that he might profit from a negotiation brought severe criticism on the part of those who were themselves anxious to secure the work which they had not wanted to do during the war. That they should take this position was unfair to Jay Cooke but at the same time it is understandable.

A refunding bill was finally passed.[59] It authorized the sale of various issues of bonds, totaling $1,500,000,000, at rates varying from $3\frac{1}{4}$ to 5 per cent and payable in from 10 to 40 years. The bonds were to be exchanged for five-twenties at par or sold at not less than par in coin, the proceeds being used for redeeming the five-twenties. A half of 1 per cent was allotted for covering all the expenses of the conversion. The measure was amended in January, 1871, to allow the issue of half a billion at 5 per cent and the payment of interest quarterly.

The conversion was not undertaken at once, however, for the crisis in Europe attendant upon the outbreak of the Franco-Prussian War made it impracticable to start operations.[60] As the financial stringency caused by the war in Europe disappeared, Boutwell continued his policy of buying bonds for the Treasury as rapidly as his surplus would permit. Jay Cooke was thoroughly disgusted with the Secretary, who had "no more spunk than to let the country drift along without even an attempt at funding the debt, & who insists upon keeping up enormous taxation for the foolish object of paying off rapidly a debt that no one wants paid off excepting gradually." [61] That this position was held by others at the time is shown by the fact that the *Commercial and Financial Chronicle*, which was independent of the Cookes, reported a growing anxiety among "financial thinkers whose experience entitles them to respect, and an apprehension that we are pushing the debt-paying policy rather too far and are hurrying it decidedly too fast." [62]

The Cookes were much concerned about what part they would be given in refunding if anything were done. They had not had the hold on Boutwell that they had had on his predecessors; in the words of one of the partners, they had not made a dollar out of the Treasury after Boutwell became secretary.[63] It is not strange, therefore, that they came to be intensely interested in the rumor in December, 1870, that the Secretary was resigning. Jay Cooke and his partners hoped that Senator Sherman would be appointed to the place.[64]

In the meantime Jay Cooke had continued to work toward getting Boutwell to accept his proposals on refunding operations.[65] Not until early in 1871, however, did the Secretary begin seriously to make plans for refunding. It then appeared that Morton, Rose & Co. might be put at the head of the operation,[66] though in the opinion of one of the New York Cookes the Mortons "don't know any more about Bonds than Hottentots. They have always been a Stock House — They are stock Brockers, through Sir John [Rose] just fledging into Bankers & selling Govt Loans."[67] There were other bankers besides Morton, Rose & Co. who also had good prospects in this connection, particularly Belmont, the Drexels, and the Seligmans. Fahnestock warned Jay Cooke that all those people had been very attentive to the President lately at Newport and Long Branch, and "we must not lose sight of the fact that influences of this kind do secure his friendly offices." [68]

Jay Cooke was fearful that the commission allowed by the refunding act was too low for a successful operation. It might have been sufficient if investors had been enthusiastic about buying the new loan or exchanging the old for the new, but there was no such enthusiasm. This was not strange since the new bonds were either to be sold at par in gold, when they were intrinsically little or no better than ten-forties, which were selling below par in gold, or to be exchanged for the 6 per cent five-twenties, which, while slightly higher than ten-forties, were still below par in gold.[69] Cooke, therefore, suggested as liberal a treatment of the loan agents as was possible under the law. To strengthen the loan, he urged, moreover, that the face of the bonds carry a statement to the effect that they were to be paid in United States coin, of the standard value of that time, and were to be exempt from taxation.[70]

The Cookes were absolutely certain that only with an aggressive and centralized organization could the operation succeed.[71] The only way in which anyone could or would manage the refunding was to be able to manipulate the market for the sale of the new and the purchase of the old bonds. One thing seemed clear, however, to the Cookes: Boutwell would never leave in the hands of the agent in charge of the loan operations a money balance sufficiently large to be of any use —"It will be quite different from 5/20 & 7/30 days, when bonds were sold for the purpose of accumulating money balances to be expended."[72]

In Boutwell's failure to give work to the Cookes or in his unwillingness to do anything which would promise profits to bankers, there was no animosity but only the desire to serve the public according to the best rules of the game. Yet it may be questioned whether the Secretary did not go too far. There were times when the Treasury needed the services of bankers, for there was then no Federal Reserve Bank to do its work. The rule applies to government, as to private individuals, that it must make its business profitable to others if it is to get their help. That this was so, Boutwell, himself, was soon to learn.

Influenced by the clamor of the press and the urgings of rival banking houses, Boutwell adopted the method which Fessenden had tried without success. When he offered $200,000,000 of the new loan in March, he entrusted the operation to national banks and to a wide number of bankers.[73] In America, Jay Cooke & Co., Fisk & Hatch, Vermilye & Co., the Clarks, Winslow, Lanier & Co (of New York), Kidder, Peabody (of Boston), and many others were appointed to aid in the sale of the loan; and in London, Jay Cooke, McCulloch & Co., Morton, Rose & Co., Seligman Brothers, and J. S. Morgan & Co. — the Barings and Rothschilds had decided not to participate.[74]

The loan went none too well. As Jay Cooke had foreseen, the commission offered proved too low to interest the agent in pushing the loan; the lack of centralization of control obviously prevented manipulation of the market in favor of the loan; and the price of the bonds was such that there would be little advantage in exchanging old bonds for new.[75] The bonds moved so slowly that Boutwell in May considered a proposal of the Cookes to form a group to take the balance of about $130,000,000,[76] but he would not accede to their proposal with regard to the length of time the funds should remain on deposit in national banks.[77] The sale of the bonds continued to be unsatisfactory.[78]

Jay Cooke, in the meantime, had made plans for a syndicate, and by August, Boutwell, on the advice of the assistant secretary who was in London, was ready to negotiate with him.[79] Jay Cooke was authorized to form two syndicates for taking the loan, one in New York and one in London. These groups should be responsible for the sale of new 5 per cent bonds to the extent, respectively, of $10,000,000 and $15,000,000 in gold, with an option on the $130,000,000 remaining of the $200,000,000 offered, with the stipulation that an average of at least $5,000,000 a month should be sold.[80] The commission was to be whatever remained of the one-half of 1 per cent allowed by the refunding act after the cost of printing and shipping the bonds and the one-eighth of 1 per cent commission to banks had been paid;[81] it was understood that the government should allow the proceeds to remain on deposit in the banks for 90 days without drawing interest, thus raising the commission without directly violating the legal limit of half of 1 per cent.[82]

In organizing the syndicate the Cookes ran into much scepticism and some rivalry. The Drexels of New York and Paris declined an invitation to join the group; Morton, Rose & Co. also declined and was reported to have grave doubts as to the success of the loan, but Morton later explained that they had

declined out of fear of offending the Barings and because they
themselves had failed in attempting to organize a syndicate;
the Barings and the Rothschilds also refused to participate.[83]
Indeed, the Cookes failed to win the support of the very strongest
bankers in both New York and London.

In making up the syndicate, Jay Cooke & Co. was forced
to lean heavily on its own organization and its friends. Of
the American subscriptions of $10,000,000, Jay Cooke & Co. and
its First National of Washington took $2,500,000 and the First
National of Philadelphia, with which the Cookes were closely
associated, took $500,000. The remaining American subscribers
included the First National of New York, which took $1,250,000
(George F. Baker's bank was thus early giving evidence of its
interest in securities); the Fourth National, which took $1,000,000;
and private bankers in New York, chiefly Jay Cooke's agents in
selling Civil War loans, that is, Fisk & Hatch, Vermilye & Co.,
Henry Clews & Co., Clark, Dodge & Co., and Leonard, Sheldon &
Foster.[84]   One sees here an interesting cleavage with Jay Cooke's
Civil War associates on the one side and the strong bankers, who
had little enthusiasm for war finance but good connections in
Europe, on the other.

Of the foreign syndicate subscription of $15,000,000, Jay
Cooke, McCulloch & Co. took $1,500,000. The other foreign sub-
scribers were principally German-Jewish bankers: in London the
Raphaels took $3,500,000 and the Cohens, $2,000,000; smaller
amounts were taken by the Seligmans, Speyers, and Bischoffsheim & Goldschmidt, of London, and by Behrens of Hamburg,
Bleichroeder of Berlin, Lippman, Rosenthal & Co. and Wertheim
& Gomperz of Amsterdam, Erlanger, Speyer, Ellison, and Seligman & Stettheimer of Frankfort and Oppenheim, Errara & Co.
of Brussels.[85]   It is significant that the Morgans, Barings, and
others strong in American business in Europe refused to participate in the European syndicate. It was not impossible, however,
that Jay Cooke might without their co-operation build up a
strong following in England and on the Continent consisting of
wealthy or aggressive Jewish banking houses.

After the two syndicates had underwritten $25,000,000,

books were opened for subscriptions to the $130,000,000 on which the syndicate had an option. By way of preparation, the editors of the "money column" of the most prominent New York dailies were "sweetened" by investments for them on the syndicate's account.[86] The American subscriptions exceeded all expectations, and the books for the loan were opened in London and Frankfort one day and closed the next.[87] By August 22 the whole amount of the $75,000,000 allotted to Europe had been taken with a great deal to spare; purchases were mostly for cash and not in exchange for old bonds.[88] By the end of August all that remained of the $200,000,000 of new fives had been sold.[89]

The task still remained of helping the subscribing banks to work off their subscriptions in such a way as to prevent any disturbance of the money market. On September 1, the Secretary of the Treasury called old five-twenties to the amount of $100,-000,000 for redemption three months later.[90] Strenuous efforts were thereafter made to induce early redemption so as to prevent a jam on December 1. To sell the loan it was necessary to create a favorable market, that is, to keep the bonds at a premium, which was not so easy because groups might unite to drive the bonds down and a gold clique was trying to drive gold upward, thus also depressing the bonds.[91]

In its efforts to peg the market for the bonds, Jay Cooke & Co. had an interest beyond that of assisting the subscribing banks and bankers to market its subscriptions. Fahnestock, always ready for a good trade in governments, wanted to be able to create a market favorable to trading in called bonds on the account of his New York house. This led to a double motive in the efforts of the Cookes to get the Treasury to interfere in the market. When the high price of gold was slowing up the market in September, Fahnestock wrote as follows to Jay Cooke: "As it is, Garland is making lots of money out of trades in the called bonds & if the Secretary will only break this high rate of gold there is no end to the money that can be made out of them during the next three months." [92]

Since the syndicate did not have adequate funds for pegging the market, it became necessary to appeal to the Treasury. But to win the Treasury to the idea of furnishing funds with which to control the market was, however, not easy; during his secretary-ship, Boutwell had consistently opposed entrusting public funds to private individuals for manipulating the gold or securities mar-ket. The gravest test came early in September, when the New York money market was in an unusually bad condition and McCulloch sent word that conditions in the London market were such that further negotiations would be impossible unless the new fives were strengthened by the sale of gold for ten-forties.[93] The Cookes pleaded for aid, but to no avail. In desperation Fahne-stock appealed to President Grant, who promised to advise the Secretary to adopt some measures to relieve the stringency,[94] and shortly thereafter Boutwell sold $4,000,000 in gold.[95]

In spite of this measure the price of gold continued upward. On September 19 the difference between gold and bonds was so considerable that, unless something were done, later attempts at refunding would in Fahnestock's opinion be utterly useless.[96] Again Fahnestock was influenced by his own needs, for his bank was at the time borrowing gold for its foreign exchange and other business at a high rate. Cooke objected strenuously to this state of affairs, saying that, if it were known, it would give their enemies a wonderful argument with the Secretary. But Fahnestock had no other recourse in the absence of a gold working capital.[97] In desperation, the New Yorker tackled Boutwell directly. The Secretary was then attending the fair at his home village, Groton, Massachusetts, where the distraught banker found "old Cin-cinnatus" superintending a plowing match; he seemed "to be the author and proprietor of nearly all the big pumpkins, big beets, and big turnips — to say nothing of the Alderneys — that are exhibited at the cattle show which is in progress there," Fahne-stock commented, somewhat sarcastically. After a twenty-minutes' conversation in a fence corner, the banker hurried off to the nearest telegraph station with the instructions to the Treas-ury which the Cookes had wanted for some time.[98]

There is no question but that it was politically risky for Bout-well thus to support Jay Cooke's operations. Jealous business men and voters were ready to complain that favors were being given, and it could not be denied that Jay Cooke's own banking houses profited from Boutwell's aid aside from their syndicate operations. Newspapers such as the *New York World* and *Herald* were strong in their denunciation of the syndicate and its relations with the Treasury. A great deal of fun was poked at the word syndicate, itself, a newcomer in the American vocabulary which was said to have been introduced by Jay Cooke. The word was defined and redefined, speculated upon, and analyzed, always with the implication that there was something sinister about it. The *Commercial and Financial Chronicle* saw in "syndicate" only a new name for old things — rings, cliques, and combinations.[99] One bit of doggerel ran thus:[100]

> Pray, what is a syndicate
> Intended to indicate?
> Is queried abroad and at home.
> Say, is it a corner,
> Where Jay Cook-e Horner
> Can pull out a very big plum?

The loan was worked off successfully. Jay Cooke watched Boutwell like a hawk to see that the deposits remained in the banks as long as had been promised.[101] Cooke's careful supervision of the drawings of the Treasury and the transferring of cash and bonds in the refunding operation were no doubt largely responsible for the fact that the transaction was carried through with so little disturbance of the money market. The most important work the Cookes did, however, in making the loan a success was the control they exercised over the money and securities markets through influencing the Treasury in buying and selling gold and through forming what they called pools or syndicates for buying and selling bonds on the market.[102]

In the final settlement of the syndicate accounts in December occurred an incident which throws some light on Jay Cooke's business character. The duplication of orders had credited the syndicate with the sale of more bonds than they actually had sold, and some of the Cooke partners urged that, since the burden of those sales would remain for the Cookes to carry, the profits of the syndicate should be cut down accordingly. But this Jay

Cooke positively opposed. "It is no argument to say that they made their money without any trouble," he said. "They took the risks and the chances." The benefit of the error was legitimately due to them — "Whether we make $30,000 more or less we must have the matter finished up in such a shape as to satisfy our own minds & conscience that we do right towards those who so fully trust in us." [103]

The closing of the syndicate brings us to a consideration of the effect of the operation on Jay Cooke's business. Even Levi P. Morton, who had refused to participate, said that "there is no wiping out the great fact: it is a wonderful negotiation, and will put Jay Cooke and Co. a head and shoulders above any American House in Europe, and make them the peers of the proudest of European houses." [104] The operation enhanced the prestige of Jay Cooke and his firms with other bankers; indeed, it put them in the way of building up a following in Europe which would be independent of the strong New York-London banking houses, such as the Barings, Morgans, and Mortons. Success also greatly raised the standing of Jay Cooke, McCulloch & Co. and gave them hope of bringing other leading houses into the Northern Pacific negotiations,[105] and it placed the London house in a better position in foreign exchange. In addition, the operation was profitable; Pitt Cooke estimated that their London and New York houses had made a quarter of a million.[106] There is no way of knowing whether this included all the profits of the Cookes; they were frankly out to make all the money they could from this "jamboree" and it is clear that the incidental tradings outside of the syndicate had been exceedingly profitable.[107] The success of the Cookes, furthermore, strengthened their hold on the government; the report of Secretary Boutwell for 1871 gave them reason to think that they would have more of such work to do. In view of the fact that this very success caused the revival of opposition to the close association of the Cookes with the Treasury, one may well question, however, whether the Treasury would continue to employ them in refunding.

It was not without significance to Jay Cooke that the syndicate operation also strengthened the credit of the United States abroad. "The foreign bankers here assure us," said the *Commercial and Financial Chronicle* in September, 1871,[108] "that there has scarcely ever been a time when they received a larger number of inquiries relative to government and railroad bonds." It would appear that conditions had become more favorable for the Northern Pacific, which had in 1871 been moving with rapid strides toward the western plains.

The developments in the organization and work of Jay Cooke & Co. in 1871 were extremely promising. The reorganization of the American houses was directed toward a more efficient functioning of the firm and toward greater safety. The employment of the underwriting syndicate had immense possibilities for securing the co-operation of other banking houses and for spreading risks. The establishment of the London house of Jay Cooke & Co. gave promise of a considerable business in foreign exchange and of being of great value in syndicating refunding loans in Europe. Most important of all, the successful handling of the refunding loan had strengthened the Cooke firms financially and had helped them to recapture some of their lost prestige. Again Jay Cooke looked toward the Rothschilds, as is indicated by a reference to the great banking house in a letter to Fahnestock: "Could you not make an alliance with them which would be permanent & give us vastly additional power? They now evidently respect us, & have a large estimate of our financial position in the world." [109]

THE NORTHERN PACIFIC BOND CAMPAIGN
OF JAY COOKE & CO. IN 1871

THOUGH Jay Cooke had said at the end of 1870 that he would not for all the money in the world undertake such a job again, the year 1871 found him planning to begin the public sale of Northern Pacific bonds. Sargent's message of December, 1870, advising that there was no hope of immediate aid from Europe, came at a time when the funds of the Northern Pacific were almost exhausted. In the summer and fall of 1870, extensive surveys had been made and construction westward from Duluth had gotten well under way. A great deal had also been spent in advertising the loan and in commissions on the $5,000,000 pool. The completion of a considerable stretch of road made it necessary soon to purchase rolling stock. As a result, the money derived from the pool was almost gone and more was needed at once. It was decided, therefore, to open the campaign for selling the bonds at home and, if necessary, to proceed without European aid.

In view of the reluctance of the market to take Northern Pacifics when offered in Europe and the lack of enthusiasm among American capitalists over the pool, it might seem that Jay Cooke should have considered waiting for a time or at least should have urged upon the management that it should for the present plan to build only to the Red River from the eastern end and as much as was necessary to meet charter requirements in Washington Territory. Such a course would have stopped expenditures on surveys elsewhere and prevented the letting of contracts and the purchase of materials far in advance of needs. It would also, no doubt, have strengthened the loan in the market, and it would have brought more enthusiastic co-operation from Jay Cooke's partners. But Jay Cooke & Co. was by that time too heavily involved in the Northwest to consider holding back the Northern Pacific.

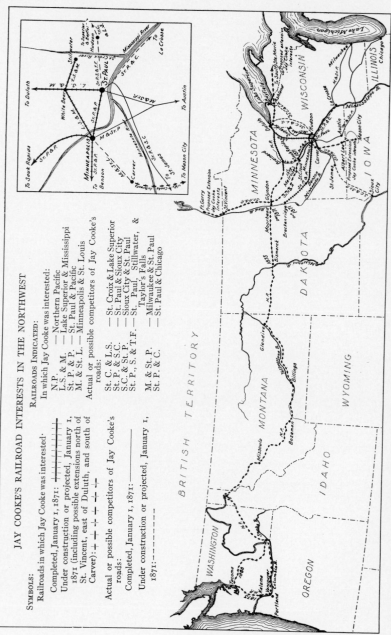

JAY COOKE'S RAILROAD INTERESTS IN THE NORTHWEST

SYMBOLS:

Railroads in which Jay Cooke was interested:

Completed, January 1, 1871: ┼┼┼┼┼┼┼┼

Under construction or projected, January 1, 1871 (including possible extensions north of St. Vincent, east of Duluth, and south of Carver): ┼ ┼ ┼ ┼ ┼

Actual or possible competitors of Jay Cooke's roads:

Completed, January 1, 1871: ─────────

Under construction or projected, January 1, 1871: ─ ─ ─ ─ ─ ─ ─

RAILROADS INDICATED:

In which Jay Cooke was interested:

N.P. — Northern Pacific
L.S. & M. — Lake Superior & Mississippi
St. P. & P. — St. Paul & Pacific
M. & St. L. — Minneapolis & St. Louis

Actual or possible competitors of Jay Cooke's roads:

St. C. & L.S. — St. Croix & Lake Superior
St. P. & S.C. — St. Paul & Sioux City
S.C. & St. P. — Sioux City & St. Paul
St. P., S. & T.F. — St. Paul, Stillwater, & Taylor's Falls
M. & St. P. — Milwaukee & St. Paul
St. P. & C. — St. Paul & Chicago

DATES: The dates at various places on the Northern Pacific and St. Paul & Pacific indicate the time when construction reached those points. As is indicated, the Northern Pacific reached Puget Sound by its own line in 1888, but five years earlier it had reached both Portland and the Sound by using the road of the Oregon Railroad & Navigation Company south of the Columbia River.

Jay Cooke & Co. Becomes Entangled in the Northwest

It is impossible to weigh exactly the various influences which had brought Jay Cooke into the Northern Pacific. The immediate and conscious reason was no doubt the expectation of securing work for Jay Cooke & Co., which then did not have enough to do. The Philadelphian probably also had an unconscious motive, one which even he himself may not have seen clearly; that was the desire to be a factor in the development of the country lying westward from Lake Superior. Jay Cooke was essentially a builder; he had a strong pioneering urge, which had its roots in his own frontier nurture. In his own lifetime he had seen the Indian country along the Great Lakes and the Mississippi develop into flourishing communities. There was no reason to think that the region west of Lake Superior would not also some day be settled and productive. To help develop it appealed strongly to Jay Cooke's imagination and talent for organization.

How far the banker was influenced, in his decision to finance the Northern Pacific, by his other interests in the region around Duluth — his lands and the Lake Superior & Mississippi Railroad — there is no way of knowing, for there is no evidence which points to any conscious relation between the two. But one thing is certain and also extremely significant at this point: by 1871 Jay Cooke had become so heavily involved in a number of projects in the Northwest that it would have been impossible for him to withdraw without heavy loss. Both his own capital and prestige and his firms' had come to be associated very closely with a number of concerns in the Lake Superior country which were faring none too well and which were somewhat dependent on the Northern Pacific. These tended to bind Jay Cooke to the Northern Pacific at a time when he might, without them, have had a desire to withdraw or at least slacken in his support of the great transportation project.

The Lake Superior & Mississippi Railroad was one of the most important links in the chain which bound Jay Cooke to the Northwest. It had been built through some 150 miles of almost untouched forest to connect the head of navigation on the Mississippi with the Great Lakes highway to the East (see map on the preceding page).

This road represented a heavy investment for Jay Cooke & Co. Its construction had been financed by the Cookes and the Clarks, both of whom had invested heavily in the project. When the road had been completed to Duluth in 1870, it was already in a weak financial condition. In order to safeguard what they had put into it, the Philadelphia bankers had made an agreement whereby Frank Clark assumed the presidency and management of the road and the two banking houses co-operated in giving financial aid. As a result of this arrangement the Cookes had by the end of 1870 tied up $300,000 in bonds for which there was scarcely any market.[1]

As so often happens in business, one investment made another necessary. If the road should carry wheat, it had to provide storage at the terminals, particularly since the Great Lakes were ice-bound almost half of the year. And so, as other railroads throughout that section had to do in the absence of storage facilities,[2] the Cookes and Clarks drew on their own resources to build elevators. In 1869 they had organized the Union Improvement & Elevator Co. which had built elevators for the storage of grain at Stillwater and Duluth, the two leading transfer points to and from the railroad. That this was done at no small cost is seen from the fact that the elevator at Duluth — which had a capacity of 550,000 bushels and had the latest equipment, including elevators run with steam power — cost $50,000.[3] It is revealing of conditions in the Middle West at the time that when the bankers were being forced by circumstance to make this investment against their will, farmer interests in Minnesota saw in the Union Improvement & Elevator Co. only another embodiment of that dangerous monster, monopoly, which they feared and hated.[4]

The wheat trade had also to be financed, an especially important matter since the grain had to be held at Duluth for months after the Lakes were closed to traffic in the fall.[5] Jay Cooke considered opening a bank in Duluth, but for some reason that was left to the Clarks, who early in 1871 announced that their bank was "prepared to make Loans on Grain stored in the Duluth Elevator, and to Negotiate Paper drawn against Shipments of Grain and Flour." [6]

This would all have been to the good if the road had secured adequate traffic, but it was not long till it was seen that the expected traffic did not come to the road. Though the forests along the Lake Superior & Mississippi were rich with pine, the lumber industry found convenient transportation to market on the rivers which cut through the forests. There was no gainsaying that the Great Lakes *via* Duluth promised economical east-bound transportation for the products of the upper Mississippi country; but, since the movement of traffic is determined by a complex relationship of business interests, transportation does not always follow the route which offers the best rates.

The Lake Superior & Mississippi suffered from that much-praised competition which is said to be the life of trade. "Our whole system," said President Clark at the beginning of 1871, "is opposed to the Milwaukee & Chicago interest, and we cannot expect friendship or aid from them." The Chicago and Milwaukee grain interests were in league with transportation lines which controlled Minnesota trade. The packet lines on the Mississippi, combined with the Milwaukee & St. Paul and the Chicago & Northwestern and subsidiary railroads, had an iron grip on the wheat trade of the region; through their hold on carriers they could even prevent Minneapolis millers from shipping *via* Duluth.[7] This combination was formidable; not only did it represent aggressive entrepreneurial and capitalistic interests in Chicago and Milwaukee but it also had a strong financial backing in New York.

The Lake Superior road was in a precarious position. It had to have traffic both to get revenue and to bring lake boats regularly to Duluth for freight. To acquire feeders and to circumvent Chicago-Milwaukee competition, the road made plans to reach out in three directions at its southern end late in 1870.[8] A branch line was projected to the St. Croix River, which was an important wheat carrier,[9] and in the fall of 1870 Jay Cooke & Co. drew on its none-too-plentiful funds to make an advance payment of

$50,000 on its subscription to the road's bonds.[10] Another branch was projected to Minneapolis.

A third attempt to reach out for trade looked southwestward toward the Missouri River. A connection was sought for the southern terminus of the Lake Superior road at St. Paul with the St. Paul & Sioux City Railroad. This road was controlled by several men from St. Paul, especially Drake and Thompson, who were railroad promoters and builders. Unfortunately for Jay Cooke's road, they were in a position to bargain, for they were able to trade on a considerable hostility to Jay Cooke's interests in Minnesota growing out of the fact that the development of Duluth was seen as a threat to the southern part of the State and to Minneapolis and St. Paul [11] and that there were those in St. Paul who did not hesitate to say that the Northern Pacific interests favored Minneapolis. The Democratic *St. Paul Pioneer Press* held in the fall of 1870 that that railroad was backing for governor a candidate who was allied with the "peculiar Minneapolis fraternity 'The Construction Company,' and the Construction Company is the double-distilled extract of the Northern Pacific Railroad Company, with Mr. Windom [candidate for the United States Senate] as its preaching apostle." [12] The construction company referred to was the King-Brackett-Windom group of Minneapolis, which succeeded in getting a contract to build a section of the Northern Pacific; [13] the Drake-Thompson-Merriam element of the St. Paul & Sioux City road hated them and lost no occasion, political or otherwise, to attack them or those with whom they were associated. The political complications in Minnesota promised nothing good for Jay Cooke's interests.

Though it would have been to the advantage of the St. Paul & Sioux City to co-operate with the Lake Superior & Mississippi in order to get an outlet for trade free from Chicago-Milwaukee control, its terms were too high for the Lake Superior road.[14] Failing to get its way with the existing road, it made plans to build a branch to the St. Croix River and to form an alliance with the projected St. Croix & Lake Superior Railroad in Wisconsin.[15]

That was the road the land grant of which Jay Cooke had asked to be restored to the market in 1869 because it was a potential rival of the Lake Superior & Mississippi.[16] The banker's action had spurred the promoters to apply for a renewal of the grant,[17] and they found support in a number of interests which looked upon Jay Cooke's projects as dangerous to them. The State of Wisconsin would not allow one of its projects to be stifled by a Minnesota road,[18] and the promoters of Superior City, on the Wisconsin side of St. Louis Bay, were afraid of Jay Cooke's activities on behalf of Duluth. Superior City had been started as a land promotion scheme before the Civil War, chiefly by southerners including Senator Breckenridge and other Kentuckians and Corcoran & Riggs, bankers of Washington; and, while it had barely survived the panic of 1857 and the Civil War, it was still maintaining a weak existence, supported mainly by a Chicago capitalist named Stinson. Jay Cooke's attack on the St. Croix & Lake Superior roused its owners to life.[19]

Duluth and certain interests which headed up there were another strong link in the chain which bound Jay Cooke to the Northern Pacific. Jay Cooke himself owned much land around Duluth and he had made some investments in the village. More important, however, was the fact that he had stood before investors as a sponsor of the place. He had encouraged individuals to invest there, and Duluth was the cornerstone of the hopes of the Western Land Association and the Lake Superior & Puget Sound Company. Two things were essential, however, to its success: that it become a railroad terminal and that it secure help in the building of harbor facilities. By maintaining a strong hold on the Lake Superior road and the Northern Pacific, Jay Cooke expected to accomplish the first object. The second required aid from the government.

Early in 1870 a bill had been introduced in Congress asking for a land grant for a Minnesota corporation organized to dredge the harbor and build a canal to give a suitable approach to Duluth. An expensive lobbying campaign had been conducted by Henry Cooke and Ignatius Donnelly of Minnesota, who had been employed to secure support for the bill. Donnelly found that Jay Cooke's enemies in Minnesota and antagonistic interests in Washington were opposing his projects.[20]

With both the Northern Pacific mortgage bill and the Duluth harbor bill before Congress, it was necessary to placate some of the opposition. Jay Cooke, therefore, proposed an alliance with the Wisconsin interests. The result was the merging of the promotion interests of Superior City and the St. Croix & Lake Superior with the Western Land Association (the affiliate of the Lake Superior & Mississippi which held land in Duluth and along the railroad) and the Northern Pacific. The Wisconsin interests were given a share in the Western Land Association and the Northern Pacific and the promise of a road from the Lake Superior & Mississippi to Superior City; Jay Cooke and his interests were, in exchange, given a hand in the affairs of the railroad enterprises designed to develop northern Wisconsin. By holding the railroad franchises under their control and building the Wisconsin railroads, Jay Cooke and those working with him expected to prevent ruinous competition. Jay Cooke's associates deposited $50,000 with the State treasury of Wisconsin as evidence of their good faith.[21]

Having conciliated the opposition in Wisconsin, the Cooke interests had in the spring of 1870 applied to Congress for the renewal of the land grant of the St. Croix road which they had earlier opposed. They had then expected also to secure the passing of the Duluth harbor bill and the Northern Pacific mortgage bill. The Wisconsin measure failed to pass,[22] however, owing chiefly, it was said, to the fact that the Northern Pacific bill was as big a dose as one Congress could swallow.[23] The Duluth harbor bill also suffered the same fate.[24]

At the beginning of 1871, Jay Cooke's interests centering in Duluth were obviously in a bad way. The Lake Superior railroad was in serious financial straits, and it was strategically in a poor position with respect to traffic. Duluth had received little of the help that had been expected to raise the value of the interests centered there. The banker believed, however, that both the road and the real-estate ventures stood to profit from the advance of the Northern Pacific. He could aid them by helping to finance the great railroad project.

In the meantime, Jay Cooke had also become involved, though

not so directly, in the Red River country. It was recognized by the banker and the promoters of the Northern Pacific that the road had to have feeders since it could not for years, if ever, secure enough traffic along its own line to be profitable. There were prospects of securing much freight on the Red River from the rich agricultural lands of its region and from the trade of the great Hudson's Bay Company, then carried between the Red and the Mississippi by the clumsy two-wheeled Red River carts.

Sometime in the spring of 1869, when he had first been considering the offer of the Northern Pacific, Jay Cooke had met a person who came to have not a little to do with his interest in transportation in the Northwest. James W. Taylor [25] was a former newspaperman who was making a profession of publicizing the Northwest; he was urging the building of railroads in the region and serving as a go-between for various individuals, Canadian or American officials, or groups which had or expected to acquire transportation interests in the Northwest.[26] He favored the annexation of the British Northwest by the United States.[27] Taylor was an impecunious publicist who would work for anyone to keep ahead of the wolf, even to the point of hiring himself out to both parties in a negotiation. He was in a real sense a forerunner of that business auxiliary whom we know today as publicity director or public relations counsel.

Shortly before Jay Cooke had signed his first agreement with the Northern Pacific, Taylor had called on him in Philadelphia, and in the fall of 1869 he had written him at length on the possible route and connections of the Northern Pacific.[28] From then on for about three years the journalist was in close communication with the banker. It is impossible to be sure to what extent Taylor influenced Jay Cooke or how far he was an instrument in the banker's hands.

It was obvious that there was a chance for the development of much traffic for the Northern Pacific in the Red River country, but there was one obstacle in the way, the St. Paul & Pacific Railroad (a part of the Great Northern of later times). This road had been chartered to run northwestward from St. Paul. A part of it, known as the First Division, had been started in two sections, one in a westerly direction toward the Red River and the other northward toward British territory (see map page 329).

The control of the First Division of the St. Paul & Pacific had been offered for sale in the summer of 1869. Moorhead had favored purchasing it, recommending that for the immediate future the Northern Pacific use the Lake Superior & Mississippi and the St. Paul & Pacific for reaching the Red River and then build westward at once from there.[29] The offer had not seriously interested Jay Cooke at the time, though he had written to James W. Taylor for full information about the road. Taylor, who was then employed to dispose of the St. Vincent Extension of the St. Paul & Pacific, not only urged the project upon Jay Cooke, Moorhead, and the president of the Northern Pacific, but also explained the advantages of an extensive railway system connecting the St. Lawrence, Mississippi, Red, and Missouri rivers in order effectually to counteract the strength of Milwaukee and Chicago in that section.[30]

Jay Cooke was not at first enthusiastic about making connections with the St. Paul & Pacific. That became Moorhead's great interest; he made movements and pledges to representatives of the road without conferring with Jay Cooke.[31] Under the influence of Moorhead and of Taylor's schemes for a great system of transportation in the Red River country, but more particularly because of the increasing evidence of conflict between the two Red River roads, Jay Cooke later came to stand out as a leader of the cause of the Northern Pacific in northwestern Minnesota.

The first step in widening the interests of the Northern Pacific in the Red River Valley was the purchase of the projected St. Vincent Extension of the St. Paul & Pacific.[32] When built, this road would give the Northern Pacific a branch northward through the Red River country to the land of the Hudson's Bay Company.

In the meantime that part of the St. Paul & Pacific known as the First Division had become a menace to the Northern Pacific. Fearing the Northern Pacific, this road had asked for a land grant down the Red River and also across Dakota Territory to the

Missouri River. Senator Becker of Minnesota, its president, tried to win the co-operation of the Northern Pacific by offering the use of his road to the Missouri River under a traffic agreement, control to remain in the hands of the St. Paul road. Jay Cooke opposed the combination and it was not accepted. As a result, Becker put forth every effort to secure the passage of the land grant bill. "As to Becker," Jay Cooke wrote to his brother, "he must be whipped, of course. It would never do for that road to have the line down the Red River to Pembina. It would injure Duluth." [33]

The outcome of the affair was that in December, 1870, the Northern Pacific purchased the franchise and property of the whole First Division of the St. Paul & Pacific. The price paid was $1,500,000 in second-mortgage bonds of the road and $500,000 in cash, one-fifth at once and the remainder to be paid in installments over two years. It was arranged that the former officers of the St. Paul & Pacific should continue to manage the First Division and also the St. Vincent Extension. The road then had 201 miles in operation and bore a bonded indebtedness of almost $13,000,000. [34]

The purchase of the St. Vincent Extension by the Northern Pacific had looked toward entrance into Canada. But the Red River region north of the 49th parallel was then in turmoil, and it was uncertain when and how a road could be built to connect with the Northern Pacific at the boundary.

In his eagerness to secure connections with the Canadian territory, Jay Cooke, probably through James W. Taylor, had become interested in the annexation of the British Northwest, to which certain Minnesotans and several members of Congress had been giving attention for some time. Early in 1870 Cooke wrote the following with regard to a certain newspaperman: "Referring to my conversation with him the other night about the Winnipeg business I should like to be one of a number to employ his services wholly in manipulating the annexation of British North America, Northwest of Duluth, to our country. This could be done without any violation of treaties, and brought about as a result of quiet emigration over the border of trustworthy men with families, and with a tacit, not legal understanding with Riley [Louis Riel] and others there. The country belongs to us naturally, and should be brought over without violence or bloodshed."[35]

Shortly afterwards he had directed his Washington brother to see President Grant and the Secretary of State about backing the "Fenians" who were causing trouble for the British authorities in the Red River district. Cooke said that if the Administration approved, he would send for some of the leaders and have the matter attended to at once.[36]   Nothing came of this suggestion at the time, but there is proof that the banker was later in touch with a leader of the Red River insurrection of 1869–70. Probably through arrangements made by Senator Ramsey of Minnesota, he saw William B. O'Donoghue in New York in February, 1871, but he apparently did not then give O'Donoghue much encouragement. It appears that the banker had come to see that, if it should become known that he was backing the filibusterers, it would embarrass him in his business in London.[37]

A quality which is not infrequently found in self-made successful business men showed itself in Jay Cooke in this instance — the belief that success in business makes almost anything possible. A success complex is a dangerous thing for a business man to have. It has sometimes led its victims to attempt the impossible outside of their own field of experience — note Henry Ford's Peace Ship. Fortunately for Jay Cooke, however, nothing came of the plan for the annexation of the British territory.

By 1871 Jay Cooke had become closely associated with those various projects which looked toward the development of a great region and the building of a great railroad empire. Although he apparently had not planned it so from the beginning, circumstance had forced him to advance step by step until he had become enmeshed in a tangle of interests. This meant not only great obligations for others but also heavy investments on the part of Jay Cooke & Co. Since the whole structure was largely dependent on the Northern Pacific, it is clear that it would not have been a simple matter for Jay Cooke to slacken in his support of that road in 1871.

THE CAMPAIGN FOR SELLING NORTHERN PACIFICS

Jay Cooke in 1871 reluctantly opened the bond campaign of the Northern Pacific in the United States. The organization he set up for selling bonds was very similar to that employed in the distribution of war securities. Nothing was done in the South, for there was no capital seeking investment in that unfortunate section still suffering under Reconstruction. But the rest of the country was divided into regions headed by some banking house, such as the Cookes' own houses; Brewster, Sweet, of Boston; Johnston Brothers, of Baltimore; the Painters, of Cleveland; and Lunt, Preston & Kean, of Chicago.[38] These banking houses were generally the more important retailers in their section, and they were expected to organize banks and bankers and look after advertising and publicity in their respective areas. They worked on commission with an allowance for traveling or other expenses.[39]

The press and the platform were again called on to assist Jay Cooke's loan campaign. Early in 1870, A. B. Nettleton was put in charge of advertising and publicity under Jay Cooke's personal direction. Nettleton was an effective writer and a man of good judgment; he had had a long experience, first as editor of the *Daily Commercial Register* of Sandusky and later as commercial editor and publisher of the *Advance*, a national religious journal published in Chicago.[40]

Advertising agencies were employed from time to time as they were needed. A small assignment was given to N. W. Ayer & Son, of Philadelphia, a firm which was just beginning to take on something of the appearance of an advertising agency though it was working chiefly with the local religious press;[41] G. P. Rowell & Co., then the outstanding agency in the United States, sent out special articles which Jay Cooke wanted broadcast by the newspapers of the whole country.[42] But these were special assignments. Jay Cooke probably did not employ the advertising agents extensively because they were still little more than space brokers, and Cooke could probably get more effective and cheaper support from the press through his own and his selling agents' influence.

Jay Cooke's organization again sought to control key positions. Henry Cooke entertained the leading newspapermen of Washington at dinner, and in the summer of 1871 a group of the most prominent editors of the country was taken into the Lake Superior-Red River region as guests of the Northern Pacific.[43] Two New York editors were engaged to help the Northern Pacific cause: Bowen of the *Independent* and Young of the *Standard*.[44] Whenever an editor attacked the Northern Pacific, the Cookes tried to "find out and capture him." [45] The bankers were in a difficult place, for it was not above the hungry press crowd to blackmail if not appeased.[46] That could hardly have been the motive, however, of Editor Bowles of the *Springfield Republican*, whom Jay Cooke believed responsible for a bitter attack by the *Cosmopolitan* and whom he tried to appease by an offer of a substantial amount of bonds. That time Cooke overshot the mark — what satisfaction Bowles must have had in refusing the banker's offer! [47]

The extent to which newspapers were used in building an opinion favorable to the Northern Pacific is shown by a statement of President Smith to a Senate investigating committee in 1872. The first prospectus of the loan — the huge advertisement entitled SAFE! PROFITABLE! PERMANENT! — was published all over the country in newspapers and journals, famous or obscure, large or small, daily, weekly, or monthly. The largest number of newspapers employed at any one time was 1,371. This extensive advertising lasted for only a few days, and by 1872 the number of newspapers used averaged about 140 a month.[48]

Various media besides the newspaper or journal were employed. The large advertisement referred to above was printed separately and was handed out by agents or distributed by post. An early pamphlet which was distributed widely was the *Northern Pacific Railroad's Land Grant and the Future Business of the Road*. The best exposition of Jay Cooke's sales arguments came in the *Northern Pacific Railroad: Its Route, Resources, Progress and Business*, published in 1871. Speeches on the Northern Pacific by prominent men, such as Wm. D. Kelley and S. Garfielde were sent out. For the more leisurely reader who loved adventure and new places, there was "Carleton" Coffin's book, *The Seat of Empire*.[49]

The exact cost of Northern Pacific advertising and publicity cannot be given since so much of it was indirect. By April, 1871, $40,000 had been spent in maps and documents and some $100,-000 had been charged directly to advertising. By May 2, 1872, the sum of $350,000 had been spent.[50]

The purpose of all this advertising and publicity was to interest the potential investor in the Northern Pacific and to prove that the road would be both safe and profitable. Nothing short of the reading of the original publications gives any idea of their extent and forcefulness. It is necessary to an understanding of Jay Cooke's relations with the Northern Pacific, however, to gain a general idea of the reasoning followed.

The bonds bore a high return — so ran the argument. They were selling for currency at their face value while they bore 7.3 per cent, both interest and principal payable in gold. This was excellent income, said a Cooke circular, when the national debt was being refunded at 5 per cent or less and interest on loanable capital "will henceforth not be much above 6 per cent." [51]

To counteract the contention that high income was a compensation for risk, the safety of the bonds was urged. There was no safer investment than first-mortgage railroad bonds: "Of the nearly one thousand railroads of our Northern and Western States, whose total bonded debt exceeds $650,000,000, it is stated that all but three are regularly paying the interest on their first mortgage bonds. . . . The author of *Poor's Railroad Manual*, a standard authority says: 'It is undoubtedly true that railroad securities have proved to be the most productive investment of capital that we have had for twenty years.'" This being true of all ordinary roads, it was doubly true of those which, like the Northern Pacific, had an immense landed property in addition. The bonds of the Northern Pacific were secured by a first mortgage on all the property and rights of the Northern Pacific Railroad Company, which would embrace on the completion of the work: "1. Over Two Thousand Miles of Road, with rolling stock, buildings, and all other equipments. 2. Over Twenty-two Thousand Acres of Land to every mile of finished road. This land [grant], agricultural, timbered and mineral, amounting in all to more than Fifty Million Acres . . . is larger than the six New England States with Maryland added." [52] Pitt Cooke reminded his brother in March, 1871,[53] that there were only 120 miles of road and only 1,400,000 acres of land in the actual control of the Northern Pacific. The Philadelphian knew this well enough, but it was characteristic of him that he did not doubt that the road would be completed and the lands thus acquired.

The Northern Pacific grant — so ran the argument [54] — was located in a region which was richly endowed by nature. There the trinity of a favorable climate, a naturally fertile soil, and sufficient moisture, in most parts, was combined. "The belt of country tributary to the Northern Pacific Road is within the parallels of latitude which in Europe, Asia, and America, embrace the most enlightened, creative, conquering, and progressive populations." This Fertile Belt was tremendously rich in resources. There was not only soil which could produce abundantly, but also timber at the eastern and western ends which would provide sufficient lumber for the whole area and for export, also; there was coal in abundance at various places; there were rich deposits of copper and magnetic iron ore near Lake Superior; and precious metals, particularly gold, enriched the Rocky Mountain area through which the Northern Pacific was projected.

The traffic possibilities of the road were naturally a major consideration. The Northern Pacific was expected to have a heavy traffic in the future, said Jay Cooke's publicity. Much work was already awaiting the road on the Columbia River, the upper Missouri, and the Yellowstone, as well as on the Red River, but this was nothing compared with what the future would bring. There were even visions of a great trade with the still-dreaming Orient in which the Northern Pacific would have a strong share because the sailing distance between Puget Sound and the ports of China was 600 to 800 miles less than between San Francisco and China, and the Northern Pacific would bring Liverpool and New York 1,400 miles nearer to the ports of China and Japan. Along its own course, however, the road would find its heaviest work. Supplemented by waterways as feeders, it would have no rival in drawing trade from an area 1,800 by 700 miles which, it was said, would some day support 30,000,000 people. The shipment of cattle over the Northern Pacific road promised to equal that upon any line in America, and the road was to open to the world's markets a region which at a very early day would furnish the bulk of the surplus wheat crop of the United States. Moreover, the shipment of supplies for the mining population and the transportation of their products eastward promised a rich traffic.

Looking backward today, we see that Northern Pacific publicity in 1871 gave a reasonably restrained picture of the prospects of the road for the long run. It contained little of that Wilkesonian exaggeration which characterized the earlier efforts.[55] It was dignified and defensible, and it was based on the soundest information then available. There was only one thing to question about it all. When would that development mature to a position where it could support a railroad?

The potential investor was not left to the influence of the press, alone. To give the Northern Pacific prestige, Jay Cooke also sought the support of prominent men. Schuyler Colfax, vice-president of the United States, was offered a connection with the Northern Pacific. "I consider it one of the highest compliments I ever received in my life," wrote Colfax to Cooke; though he was unable to accept as long as Congress was in session, he offered to do all he could to help the project, such as to aid in securing appropriations for surveys.[56] Jay Cooke wrote to Colfax that the road would not appeal to Congress for aid nor "have any complications with its good father the Government," and promised to keep the enterprise "pure and free from all entanglements of every kind," building "with close economy, without clique, credit mobilier, private contracts, or anything of the kind."[57] Though Colfax never became directly connected with the project, he wrote an article on the Northern Pacific which first appeared in Bowen's New York *Independent* early in 1871 and was copied far and wide by newspapers and broadcast in the form of pamphlets; 75,000 copies were distributed by an insurance company.[58]

Other prominent figures were also employed by the Cookes. Garfielde, delegate in Congress from Washington Territory, delivered a lecture on the climate of the great Northern Pacific Northwest which was printed as a pamphlet in 1872 under the title of *Climates of the Northwest*. Ex-Governor Marshall of Minnesota wrote for publication what he saw on expeditions westward into the Fertile Belt; [59] and Senator Windom of Minnesota was in the service of the road. [60] None less than former Senator Benjamin Wade was chosen to be attorney for the Northern Pacific in Washington, to aid in getting appropriations for surveys, secure title to lands under the grant, and manage other matters in which the Northern Pacific had dealings with the government. [61]

One of the most spectacular episodes in the Northern Pacific campaign was a meeting held in Philadelphia in June, 1871. Wm. D. Kelley — ranking Republican orator in Congress and for 20 years chairman of the Committee on Ways and Means [62] — was invited by the Commercial Exchange of Philadelphia to speak "on the development of the Northwest section of the Continent by the building of the Northern Pacific Railroad." (The hands were the hands of the Commercial Exchange, but the voice was clearly that of Jay Cooke!) Four thousand gathered in the Academy of Music on the occasion. Governor Geary of Pennsylvania was elected chairman, and 323 of Philadelphia's solid men of business were elected vice-presidents!

Congressman Kelley spoke with the utmost intensity and fervor for two hours. He traced the history of transportation projects to the Pacific; he stressed the favorable location of the Northern Pacific in world trade; and he grew eloquent over the prospects of the Northern Pacific Empire. The ardent humanitarian visioned the Northern Pacific in a great rôle: it "will open to settlement . . . a territory that would accommodate all the peasantry of Europe, and, by the development of its boundless and varied mineral and agricultural resources, lift millions of men from poverty to wealth, and enable many who are burdens upon society to bless it by their prosperity!" Kelley's speech was printed and scattered far and wide in support of the project for which he had spoken.

Though the object of Northern Pacific publicity was to influence the potential investor to buy bonds, to Jay Cooke and his banking house it came to have a further meaning. It became one of the strongest links which bound Jay Cooke & Co. to the Northern Pacific, for it made the banking house stand in the opinion of the investor as a sponsor of the railroad. Under their contract with the railroad, the Cookes did not underwrite the bond issue; but because of their extensive advertising and publicizing of the project, their prestige virtually came to be pledged in support of the enterprise.

THE BONDS AND THE LANDS OF THE NORTHERN PACIFIC SELL SLOWLY

In spite of Jay Cooke's vigorous selling campaign, the results were distinctly disappointing. By July 1, 1871, the bonds sold totaled less than $2,500,000 above the pool subscription of $5,000,000.[63] Already in March the disappointment of the partners with the sales was quite evident; Henry Cooke expressed his regret that Jay was having so much trouble over the Northern Pacific since he had gone into it largely to help his brothers.[64] By June, Moorhead was urging Jay to build up a reserve to meet costs and interest in the first few years: "I write you because we so seldom have a chance to talk & you get excited thinking I am wrong & you right all the time. I implore you to think calmly & earnestly over this matter & of your condition in the event of failure of N. P., or, of payment of coupons on bonds, sold on your personal recommendation, and faith in your judgment & integrity." [65]

In the month of July about $700,000 of bonds were sold, but at the same time $600,000 were repurchased from Budge, Schiff & Co. In August, sales picked up, and still more were sold in September. In October, the near-panic following upon the Chicago fire depressed sales again, but in November sales exceeded a million. Late November and December saw a tight money market. The New York house then feared that their bonds were getting to be an "old story," and that nothing could be done until the road had something tangible to show. So discouraging was the year on the whole that at the end of December Jay Cooke wrote to the treasurer of the Northern Pacific: "My experience is that if we succeed beyond what we have already done, it will be almost at the expense of my health. . . . I would not again undertake such a job for all the money in the whole world." [66]

The weakness of the Northern Pacific bonds cannot be blamed to any great extent on the condition of the money or bond markets in 1871; the situation was then, on the whole, more favorable to railroad financing than had been the case for at least two years. But the great northwestern transportation project was not in a condition to make a strong appeal.

The sale of Northern Pacifics was weakened by the fact that subscribers were expected to hold the bonds for income. Obviously, investors who wanted to keep their assets liquid would not tie up funds where they could not be turned. The reason for the rule was that Jay Cooke wished to prevent the bonds from returning to the market to depress the price. The alternative was to be prepared to support the bonds on the market, but Jay Cooke could not do that because his working capital was too small. "I am looking forward to the time," he wrote in December, 1871,[67] "when we shall have so much money in hand, that we can come down on the market and stiffen it up, and make people sorry they did not buy more bonds at par. But at present we prefer only to sell to those who expect to hold the bonds a reasonable time."

The greatest obstacle the loan campaign had to meet was unquestionably the fact that there were no prospects that the Northern Pacific would soon be a paying concern. Jay Cooke had from the first seen the necessity of aggressive sale of the land, both to bring in money from land sales and to provide traffic.[68] He had expected that by the fall of 1871 the selling of land would be sufficiently well under way to help the Northern Pacific treasury, but this did not come to pass. One thing stood immediately in the way of selling the road's acres and building settlements; the Northern Pacific acquired its lands only as a 25-mile section of the railway was completed. Since most of the line in Minnesota was through dense forest, there was no agricultural land available for settlement before the Red River Valley was reached. The settlement of the road's lands had, therefore, to wait until a long section of railway had been constructed.

The land department of the Northern Pacific was not organized until the spring of 1871. John S. Loomis, who had been notably successful in directing the colonization of the lands of a railroad in Kansas,[69] was made land commissioner, and he immediately set to work to inspect the lands and to do the preliminaries necessary to selling and colonizing them.[70] A commissioner of immigration was also appointed to bring in settlers.[71]

A large organization was thus set up and far-seeing policies were adopted for settling the lands, but the project could not bear immediate fruit. It took time to reach prospective settlers and to bring them into the West. It is not strange, therefore, that those efforts succeeded in bringing few settlers to the Fertile Belt in 1871. The failure to sell much land was extremely unfortunate, for the income from land sales and traffic was very much needed. The real question was whether the Northern Pacific could carry the burden of the lag between the construction of the road and settlement.

By then it was clear that Jay Cooke had made a grave error in relying so heavily on the lands. Again it must be observed that it was his timing which was wrong — it is doubtful that the best of plans could have settled the best of lands under the best business conditions in so short a time as would have been necessary in order to help the Northern Pacific.

It must not be concluded that there was no settlement along the Northern Pacific. By 1871 there was a considerable movement into the Red River Valley.[72] Those settlers probably, however, took government land; and the Red River Valley was a large region. Eventually, of course, such a movement would inevitably fill the Northern Pacific lands; it was only a question of time, but in business, time is very important.

As for the bonds of the Northern Pacific, they were obviously in no condition to attract investors in so highly competitive a bond market as existed in 1871. The market was then offering a large amount of bonds of sound railroads which yielded well for conservative investments. The older railroads in the more settled sections had come into their own, and some of them were enjoying the fruits of careful management and a developed traffic.

For the more speculative, there were many new roads from which to choose.[73] Among them was the Chesapeake & Ohio, which was offering the $4,000,000 remaining of $15,000,000 of bonds at 94; out of the 427 miles projected, 322 had already been built. The St. Joseph & Denver City Railroad was offering $5,500,000 of 8 per cents at $97\frac{1}{2}$; this road which was planned to be 170 miles long was to complete a line connecting Missouri with the Union Pacific. The Louisville & Nashville was offering $8,000,000 of 7 per cent bonds at $92\frac{1}{2}$. The Burlington, Cedar Rapids & Minnesota was offering 7 per cent gold bonds at 90. The Peoria & Rock Island the same. The West Wisconsin Railway was selling $4,000,000 bonds on 154 miles of railroad at 90. Compare these with the Northern Pacific, which was offering $100,000,000 on 2,000 miles of road at 100!

It is significant to note the amount of mortgage per mile of some of the new roads. The Chesapeake & Ohio, uniting somewhat developed trade and production areas, was mortgaging itself $35,000 a mile; the St. Joseph, connecting a completed road with an older section and having a substantial land grant, $49,107 a mile; the West Wisconsin, which had a respectable land grant, was offering about $25,000 of bonds a mile; the Mobile & Montgomery, $13,000; and the Omaha & Northwestern, another land-grant road, $16,000. Again compare these with the Northern Pacific, a land-grant road, which was offering bonds for $50,000 a mile.

Nothing can possibly show more effectively than the above comparisons with other railroads why the Northern Pacific bonds went so slowly. It is probably accurate to say that but for the prestige of Jay Cooke and his firms the bonds would hardly have sold at all. But even with their best efforts the sales fell far short of what the road needed.

DIFFICULTIES WITH THE EXECUTIVES OF THE NORTHERN PACIFIC

Though Jay Cooke had no intention of taking a hand in the management of the Northern Pacific, it was not long before he discovered that its officers lacked both energy and reliability. Rumors came to him of irregularities in the road's management,[74] and such substantial railroad men as S. M. Felton and J. Edgar Thomson urged that construction had to be planned and supervised more carefully.[75] But of greatest importance to Jay Cooke & Co. was the fact that from the first there was a dangerous lack of co-operation on the part of the officers of the Northern Pacific with the bankers.

Several points of contention arose between the Northern Pacific management and the road's financial agent. One was the way in which iron was purchased. The bankers, as authorized by the contract with the Northern Pacific, wanted to have charge of purchasing for the road, for then they could keep the amount bought within their means to pay and they could use bonds in payment. But the Northern Pacific executives preferred to manage purchasing. Jay Cooke repeatedly urged that arrangements be made to take payment in bonds and that he be consulted in advance of purchases so he could be prepared.[76]

The crux of the whole difficulty was that the Northern Pacific was drawing on Jay Cooke & Co. faster than it could sell bonds. As early as January, 1871, Jay Cooke was urging the road to cut drafts on his house; on August 23, the company was overdrawn about $600,000, which exceeded the limit provided by the contract with the road.[77] During the depression in the fall of 1871 following the Chicago fire, Jay Cooke requested the temporary suspension of purchases and of the making of new construction contracts, but President Smith held that they had to order iron long in advance to be certain of having it in time to meet the charter requirements on construction and that it would look bad if work on the road were slackened.[78]

At this time Jay Cooke urged President Smith to be cautious:[79]

It won't answer to create liabilities before we have the money on hand. *You must not do it* for I cannot carry with my partners a greater advance than the contract calls for. I have over and over pledged myself to them to advance no more — & this amount I fear will be needed to pay interest next January — if we don't sell bonds. There is no need of pushing things until we know how the times will turn. . . . I will do all that mortal man — trusting in his God — can do to sell Bonds, but it is not wise to launch out into a big contract like this one to Red River, when we have so much to finish up of old work, interest to pay, &c. . . . I am not an alarmist and have more courage than is good for me, but my sober common-sense tells me we are to have a bad, *bad* time — tight money and general distrust.

Jay Cooke warned that "I have frankly & honestly advised you as above and if you go ahead without the means provided, it will not be my fault if you have trouble."

In November Jay Cooke protested against additional overdrafts. "Do not yet know where the money is to come from. The account is already overdrawn $100,000, the bonds are not selling to any extent, and it is impossible to force sales. Have had to buy back to sustain the market already within a few days, or the whole fabric would go to ruin." [80] Two weeks later he again complained: "Phew! Phew!! Phew!!! That dose of $400,000 in addition to amount already paid is a big thing to swallow. You must stave off the Minnesota Construction people until next week — a part of it, and let them draw short sight drafts & all the others that you can." [81] By December Cooke was warning the treasurer of the necessity of keeping the road's finances in such a shape as to avoid dishonoring its credit.[82]

Jay Cooke, remembering the wasteful building of the Lake Superior & Mississippi, was also disturbed over the high cost of the road and was pleading for more economical construction. He felt that the heavy expenditures proposed in the new Dakota contract were beyond all necessity; that the costs were far above the costs of other roads. "I beg of you, Dear Governor, to take the bull by the horns to see whether we cannot do work for the Northern Pacific as economically as it can be done in Iowa & other parts of the country." [83]

The banker pointed to a weakness in Northern Pacific management. He wrote President Smith that "the President, Directors, &c, — every one of whom has five times as much business as any one man ought to do are entirely insufficient to watch the leaks in the expenditures & estimates." He did not believe that all the men working for the road would be honest or would show the best judgment, and he therefore urged upon President Smith that someone in a responsible position should be in Minnesota to supervise the work and thus prevent extravagant expenditures. If something in this direction were not done, he would prefer that his firm resign from their position as financial agent of the road: "You must remember that my responsibility is greater than that of all the rest put together, as the money thus to be expended comes in 90 cases out of a hundred from those who purchase simply on my word, not on the word of Jay Cooke & Co. in this case so much as my personal reputation. If failure should occur, scarcely a word would be said or an imputation be cast upon any director or upon anybody but myself." [84]

The point that failure would reflect on Jay Cooke is extremely significant. He had fallen into the trap of which his partners had warned him. How far he had gone in endorsing the Northern Pacific can best be shown by quoting from one of the many letters he wrote to prospective bond buyers: [85]

First. I regard 1st Mortgage R.R. bonds, as next to governments the best security in the land. I have been selling the first mortgage bonds of railroads for over 30 years, and not one of these has failed to pay interest promptly and most of them are now worth more than when I sold them. I think the Northern Pacifics the best railroad bond we have ever sold. I have taken great pains individually in connection with the eminent Board of Directors, and with other members of my firm, to make this mortgage bond perfectly secure, as I knew great numbers would invest solely upon our reputation as bankers, and because we recommended them. Therefore, we have required the Company to give to the 1st Mortgage bond holders all their property, road rolling stock, depots, telegraph lines and all the immense land grant which the government has donated.

This is entirely different from the course usually pursued. The Union & Central Pacific Roads have not given any of their lands in security for their 1st Mortgage bonds but have sold their land grant bonds separately — We also give bond holders 1 3/10 % more than the dividend over the stockholders — This has been done because the bulk of the money to build the road comes from the bondholders and we think it right as a further security to them.

I requested that I should be made Trustee in connection with J. Edgar Thomson, President of the Penna R.R. of the bonds, and all the lands pass through our hands, Not an acre can be diverted, but all the proceeds must be used in paying the interest and principal of the bonds now issued. We all think that after the bondholders are provided for abundantly, and a large portion of the debt paid off, the stockholders will have an immense property as a reward for their time, talent and many years devotion to the interests of the road.

I would not advise you to put all you have in the world into any one thing, even into governments — If $15,000 is all you have, you ought not to put over 7 or $8,000 in the Northern Pacific, but if you have other resources to an equal extent, I would not hesitate to advise you to put the whole $15,000 in these 7 3/10 % bonds, I believe that interest will be punctually paid — During the construction of the road, and probably for a year or so afterwards, this interest is paid partially out of the proceeds of the bonds sold, the basis of all being the road and the enormous amount of splendid lands, all of which are available for the payment of interest and principal.

This letter is extremely indicative of what was happening to Jay Cooke. The very words he used reveal a subconscious feeling that he was getting in too deeply. He was striving hard for arguments with which to support the Northern Pacific, but the sum of them all was that he stood behind the enterprise. He clearly recognized that the road, itself, had nothing to stand on.

It is well to stop here to note how complicated Jay Cooke's relations with the road really were. He and his houses had invested in the Northern Pacific; in making advances to the road he was using the deposits of other people in his banks; he was pledging his own word heavily in support of the project; and, lastly, he was one of the two trustees of the mortgage bondholders, so that he was legally and morally bound to defend their interests. A more complicated set-up of conflicting responsibilities can scarcely be imagined: Jay Cooke was investor, trustee of bondholders, banker responsible for deposits, and salesman, all in one. Which of these responsibilities was to win in case of trouble? The problem was not a simple one.

THE LOAN CAMPAIGN IN EUROPE

The hope of a successful European negotiation helped to sustain Jay Cooke's courage throughout 1871. In the early part of the year conditions were none too hopeful; but in May the agreement of the United States and Great Britain to submit the *Alabama* Claims to arbitration and the settlement between France and Prussia gave promise of peace. Both in England and in Germany capital became more confident than it had been for some time and the interest in railroad bonds increased. The New Germany, especially, was ready to put its young strength and the French indemnity into whatever promised good returns.

About the time that those international complications were settled, Jay Cooke's representatives undertook a foreign negotiation which extended throughout the remainder of the year 1871. Through a representative of Bischoffsheim & Goldschmidt of London, who had agreed to help negotiate the sale of Northern Pacifics, they opened negotiations with the Oppenheims of Cologne, one of the oldest and wealthiest banking firms in all Germany. Encouraged by conditions at home, the Oppenheims and the great *Bank für Industrie und Handel* of Darmstadt were said to be ready to sign a contract to undertake the placing of the Northern Pacific loan.[86] By the time Fahnestock arrived in Cologne, however, the Oppenheims had learned that the loan had been turned down by the Rothschilds and had for a year been in the hands of the Budges, who had no standing as bankers.[87]

Though the old Baron Oppenheim hesitated, "being too rich and independent to go into anything involving responsibility and work without the cooperation of A1 parties," the junior Oppenheims were willing to seek others to undertake the project with them. They recommended the *Union Bank* of Vienna, which they believed would "take five or six million francs" because it had plenty of money and needed business. The *Union Bank* was interested. It suggested an association with the *Deutsche Bank* of Berlin, the *Sachsse Credit Bank* of Dresden, the *Vereins Bank* of Munich, Erlanger's Bank of Frankfort, and the *Banque des Pays-Bas* of Amsterdam and Brussels.

The negotiations could, however, go no further without the consent of Bischoffsheim & Goldschmidt of London under the terms of the contract with them. After a considerable delay, the contracts with both Bischoffsheim & Goldschmidt and the Budge associates were finally cancelled. This was a relief to Jay Cooke & Co. The Bischoffsheims had shown no disposition to sell bonds; their only object had evidently been to maintain a connection with Jay Cooke & Co. so as to get a hand in refunding the Civil War debts.[88] And the Budges had threatened to throw their Northern Pacific bonds on the market. Reluctantly, Jay Cooke & Co. repurchased bonds for $600,000 from them in July.[89]

Fahnestock was hopeful over the prospect of winning the aid of the Viennese bank. The Viennese had a great deal of capital seeking investment and America would be a new field for them. "The Union Bank," reported Fahnestock, "controls the Press of Austria completely & are very sanguine that they can place not only a large amt of the loan but put the whole of it in their own circle." Yet the ghosts of earlier mistakes haunted Fahnestock.

His fears were justified. The *Union Bank* finally made an agreement with Jay Cooke & Co. to join Jay Cooke, McCulloch & Co. and Bischoffsheims' solicitor (who had opened the negotiation) as sole and exclusive agent in Europe for placing $50,000,000 of bonds, the *Union Bank* undertaking to organize a group to manage the sale of bonds in Germany.[90] Fahnestock was finally enthusiastic. "I like the snap of these fellows but their acquisitiveness is overwhelming," he wrote from Vienna to his London partners.[91] He was certain this arrangement could not fail as "they own the press body & breeches"— the only thing to be feared was that they might be excessive in their statements! Then came word that the Viennese had cancelled their contract because of Frankfort influence and the new French loan.[92] Again, the shadow of the Budge associates and the Franco-Prussian War!

The *Union Bank* and its associates would not give up the project altogether but wanted to send a committee to investigate the Northern Pacific. Five commissioners, prominent engineers and bankers, arrived in the United States in the summer of 1871. Jay Cooke gave stern orders that they should be treated as plain men who should be met with frank discussion rather than with the methods of diplomacy and secret statecraft, such as Sargent had unfortunately employed in Europe.[93]

The commissioners were conducted over the eastern and western sections of the Northern Pacific by Engineer Roberts and Sargent. The prospects seemed good. Jay Cooke, who was then in high spirits over the syndicating of the government loan, felt certain that seeing the great Northern Pacific country and the rapid advance of the road would convince the commissioners of the feasibility of the project.[94] Even Fahnestock believed that "the effect of this great 'coup de etat,'" the syndicating of the government loan, would be to ensure success to any loan they would bring out under fair conditions.[95] Though McCulloch was lukewarm, he wrote Jay Cooke that "with a favorable report from the Commission we will see if we cannot place the Bonds before the public in a manner which will insure their being taken." [96] To the great disappointment and chagrin of Jay Cooke, it soon became evident that the commissioners were not to be convinced easily. From the time of their arrival, they had questioned the feasibility of paying interest in the first few years without traffic, and by the time they were returning eastward, the Philadelphia banker was thoroughly irritated with their views.[97]

Though the commissioners would not report before sailing, Jay Cooke and his partners were not altogether discouraged. Their success with the government loan in 1871 had raised their standing sufficiently in England so that there was some hope of arranging the syndicating there of $10,000,000 or more Northern Pacifics [98] — "everything is being prepared for putting the bonds out in England, if the Germans don't take hold."[99] November and December passed. The year ended and no decision came from the Germans. By that time Jay Cooke and his partners were very much disturbed, and Cooke was tempted to withdraw the whole negotiation from Europe —"We can most certainly sell all the bonds here with a little time and patience." [100]

PERSONAL LOSSES IN 1871 ACCENTUATE JAY COOKE'S BUSINESS DIFFICULTIES

His business, his church and charities, and his family had been Jay Cooke's greatest interests. In them he had found a rich and satisfying life. But those old interests were all slipping away from him.

By the end of 1871, Jay Cooke's business had become burdensome and disappointing and his prestige as a banker had fallen considerably. The confidence and loyalty of his partners were, moreover, changing to distrust and ill-feeling. There was clearly a growing division in the Cooke firms. McCulloch was dissatisfied over the turn of events in the London house; he maintained that his firm had not been given the independence of action which it had been promised and he felt bitterly over the fact that the Northern Pacific had done so much to discredit it.[101] Fahnestock was less co-operative than ever; he completely dominated the New York house and the relations of Jay Cooke & Co. with its foreign affiliate. Jay Cooke definitely had the support of only the weaker members of his two firms.

He had been losing in other ways. His generous heart had come to be restrained by a cautious hand. He had been forced to cut his gifts to charities and educational institutions. His firms gave liberally to help the relief work after the Chicago fire,[102] but, aside from that, most of their gifts went into the Northern Pacific country. Jay Cooke encouraged the work of the Home Missionary Society, the American Sunday School Union, the Y. M. C. A., and the cause of "temperance," and he aided particularly in the building of churches along the Northern Pacific.[103] The main object of this aid was apparently "to civilize the country lying along our roads." [104] It is significant that even his gifts to church and charity had come to be dominated by a business motive.

Jay Cooke's relations with the Church, which had always meant so much to him, were also slipping. In 1871 he drifted into an impasse with the Episcopal Church over its exclusiveness and high-church tendencies.[105] The questions at issue were closed communion and the exclusion of other Protestant ministers from the Episcopal pulpits. "My dear Bishop," wrote Jay Cooke to a Bishop Lee in 1871, "the *whole* prayer book should be taken hold of by *conscientious, evangelical* hands and remodelled to suit the *Protestant* feelings of America, and everything that look like priestcraft, apostolic succession dogmas, regeneration dogmas, exclusive dogmas, uncharitable, unchristian, inhospitable dogmas — all should be stricken out. We should come down to the basis, and put our feet on the rock Christ Jesus and go ahead!"[106]

His third great interest, his singularly happy home, was also broken up at the same time. Jay Cooke had never been a student nor an extensive reader nor a club man. The social connections of the Cookes had been very narrow, just a few friends. The Cooke home was a hospitable place, but so far as Jay Cooke was concerned, that was a matter of business or merely a way of satisfying his generous nature; it was not an important element in his life. His family, however, had been everything to him, and he and Mrs. Cooke showed a rare devotion to each other. Yet this fine family relationship was in a short time broken. The children grew up and acquired their own interests. Jay Cooke, Jr., and Laura by 1871 had homes of their own, the latter having become the wife of Charles D. Barney, a young clerk in the Philadelphia Cooke bank; the second daughter was also married in the fall of 1871; and the youngest son was away at school. In July, 1871, as a climax to this breaking up of the family, when the government loan and the Northern Pacific were resting especially heavily on Jay Cooke, his wife died.[107] This was a heavy blow. How much it may have affected him, there is no way of knowing— his Christian philosophy and the pressure of business made him appear adjusted to the loss. Yet it must have left a great void and have taken away some of the incentive and the spirit that had earlier actuated him.

Jay Cooke was no longer the buoyant, masterful man that he had been, though he was only fifty years of age and should still have been in the prime of his strength. He was, instead, tired and irritable, and he lacked the decisiveness that had earlier characterized his work. He had gotten his firms into a difficult place. The banker himself and his banking house had become deeply involved in railroads, land ventures, and politics. Jay Cooke & Co. had tied up many hundreds of thousands of dollars in other railroads than the Northern Pacific. Even without the great transcontinental road, they would have been in no happy situation. They were in a serious predicament: they could not go backward without serious loss, nor yet go forward, it seemed, without taking on too heavy burdens.

INCREASING DIFFICULTIES WITH THE NORTHERN PACIFIC IN 1872

IN SPITE of the stresses and strains which the year 1871 had brought, it was on the surface the most profitable year Jay Cooke's firms had ever had. The Northern Pacific had yielded them generous commissions; the syndicating of the government loan was the biggest single negotiation that had come their way since the war; and the foreign commercial banking of the New York and London houses had been exceedingly profitable. The new London house earned in 1871 the handsome sum of £100,000. The New York house, which had declared no dividends since 1868, divided $650,000 at the end of the year, 10 per cent of which went to the Old Patriarch Jacob, leaving the neat sum of $585,000 for the partners. The Philadelphia house divided $500,000, that is, $50,000 to the Old Patriarch and $450,000 to the partners. The Washington house alone had nothing to divide.[1]

There was much that was promising at the beginning of the year 1872. There were then excellent grounds for the expectation of Jay Cooke and his partners that they would soon be given further refunding to do for the Treasury. And there was real cause for rejoicing in the fact that the Northern Pacific at the end of 1871 had reached the Red River; for the first time there was some hope of traffic and of income from the sale of lands. Yet there were troubles ahead. The years 1872 and 1873 were to be far different from 1871. The foreign exchange business continued to be profitable, but in their other work the Cookes were to meet only disappointment and frustration. Underneath it all was a tightening of the money market and a slowing up of business in general.

REFUNDING IS BLOCKED IN 1872

The successful syndicating of the government loan of 1871 had led the Cookes to believe that they would be given the management of another issue. They had reason to think that the Rothschilds would co-operate with them on equal terms; and they continued to hope that success in selling government bonds would lead to securing aid in the sale of Northern Pacifics. Jay Cooke, therefore, proposed to the Secretary of the Treasury that Jay Cooke & Co., Jay Cooke, McCulloch & Co., and the Rothschilds be given a new $600,000,000 loan to sell, a part to bear 4½ and a part 5 per cent, interest to be paid in Europe.[2]

The proposal was not accepted by the Treasury. Strong opposition to the employment of the Cookes stood in the way. The opposition took the form of criticism of Secretary Boutwell for his handling of the syndicate loan in 1871. He was accused of allowing compensation exceeding the maximum set by the refunding act by allowing the proceeds of bond sales to remain for three months without interest in the hands of participating banks. Though both the Committee on Ways and Means and the House of Representatives upheld the Secretary, the publicity given the matter pointed to the great profits of the syndicate.[3]

Another complication grew out of the fact that Morton, Rose & Co. and Drexel, Morgan & Co., particularly, wanted to get a hand in the loan. Jay Cooke admitted that, in view of the part played by Sir John Rose in bringing about the Treaty of Washington, the Mortons should be given some consideration. Though he would allow others to participate in the loan, he insisted that it be managed by his own firms and the Rothschilds.[4]

Nothing came of the proposed syndicate in 1872. The attacks on Secretary Boutwell and his refunding plans delayed action until concern over the coming election made the administration postpone the matter until the presidential election was over. The Cookes continued to stay close to the President and the Secretary, and they were given reason to believe that they would be assigned the leading part in the refunding operations to be resumed after elections.[5]

It was extremely unfortunate for Jay Cooke & Co. that their plans for selling a refunding loan in 1872 did not go into effect, for it is reasonable to suppose that they would have been successful. Success would have bound the Rothschilds to them and would presumably have brought enormous profits. Both the prestige and the profits would have strengthened Jay Cooke & Co. in its other business and would have given it greater means with which to meet the needs of the Northern Pacific. Frustration in this government loan matter was a major tragedy for Jay Cooke & Co.

An Error in London

Having failed in two and a half years of effort to get a European house to sponsor the Northern Pacific loan, the Cookes had become convinced that they themselves would have to introduce the bonds in Europe. That was, accordingly, done in January, 1872. Jay Cooke, McCulloch & Co. offered bonds to the amount of £4,000,000 to syndicate subscribers at a price that was expected to be very attractive. Only £500,000 were actually taken, however, though as much again was subscribed but was merely speculative and not in accordance with the aim to sell the bonds to investors and was, therefore, not allotted.[6]

Since the syndicate had an option on the remainder of the issue, Jay Cooke, McCulloch & Co., presumably representing the syndicate, tried to sell the remainder of the loan to the public. In so doing they made an error which proved embarrassing. Because of a misunderstanding with Jay Cooke, which seems to have risen out of the difference in the currency and sterling value of the dollar, they offered the loan to the public at the syndicate or wholesale price. That price was about 10 per cent below the price for which it was being sold in the United States though it was all they could hope to get in London. The difference in price in favor of the British was severely criticized in the United States and proved extremely embarrassing. Jay Cooke, therefore, ordered the repurchase of the bonds and the abrogation of the syndicate. All but £50,000 of the £500,000 was repurchased, at a loss on the transaction of close to £40,000.[7]

The loans were then offered in London at close to par in currency. The plan was for Jay Cooke, McCulloch & Co. to manipulate the market for Northern Pacifics. But, as the London partners had predicted, the price proved too high. A report of the transaction as of April 6 showed that, at a cost of £32,874, net sales of £88,640 had been made. In this matter, thereafter, practically nothing was accomplished for the Northern Pacific in London.[8]

THE HOME MARKET TAKES NORTHERN PACIFICS SLOWLY IN 1872

The situation in the home market was far from satisfactory in the winter of 1872. It is true that sales totaled $1,500,000 in January, but in February they fell off to $1,000,000, and in March they were much smaller. Jay Cooke had believed that the completion of the road to the Red River would help sales; and the establishment of Yellowstone National Park was looked upon by the Cookes as recognition of their claims for the Northern Pacific country.[9] At the same time, however, things occurred which worked very strongly against the road. Word of the failure of the German negotiation had its effect, though the report of the commissioners was not made public. It is interesting to note that the report was in many ways very favorable to the Northern Pacific; but it asked for one impossible change, the establishment of a reserve fund to carry interest until traffic had developed sufficiently.[10] The Banks Resolution in Congress, proposing an investigation of the Northern Pacific, proved to have a serious effect on sales even though the attack was cleverly turned into favorable publicity.[11] The Cookes, who had been saying that the lands of the Northern Pacific were worth from $2.50 to $10.00 an acre, were very much embarrassed by the statement of Senator Wilson of New Hampshire that the lands were not worth 5 cents an acre.[12] Having contributed $10,000 to Wilson's party for campaigning in New Hampshire, Jay Cooke & Co. asked the Senator for the "amende honorable." "It is wrong of course," said Jay Cooke, "and if he does not correct it we will smash him flatter than a pancake." Wilson hastily made an acceptable explanation, and he was requested by Jay Cooke to sketch in his future speeches the progress of the Northern Pacific. [13]

As if driven by adversity, Jay Cooke at this time became more aggressively enthusiastic over the Northern Pacific than ever before. That enthusiasm was mixed with not a little irritability — his nerves were obviously becoming ragged. He was impatient with Fahnestock and Moorhead for what he considered their lukewarmness. To the London partners, to selling agents, and bond buyers, he wrote most glowing accounts of the Northern Pacific country. The completion of the road to the Red River and its advance toward the Missouri, together with progress between the Columbia River and Puget Sound, provided him a happy theme. He continued to emphasize the great value of the land grant: "there is really nothing on the market as secure as these Northern Pacific bonds, based as they are upon the double security of the road & land grant." Jay Cooke criticized the engineers' reports on the lands: "Of course we must stick to the truth, but there are several ways of stating the truth. I would have it enthusiastically stated and a reasonable allowance made for all new countries and for all difficulties in the way of their settlement." So far did he go in the praise of Northern Pacifics as to say that "there is no bond like them in the United States, none half so secure and that has half so many privileges." [14]

Toward the end of March the banker became panicky. Sales promised to be not over $400,000 for the month, "about as much as will pay accumulated interest." He saw all their enemies closing in upon them, the St. Croix people, banking and newspaper cliques in Philadelphia and New York, and even the Union Pacific —"We are denounced as swindlers, our roads, route, & lands ditto not only in England but Canada, and by secret circulars all around." [15]

The Cookes were not only denounced but also ridiculed for their relations with the Northern Pacific. Some wit dubbed the region the road was to traverse—which the publicity of Jay Cooke & Co. had called the Fertile Belt and had represented on the map of the Northwest as a yellow band extending from Lake Superior to the Coast — the "Banana Belt." A New York broker wrote a parody on the Northern Pacific advertisement, SAFE! PROFIT-

ABLE! PERMANENT!, which, though humorous, had much truth in it.[16] For those who might be interested in securing Northern Pacific bonds, this "advertisement" announced that they would be supplied by "your nearest Bank or Banker, Butcher or Baker, Apple-woman or Peanut-man, Paper-vender or Billposter." It referred the investor to various sources giving information on the region, including a map giving "a correct census of the inhabitants, including Indians, foxes, muskrats, white bears, black bears, grizzly bears, green bears, polar bears, Wall-street bears, bisons, stationary herds of roving buffaloes . . ., grasshoppers and wheat fields." As for the land grant, it was larger than the "nine" New England States, with the northern part of European Russia, all of France, except Alsace and Lorraine, Turkey, a portion of New Jersey, and Coney Island added, or as large as the "two States of Delaware combined." With a railroad built through these lands, "their price could only be estimated by multiplying the present value of the Broadway Boulevard lots by six, and adding the cost of the new site for the capital, west of the Mississippi." In a style reminiscent of Wilkeson, all the points considered in the original advertisement were discussed: the income from the bonds, the emigration scheme, the future business of the road. "Branch lines or 'feelers' will be built from the main trunk, Eastward, Westward, Northward, and 'Sou-Sou-West by Southward,' stopping at all the important points on both Hemi-spheres going and returning, so as to drain the entire known world, and render valueless all the other railroads on the face of the Globe." Altogether it was a nonsensical performance but a pointed one.

The sale of Northern Pacific bonds continued to be low throughout 1872. Danger of trouble with England over the *Alabama* Claims weakened the market in April and May. In the latter month sales began to pick up, and June was not so bad. July sales were reported to have been a million, but more than a tenth was taken by Jay Cooke & Co. in order to be able to say that a million had been sold. Thereafter, sales continued to be low — pitifully and dangerously low for the Cookes until the end of the year.[17]

The Northwest Grows More Troublesome

Jay Cooke's burden in 1872 was greatly increased by the difficulties met in the Northwest. In 1871 matters had turned for the worst, and in 1872 several of Jay Cooke's interests beyond Lake Superior reached something of a crisis and the transportation system supported by Jay Cooke & Co. and the Northern Pacific began to disintegrate.

The Lake Superior & Mississippi continued to make desperate efforts to secure traffic. President Clark even started to run Sunday excursions from St. Paul to White Bear Lake, but in that effort he did not succeed, for his plea for those who needed rest in the country did not serve to overcome Jay Cooke's stand against such a desecration of the Sabbath.[18] More serious was the road's failure to come to terms with its rivals. Having failed in a long and expensive effort to come to some agreement with the Milwaukee-Chicago interests, the Lake Superior road had been forced to fight for traffic. In the summer of 1871 it had leased a boat and barges on the Mississippi and St. Croix rivers to compete with the Milwaukee-Chicago packets for wheat to be loaded on its cars at Stillwater.[19] Also having failed to conciliate the St. Paul & Sioux City, which ran into the prairie country in southwestern Minnesota, the Cookes and Clarks had agreed to take $340,000 of bonds of the Minneapolis & St. Louis, a road projected to be built from the branch of the Lake Superior & Mississippi at Minneapolis to Carver on the Minnesota River.[20] In 1872 the Northern Pacific agreed to join the North Missouri in financing construction of an extension from Carver to meet the Central of Iowa, which extension the Northern Pacific pledged itself to lease.[21] The project was not realized, but the plans show how far Jay Cooke's interests were going in their attempt to secure traffic.

In the meantime, the Lake Superior & Mississippi had continued to go backward financially, and in the fall of 1871 President Clark expressed his inability to manage it any longer. To cover interest due, floating debt, and operating expense above income in the year 1872, he estimated that the sum of $750,000 would be needed. The Clarks refused to do anything further in a financial way and they left to Jay Cooke the responsibility of finding a way out, suggesting that the Northern Pacific ought to be interested.[22]

Jay Cooke's firm was too heavily invested in the Superior road to let it go — the Philadelphia and New York houses had a total of $2,135,237 in the road and its branches.[23] Jay Cooke, therefore, urged upon the Northern Pacific the advisability of securing control of the Lake Superior & Mississippi. The Northern Pacific refused to purchase the road but, instead, leased it and its branches to Minneapolis and Stillwater. The lessee assumed full responsibility for supplying funds to meet maturing coupons as well as for operating and maintaining the Lake Superior road. So favorable was the deal to the lessor that it was feared it might injure the sale of Northern Pacific bonds.[24]

Jay Cooke & Co. continued to have troubles on its hands in Wisconsin. It is recalled that Jay Cooke had in 1870 formed an alliance with certain interests in that State. In keeping with their promises, they had tried to secure a renewal in Congress of the land grant of the projected St. Croix & Lake Superior Railroad. The measure had failed in the summer of 1870 but had been brought up again in the following session. The Cooke forces then met an attack which they did not know how to parry.

The occasion was a speech given by Representative J. Proctor Knott of Kentucky on January 27, 1871, during the debate on the St. Croix land-grant question. This speech rates as one of the most conspicuous of its kind in the history of Congress. Its withering satire was all directed at Duluth and at Jay Cooke's great projects. Taking first a quip at "those vast and fertile pine barrens, drained in the rainy season by the surging waters of the turbid St. Croix," Knott next delighted his colleagues in the House by taking a turn at certain members from Pennsylvania who were intensely interested in the measure: "I knew they were looking forward with the far-reaching ken of enlightened statesmanship to the pitiable condition in which Philadelphia will be left unless speedily supplied with railroad connections in some way or other with this garden spot of the universe."

After many clever sallies which delighted his hearers, Knott came to the climax of his speech. Not only, said the orator, did Duluth have a climate which was "unquestionably the most salubrious and delightful to be found anywhere on the Lord's earth," but its commercial possibilities were "simply illimitable." In the hinterland of the Zenith City of the Unsalted Seas, as he named the city at the westernmost point of Lake Superior which had come to be looked upon almost as Jay Cooke's own creation, "are inexhaustible mines of gold, immeasurable veins of silver, impenetrable depths of boundless forests, vast coal-measures, wide, extended plains of richest pasturage, . . . immense wheat fields . . . , vast herds of buffalo," — he could see them then, "with their heads down, their eyes glaring, their nostrils dilated, their tongues out, and their tails curled over their backs, tearing along towards Duluth, . . . the stock-yards of Duluth!"

The Congressmen rocked with laughter. But they did not renew the land grants. And Knott's ridicule of Duluth spread like wildfire over the country. It was too good to be forgotten by Jay Cooke's enemies.

Unfortunately for Jay Cooke's interests, his plans for Wisconsin were not carried out in 1871. The burden proved too heavy. The weakness of the banker-railroad alliance gave to the St. Paul & Sioux City the opportunity to ally itself with the Wisconsin group to fight them. Jay Cooke himself felt that the old rivalries would again arise and would result in "the ultimate gobbling up of this noble system of roads by the Erie R. R. people or the Vanderbilts and the building of a narrow gauge road at one-fourth the cost of the Lake Superior." [25] Here the banker was expressing that fear of another railroad group, such as was later to become a dominant factor in the history of many of the great American railroad systems.

The St. Croix fight was again resumed in 1872, this time under the leadership of the St. Paul & Sioux City, which hoped, Jay Cooke believed, to force the Lake Superior & Mississippi to buy the St. Paul road. The Cookes feared that Minnesota's representatives in Congress, because of the strength of Drake and Thompson of the St. Paul & Sioux City, would support the move with the aid of Wisconsin. Jay Cooke tried to gain the support of Wisconsin's governor but refused to have anything to do with lobbying in Congress, though he authorized President Clark of the Lake Superior road to draw on his firm for money with which to fight. He hoped again to draw the Wisconsin interests to his side, but he met the additional opposition of Ezra Cornell, who had given lands in Wisconsin to the college in New York State named after him.[26] Jay Cooke finally made two suggestions which he thought would interest Wisconsin: he proposed a road up the Chippewa Valley to Lake Superior with a branch swinging over to the St. Croix, and the building of another road eastward from Superior City to Ashland and the Montreal River, which had long been talked of by the Northern Pacific.[27] But by that time the Wisconsin legislature and governor were avowed enemies of Jay Cooke and his projects.[28]

Jay Cooke was more successful in the promotion of Duluth. He succeeded in getting the Northern Pacific Railroad to proceed with the development of that lake village. In the summer of 1871 the board of directors of the railroad had taken the first steps toward making Duluth the eastern terminus of the Northern Pacific by building terminal facilities there. Jay Cooke was disturbed, however, that the company did not provide for the building of docks and in general pursue a more aggressive policy in Duluth. He even threatened to resign, saying that the road had promised to meet his wishes with respect to Duluth, which was "part of my defence in undertaking this gigantic matter, and was the principal motive, I can assure you, at the beginning." The banker was not after direct personal gain in Duluth; he had purchased no property there since joining the Northern Pacific and he was willing to give the road all that he held, but he was determined that his good faith and statements should not be dishonored by anyone.[29]

The Northern Pacific thereafter took even a stronger hand in developing Duluth. In August, 1872, Jay Cooke stated that the road had, directly or indirectly, paid out not less than $300,000 "in canals, dykes, wharves, and various other things in Duluth."[30]

The question may well be asked whether Jay Cooke had properly reckoned the cost to the road of such expenditures. And yet it was necessary to prepare the harbor for handling the expected trade.

There continued to be trouble, however, with Superior City, particularly after the alliance with the Wisconsin interests had broken down. Superior objected to the improvement of the Duluth inner harbor, on the grounds that its harbor was injured thereby, and it brought suit to have the dike removed. More serious was its attempt to force the Lake Superior & Mississippi and the Northern Pacific to allow the building of a cut-off to Superior which would divert traffic from Duluth. The Northern Pacific wanted to build to Superior City but only as an extension eastward to Sault Ste. Marie and as a part of a system of roads heading up in Duluth. After much trouble, an arrangement was finally made whereby the Northern Pacific agreed to build a line from Duluth to the wharves and docks of the rival town.[31]

Of Jay Cooke's projects, none proved more disappointing than the Lake Superior & Puget Sound Land Company. The banker was continually called upon to settle one problem after another arising out of the affairs of that concern.[32] The Puget Sound officers were, unfortunately, none too reliable and efficient, and there was much criticism of their policies, which were said to discourage business men from settling in Northern Pacific towns.[33] Furthermore, there was much criticism of the fact that the land company was informed of every move made by the Northern Pacific so that it had an advantage in buying both the railroad and government lands.[34] The idea came to be held widely by outsiders that a small coterie of bondholders of the Northern Pacific, who were also stockholders in the Puget Sound Company, was profiting at the expense of the other bondholders of the road.

Most serious of all the troubles of the Northern Pacific in 1872 were those which arose out of its connection with the St. Paul & Pacific Railroad operating between St. Paul and the Red River. A committee of the Northern Pacific, headed by William Moorhead, managed construction on the new acquisition. By the end of 1871 the main line had been completed to the Red River, and in 1872 construction was rushed toward Canada on the St. Vincent Extension and some work was also done on the line following the Mississippi River toward its junction with the Northern Pacific.[35]

This work placed a heavy financial burden on the Northern Pacific and on Jay Cooke & Co. Arrangements had been made with Lippman, Rosenthal of Amsterdam, who had invested over $10,000,000 for themselves and others in the road, to sell bonds for paying interest and financing construction. But the sales of the Dutch proved inadequate, and Jay Cooke & Co. was forced to make advances for the Northern Pacific. Already in the fall of 1871 Jay Cooke had become fearful of the St. Paul & Pacific; by September several hundred thousand dollars had been advanced, and by November Cooke threatened to protest as trustee of the bondholders of the Northern Pacific. By April, 1872, the advance stood at over $1,000,000. The banker then ordered the treasurer of the road not to pay the interest due on the St. Paul & Pacific's mortgage bonds and urged disposing of the road. The situation reached a climax when Lippman, Rosenthal in August refused to accept a bill for £50,000 drawn by Jay Cooke & Co. The result was that in September, 1872, the road failed to pay its construction company, which had "borrowed half a million from the banks and put off the men for the last two months."[36]

In 1872 still another of Jay Cooke's railroad plans met defeat. He had for some time been interested in a road up the Red River to Winnipeg and thence westward, and James W. Taylor, who had been appointed United States consul to Winnipeg, had worked zealously to secure a charter for such a railroad. His plans had, however, been overshadowed by the possibility of co-operation with a great project of Sir Hugh Allan.[37]

Allan had a great scheme for building a Canadian railroad to compete with the Canadian Grand Trunk for western traffic. His plan was to build a road from Quebec and Montreal westward, north of Georgian Bay and Lake Huron. Late in 1871, Jay Cooke had been approached on the question of co-operating with the Canadian road. Negotiations had followed which ended in an agreement whereby certain Americans, most of whom were connected with the Northern Pacific, subscribed to a large portion of the stock of the proposed Canadian Pacific. It was planned that the road should connect with an extension of the Northern Pacific at Sault Ste. Marie, between lakes Huron and Superior, and continue from the railhead of the St. Paul & Pacific at Pembina on the Red River up to Fort Garry and from thence westward to the Coast.[38]

But the plan was killed by Allan's failure to get Canadian support for his project. It was alleged that the prominent position occupied by Americans in the organization made the Canadian government turn it down, but the real reason was probably the hostility of the Grand Trunk Railway, which had a powerful backing both in Canada and in London. That road, which was connecting with the West through Michigan, feared the competition of the proposed road for traffic coming from the West. It was especially fearful of Allan for the reason that he had a line of steamers plying between Liverpool, Portland, Halifax, Quebec, and other ports. Forced by opposition in Canada, Allan excluded the American interest from his project, formed a company which met the objections of the rival concern, and then sought financial aid in London. But his project again failed.[39]

Jay Cooke had believed that union with the Canadian Pacific would strengthen the Northern Pacific in London,[40] but in reality the effect was the reverse. The banker apparently did not realize that he had a weak ally compared with the old and established group centering in the Grand Trunk. Several London banking houses, including Barings and McCalmonts, had helped finance the Grand Trunk; and Sir John Rose, of Morton, Rose & Co., saw in Allan's Canadian Pacific an invasion by Jay Cooke & Co. of his own Canadian preserves. The opposition of Morton, Rose & Co., coupled with the repercussion from the considerable feeling which arose in Canada against American participation, actually injured the standing of Jay Cooke's interests in London.[41]

With all these difficulties, it would seem that Jay Cooke & Co. and the Northern Pacific should not have assumed further burdens. But the Oregon Steam Navigation Company was too tempting. This concern was engaged in transportation on the Columbia River and its branches, the Cowlitz and the Willamette. It had steamers and towboats, machine shops, wharves, and real estate in Portland, and 26 miles of railroad around the Dalles of the Columbia [42] (see map page 329).

The owners of the Oregon Steam Navigation Company, having become afraid that the Northern Pacific would take their trade,[43] offered to sell control to the railroad. The officers of the Northern Pacific were interested. First of all, the enterprise would help greatly in reaching the western terminal on Puget Sound; the Oregon company would afford transportation for hundreds of miles down the Columbia past Portland and from thence up the Cowlitz to connect with a section of the Northern Pacific being built to the Sound. It was also expected that the purchase of the concern would win to the support of the Northern Pacific its owners, Ainsworth, Thompson, and Reed, three strong business men of the region.[44] The Northern Pacific also hoped through the Oregon Steam Navigation Company to exclude the Union Pacific from the Columbia River country.[45]

Jay Cooke opposed the purchase because he did not see where the money was to come from; but Fahnestock, whose house would earn rich commissions from the deal, favored it.[46] Against the Philadelphian's advice, the Northern Pacific purchased three-fourths of the capital stock of the Oregon Steam Navigation Company. Payment was to be made in the form of bonds of the Northern Pacific to the amount of $750,000, $250,000 out of the net earnings of the company purchased and $500,000 in gold to be paid in installments over nine months. The former owners, who retained one-quarter of the stock, were to continue managing the concern.[47]

The purchase of the Oregon Steam Navigation Company gives further evidence of both the strength and the weakness of Jay Cooke's railroad interests. Strategically it was an excellent move, as others in the Lake Superior-Red River country had been. Moreover, it provided hundreds of miles of transportation in Washington Territory. But it was a serious thing to pay out half a million in gold for a concern which was earning little at a time when the Northern Pacific was financially embarrassed.[48]

Jay Cooke had thus been drawn into one project after another which he had not planned from the first to take on. For all of them there was a great deal of logic. But the total effect was to bring him to a point of embarrassment when the market turned in the direction of stringency.

JAY COOKE & CO. HAS DIFFICULTY WITH NORTHERN PACIFIC EXECUTIVES

Had the original understanding with the Northern Pacific, that the road should be built only as fast as the sale of bonds provided the means and that it should never require an advance from the bankers of over $500,000, been adhered to, the slow sale of bonds would have made no material difference to Jay Cooke & Co. except for commissions. But this stipulation was disregarded. The Northern Pacific officers made their plans and entered into contracts for construction far ahead of the sale of bonds and expected Jay Cooke & Co. to meet payments as they became due.

An inexcusable lack of co-operation on the part of the road with its financial agent had appeared in 1871. During the winter of 1872, when sales were better and drawings of the road relatively less, the situation righted itself somewhat. But in March the old trouble returned. Jay Cooke objected to heavy drafts for cash payments to the construction company.[49] He urged that a part of the payment should be deferred and that such big sums should not be disbursed without consultation with him. The company had also purchased iron for use on the West Coast a year before it was needed, and payment of $800,000 in cash was due on May 1. This was a fearful sum to Jay Cooke. The utter disregard of his wishes as to full consultation in regard to purchases and payments led him to believe that even the St. Paul & Pacific might lay violent hands upon some of the Northern Pacific's money. "This must not be," he pleaded, "I must have some cooperation in regard to finances, or I shall feel like giving up." He urged reconsideration of all the plans of the Northern Pacific.[50]

The Northern Pacific overdrafts became worse as the spring and summer of 1872 passed. Jay Cooke objected to spending heavily for running a railroad where there were no receipts and for purchasing a steamboat on the Missouri long before the Northern Pacific reached that river. But the overdraft continued to increase, passing $1,500,000 in August. The banker then asked the directors of the Northern Pacific to cover the sum with their personal notes. The notes were discounted by the Cookes, however, and these, together with further drafts, made the advance close to $2,000,000 before a month had passed. At that time bond sales were hardly sufficient to pay for advertising.[51]

Jay Cooke protested, but to little avail. A letter of the treasurer of the road to the banker, dated September 16, shows how futile were the protests: "The instructions to Mr. Newport sent under your direction to make no drafts whatsoever are still in force, but I shall expect you to take the responsibility of any consequences that may result from the non payment of accounts." [52]

It was no simple matter, it is true, to stop payments at the time. Work had been discontinued on the St. Paul & Pacific, and the workers threatened to destroy bridges and other property if they were not paid.[53] Jay Cooke conceded that payrolls would have to be taken care of, but he maintained that contractors in Minnesota would have to wait as other contractors had to do. He was well aware that the consequences of the failure of the Northern Pacific to pay any of its obligations would have been bad, but he saw that there might be worse evils.

The trouble was that the executives of the Northern Pacific had committed themselves to expenses prior to bond sales. The reason for this state of affairs is not hard to find. While the officers of the road should, by virtue of their contract with Jay Cooke & Co. and from the nature of the case, have conferred with the bankers before incurring any heavy expenses, that was not done.

It is obvious that Jay Cooke did not have the co-operation or sympathy of the leading executives of the Northern Pacific. When he on one occasion reminded the treasurer of the stipulation in the contract that the financial agent should be consulted in advance about expenditures, the treasurer replied that neither the president nor the board had instructed him to that effect.[54] Most illuminating is a reference in a letter of the treasurer to President Smith to Jay Cooke's protests against heavy overdrafts: "There is the usual growl from Philadelphia, otherwise all is serene." [55] So nonchalantly did the officers look upon the predicament of the banker, whose banking firm was actually embarrassed at the time by the payment of interest on Northern Pacific bonds and by drafts for construction or other expenses!

The chief responsibility for this state of affairs must rest with President Smith. There is evidence on every hand that he failed to give adequate attention to the Northern Pacific. Smith was rarely at his office in New York, judging by the correspondence in the Jay Cooke Papers and the Northern Pacific Papers. The Cooke partners frequently complained of their inability to see him. Even the treasurer of the road wrote about a visit of the president to his office: "Your stay here was so short that I found no time to talk up with you many matters relating to the organizing of the business of the road." [56] One reason for Smith's neglect of the western road was that he was very heavily involved as president of the board of managers of the Vermont Central, which was still having an extremely difficult time. But that is not a sufficient explanation. Many executives have handled two heavy jobs. They have been able to do this by having an organization which could be entrusted with details. It is not impossible that Smith neglected the Northern Pacific for the reason that under Jay Cooke's scrutiny the road did not yield such great opportunities for irregular profits.

That the Northern Pacific was badly managed was obvious to others than the Cookes. President Becker of the St. Paul & Pacific held that the management of the road was not a "business affair" and predicted that it would come to a bad end.[57] The opinion of W. Milnor Roberts, chief engineer of construction, concerning the management of the Northern Pacific must be regarded as the judgment of an able and fair-minded man who was in the best position to observe how things were done. He held that the road could not be properly located and planned or economically and honestly built "under the total absence of sound system, or under the curious spasmodic system now prevailing." The concern was shot through with personal antagonisms, indefiniteness, and lack of efficient organization — "It will never be remedied until your President can give his whole time to the road; or in lieu of that, that others have authority to make and keep up systematic instead of spasmodic action." [58] This is an interesting example of the sense of efficiency which the engineer was bringing into American business.

The board of directors of the Northern Pacific should have had some check on the affairs of the road. Such names as Cass, Rice, Ogden, Felton, Cheney, Stinson, and Moorhead — men of wide experience in business and particularly in transportation — should have meant something in the way of a guarantee of careful management. Yet this board of outstanding men ratified one plan after the other for heavy expenditures without regard for the financial condition of the road.[59]

Here we are given a glimpse into a change which was coming in American corporate management which had a wide significance. Prior to the Civil War, the directors of American railroads had often been concerned with management. The directors frequently lived along the railroad with which they were concerned; they had themselves invested in the road; and their prestige in their own communities was in a measure dependent on the success of the road. The directors of the Northern Pacific were of another kind. They had secured control of the stock with very little investment; their prestige was hardly dependent at all on the success of the Northern Pacific, which was a minor consideration in their business activities; and they were too far removed from the Northern Pacific's roadway and too busy with their own affairs to pay much attention to their duties as directors. What actually happened was that they took the word of the executives. That is to say, they were not managing directors but policy-forming directors who voted on evidence and recommendations submitted by the executives. It is clear that they did not recognize their responsibilities and failed to check plans against costs and resources.

An accurate financial statement of the Northern Pacific at this time would throw some light on the question of irresponsibility of management — whether it grew out of incompetence, neglect, or dishonesty — but such a statement does not exist and could probably not be constructed from existing material. The annual reports of the Northern Pacific [60] have no meaning except to suggest that, as was then the rule, the road's accounting was very bad. It is impossible to derive from the information given even an approximate idea of the cost per mile of road built.

It is difficult to understand why a man of Jay Cooke's ability should have allowed himself to be put in a position where he had to meet demands over which he had no control. This does not mean that he should have held a controlling hand on Northern Pacific management; even today there is by no means unanimity of opinion as to how far investment bankers should go in the management of corporations whose securities they sell, and obviously Jay Cooke had neither the necessary experience nor the time to take a directing hand in management. Jay Cooke was clearly at fault, however, in two respects: in associating his firm with a concern whose management was questionable; and, perhaps even more significant, in so strongly recommending the Northern Pacific as to become almost morally bound to support it.

The only plausible explanation of Jay Cooke's failure to foresee the difficulties into which he drifted was the newness of the situation. The railroads with which he had previously been closely connected had been mostly of the old kind where administrative responsibility was much greater and where the chances for plunder were very much less. Moreover, Jay Cooke had never had experience with a concern whose fixed costs were so heavy, which had such a burden of interest. Indeed, the whole field of railroad finance was undergoing changes which business men did not have adequate experience to understand.

DISSENSION WITHIN JAY COOKE & CO. OVER THE NORTHERN PACIFIC

The New York house of Jay Cooke & Co. had always served as a depository for the unemployed funds of the whole firm, and it had generally held large balances for the Philadelphia house. But as Jay Cooke & Co. became more and more involved with the Northern Pacific, the balances of the older house with the younger decreased, disappeared, and were finally changed to a considerable indebtedness. The New Yorkers had warned the Philadelphians earlier, but in March, 1872, when the balances of the Philadelphia house in New York were unusually low,[61] they began to make strong appeals to Jay Cooke out of fear of the consequences of too heavy advances to the railroad.

Fahnestock urged that they take an appraisal of the whole business of the firms. He pleaded for consideration for the London house and the need of a handsome gold capital there; "in a year our bills shall be unequivocally prime & shall rate always with the four bills in this city classed as such." He did not complain of Lake Superior and other heavy advances already on their books, and he said his house could carry itself without assistance. "But I do insist," he said, "that the business of the Phila House must be run upon a self-sustaining basis & that we shall not be forced, as we were last season, to make large money advances to you when our own current balances are reduced by heavy drawings of correspondents and our money markets are stringent."[62]

Instead of taking a firm stand with the Northern Pacific, which was the root of the trouble, Jay Cooke characteristically attempted to patch up the situation. On one day he wrote five very significant letters in response to the complaints of Fahnestock and Pitt Cooke:[63] he warned the treasurer of the road that funds were low and that enormous payments were immediately ahead; he requested the president to try to sell to the Union Pacific the iron ordered for the western division; he appealed to Fahnestock to secure another government draft for the Navy account in London; he wrote with great enthusiasm to McCulloch of the remarkable progress of the Northern Pacific, saying that, if the

London house could sell $10,000,000 of bonds in the spring and
the same in the fall, the whole line could be put under contract;
and he appealed to Puleston again to seek the co-operation of the
London Rothschilds. Nothing could bear more eloquent witness
of Jay Cooke's inability to retrench than those letters.

The responses to the appeals were not very helpful. Fahnestock reported that it was impossible to ask for another Navy
draft since the balance was still large. Nearly a month later the
Northern Pacific bond account of the London house showed for
the three preceding months that bonds to the amount of £610,500
had been sold and £521,860 had been repurchased, while the
whole proceeds after expense totaled £42,470.[64] There was only
one positive gain; most of the iron for the western division was
sold.

The New York partners of Jay Cooke became fearful about
their own house during the near-panic in the money market in
April and May, 1872. The country was then financially in an un-
healthy state. The great obligations to Europe and the rapid
tying up of capital in fixed and unproductive investments were
regarded as possible sources of danger. The failure of funds to return to New York from the inland as rapidly as usual in the
spring served to aggravate fears that danger was ahead.[65] Indeed, so bad was the situation early in May that one of the New
York partners feared a repetition of Black Friday.[66]

By June Fahnestock had become thoroughly alarmed over his
firm's relations with the Northern Pacific, and he pleaded with
Jay Cooke to do something about it. He made a scorching indict-
ment of the relations of Jay Cooke & Co. with the project. He
said, "the present actual condition of the N. P. if it were understood by the public would be fatal to the negotiation of its securities." He pointed to the weakness of the management of the concern and its extremely bad financial condition.

Jay Cooke & Co., according to Fahnestock, had become so
closely identified with the Northern Pacific as to have become
responsible for the road. Jay Cooke's position as one of the two
trustees of the bondholders made him morally, if not legally, responsible for the economical use of the money received and for

the truth of the publicity endorsing the bonds. Yet, held Fahnestock, the publicity could not stand the test of truth: Jay Cooke & Co. had assured the bond buyers of the intelligence and economy of Northern Pacific management while they knew it was inefficient, inattentive to its responsibilities, and extravagant to the last degree; they had given assurance of the superiority of the lands in the Northern Pacific country, while they knew a large proportion was practically valueless; their publications had promised a rapid marketing of the road's lands, but the aggregate cash result to date totaled $338.76; and their publications had enlarged upon the comprehensive and perfect system of immigration for purchasing and selling the lands, but there had as yet been no results worth mentioning. The effect of this extravagant picture of the enterprise and of its dependence on promoters had been to prejudice the securities in the minds of "capitalists & people whose *judgment* governs their investments."

Fahnestock referred very pointedly to an extremely important aspect of the bond campaign: "If the bonds had been sold at a price commensurate with the experimental character of the undertaking, they would have been taken largely by moneyed men." Such a procedure would have cut the expense of selling so that the net for each bond might have been the same as under the method followed, while more bonds would presumably have been sold. Here was a major question of policy which Jay Cooke seems never to have faced squarely; he had modified it only in offering bonds for syndicating in London, but the general price to the public was at par. He had succeeded with such a price policy in selling the war bonds, and he similarly expected with aggressive selling to maintain the Northern Pacifics at par. This is one more illustration of the fact that Jay Cooke had not adapted himself to the realistic needs of private business as distinct from the emotional conditions prevailing during the war.

The New York partner urged that the issue be faced squarely. Radical changes were "necessary to save the company from ingloriously breaking down within the next year and involving us in discredit if not in ruin." He recommended that Jay Cooke & Co. be so divorced from all but the finances as not to be responsible for the mistakes of the company. It should stand in relation to its road merely as brokers. He also recommended that a more capable management be secured for the Northern Pacific. As an example of what could be done with careful management and without guarantees, Fahnestock pointed to the Missouri, Kansas & Texas, which had in three years built and equipped 433 miles with an aggregate indebtedness of only $10,000,000 and which was netting 83 per cent of interest from traffic.[67]

This letter was an amazingly searching examination of the whole operation, and Fahnestock's request that advances to the Northern Pacific be curtailed was sound. Had Jay Cooke's first consideration been for Jay Cooke & Co. and for its depositors, he should have announced to the Northern Pacific in the summer of 1872 a reversal of policy on advances. He would have been well within his rights if he had refused to advance any further to pay the road's expenses. He would no doubt have been severely criticized by holders of some $15,000,000 of Northern Pacific bonds for thus endangering the road,[68] and Jay Cooke & Co. would have had to carry the load of advances already made. But the taking of a definite stand in the summer of 1872, when the money market had recovered somewhat, would probably have sufficiently strengthened the Cookes with moneyed men to enable them to stand the shock attendant upon such a step.

Jay Cooke must have been deterred from such action by the sacrifices involved. By 1872 it was no longer a question of profits; it was merely a question of seeing the project through. Jay Cooke himself was tired and worn, and he would gladly have been relieved.[69] But his prestige with his partners, with business men in general, and with the bond buyer would have suffered greatly by a confession of misjudgment and failure. There is no way of knowing how much Jay Cooke's pride really influenced him in continuing with the Northern Pacific in the hope that he could prove to his critics that they were wrong. His feeling that he was on the defensive so far as some of his partners were concerned may have had a strong effect on him. Such intangible things as personal factors, while they are often extremely important in business, cannot be measured. There was the further consideration that Jay Cooke felt a genuine responsibility for the bondholders, who had bought Northern Pacifics largely on the strength of his recommendation, and he had some moral responsibility as trustee. Since there was little local trade beyond the Missouri and so much depended on reaching the Coast, it must be recognized that to have stopped part way would have endangered all that had been accomplished. We may ask why the banker did not feel a similar responsibility for the depositors of Jay Cooke & Co. Had the issue been clearly that of saving his banking firm or the bondholders, Jay Cooke's previous career leads to the conclusion that he would probably have chosen the former. In his opinion, however, there was still a chance of saving both. If the management of the Northern Pacific were improved, if Jay Cooke & Co. were given the work of refunding the government loan, or if settlement and traffic or government aid should strengthen the Northern Pacific, the threat of failure might turn to success. Even if everything else failed, improvement in general business conditions would help to save both the road and the banking house.

The hope of some improvement in the situation influenced Jay Cooke to continue carrying the Northern Pacific. A less sanguine man or one with a keener insight into general business conditions might have had less faith. Yet it must be remembered that many a concern which has in reality been insolvent has actually been saved from bankruptcy by some favorable turn in conditions beyond its control. It was not impossible that such might be the good fortune of Jay Cooke & Co.

THE FALL OF THE BANKING HOUSE OF
JAY COOKE, 1872–1873

EARLY in September, 1872, Fahnestock, then in London, sent to Jay Cooke a last appeal to stop advances to the Northern Pacific. In his opinion it was cruelly unjust to their depositors to hazard "their money in such an unbusiness like way," and unpardonably stupid to wreck themselves when they could control the finances of the Northern Pacific.[1] However unpleasant would be the embarrassment of the Northern Pacific after the extraordinary recommendations of their house, they could still survive the odium of its failure. Neither Jay Cooke's pride nor his interest in the road, urged Fahnestock, should stand in the way. His solution was that the Northern Pacific should go into the market to borrow at whatever rates would secure loans.[2]

The near-panic in the money market of September, 1872, made it absolutely impossible to follow Fahnestock's advice. All that Jay Cooke could do was to wait for some favorable turn. But that never came. As if driven by an inexorable fate, the various possibilities of a fortunate solution of the difficulties of Jay Cooke & Co. failed in the year which followed. Finally came the panic of the fall of 1873. Leveling many business firms, it also destroyed the once proud and great banking house of Jay Cooke & Co. Altogether this is not a pleasant story, but it is one that is full of meaning. It shows what happened to a promoter-banker who had not looked adequately to his defences.

THE MONEY MARKET THREATENS JAY COOKE & CO.

The stringency in the money market of September, 1872, caught the New York house of Jay Cooke & Co. in a fearful condition. It held no balance for the Philadelphia house; Washington was overdrawn; and its own advances to railroads stood at about $2,600,000. It tried to borrow but found that "money can hardly be raised on Govts — let alone paper of a R. R. Co. in these times." [3]

Again we see the familiar figure of the Treasury stepping into the breach.[4] Jay Cooke, who was at the time entertaining Assistant-Secretary Richardson at Ogontz, prevailed upon the Treasury to purchase government bonds for $3,000,000 in time to relieve the money market. Cooke, like others,[5] attributed the stringency to a conspiracy to lock up greenbacks, and he considered it the duty of the government always to be in a position to check and discourage such efforts. He even advocated that, if necessary, the Treasury should use the $40,000,000 of greenbacks held since McCulloch had withdrawn them from circulation. Indeed, at this time he came to think that "we need to increase currency every year to meet increase in population & business but not enough to cause inflation." [6] Fortunately for Jay Cooke & Co., the Treasury, watched daily and even hourly by Henry Cooke, continued to help keep the wolf at bay during the two weeks or so in which the severe condition in the money market lasted.[7]

Jay Cooke & Co. was then close to breaking. On October 4 Pitt Cooke reported the condition of the New York house as follows: it had by then advanced $3,000,000 on railroads; on October 3 and 4 its deposits had been drawn down through the clearing house to the extent of $900,000; on October 4 the St. Paul & Pacific had drawn $100,000 and another draft of the same amount was coming in the next day. George F. Baker had proved the friend in need: "Garland managed to have H. D. stir up Comptroller Knox to date the Banks Statement as of Yesterday Thursday 3 Oct. & that let Baker of 1st [National] loose & we took 500,000 of him at ¼ to 3 [fourths] which just let us squeak through."

This situation frayed still more the ragged nerves of Jay Cooke and his partners. Fahnestock and Moorhead both attacked the senior partner severely.[8] He had failed to hold investors and capitalists, and now he was even losing his hold on his partners. In defence of himself Jay Cooke turned upon the London house.[9] Refusing to admit that the Londoners or Fahnestock had a right to complain of advances to the Northern Pacific, for "strictly speaking, taking on our profits, we are within that limit [of $500,-000] now," he turned upon London for not supporting his project: "If the London house is to be of no use to us in tight times or pinches, if it is to have all the advantages of the large Navy A/C. and the capital they have made . . . without our occasionally using our credit in a pinch, we might as well not have any house there. . . . Let them keep a stiff upper lip, attend to this legitimate business, sell all the bonds they can, & have a little faith & confidence in the partners here, and all will be right."

The resident London partners, whose house was largely dependent on the American firm's standing, accepted the challenge. Puleston defended his house against the charge of indifference to the Northern Pacific, saying that "apart from N. P. itself the market for over a year in American Railways has been most unsatisfactory — at least half a dozen put out here in the glowing prospectuses are knocking about discredited by non payment of interest." To Jay Cooke's request that they borrow £500,000 to help carry the Northern Pacific, Puleston replied that because they had been constant borrowers, while all other London bankers in good standing were constant lenders, their borrowing had counted seriously against them.[10]

The good banker McCulloch replied to Cooke in a tone of alarm, mortification, and deep regret.[11] The connection of Jay Cooke & Co. with the Northern Pacific, he said, had caused them great difficulty in London. Careful men had been apprehensive that the road might break the Cooke firms, but the London partners had tried to allay their fears with the statement that advances to the road should never exceed $500,000. When McCulloch learned that the limit had been exceeded and that the Cooke houses had not a large capital, he had become alarmed, especially since "you were in danger of using in sustaining the road the money of your depositors & regarding as I do, Bankers as Trustees of the moneys of their customers and culpable for any illegitimate use that may be made of them, I confess I was alarmed at the step you had taken." McCulloch recommended an assessment on the private means of the partners — little did he realize how small the chance was of getting anything that way!

The protests of the partners were thoroughly justified, but as conditions were then it was impossible to do much to improve matters. The least effort to rid Jay Cooke & Co. of some of the burden of the Northern Pacific — even refusing to pay construction contractors, at a time when the firm was without available reserves and the money market was bad—would have invited disaster. Jay Cooke was caught in a trap; the only thing to do was to try to save the firm without letting its weakness be known. "If we can only now manage to wriggle along until we reach the Missouri River, all will come out right." It was his plan then to throw the whole responsibility onto the Northern Pacific, itself.[12] But that would not be for some months. Jay Cooke's decision to change his position when the Missouri was reached had in mind the fact that existing contracts for construction would then be fulfilled; he did not mean that the road would become self-sustaining at that point.

In the meantime, Jay Cooke continued to patch up matters as best he could. He kept a strong hand on the United States Treasury. He urged the treasurer of the Northern Pacific to dispose of iron not yet used and to stave off payments, both of which were done with some success.[13] He also appealed to agents to take bonds, with the promise that Jay Cooke & Co. would take the securities back if not sold in six months.[14] There was little hope of getting financial assistance from banks or others for any length of time; they had even gotten all they could get from the National Insurance Company of the United States of America, which they had always been able to rely on for something handsome.[15] The only real gain was the sale of the South Mountain iron property, which brought them $200,000 of fresh means.[16]

REVAMPING THE NORTHERN PACIFIC ORGANIZATION

By the fall of 1872 some improvement had come in the administration and management of the Northern Pacific which promised to help matters somewhat. Early in the year a committee of three, including William Moorhead, had been appointed to draw up suggestions for reforms.[17] This bore two important

results. Certain officers were appointed to reside on the line of
the Northern Pacific; they were assigned definite responsibilities
with a view to securing more systematic and economical construction and operation.[18] More important from the point of view of
the larger administrative policies and problems were the changes
which were effected at the top. In March, 1872, the executive
committee was cut to five members, four directors and the president, and was empowered to act in place of the board; [19] this provided an organization that could act quickly. William Moorhead,
Wright, Cass, Billings, and President Smith were the members of
the new committee.[20] These four directors were all conservative
and cautious men, and the three first-named were close to Jay
Cooke and were sympathetic with his policies.

The main problem, in Jay Cooke's opinion, was to secure the
removal of President Smith. In May he had suggested that
Smith go abroad in the interests of the Northern Pacific,[21] but in
June Smith resigned.[22] That did not, however, settle the matter.
His western friends, such as Senator Windom of Minnesota and
William King of Minneapolis, who had apparently made high
profits out of construction contracts on the Northern Pacific,
tried to block the acceptance of the resignation by the board.
Action was finally secured, however, on the insistence of Wm. B.
Ogden of Chicago and Moorhead of Jay Cooke & Co. But
Smith's resignation did not take effect until November 1, an un-
fortunate postponement of a vital change.[23]

George W. Cass, the choice of Jay Cooke for the position, was
elected to succeed Smith. General Cass was a man of strength of
character, wide experience, and superior ability in railroad administration.[24] He had been reared by his uncle, the well known
Lewis Cass of Michigan, and he had been graduated from West
Point with honors. After a miscellaneous engineering experience,
he had become associated with the Pittsburgh, Fort Wayne &
Chicago, which road he served as president for 25 years, leading it
through a long period of construction to a strong position and final
absorption by the Pennsylvania. He was president of this road
as well as director of the Northern Pacific when he became president of the latter.

The appointment of Cass to the presidency of the Northern Pacific was regarded by Jay Cooke as relieving him of much responsibility. But, unfortunately, Cass hesitated and postponed entering upon the duties of the office until near the close of the year. He then asked Jay Cooke whether the enterprise could meet its obligations, explicitly stating that he would assume no financial responsibility except to see that the concern was honestly managed.[25] It was probably Jay Cooke's assurance of the feasibility of the enterprise which finally encouraged Cass to take hold,[26] but that very assurance in a real sense placed on the banker the responsibility he had hoped to shift.

Looking toward a more systematic and economical management of the road, the executive committee had in the summer and fall of 1872 entered upon a policy of retrenchment. They cut salaries and dismissed unnecessary engineers and laborers. It was decided not to undertake any further construction beyond what was being done in Washington Territory.[27] In December a committee was appointed to study the condition of the company and to use its credit and assets for improving its finances.[28]

Thus was accomplished in a measure what Jay Cooke and his partners had urged. The changes effected were reassuring to them and made them hopeful that the Northern Pacific might be strengthened. There was good reason to believe that they might thereby be relieved of some of their burden. But they were meeting very late a situation which they should have foreseen from the beginning. Under the circumstances, the Cookes should have heeded Baron Rothschild's rule not to become concerned with anything that required risk or trouble in management.

Supporting President Grant and the Republicans in the Election of 1872

Jay Cooke was convinced that it was absolutely essential to his firm that the Republican party should be retained in control of the government in the election of 1872. In view of the gathering clouds of economic and social discontent, which were taking on an especially portentous color in the West where Grangerism was rampant, and the real, but not clearly expressed, fear of the future on the part of business men, Cooke felt that it was almost a matter of life and death to re-elect Grant and the Republicans.[29] He was especially fearful that Horace Greeley might be elected to the presidency. Jay Cooke, moreover, was convinced that his firm had a better chance of obtaining favorable action from the President and his party than from anyone else — the Cookes believed they had the promise of refunding if Grant were re-elected.[30]

Jay Cooke and his partners, therefore, exerted themselves to the utmost in helping Grant and the Republicans. Jay Cooke himself collected a generous amount in his own State for the campaign chest,[31] and the Republican National Committee preyed like a hungry wolf on the diminishing resources of the Cooke firm.[32] At the same time that it was making heavy contributions in money, Jay Cooke & Co. was co-operating with the Treasury in keeping the pre-election money market steady.[33] It is quite possible that Cooke was showing a strong hand at many places so as to cover up the fundamentally weak financial position of the firm.

ON THE BRINK OF FAILURE, DECEMBER, 1872, TO JANUARY, 1873

The evils responsible for the predicament of Jay Cooke & Co. were too deeply entrenched to give way immediately before such things as changes in the administration and management of the Northern Pacific or the return of the Republicans in the federal administration. The money market continued to be bad, the obligations of the Northern Pacific continued to mature, and Jay Cooke & Co. became more and more poverty stricken until insolvency, inevitable since September, was imminent in December.

The bills of the Northern Pacific presented for payment in the fall of 1872 were very large,[34] and, since bond sales were negligible, the overdrafts on the road's financial agent increased. Besides a difficult money market and a reluctant bond market, Jay Cooke & Co. had to face ugly rumors about the Northern Pacific, particularly after its refusal further to meet the obligations of the St.

Paul & Pacific. The colored messenger of the New York house heard someone say Jay Cooke & Co. would smash up because it was stuck with the Northern Pacific. One depositor who had had $250,000 with the New York house for a long time drew most of the sum because he had heard it said that Jay Cooke & Co. was badly crippled by the Northern Pacific.[35]

The Philadelphia house had to overdraw on New York, which was also burdened with the overdrafts of Washington. On October 28 New York stood $550,000 in advance to the Northern Pacific and it was carrying overdrafts of $450,000 for the Philadelphia house and $147,000 for the Washington house. A month later the overdrafts were even larger.[36]

December proved to be the most difficult month Jay Cooke & Co. had ever known. The New York house, in which all the business of the firm centered, was in a position where the least run on its deposits would have been fatal. It was paying 5 per cent, compounded monthly, on demand deposits, while no other respectable private bank and only the Importers and Traders Bank among the chartered institutions, according to Fahnestock, was paying over 4 per cent.[37] On the evening of December 9 the New Yorkers were overdrawn $140,000 on the Bank of Commerce, with no balance to meet next morning's clearings and absolutely no collateral in the house — "without any exaggeration we are in a perfectly helpless position." The London house was at the same time in desperate need of funds — "they do not at all exaggerate the miserable poverty of the concern," said Fahnestock — and McCulloch was constantly worrying the New Yorkers with letters and cables pleading for help. During the last week of December, the deposits of the New York house fell off heavily.[38] But somehow they managed to keep going. Early in January the Northern Pacific gave to Jay Cooke & Co. four months' notes totaling $1,400,000, covered by $3,500,000 in stock of the Oregon Steam Navigation Company as collateral.[39]

At this time we observe something that is both strange and significant. Though 1872 had been a difficult year, Jay Cooke & Co. had made excellent profits. The Washington house had nothing to show for the year, but Philadelphia divided $500,000,

London had earned a profit of £100,000, while New York reported earnings of $628,222.70 and expenses of $122,692.99, which left net earnings of $505,528.71.⁴⁰

It is significant to note the kinds of business which had brought such profits. The Philadelphia house apparently made most of its gains from commissions on the sale of Northern Pacifics; because of advances to the road, these profits cannot be said actually to have been realized. The dividend of Jay Cooke, McCulloch & Co. speaks eloquently of the success of the London house in banking growing out of foreign trade. The earnings of the New York house, as shown by the table below, are most interesting of all:

Type of Business	Amount of Profit
Governments	$216,965.19
Northern Pacifics	39,721.09
Interest	89,302.95
Commissions	12,817.05
Gold Department	80,516.42
Iron Business (estimated)	100,000.00
Foreign Exchange	88,900.00
	$628,222.70

Unfortunately, complete records of the work of the New York house have not survived. Until about 1869, Fahnestock reported frequently to Jay Cooke, and it is possible to gain from his letters in the Jay Cooke Papers a fair picture of what his house was doing. But from about late 1869 till the closing of the firm, the New Yorker reported very little to the Philadelphian. It appears that thereafter each of the two houses went its own way. The work of the New York house was so different from that of Philadelphia that it was altogether reasonable that Fahnestock should act more on his own responsibility. But because of his failure to confer with Jay Cooke, there has survived little evidence of the work of his house in its last years.

The above table, which was included in an annual statement to Jay Cooke on the disbursement of earnings to partners, is, therefore, all the more valuable as an indication of what was being done in New York. It indicates clearly why Fahnestock, aside from his fear of overdrafts, had no enthusiasm for the Northern Pacific; and it shows that the road's bonds must have had little standing in New York. The substantial profits in governments point to a considerable revival in the trading in government securities on the part of the New York house. It would be extremely interesting to know the source of the profits on the interest account, particularly since the house was paying 5 per cent on demand deposits; some of it came, of course, from advances to the Northern Pacific. The iron business consisted of the importing of English iron on commission, which the head of the New York house had built up. Fahnestock reports a significant fact with respect to the foreign-exchange account. The work of his house in foreign exchange during 1872 had brought earnings of $215,278, shared equally on joint account with the London house. But in the period of stringency in October, 1872, the London house had been caught so short of funds that the New Yorkers had to remit in a very difficult exchange market at a loss of $37,474.81. This loss, wrote Fahnestock to Jay Cooke, "resulted only from the condition in which we were obliged to keep the account because of the other enforcements of which you know (that in N. P.)." [41]

This situation points to a great weakness in the organization of Jay Cooke & Co. The New York house was doing ten times the banking business done by the Philadelphia house, in the judgment of Mr. Charles D. Barney of Philadelphia, who was with the parent house in the 1870's. New York had little to gain from Philadelphia because the latter had in the 'seventies no idle funds for New York to use, and its business, chiefly in Northern Pacifics, brought very little work to the New York house. As an integral part of Jay Cooke & Co., New York was subject to the drawings for the Northern Pacific, an extremely dangerous situation since New York held very extensive deposits of inland bankers. The result was that the investment part of the business of Jay Cooke & Co. was in a position where it could draw heavily on the commercial banking part, which fact made it possible to go much farther in carrying the Northern Pacifics than could otherwise have been done and which put the New

York house in an extremely dangerous condition. Jay Cooke & Co. had fallen into the common American error of tying up deposits in the investment business.

Altogether, the year 1872 had been a strange one for Jay Cooke's firms. Though they had made very good profits, they were on the verge of bankruptcy. There was no going backward at this stage; Jay Cooke & Co. was too heavily invested in railroads, and the money market was not favorable to readjustment. Jay Cooke & Co. could only wait, hoping that something would occur to help them.

DISAPPOINTMENTS AND DIFFICULTIES OF THE WINTER AND SPRING OF 1873

As long as there was hope of refunding, there was still hope of saving Jay Cooke & Co. At the beginning of 1873 there was every reason to believe that the Rothschilds would join in such an undertaking. Fahnestock considered the syndicating of the loan with the co-operation of the Rothschilds "as the greatest card our house has ever played, and one, which, advantageously managed, ought to put our house head and shoulders above everybody else, and outside from our own immediate interests it will do more for N. P. than any other agency possibly could." [42] The same pathetic refrain that had for several years run through the correspondence of Jay Cooke and his partners!

But the plum was too big and the opposition too strong for Jay Cooke & Co. to get the work without a struggle. Morton, Bliss & Co. put in a bid for $100,000,000 for itself and Morton, Rose & Co., the Barings, and Morgans. Jay Cooke & Co., fighting for its very existence, struggled with the Treasury and secured what it believed to be the promise of the negotiation through a syndicate. [43] Before the contract was signed, however, the opposition succeeded in blocking the move. The leading spokesman of the opposition was Joseph Patterson of Philadelphia. Patterson was of a group of Philadelphia bankers who supported Drexel but opposed Jay Cooke; he was in good standing with the Administration and it had even been rumored that he was being supported by Drexel to succeed Boutwell as secretary of the Treasury.[44]

Patterson attacked Jay Cooke's refunding plan before the House Committee on Ways and Means. He explained at length to the committee the high cost of refunding under Jay Cooke's plan and the very grave danger of giving to a syndicate power with which to control the exchanges and disturb the business of the country. He suggested a method of refunding which had long since proved itself to be ineffective,[45] that is, to carry on the operation through banks on commission. There was sufficient evidence to indicate that the Drexels were behind Patterson's attack.[46]

The Secretary of the Treasury was forced to recognize the opposition.[47] The result was that Jay Cooke & Co. had to agree to share this work with its rivals.[48] The Cookes signed an agreement to co-operate with the other parties in negotiating the sale of $300,000,000. They expressed the belief that the combination would be invincible, but they were uncertain and somewhat apprehensive about who should manage the operation.[49]

The syndicate group subscribed outright to $10,000,000 in 5 per cents, with the right to take the whole $300,000,000 before December 1.[50] The syndicate was to get the one-half of 1 per cent commission allowed by the act covering the loan and was to hold the proceeds of the negotiation without interest for three months, which meant an additional $1\frac{1}{2}$ per cent.[51] Jay Cooke & Co., representing N. M. Rothschild & Sons and Jay Cooke, McCulloch & Co., subscribed for one-half; and L. P. Morton and J. Pierpont Morgan, representing Baring Brothers, J. S. Morgan & Co., Morton, Rose & Co., Morton, Bliss & Co., and Drexel, Morgan & Co., subscribed for the other.

Books were opened for subscriptions in London and New York on February 4, 1873, with the understanding that they should close on the 7th.[52] At the end of the second day, nine-tenths of the American subscriptions had been taken by Jay Cooke & Co.[53] On February 6, McCulloch reported that the European subscriptions were not likely to be successful.[54] It was by then apparent that the subscription would be small.

Fearing the failure of the operation, Jay Cooke on his own responsibility advised Secretary Boutwell to call $100,000,000 in old bonds to be paid March 1, with the expectation that such a call would help the negotiation. Jay Cooke was gambling again in a big way! One may wonder why he took the risk of this step without consulting with the other syndicate members. His statement to the effect that he was ready to complete the negotiation alone, if they would not support such a large call,[55] suggests that it may have been a move toward getting control of the operation. Instead of withdrawing, however, the Rothschilds and the other London members of the syndicate to a man voted their disapproval of Jay Cooke's action.[56] The outcome was that the call was rescinded and another was issued on March 1 calling only $50,000,000.

The results of the effort were extremely disappointing to Jay Cooke. New bonds to the amount of $28,500,000 were sold in Europe for cash, and $8,000,000 for cash and $13,000,000 for old bonds in America.[57] This was far less than $300,000,000.

The failure of this attempt to syndicate the whole refunding loan in a short time leads to some very interesting speculations. First comes the question as to why the operation failed. The market was not too good, it is true. Yet there is no reason to believe that it had changed noticeably for the worse between the time the operation was agreed upon and the days in which subscriptions were received. Various explanations were given of the failure of the syndicate at the time. The *Commercial and Financial Chronicle*[58] held that, with their control of the secret springs of finance, the Rothschilds could have sold $500,000,000 or $600,000,000 of the loan. It believed that the European houses made no effort to secure subscriptions because they had an option on the loan till December 1, 1873. Some of the members of the London syndicate attributed the failure to float the loan immediately to the antagonism of the associates in the earlier syndicate, who, disappointed in being left out, sold their United States bonds and broke the market. Jay Cooke held that such a result should have been expected when they deserted their friends and went over to their enemies.[59]

Jay Cooke and his partners attributed the failure of the loan to the fact that there was no central management of it.[60] There is no evidence of any attempt in this case to influence the market, on which action much of the Cookes' earlier success had been based. Undoubtedly this was an important factor in the failure.

It is clear that the loan was sold neither aggressively nor enthusiastically. There is nothing in the correspondence or other material at hand which suggests that the associates of Jay Cooke & Co. purposely neglected the operation. The explanation probably is that their methods were different from Jay Cooke's. The refunding which was handled by the Rothschilds, Mortons, Seligmans, Morgans, and Belmont in the next four years was done slowly and cautiously.[61] Those conservative houses did not have Jay Cooke's way of doing a big job in a hurry. There was, moreover, no reason why they should hurry the loan of 1873; they had an option on $300,000,000 which was good until December 1, 1873.

The failure to sell the loan as expeditiously as had been done earlier weakened Jay Cooke's position in the refunding business. It was unfortunate for his firms that the loan was handled as it was. Had they controlled the operation and managed it as they had done in 1871, with the support of their old friends in New York and their European supporters of the loan of 1871 — rich Jewish bankers of London and the Continent, it is not unlikely that they would have had a considerable if not a complete success. But not only did the great Civil War banking house fail in this operation; by deserting its former friends, it also destroyed the support which had made earlier success possible. In being forced to co-operate with their enemies, Jay Cooke and his firms were driven into an impossibly weak position. With this failure vanished all hope of saving Jay Cooke & Co. by means of work for the government.

There remained just a shred of hope that Congress might still come to the aid of the Northern Pacific. Late in 1872 Jay Cooke had been encouraged in this hope by Thomas A. Scott, president of the Texas & Pacific, who proposed that the Northern and Southern Pacific roads should unite in seeking federal endorsement of the interest on bonds to the extent of $40,000 a mile.[62] Jay Cooke and his partners realized that Congress was in no mood to aid; yet, as the former said, "a year's delay might find us in quite a different position which might be avoided by some boldness now." [63] Whatever hopes the two Pacific roads may have had were soon blasted by the turn of the Crédit Mobilier investigation by Congress.[64] So glaring were the revelations of corruption in the building of the Union Pacific that all possibility of getting aid for the other Pacific railroads vanished. Indeed, Crédit Mobilier and Erie were so shamelessly corrupt that railroads lost standing not only in Congress but also in the bond market. The situation was not improved for Jay Cooke & Co. by revelations of corruption in the affairs of the District of Columbia, of which Henry Cooke had been governor.[65]

In the winter and spring of 1873 the condition of the money and securities markets would have made the sale of railroad bonds difficult regardless of other matters. The purchase of American railroad securities was slowing up both in Europe and the United States. The stringency which had appeared in the American money market in September, 1872, continued after a slight let-up in the winter. This was described by the *Commercial and Financial Chronicle* in April as the "most protracted monetary pinch which has been known for a quarter of a century." [66] It was believed by some that speculators in New York were again at work locking up greenbacks. Jay Cooke proposed that a flexible currency be established for the purpose of curbing them; he suggested that the $44,000,000 of greenbacks in the Treasury, which had been withdrawn by McCulloch, be held as a reserve to checkmate the speculators, or that the National Bank Act be so modified as to make the issue of notes more flexible.[67] But nothing was done. Money rates rose to an unusual height; New York bank reserves fell; inflation was widely urged as a remedy; and fear settled upon business.[68] The *Commercial and Financial Chronicle* suggested in March, 1873, that there might soon be a panic.

In such a market it was hopeless to float new bonds which were not of the highest security. Yet there were twenty new issues on the market according to the *Commercial and Financial Chronicle*.[69] Of these the Northern Pacific bonds offered the highest interest, 7.3 per cent in gold; the common interest was 7 per cent in gold, only a few bearing the same in currency. The New York & Oswego Midland, bearing 7 per cent, and the Northern Pacific offered their bonds at 100, while the others were offered at from 75 to 92½, most generally, however, at 90. The amount of bonds to be issued per projected mile by the Northern Pacific was $50,000, while the next highest was $28,000 and the most common about $20,000. Only two had land grants, the Northern Pacific with a grant of 23,000 acres a mile and the Houston & Texas Central, which had 10,240 per mile. The only far-western road among the twenty was the Northern Pacific; the others were mostly in somewhat developed regions, chiefly in the interior, and all but three were planned to be less than 500 miles in length.

It is not strange that Northern Pacifics, like most other railroad bonds, sold slowly under such conditions. In February about $320,000 Northern Pacifics were sold. In March J. V. Painter of Cleveland, one of the most faithful of Northern Pacific bond agents, complained that the subagents in the Cleveland district were doing nothing. At the same time Lunt, Preston & Kean, agents for the Chicago district, asked that arrangements be made for buying back bonds; they said that it was of no use even to try to offer Northern Pacifics in Chicago. Jay Cooke was heavily disappointed that the chance of getting a group of capitalists on the Pacific Coast to finance the extensive construction in Washington provided for by a new contract was dimmed by the tightness of money out there. Very portentous was the fact that it became necessary to repurchase several original interests in the $5,000,000 pool and also other Northern Pacifics thrown on the market.[70] This development was extremely serious because Jay Cooke & Co. did not have the means with which to support the railroad bonds.

It was not only the Northern Pacifics that were going slowly. Most new issues were having a difficult time. And other bankers were having the same trouble as Jay Cooke & Co.; they were endeavoring to support their roads by advances to them. If the internal situation in the different railroad banking houses were known, it would probably be seen that many of them were also near the breaking point in the winter and spring of 1873. It is doubtful, however, that any other house was as heavily loaded in proportion to its available assets as Jay Cooke & Co.

Progress of the Northern Pacific

Amid all the disappointments and difficulties of the winter of 1872–73 was the one encouraging fact that the Northern Pacific was making rapid progress in the West. The building of the railway was making remarkable headway; about 10,000,000 acres of the richest forest and agricultural land had been earned;[71] and settlement was becoming a reality in the Northern Pacific country.

In Washington Territory a great deal of progress had been made. The Columbia River-Puget Sound division, started at Kalama below Portland on the Columbia, was nearing Puget Sound.[72] Through its ownership of the Oregon Steam Navigation Company, the Northern Pacific also was prepared to carry passengers and freight up the Columbia River into eastern Washington. The road was well ahead of the requirements of its charter in Washington Territory.

On the eastern section of the Northern Pacific built westward from Duluth, even greater strides had been taken. By June 3, 1873, the great railway reached the Missouri;[73] there it provided a cheap outlet by rail for the rich mineral treasures and the cattle that the Dakota-Montana country was already sending eastward. These products offered some freight to the new railway, as also did the troops and supplies for government forts in the Indian country, whose transportation needs the Northern Pacific in the spring of 1873 was ready to supply.

The railhead halted on the Missouri. The junction point was promptly named Bismarck with an eye to German immigration.[74] But the railway was eager to march on westward. Surveying parties had already pierced the Bad Lands, and the route had been located to the Yellowstone River in eastern Montana.[75]

Everything except the funds was in readiness for the drive toward the mountains.

The Northern Pacific had become the owner of a very substantial property in land. "The 10 Million acres which are now due the Company," according to Jay Cooke, "contain nearly 2 Million acres on Puget Sound, which the President and Land Commissioner [of the Northern Pacific] give as their opinion are worth, for the lumber upon it alone, 100 Million Dollars. We have vast pine tracts in Minnesota which, if they sell at one-third the price the Grand Rapids is getting for similar tracts in Michigan, will pay off all the bonds speedily." [76]

"All that this country needs now is settlers," wrote Engineer Roberts to Jay Cooke from the Missouri River on May 30, 1873. The Northern Pacific had opened up a rich region: between Lake Superior and the Missouri lay 450 miles of prairie country and forest. With the building of the railroad, the Indian moved on toward the sunset and the white man came to make a home in the Red Man's wilderness haunts. Settlement was well under way in the Minnesota Red River country, and an agreement with the Wahpeton-Sisseton Indians opened to settlers eastern Dakota, where in the spring of 1873 claim shanties, barns, and wagon camps were already appearing.[77] In addition to individuals who were seeking a home in that region, there was the promising development of settlement by colonies.[78] In 1872 a small New England group had settled at Detroit Lake on the Northern Pacific and another at Glyndon. In the spring of 1873 were started the Yeovil and Furness colonies, both of which came from England and founded communities which came to center about Hawley and Wadena in Minnesota.

Behind this movement was the very elaborate immigration department of the Northern Pacific. It advertised the lands of the road at home; and through agents and lecturers it worked out from a central office in London into the English countryside, Holland, Germany, and the Scandinavian countries. The movement to the Northern Pacific lands was well under way and gave promise in the near future of the fulfillment of Jay Cooke's dream of happy and prosperous communities.

That settlement was beginning to bear fruit for the Northern Pacific is shown by a new item in the report for the year ending June 30, 1873. Passenger and freight receipts for the year were given for over half a million dollars. Jay Cooke's promises for the road were being realized, and it looked as though settlement might at least have a chance of defeating the forces which were working against Jay Cooke & Co. and the railroad it was financing.

THE NINE-MILLION NORTHERN PACIFIC SYNDICATE

The progress of the great railroad was not yet, however, bringing in enough returns to give much aid in meeting overhead, construction costs, or interest on the bonds. With the decrease in bond sales in the winter and spring of 1873 and the very difficult bond and money markets, the situation became extremely serious. It became evident that only the boldest strategy might suffice to ease matters for Jay Cooke & Co. In the difficult days of April, therefore, Jay Cooke undertook to close the issue of Northern Pacific seven-thirties at $30,000,000, organizing a syndicate to take the $9,000,000 still remaining unsold. If this effort were successful, the funds obtained would presumably, in part at least, be used to relieve Jay Cooke & Co. of some of the burden of its advances to the Northern Pacific and to take care of other obligations of the road already incurred. Jay Cooke would then be in a position to throw the responsibility on the road, as he had planned, when the Missouri was reached.

The reason given for the proposed closing of the seven-thirty loan was that, since the Northern Pacific had made such progress, it was no longer necessary to pay 7.3 per cent interest, and, therefore, later issues would bear only 6 per cent.[79] Thus limiting the issue of bonds bearing 7.3 per cent should, according to Jay Cooke, strengthen the bonds already on the market. To expect that Northern Pacifics would sell at 6 per cent was a bold position to take when the loan would hardly sell at all at the higher rate. Jay Cooke must have realized that the reasons given would not impress capitalists, but he was undoubtedly hoping that they would appeal to the smaller investors. Indeed, the operation looks very much like a resort to bluffing after other means had failed.

Perhaps Jay Cooke's real reason for closing the issue at $30,-000,000 was to get an excuse to organize a syndicate for taking the bonds on favorable terms. The syndicate offer was made very attractive. Jay Cooke & Co. arranged to take the $9,000,000 from the Northern Pacific at 88 and accrued interest with an allowance of 5 per cent for advertising, thus making the net cash cost of the bonds 83 per cent plus interest. The bonds were offered to syndicate subscribers at 83 and accrued interest, with a 50 per cent stock bonus. The bonds were to be held by the subscribers or sold at par, subscriptions to be paid in eight monthly instalments.[80] The syndicate offer was made early in May.

The month of May, 1873, was an extremely bad time to secure bond subscriptions even on such favorable terms. The market was then in its eighth month of stringency and discouragement and in an especially nervous condition. The panic in Vienna and other Continental cities frightened the American market. Thousands of merchants were going down. Jay Cooke had been disturbed in April that the government was not acting: "What is the use of having a Government and a Treasury when such things can for months be permitted to exist and the power that would correct them remain inactive?" [81] He expected, however, that the excellent terms would sell the loans even under the stress of such times. "The proposition now made is the prettiest speculation for a syndicate that we know of," wrote Jay Cooke, urging subscription in London, and "the affairs of the Company never looked so bright as at present." [82]

Then came disappointment. Brewster, Sweet of Boston, Painter of Cleveland, and even the Johnstons of Baltimore, all failed to subscribe. The Johnstons, old friends and supporters of Jay Cooke, refused because of the shrinking of their deposits.[83] Jay Cooke pleaded with them to take something, as the absence of their name would hurt Jay Cooke & Co. "I cannot agree with any one," he urged, "who prognosticates in this glorious country, which is receiving some days as high as 10,000 rich emigrants, that there can be anything like a permanent financial crisis here." If the Johnstons would subscribe for $100,000 or $200,000, Jay Cooke would agree to take back any bonds unsold on the next January 1.[84] A similar offer was made to the Fourth National of New York, the bank for whose organization Jay Cooke had been largely responsible.[85] Then came the last offer to Europe and the Rothschilds. Jay Cooke wrote to A. G. Cattell, who was then in London as representative of the Treasury in the settlement of the recent syndicating of the government loan and whose office was in the Rothschilds' bank. With 165 miles nearing completion in Washington Territory and 450 at the eastern end, with 10,000,000 acres of land already actually earned, and with 9,000 emigrants arriving at Castle Garden each day, the Northern Pacific, wrote Cooke, looked better and better every hour. "Oh, if Messrs. Rothschilds would only take hold of this matter with us! We could make more millions for them than they have now in their possession." [86]

The nine-million syndicate was a decided failure. The Cookes pointed with pride to one subscription, that of Charlemagne Tower, the Pennsylvania iron manufacturer. Jay Cooke had secured for Tower one of the original 24 shares, which gave him the right to appoint one director of the Northern Pacific; and Tower subscribed $250,000 to the new syndicate, but, since the Cookes promised to advance credit for his payments, this was not so great a deal as it might seem.[87] C. B. Wright, a Pennsylvanian who had recently become vice-president of the Northern Pacific, also subscribed for $250,000. The total subscription, outside of that of Jay Cooke & Co., was less than $2,000,000.[88] Most of the subscribers were banks or bankers in smaller towns, and, with the exception of the subscriptions of Tower and Wright, most of the subscriptions were small. Jay Cooke's last courageous stroke failed. Only one thing could help the Northern Pacific and Jay Cooke & Co. As Blücher saved the day for the English at Waterloo, so a very considerable improvement in the money market might still save the banker and his railroad and banking house.

The Fall of the Banking House of Jay Cooke

At the very time that the syndicate effort was failing, business was taking a turn for the better in the United States. The improvement continued well into the summer. Money became easier and bank reserves in New York reversed their downward trend. Exports rose relatively to imports. The bond market picked up slightly. Business men hoped that this was really the beginning of a considerable upturn. But underneath was grave fear of what the autumn would bring.

Though business improved somewhat, there was no favorable turn in the sale of Northern Pacifics. Jay Cooke & Co. continued to press the sale of their $9,000,000 loan. They had 1,500 agents selling on commission. But very little was accomplished. At the same time, dangerous amounts of Northern Pacific bonds were returned to the market, and brokers quoted them considerably below par.[89] "I wish," said Jay Cooke, "we cᵈ see our way clear to buy up the floating bonds, & stiffen up the market to 95." [90]

Under its changed management the Northern Pacific tried to economize. Construction was curtailed considerably in 1873; only on the Columbia River-Puget Sound division was there much advance.[91] But there were prior commitments, overhead, and fixed costs about which little could be done. Payments had to be made for the Oregon Steam Navigation Company; interest on bonds had to be met as due; and the executive and managerial personnel had to be maintained. The result was that the overdraft on Jay Cooke & Co. grew at a rapid rate. It is amazing to see how a banking firm like Jay Cooke's could get into such a position of responsibility when it was so well aware of the dangers. It must be remembered, however, that since the fall of 1871 there had been no considerable period of time in which the money market had not been heavy.

On August 15 the accounts of the Northern Pacific and the Lake Superior & Mississippi with the Philadelphia and New York houses stood as follows:[92]

(1) Lake Superior & Mississippi Railroad Company

	Cr.	Dr.
Advanced on first mortgage bonds		$ 296,873.73
" " second " "		1,139,350.07
" " third " "		106,434.70
Balance on book account, Philadelphia		56,875.43
" " " " New York		1,347.50
Stumpage account		264,565.38
Total		$1,865,446.81

(2) Northern Pacific Railroad Company

	Cr.	Dr.
Balance on book account, Philadelphia		$1,910,359.79
" " " " New York $116,454.17	
Notes, New York		1,898,240.00
" Philadelphia		1,400,000.00
		$5,208,599.79
		116,454.17
Total		$5,092,145.62

The two accounts showed a total indebtedness of $6,957,592.43 to Jay Cooke & Co.

Two attempts to help the Northern Pacific in the summer of 1873 were pathetically futile under the circumstances. President Cass tried to free the road from the criticism arising out of the nature of its connection with the Lake Superior & Puget Sound Land Company. Jay Cooke had also come to see that the land company's interests should be made secondary to the railroad's. The consolidation of the two concerns was recommended in May but it was opposed by some stockholders of the land company. Finally on September 17, 1873, the Northern Pacific offered to purchase the unfortunate company.[93]

The St. Paul & Pacific had also become so difficult a problem that in May the Northern Pacific offered its equity in the road for sale. In June President Cass offered to sell to an English group, with the understanding that the buyers should complete the two lines of the St. Paul road to Brainerd and Pembina and enter into a contract with the Northern Pacific to interchange traffic on the footing of the most favored road. But the two parties failed to agree on terms. In August the St. Vincent Extension and the line from Watab to Brainerd went into receivership.[94]

The acquisition of the St. Paul & Pacific had been extremely unfortunate for the Northern Pacific; it had involved the road in political controversy, in suits at law, and in great financial loss. If the Northern Pacific had had a few million to put into the other road, it could have built a magnificent system of railroads in the Red River Valley. But the attempt failed, and in failing weakened seriously the Northern Pacific itself.

The improvement in business of which there was some promise in the summer failed to materialize. Instead of becoming better, business became worse. Both the European and the American markets for new railroad issues were heavy. Prices of commodities and of government bonds and railroad stocks, which had begun to fall earlier in the year, continued their downward course.[95] In the summer, gold exports increased.[96] Long-time loans had been difficult to get since spring, but in August commercial paper began to tighten, and even call-loan rates rose considerably.[97] The seasonal westward movement of money, beginning in August, drew down New York bank reserves relatively to deposits.[98] At the same time it became known that the St. Joseph & Denver and the Oswego & Midland railroads were in trouble; and fear was expressed concerning savings banks and trust companies, many of which were supposed to have been loaded with unsalable bonds.[99] It was unfortunate that at that very time the Granger movement should have inspired investors with fear of railroads in the West, and that confidence in political and business morals should have reached such a low point under the impact of the exposure of the corruption of Crédit Mobilier, Erie, and the Tweed Ring.[100]

In the second week in September the storm broke. First went the New York Warehouse & Security Company, which had undertaken to finance the Missouri, Kansas & Texas Railroad for which it had assumed too heavy burdens.[101] Next went

Kenyon, Cox & Co., in which astute old Daniel Drew was a partner, which had endorsed paper for the Canada Southern to the extent of $1,500,000.

Jay Cooke later said he was unaware of the imminence of serious trouble at the time. This seems to have been true of many business men. It is difficult to understand how they could have expected to continue to build thousands of miles of railroad a year, much of it without any immediate prospect of being profitable, and thus tie up the available capital of the country and large amounts from Europe, without sometime running into difficulty. How much actually went into railroads is not definitely known. According to Poor's *Manual* the total capital account of railroads in the United States rose from about two billion dollars in 1869 to well on toward four billion in 1873.[102] Those figures have, of course, little meaning in themselves, as the stocks of many roads were highly inflated, but compared with each other they do give some indication of what had been happening in railroad finance.

One looks in vain to the business men of the early 'seventies for a clear recognition of the cyclical movement of business. One may wonder why Jay Cooke did not remember that what had happened in the past might happen again. He had at best only a faint recollection of 1837, but the panic of 1857 had impressed itself strongly on him and he must have known something of England's experience in 1866, when the weaknesses in her business structure were so similar to those in the United States in 1873. When 1929 is called to mind, however, it does not seem strange that Jay Cooke and his contemporaries should have been mistaken. Not only did they not have the knowledge of the cyclical movement of business which we have today and the help of various informational and forecasting services — the first crude American attempt of this type appeared in 1875 [103]— but they also looked upon business prosperity as a more or less certain result of the potential productiveness of the United States. True to the pioneer spirit, those promoters in the United States of the early 1870's were taking a long-time point of view. It is very easy to confuse long-time economic progress with the well-being of business. The two do not always parallel each other; indeed, they may even for a time go in opposite directions. Jay Cooke made the common mistake of seeing the one and taking the other for granted.

In one way, and a very significant one, Jay Cooke and many of his contemporaries made a grave error which is not altogether excusable. They forgot that they were bankers and became promoters. They allowed the assets of their houses — even their deposits — to be frozen in advances to and investments in great concerns which gave no promise of immediate returns. In such a condition they could not stand under a strain. The same thing happened to them that had occurred so often before — for instance in the Overend, Gurney panic in England in 1866 — and has so often happened since.

The first break in Jay Cooke & Co. came in New York, as would be expected from its position at the center of financial affairs. For several weeks there had been a steady diminution of deposits in the New York house, owing to the seasonal westward movement of money and, particularly, to the prevailing uneasiness over railroad securities. At the same time the Philadelphia house had continued to draw on New York. The New Yorkers had used everything that looked like cash and converted everything possible into cash so that when trouble came they had nothing to fall back upon.[104] The First National Bank of Washington had even been drawn on in the last weeks; its advances to Jay Cooke & Co. from August 18 to September 18 totaled over half a million.[105] As a last reminder of their former strength was the part the New York house took in the transfer of the Geneva awards for the *Alabama* Claims from England to the United States Treasury; the negotiation, which was handled by a syndicate consisting of Jay Cooke, McCulloch & Co., J. S. Morgan & Co., and Morton, Rose & Co., was completed when payment was made to the United States Treasury on September 13.[106] By the morning of September 18, things had come to such a pass in the New York house of Jay Cooke & Co. that Fahnestock called in the heads of several of the leading banks in New York to advise him as to what should be done.[107] The result was that, just before eleven o'clock of the same morning, Jay Cooke & Co. of New York was closed.[108]

Jay Cooke first knew of the closing of the New York house after it was an accomplished fact. His partners had finally taken matters into their own hands. It would probably not have happened in that way if Pitt Cooke had not been absent at the time— he was on board ship returning from Europe. The result, however, could hardly have been different had the senior partner been informed of the state of affairs. There was no chance of getting advances on the paper of Jay Cooke & Co. in such a money market as then existed. The Clarks, who might have aided them, also suspended the same day. Indeed, the friends of Jay Cooke & Co. were like themselves heavily involved in railroads. The Philadelphia house of Jay Cooke & Co. was closed at eleven, and a little later the Washington house and the First National Bank of Washington, D. C.

The failure of Jay Cooke & Co. came at the beginning of a severe panic in New York. It was difficult to convince the "Street" that the "foremost American banking-house" was unable to meet its obligations, and, when it was realized, "dread seemed to take possession of the multitude."[109] On the announcement that Jay Cooke's Philadelphia house and the First National Bank of Washington had suspended, the scene became indescribable on Wall Street. The stock market broke and securities were sacrificed in the most ruthless manner.[110] Depositors drew their money. Loans were called. Business became paralyzed.[111] On September 20, for the first time in its existence, the New York Stock Exchange was closed.

Mercantile houses and savings banks escaped fairly well, but bankers and brokers fell under the burden of advances to railroads or heavy investments in their bonds. Several of Jay Cooke's faithful friends in war finance had to close, investment houses which like his own had turned to railroads when the government business had declined, including E. W. Clark & Co., Fisk & Hatch, and Henry Clews & Co.[112] The internal condition of those houses was that they had bought too many railroad bonds or had made too heavy loans in proportion to their own capital and their deposits; when trouble came, the depositors demanded their money in order to make themselves secure. Many other concerns went down in New York, among them Howes & Macy, Robinson & Suydam, and Richard Schell, brokers, and the National Bank of the Commonwealth and the Union Trust, all too heavily loaded with railroad investments or advances. The shock in New York soon spread throughout the country and bankruptcy became epidemic.

Jay Cooke has often been credited with bringing on the panic of 1873. While the failure of his house was not the cause of the trouble, nor even the first of the failures, it was the element which precipitated a general panic. Jay Cooke & Co. performed the function in 1873 which William Duer had performed in 1792 and the Ohio Life & Trust Co. in 1857, and which the Knickerbocker Trust was to perform in 1907. They all provided the dramatic event which broke confidence in a business situation which was ready to collapse.

On the closing of his banking houses, Jay Cooke thought that the assets were so much larger than the liabilities that it would be possible soon to reopen.[113] The panic and depression made an immediate settlement impossible, however, and it soon became evident that Jay Cooke & Co., which had been the foremost banking house in America, had definitely failed.

There was some question at first as to the cause of the failure. It was said that the Cookes had been speculating, but that was soon disproved. The records show that Jay Cooke & Co. broke under the weight of its many investments in and advances to railroads, including the Northern Pacific, the Lake Superior & Mississippi, and other smaller roads, which had been accumulating in the years immediately preceding the failure. Under the stress of the growing reluctance of the bond buyer and increasing stringency in the money market, it proved impossible to carry the load at a time when the depositors were demanding their money.

The failure of Jay Cooke & Co. marked the close of an important movement in American business, the speculative promotion of railroads beyond a reasonable expectation of returns under the drive of post-war conditions. The movement had deep roots: it was made possible by the large amount of war savings and government bonds in the United States after the war, which could readily be converted into railroad investments; and it was driven by the need of the bankers, who had been engaged in government finance, for new work and by the speculative spirit of the time.

Thus ended Jay Cooke's work as a railroad financier. He had helped significantly in providing the transportation necessary for the conversion of a great wilderness into productive forests, farms, and mines. But this effort had destroyed his banking firms, brought loss to many of his customers, and contributed to the bringing on of the panic and depression which ended the great post-war boom in 1873. This outcome of Jay Cooke's work in railroad promotion is typical of American history. Since the time when certain London merchants invested their own and their friends' funds in the business enterprise of establishing the Virginia colony in 1607, which failed to make profits but laid the foundations of the United States, business men and investors have again and again paid the same price for the rapid development of the American Continent.

JAY COOKE CARRIES ON

THERE is a remarkable continuity in human institutions which defies the forces that tend to destroy. This is as true in business as in social and political life. The individual institution disappears, but the greater Institution lives on. It lives because its essentials are men and techniques and efforts and results, and these always in some measure survive the single institution, which passes away.

Jay Cooke, the banker, was never to return to banking — his prestige was gone and hence his leadership and strength. He was to turn to the building up of a personal fortune and before long to retire from business altogether. His younger partners, however, men who had received their training and experience with Jay Cooke and his firm, were to enter other important banks, where they were to carry on till the end of the century or longer. Much of the work of Jay Cooke & Co., its technique and policies, which served the needs of the time, had already entered upon a broader activity and had become a part of that greater Institution, American banking. Jay Cooke & Co. was dead — and yet Jay Cooke & Co. lived on.

CLOSING OUT JAY COOKE'S BANKING FIRMS

Jay Cooke was closely involved in three banking firms, the one which bore his name, including the Philadelphia, New York, and Washington houses, Jay Cooke, McCulloch & Co., of London, and the First National Bank of Washington, D. C. All of these firms were liquidated as a result of the failure of Jay Cooke & Co.

The banker at first attempted to settle the affairs of Jay Cooke & Co. without bankruptcy. It was his belief that the matter could be handled more profitably for both the creditors and the members of the firm if left in the hands of those who were familiar with the business. About ten days after suspension, a statement was handed to the Associated Press on the assets and liabilities of the firm which seemed to indicate that such a settlement might be possible. The assets were said to total $15,875,120.04 and the liabilities $7,937,409.26, showing, as it was pointed out, that without counting advances to the Northern Pacific, assets were "amply sufficient to secure all its creditors against loss." [1] A plan was devised for settling without bankruptcy. Jay Cooke & Co. and its members turned the firm's and the partners' individual assets over to E. A. Rollins of Philadelphia as trustee for settlement with the creditors.[2] Rollins, a friend of the Cookes who had been associated with the National Life Insurance Company, was to be responsible to a committee of three prominent business men of Philadelphia who were to appraise all the property and assets available for settlement. It was necessary to secure the unanimous consent of the creditors for any plan of settlement short of bankruptcy.

Jay Cooke worked hard to gain approval for this plan. He was supported in this effort by his Washington brother [3] but opposed by his New York brother, Fahnestock, and Moorhead. Pitt Cooke, impatient with his brother's concern for the creditors and apparently speaking for the New Yorkers, urged that, in the absence of assets which could in a reasonable time be converted into cash, his plan was not feasible and that it would be better for the partners to settle at once through bankruptcy.[4] Though Jay Cooke secured the consent of a large number of the creditors to his plan, it was impossible to make it unanimous.

In the meantime a creditor had requested that Jay Cooke & Co. be adjudged bankrupt. When it was seen that it would be impossible to settle by another method, the United States District Court for eastern Pennsylvania, on November 26, 1873, adjudged Jay Cooke & Co. and its partners bankrupt. Jay Cooke, thereupon, attempted to secure an amendment of the federal bankruptcy law which would have given the Cookes a measure of control over the settlement; but in this he also failed.[5] The matter was therefore left to a trustee in bankruptcy under the existing law.

After the appointment of the receiver, a careful investigation was made of the assets and liabilities of the firm and a summary statement was made. By that time, of course, the value of the estate had fallen greatly. After a careful investigation the total liabilities were then reported as being $11,134,878.94, and of this $8,481,646.05 were unsecured.[6] Assets definitely appraised, consisting of $130,332.51 in cash, bills receivable, and well over a million due on book accounts, bank shares, pig iron, and various bonds and stocks, amounted to $3,310,009.77. The homes of the partners and miscellaneous real estate in Ohio and the East, almost 90,000 acres of land in the Middle West, various railroad securities, particularly bonds of the Sterling Iron & Railway Co. and the Northern Pacific Railroad, and a miscellany of other things, were given an uncertain appraisement of $3,930,018.09. There remained, unappraised, thousands of shares of stock in various concerns, railroad bonds, town lots, and sundry other things.

The settlement of the estate in bankruptcy was complicated by the involved relationship of Jay Cooke & Co. and its partners. For a time there was uncertainty concerning the relations of the American firm with Jay Cooke, McCulloch & Co. The double liability of the Cooke partners for three-fourths of the stock of the First National Bank of Washington threatened to absorb a large part of the assets that could be liquidated without too great a loss. The fact that Fahnestock, Moorhead, and Henry Cooke had turned a considerable amount of property over to their wives was investigated. Action was taken against Fahnestock, who, at the very time when Jay Cooke had begun to protest seriously against the overdrafts of the Northern Pacific, had assigned to his wife $100,000 in United States ten-forties and $2,500 in shares of a New York concern.[7] Most serious in the settlement of the affairs of Jay Cooke & Co. was the fact that liquidation had to come during the period of severe deflation in values which followed in the wake of the panic of 1873.

The settlement of the bankruptcy estate was not completed until 1890. By then the creditors had received a total of $15\frac{1}{2}$ per cent in cash, 15 per cent in asset scrip, and, for each $1,000 of liabilities, 8 shares of Northern Pacific preferred, $3\frac{1}{2}$ shares in

the Oregon Steam Navigation Company, and three-fourths of a
share of St. Paul & Duluth preferred and half a share of common.[8]
It would be interesting to know to what extent the monetary loss
suffered by the creditors of Jay Cooke & Co. was actually made
up. It is rather obvious that it would be extremely difficult, if not
altogether impossible, to arrive at even an approximate conclusion. Jay Cooke's own opinion was that those who held on to their
securities ultimately received much more than their claims.[9]

The life of Jay Cooke, McCulloch & Co. was very short after
the closing of the parent house. Under the original agreement
the co-partnership expired at the end of 1873, but at first the
London partner proposed to reorganize in order to continue in
London.[10] This it was found impossible to do, since, with the
breaking of Jay Cooke & Co., the source of its working capital
and much of the business of Jay Cooke, McCulloch & Co. disappeared.[11] Thus ended a house which had in less than three years
in London become firmly entrenched and fairly profitable.

The settlement of the affairs of the First National Bank of
Washington proved very difficult. Jay Cooke & Co. owed the
Washington bank $827,000, only a small portion of which was
secured. And the bank had been too lenient in its loans to needy
politicians who had little security. Furthermore, the Cookes
held almost three-quarters of the stock of the national bank,
which meant that an equivalent percentage of possible levies on
stockholders was tied up in the bankruptcy of the Cooke firm.
Before it was adjudged bankrupt, Jay Cooke & Co. attempted to
purchase the claims of other national banks against the First
National by a payment of 50 per cent in cash and the remainder
in Northern Pacific bonds, but this effort failed. Through its receiver, the bank's affairs were finally settled and its liabilities
were met in full in 1876.[12]

THE NORTHERN PACIFIC IS COMPLETED

Jay Cooke's career as a banker ended in failure. Yet the work
he had done as a promoter of railroads was to bring important
results in the development of the Northwest. Time has showed

that the Northern Pacific country, so derisively named the Banana Belt by Jay Cooke's critics, had great potentialities for production and settlement. The system of roads planned by Jay Cooke has become a reality.

Within fifteen years after Jay Cooke's failure the Northern Pacific was completed. The company had carried on for a few months after the closing of Jay Cooke & Co., but reorganization was inevitable. Under the plan of reorganization adopted the old stockholders were given $49,000,000 in common stock for their $100,000,000, with limited rights. The bondholders were given the right to change their $30,000,000 of bonds plus unpaid interest into 8 per cent preferred stock. In the meantime, expenses had been cut to the minimum and interests in other transportation concerns had been sacrificed. This was followed by a slow improvement in the condition of the company. In the year 1876, earnings for the first time exceeded expenditures. In the late 1870's, projected branches and connections in Minnesota and the Red River Valley were completed essentially as had been planned, so that the Northern Pacific reached to both St. Paul and the Canadian boundary. In the meantime some advance had been made westward. Settlement was growing in the Red River country, which Cass and Cheney, former directors of the road, were so dramatically advertising by means of their bonanza wheat farms; and the pine of Minnesota was being carried westward by the Northern Pacific to build homes for the settlers. Considerable traffic was thus provided for the road.[13]

By 1880 the Northern Pacific was not only a substantial property with considerable additions to the 600 miles of railway and the 10,000,000 acres of rich forest and agricultural lands which it had acquired with the help of Jay Cooke. The company had also, like so many other roads at the time, rid itself of heavy fixed interest charges by reorganization. And it was making progress with its earnings. This change over a few years in the fortunes of the Northern Pacific illustrates the generalization about American transportation history that the railway went into bankruptcy and became a railroad.

The road was by 1880 in a condition to attract capital. An

A Tribute to a Pioneer

Statue of Jay Cooke on the shore of Lake Superior at Duluth

agreement was, as a result, made with Winslow, Lanier & Co. of New York, A. Belmont & Co., and the Drexel-Morgan houses of Philadelphia, New York, and London to furnish funds for the completion of construction to the Coast.[14] In the meantime, Henry Villard, who had been reorganizing the transportation system in the Oregon country, an important part of which was the Oregon Steam Navigation Company earlier purchased and lost by the Northern Pacific, had become interested in the road because of its threat of becoming a competitor of his system. Villard succeeded in purchasing control of the Northern Pacific.[15] He was elected its president and brought into its directorship J. Pierpont Morgan and August Belmont. With its new management and financial backing the Northern Pacific reached Puget Sound on the Pacific Coast in 1883, *via* the Oregon Railway & Navigation Co. along the Columbia River; its own line to Tacoma on the Sound was completed in 1888.[16]

Jay Cooke felt vindicated by the completion of the great transcontinental road. In 1891 he went as the guest of the railroad over the whole line to Tacoma, the western terminus. In the Gibraltar Records on his return he wrote the following paragraph, which epitomizes the significance of the road for which he had stood as financial sponsor:

My sensations as day after day I passed over this road & through this wonderful country now so rapidly developing & which now contains 6 Millions of people where only 20 years ago the Indian & Buffalo held full sway were such as few have ever experienced — It was in a measure the fulfilment of prophecies which I uttered long ago, I felt that I was fully justified.

The completion of the Northern Pacific does not tell the whole story of the fulfillment of Jay Cooke's plans for the great country beyond Lake Superior. The larger railroad system which he had visioned also eventually came into being. Finally, James J. Hill succeeded where Cooke had failed. In 1876 Hill gained the assistance of Donald Smith, who later became Lord Strathcona, and of other Canadian interests in building the Great Northern (as the St. Paul & Pacific came to be called), which reached the Coast in 1893, and the Canadian Pacific, which was finished in

1886.[17] He later secured control of the Northern Pacific with the aid of Morgan, thus uniting the two roads Jay Cooke had tried to carry. Hill succeeded where Cooke had failed. But Hill worked under entirely different conditions from those which had confronted Jay Cooke: he lived in the Northwest and was in a position properly to manage his property, and in railroad operation and finance he was a superb master; he was able to secure strong financial backing, which Cooke had failed to do; he worked in a country which was developed and which furnished traffic for his roads, as compared with the virgin West of Cooke's time; and he was fortunate enough, in his later and most successful years, to have worked at a time when business was on the upgrade, as compared with the downward trend of the early 1870's.

Business history is strewn with situations of this kind. The pioneer may plan well for the long-run but in advance of his time, so that he fails to gather the fruits of his efforts. He first plows the virgin soil and wins praise or blame. The next generation reaps the financial harvest.

JAY COOKE'S PARTNERS CARRY ON IN BANKING

With the declaration of the bankruptcy of Jay Cooke & Co., the founder of the firm left banking never to enter it again. After 34 years in finance, after almost a decade of striking leadership in American banking and a few years of intense struggle to protect his position, Jay Cooke retired from the work which had given him wealth, prestige, and, finally, failure. It is clear why he did not go on. With his fortune went his prestige, and he had not the will to enter again upon the work which would be required to re-establish himself. He had been up the tower, he once said, speaking of business; he had seen what there was to see and he was satisfied.[18]

Jay Cooke's older partners also retired from banking. Pitt Cooke returned to his former home, Sandusky, where he spent his few remaining years in the real-estate business, putting into effect a plan for supplying cheap homes for working men.[19] Henry Cooke, no longer engaged in the politics of finance, lived on in Washington where he died in 1881.[20] William Moorhead never re-entered business nor regained his fortune; he lived the remainder of his days from the property he had assigned to his wife.[21] Hugh McCulloch returned to America where he again served for a short time as secretary of the Treasury; he spent the last years of his life on a country place near Washington, D. C.[22]

Except Puleston and Evans, who remained in England, the younger members of Jay Cooke & Co. carried on in American banking. What knowledge they had gained from Jay Cooke and from their years in his firm was thus put to work in various other institutions.

George C. Thomas, who had risen to rank next to the senior partner in the parent house of Jay Cooke & Co., entered a brokerage firm in Philadelphia in which he became a partner. In 1883 he was invited to join the three banking houses of Anthony J. Drexel, and in 1894 he became the senior resident in the Philadelphia house.[23] It is interesting that a man trained by Jay Cooke should become the head of Anthony J. Drexel's bank. Thomas acquired a considerable fortune. He contributed liberally to charitable institutions and to the Church, and he became somewhat of a collector of rare manuscripts and books and works of art. He is thus representative of that great number of American business men of his generation who contributed so much, through their collecting, to the great American libraries and museums.

Jay Cooke & Co., of New York, was taken over almost bodily by the First National Bank. This bank had been established in 1863 under the leadership of John Thompson, a former publisher of a bank-note detector. George F. Baker, only 23 years of age at the time, had become its first cashier.[24] The First National Bank had prospered. Though its capital was only $500,000, small compared with that of some of the national banks in New York, the bank had become important in commercial banking; in the early 1870's it held bankers' deposits of from $4,000,000 to $5,000,000.[25]

Baker and Fahnestock had for some time been close friends. For years they had gone on fishing trips together, according to letters in the Jay Cooke Papers. Fahnestock had even at one time hoped to bring Cashier Baker into Jay Cooke & Co., as the following letter shows:

> Banking house of
> Jay Cooke & Co
> Cor. Wall & Nassau Sts
> New York Sept 15 '68

Dear Jay

Only one word privately to think over. George F. Baker of 1st Nat Bank here (Cashier) is a good man to *think* of without saying anything. He is about 30. Irreproachable — smart & we all like him. *Don't speak of him* but we will talk hereafter when the time comes.

He now has a salary of 5000 or 6000 & has once or more intimated to me that when the *right time* comes he will transplant himself

Besides a good knowledge of business here, he has kept a London a/c & done some Ex business

He is son of Baker Chf clk State Dept now & for many years

> trly
> H. C. F.

Though there is no evidence to show that Baker ever seriously considered joining Jay Cooke & Co., after the bankruptcy of the Cooke firm his First National Bank almost at once took in Fahnestock and Garland and ten of the clerks of Jay Cooke & Co., of New York.[26]

Fahnestock and Garland were a valuable acquisition to the First National. Garland was an excellent broker — said to have been one of the best on the Street.[27] He later was concerned in the founding of the Lincoln National Bank. Fahnestock was well equipped in three lines: he was known as one of the best "traders" in government bonds on the Street;[28] he was no less at home in railroad finance; and he had led the New York office of Jay Cooke & Co. through a considerable development in foreign exchange. Jay Cooke's former partner was made head of the bond department of the First National, and as such he directed a considerable business during the subsequent refunding of the war debt, in which the First National Bank played a considerable part. In 1877 Fahnestock was elected director and vice-president and George F. Baker, president. The Thompsons retired at the time and organized the Chase National Bank.

As the government business dwindled with the completion of refunding on a large scale, Fahnestock returned to transportation finance, seizing the opportunities offered by the receivership of companies in distress. While reorganizing the West Shore Railroad, he was a partner in Winslow, Lanier & Co., private bankers. Among the other railroads with which he came to be associated were the Southern, the Central of New Jersey, and the Delaware, Lackawanna & Western. He became prime mover in the Tide Water Oil Company, gained control of the Jersey Water Properties, and became director in numerous other companies, among which were the American Cotton Oil Company and Western Union.[29]

Fahnestock thus carried on in the fields which had been the chief interest of Jay Cooke & Co., that is, in government bonds and railroad finance. But his was no longer the work of the pioneer and builder; it was rather that of the reorganizer who reaped the financial rewards of the earlier efforts. He was representative of the new era, the age not so much of railroad promotion as reorganization and consolidation and the age of emphasis on operation and management.

CHAS. D. BARNEY & CO.

The direct business heir of Jay Cooke was his son-in-law, Charles D. Barney. Mr. Barney had been in charge of the department in the Philadelphia house of Jay Cooke & Co. which handled small orders for stocks and bonds other than governments, the so-called stock department. Shortly after the closing of Jay Cooke & Co., Mr. Barney opened an office to do a business in securities.

The new house was started in December, 1873, with Mr. Barney as the sole legal member. Jay Cooke, Jr., who worked with Mr. Barney from the first, was admitted to partnership in Chas. D. Barney & Co. as soon as he received his discharge from bankruptcy. A messenger boy or page completed the personnel of the concern. This new enterprise was at first housed in a small office on South Third Street in Philadelphia.

Chas. D. Barney & Co. soon outgrew its original quarters. The day after it opened, it received a large order in Philadelphia City 6 per cent bonds. In two months it moved into the old home of Jay Cooke & Co. It occupied, however, only a corner of the proud home of what had been America's greatest banking firm — the rest of the big and pretentious office of Jay Cooke & Co. was at one time sublet to as many as five tenants. In February, 1874, Mr. Barney bought a seat on the Philadelphia Stock Exchange for $800. J. Horace Harding, who had been trained for the printer's trade, became a clerk in the young firm in 1885 and soon thereafter a partner. He was put in charge of the New York house of the firm when it was established in 1902. On the retirement of Mr. Barney in 1905, Harding became the leading partner.

Chas. D. Barney & Co. started as a brokerage firm, dealing in stocks and bonds. At first it kept deposits for the members' families and for a few banks, but it did not make loans and it did no underwriting; but gradually it took on the additional functions of underwriting and making loans to customers for carrying securities on margin. It dealt at first in railroad bonds, Northern Pacifics, "Pennsys," Readings, and others, but it did very little work in governments. As time passed its interests expanded. Its more important work in the earlier period of expansion had to do with the consolidation of a number of breweries and the sale of their bonds, and in the syndicating of electric railroad construction and consolidation in the Cleveland district.[30] It eventually took on all the work of a fully developed investment bank, that is, underwriting, distributing and dealing in stocks and bonds, and the brokerage business.

The firm continues in the same business today (1936). Its headquarters are in New York, where it occupies the very site on which Jay Cooke & Co. was located. By means of six branches and correspondents, all connected by private wire, it reaches a large part of the United States. Among its twenty partners are one grandson of Jay Cooke, Henry E. Butler, and three great-grandsons, one who bears Jay Cooke's name and Charles Barney Harding and William Barclay Harding, sons of J. Horace Harding and grandsons of Charles D. Barney.

JAY COOKE HIMSELF BECOMES AN INVESTOR

Jay Cooke was at first very much stunned by the failure of his house. He said he had not expected it. He may have meant by this that, when the blow came, it gave no immediate warning; but it may be that he had really believed his firm could carry its railroad burden. Jay Cooke was of a sanguine nature; his robust and energetic physique, his lively imagination, his warm and hopeful spirit buoyed up by a childlike faith in God, all tended to give him a positive outlook. Moreover, experience had been kind to him; until 1873 his successes had been great and his failures small, a fact which no doubt gave him a false sense of strength. Of fundamental importance was the fact that he had a faith in his own strength and in the power of the individual which made him somewhat blind to the great forces in business beyond the individual's control — he did not know the fatalistic philosophies reborn in his day, which were to influence greatly the thought of the generation to follow, and his was a world in which man, by the grace of God, dominated. These were the sources of the banker's strength and also the sources of his failure.

Jay Cooke's first reaction to his failure was to place much blame on others. He was particularly bitter toward Fahnestock for closing the New York house without consulting the head of the firm;[31] he believed that, had he known of the condition of the New York house, he could have saved it by securing credit to tide it over. Jay Cooke believed that he could have gotten help from his friends, such as the Clarks; but since his friends were themselves in trouble, their help in the panic would have melted like snow before the summer's sun. Urged on by Sargent, who was seeking an explanation of his own failure with Northern Pacifics in Europe,[32] Jay Cooke also blamed the London partners for contributing to the failure by their lack of enthusiasm for the Northern Pacific. As for the money market, the source of its continuous stringency he found in McCulloch's policy of contracting the currency by the withdrawal of greenbacks while at the head of the Treasury.[33]

As time passed, however, Jay Cooke came to see that his own

policy had been wrong. He recognized that his firm had been seriously overextended, considering the condition of the money market. Not only had it made heavy advances to the Northern Pacific, but it had also become loaded with securities of the Lake Superior & Mississippi and its branches and the Iowa Central, besides having immense dealings in railroad iron. He also recognized that a fundamental error had been made in the failure to build up an adequate capital for his firm.[34]

Jay Cooke received his discharge from bankruptcy on August 7, 1876.[35] Up to that time he had given fully of his time and energies to aid in the settlement with the creditors. He had a desk in the office of Chas. D. Barney & Co., but he had no interest in re-entering upon business in any permanent way. Yet he was not to retire from it so soon. It has been noted again and again that Jay Cooke's firm belief in the prosperity of the United States was based on the great resources of this country. Appropriately enough, it was the exploitation of those resources which was the source of the rebuilding of his fortune.

It began with the Horn Silver Mine in Utah. A certain Lycurgus Edgerton, who had appeared in a rather futile way in the Northern Pacific negotiations, in 1878 called to Jay Cooke's attention the possibilities of the Horn Silver Mine.[36] This mine, to which four prospectors without capital had acquired the claim in 1876, was in the San Francisco mining district in Utah, 225 miles southwest of Salt Lake City and 150 miles from a railroad.[37] Cooke had a careful examination made of the situation and went out to see the mine, himself. Finding everything satisfactory from the point of view of both silver and law, he agreed with the owners to furnish railroad connections.

The former banker had no capital with which to finance such an enterprise, but he still had his ability to organize, his convincing personality, and some prestige. He succeeded in arranging for the building of the road without any difficulty. The four mine owners took a 25 per cent interest; a Salt Lake City group took another quarter; and the remaining half was taken by Dillon of the Union Pacific, who promised to furnish the capital for building the road.[38] The Utah Southern was immediately put under construction and was completed in 1880.[39]

The Horn Silver Mining Company was organized in February, 1879, with a capital stock of $10,000,000 divided into 400,000 shares.[40] In return for arranging for the building of a railroad to the mine and for negotiating the sale of the mining property, Jay Cooke was given 40,001 shares of stock plus commissions. Though there were then hundreds of such enterprises seeking a market, this mine was rated by a contemporary mining journal as "unquestionably the richest silver mine in the world now being worked." [41]

Jay Cooke sold the larger part of the stock in the Horn Silver Mining Company to Charles G. Franklyn and Frank G. Brown, who expected to sell to others.[42] His portion of the stock which was sold in January, 1880, brought him something over $800,000.[43] This together with commissions on the sale and dividends netted Jay Cooke close to a million on the transaction. In this way the bankrupt banker, past the meridian of his life, laid the basis for another fortune.

Jay Cooke was again on the road to riches, and success brought greater success. He was soon overwhelmed with offers from other mining properties which were seeking a buyer.[44] The sale of some of those, such as the St. Eulalie in Mexico and the Great Republic in Montana Territory, he undertook to negotiate, and the work brought him considerable amounts. But it is significant to observe that in none of them would he assume responsibility for management.[45] When asked to become associated with mining companies, he emphatically stated that he would have no responsibility for management. He was not to be caught again.

With some means again at his command, Jay Cooke turned to the task of regaining some of the property he had lost in his failure, when he had given up everything to his creditors except personal effects and a few objects treasured for sentimental reasons and had moved into the home of his daughter, Laura Barney. His first repurchase was the Ogontz estate. The furnishings could not all be restored, however, and it was impracticable for him to return to his old home. The mansion and the immediate grounds were, therefore, leased to a private school. Much of the estate was sold at excellent prices to prominent Philadelphians, and Ogontz became the heart of Philadelphia's most wealthy and most fashionable residential district. Another property of which the Philadelphian regained control was the St. Louis water-power site on the St. Louis River near Duluth. The St. Louis River Water Power Co. was organized in the 'eighties, Jay Cooke and his family owning two-thirds of the shares.[46] This concern was eventually sold to a large power company at a good profit,[47] and today (1936) it supplies the cities of Duluth and Superior with power. Various other properties were also regained, among them the South Mountain Iron Co. in Pennsylvania.

Jay Cooke did not take a very active part in the management of his investments. His son-in-law, John M. Butler, was his assistant from the early years after the bankruptcy, and later both Mr. Barney and J. Horace Harding, Mr. Barney's son-in-law and partner, aided in the management of his affairs. Thus he shifted from active business to the passive position of the investor.

Free from concern over business and with an ample fortune, Jay Cooke enjoyed his later years in the way that one of his nature would. His was not a philosophic old age. Though sometimes, as American business men will do, he discoursed with reporters on such things as the faults of a college education or the virtues of free silver, as to the deeper philosophic problems of the individual he continued to the end of his days firm in his simple Christian faith. His social and generous nature found many satisfactions. He was liberal in his gifts; and he enjoyed his friends and family, his fishing cronies, and the girls at the Ogontz School, to whom he was like a jolly grandfather. His was one of those rare spirits which grow mellow with age. Fishing was his great indulgence, and his fishing lodge in the Pennsylvania mountains and his old home on the island of Gibraltar in Lake Erie, which were both restored to him, provided many a happy occasion for his later years.

But time was passing. In the fall of 1904, Jay Cooke made his regular visit to Gibraltar. "*Goodbye* dear old Gibraltar," he wrote for the last time in the Gibraltar Records on October 26, "we thank God for permitting us to enjoy such a glorious visit and hope to come again — we feel that the visit has done us good — & that health has been much improved thereby." [48] Indeed, for several years, Jay Cooke had had warnings of an apoplectic nature that all was not well with his health. Yet he continued his usual activities. On an evening in February, 1905, he gave his annual reception to the girls at the Ogontz School, enjoying it all, even to juggling oranges to the delight of the girls. Only the second day thereafter, came, quietly and peacefully, the end of a happy and for many years an influential life. [49]

JAY COOKE'S PLACE IN THE HISTORY OF AMERICAN BUSINESS

In the history of American business, Jay Cooke ranks as an outstanding leader. Not that he always built well; like the typical pioneer he was likely to advance ahead of his time — even as a banker he was still in his heart a frontiersman always eager to push on westward. But he towered high in his generation and left his mark on American business, both in the work he did and in the practices and institutions which he handed down to the generation which followed him. Jay Cooke's part in the financing of the Civil War still stands as a remarkable financial achievement and a great patriotic service, and his work in railroad finance contributed to the development of the Northwest. His importance in the history of American business lies especially, however, in his leadership in a very significant transition that came in investment banking in the 1860's and 1870's. He was the first in America to stand out dramatically and effectively as an active investment banker operating on a large scale. Though his firm was destroyed in his effort to finance the Northern Pacific, he demonstrated the possibilities of aggressive investment banking, revealed some of its problems, and pointed to their solution. Though he himself failed, those who later followed his general strategy succeeded.

It was the Civil War which turned Jay Cooke in the new direction. When the leading bankers of the country, men of experience and considerable resources who lived by the old tradition, had showed that they could no longer furnish the government with sufficient means for conducting the war, Jay Cooke, almost single-handed and without much prestige or capital or even much encouragement from the leading bankers, conducted loan campaigns which supplied the Treasury with adequate funds.

The investment banker operating on a large scale must have a considerable market and a good distribution system. Jay Cooke succeeded in getting both in war finance. Contrary to both American and English practice, he turned to the people, rather than the big bankers, in the sale of the war loans. By his results he demonstrated to American bankers the importance of the small investor. He brought the great democracy into the bond market; in the language of today, he popularized the baby bond. To reach the small investor it was necessary to develop a new method of security distribution. Bankers and capitalists could be reached directly, but it took entirely different methods to reach the small buyer. Jay Cooke, accordingly, introduced aggressive advertising and publicity into security selling; he brought thousands of small bankers, insurance men, and leading citizens into his selling organization, and he even used traveling agents, forerunners of our door-to-door salesmen. Thus arose large-scale, high-pressure selling of bonds in the United States. The development of this new method of retail distribution was an important contribution to American investment banking technique.

Driven by necessity and by his success in the war, Jay Cooke was caught in the post-war railroad boom. Like two earlier leaders in national finance, Robert Morris, the financier of the Revolution, and Nicholas Biddle of the second Bank of the United States, both of whom had made a great reputation and had acquired great self-confidence, Jay Cooke turned to speculative promotion. In financing the Northern Pacific, he used the methods which had proved so successful during the war. Though Jay Cooke as railroad financier was less successful than as war financier, it was in the railroad field that he did his most significant experimenting in the new rôle of the active investment banker.

Jay Cooke was right in believing that only aggressive methods would succeed in selling Northern Pacifics. But he evidently did not have a clear comprehension of the necessity of protecting his own organization from the heavy risks which such a method would involve. He made the mistake of committing his own firms to the project before he had built proper defences against failure. In his feeling out for new devices he was a leader; his weakness lay in not perfecting the mechanism required by the new type of leadership.

In his handling of the big bankers he was especially unfortunate. He tried to win the support of the Rothschilds before he finally committed himself to the project, but they were of the old, passive type of investment banker and would have nothing to do with a promotion scheme like the Northern Pacific. Jay Cooke, therefore, fell back upon the old practice of relying on bankers as distributors only. That he did not have a clear comprehension of his problem is seen from the fact that he was willing to go ahead without any guarantee of support from bankers. He even failed to enlist the aid of strong bankers as distributors. He had clearly overestimated his own strength with bankers, both at home and abroad. In forming our final judgment of Jay Cooke as a financier, we should remember that, while he stood high among the smaller people in finance, he never gained leadership among leaders. In the Northern Pacific, as in the war, his work was grounded on faith rather than on economic reality, which not only made no appeal to his realistic compeers but must even have made them suspicious of the Philadelphian. Moreover, the outstanding bankers, both in America and Europe, were of the passive type which was suspicious of the banker who took so aggressive a position in the promotion of a large enterprise.

Failing to secure the aid of the bankers, Jay Cooke fell back on the market on which he had depended during the war. But with the small investor, also, he overestimated his influence. The war securities had appealed to patriotism in a national crisis, while the railroad bonds were judged on the strength of their investment value. In the earlier instance, moreover, increasing incomes from an inflated war business made people ready to purchase securities, while in the later case Jay Cooke had to work against the decreasing investment power of the small investor who was suffering from post-war deflation in many lines of business and decreased income.   Jay Cooke not only failed to realize where business was in reference to the cycle, but he also failed to see that we were in a long-time downward trend.   In fairness to him it must be noted that this observation is based on information which he did not have.

After he had failed to win the support that he had anticipated, Jay Cooke should have withdrawn from active promotion of the Northern Pacific, but by that time he and his firms had virtually become underwriters of the road.   Their contract with the Northern Pacific actually placed only a moderate amount of responsibility on Jay Cooke & Co., but Jay Cooke's handling of his firm's banking relations with the road led them into a position which had not clearly been defined from the beginning and from which it would have been dangerous, if not impossible, to withdraw.

Jay Cooke made a grave mistake in assuming responsibility for such a venture as the Northern Pacific.   The project was a rank promotion scheme; the road had an extensive land grant but it had no capital and no immediate prospect of traffic or income from the sale of land.   In judging Jay Cooke it must be remembered that, with the great resources of the United States, its heavy immigration, and the rapid technological advance then in progress, he saw good times ahead for business.   He made the common error of confusing the well-being of business with social and economic growth.

Though only the most able management could under the circumstances have carried the project to success, the Northern Pacific had neither responsible nor efficient heads.   Jay Cooke had not foreseen that, in assuming such an active position in the sale of the road's bonds, he might have to give consideration to its management.   He had no intention, at the beginning, of participating in the management of the concern, and in this he was rightly recognizing the limitations of his own experience and energies. Under those circumstances he should have followed the Rothschilds' rule not to undertake to sell securities for any project which might involve risk or trouble in management. What long experience had taught the Old-World bankers, Jay Cooke had not yet learned.

The situation was made especially difficult because Jay Cooke had allowed himself and his firm to become enmeshed in several conflicting responsibilities. As investor through the direct investments of Jay Cooke & Co. in the Northern Pacific and other railroads and through loans to them, as leader of a group of partners, as a banker and as a holder of extensive deposits, as sponsor and virtual underwriter of the enterprise, and finally as trustee for the bondholders, Jay Cooke found himself in a serious dilemma when trouble came. He has been severely criticized for sacrificing the depositors of his banking firm to the bondholders of the Northern Pacific; it is very important to remember that as a trustee he had not only a moral but also a legal responsibility for the interests of the bondholders. His mistake was not so much in choosing between conflicting responsibilities when trouble arose as in assuming them in the first instance.

By the time Jay Cooke had realized the full implications of his position, it became almost impossible for him to save himself. A long-continued and increasing stringency in the money and bond markets drove him to support the road by loans from Jay Cooke & Co. At this point the Cookes felt the full force of a fundamental weakness in their set-up: they did not have an adequate firm capital for the business they were doing. This arose, Jay Cooke explained in his Memoirs, from an injudicious mode of distributing annual profits. Instead of being retained by the firm in the form of cash securities, their profits had been distributed among the partners, who had made them unavailable for emergencies. So strongly did Jay Cooke feel later about this weakness of his firm that he said that, if he were to pass through the same experience again, he would capitalize all profits except moderate living expenses and thus acquire large and independent means for his business. It is a significant commentary on American business that this weakness has prevailed so extensively in American banking. It remains to be seen whether the Banking Act of 1935, which places limits on the disbursement of profits until a fair surplus has been established, will provide something in the way of improvement.

The lack of an adequate capital forced the Cookes to depend largely on their deposits for working capital. Since they followed the common practice of paying interest on demand deposits, the New York house, especially, had come to hold deposits which were virtually the reserves of inland banks. The employment of those deposits in advances to the Northern Pacific could lead only to trouble under the condition of business in 1873. Here was a striking instance of that use of bank reserves in investment banking which has caused so much trouble in American business. This evil has been strongly attacked in the Securities Act of 1933. It is to be hoped that this measure will help materially to correct the practice which proved so dangerous to Jay Cooke & Co. and many other bankers from the 1850's to 1929.

The way in which Jay Cooke became involved in the affairs of the Northern Pacific demonstrated forcibly the vulnerability of the banker as promoter. It showed that one house could not alone stand the risk of sponsoring so great an enterprise. Bankers could, of course, in the future desist from active participation in promotion, but that was not to be in keeping with the opportunities nor the spirit of the time. The bankers had seen what could be done, and they would not turn back if it were possible to go forward.

Jay Cooke had pointed the way along which they could go forward with some degree of safety. Through his experience he had not only demonstrated that the active investment banker would have to look to his own defences by strengthening the base on which he stood and by establishing some control over the project which he was financing; in his successful use of the underwriting syndicate in the government loan of 1871 he had also showed how bankers could, by co-operating in risk-bearing and aggressive marketing, go far toward minimizing the dangers in the promotion of large enterprises.

The full significance of the work of Jay Cooke and other contemporary bankers of his type can be seen only through developments after 1873. Then came a most rapid exploitation of American resources, an unprecedented increase in wealth, and a remarkable growth in business activity and organization. Whether or not this rich economic development was healthy, it is not the function of this study to consider. It is important to observe, however, that in this remarkable period the active bankers played a significant, even a dominant, rôle. The leaders among these bankers were the Morgans, Drexels, Mortons, Seligmans, and Kuhn, Loebs, all of whom had strong support abroad. They particularly developed the technique for protecting themselves, spreading their risks by the use of the underwriting syndicate and employing aggressive marketing methods. They also reached out for a measure of control of management and thus brought a degree of order into a chaotic competitive system. By such means, men like J. Pierpont Morgan and Jacob H. Schiff raised the active banker to his highest power and effectiveness in the United States. They built on the foundation which Jay Cooke had helped to lay.

REFERENCES AND NOTES

REFERENCES AND NOTES

In order to save space the notes have been made as brief as possible. All the letters or other manuscripts the location of which is not indicated are from the Jay Cooke Papers, Historical Society of Pennsylvania. Abbreviations have been used freely. Where mention is made of the Jay Cooke Papers, Historical Society of Pennsylvania, they are designated as CP, and the Jay Cooke Papers, Baker Library, Harvard University, are referred to as CH. Initials, instead of the full name, are given in referring to Jay Cooke, Pitt Cooke, Henry Cooke, Harris Fahnestock, William Moorhead, and George Thomas, all partners in Jay Cooke & Co. whose letters are frequently cited. Lb. is used instead of letter book.

CHAPTER I

1. Salem Vital Records, 1839; Salem Deed Book, no. 21. Subsequent appearances in the court records are: *Records and Files of the Quarterly Courts of Essex County, Massachusetts*, vol. i, 1636–56 (Salem, 1911), pp. 35, 115, 152, 180, 183, 244, 257, 349.

2. Henry's son, Samuel, moved to New Haven and later to Wallingford, Conn. His grandson, Asaph, moved to southwestern Massachusetts, and, after the Revolution, to Granville, New York, with his son, Asaph, the father of Eleutheros Cooke, who was born in 1787. I am indebted to Marian Watts DeWolf, a great-granddaughter of Jay Cooke, for the use of a manuscript Genealogy of the Cooke Family which she has compiled with great care from the original sources, most of which I have checked.

3. Jay Cooke's Memoirs, CH. Unless otherwise stated the information in this chapter on Jay Cooke's early life is from his Memoirs.

4. Jay Cooke's Memoirs describe the trip briefly.

5. Travel on the Ohio at this time is interestingly described in C. H. Ambler's *History of Transportation in the Ohio Valley* (Glendale, California, 1932), pp. 38–49.

6. The village was plotted and named Portland in 1817 but became Sandusky City in 1818 (Harriet T. Upton, *Western Reserve*, vol. i, Chicago and New York, 1910, p. 394).

7. John Sherman, *Recollections of Forty Years in the House, Senate and Cabinet* (Chicago, 1895), vol. i, pp. 12–13.

8. The *New York Sunday Advertiser*, Sept. 16, 1890; series of articles by "Gath" (G. A. Townsend) in the *Cincinnati Enquirer*, June, 1890.

9. *Records and Files of the Quarterly Courts of Essex County, Massachusetts*, vol. i, p. 152; *Probate Records of Essex County, Massachusetts*, vol. i, 1635–64 (Salem, 1916), inventory of estate of Henry Cooke, 1661; Salem Deed Book, no. 21.

10. According to Marian Watts DeWolf's Genealogy of the Cooke Family.

11. *Ibid.*; Jay Cooke's Memoirs.

12. The material for the above characterization of Eleutheros Cooke was a photograph and many of his own letters in CP, his speeches in Congress, and Jay Cooke's Memoirs.

13. *Ibid.*, and letters written by E. Cooke, in CH and CP.

14. According to B. H. Meyer, *History of Transportation in the United States* (Washington, 1917), pp. 489 and 495, the first railroad charter granted by Ohio was given to the Ohio and Steubenville in 1830, and in 1831–32 twelve acts were passed incorporating railroads, including the Mad River and Lake Erie. The Mad River was the only one of the thirteen projected roads ever built.

15. E. Cooke to N. M. Standart, Feb. 3, 1832, CH.

16. My information about Martha Cooke has come chiefly from her descendants, especially her granddaughter, Mary Cooke, of Sandusky, Ohio, and her grandson-in-law, Mr. Charles D. Barney of Philadelphia, both of whom knew her personally.

17. Jay Cooke's Memoirs and manuscript draft of a speech delivered by Jay Cooke in 1900 before the Firelands Historical Association. This manuscript is in the possession of Mr. Charles D. Barney.

18. Upton, *op. cit.*, p. 400.   19. Memoirs and speech cited above.

20. *Ibid.*   21. Upton, *op. cit.*, p. 406.

22. Letter, Jay to his brother Pitt, Nov. 23, 1833, quoted in E. P. Oberholtzer, *Jay Cooke, Financier of the Civil War* (Philadelphia, 1907), vol. i, pp. 27–28.

23. Miss Mary Cooke of Sandusky, Ohio, says that this was the explanation accepted by the family.

24. Jay Cooke's Memoirs. Actually it must have had a larger population, for the *Census* of 1840 credits the city of St. Louis with over 16,000.

25. Besides Jay Cooke's Memoirs, the only records of his experiences in St. Louis are his letters home found in Oberholtzer, *op. cit.*, pp. 34–39.

26. Jay Cooke's Memoirs. The bank loaned to a number of such Pennsylvania projects (see 26th Cong., 2nd Sess., 1840–41, *House Ex. Docs.*, no. 111, p. 155).

27. *Poulson's American and Daily Advertiser*, Apr. 10, 1838.

28. Told to the writer by Mr. Charles D. Barney.

29. *Poulson's American and Daily Advertiser*, Apr. 10, 1838.

30. *Ibid.*, June 21, 1838.   31. Oberholtzer, *op. cit.*, p. 50.

32. Jay Cooke's Memoirs.

CHAPTER II

1. "State Banks and Banking Companies," 24th Cong., 1st Sess. (1835–36), *House Ex. Docs.*, no. 42, p. 91, gives the number of banks in each State in 1811.

2. J. B. McMaster, *The Life and Times of Stephen Girard* (Philadelphia, 1918), vol. ii, pp. 240–251.

3. On this subject I have consulted the Girard Papers, Girard College. For a more detailed consideration of Girard's work in financing the War of 1812, see McMaster, *op. cit.*

4. Stephen Girard to Albert Gallatin, Mar. 2, 1813, Girard Papers.

5. David Parish and Stephen Girard to Albert Gallatin, Apr. 4, 5, 1813, Girard Papers; K. W. Porter, *John Jacob Astor: Business Man* (Cambridge, 1931), vol. i, pp. 331–332; McMaster, *op. cit.*, pp. 248–250.

6. Richard Ehrenberg, *Capital and Finance in the Age of the Renaissance* (New York, 1928).

7. A. B. Kerr, *Jacques Coeur* (New York, 1927).

8. For a more detailed story of the work of the Allens, see Henrietta M. Larson, "S. & M. Allen — Lottery, Exchange, and Stock Brokerage," *Journal of Economic and Business History*, vol. iii (May, 1931), pp. 424–445. The article is based principally on material from newspapers, such as the *Register*, the *Gazette*, and the *Argus*, of Albany, the *New York Commercial Advertiser*, the *New York Gazette and General Advertiser*, and *Poulson's American and Daily Advertiser*, of Philadelphia.

9. On Enoch W. Clark's early business career see Henrietta M. Larson, "E. W. Clark & Co., 1837–1857," *Journal of Econ. and Bus. Hist.*, vol. iv (May, 1932), pp. 429–436.

10. According to Samuel Hazard, *Register of Pennsylvania*, vol. xiv (1834), p. 199, there were in Philadelphia 3 lottery offices in 1809, 60 in 1827, 127 in 1831, and 200 in 1833.

11. E. C. Stedman, editor, *The New York Stock Exchange* (New York, 1905), vol. i, pp. 62–66.

12. R. C. H. Catterall, *The Second Bank of the United States* (Chicago, 1903), p. 507.

13. Since there is a tradition in the Clark family that this enterprise ended in debt, I have made a careful search of Rhode Island court records for insolvency assignments. None was found, which, however, proves little, as the Rhode Island laws on insolvency were then so lenient.

14. *New York Journal of Commerce*, Feb. 14, 1834.

15. *Ibid.;* Allan Nevins, editor, *Philip Hone's Diary* (New York, 1927), vol. i, p. 114.

16. Moses Allen *vs.* George H. Paddock and Laban Paddock, Chancery Court, Oct. 3, 1846, Hall of Records, New York City.

17. *United States Gazette*, Jan. 2, 1837; *New York Commercial Advertiser*,

Sept. 4, 1837; *Poulson's American and Daily Advertiser*, Sept. 5 and Oct. 25, 1837.

18. Judging by the indenture of assignment turned over to the trustees of the creditors four years later. A copy of the original indenture is filed with a petition of Moses Allen to the Supreme Court of the State of New York, Mar. 3, 1848, Hall of Records, New York City.

19. *United States Gazette*, Feb. 16, 1837.

20. Memorandum, July 18, 1853, signed by the Clark partners, CH.

21. Letter of Edward W. Clark to Crawford, Aug. 13, 1895, in the possession of George C. Clark, of Clark, Dodge & Co., New York.

22. "Condition of the State Banks," 26th Cong., 1st Sess. (1839–40), *House Ex. Docs.*, no. 172, p. 1005.

CHAPTER III

1. Oberholtzer, *op. cit.*, vol. i, pp. 53, 57.

2. In this description I am relying chiefly on Mr. Charles D. Barney.

3. Oberholtzer, *op. cit.*, p. 70, quoting a man who knew Jay Cooke in his early days with the Clark firm.

4. Letter of H. H. Wainright to E. W. Clark & Co., Feb. 17, 1914, in the possession of E. W. Clark & Co., of Philadelphia.

5. Mar. 9, 1840, and thereafter for months.

6. A manuscript, in the possession of E. W. Clark & Co., Philadelphia, records the agreement between the Clarks and a bank. A Clark advertisement in the *North American and Daily Advertiser*, July 19, 1841, announced that they would redeem at 3/4 of 1 per cent discount the notes of the Berks County Bank.

7. *Ibid.*, and thereafter.   8. Oberholtzer, *op. cit.*, pp. 57, 59.

9. *Ibid.*, pp. 57–58, 69–71.   10. Jay Cooke's Memoirs.

11. 26th Cong., 1st Sess. (1839–40), *House Ex. Docs.*, no. 172, p. 288.

12. L. H. Jenks, *The Migration of British Capital, to 1875* (New York, 1927), pp. 88–98; 26th Cong., 2nd Sess. (1840–41), *House Ex. Docs.*, no. 111, pp. 154–157.

13. See R. C. McGrane, *Foreign Bondholders and American State Debts* (New York, 1935).

14. Oberholtzer, *op. cit.*, pp. 57, 59. Unless otherwise stated the remainder of this chapter is based on *ibid.*, pp. 53–65.

15. *The Biographical Encyclopaedia of Pennsylvania of the Nineteenth Century* (Philadelphia, 1874).

16. Jay Cooke's Memoirs, and *Daily Chronicle*, May 5, 1840, and thereafter.

17. Jay Cooke's Memoirs.

18. An article in the *Detroit Free Press*, Oct. 5, 1902, based on an interview with Jay Cooke, states that Jay's salary was at first $30 a month.

CHAPTER IV

1. J. R. Cable, *The Bank of the State of Missouri* (New York, 1923), pp. 124–133.

2. G. W. Dowrie, *The Development of Banking in Illinois, 1817–1863* (Urbana, 1913), pp. 61, 109, 112, 123–124, 127.

3. 30th Cong., 1st Sess. (1847–48), *House Ex. Docs.*, no. 77, p. 593.

4. *Ibid.;* H. H. Preston, *History of Banking in Iowa* (Iowa City, 1922), chap. II.

5. Whereby banks could be established on filling certain requirements stated by law without having to secure a charter by act of the legislature.

6. *Private Laws of the State of Illinois*, 1851, p. 144; Dowrie, *op. cit.*, pp. 135–139; Horace White, "National and State Banks," *Sound Currency*, vol. ii (Dec., 1894), p. 8. A free banking act was passed in Iowa in 1858, but no banks were established under it (Preston, *op. cit.*, pp. 74–82); a State bank was established in 1858 (*ibid.*, p. 84).

7. Vol. viii, pp. 79–80 and 563. See also D. R. Dewey, *State Banking before the Civil War* (Washington, 1910), p. 180.

8. See above, p. 24. 9. Vol. iv (n.s.), pp. 19 ff.

10. Memorandum, July 18, 1853, and Jay Cooke's Memoirs, CH.

11. Cable, *op. cit.*, pp. 227 ff.

12. Letter of W. C. Little, St. Louis, to E. W. Clark & Co., Nov. 4, 1912, in the possession of E. W. Clark & Co., Philadelphia. The information it contains was secured from two men who had been with the St. Louis house in the 'fifties.

13. Memorandum, July 18, 1853, CH.

14. Margaret G. Myers, *The New York Money Market* (New York, 1931), *passim.*

15. Memorandum, July 18, 1853, CH. This firm is listed in Doggett's *New York Directory* for the first time in 1846–47, which was corrected to May 19, 1846.

16. Memorandum cited above. In 1846 the interest of the New Orleans partnership went to the St. Louis house.

17. Letter of W. C. Little to E. W. Clark & Co., Nov. 4, 1912, and of R. M. Hubbard (teller in the St. Louis house in the 'fifties) to E. W. Clark & Co., Nov. 16, 1912, in the possession of E. W. Clark & Co. H. H. Wainright stated in his letter to E. W. Clark & Co., Feb. 17, 1914, that the partners in the Burlington house were Enoch W. Clark, Luther C. Clark, Jay Cooke, and a resident partner.

18. Three certificates of incorporation were registered (filed in office of the auditor of the State of Illinois at Springfield) for Clark's Exchange Bank in 1852. The first provided for a bank with a capital of $100,000, all to be held by three Clark partners; the second substituted N. H. Ridgely of Springfield for Enoch Clark as a stockholder; the third provided for a bank

with a capital of $500,000, one-tenth subscribed by Ridgely and the rest by L. C. Clark and Edward Dodge. The banks authorized by the second and third certificates of incorporation were consolidated into one bank in 1853 (*Private Laws of the State of Illinois*, 1853, pp. 539–540).

19. Dowrie, *op. cit.*, p. 139. In the *Report of the Bank Commissioner of the State of Illinois*, 1858, p. 14, the capital stock paid in was stated as $5,250.

20. Dowrie, *op. cit.*, pp. 67, 109, 112, 120–123, 127; *Montague's Illinois and Missouri State Directory* (St. Louis, 1854), p. 57.

21. *North American and Daily Advertiser*, Jan. 4, 1843. Memorandum, July 18, 1853, CH.

22. Cooke Family Genealogy compiled by Marian Watts DeWolf.

23. The following papers have been searched for information on the Clarks for those years: *New York Journal of Commerce* and *New York Daily Advertiser*, 1845–57, and occasionally the *Tribune* and *Evening Post;* the *Philadelphia Public Ledger* to 1847, and the *North American and United States Gazette* to 1858; the *Boston Daily Atlas* to 1854; and the St. Louis *Daily Missourian, Missouri Reporter*, and *Missouri Republican* for short periods. The New York firm did not advertise in the above-listed New York papers from 1850 to 1857.

24. Letters of Oct. 26, Nov. 20, and Dec. 29, 1854.

25. Note that though the Philadelphia and New York Clarks had no ownership in the Boston house, the Boston firm was still important in their business.

26. These are from vols. viii and ix, published in 1845 and 1846.

27. A letter of W. C. Breckenridge, vice-president of the Missouri State Historical Society, to E. W. Clark & Co., Sept. 11, 1915, in the possession of E. W. Clark & Co., describes one such copy consisting of 76 pages.

28. Based on Corcoran & Riggs correspondence in the Riggs & Co. Papers, Library of Congress.

29. For instance, Corcoran & Riggs to Clark, Dodge & Co., Feb. 16 and July 3, 1846, and May 13, 1847, Riggs & Co. Papers, Library of Congress.

30. Riggs & Co. Papers, Library of Congress.

31. The best evidence on this whole question is the Clark and Corcoran & Riggs correspondence in *ibid*.

32. Enoch W. Clark & Others *vs.* James B. Martin & Others, Feb. 29, 1844, Chancery Court Records, Hall of Records, New York.

33. In directories, advertisements, etc. The first Clark house to call itself a "Banking House," in the advertisements examined by the writer, was that of St. Louis, advertising in the *Missouri Reporter* (St. Louis), Feb. 3, 1845.

34. See Dewey, *op. cit.*, pp. 43 ff., for a discussion of the scope of the business of the early banks.

35. Catterall, *op. cit.*, chap. VI.

36. Letters of H. H. Wainright to E. W. Clark & Co., Feb. 17, 1914, and

R. M. Hubbard to E. W. Clark & Co., Nov. 16, 1912; also, *The History of the First National Bank in the United States* (anonymous, Chicago, 1913), p. 17. Hubbard, who was teller in the St. Louis house in the 'fifties, stated that he thought those issues totaled two million or more. E. W. Clark & Co. have a number of the drafts.

37. J. J. Knox, *A History of Banking in the United States* (New York, 1900), pp. 726–727.

38. Dowrie, *op. cit.*, pp. 135–136.

39. Letter of William Ridgely to E. W. Clark & Co., Oct. 25, 1912, in the possession of E. W. Clark & Co. Also *Bankers' Magazine*, vol. vi (n.s., 1851–52), p. 1015.

40. Statement on the condition of Clark's Exchange Bank, Nov. 30, 1858, in *Reports made to the General Assembly of the State of Illinois*, 1859, pp. 136–140.

41. Ridgely to E. W. Clark & Co., Oct. 25, 1912.

42. *Missouri Reporter*, Jan. 1, 1854.

43. E. W. Clark to E. W. Clark, Dodge & Co., Jan. 3, 1854. This letter is in the possession of G. C. Clark of Clark, Dodge & Co., New York.

CHAPTER V

1. G. H. Evans, "Early History of Preferred Stock in the United States," *Amer. Econ. Review*, vol. xix (1929), pp. 43–58.

2. Letter books and account books, Bryant & Sturgis Papers, and J. P. Cushing Papers, Baker Library, Harvard University; Henrietta M. Larson, "A China Trader Turns Investor," *Harvard Bus. Review*, vol. xii (1934), pp. 345–358.

3. Jenks, *op. cit.*, pp. 69–71.

4. An excellent study of one such English banking house in American trade and investments at this time is R. W. Hidy, "The House of Baring and American Trade, 1830–1842," a manuscript thesis in Widener Library, Harvard University.

5. Photostats from Baring Papers, Canadian Archives, Ottawa; Jenks, *op. cit.*, p. 359, notes 12, 13.

6. *Ibid.*, pp. 88–98.

7. *Ibid.*, pp. 85–88, 99–108; McGrane, *op. cit.*, chap. XIII.

8. *Hunt's Merchants' Magazine*, vol. vii (1842), p. 288.

9. *Ibid.*, p. 363.

10. Regular advertisements to this effect appeared in the Philadelphia *North American* and the *New York Journal of Commerce*.

11. E. W. Clark & Co. to Corcoran & Riggs, Feb. 15, 1845, Riggs & Co. Papers, Library of Congress.

12. Authorized by the acts of Jan. 28, 1847, and Mar. 31, 1848 (9 *U. S. Statutes*, pp. 118 and 217).

13. Jay Cooke's Memoirs; Sec. of the Treas., *Annual Report*, 1846–49, pp. 134, 215–216, 224, 302, 325, and 336–337.

14. *Ibid.*, pp. 215 and 325; Jay Cooke's Memoirs.

15. This I am presuming from the fact that correspondence in Riggs & Co. Papers indicates that Corcoran & Riggs sold theirs thus.

16. The following descriptions of exchange operations in handling the loan is from Jay Cooke's Memoirs.

17. Jenks, *op. cit.*, pp. 169, 190; *Hunt's Merch. Mag.*, vol. xxii (1850), p. 644, and vol. xxiii (1850), p. 204. The American *Bankers' Mag.*, vol. v (1850–51), p. 83, says almost half of a three-million Ohio State loan of 1850 was taken on foreign account.

18. Jenks, *op. cit.*, pp. 126–192; American *Bankers' Mag.*, vol. vi (n.s., 1856–57), pp. 194–195, 227; Josef Kulischer, *Allgemeine Wirtschaftsgeschichte*, vol. ii (Munich and Berlin, 1929), p. 537.

19. As early as Jan., 1850, the *Hunt's Merch. Mag.*, vol. xxiii (1850), p. 205, commented on the increase in capital due to California's gold.

20. A. H. Cole and Edwin Frickey, "The Course of Stock Prices, 1825–1860," *Review of Economic Statistics*, 1928, pp. 117–139; W. B. Smith and A. H. Cole, *Fluctuations in American Business, 1790–1860* (Cambridge, 1935), pp. 171–184.

21. Advertised in the Philadelphia *North American and U. S. Gazette*, Feb. 13, 1850, and almost daily throughout the year 1851.

22. Correspondence of the Clark partners in CP.

23. *North American and U. S. Gazette*, Jan. 16, 1854, and Apr. 21 to Aug. 15, 1857.

24. *Report of the Pennsylvania Rail Road Company*, 1855, p. 3.

25. J. T. Scharf and T. Westcott, *History of Philadelphia* (Philadelphia, 1884), vol. iii, p. 2195; *Report of the Pittsburgh, Fort Wayne, and Chicago Rail Road Company*, 1857, pp. 5, 14.

26. Meyer, *History of Railroad Transportation in the U. S.*, p. 393.

27. Statement authorizing E. W. Clark & Co. to sell stock of the Chartiers Valley Railroad on the Philadelphia Board, signed by J. K. Moorhead, Mar. 1857, CP.

28. *Report of the Northern Central Railway Company*, 1854, p. 5.

29. *Report of the Special Committee of the Common Council in Relation to the Sunbury and Erie Rail Road*, 1854, p. 22.

30. Chartered by Missouri to be built westward from St. Louis and aided by bonds of the State of Missouri and the city and county of St. Louis (Meyer, *op. cit.*, p. 550).

31. Chase to J. C., June 20, 1856. The Grayville bank was closely associated with the Clarks. A letter of Hubbard (teller in the St. Louis house to E. W. Clark & Co., Nov. 16, 1912) said it was a branch of the Clark banks, but it was never listed as a branch in the contemporary material I have examined.

32. May 6, 1812, July 27, 1842, Feb. 11, 1847, and June 26, 1848.

33. Sec. of the Treas., *Annual Report*, 1848, p. 2.

34. In the *New York Journal of Commerce*, May 6, 1848, and thereafter; in the *Boston Daily Atlas*, Jan. 4, 1849, and thereafter; and in the *North American and U. S. Gazette*, Jan. 7, 1850, and thereafter.

35. Wainright, *loc. cit.;* will of Enoch W. Clark, book 36, p. 332, Office of Wills, City Hall, Philadelphia.

36. Letters of N. H. Ridgely to L. C. Clark and E. W. Clark, 1862–79, and other miscellaneous material, in the possession of E. W. Clark & Co., are concerned with the lands in and about Galena.

37. N. H. Ridgely to L. C. Clark, Feb. 14, 1863, E. W. Clark & Co.

38. There are many letters in CP written from Iowa by Pitt Cooke to Jay Cooke from 1855 to 1857.

39. P. C. to J. C., Aug. 13, 1856.

40. H. C. to J. C., Apr. 24, 1856; W. J. Barney to J. C., Dec. 26, 1856.

41. W. M. (Munich, Germany) to J. C., June 5, 1857; and P. C. to J. C., Nov. 23, 1857.

42. *Ibid.*, Apr. 25 and Aug. 18, 1856, and May 9 and 11, 1857.

43. W. J. Barney to J. C., Dec. 16, 1856, and another Dubuque land firm, June 13, 1856, offering to sell Cooke's lands at a good profit. P. C. reported from time to time that he could sell their lands at a considerable gain.

44. Miscellaneous Account Book. 45. P. C. to J. C., May 19, 1855.

46. Wainright, *loc. cit.*

47. E. W. Clark to E. W. Clark, Dodge & Co., Jan. 3, 1853, in the possession of G. C. Clark, of Clark, Dodge, & Co., New York.

48. Hubbard, *loc. cit.*

49. *North American and U. S. Gazette*, July 16, 1852, and Feb. 16, 1853.

50. *Hunt's Merch. Mag.*, vol. xxxi (1854), pp. 207–208.

51. E. Cooke to J. C., Nov. 9, 1854.

52. The partners of the other firms frequently complained of the way in which the Boston house got itself into difficulties and then depended on the others for aid.

53. Copy, J. C. to J. W. Clark, July 14, 1854.

54. E. Dodge to J. C., July 13, 1854.

55. Copy, J. C. to J. W. Clark, July 14, 1854.

56. Oberholtzer, *op. cit.*, pp. 83–84.

57. Will of Enoch W. Clark, *op. cit.; North American and U. S. Gazette*, Aug. 5, 1856. He is said to have left an estate worth $800,000 (*New York Times*, Oct. 5, 1857).

58. Memorandum, July 18, 1853, CH.

59. MS. Firm History (1928), in the possession of E. W. Clark & Co.

60. Correspondence between J. C., P. C., W. M., and the Clarks.

61. The earliest statement I have found to the effect that they paid interest on deposits was in the advertisement of E. W. Clark & Brothers, St.

Louis, in the Sunday *Republican* (St. Louis), Jan. 1, 1854. The other houses may well have paid interest on such deposits earlier.

62. Edward Clark to J. C., Sept. 29, 1857.

63. Chase to J. C., Oct. 7, 1857.

64. E. Cooke to J. C., Oct. 2, 1857.

65. Myers, *op. cit.*, vol. i, chap. VII. Boston, especially, complained of the failure of New York banks to keep reserves commensurate with their responsibilities (*Hunt's Merch. Mag.*, vol. xxxvii, 1857, pp. 593–595).

66. *Bankers' Mag.*, vol. xii (1857), p. 419.

67. *New York Times*, Oct. 5, 1857.   68. Wainright, *loc. cit.*

69. *Bankers' Mag.*, vol. xii (1857), p. 418.

70. Circular notice of E. W. Clark & Co., Oct. 13, 1857, in possession of E. W. Clark & Co.; *North American and U. S. Gazette*, Oct. 14, 1857.

71. Wainright, *loc. cit.* White, Cook & Co., of Burlington, of an Iowa chain, may be considered their local successors.

72. A card of the Ridgely National Bank in the possession of E. W. Clark & Co., of Philadelphia, gives 1859 as the date of the organization of N. H. Ridgely & Co., the successor of Clark's Exchange Bank. This bank was not important to the Clark system for some time before the panic. The *Report of the Bank Commissioner of the State of Illinois*, 1858, pp. 14–19, states that in Oct., 1856, the bank had $5,250 in stocks deposited to secure a circulation of $4,818 and specie on hand totaling $1,000.

73. Letters of P. C. and E. Cooke to J. C., Oct., 1857, and E. Dodge to J. C., Oct. 7, 1857.

74. P. C. to J. C., Aug. 18, 1856.

CHAPTER VI

1. P. C. to J. C., Oct. 6, 1857.   2. E. Cooke to J. C., Oct. 6, 1857.

3. Jay Cooke's Memoirs.

4. André Liesse, *Evolution of Credit and Banks in France* (Washington, 1909), pp. 96–108.

5. J. Riesser, *The German Great Banks* (Washington, 1911), pp. 27–69.

6. Jenks, *op. cit.*, p. 245.

7. *The Biographical Encyclopaedia of Pennsylvania*, pp. 356–357.

8. *Ibid.*, p. 572, and *Dictionary of American Biography*.

9. *Supreme Court in Equity, the Sunbury & Erie Railroad Co.* vs. *Lewis Cooper* (undated pamphlet published in Philadelphia in the 'fifties), p. 1; *Proceedings of the Citizens of Philadelphia relative to the Rail Road to Erie, and the Convention at Williamsport*, 1836, pp. 3–15.

10. W. B. Wilson, *History of the Pennsylvania Railroad Company* (Philadelphia, 1899), vol. i, p. 249.

11. *Report of the Joint Special Committee on the subject of a proposed Sub-*

scription by the Councils of the City of Philadelphia to the Capital Stock of the Sunbury and Erie Rail Road Company, 1853, p. 7.

12. Wilson, *op. cit.*, p. 252; *Report of the Special Committee of the Common Council in Relation to the Sunbury & Erie Rail Road*, 1854, p. 22.

13. In building a section between Sunbury and Lock Haven, the Moorheads received in payment for materials and work 80 per cent in bonds of the road and 20 per cent in stock (*Report of the Special Committee appointed by Select Councils to examine the Sunbury and Erie Railroad Company*, 1854, p. 21). A similar arrangement was made in the agreement of Feb. 16, 1855, between the Moorheads and the president of the road (CP).

14. There are many letters in CP for July, 1854, from banks which unequivocally refused them loans.

15. *Report of Special Committee of the Common Council*, *op. cit.*, pp. 22–28.

16. W. M. to J. B. Moorhead, Aug. 24, 1854; *Report of the Joint Special Committee*, *op. cit.*, 1853, p. 8.

17. *Report of the Special Committee of the Common Council*, *op. cit.*, pp. 10–11, 40; memorandum signed by W. M. and J. B. Moorhead, Sept. 4, 1854.

18. Wilson, *op. cit.*, p. 253.

19. Memorandum signed by W. M. and J. B. Moorhead, Sept. 27, 1854.

20. Copy of letter of Moorheads to M. S. Wickersham, Sept. 27, 1854.

21. *Report of Special Committee of the Common Council*, *op. cit.*, pp. 22, 28.

22. By 1858 (said the Philadelphia *Public Ledger*, Feb. 9, 1858), $2,000,-000 had been sold.

23. Wilson, *op. cit.*, pp. 253–254.

24. *Public Ledger* (Philadelphia), Feb. 9, 1858.

25. *The Sunbury and Erie Railroad and the State Legislature*, 1860, p. 7.

26. *Laws of Pennsylvania*, 1858, pp. 414–419.

27. *The Sunbury and Erie Railroad and the State Legislature*, 1860, p. 7; Wilson, *op. cit.*, p. 256.

28. *Ibid.*, pp. 257–258.   29. Misc. Account Book.

30. *Report of Board of Canal Commissioners, Penn.*, 1857, pp. 6–9.

31. "Message of Gov. Pollock to the Legislature," Penn. *Ex. Docs.*, 1858, p. 8; *Supreme Court in Equity, the Sunbury & Erie Railroad Co.* vs. *Lewis Cooper*, p. 11.

32. *Report of Board of Managers of the Sunbury and Erie Railroad Company*, 1859, p. 7; many letters in CP, 1858–59; records of dealings in securities in Misc. Account Book.

33. *Report of Delaware Division Canal Company of Pennsylvania*, 1859, p. 3; *Daily Express* (Easton), Nov. 24, 1858.

34. C. L. Jones, *The Economic History of the Anthracite-Tidewater Canals* (Philadelphia, 1908), pp. 67–68.

35. *Report of Del. Div. Canal Co. of Penn.*, 1860, p. 12.

36. *Ibid.; Report of Lehigh Valley Railroad Co.*, 1855–63 (New York, 1899), p. 27.

37. *Report of Board of Managers of the Sunbury and Erie Railroad Company*, 1859, p. 7; *U. S. Railroad and Mining Register*, Feb. 26, 1859; W. H. Falcord to J. C., July 21, 1858.

38. *U. S. Railroad and Mining Register*, Feb. 26, 1859; *Supreme Court in Equity, The Sunbury & Erie Railroad Co. vs. Lewis Cooper*, p. 54.

39. Jay Cooke's Memoirs. See *Report of Del. Div. Co.*, 1859, p. 13.

40. *U. S. Railroad and Mining Register*, Feb. 26, 1859.

41. *Report of Del. Div. Canal Co.*, 1859, pp. 12–13; *ibid.*, 1860, pp. 21–22.

42. *Laws of Penn.*, 1858, p. 619 (referring to Act of May 12, 1857).

43. *Annual Railroad Reports of Penn.*, 1863, p. 73.

44. *Laws of Penn.*, 1858, p. 619, and 1859, pp. 20–22; H. F. to J. C., July 1, 1859.

45. H. F. to J. C., Dec. 7, 1858, about the candidacy of one of the purchasers for State treasurer in 1858: "It is very reasonable to conclude that, with the business connections now growing up between A. J. J. and yourselves, it would be mutually advantageous to assist his election. . . . You may be in a position to influence some of your city members, and if so should go at it at once." Fahnestock suggested that the Moorheads might help Jones in western Pennsylvania.

46. *Laws of Penn.*, 1859, pp. 20–22, gives details on stocks and bonds issued.

47. A. Armstrong to E. W. Clark & Co., Jan. 14, 1859; James Mason to E. W. Clark & Co., Dec. 31, 1858; telegram of Armstrong and Mason to E. W. Clark & Co., Jan. 25, 1859; A. B. Wingard to E. W. Clark & Co., Jan. 3, 1859.

48. There are many letters in CP to Jay Cooke which deal with the purchase of materials.

49. *Annual Railroad Reports of Penn.*, 1863, p. 73.

50. A. J. Jones to J. C. and E. W. Clark & Co., Mar. 11, 1859, and O. N. Lull to J. C., Jan. 7, 1862.

51. *Laws of Penn.*, 1861, p. 539.

52. O. N. Lull to J. C., Nov. 3, 1860.

53. *North American and U. S. Gazette*, July 17, 1860; *Laws of Penn.*, 1859, pp. 739–740; *Report of Board of Managers of the Ironton Railroad Co.*, 1861, pp. 1–2.

54. *Ibid.*; Misc. Account Book records dealings with Jeter.

55. J. K. Moorhead to J. C., July 16, 1860.   56. *Ibid.*, Apr. 30, 1859.

57. Misc. Account Book.   58. *Ibid.*

59. Letters to J. C. on his relations with the Southern Pacific: J. Fowlkes, Mar. 13 and Dec. 2, 1858, and May 7, 1859; W. C. Wilder, Jan. 19 and Nov. 18, 1859; Shreve & Tucker, Jan. 18 and Feb. 28, 1860.

60. Gibson to J. C., Jan. 12 and 17, July 9, 1859; Gilliat to J. C., Mar. 8, 1860.

61. On these loans there are scores of letters to J. C. from the cashiers Messersmith of Chambersburg and Weir of Harrisburg. The following from the Harrisburg bank, Nov. 7, 1860, is typical: "John W. Weir will hand you $30,000 of our notes, and receive from you note and collaterals as proposed. $1850 of the issue has not come in yet and in lieu I send you our own notes not marked; which *please circulate*. If you scatter them *where the others went* may be they, also, wont come back till 60 days after . . . [illegible]. There is a pretty fair prospect that the originals of these . . . will not soon trouble you."

62. *Report of Directors of the Vermont Central Railroad Company*, 1850, p. 15.

63. The reports of the road's earliest years spoke in optimistic terms of the future of the road as a carrier helping to connect important producing areas and trading centers.

64. *Report of Directors and Treasurer of the Vermont Central Railroad Company*, 1851, p. 14; *Report of Directors of the Vermont Central Railroad Company*, 1850, p.15.

65. *Report of Directors and Treasurer of the Vermont Central Railroad Company*, 1851, list of officers and directors; *Railroad Charters and Mortgages of the Vermont Central Line*, charter of Vermont & Canada.

66. *Ibid.*, pp. 31–35.

67. A manuscript record of Engineer Wm. E. Morris, June 6, 1856, CP. Considerable detail can be found in *Charters, Decrees, and Leases of the Central Vermont Railroad* (St. Albans, 1875), pp. 61–74.

68. A record of the various legal proceedings is given in *ibid.*

69. *Report of the Directors of the Vermont Central Railroad Co.*, 1855, p. 10.

70. *Report of the Committee on Consolidation of the Vermont & Canada Rail Road Co., and Vermont Central Rail Road Co.* (Sept., 1856), pp. 9–17; Camp to J. C., Sept. 5 and 18, 1856, CP.

71. *Ibid.*, Nov. 26, 1856.   72. Gibson to J. C., Jan. 2, 1858.

73. *Ibid.*, June 16, 1858; Hard to J. C., May 14, 1859.

74. Misc. Account Book.

75. The Jay Cooke Papers in Philadelphia contain scores of letters from bankers and others in Boston who were purchasing bonds for Jay Cooke.

CHAPTER VII

1. W. M. to J. C., Sept. 7, 1856.   2. H. C. to J. C., Dec. 18, 1860.

3. Jay Cooke's Memoirs.

4. *In the Matter of . . . Jay Cooke & Co., Bankrupts* (In the District Court of the United States for the Eastern District of Pennsylvania, Philadelphia, 1875), "Statement of Bankrupts as to Causes of Insolvency of Firm," pp. 83, 93–94.

5. H. D. Moore to W. M. and J. C., Mar. 1, 1871.

6. Vol. x, p. 952.   7. *Philadelphia Inquirer*, Jan. 9, 1866.

8. Opening announced in the *U. S. Railroad and Mining Register* and the *Philadelphia Inquirer* for some time after establishment of Jay Cooke & Co.

9. *Bankers' Mag.*, vol. x (1860–61), p. 988.

10. *Hunt's Merch. Mag.*, vol. xliv (1861), pp. 95–202, 327–331.

11. Sec. of the Treas., *Report on the State of the Finances*, 1861, pp. 2, 3, 18.

12. *Ibid.*, pp. 19–49.

13. J. C. to H. C., Apr. 8, 1861, in Oberholtzer, *op. cit.*, p. 134.

14. Jay Cooke's Memoirs.   15. E. Cooke to H. C., Jan. 2, 1843.

16. H. C. (Aspinwall, New Granada) to J. C., Dec. 30, 1853, letter in the possession of Mr. Charles D. Barney.

17. *In the Matter of . . . Jay Cooke & Co., Bankrupts*, *op. cit.*, p. 123.

18. H. C. to J. C., July 1, 1856; P. C. to J. C., Nov. 8, 1856, and Dec. 1, 1857.

19. H. C. to J. C., Apr. 24, 1856.   20. *Ibid.*, July 6, 1859.

21. P. C. to J. C., Mar. 12, 1860.   22. H. C. to J. C., Mar. 8, 1861.

23. The letter is undated, but its contents place it about Mar., 1861.

24. Oberholtzer, *op. cit.*, pp. 132–133.

25. Sec. of the Treas., *op. cit.*, 1861, pp. 50–51.

26. *Ibid.*, p. 52.   27. H. C. to J. C., May 17, 1861.

28. Sec. of the Treas., *op. cit.*, 1861, pp. 54–59.

29. J. C. to H. C., May 24, 1861.   30. May 23, 1861.

31. June 1, 1861.

32. Provided for by an act of May 15, 1861, of the State legislature.

33. H. D. Moore to J. C., Sept. 15–27, 1873, in Oberholtzer, *op. cit.*, pp. 116–120.

34. Moore to W. M. and J. C., Mar. 1, 1871.

35. Jay Cooke's Memoirs; numerous letters in CP on selling this loan.

36. Jay Cooke's Memoirs give $200,000, but a copy of the list of subscribers in Oberholtzer, *op. cit.*, pp. 112–116, credits Mercer's bank with $300,000.

37. Moore to J. C. and W. M., Mar. 1, 1871.

38. Letters and memoranda in CP on the paying of the troops, etc.

39. Moore to J. C., Sept. 15–17, 1873, in Oberholtzer, *op. cit.*, pp. 116–120.

40. Jay Cooke's Memoirs.   41. H. C. to J. C., July 9, 1861.

42. *Ibid.*   43. J. C. to Chase, July 12, 1861.

44. J. C. to H. C., July 12, 1861.   45. J. C. to Chase, July 12, 1861.

46. I have searched for information on this matter since a group of Philadelphians living today (two of whom I have talked with at length about this matter) assert that Jay Cooke was not concerned with this event. Their arguments are stated in a manuscript in the Library of Congress, entitled, "History of the Banks in 1861," written by Theodore Cuyler Patterson of Philadelphia. Some of the arguments put forth in this paper I

have been unable to prove or disprove. The statement that the heading, or contract, preceding the signatures of the subscribers was written by Joseph Patterson cannot stand against the obvious fact that the handwriting is Jay Cooke's. The original subscription list is reproduced in Oberholtzer, *op. cit.*

47. The group referred to in note 46, above, also questions Jay Cooke's part in these loans. A letter of Chase to J. C. (Aug. 12, 1861) shows that Chase sought Cooke's advice.

48. There is no evidence of such participation in the records of the clearing-house associations concerned or in the reports of their meetings in the *Bankers' Mag.*

49. D. C. Barrett, *The Greenbacks and Resumption of Specie Payments, 1862–1879* (Cambridge, 1931), pp. 42–44.

50. The report of the loan committee of the New York banks is given in 37th Cong., 3rd Sess. (1862–63), *House Ex. Docs.*, vol. v, no. 23, pp. 125–142.

51. Sec. of the Treas., *op. cit.*, Dec., 1861, pp. 8–10.

52. W. C. Mitchell, *A History of the Greenbacks* (Chicago, 1903), p. 24.

53. 38th Cong., 1st Sess. (1863–64), *House Ex. Docs.*, no. 66, p. 2.

54. Jay Cooke's Memoirs.

55. 38th Cong., 1st Sess., *House Ex. Docs.*, no. 66, p. 2.

56. Mitchell, *op. cit.*, pp. 26–27.

57. *Ibid.*, pp. 25–26; Barrett, *op. cit.*, pp. 29–36, 49–50.

58. Sec. of the Treas., *op. cit.*, Dec., 1861, pp. 9–21.

59. *Bankers' Mag.*, vol. xvi (1861–62), pp. 625–631; Sec. of the Treas., *op. cit.*, 1862, p. 7.

60. *Op. cit.*, p. 42.

61. E. Cooke to J. C., Dec. 22, 1861, Oberholtzer, *op. cit.*, p. 185.

62. *In the Matter of . . . Jay Cooke & Co., Bankrupts, op. cit.*, p. 116; J. C. to H. C., Mar. 3, 1862.

63. For some time after Henry Cooke joined Jay Cooke & Co. he was paying debts incurred before he joined the firm.

64. Information obtained from his son, William Fahnestock.

65. Chase to J. C., Mar. 7, 1862.

66. MS. Treasury Records, quoted by Oberholtzer, *op. cit.*, p. 194; J. C. to H. C., Mar. 4, 1862; Chase to J. C., Sept. 27, 1862.

67. J. C. to H. C., Mar. 4, 1862.   68. *Ibid.*

69. Vol. xx, pp. 1149–1150.   70. Barrett, *op. cit.*, pp. 45–48.

71. Mitchell, *op. cit.*, p. 48.

72. On the question of the necessity of the greenbacks, see Barrett, *op. cit.*, chap. II. Also, Mitchell, *op. cit.*, pp. 68–81, and Sec. of the Treas., *op. cit.*, 1862, pp. 8–9.

73. *Ibid.*, p. 11.   74. Mitchell, *op. cit.*, p. 73.   75. *Ibid.*, pp. 83–88.

76. 12 *U. S. Statutes at Large*, p. 345.

77. Chase to J. C., Oct. 23, 1862 (letter quoted in full in Oberholtzer, *op. cit.*, pp. 218–220); also, Sec. of the Treas., *op. cit.*, 1862, p. 52.

78. *Ibid.*, 1861, p. 9.

79. August Belmont to Chase, Oct. 31, 1861, Chase Papers, Hist. Soc. of Penn.

80. Sec. of the Treas., *op. cit.*, 1862, p. 25.

81. 38th Cong., 1st Sess., *House Ex. Docs.*, no. 66, pp. 2–3.

CHAPTER VIII

1. 38th Cong., 1st Sess. (1863–64), *House Ex. Docs.*, no. 66, pp. 2–3; auditors certificates in the General Accounting Office of the United States Treasury.

2. E. Vidal, *The History and Methods of the Paris Bourse* (Washington, 1910), p. 173.

3. Clippings from special supplement of Imlay & Bicknells' *Bank Note Reporter*, Dec. 5, 1862 (in a scrapbook now in the United States Treasury, sent by Cooke to Chase); *North American and U. S. Gazette*, Feb. 22, 1860.

4. Circular entitled, "An Hour at Jay Cooke and Co.'s," CP.

5. The CP contains hundreds of letters and many telegrams from H. C. to J. C.

6. J. C. to Chase, July 16, 1863; a scrapbook on the five-twenty loan in the United States Treasury contains numerous handbills and circulars of these agents.

7. *Bankers' Mag.*, vol. xvi (1861–62), p. 971; H. E. Fisk, "Fisk & Hatch, Bankers and Dealers in Government Securities, 1862–1885," *Journal of Econ. and Bus. Hist.*, vol. ii (1930), p. 707.

8. Henry Clews, *Twenty-Eight Years in Wall Street* (New York, 1888), p. 77; W. W. Fowler, *Inside Life in Wall Street* (Hartford, 1873), p. 581.

9. Robert Clarkson to J. C., Dec. 15, 1862.

10. There are many letters from the agents to J. C. in CP.

11. 38th Cong., 1st Sess. *House Ex. Docs.*, no. 66, p. 3; J. C. to Chase, Jan. 16, 1864, Division of Loans and Currency, U. S. Treasury.

12. J. D. Reid, *The Telegraph in America* (New York, 1886); 41st Cong. 2nd Sess. (1869–70), *Reports of Committees*, no. 114, pp. 82–83; *Report of the President of the Western Union Company*, 1869, pp. 1–8.

13. Bankers' & Brokers' Telegraph Co. to J. C., Sept. 14, 1863.

14. Oberholtzer, *op. cit.*, pp. 286–287.

15. W. M. to J. C., Oct. 25, 1863.

16. William Evans to J. C., Feb. 10, 1864.

17. A. E. Taylor, "Walker's Financial Mission to London on Behalf of the North, 1863–64," *Journal of Econ. and Bus. Hist.*, vol. iii (1930–31), pp. 296–320.

18. Jay Cooke's Memoirs; copy, J. C. to Artemus Ward, Dec. 28, 1872;

J. H. Appel, *The Business Biography of John Wanamaker* (New York, 1930), pp. 41–44.

19. S. N. D. North, *History and Present Condition of the Newspaper and Periodical Press of the United States* (Washington, 1884), pp. 101–102.

20. The *United States Census*, 1860 and 1870, records increase in circulation from 13,663,409 to 20,842,475.

21. 41st Cong., 2nd Sess., *House Reports*, no. 114, pp. 102–103.

22. On early agencies I have used the manuscript of R. M. Hower on "The History of an Advertising Business," pp. 10–12, and G. P. Rowell, *Forty Years an Advertising Agent*, 1865–1905 (New York, 1926), p. 138.

23. Undated clipping in a scrapbook, CP.

24. In the opinion of Rowell, as expressed in *op. cit.*, p. 138.

25. Stephen Girard to Albert Gallatin, Sec. of the Treas., Mar. 2, 1813, Girard Papers, Girard College.

26. S. M. Pettingill to J. C., Dec. 2, 1863; Fisk & Hatch to J. C., Dec. 3, 1863. Pettingill's first work was to send an article to 200 newspapers in New York State (S. M. Pettingill & Co. to J. C. & Co., Dec. 7, 1863).

27. A scrapbook in the U. S. Treasury, prepared by Jay Cooke & Co., contains clippings from 86 newspapers or periodicals published in Pennsylvania in Nov. and Dec., 1862, in many of which advertisements appeared regularly and frequently. Among these publications were several German newspapers and trade papers. The examination by the writer of scores of newspapers from various sections of the country has proved the comprehensiveness of five-twenty publicity.

28. Posters, handbills, etc., in the U. S. Treasury and in CP.

29. In the *Public Ledger*, Mar. 27, 1863, and numerous other papers.

30. *City Item* (Philadelphia), Mar. 21, 1863.   31. *Ibid.*, May 16, 1863.

32. *North American and U. S. Gazette*, May 11, 1863.

33. *City Item*, May 7, 1863.   34. *Philadelphia Press*, May 2, 1863.

35. *Philadelphia Bulletin*, Apr. 8, 1863.

36. *The Daily Conservative* (Leavenworth, Kentucky), Jan. 5, 1864.

37. Oberholtzer, *op. cit.*, p. 244.

38. *Philadelphia Inquirer*, Apr. 9, 1863.

39. *Evening Bulletin* (Philadelphia), June 1, 1863; Oberholtzer, *op. cit.*, pp. 248–249.

40. *Philadelphia Inquirer*, Apr. 9, 1863.

41. *Philadelphia Press*, Apr. 8, 1863.   42. July 18, 1863.

43. J. K. Medbery, *Men and Mysteries of Wall Street* (Boston, 1870), p. 245.

44. See Mitchell, *op. cit.*, pp. 187–210.   45. H. C. to J. C., Dec. 1, 1863.

46. Jay Cooke's Memoirs.   47. *Ibid.*

48. Sec. of the Treas., *Report on the State of the Finances*, 1862, p. 12.

49. Quoted in Oberholtzer, *op. cit.*, p. 377.   50. *Ibid.*, pp. 378–379.

51. There is an excellent chapter on this in Mitchell, *op. cit.*, pp. 100–118.

52. Jay Cooke recognized the importance of taxation, and in a letter to Chase (Mar. 13, 1863, Chase Papers, Library of Congress) urged that he take steps toward a better enforcement of revenue laws. Cooke held that by explaining through the press the law on internal taxation, by prosecuting a few notorious tax evaders, and by having one active and intelligent agent in each State, he could bring in enormous sums now lost.

53. Jay Cooke's Memoirs explain fully Jay Cooke's part in establishing the national banking system.

54. *Ibid.*, and copy, J. C. to Chase, Feb. 2, 1863, and undated letter to Chase.

55. Chase to J. C., Feb. 13, 1863.

56. See chap. XII of Hugh McCulloch, *Men and Measures of Half a Century* (New York, 1889).

57. "Report of the Comptroller of the Currency," 39th Cong., 1st Sess. (1865–66), *House Ex. Docs.*, no. 4, p. 86; Jay Cooke's Memoirs.

58. Directors' Minutes, the First National Bank of Philadelphia, p. 1.

59. C. H. Chaffee, vice-president and cashier, First National Bank of Philadelphia, to the author, May 19, 1933, quoting from the bank's records; articles of association, Stockholders' Minutes, First National Bank of Philadelphia; and *ibid.*, Mar. 13, 1865. Jay Cooke was not an original stockholder.

60. *Ibid.*, Jan. 12, 1864.   61. *Ibid.*, Jan. 9, 1866.

62. Directors' Minutes, *op. cit.*, Oct. 9, Nov. 19, Dec. 22, 1863.

63. *Ibid.*, Oct. 28, 1864.   64. Sec. of the Treas. *op. cit.*, 1863, pp. 60–61.

65. Oberholtzer, *op. cit.*, pp. 342–343.

66. Sec. of the Treas., *op. cit.*, 1863, pp. 60–61; *Bankers' Mag.*, vol. xviii (1863–64), p. 384.

67. "Proceedings of the Meeting in Relation to the Establishment of a Large National Bank in this City," in the *Bankers' Mag.*, vol. xviii (1863–64), pp. 444 ff.

68. *Ibid.*, p. 827.

69. The powerful Bank of Commerce joined the national ranks shortly after the passage of the bill (*Bankers' Mag.*, vol. xix, 1864–65, p. 840), and was soon followed by almost every State bank in New York (*ibid.*, vol. xx, 1865–66, pp. 221–222). "Report of the Comptroller of the Currency," *op. cit.*, 1865, p. 4.

70. T. F. Shewell to J. C., Oct. 17 and Nov. 9, 1863, and H. C. Storms to J. C., Oct. 15 and 29, Nov. 14 and Dec. 16, 1863.

71. William Poulterer to J. C., Oct. 18, 1863.

72. Sec. of the Treas., *op. cit.*, 1863, p. 60, and 1864, p. 47; and "Report of the Comptroller of the Currency," *op. cit.*, 1865, p. 135.

73. *The Economist*, vol. xxi (Mar. 1, 1863), p. 318.

74. Mitchell, *op. cit.*, p. 202.

75. Sales were reported daily in the *Philadelphia Inquirer* and other newspapers.

76. J. C. to H. C., May 4 and 29, 1863; *Philadelphia Inquirer*, May 15, 1863.

77. J. C. to H. C., May 28, 1863.

78. Sec. of the Treas., *op. cit.*, 1863, p. 35.

79. 12 *U. S. Statutes at Large*, p. 345; Mitchell, *op. cit.*, pp. 115–116.

80. Joshua Hanna to Chase, June 27, 1863, Chase Papers, Library of Congress.

81. June 2, 1863.   82. H. C. to J. C., Oct. 3 and 29, 1863.

83. J. C. to H. C., Nov. 30, 1863.

84. Hanna to Chase, June 27, 1863, Chase Papers, Library of Congress.

85. 38th Cong., 1st Sess. (1863–64), *Cong. Globe*, pp. 1046–1048, reply of Senator Sherman to a criticism of Jay Cooke.

86. J. C. to H. C., Nov. 21, 1863.   87. *Ibid.*

88. H. C. to J. C., Nov. 27, 1863.

89. Copy of letter of J. C. to Chase, Jan. 16, 1864.

90. On that day subscriptions totaled $11,000,000 more than the limit set, and a special act of Congress (Mar. 3, 1864) had to be passed to legalize the issue of bonds to cover the oversubscription.

91. Jay Cooke's vouchers and certificates of the first auditor, General Accounting Office, U. S. Treasury.

92. Letter of Secretary Chase to Schuyler Colfax, 38th Cong., 1st Sess. (1863–64), *House Ex. Docs.*, no. 66, p. 4.

93. *Ibid.*, pp. 3–4.

94. *Ibid.*; George Harrington, acting sec. of the Treas., to J. C., Oct. 17, 1864, CH.

95. Chase to Colfax, *op. cit.*, p. 3. This total checks with Jay Cooke's vouchers and auditor's certificates in the General Accounting Office, U. S. Treasury.

96. Chase to Colfax, *op. cit.*, p. 3.   97. Oberholtzer, *op. cit.*, p. 325.

98. Chase to J. C., Oct. 23, 1862; H. C. to J. C., Aug. 12, 1863.

99. Circular letter of J. C., July 1, 1863; telegram of J. C. to H. C., Sept. 4, 1863.

100. H. C. to J. C., June 29, 1863.   101. Oberholtzer, *op. cit.*, p. 278.

102. Draft of a long letter, probably used as a model but not sent, to Chase, Oct. 16, 1863.

103. Hanna to Chase, June 27, 1863, Chase Papers, Library of Congress.

104. Chase to Colfax, *op. cit.*, p. 4. It would be interesting to compare the cost of selling the Civil War loans with the United States loans in the recent war, but that is impossible. Beyond the one-tenth or one-fifth of one per cent on sales appropriated for direct expenses by the Treasury for the earliest War loans (Sec. of the Treas., *Report on the Finances*, 1917, pp. 86,

96), there were the costs incurred by the Post Office and other government agencies which it is impossible to estimate.

105. Robert Clarkson to J. C., Jan. 16, 1863.

106. H. C. to J. C., Jan. 13, 1863.

107. *In the Matter of . . . Jay Cooke & Co., Bankrupts, op. cit.*, p. 21.

108. There are many congratulatory letters from agents in CP.

109. Report showing the extent of the business of banks and bankers in the United States, 38th Cong., 1st Sess. (1863–64), *Senate Ex. Docs.*, no. 50.

CHAPTER IX

1. Letters to J. C., of John G. Camp, Apr. 8, 1861; P. W. Sheafer, Apr. 11, 1864; I. Rosenfeldt, May 2, 1864.

2. A number of letters in CP written in Apr. 1864, and one by Geo. Harding to J. C., Sept. 28, 1864.

3. List of subscribers, dated July 1, 1864, CH.

4. David Crawford to J. C., Mar. 4, 1864.

5. J. C. to Chase, undated, 1865.

6. *Bankers' Mag.*, vol. xix (1864–65), p. 251.

7. The investments in oils are treated in Oberholtzer, *op. cit.*, vol. i, pp. 439–441. Also, J. C. to H. F. and H. C., Jan. 23, 1865; H. C. to J. C., Jan. 23, 1865; H. F. to J. C., Jan. 24, 1865.

8. R. B. Warden, *An Account of the Private Life and Public Services of Salmon Portland Chase* (Cincinnati, 1874), p. 519.

9. Oberholtzer, *op. cit.*, pp. 437–438.

10. Medbery, *Men and Mysteries of Wall Street*, p. 241.

11. 13 *U. S. Statutes at Large*, p. 404.

12. H. C. to J. C., and J. C. to H. C., Mar. 8, 1864, in Oberholtzer, *op. cit.*, p. 400.

13. J. W. Schuckers, *The Life and Public Services of Salmon Portland Chase* (New York, 1874), pp. 357–358; *Bankers' Mag.*, vol. xviii (1863–64), p. 925; *Hunts' Merch. Mag.*, vol. l (1864), pp. 362–363.

14. Jay Cooke's Memoirs.   15. Schuckers, *op. cit.*, p. 558.

16. H. F. to J. C., Apr. 28, 1864, quoted in Oberholtzer, *op. cit.*, p. 406.

17. In his Memoirs Jay Cooke gives the figures in the 200's, which is obviously wrong as they never rose to 200 during Chase's secretaryship (*Hunts' Merch. Mag.*, vol. lii, 1865, p. 64). His figures are approximately correct when interpreted as above 100 instead of 200.

18. Jay Cooke's Memoirs.

19. The government had been withdrawing greenbacks for some time by selling ten-forty bonds and gold certificates (*Hunts' Merch. Mag.*, vol. l, p. 363).

20. Stedman, *The New York Stock Exchange*, pp. 185–186.

21. Schuckers, *op. cit.*, p. 359.   22. J. C. to Chase, Apr. 21, 1864.

23. J. C. to Chase, Apr. 22, 1864.

24. Chase to J. C., May 30, 1864; J. C. to Chase, May 31, 1864.

25. *Bankers' Mag.*, vol. xviii (1863–64), p. 1005.

26. Mitchell, *op. cit.*, p. 228 (refers to *New York Times*, May 20, 1864).

27. 13 *U. S. Statutes at Large*, p. 132.   28. Mitchell, *op. cit.*, p. 427.

29. *Bankers' Mag.*, vol. xix (1864–65), p. 77; Warden, *op. cit.*, p. 607.

30. 13 *U. S. Statutes at Large*, p. 344.

31. Mitchell, *op. cit.*, pp. 220–224.   32. Oberholtzer, *op. cit.*, p. 415.

33. 38th Cong., 1st Sess. (1863–64), *House Journal*, Jan. 5, 1864, p. 103.

34. 38th Cong., 1st Sess. (1863–64), *Cong. Globe*, p. 1046.

35. 38th Cong., 1st Sess. (1863–64), *House Ex. Docs.*, no. 66; *Cong. Globe, op. cit.*, p. 1046.

36. Schuckers, *op. cit.*, p. 416.

37. Sec. of the Treas., *Report on the Finances*, 1864, p. 7; A. S. Bolles, *The Financial History of the United States* (New York, 1886), p. 105.

38. Sec. of the Treas., *op. cit.*, 1864, pp. 44–45; Bolles, *op. cit.*, p. 104.

39. Chase to J. C., Apr. 8, 1864.   40. J. C. to Chase, Aug. 3, 1864.

41. Sec. of the Treas., *op. cit.*, 1864, p. 31.

42. *Ibid.*, p. 19, and 1865, p. 19.

43. H. C., especially, and J. C. had aided a movement in 1863–64 to nominate Chase for the presidency (Oberholtzer, *op. cit.*, pp. 363–365).

44. J. C. to Chase, Aug. 3, 1864.

45. Ketchum to Hugh McCulloch, May 16, 1864, McCulloch Papers, Library of Congress.

46. Ketchum to Fessenden, Aug. 24, 1864, Fessenden Papers, Library of Congress. Ketchum had for some time been friendly toward Fessenden (*ibid.*, Dec. 18, 1864).

47. J. C. to Chase, Sept. 20, 1864.

48. Memorandum, July 21, 1864, printed in Oberholtzer, *op. cit.*, pp. 429–430.

49. They are summarized in his *Report on the Finances*, 1865, pp. 20–42.

50. Oberholtzer, *op. cit.*, p. 450; H. C. to J. C., Nov. 14 and 25, 1864.

51. *Ibid.*, Nov. 25 and 26, 1864.   52. *Ibid.*, Nov. 26, 1864.

53. Oberholtzer, *op. cit.*, pp. 458–459.

54. J. C. to Fessenden, Dec. 2, 1864.   55. Oberholtzer, *op. cit.*, p. 460.

56. Lewis Corey, *The House of Morgan* (New York, 1930), pp. 59–60, 66–68; *Bankers' Mag.*, vol. xx (1865–66), pp. 250, 742.

57. Copy, J. C. to Fessenden, Nov. 19 and Dec. 2, 1864, and Jan. 28, 1865; Fessenden to J. C., Jan. 28, 1865.

58. H. C. to J. C., Jan. 23, 1865.   59. Fessenden to J. C., Jan. 28, 1865.

60. J. C. to H. C., Feb. 3, 1865.

61. Circular letters to banks and bankers, Jan. 28, 1865.

62. J. C. to H. C., Feb. 8, 1865.

63. The names of 24, with the territory assigned to each, were given on

Jay Cooke & Co. stationery used for a letter dated June 13, 1865. Circular letter of J. C. to traveling agents, Apr. 25, 1865, and letters of agents to J. C.

64. Edward Roward to J. C., May 3 and 29, 1865; Richard Randolph to J. C., Apr. 13, May 18, and July 3, 1865; *New York Herald*, Mar. 20, 1865.

65. *Ibid.; San Francisco Bulletin*, May 18, 1865; *Placer Herald*, Apr. 29, 1865.

66. According to signed receipts dated July 14 and 30 and Aug. 14, 1865.

67. J. Edgar Zug's report to J. C. in the spring of 1865.

68. Julian Brewer to J. C., Mar. 21, 1865.

69. J. C. to H. C., Mar. 30, 1865.

70. J. W. Schuckers to J. C., May 23, 1865, and J. R. Young to J. C., June 5 and 6, 1865. Eleven agencies in greater New York were listed in *New York Tribune*, July 17, 1865.

71. Wilkeson writing in *ibid*.

72. W. M. Clark to J. C., Mar. 30, 1865; circular to agents dated June 10, 1865.

73. *New York Tribune*, Mar. 7, 1865.

74. Report of Zug to J. C., spring of 1865.

75. Circular letter of J. C. to agents, Apr. 25, 1865.

76. *New York Tribune*, Mar. 7, 1865.

77. *Constitutional Union*, Feb. 15, 1865.   78. Feb. 7, 1865.

79. Jay Cooke frequently went to New York for this purpose, as he notes in a letter to H. C. of April 23, 1865.

80. Circular letter of J. C. to traveling agents, Apr. 25, 1865.

81. Circulars of Peaslee & Co. to editors, especially Feb. 6 and June 28, 1865; Rowell, *Forty Years an Advertising Agent*, p. 138.

82. Such a statement is in the CP.

83. There are literally hundreds of clippings on this campaign in CP. Circular of Peaslee & Co., sent to newspapers, dated Feb. 6, 1865.

84. Many of these are in CP.

85. Copies of these pamphlets are in CP.

86. The most vehement was the *New York Herald*.

87. An example is given in Oberholtzer, *op. cit.*, pp. 652-653.

88. Francis Lieber to J. C., June 20, 1865.

89. Jenks, *op. cit.*, pp. 264-265, referring especially to Carl Dietzel (*Das System der Staatsanleihen*, Heidelberg, 1855) and Lorenz Stein (*Lehrbuch der Finanzwissenschaft*, Leipzig, fifth edition, 1886).

90. J. C. to Nettleton, Apr. 23, 1865.

91. *Com. and Fin. Chron.*, vol. i (July, 1865), p. 2.

92. *Richmond Examiner*, Feb. 20, 1865.

93. Sec. of the Treas., *op. cit.*, 1865, pp. 54-55.

94. F. H. Evans to J. C., Mar. 18, 1865.

95. CP has much material on this, especially on the Pittsburgh case.

96. D. Crawford, Jr., to J. C., Mar. 22, 1865, and J. C. to H. C., Mar. 27

and Apr. 15, 1865; John A. Stewart to McCulloch, Mar. 22 and 23, 1865, McCulloch Papers, Library of Congress; Oberholtzer, *op. cit.*, pp. 564–566.

97. J. C. to H. C., Mar. 27, 1865.

98. Sec. of Treas., *op. cit.*, 1865, p. 36. 99. *Ibid.*

100. Circular letter of Jay Cooke to agents, July 27, 1865.

101. Sec. of Treas., *op. cit.*, 1865, pp. 17, 36. 102. *Ibid.*

103. Undated manuscript in CP, giving quotations from agents' letters.

104. Clipping from *Republican*, Feb. 4, 1865, CP.

CHAPTER X

1. *In the Matter of . . . Jay Cooke & Co., Bankrupts*, "Statement of the Bankrupts as to Causes of Insolvency," pp. 21–23. Though the statement of the Washington house does not so specify, I am assuming that this total included the O. P. J. allotment, which made the actual disbursement to partners one-tenth less.

2. *Ibid.*, pp. 81, 84, 94, 95. The approximate holdings of Jay Cooke and Moorhead, the principal partners, was about $3\frac{1}{2}$ million on Jan. 1, 1868. The years 1866–68 were very profitable so that the value was much less in 1866.

3. *In the Matter of . . . Jay Cooke & Co., Bankrupts*, "Schedules of the Bankrupts," pp. 60–61.

4. Jan. 9, 1866. The description which follows is taken from the *Philadelphia Inquirer* and an unidentified clipping in CP.

5. *Philadelphia Inquirer*, Jan. 9, 1866.

6. A. Robinson and J. G. Ogden to J. C., Dec. 22, 1865.

7. J. C. to H. C. and H. F., Jan. 2, 1866.

8. J. C. & Co., N. Y., to J. C. & Co., W., Mar. 1, 1866.

9. J. C. to H. F., Dec. 19, 1865, quoted in Oberholtzer, *op. cit.*, vol. ii, p. 17.

10. Corey, *op. cit.*, pp. 42–43. The George Peabody Papers are in the Essex Institute, Salem.

11. The Baring Papers at Ottawa contain the Barings' correspondence with American agents. Also, Corey, *op. cit.*, pp. 42, 48; *Dict. of Amer. Biog.*

12. Articles on the Seligmans in *ibid.* 13. Corey, *op. cit.*, pp. 42, 49, 57.

14. P. I. Instree to J. C., Mar. 22, 1866, and George Sauer (American Consul to Brussels) to J. C., Mar. 29, 1866.

15. J. C. to H. F., Dec. 8, 1866.

16. F. H. Evans to J. C. & Co., June 9, 1866; H. C. to J. C., Aug. 30, 1866.

17. A letter of Evans to J. C., Apr. 11, 1866, acknowledged Jay Cooke's proposal that they form a London house. There were others who wanted a hand in the London house: among them Gilead A. Smith, a London iron export merchant, and Chief Justice Chase, who played with the idea of becoming a "sleeping" partner in London (Chase to J. C., Dec. 28, 1868).

18. William Evans to J. C., Mar. 1, 1865, and Jan. 10, 13, and 27, 1866; F. H. Evans to J. C. & Co., Jan. 6, Feb. 26 and 28, Apr. 11 and 14, 1866.

19. Walter Bagehot, *Lombard Street* (New York, 1874), p. 27.

20. *In the Matter of . . . Jay Cooke & Co., Bankrupts*, "Statement of Bankrupts as to Causes of Insolvency," p. 4.

21. Oberholtzer, *op. cit.*, vol. ii, pp. 17–18 (quoting J. C. to H. F., Dec. 19, 1865), and p. 20.

22. *In the Matter of . . . Jay Cooke & Co., Bankrupts*, "Statement of Bankrupts as to Causes of Insolvency," p. 22.

23. P. C. to J. C., Mar. 2, 1866.

24. *In the Matter of . . . Jay Cooke & Co., Bankrupts*, "Statement of Bankrupts as to Causes of Insolvency," pp. 127, 132–133.

25. There is on this subject some correspondence between J. C. and his brother in the CP (for instance, P. C. to J. C., Dec. 11, 15, 26, 1862).

26. *In the Matter of . . . Jay Cooke & Co., Bankrupts*, "Statement of Bankrupts as to Causes of Insolvency," pp. 132–133.

27. There are scores of personal letters in CP written by P. C.

28. The statement of his own personal finances, *In the Matter of . . . Jay Cooke & Co., Bankrupts*, "Statement of Bankrupts as to Causes of Insolvency," pp. 122–126, and scores of letters of H. C., J. C., H. F., and P. C., in CP, bear witness to these assertions.

29. *In the Matter of . . . Jay Cooke & Co., Bankrupts*, "Statement of Bankrupts as to Causes of Insolvency," pp. 4, 22, 137; J. C. to H. C. and H. F., Jan. 2, 1866; *Philadelphia Inquirer*, Jan. 9, 1866. In the absence of Jay Cooke, Thomas assumed the responsibility of directing the house, reporting fully to Cooke.

30. There are hundreds of such letters and statements in CP.

31. The tycoon was a name for the *shogun* of Japan, which made its appearance about the time when Perry first visited that country in 1854.

32. Henry Cooke was especially prone to get tied up with projects which Jay Cooke said wanted to trade on the name of Jay Cooke & Co. J. C.'s chief objection to such investments was, however, that they jeopardized the firms' capital. On Jan. 23, 1865, J. C. wrote H. C. he hated to have people ask him about the poor projects his brother was in. On May 5, 1864, J. C. wrote a strong letter to H. C. urging him to economize. Such letters continued to be written until the partnership was dissolved. Pitt was reprimanded by J. C. in a letter of May 11, 1867.

33. J. C. to H. C., May 12, 1866; Huntington to J. C., Oct. 24 and 29, 1866; J. C. to Huntington, Oct. 24, 1866. In his reply to Cooke, Huntington admitted that he had gone reluctantly, "for I'd be *ashamed* to be seen riding so on Sunday and moreover to be doing anything that would look 'fast' or 'cutting a swell.'"

34. P. C. to J. C., Dec. 14, 1859.   35. W. Geddis to J. C., Oct. 26, 1856.

36. B. S. Russell to J. C., Mar. 30, 1858.

37. Stationery of A. C. C., letter dated Apr. 16, 1869; S. B. Howell to J. C., May 28, 1867; C. MacMichael to J. C., Oct. 15, 1866.

38. He gave Dartmouth and the Academy of Natural Sciences each $1,000 in 1866 (J. C. to Chase, July 2, 1866, Chase Papers, Library of Congress; W. M. Rauschenberger to J. C., letter dated 1866).

39. An interesting manuscript history of the Chelten Hill section, in CP.

40. Oberholtzer, *op. cit.*, vol. ii, chap. XIX gives a full account of his charities.

41. A little leather account book, CP, kept by the Rev. R. J. Parvin for July 6 to Sept. 14, 1868, shows that 47 preachers spent 10 days at Gibraltar, the Cookes' summer home in Lake Erie. Thirty-nine of these had their traveling expenses paid by Jay Cooke at a total cost of $2,210.60.

42. J. R. Mann to J. C., Mar. 13, 1866.

43. He gave a thousand dollars to Wanamaker's Sunday school building (John Wanamaker to J. C., Dec. 31, 1866).

44. John McCullough to J. C., Sept. 25, 1868.

45. Oberholtzer, *op. cit.*, vol. ii, p. 501.

46. Jay Cooke's Memoirs. He was "low church" and stood for the "simple & unequivocal teachings of the Bible," according to a letter of a rector, John Hocherly, to J. C., Mar. 13, 1868.

47. His Memoirs give an intimate picture of his faith. His letters to his partners often spoke of God's goodness and the duties of a Christian.

48. According to Mr. Charles D. Barney. Mr. Barney was Jay Cooke's son-in-law.

49. One instance of this is seen in the following letter of J. C. to H. C., Apr. 16, 1866: "Enclosed is a letter from Mr. Weir & it is a great outrage if this subterfuge is used in order to let passenger railway run cars on the Sabbath. It is against public opinion & public morals. Kimble the leading man in the Union Passenger RWay is State Treasurer & one of our depositors but I shall not hesitate if thought best to urge the Postmaster Gen'l to rescind at least that portion of the contract which allows them to run cars on the sabbath."

50. So strong was this faith in God that he believed He would protect his children from a contagious disease even though they were exposed to it (J. C. to H. C., Feb. 13, 1866).

51. *Ibid.*, Feb. 4, 1868.   52. Jay Cooke's Memoirs.

53. Mrs. Anna McMeens to J. C., Nov. 7, 1867, and Mar. 11, 1868; J. C. to H. C., Oct. 31, 1867, and July 20, 1868, and to L. B. Caldwell, Aug. 29, 1868.

54. The Gibraltar Records, in the possession of Mr. Charles D. Barney, reveal much about life on Gibraltar Island. They have recently been edited by J. E. Pollard and published (Columbus, 1935) as *The Journal of Jay Cooke, or The Gibraltar Records, 1865–1905.*

55. To H. C., June 9, 1866.

56. From an interesting chapter on fishing in Jay Cooke's Memoirs.

57. The house has long since given place to another, but I have been told much about it and life within it by members of the Cooke family and others who knew Ogontz, especially Mrs. Fancher Eaton Heard, Graduate School of Business Administration, Harvard University.

58. Ogontz Records, in the possession of Mr. Charles D. Barney of Philadelphia.

59. Feb. 6, 1867.

60. Undated letter which was, according to internal evidence, written at Christmas, 1866.

CHAPTER XI

1. Vol. xxiii (Dec. 23, 1865), p. 1550.

2. P. C. to J. C., Nov. 5 and 27, 1868; J. C., Jr., to H. C., Feb. 25, 1869; and H. C. to J. C., Mar. 2 and 10, 1869.

3. H. F. to J. C., Feb. 19, 1869.

4. For instance, H. C. wrote J. C., Nov. 13, 1865, that McCulloch wanted J. C. to come to Washington to advise him "*upon the line* of *policy which* he *will recommend* to *Congress in his report*," and on Apr. 8, 1867, that "the Sec'y wants to have a full exchange of views with you about future movements." McCulloch wrote to J. C. (Aug. 24, 1866) asking Cooke to get the press to protect the Treasury.

5. The *Philadelphia Inquirer*, Jay Cooke's spokesman, was one of McCulloch's strongest supporters.

6. Chandler resigned his position in a letter to Hugh McCulloch, May 31, 1867, McCulloch Papers, Library of Congress. There are many letters of H. C. to J. C. in the CP about relations with Chandler.

7. H. F. to J. C., Feb. 11, 1867.

8. *Ibid.*, Aug. 17 and 21 and Sept. 4, 6, 11, 17, 1867; H. C. to J. C., Oct. 17, 1867.

9. P. C. to J. C., Nov. 24 and Dec. 3, 1868; J. C. to H. C., Feb. 27 and Mar. 2, 1869.

10. *Ibid.*, Mar. 2, 1869.

11. *Ibid.*, Jan. 9 and 11 and Feb. 4 and 16, 1869; H. C. to J. C., Feb. 2, 8 and 13, 1869; J. C., Jr., to H. C., Mar. 11, 1869.

12. H. C. to J. C., Mar. 11, 16 and 19, 1869. The *Inquirer*, Mar. 12, 1869, spoke enthusiastically about the appointment.

13. There are numerous letters and telegrams in CP from "Star," dealing with impeachment, funding bills, and other matters.

14. P. C. to J. C., Feb. 18, 1869.   15. See below, pp. 212–213.

16. See Sec. of the Treas., *Report on the Finances*, 1867, p. xiii, and 39th Cong., 2nd Sess. (1866–67), *House Reports*, no. 14.

17. An article in *Harper's Weekly*, Aug. 4, 1866, gave the common arguments used about how Cooke had won great wealth from war finance.

18. H. C. to J. C., Nov. 30, 1869. 19. *Ibid.*, Feb. 15 and Mar. 26, 1866.

20. In a letter to J. C. of Sept. 2, 1867, H. C. wrote interestingly on Grant's position on Johnson's reconstruction policy. J. C. answered on Sept. 9, 1867: "Tell Genl Grant from me that we all look to him to save to the country the legitimate results & fruits of the War." This seems to have marked the rise of a strong feeling of the Cookes for Grant. J. C. offered to undertake to support Grant through the press (J. C. to H. C., Sept. 3, 1867).

21. H. C. to J. C., Oct. 12, 1867, CP, and to John Sherman, Oct. 24, 1867, John Sherman Papers, Library of Congress.

22. Chandler to J. C., Sept. 1, 1867.

23. H. C. to J. C., Jan. 7, 1869.

24. Jay Cooke's Memoirs; article on resumption in *The Advance*, Sept. 1869.

25. Letter in defence of national banks in *Sandusky Register*, Oct. 17, 1867. This defence of the system was widely copied by other papers and it was distributed as a pamphlet by the Cookes.

26. J. C. to H. C., Mar. 14, 1866.

27. *Ibid.*, Feb. 5, 1869. H. C. favored leaving national bank notes to supply and demand, removing all restrictions (H. C. to J. C., Nov. 20, 1869), but I have no reason to think Jay Cooke went that far.

28. The *Philadelphia Inquirer*, presumably speaking for Jay Cooke, consistently interpreted attacks on McCulloch as emanating from New York speculators. An officer of the City Bank, of New York, wrote to McCulloch on Oct. 10, 1867 (McCulloch Papers, Library of Congress), to the same effect.

29. Sec. of the Treas., *op. cit.*, 1865, p. 36; Barrett, *The Greenbacks and Resumption of Specie Payments*, pp. 129–130; and the *New York Tribune* in the fall of 1865. Cooke's position was much criticized by newspapers opposed to resumption.

30. E. G. Spaulding to J. C., Mar. 15, 1866; *New York Herald*, Nov. 15, 1866.

31. J. C. to J. K. Edgerton, Mar. 20, 1867, speaking of his plans for resumption in the fall of 1867.

32. Barrett, *op. cit.*, pp. 131–137. 33. J. C. to H. C., Sept. 20, 1867.

34. H. F. to J. C., Nov. 4, 1867.

35. Sec. of Treas., *op. cit.*, 1868, pp. iii–vii; H. C. to J. C., Nov. 20, 27, 29, and 30, 1869.

36. Nov. 20, 1869. 37. J. C. to H. C., Nov. 23, 1869. 38. *Ibid.*

39. This was proposed in an article in *The Advance* in Sept., 1869, the ideas of which were Jay Cooke's (H. C. to J. C., Sept. 11, 1869). The article was copied in other important newspapers.

40. As he called it in a letter to J. K. Edgerton, Mar. 20, 1867.

41. In the funding bill reported from the finance committee of the Senate.

42. Mar. 19, 1868.

43. Mar. 2, 1868, John Sherman Papers, Library of Congress.

44. July 6, 1868.

45. Bolles, *The Financial History of the United States, 1861–1885*, p. 319.

46. Jay Cooke's Memoirs.

47. At least so the Cookes thought, according to H. C. to J. C., Jan. 2, 1868.

48. Sec. of the Treas., *op. cit.*, 1865, p. 17. Page 20 gives the balance in the Treasury at the time as $67,158,515.44.

49. The *National Intelligencer* of Nov. 12, 1869, said that R. J. Walker sold $250,000,000 of five-twenties in Europe during the war. I have found no substantiation of this statement. A recent article on Walker (Taylor, *op. cit.*, pp. 296–320) makes no such claim. On Germany some information is found in the reports (Dec. 2, 1862; Sept. 16 and Dec. 21, 1863; Jan. 21 and Apr. 25, 1864; and Feb. 20, 1865) of W. W. Murphy, consul general at Frankfort.

50. R. H. Lutz, *Die Beziehungen zwischen Deutschland und den Vereinigten Staaten wahrend des Sezessionskrieges* (Heidelberg, 1911), p. 87.

51. Vol. ii (Apr. 14, 1866), p. 450.

52. Bagehot of the *Economist* and Gladstone were strong in their praise of our desire and our capacity to pay our debts.

53. *Economist*, vol. xxiv, pp. 553–554 (May 12, 1866), and pp. 581–583 (May 19, 1866); *Com. and Fin. Chron.*, vol. ii (June 2, 1866), p. 673; Jenks *op. cit.*, chap. VIII.

54. H. C. to J. C., Jan. 24, 1866.

55. *Ibid.*, and Feb. 10 and Apr. 9, 1866. Sherman explained his stand in his *Recollections of Forty Years*, p. 320.

56. H. C. to J. C., Feb. 9, 15 and Mar. 26, 1866.

57. *Ibid.*, Feb. 9, 1866.   58. *Ibid.*

59. J. C. to H. C., Jan. 19, 24 and 30, 1866; H. C. to J. C., Jan. 29, 1866.

60. 14 *U. S. Statutes at Large*, pp. 31–32; Bolles, *op. cit.*, pp. 308–311.

61. A copy of the memorandum is in CP.   62. CP.

63. H. C. to J. C., Mar. 10, Apr. 7, 24 and May 12, 14, 19, 1866.

64. *Com. and Fin. Chron.*, vol. ii (May 5, 1866), p. 553.

65. West (J. C.'s secretary) for J. C. to H. C., May 3, 1866.

66. H. C. to J. C., May 19 and June 20, 1866. Also, *ibid.*, Apr. 24, May 9, 12, 14, 1866.

67. H. C. to J. C., May 9, 1866.   68. *Ibid.*

69. West, for J. C., to H. C., May 3, 1866.

70. *Ibid.*, H. C. to J. C., May 3, 1866.

71. H. F. to J. C., May 3, 1866. In a letter to J. C., Jan. 26, 1866, Hennessey had pledged his allegiance to the Morrill bill and gratefully thanked Jay Cooke for Cooke's venture in his behalf.

72. I have examined the important papers for the week after May 3.

73. For instance, the issue of May 12, 1866, p. 577.

74. Shattuck to J. C., May 4, 1866.   75. J. C. to H. C., June 9, 1866.
76. Sherman's *Recollections*, p. 328.   77. June 21, 1866.
78. H. C. to J. C., Nov. 30 and Dec. 10, 1866.
79. Agreement signed by the members of the New York group and J. C., Dec. 6, 1866. Also, J. C. to H. C., Dec. 12, 1866.
80. H. F. to J. C., Dec. 11, 1866.
81. On Dec. 18, 1866, J. C. wrote H. C. that the "German" document had been returned to New York "with my recommendation to treat them courteously." According to H. F. to J. C., Feb. 2, 7, 1867, Biedermann, however, continued to work for the loan in Washington, familiarizing members of Congress with the idea of a foreign loan (H. C. to J. C., Feb. 27, 1867).
82. H. F. (in Paris) to J. C., Nov. 8, 1868; undated note, P. C. to J. C.; and C. H. Clark to J. C., Oct. 19, 1868. Chase offered to become a "sleeping" partner in London (Chase to J. C., Dec. 28, 1868). According to H. C. to J. C., June 6, 1868, McCulloch was strongly in favor of the sale of a 5 per cent 30-year loan.
83. H. F. to J. C., Nov. 8, 1868.

CHAPTER XII

1. A copy of a letter from J. C. to McCulloch in CP (May 7, 1866) states that at the time the operations of the Cooke firms in governments were ten times their operations in any other securities.
2. *Report of the Special Commissioner of Revenue*, 1869, p. xxxi.
3. Robert McElroy, *Levi Parsons Morton* (New York, 1930), pp. 33–40, 44–48; circulars of L. P. Morton & Co. in Baker Library.
4. Corey, *The House of Morgan*, pp. 49, 57.
5. *Dict. of Amer. Biog.* Belmont was the American representative of the Rothschilds.
6. *New York Tribune*, July 2, 1899; *New York Commercial Advertiser*, Apr. 23, 1894; Jesse Seligman, *In Memoriam* (New York, 1894). Max J. Kohler, who wrote the articles on Jesse and Joseph Seligman for the *Dict. of Amer. Biog.*, generously gave me information on the Seligmans and early German-Jewish bankers in the United States.
7. Cyrus Adler, *Jacob H. Schiff: His Life and Letters* (New York, 1929), pp. 7–9.
8. Compiled from the Secretary's *Report on the Finances*, 1866, p. 2; 1867, pp. xliv, xlviii; 1868, pp. xlvi, l; 1869, pp. xxxi, xxxv. The amounts of the various debts are given in the reports quoted.
9. 39th Cong., 1st Sess. (1865–66), *House Ex. Docs.*, no. 134, pp. 2–7; H. F. to J. C., Aug. 29, 1866.
10. This seems to have been $\frac{1}{8}$ of 1 per cent on single transactions, making $\frac{1}{4}$ on conversions.
11. Sec. of the Treas., *op. cit.*, 1868, p. xliii.

12. P. C. to J. C., Oct. 9, 1867; and H. F. to J. C., Oct. 10, 1867.

13. Sec. of Treas., *op. cit.*, 1868, p. xliii; H. C. to J. C., Jan. 12, 1867.

14. Medbery, *Men and Mysteries of Wall Street*, p. 256.

15. Nov. 6, 1868.   16. P. C. to J. C., Nov. 7 and 10, 1868.

17. J. C. to H. C., Oct. 5, 1869.   18. *Ibid.*, Sept. 24, 1869.

19. 39th Cong., 1st Sess. (1865–66), *House Ex. Docs.*, no. 134, p. 3.

20. *Philadelphia Inquirer*, Nov. 18, 1868.

21. J. C. to H. C., Mar. 11, 1869.

22. McCulloch gives an excellent explanation (Sec. of Treas., *op. cit.*, 1868, pp. xli–xliv) of his employing few agents and keeping the operations secret.

23. For instance 39th Cong., 2nd Sess. (1866–67), *House Reports*, no. 14.

24. *Com. and Fin. Chron.*, vol. iv (Feb. 16, 1867), p. 198.

25. 40th Cong., 2nd Sess. (1867–68), *Cong. Globe*, p. 1972. H. C. to J. C., Feb. 21, 22, 25, and Mar. 5, 1868; J. C. to H. C., Feb. 24, 1868.

26. Feb. 17, 1869. The *Inquirer* answered the *Ledger's* attacks. The *Ledger* had consistently opposed the Treasury's policy of secrecy. As early as June 22, 1866, it had urged leaving the price of gold to natural laws of trade.

27. J. C. to Drexel, Feb. 17, 1869.

28. Drexel to J. C., Feb. 17, 1869; Wm. McKean to J. C., Feb. 18, 1867.

29. Feb. 17, 1869.   30. H. C. to J. C., Mar. 1, 1869.

31. H. F. to J. C., Aug. 2, 1869.

32. The Cooke correspondence contains frequent references to other firms' attempts to get government business (for instance, West for J. C. to H. F., Apr. 14, 1866; H. F. to J. C., Nov. 12, 1866, and Jan. 22, 1867; H. C. to J. C., Mar. 22, 1867).

33. Sec. of the Treas., *op. cit.*, 1868, p. xliv.

34. *Ibid.*, 1867, pp. xliii–xliv; 1868, p. xlvi; 1869, p. xxxi.

35. *Ibid.*, 1868, pp. xxii–xxiii.   36. H. C. to J. C., June 25, 1868.

37. H. F. to J. C., Nov. 8, 1868.   38. Vol. vii (1868), pp. 326, 357.

39. P. C. to J. C., Mar. 26, 1869; H. F. to J. C., Aug. 2, 1869.

40. P. C. to J. C., Mar. 26, 1869.

41. J. C. to J. C. & Co., Washington, Mar. 11, 1867, and E. W. Clark & Co. to J. C. & Co., Apr. 20, 1867; advertisements in *Ledger*, Apr. 3 and June 1, 1867; *U. S. Railroad and Mining Register*, July 27, 1867; and *Inquirer*, Aug. 9, 1867; and scores of bids for the loans in CH.

42. P. C. to J. C., Oct. 27, 1866.   43. H. F. to J. C., Apr. 2, 1868.

44. According to a letter of H. F. to J. C., Jan. 4, 1867, the New York house paid 6 per cent on partners' deposits.

45. According to J. C. (West to H. F., Apr. 14, 1866), three things were expected from the government business: profits, prestige, and deposits. J. C. to H. C., Mar. 18, 1867: I have feared that "stoppage of our arrange-

ment at Treasy — will cut off all but a very small deposit — too small to be worth much — This is unfair & wrong — for we have always done well for them & what balances we have had have been of no loss to the Treasy."

46. The Cookes tried to derive such an advantage from a controlling interest in the National Bank of Commerce, of Georgetown, near Washington. Of a total capital of $100,000 the Cookes took $55,000 (H. C. to J. C., Aug. 30, 1866). The bank proved unsuccessful and was finally wound up at a considerable loss (H. C. to J. C., Jan. 27, 1869; Huntington to J. C., Feb. 9, 1869; H. F. to J. C., Feb. 10, 1869).

47. *Report of Comp. of Currency*, 1865, p. 124; 1866, p. 129; 1867, p. 371; 1868, p. 372; 1869, p. 366.

48. *Ibid.* On May 7, 1866 (H. C. to J. C., May 7, 1866), this account was about 3/4 million, while the Treasury reported $74,117.34 on Oct. 1 (*Report of Comp. of Currency*, 1866, p. 129).

49. Weekly statements of the bank to J. C. in CP. It was easy to decrease the deposits when a report was imminent. That they actually did so on occasion is proved by H. C. to J. C., May 7, 1866, and Mar. 16, 1867. Also, *Com. and Fin. Chron.*, vol. viii (June, 1869), p. 741.

50. In the many and bitter attacks on the national banking system in Congress, Jay Cooke stood as a champion of the system which he had helped establish. His article, which appeared in the *Sandusky Register*, Oct. 19, 1867, and was copied widely, was an admirable defence of the system.

51. *New York Herald*, May 11, 1866; *Ledger*, May 14, 1866; J. C. to H. C., May 6, 1866; H. C. to J. C., May 14, 1866; Wilkeson to J. C., Jan. 18, 1868.

52. *Ledger*, Jan. 31, 1868.

53. Feb. 20, 1868; H. C. to J. C., Feb. 3, 1868.

54. H. F. to J. C., July 1, 1868.

55. H. C. to J. C., Mar. 16, 1867: "We owed him [Huntington of First National] last week over 1,300th[ousand] and *now* only 600th, and we intend to cut it down early next week to 300th. You know *we* haven't a big line of outside depositors nor can we get money on call as you do in Phil[a] and New York, and the Bank is one of our main reliances." This bank, wrote H. F. to J. C., Jan. 7, 1868, "can be and must be managed chiefly as a convenience to our several houses."

56. J. C. to H. C., Nov. 2, 1866; copy of letter of H. F. to Huntington, Feb. 17, 1869.

57. Statements of the bank sent to Jay Cooke.

58. J. C. to H. C., Aug. 28, Sept. 7 and Oct. 11, 1866; and P. C. to J. C., Nov. 21, 1868.

59. 43rd Cong., 1st Sess. (1873–74), *House Reports*, no. 300.

60. For instance on Apr. 27, 1866 (J. W. Sexton to J. C.), they held $422,000 for J. C. & Co. of N. Y., $264,000 for Vermilye & Co., $121,000 for Clark, Dodge & Co., and $296,000 for Fisk & Hatch.

61. I have been unable to find any of the firm's account books for those years. Mr. Charles D. Barney, who was in the Philadelphia house in the late 'sixties, has given me much information on various aspects of the business.

62. J. C. to H. D., Oct. 29, 1866, and May 20, 1867; copy, H. F. to Flynt, Jan. 24, 1868; H. C. to J. C., Jan. 13, 1869.

63. H. F. to J. C., Mar. 23, 1867.

64. Illustrations of the practice of the Philadelphia house: On Sept. 21, 1866 (Thomas to J. C.), they had $750,000 in government bonds, a balance of $650,000 with other banks in Philadelphia, $645,000 with the First National and J. C. & Co. in Washington, $700,000 with their firm in New York, and $200,000 with other New York banks. On Mar. 18, 1867 (ibid.), they had $590,000 in governments, $450,000 with other banks in Philadelphia, and $400,000 with their New York firm. On June 23, 1868 (ibid.), they had $100,000 in governments, $350,000 with other banks in Philadelphia, $1,600,000 with the New York firm, $90,000 with the First National of Washington, $200,000 on call, $100,000 loaned on Delaware & Hudson paper, and $70,000 in notes due in July and August.

65. In a letter to Thomas of the Philadelphia house, Oct. 15, 1869, Jay Cooke when on vacation instructed loans should be made only on governments and Reading and Pennsylvania bonds but not on stocks. Also references in note 64, above.

66. J. C. to H. C., Sept. 10, 1867, and G. T. to J. C., Sept. 30, 1869.

67. J. C. to H. C., Jan. 26, 1867: "The Boys from New York write that they are perfectly snug. I give them a dig every day or two on the subject of loans so that I have no doubt they will keep their eyes open." Also, H. F. to J. C., Oct. 27, 1866.

68. Ibid., Oct. 27, 1866.

69. P. C. to J. C., Dec. 30, 1868, and Jan. 18, 1869. Sometimes they bought good commercial paper, but not when money was tight: "We can always raise money on our loans on Call & we do Call all we have *Every* day & loan over again, more or less next morning whatever we may have to loan. Thus Constantly keeping Easy but Packers paper, or anybody Elses paper, with *JC&CO over it*, or *anybody else* for 15 or 30 days would not sell in such a market. . . . As for selling long winded paper here as a way of using balances you must educate us to see it." (P. C. to J. C., Dec. 30, 1868.)

70. P. C. to J. C., Mar. 29, 1867.   71. *Ibid.*, Dec. 30, 1868.

72. *Ibid.*, Nov. 17, 1868.

73. In 1866 Dodge loaned considerably on stocks (P. C. to J. C., Nov. 22, 1866, and Jan. 2, 1867). Fahnestock objected to his loaning on weak stocks (to J. C., Jan. 24, 1867), though he loaned only a little over two-thirds of the market value (Jan. 26). In the fall of 1868, P. C. complained strongly of Dodge's loans on stock (to J. C., Oct. 28, 31, Nov. 6, 13, 1868, and Jan. 4, 1869). On Nov. 6, 1868, reported P. C. to J. C., the loans of the New York house were as follows: $100,000 on different railroad stocks valued at

$127,000 under the existing panic conditions; $150,000 on $214,000 in railroad stocks; $350,000 on $446,400 in railroad stocks; $100,000 on $117,000 N. Y. Central stock, $50,000 on $110,550 in railroad stock. On Feb. 2, 1869, H. F. complained to J. C. of risky stock loans. On Feb. 5, he informed J. C. that stock loans were down to $1,200,000.

74. P. C. to J. C., Nov. 6, 1868. 75. H. F. to J. C., Feb. 9, 1869.

76. For instance, P. C. to J. C., Mar. 13, 1867.

77. If Washington demanded more than 4 per cent, wrote J. C. to H. C., Apr. 21, 1866, Philadelphia would return the million they held. Sometimes the question of interest caused ill feeling. On Feb. 19, 1867, the New Yorkers wrote to the "rural" Philadelphians: "while money was worth 3 % here & we were paying you 6 % Int. your balance was *1,800th* & now on a *very* tight & panicky market when money is worth 7. % — & a com — your balance is drawn down to one million."

78. This is illustrated by a letter of the New Yorkers to the Philadelphia house, Feb. 19, 1867: "We have just paid your 3 drft 200th 10th & 50. *$260,000* without advice You must agree with us that this is irregular; not to say Exceedingly inconvenient to us. Frequently large Drfts, drawn by you without advice, are presented just before 3 P.M. and it places us in an exceedingly unpleasant fix, to provide for the payment of Such large amounts on a moments notice, in a tight money market. . . . Your Dfts today came in late, and to meet them we had to Call in Loans later in the day than is Customary, which we are very reluctant to do."

79. When a certain house was in a tight place, it warned the others not to draw their balances (J. C. & Co., N. Y., to J. C. & Co., Phila., Oct. 4, 1867; H. F. to J. C., Apr. 2, 1868).

80. P. C. to J. C., Feb. 5 and Dec. 3, 1868; H. F. to J. C., letters of Aug., 1868, and Nov. 29, 1869.

81. Illustrations at random: April 27, 1866, $422,000; June 19, 1866, $906,000; Sept. 21, 1866, $700,000; Mar. 18, 1867, $400,000; June 23, 1868, $1,600,000; Sept. 30, 1869, $350,000. These were taken from letters from Sexton and Thomas to Jay Cooke reporting to him (when away from Philadelphia) the condition of the house.

82. See above p. 139 and below, p. 239. Shortly after the insurance company had been formed, it loaned half a million to Jay Cooke & Co. (receipt for collateral, Sept. 3, 1868).

83. The following quotation from a letter of Thomas of the Philadelphia house to J. C., Sept. 28, 1868, illustrates the loaning and borrowing of the Philadelphia house: "Yesterday I sold 7th National $100,000 5/20^8 99 1/8 bought them at 99 & carry them at 5 % payable on call any time after 10 days. I then borrowed $100,000 from Bank of North America at 4 % & took National Bank notes at 4 Days flat, these notes I immediately deposited in our banks; today I took $200,000 Nationals from Philada National at 30 Days flat & sent them to New York office who credit us after 4 days Pretty

good wasn't it? It is really fine to have some business to do after such a dull spell."

84. J. C. to H. C. and H. F., Jan. 3, 1866; H. F. to G. T., July 28, 1869; H. F. to J. C., Sept. 13, 1869; G. T. to J. C., Oct. 7, 1869. They frequently complained that they did not have more governments for collateral.

85. P. C. to J. C., Nov. 3, 1868: "These Stocks belonged mostly to customers who have left them here for sale & who have bought & paid for them & left them with us, & we used them at Park Bk to borrow Gold on — which Gold we *lent*. . . . We had these stocks laying idle & we took this way to make them earn a 'living.'"

86. P. C. to J. C., Mar. 25, 1867.   87. According to Mr. Barney.

88. According to Harvey E. Fisk, 37 Madison Avenue, New York City. Mr. Fisk entered his father's bank in the 'seventies.

89. H. F. to J. C., Jan. 26, 1867, and July 23, 1867; P. C., to J. C., Oct. 28, 1868; G. S. Kimball to J. C., Nov. 3, 1868.

90. According to Mr. Barney.

91. The weekly statements of the First National to Jay Cooke show that the bank really went into governments to a surprising degree. Also, J. C. to H. C. and H. F., Jan. 7, 1866; H. C. to J. C., June 18 and Oct. 16, 1866; J. C. to H. C., Feb. 13, 1869.

92. In Philadelphia they traded much with D. C. Wharton, Smith & Co.

93. J. W. Sexton to J. C., Apr. 11, 1866; West (for J. C.) to H. C., Apr. 14, 1866; J. C. to H. C., May 6, 1866; G. T. to J. C., June 6 and Sept. 21, 1866. In their correspondence they spoke frequently of turning the securities quickly.

94. H. F., Aug. 1, 1866.

95. The *Com. and Fin. Chron.* often spoke of the nervous money market.

96. H. F. to J. C., Aug. 6, 1867.

97. Notably the currency corner of Nov., 1868, and the Gold Panic of 1869.

98. H. F. to J. C., Dec. 10, 1866.   99. *Ibid.*, Jan. 12, 1867.

100. J. C. to H. C., Mar. 12, 1867.   101. *Ibid.*, Nov. 27, 1866.

102. P. C. to J. C., July 10, 1867.

103. H. F. to J. C., Oct. 11, 1866. Fahnestock's cryptic figures refer to individual issues or kinds of bonds, such as one issued under an act of 1862, another due in 1881, compound-interest notes, the ten-forties, etc.

104. H. F. to J. C., Mar. 12, Aug. 11 and 14, 1866; and P. C. to J. C., May 22 and 30 and June 21, 1866.

105. H. F. to J. C., Jan. 23, 1867.

106. For instance, *ibid.*, Jan. 9 and Apr. 24, 1867; and P. C. to J. C., July 20 and Dec. 21, 1867.

107. According to letters in CP, on Mar. 12, 1868, their stock of governments stood reduced to 3 million; on Mar. 16 they had only $20,000; on Apr. 1,

governments were down to zero where they would keep them as long as money was hard to get.

108. In his absence, P. C. had charge of his department. Pitt was by nature a bear.

109. P. C. to J. C., Dec. 29, 1868.   110. H. F. to J. C., Jan. 25, 1869.

111. On Aug. 1, 1866, he wrote Cooke that those who were where they could feel the market knew best how to act, and on July 10, 1868, that Cooke must trust him.

112. In a letter to J. C., Nov. 5, 1870, reviewing their trading.

113. H. F. to J. C., Apr. 8, 1869.   114. *Ibid.*, Feb. 25, 1869.

115. *Ibid.*, Aug. 28, 1869.   116. H. F. to G. T., July 28, 1869.

117. H. F. to J. C., Aug. 10, 1869.   118. *Ibid.*, Aug. 28, 1869.

119. *Ibid.*, Sept. 1, 1869.   120. *Ibid.*, Sept. 30, 1869.

121. *Ibid.*, Aug. 10, 1869.   122. *Ibid.*, Nov. 5, 1870.

CHAPTER XIII

1. *Minneapolis Tribune*, Jan. 7, 1868.

2. *Report of the Commissioner of Patents*, 1867, no. 67,052.

3. E. J. Hill to J. C. (with refusal in J. C.'s hand), Nov. 8, 1867.

4. J. R. Brown to J. C. (with refusal in J. C.'s hand), Nov. 24, 1869.

5. R. Johnson to J. C., Apr. 25, 28, and May 1, 1866.

6. N. Murphy to J. C., June 15, 1866, and I. W. Pendleton to J. C., June 13, 1867. On both these letters are notes in Jay Cooke's hand to guide his secretary in answering them.

7. Letters to J. C.: G. B. Walter, June 25, 1866; John Sherman, July 15, 1866; J. A. Stewart, July 27, 1866; Huntington, May 6, 1868; Elisha Wilson, Jan. 21, 1869. The shares of the East India Telegraph, for which Jay Cooke refused to work, were sold by the Drexels (*Philadelphia Inquirer*, Sept. 12, 1868). Anson Burlingame, who secured from China the treaty allowing the company to lay its cables to important Chinese ports, spent a week with Cooke at Gibraltar (H. C. to J. C., July 25, 1868; A. Burlingame to J. C., July 27, 1868).

8. H. C. to J. C., May 9, 1866; Antoine de Gagorza to J. C., May 15 and 20, 1866; unsigned letter and memorandum of May 18, 1866.

9. C. K. Knight, *The History of Life Insurance in the United States to 1870* (Philadelphia, 1920), p. 141.

10. J. C. to H. F., Sept. (undated), 1871.

11. C. H. Clark to J. C., Dec. 18, 1867; Knight, *op. cit.*, pp. 143–144.

12. This company advertised as the original joint-stock life insurance company of the United States (*The Insurance Times*, vol. i, Dec., 1868, p. 544).

13. Knight, *op. cit.*, pp. 143–145.   14. H. C. to J. C., Jan. 7, 1868.

15. This point was stressed in the company's insurance.

16. H. C. to J. C., July 22, 1868.

17. It was a question considered in the *Report of the New York Supt. of Insurance*, 1868, and the *Massachusetts Insurance Commissioners' Report*, 1868.

18. H. C. to J. C., July 22, 24, 25, 1868.

19. H. F. to J. C., Nov. 22, 1869; H. C. wrote J. C., Aug. 15, 1868; J. C. to H. C., Jan. 21, 1869.

20. Comparison of directors of various companies in *The Insurance Times*. Banking and insurance had been closely connected a generation earlier, as in the Manhattan Company, but the connection had not been lasting.

21. *The Insurance Times*, vol. i, pp. 334-335.

22. Among the directors were a former assistant secretary of the Treasury, commissioner of internal revenue, and superintendent of public printing. On the medical advisory board were the surgeons general of the army and navy and the director of a war hospital in Washington (*U. S. Railroad and Mining Register*, Aug. 8, 1868; the *Philadelphia Inquirer*, Aug. 3, 1868; and *The Insurance Times*, vol. i, pp. 334-335).

23. *Ibid.*, pp. 334-335.

24. J. C. to H. C., July 31, 1868, and Mar. 15, 1869.

25. C. H. Clark to J. C., Oct. 5, 1868; W. M. to J. C., Oct. 27 and Nov. 22, 1869; W. Smith to W. M., Nov. 2, 1869.

26. An illustration of the earliest advertising and publicity of the company is found in *The Insurance Times*, vol. i (Aug., 1868), pp. 307, 334-335.

27. There is a premium book for 1871 in CP. *The Insurance Times*, vol. i, pp. 334-335.

28. J. C. to H. C., Aug. 6, 1868, Jan. 19 and Feb. 4, 1869; J. C., Jr., to H. C., Aug. 4, 1868; P. C. to J. C., Oct. 31, 1868; H. C. to J. C., Feb. 5 and Dec. 9, 10, 1869; H. F. to J. C., Mar. 5, July 21, and Aug. 28, 1869; C. H. Clark to J. C., Jan. 15, 1870.

29. Detailed statements of the company for Aug. 1, 1869, Jan. 1 and Aug.1, 1870; S. A. Kean to J. C., Nov. 1, 1869.

30. Statements in note above. Expenses were commissions, $261,034.60; advertising, $136,420.22; salaries, $91,605.34; printing, $45,714.61, etc.

31. J. C. to H. F., Sept. (undated), 1871.

32. J. C. to McCulloch, Nov. 23, 1871, lb.; H. D. Moore to J. C., May 7, 15, 1866, and May 5, 1868; Moore to W. M. and J. C., Mar. 1, 1871.

33. Moore to J. C., May 18 and June 5, 1866; Peter Roberts, *The Anthracite Coal Industry* (New York, 1901), p. 104; J. I. Bogen, *The Anthracite Railroads* (New York, 1927), p. 50.

34. Roberts, *op. cit.*, p. 75, shows a drop in the price of coal in Philadelphia from $8.39 a ton in 1864 to about $3.85 in 1868. H. D. Moore, who was closely associated with the Cookes in Preston, diagnosed the general situation thus, in a letter to J. C., June 5, 1868: "People got crazy about

Coal Lands, and almost every acre of Coal Land (Anthracite) that could be bought or leased was taken up in '64 and 65 and mines opened and Improvements put up, so that in '66 there were more mines in operation than ever before, and that year there was *three million one hundred thousand Tons* more coal produced than the year previous. . . . The market was glutted, prices commenced receding and have been going down ever since." The demand for coal, said Moore, had for twenty years shown an annual increase of about 10 per cent: the production of '66 was 30 per cent above that of the previous year. Annual coal production figures are given on p. 27 of "Business and Financial Conditions following the Civil War in the United States," *Review of Economic Statistics*, Supplement, 1920. Also, J. C. to H. C., Jan. 27, 1868.

35. P. C. to J. C., Jan. 27, 1869; J. C., Jr., to H. C., Mar. 1, 1869.

36. J. C. to H. C., Jan. 15, 1869; Moore to W. M. and J. C., Mar. 1, 1871.

37. J. C. to McCulloch, Nov. 23, 1871, lb.

38. W. M. to J. C., Feb. 27, 1866.

39. Statement of J. C., signed by J. K. Moorhead, W. M., P. C., H. C., and H. F., Sept. 14, 1867.

40. W. M. to J. C., Feb. 27, 1866; H. C. to J. C., June 6, 1867.

41. W. G. Neilson to J. C., June 1, 1868.

42. B. J. Hendrick, *Life of Andrew Carnegie* (Garden City, 1932), vol. i, chap. VIII.

43. H. D. Cooke had a weakness for new projects — a stone quarry, gas company, ferry, gold mine, engraving concern, etc. His partners protested, but it was all "colouer de rose" to Harry, according to Pitt (P. C. to J. C., May 15, 1869).

44. A revealing letter of Moore to W. M. and J. C., Mar. 1, 1871, reviews their experiences with a number of those concerns.

45. This was the reason for trying to sell some of those properties in 1869 (J. C. to H. C., Jan. 15, 1869).

46. Poor's *Manual of the Railroads of the United States*, 1873–74, p. xxvii: 1865, 1,177; 1866, 1,742; 1867, 2,449; 1868, 2,979; 1869, 5,118; 1870, 5,525; 1871, 7,779; 1872, 6,427.

47. P. C. to H. C., Apr. 3, 1866.

48. J. C. to H. C. and H. F., Feb. 17, 1866.

49. Memorandum dated June 5, 1866; copy of letter of J. Edgar Thomson to Edward Miller & Co., July 24, 1866; Moore to J. C., Aug. 21, 1867; J. C. to Chase, July 10, 1868, Chase Papers, Library of Congress; statement of J. C. & Co. of Phila., Jan. 11, 1867; J. H. Ewing to J. C., Mar. 26, 1866; J. K. Moorhead to J. C., Apr. 7, 1866; John D. Scully to J. C., Aug. 9, 1866; *Com. and Fin. Chron.*, vol. iii (Dec. 22, 1866), p. 801.

50. *Ledger.* (Philadelphia), July 31, 1867, and *Philadelphia Inquirer*, June 27, 1867; H. C. to J. C., June 6, 1867.

51. Wilson, *History of the Pennsylvania Railroad Company*, vol. i, *passim;* Bogen, *op. cit.*, chaps. III, IV, V, VII.

52. H. F. to J. C., Nov. 29, 1869.

53. F. H. Evans to J. C. & Co., Feb. 26 and 28, Mar. 3, 17, 21, 28, 1866, and Feb. 10, Mar. 3 and 12, 1869.

54. P. C. to J. C., Apr. 3, 1866, Feb. 5, Oct. 30, and Nov. 2, 1868; Edgerton to J. C., July 26, 30, Nov. 1, 1866, and June 11, 1868.

55. H. C. to J. C., Jan. 23, 1865, and Jan. 13, 1866.

56. H. F. to J. C., Feb. 27, 1866.

57. W. I. Palmer to J. C., Mar. 16 and June 26, 1866, CP, and Mar. 17, 1866, CH. Jay Cooke & Co. became the New York agents for the payment of interest on the Union Pacific bonds (*Philadelphia Inquirer*, July 20, 1866).

58. *Philadelphia Inquirer*, July 17, 1866; *New York Tribune*, Sept. 8, 1866; *U. S. Railroad and Mining Register*, editorial, July 28, 1866, and advertisement, July 28, 1866–Jan. 19, 1867.

59. *Philadelphia Inquirer*, July 17, 1866.

60. Signed agreement, July 6, 1866. Also, J. C. to H. C., Aug. 28, 1866.

61. Letters to J. C.: Semple & Jones (Pittsburgh), July 23, 1866; John Ellis (Cincinnati), July 23, 1866; Bartlet & Smith (Columbus, Ohio), Aug. 11, 1866; H. F., Dec. 11, 1866.

62. J. C. to H. C., Dec. 20, 1866; Isaac Sturgeon to J. C., Jan. 24, Mar. 4, June 26, 1867; Champlin Smith & Co. to J. C., Feb. 25, 1867.

63. P. C. to J. C., Mar. 23 and May 15, 1867.

64. *Philadelphia Inquirer*, July 16, 1867.

65. P. C. to J. C., July 16, 1867.

66. Sturgeon to J. C., Aug. 9, 1867; advertisement in *U. S. Railroad and Mining Register*, Aug. 24, 1867–July 4, 1868.

67. Hume to J. C., Nov. 23, 1867; Barton Bates to J. C., Dec. 10, 1867. Also, *Com. and Fin. Chron.*, vol. vi (June 27, 1868), p. 804.

68. J. C. to H. C., Dec. 20, 1866.

69. Durant to J. C., Sept. 28, 1866.

70. P. C. to H. C., Nov. 2, 1866; H. C. to J. C., Nov. 3, 1866.

71. H. F. to J. C., Feb. 20, 1867; P. C. to J. C., Mar. 9, 1867.

72. *Ibid.*, Mar. 12, 1867.

73. Early advertisement of the Ciscos, *Com. and Fin. Chron.*, vol. iv (June 1, 1867), p. 676.

74. Interview with Harvey E. Fisk, New York City, Oct. 19, 1933; Fisk, "Fisk & Hatch, Bankers and Dealers in Government Securities," *op. cit.*, pp. 711–712.

75. Poor's *Manual of Railroads*, 1870–71, pp. 416, 424.

76. Jay Cooke considered buying Kansas land but never purchased any (W. J. Barney to J. C., Feb. 27, 28, 1866, and Jan. 18, Feb. 3 and Apr. 1, 1868; S. H. Kean to J. C., Apr. 20, 1868).

77. Agreement of Sept. 16, 1866, for the purchase of the land, CH.

78. Letter and statement of the account of Rice Harper to J. C., Nov. 9,

1869, CH. Most of the land scrip was purchased for 58 cents an acre (statement above, and P. C. to J. C., Sept. 18, 1866).

79. A statement of the amount and location of these lands and of all the others purchased is given in CH. Also, W. B. Banning to J. C., Nov. 15, 1866.

80. J. C. speaks at length in his Memoirs of this trip to Duluth. He is mistaken in saying it happened in 1867 as he wrote a long letter to H. C. from Superior, Wisconsin, June 18, 1868.

81. There is a letter in CH, Mar. 17, 1866, on the legality of the charter of the L. S. & M. R. R. Co., and a copy of the engineer's report on the road, Dec. 10, 1866, in CP.

82. Circular from the executive committee to the stockholders, Feb. 1, 1869, CH.

83. Henrietta M. Larson, *The Wheat Market and the Farmer in Minnesota* (New York, 1926), p. 59.

84. Their purchase totaled $138,825.41 (statement of subscription, Sept. 17, 1868, CH).

85. Numerous telegrams and letters dated Sept. 14, 1868, CP.

86. They went to London, Frankfort, Amsterdam, Berlin, and Paris (P. C. to J. C., Nov. 21, 1868). Clark to J. C., Oct. 6, 1868, quoting a cable from J. Hinckley Clark from London; H. F. to J. C., Oct. 13, 17 and Nov. 8, 1868.

87. Oct. 13, 1868, referring no doubt to the Atlantic & Great Western and the Erie. On Feb. 10, 1869, Frank Evans wrote to J. C. from London that the British public was thoroughly frightened of American securities. "This Erie business with its awful disclosures of corruption existing in your state courts has added tenfold to the distrust. Look at the Penn^a Central issuing its mortgage six per cents at *85 per* cent & even *now* all not taken though issued by, & energetically aided by, every American broker."

88. Signed agreement of Feb. 10, 1869.   89. P. C. to J. C., Feb. 3, 1869.

90. Agreement of E. W. Clark & Co. and Jay Cooke & Co., Feb. 10, 1869, CH. One-half of their commission and stock bonus was credited to a joint account and one-half retained by the house making the sale.

91. G. T. to J. C., Mar. 5, 1869; E. G. Townsend to J. C., Mar. 18, 1869.

92. J. C. to H. C., Mar. 25, 1868.

93. *Ibid.*, Feb. 25, 1869. Wilkeson was paid $6,200 and Painter $1,000 for their services (H. C. to J. C., Apr. 30, 1869).

94. P. C. to J. C., Feb. 23, 1869.   95. H. F. to J. C., Mar. 16, 1869.

96. P. C. to J. C., Mar. 18 and 29, 1869.

97. H. C. to J. C., Mar. 17, 18, 1869.

98. Wilkeson to J. C., Mar. 10, 17, 1869.

99. P. C. to J. C., Mar. 20, 1869.   100. H. F. to J. C., Mar. 13, 1869.

101. J. C. to H. C., Mar. 22, 1869; H. C. to J. C., Mar. 22, 1869.

102. Statement of bonds delivered, Apr. 12, 1869, CH. A large proportion of their sales were on time, wrote H. F. to J. C., Apr. 1, 1869.

103. H. F. to J. C., Mar. 22, 1869.

104. J. C. & Co. circulars, Apr. 19, May 20, and Aug. 2, 1869, CH; H. F. to J. C., Mar. 29, May 18, Sept. 1 and 7, 1869; J. C. to H. C., Apr. 15, May 22, 1869; G. T. to J. C., May 26, Nov. 5, 1869.

105. Receipt signed by Robt. H. Lamborn, Mar. 13, 1869, CH.

106. Statement of Joint Account, dated from May 18, 1869, CH.

107. P. C. to J. C., Nov. 23, 1868; Sargent to J. C., Mar. 1, 1869. Sargent's advertisements were conspicuous in the Duluth papers, and he rates as one of Duluth's important pioneers.

CHAPTER XIV

1. D. A. Wells, *Report of the Special Commission of the Revenue*, 1869, p. xxviii.

2. H. F. to J. C., May 19, 1869; P. C. to J. C., May 18, 1869.

3. H. C. to P. C., Mar. 20, 1869.

4. H. F. to J. C., May 19, 1869. In his report to the receiver in 1873 (*In the Matter of . . . Jay Cooke & Co., Bankrupts*, "Statement of the Bankrupts as to Causes of Insolvency," p. 124), H. C. stated that the two properties cost $230,000.

5. H. F. to J. C., May 19, 1869.

6. *Ibid.;* P. C. to J. C., May 18, 1869; J. C. to H. C., May 22, 1869.

7. H. C. to J. C., May 24, 1869.

8. *In the Matter of . . . Jay Cooke & Co., Bankrupts*, "Statement of Bankrupts as to Causes of Insolvency," p. 122.

9. P. C. to J. C., undated letter of July, 1869, and H. C. to H. F., July 1, 1869.

10. H. F. to J. C., Feb. 25, 1869.

11. Poor's *Manual of Railroads*, 1870–71, p. xlvi.

12. *Com. and Fin. Chron.*, vol. viii (Jan.–June, 1869), pp. 685 and 689, and weekly reports of sales in the issues of April and May.

13. Advertisements in *ibid.*, 1869.   14. Fisk, *op. cit.*, p. 712.

15. Poor's *Manual of Railroads*, 1870–71, pp. 145, 354, 385–389, 460. Horace F. Clark of the Lake Shore and Michigan was a son-in-law of Vanderbilt of the New York Central.

16. E. V. Smalley, *History of the Northern Pacific Railroad* (New York, 1883), chaps. VII–X; *Letter of Isaac I. Stevens to the Railroad Convention of Washington and Oregon* (Washington, 1860).

17. Smalley, *op. cit.*, chap. XIII; *Northern Pacific Railroad Company, Charter, Organization, and Proceedings* (Boston, 1865).

18. Com. of Boston Board of Trade, *Report on the Northern Pacific Railroad* (Boston, 1865).

19. H. A. Innis (*A History of the Canadian Pacific Railway*, Toronto, 1923, p. 79) says that Allan "had about $3,000,000 invested in sea-going steamers alone."

20. Smalley, *op. cit.*, p. 134.

21. 40th Cong., 2nd Sess. (1867–68), *Senate Misc. Docs.*, no. 9, p. 1.

22. Smalley, *op. cit.*, pp. 137–139.

23. *Ibid.*, pp. 142–144; manuscript copy of agreement in vol. vii of "Archives," a collection of miscellaneous materials on the N. P. in CH.

24. Smalley, *op. cit.*, pp. 144–145.

25. 40th Cong., 2nd Sess., *Senate Misc. Docs.*, no. 9.

26. 40th Cong., 3rd Sess. (1868–69), *Senate Reports*, no. 219.

27. 15 *U. S. Statutes at Large*, p. 346.

28. A signed duplicate of the original agreement is in CH.

29. P. C. to J. C., May 22, 1869.

30. Roberts, civil engineer for the U. S. government in charge of Ohio River improvement, had been active in Pennsylvania railroad construction; he had also been in Brazil for several years and had been engineer in the building of the Mississippi bridge at St. Louis (Roberts to W. Canfield, June 26, 1869; Roberts to J. C., July 31, 1869).

31. H. C. to J. C., June 25, 1869; *St. Paul Pioneer Press*, July 7 and 28, 1869.

32. Wilkeson to J. C., July 11, 25, 28, and Aug. 19, 1869.

33. Numerous letters in CP from Roberts reporting on the trip.

34. W. Milnor Roberts, *Special Report of a Reconnoissance of the Route for the Northern Pacific Railroad*, 1869.

35. His articles were collected and published (Boston, 1870) in *The Seat of Empire*.

36. Samuel Wilkeson, *Notes on Puget Sound* (pamphlet published in 1869), p. 10.

37. H. F. to J. C., May 18, 1869.

38. There was a lack of understanding between Moorhead and his brother-in-law partners which was if anything heightened by the fact that Moorhead remarried soon after the death of his first wife, Sarah Cooke (H. C. to J. C., June 18, 1869).

39. W. M. to J. C., July 22, 1869.   40. H. F. to J. C., July 26, 1869.

41. Undated letter of W. M. to J. C., about Aug. 11, 1869.

42. Prof. L. H. Jenks, author of *The Migration of British Capital, to 1875*, has generously given me some information about the British loan market at the time.

43. Lucien Wolfe, biographer of Baron Nathan Rothschild, had a careful search made in the Rothschild records in London on these negotiations,

but nothing was found. This was not surprising, for so much of the Rothschild business was done in private conference and was not recorded.

44. W. M. to J. C., July 22 and Aug. 2 and 9, 1869.

45. H. F. to J. C., Aug. 16, 17 and Sept. 18, 1869.

46. Copy of letter of J. C. to W. M., Aug. 13, 1869.

47. W. M. to J. C., Oct. 6, 1869.

48. *Ibid.* (London), undated letter of Oct., 1869.

49. H. F. to J. C., Sept. 18, 1869.

50. J. C. to W. M., Aug. 13, 1869; Chase to J. C., Aug. 14, 1869.

51. Even the Clarks declined an invitation to join in the project (J. H. Clark to J. C., Oct. 27, 1869).

52. "Gold Panic Investigation," 41st Cong., 2nd Sess. (1869–70), *Reports of Committees*, no. 31, pp. 13, 15, and 36.

53. W. W. Fowler, *Ten Years in Wall Street* (Hartford, 1870), pp. 520 and 524; *Bankers' Mag.*, vol. xxiv (Nov., 1869), pp. 385–387.

54. "Gold Panic Investigation," *op. cit.*, pp. 13, 15, 179–180; H. F. to J. C., Jan. 12, 1871.

55. "Gold Panic Investigation," *op. cit.*, pp. 16, 448.

56. H. F. to J. C., Sept. 24 and Oct. 16, 1869, and Jan. 12, 1871; H. C. to J. C., Sept. 28, 1869.

57. H. C. to J. C., Sept. 23 and 24, 1869.

58. "Gold Panic Investigation," *op. cit.*, pp. 15–17.

59. *Ibid.*, pp. 11, 16; H. C. to J. C., Sept. 24, 1869.

60. Fowler, *op. cit.*, pp. 528–529; and *Bankers' Mag.*, vol. xxiv, pp. 386–389.

61. H. C. to J. C., Sept. 25, 1869.   62. *Ibid.*, Sept. 27, 28, and 29, 1869.

63. J. C. to H. C., Sept. 24, 1869.   64. P. C. to J. C., Sept. 29, 1869.

65. *Ibid.*, Oct. 8, 1869.

66. H. F. to J. C., Oct. 16, 1869, and Jan. 12, 1871; P. C. to J. C., Oct. 4, 1869.

67. H. F. to J. C., Sept. 30, 1869.

68. P. C. to J. C., Sept. 30 and Oct. 1, 4, and 6, 1869.

69. J. C. to G. T., Oct. 5, 1869; Gibraltar Records, in the possession of Mr. Charles D. Barney.

70. J. C. to G. T., Oct. 20, 1869.   71. H. F. to J. C., Nov. 29, 1869.

72. W. M. to J. C., Nov. 26, 1869; H. F. to J. C., Dec. 18, 1869.

73. H. C. to J. C., Mar. 26, Apr. 2, 3, 10, Sept. 27, Dec. 17, 18, 1869; W. L. Banning to J. C., Sept. 15, Oct. 13, 1869; H. C. to G. T., Oct. 19, 1869; J. C. to H. C., Mar. 25, Sept. 25, 1869.

74. J. W. Taylor to J. C., Nov. 28, 1869; R. H. Lamborn to J. C., Nov. 3, 1869.

75. *U. S. Railroad and Mining Register*, Dec. 4, 1869, quoting *Duluth Minnesotian*; J. C. to G. T., Oct. 20, 1869.

76. H. C. to J. C., Dec. 13, 1869.

77. H. F. to J. C., Nov. 29 and Dec. 7, 1869.

78. J. C. to G. T., Oct. 15, 1869.   79. H. C. to J. C., Sept. 11, 13, 1869.

80. W. M. to J. C., Nov. 13, 1869.   81. H. F. to J. C., Sept. 18, 1869.

82. H. C. to J. C., Aug. 23, Oct. 27, Dec. 1 and 2, 1869.

83. *Ibid.*, Nov. 13 and 29, 1869.   84. H. F. to J. C., Dec. 9 and 11, 1869.

85. The Memphis, El Paso & Pacific (Poor's *Manual of Railroads*, 1869–70, p. 438).

86. Blaine's speech and letters in 44th Cong., 1st Sess. (1876), *Cong. Record*, pp. 3604 ff.; and contract and memorandum book in *Mr. Blaine's Record*, published by Committee of One Hundred, 1884. The memorandum book shows that for selling bonds and stock for $130,000 in cash Blaine received $130,000 in 7 per cent currency land bonds and $32,500 in 6 per cent gold first-mortgage bonds, and for other sales received substantial amounts in cash.

87. H. C. to J. C., Oct. 16 and Nov. 1, 1869.

88. J. C. to H. C., Nov. 2, 1869; Blaine to J. C., Nov. 10, 1869.

89. The original letter, dated Nov. 10, 1869, is in CP.

90. J. C. to H. C., Dec. 30, 1869.   91. *Ibid.*, and Apr. 16, 1870.

92. H. F. to J. C., Mar. 13, 1872, speaking of new loan added to previous loan. At the time of the bankruptcy of J. C. & Co., the Washington house held Blaine's notes for $33,333.33 (*In the Matter of . . . Jay Cooke & Co., Bankrupts*, "Schedules of the Bankrupts," p. 71).

93. H. F. to J. C., Dec. 11, 1869.

94. J. G. Smith to J. C., urging a decision, Aug. 18, Sept. 16, Oct. 22, 1869, etc.

95. Taylor to Geo. L. Becker, Oct. 2, 1869, Taylor Papers, Minn. Hist. Soc.

96. Smith to J. C., Nov. 23, 1869. Also correspondence in the Taylor Papers, Minn. Hist. Soc., on the efforts of the St. Paul & Pacific Railroad.

97. H. F. to J. C., Nov. 29, 1869.

98. P. C. to J. C., Mar. 26 and Apr. 11, 1869.

99. *Ibid.*, Dec. 13 and 16, 1869.

100. W. M. to J. C., from Paris, Dec. 14, 1869.

101. H. C. to J. C., Dec. 1, 1869.

102. This summary of his position is taken from a letter of Smith to A. H. Barney, treasurer of the Northern Pacific, Dec. 6, 1869, Smith lb., Northern Pacific Papers, Northern Pacific Office, St. Paul, Minnesota.

103. W. M. to J. C., Dec. 15, 21, 1869.

104. Wilkeson to J. C., Dec. 22, 1869.

105. The agreement, on parchment, is in CP; there are signed copies of agreements of May 20, 1869, and Jan. 1, 1870, in CH.

106. P. C. to J. C., Nov. 1, Dec. 16, 1869; H. F. to J. C., Dec. 27, 31, 1869; W. M. to J. C., Dec. 21, 1869.

107. H. F. to J. C ., Dec. 27, 31, 1869.

108. *In the Matter of* . . . *Jay Cooke & Co., Bankrupts*, "Statement of the Bankrupts as to Causes of Insolvency," p. 22.

CHAPTER XV

1. See letter on p. 352.   2. J. C. to Wilkeson, Sept. 20, 1871.

3. This program was stated in H. F. to W. M., Dec. 3, 1869, and repeated in H. F. to J. C., June 22, 1872.

4. Several copies of the pool agreement signed by subscribers are in CH.

5. J. C., Jr., to H. D. Faulkner, Jan. 29, 1870, lb.

6. H. F. to J. C., Jan. 3 and 5, 1870; Wilkeson to J. C., Jan. 7, 1870.

7. Oberholtzer, *op. cit.*, vol. ii, p. 166.   8. H. F. to J. C., Jan. 22, 1870.

9. *Ibid.*, Jan. 26, 1870.   10. *Ibid.*, Jan. 28, 1870.

11. Oberholtzer, *op. cit.*, vol. ii, p. 167.

12. 15 *U. S. Statutes at Large*, p. 346.

13. 41st Cong., 2nd Sess. (1869–70), *Cong. Globe*, p. 1097.

14. J. C. to H. C., Feb. 9, 26, Mar. 2, 1870, etc.

15. J. C. to Marshall, Feb. 9, 1870; Marshall to J. C., Mar. 24, 1870.

16. There are many letters in CP of Donnelly to J. C. for 1870.

17. H. C. to J. C., Jan. 29, 1870.   18. *Ibid.*, Feb. 5 and 8, 1870.

19. J. C. to H. C., Apr. 11, 1870.   20. H. C. to J. C., Mar. 14, 1870.

21. J. G. Smith to J. C., Apr. 15, 1870.

22. 41st Cong., 2nd Sess., *Cong. Globe*, pp. 1584–1585, 1624–1625.

23. H. C. to J. C., Mar. 1 and 3, 1870.

24. 41st Cong., 2nd Sess., *Cong. Globe*, pp. 2569–2571, 2867–2869; J. C. to H. C., Apr. 12, 1870.

25. J. C. to Wilkeson, Mar. 2, 1870, lb.

26. J. C. to H. C., Apr. 14, 1870.

27. The negative votes came from California, Tennessee, Kentucky, Missouri, Iowa, Indiana, West Virginia, and Delaware.

28. J. C. to H. C., Feb. 21 and Apr. 19, 1870.

29. J. C. to H. C., Apr. 23, 1870.

30. H. C. to J. C., Apr. 23 and May 10, 1870; J. C. to H. C., May 2 and 7, 1870; Chandler to J. C., May 11, 1870.

31. Letter to J. C., May 5, 1870.   32. Donnelly to J. C., May 6, 1870.

33. 41st Cong., 2nd Sess., *Cong. Globe*, pp. 3343–3348, 3365–3368; Chandler to J. C., May 11, 1870.

34. Donnelly to J. C., May 5 and 11, 1870.

35. J. W. Geary to J. C., May 21, 1870; H. C. to J. C., May 26, 1870.

36. H. F. wrote to J. C. (May 10, 1870) that Young of the *Tribune* had suggested this move to the President.

37. Telegrams in CP.

38. 41st Cong., 2nd Sess. ,*Cong. Globe*, pp. 3786 and 3853; 16 *U. S. Statutes at Large*, pp. 378–379.

39. J. C. to H. C., May 31, 1870. 40. Donnelly to J. C., May 25, 1870.

41. On this, see Jenks, *Migration of British Capital*, chap. IX; *Bankers' Mag.* (London), vol. xxx (1870), pp. 329–330, 421, 611–614, 633, and vol. xxxvi (1876), pp. 424–430, 517–522.

42. *Ibid.*, vol. xxx (1870), p. 77.

43. *Ibid.*, and *Economist* for 1870.

44. Adler, *Jacob H. Schiff: His Life and Letters*, pp. 7–8.

45. J. C. & Co. to Budge, Schiff & Co., M. Budge, and Robert Thode & Co., Feb. 25, 1870.

46. H. F. to J. C., Feb. 18 and 24, 1870. 47. *Ibid.*, undated, Feb., 1870.

48. *Ibid.*, Mar. 19, 1870.

49. Copy of contract of Apr. 15, 1870, in CP.

50. Sargent to J. C., Apr. 15 and 27, 1870.

51. There is an extensive correspondence in CP on Sargent's efforts.

52. H. Budge and M. Goldschmidt to J. C., May 25, 1870.

53. J. C. to H. C., May 2, 1870; H. C. to J. C., June 3, 1870.

54. Announced in Berlin papers, May 3 and 4, 1870.

55. The *Ledger* articles of Apr. 19 and 25 were, according to Fahnestock, mailed to bankers in the United States and Europe (H. F. to J. C., Apr. 29 and May 2, 1870). H. C. informed his brother (June 3, 1870) that he had received a letter from W. W. Murphy, veteran counsel at Frankfort, enclosing a slip printed by the *Ledger*.

56. Sargent to J. C., Apr. 30 and May 18, 1870.

57. W. M. to J. C., May 10, 1870.

58. Sargent to J. C., May 18 and June 11, 1870.

59. *Bankers' Mag.* (London), vol. xxx (1870), pp. 489–490.

60. Sargent to J. C., May 5, 12, 18, 1870; Sargent to Fahnestock, July 6, 1870; H. Budge to J. C., May 25, 1870; H. F. to J. C., June 28, 1870.

61. See Drummond Wolff in chap. IX of Jenks, *op. cit.*

62. Sargent to H. F., July 6 and 23, 1870; Sargent to J. C. & Co., July 16, 1870.

63. *Economist*, Aug. 1870; Sargent to J. C., July 16, 1870; H. C. to J. C., July 16, 1870.

64. Sargent to J. C. & Co., July 21, 1870.

65. Sargent to J. C., Oct. 1 and 3, 1870; Sargent to H. F., July 23, 1870; H. F. to J. C., Oct. 5, 1870.

66. Sargent to J. C., July 26 and Aug. 8, 1870; Robert Thode to J. C., July 20 and Sept. 10, 1870; H. Budge to Sargent, Aug. 4, 1870.

67. Jenks, *op. cit.*, pp. 269–270; and the *Jewish Encyclopaedia*.

68. Jenks, *op. cit.*, p. 270; *Bankers' Mag.* (London), vol. xxx (1870), p. 631.

69. Jenks (p. 292) refers to criticism of them in the report of a committee of the House of Commons on foreign loans in 1875.

70. Sargent to H. F., Nov. 8, 1870.

71. Copy of proposed terms of agreement with Bischoffsheim and Gold-schmidt, dated Oct. 22, 1870; H. F. to J. C., Nov. 15 and 22 and Dec. 9, 1870.

72. Sargent to H. F., Nov. 8, 1870; H. F. to J. C. (letter and telegram), Nov. 15, 1870.

73. Sargent to J. C., Dec. 29, 1870.

74. J. C. to A. H. Barney, Dec. 30, 1870, lb., Northern Pacific Papers.

CHAPTER XVI

1. H. F. to J. C., Sept. 15, 1871.

2. *Ibid.*, Sept. 20 and Oct. 28, 1870; Smith to J. C., Nov. 1, 1870; McCulloch to J. C., Oct. 27, 1870.

3. H. F. to J. C., Oct. 28, 1870; H. C. to J. C., Nov. 1, 1870.

4. *Ibid.*, Oct. 7, Nov. 1 and 26, 1870.

5. *Ibid.*, Dec. 23, 1870.　　　　6. H. C. to J. C., Mar. 1, 1871.

7. The articles are given in full in *In the Matter of . . . Jay Cooke & Co., Bankrupts*, "Statement of the Bankrupts as to Causes of Insolvency," pp. 13–16.

8. Dodge to J. C., Aug. 6, 1870.

9. H. F. to J. C., Aug. 12, 1869; P. C. to J. C., Oct. 16, 1869.

10. W. M. to J. C., Oct. 12 and Dec. 17, 1870; articles of co-partnership referred to above.

11. Mr. Charles D. Barney and Mr. Harvey E. Fisk. Also, H. F. to J. C., Sept. 23, 1871.

12. *In the Matter of . . . Jay Cooke & Co., Bankrupts*, "Statement of the Bankrupts as to Causes of Insolvency," p. 15.

13. This figure was compiled from statements of partners in *ibid.*, pp. 83 ff.

14. *Ibid.*, p. 23; H. F. to J. C., Jan. 12, 1871.

15. *Ibid.*　　　　16. *Ibid.*, Jan. 31, 1870.

17. *Ibid.*, Nov. 14 and 15, 1870; J. C. to Puleston, Dec. 15, 1871; H. F. to Baring Brothers, Mar. 17, 1870. There is a draft of this letter in CP; the original is in the Baring Papers, Ottawa. I have used photostats of letters from the Baring Papers.

18. Copy, H. F. to Evans, Feb. 2, 1871, CH.

19. H. F. to Baring Brothers, Mar. 17, 1870, referred to above.

20. H. F. to J. C., Mar. 28, 1870.　　21. *Ibid.*

22. A copy of a letter of J. C. & Co. to S. G. & G. C. Ward, Mar. 4, 1870, is in the Baring Papers, Ottawa, Canada.

23. *Ibid.*

24. S. G. & G. C. Ward to Baring Brothers & Co., Mar. 5, 1870, Baring Papers, Ottawa.

25. J. C. & Co. to Baring Brothers & Co., Mar. 17, 1870, Baring Papers, Ottawa; H. F. to J. C., Apr. 13, 1870.

26. American *Bankers' Mag.*, vol. xxiv (1870), pp. 909, 911; *Bankers' Mag.* (London), vol. xxx (1870), p. 489.

27. McCulloch to J. C., July 13, 1870; J. C. to H. C., July 30, 1870; H. F. to J. C., June 3, 1870.

28. *Post Office London Directory*, 1869.   29. H. F. to J. C., July 14, 1870.

30. *In the Matter of . . . Jay Cooke & Co., Bankrupts,* "Statement of Bankrupts as to Causes of Insolvency," pp. 16–20. Garland was at first a partner but later resigned because partnerships over ten members were under English law in the class of joint-stock companies (P. C. to J. C., Aug. 16, 1871).

31. McCulloch to J. C., Dec. 3, 1870.   32. Puleston to J. C., Jan. 5, 1871.

33. J. C. to H. C., June 14, 1870.

34. H. C. to J. C., Feb. 14, 1871; H. F. to J. C., Aug. 20, 1870.

35. H. C. to J. C., May 26, 1871.   36. *Ibid.*, Feb. 8, 1871.

37. *Ibid.;* H. F. to J. C., Nov. 11 and Dec. 27, 1871; J. C. to H. F., Dec. 26, 1871, lb.

38. H. C. to J. C., May 20, 31, 1871.

39. *Ibid.*, June 7, 12, 16, 1871; J. C. to McCulloch, Feb. 6, 1872, lb.; H. F. to J. C., Aug. 12, 1871.

40. J. C. to H. C., May 29, 1871.   41. *Ibid.*, May 22, 1871.

42. F. D. French to J. C., Dec. 15, 1871. One million was for 3 days' sight; one for 60; and one for 90 days.

43. H. F. to J. C., Nov. 11, 1871.   44. *Ibid.*, Apr. 27 and May 1, 1871.

45. *Ibid.*, Aug. 1, 18, 20, 1870.   46. *Ledger*, July 1, 1871.

47. Vol. xiii (1870), p. 11.   48. H. F. to J. C., Oct. 19, 1871.

49. *Ibid.*, Sept. 1 and 5, 1871; J. C. to P. C., Nov. 1 and to H. C., Nov. 23, 1871.

50. H. F. to J. C., Sept. 7 and Oct. 19, 1871.

51. J. C. to Johnston, Aug. 11, 1871, lb.

52. J. C. to Thomas Squires & Son, Dec. 8, 1871, lb.; P. C. to J. C., Oct. 17, 1871.

53. J. C. to Puleston, Dec. 15, 1871. The occasion was the discovery that Jay Cooke, McCulloch & Co., of London, had carried the London account of the Emma Mining Company, a scandalous enterprise (J. C. to P. C., Nov. 24, 1871; J. C. to H. C., Dec. 15, 1871; H. F. to J. C., Dec. 7, 1871, lb.).

54. This was maintained throughout Northern Pacific publicity.

55. Compiled by the National Bureau of Economic Research, *Standard Statistical Bulletin, Base Book*, Jan. 1932, p. 134.

56. Copy of letter of J. C. & Co. to Edmund Smith, vice-president of the Pennsylvania Railroad, Mar. 18, 1870, and copy of the reply of the same date, both in CP.

57. The original signed agreement is in CP.   58. *Ledger*, Feb. 14, 1870.

59. 16 *U. S. Statutes at Large*, pp. 272–274.

60. *Com. and Fin. Chron.*, vol. xi (1870), p. 101; Sec. of the Treas.,

Finance Report, 1870, p. vi; H. C. to H. F., P. C., and J. C., July 27, 1870; H. C. to J. C., Nov. 19, 1870.

61. J. C. to H. C., Dec. 15, 1870.

62. *Com. and Fin. Chron.*, vol. xi (1870), p. 293. Also, vol. xii (1871), p. 5.

63. H. F. to J. C. and H. C., Jan. 25, 1871.

64. J. C. to H. C., Dec. 15, 1870; H. C. to J. C., Dec. 19, 1870.

65. H. F. to J. C., Aug. 1, 1870; H. C. to J. C. and H. F., July 27 and Nov. 9, 1870; H. D. to J. C., July 30 and Aug. 1, 1870; J. C. to H. D., July 30, 1870.

66. H. F. to J. C., Jan. 25, 1871; H. C. to J. C., Feb. 14, 1871.

67. P. C. to J. C., Mar. 30, 1871. 68. H. F. to J. C., Feb. 23, 1871.

69. *Ibid.*, Jan. 25, 1871.

70. H. C. to J. C., Feb. 6, 1871; memorandum, Jan. 25, 1871.

71. H. F. to J. C., Aug. 1, 1870. 72. *Ibid.*, Jan. 25, 1871.

73. Sec. of the Treas., *op. cit.*, 1871, p. xvii.

74. H. F. to J. C., Mar. 27, 1871.

75. *Com. and Fin. Chron.*, vol. xii (1871), p. 167; New York *Journal of Commerce*, quoted by the *Ledger*, July 12, 1871.

76. H. C. to J. C., May 18, 20, 24, 1871. There is a partial copy of their proposal, dated May 22, 1871, in CP.

77. Boutwell to J. C., May 29, 1871; J. C. to Boutwell, May 31, 1871, lb.

78. *Com. and Fin. Chron.*, vol. xii (1871), p. 741; Sec. of the Treas., *op. cit.*, 1871, p. xvii.

79. H. C. to J. C., June 13, 1871; Sec. of the Treas., *op. cit.*, 1871, p. xviii; *Com. and Fin. Chron.*, vol. xiii, p. 741; copy of Richardson's cables, CH.

80. National banks could subscribe for $51,000,000 of the remainder.

81. Abstract of agreement with Jay Cooke & Co. and memorandum of agreement between the Sec. of the Treas. and J. C., Aug. 14, 1871, CP.

82. Undated letter of J. C. to H. C.; Sec. of the Treas., *op. cit.*, 1871, p. xix.

83. Drexel, Morgan & Co. to J. C. & Co., Aug. 11, 1871, and Drexel, Harjes to Jay Cooke, McCulloch & Co., Aug. 18, 1871; L. P. Morton to H. F., Aug. 12, 1871, CH; H. F. to J. C., Aug. 12, 1871; J. C. to McCulloch, Feb. 6, 1872, lb.

84. List of subscribers to the American syndicate in CH; *Com. and Fin. Chron.*, vol. xiii, p. 237.

85. *Ibid.; New York Times*, Aug. 15, 1871.

86. H. F. to J. C., Aug. 18 and 26, 1871; J. C. to H. F., Aug. 19, 1871, lb.

87. *Com. and Fin. Chron.*, vol. xiii, pp. 237 and 269.

88. H. F. to J. C., Aug. 22, 1871; *Money Market Review*, Aug. 26, 1871, p. 233; *Com. and Fin. Chron.*, vol. xiii, p. 301.

89. Sec. of the Treas., *op. cit.*, 1871, p. xviii.

90. *Ibid.*, p. xix; H. F. to J. C., Aug. 30, 1871.

91. J. C. to H. F., Aug. 30, 1871, lb.; H. F. to J. C., Sept. 14, 1871.

92. *Ibid.*, Sept. 9, 1871. 93. McCulloch to J. C., Sept. 9, 1871.

94. H. F. to J. C., Sept. 8, 1871.

95. *Com. and Fin. Chron.*, vol. xiii, pp. 357–358.

96. H. F. to J. C., Sept. 19, 1871.

97. *Ibid.*, Sept. 22, and J. C. to H. F., Sept. 21, 1871.

98. H. F. to J. C., Sept. 21, 1871. 99. Vol. xiii, p. 227.

100. Quoted by Oberholtzer, *op. cit.*, vol. ii, p. 275.

101. J. C. to H. C., Nov. 6, 8, 25, 29, 1871; J. C. to P. C., Nov. 10, 1871; J. C. to Boutwell, Nov. 6, 1871, lb.

102. J. C. to H. C., Aug. 19 and 29, 1871; H. F. to J. C., Aug. 22, 1871.

103. J. C. to Garland, Nov. 24 and 27, Dec. 8 and 9, 1871, and to A. T. Huntington, Dec. 15, 1871, lb.; J. C. to P. C., Nov. 27, 1871.

104. Reported to H. C. by General Porter (H. C. to J. C., Sept. 1, 1871).

105. McCulloch to J. C., Dec. 2, 1871.

106. P. C. to J. C., Dec. 30, 1871.

107. H. F. to J. C., Aug. 13 and 22, 1871, and to Jay Cooke, McCulloch & Co., Oct. 10, 1871.

108. Vol. xiii, p. 359.

109. J. C. to H. F., Nov. 13, 1871, lb., CP. The *Com. and Fin. Chron.* (vol. xiii, p. 826) estimated the profits to the syndicate at $3,000,000.

CHAPTER XVII

1. *Report of L. S. & M. Railroad*, 1871, p. 5; F. D. Clark to J. C. & Co., Dec. 6, 1870.

2. Larson, *The Wheat Trade and the Farmer in Minnesota*, chap. III.

3. C. S. Hinchman to J. C., Aug. 22, 1870; *St. Paul Pioneer Press*, Sept. 24, 1870; C. B. Newcomb to J. C., Aug. 22, 1870, and Sept. 11, 1871.

4. *Owatonna Journal* (Minnesota), Sept. 15, 1871.

5. W. L. Banning to J. C., Aug. 13, 1870.

6. J. C. to H. C., Nov. 16, 1870; H. C. to J. C., Nov. 17 and 19, 1870; H. R. Hubbard to J. C., Nov. 26, 1870; printed notice, Mar. 25, 1871, in letter of B. S. Russell to J. C., Mar. 30, 1871; *Duluth Minnesotian*, Mar. 25, 1871.

7. *Report of the L. S. & M. Railroad*, 1871, p. 5, and 1872, pp. 15–18; Clark to J. C. & Co., Dec. 6, 1870, and to J. C., Jan. 11, 1871; Larson, *The Wheat Trade and the Farmer in Minnesota*, chap. II.

8. Clark to J. C., Oct. 14, 1871; *Report of the L. S. & M. Railroad*, 1871, p. 16.

9. *Ibid.*, 1871, p. 10.

10. Receipts made out to J. C. & Co., signed by R. L. Lamborn, Nov. 3 and 18, 1870.

11. T. B. Walker to J. C., May 2, 1870.

12. *St. Paul Pioneer Press*, Nov. 5, 1870.

13. Banning to J. C., Sept. 23, 1870; Marshall to J. C., Oct. 1, 1870.

14. J. C. to H. C., Nov. 28, 1871, and Jan. 23, 1872.

15. J. W. Bishop, *Sketch of the St. Paul & Sioux City Railroad* (St. Paul, 1903), pp. 6–7.

16. *Acts of the Legislature of Wisconsin and of the Congress of the United States Relative to the St. Croix & Lake Superior Railroad Company* (New York, 1865), p. 34; Banning to J. C., Sept. 15 and Oct. 13, 1869; J. C. to H. C., Sept. 25, 1869; H. C. to J. C., Sept. 25, 1869, and July 6, 1870, and to G. T., Oct. 19, 1869.

17. H. C. to J. C., Dec. 17 and 18, 1869.

18. *Ibid.*, Feb. 3, 1870.

19. *Ibid.*, Mar. 22, 1870.

20. The CP contain dozens of letters from Feb. to July, 1870, on this measure (the letters of Mar. 21 and Apr. are especially important). The Donnelly Papers in the Minn. Hist. Soc. contain copies of a number of letters written in this connection, especially his letters of Mar. 8 to Minnesota senators.

21. J. C. to Ritchie and Bright, Feb. 5, 1870, to Magoffin, Feb. 7, 1870, and to Felton, Apr. 1, 1872, lb.; J. C. to H. C., Feb. 2 and 24, May 7, and June 10, 1870; Stinson to J. C., Jan. 27, 1871, and H. C., Mar. 22, 1870. There is an undated and unsigned paper in CP which gives in detail the plans for joining the Superior interests to the Western Land Association.

22. J. C. to Lucius Fairchild, June 14, 1870, Fairchild Papers, Wis. Hist. Soc.; Fairchild to J. C., June 20, 1870; H. C. to J. C., Mar. 22 and July 6 and 11, 1870; Banning to J. C., June 15, 1870; J. C. to H. C., May 7, 1870; 41st Cong., 2nd Sess. (1869–70), *Cong. Globe*, p. 5470.

23. H. D. to J. C., July 2, 1870.

24. 41st Cong., 2nd Sess., *Cong. Globe*, p. 5476.

25. There is an excellent article by T. C. Blegen on Taylor in *Minn. Hist. Bulletins*, vol. i (Nov., 1915). Also Taylor to J. C., Apr. 2, 1869.

26. There are in the Taylor Papers, Minn. Hist. Soc., numerous clippings or copies of articles published in such papers as the *Toronto Globe*, the *New York Tribune*, and the *Chicago Tribune*.

27. Copy of letter to President Grant, May 5, 1869, Taylor Papers, Minn. Hist. Soc.

28. *Ibid.;* Taylor to J. C., May 8 and Oct. 12, 1869; Taylor to G. L. Becker, Oct. 2, 1869, Taylor Papers, Minn. Hist. Soc.

29. W. M. to J. C., Oct. 16, 23, 27, 1869.

30. W. M. to J. C., Oct. 23 and 27 and Nov. 22, 1869; Taylor to J. C., Oct. 7 and Nov. 28, 1869; pencil notes of Taylor to Becker, Oct. 23, 1869, and to W. M. and Smith (undated), in Taylor Papers, Minn. Hist. Soc.

31. J. C. to H. F., Mar. 19, 1872, lb.

32. H. F. to J. C., Feb. 28, 1870, and J. C. to H. F., Mar. 1, 1870; memorandum, Mar. 8, 1870, signed by J. C. and M. L. Sykes, CH; *Book of Refer-*

ence, N. P. Railroad, p. 62, exec. com., Apr. 7, 1870. The original agreement with Rice, Oct. 22, 1870, is in CP and a copy is in CH.

33. Becker to Taylor, Jan. 10, 19, 20, Feb. 5, Mar. 20, and Apr. 5, 1870, Taylor Papers, Minn. Hist. Soc.; J. C. to H. C., Mar. 2, 1870.

34. *Book of Reference, N. P. Railroad*, pp. 68–69, exec. com., Dec. 7, 1870; Poor's *Manual of Railroads*, 1871–72, pp. 480–481, 1872–73, p. 577, and 1873–74, p. 355; Becker to Taylor, Dec. 2, 1870, Taylor Papers, Minn. Hist. Soc.

35. J. C. to Sargent, Feb. 25, 1870.   36. J. C. to H. C., Apr. 14, 1870.

37. J. P. Pritchett in "Notes and Documents," *North Dakota Hist. Quart.*, vol. v (1930), p. 51; W. B. O'Donaghue to "J. Cooke," Mar. 29, 1871 (reproduced in full in Pritchett, *op. cit.*, pp. 52–53). An excellent picture of the Red River troubles is given in Pritchett, "The So-Called Fenian Raid on Manitoba," *Canadian Hist. Review*, vol. x (1929), pp. 23–42.

38. There is much correspondence in CP between the Cookes and these agents.

39. These ran into hundreds of dollars for each house for a few months, according to a statement of expenses, Apr. 1, 1871, in CP. At first Jay Cooke sent out traveling agents from Philadelphia, but they were soon dropped as their cost was out of proportion to the results obtained (statement of expenses, Apr. 1, 1871, and J. C. to Hugh McCulloch, Jr., Nov. 27, 1871, lb.).

40. A. B. Nettleton to J. C., Mar. 29, 1870; J. C. to Wilkeson, Sept. 30, 1871, lb.

41. Ledger, 1871, Ayer Collection, N. W. Ayer & Son, Inc., Philadelphia.

42. J. W. Orvis to J. C., Jan. 1, 1871.

43. H. C. to J. C., Jan. 17, 1871; J. C. to Nettleton, undated, summer of 1871, lb. Also, Nettleton to Taylor, July 7, 1871, Taylor Papers, Minn. Hist. Soc.

44. Memoranda of the expenses incurred in selling the loan (Apr. 1, 1871) list $13,440 paid to Bowen and $20,975.37 to Young. Also, Young to J. C., Sept. 10, 1871, and J. C. & Co. to Bowen, Dec. 18 and 19, 1870, CH.

45. J. C. to H. C., and J. C. to H. F., Sept. 5, 1871, lb.

46. Young to J. C., Feb. 6, 1871.

47. H. F. to J. C., Jan. 10, 1871; Smith to J. C., Mar. 16, 1871; J. C. to S. Bowles, Apr. 20, 1871, lb.; Bowles to J. C., Apr. 24, 1871, CP.

48. 42nd Cong., 2nd Sess. (1871–72), *House Misc. Docs.*, no. 228, p. 28.

49. Copies of these publications are not rare. Several are in the Library of Congress, the Hist. Soc. of Penn., and Baker Library at Harvard University.

50. According to statements of expenses and memorandum, Apr. 1, 1871, and J. C. to H. C., May 2, 1872, lb.

51. A Cooke circular in the Library of Congress.

52. The circular, SAFE! PROFITABLE! PERMANENT!, a copy of which is in CP.

53. P. C. to J. C., Mar. 17, 1871.

54. *The Northern Pacific Railroad: Its Route, Resources, Progress and Business* (1871), pp. 4, 21–24.

55. For instance, *The Northern Pacific Railroad's Land Grant and the Future Business of the Road*, 1870.

56. Colfax to J. C., Jan. 27, 29, and 31, 1871.

57. Copy, J. C. to Colfax, Jan. 30, 1871.

58. Colfax to J. C., Apr. 1, 1871.

59. J. C. to Marshall, Sept. 26, 1871, lb.

60. Windom to J. C., Aug. 12, 1871. Also, W. Goddard to Windom, May 25, 1871, treasurer's letterbooks, N. P. Papers.

61. Report of meeting of board of directors of N. P. Railroad, Nov. 14–16, 1871; J. C. to F. Billings, Oct. 28, 1871. According to treasurer's letterbooks, N. P. Papers, Wade had a salary of $500 a month with $100 for expenses.

62. *Dict. of Amer. Biog.*

63. Copy of the Annual Report of the Northern Pacific Railroad, for year ending July 1, 1871, in N. P. Papers.

64. H. C. to J. C., June 20, 1871.   65. W. M. to J. C., June 23, 1871.

66. J. C. to Goddard, Aug. 3, 1871, and to Barney, Dec. 30, 1870, N. P. Papers; J. C. to H. F., Aug. 23, 1871, to McCulloch, Sept. 25, 1871, and Smith, Dec. 1, 1871, lb.; Holmes to J. C., Nov. 28, 1871.

67. J. C. to W. C. Kibbe, Dec. 9, 1871, lb.

68. A circular issued Oct. 20, 1869, by J. C. & Co.

69. J. B. Hedges, "The Colonization Work of the Northern Pacific Railroad," *The Miss. Valley Hist. Review*, vol. xiii (1926), p. 314.

70. *Report of John S. Loomis, Land Commissioner* (New York, 1871), pp. 3–4; *Letter of John S. Loomis to F. Billings* (New York, 1871).

71. G. B. Hibbard, *Land Department of the Northern Pacific Railroad Company* (New York, 1871).

72. Quoted by *Com. and Fin. Chron.*, vol. xiii (1871), p. 11.

73. *Ibid.*, p. 695.

74. Roberts to J. C., July 8, 1871; Nettleton to J. C., Aug. 12, 1871.

75. Felton to J. C., Jan. 15, 1871; Thomson to J. C., Mar. 22, 1871.

76. J. C. to H. F., Aug. 31, 1871, to Smith, Sept. 21, 1871, and to Barney (treasurer of Northern Pacific), Mar. 3 and Nov. 2, 6, 23, 1871, lb.

77. J. C. to Barney, Jan. 26, 1871, and to Goddard, Aug. 23, 1871, N. P. Papers.

78. J. C. to Barney, Oct. 13, 1871; Smith to J. C., Oct. 16, 1871.

79. Copy, J. C. to Smith, Oct. 19, 1871.

80. J. C. to Smith, Nov. 2, 1871, lb.

81. J. C. to Barney, Nov. 17, 1871, N. P. Papers.

82. *Ibid.*, Dec. 1, 1871.   83. J. C. to Smith, Dec. 22 and 23, 1871, lb.

84. *Ibid.*   85. J. C. to M. W. Fairwell, Sept. 1, 1871.

86. *Ibid.*, and H. F. to J. C., May 30, 1871.

87. The account of what happened is given in Puleston to J. C., May 23, 1871, and H. F. to J. C. & Co. of N. Y., May 30, 1871.

88. H. F. to J. C., Apr. 19 and May 30, 1871; Puleston to J. C., Jan. 5 and May 23, 1871.

89. Oberholtzer, *op.cit.*, vol. ii, p. 216; P. W. Holmes to J. C., May 13, 1871, and J. C. to Budge, Schiff & Co., July 14, 1871, lb. And from CH: Budge, Schiff & Co. to J. C. & Co., July 7, 1871; J. C. & Co., N. Y., to J. C. & Co., Phila., July 8, 1871; copy of agreement, July 7, 1871, between contracting parties, signed by J. C. & Co. and representatives of Budge, Schiff & Co., Robert Thode & Co., and Moritz B. Goldschmidt; and copy of agreement with representative of Moritz Budge.

90. Memorandum of agreement, June 7, 1871.

91. H. F. to "Puleston et al," June 7, 1871.

92. H. F. to J. C., June 29, 1871.

93. Nettleton to J. C., Feb. 8 and July 28, 1871; J. C. to Sargent, Aug. 3, 1871.

94. J. C. to Johnston Bros. & Co., Aug. 26, 1871, to H. F., Aug. 23, 1871, and to McCulloch, Sept. 4, 1871.

95. H. F. to J. C., Aug. 23, 1871.

96. McCulloch to J. C., Apr. 24 and Sept. 9 and 13, 1871.

97. Roberts to J. C., Sept. 14, 1871; Sargent to J. C., Sept. 14, 1871; J. C. to Roberts, Sept. 21, 1871, lb.

98. J. C. to McCulloch, Sept. 20, 1871, to Evans, Nov. 7, 1871, and to Moorhead, Dec. 9, 1871, lb.; Puleston to J. C., Nov. 4, 1871; H. F. to J. C., Nov. 18, 1871.

99. J. C. to H. F., Nov. 4, 1871, and to Sanford, Dec. 26, 1871, lb.

100. J. C. to McCulloch, Jan. 2, 1872, lb.

101. McCulloch to J. C., Apr. 24 and Sept. 9 and 13, 1871.

102. S. A. Kean to J. C., Oct. 18, 1871.

103. D. Paulson to J. C., July 20, 1871; J. C. to Sanford, Dec. 26, 1871, lb.

104. J. C. to superintendents of the St. P. & P., the N. P., and L. S. & M. railroads, Dec. 11, 1871, lb.

105. J. C. to W. J. Bedford, Sept. 16, 1871; J. C. to W. W. Billson, Apr. 20, 1872, lb.

106. J. C. to the Rt. Rev. Henry W. Lee, Dec. 2, 1871, lb.

107. J. C. wrote to his Washington brother and his wife on July 22, 1871, about the passing of Mrs. Cooke.

CHAPTER XVIII

1. H. F. to J. C., Jan. 2, 1872; P. C. to J. C., Jan. 4, 1872; Garland to J. C., Jan. 4, 1872; *In the Matter of . . . Jay Cooke & Co., Bankrupts,* "Statement of the Bankrupts as to Causes of Insolvency," pp. 22–23.

2. H. F. to J. C. and H. C., Nov. 23, 1871; J. C. to Boutwell, Dec. 16, 1871, and to H. F., Dec. 22 and 26, 1871, lb.; J. C. to H. C., Dec. 28, 1871; *Financier*, vol. i (1872), pp. 42–43.

3. 42nd Cong., 2nd Sess. (1871–72), *Cong. Globe*, pp. 12, 21, 22, 60, 737–743, 750, 768; *Ledger*, Feb. 5, 1872; J. C. to H. C., Jan. 29 and Feb. 1, 1872, lb.

4. P. C. to J. C., Feb. 5 and Mar. 8, 1872; J. C. to P. C., Jan. 15 and Feb. 6, 1872, and to McCulloch, Feb. 6, 1872, lb.

5. J. C. to H. F., Aug. 10 and Apr. 16, 1872, and to H. C., May 18, Aug. 15, and Oct. 25, 1872, lb.; H. C. to J. C., Aug. 15 and 16, 1872.

6. Copy of cables from London to New York, in letter of H. F. to J. C., May 1, 1874.

7. There arose in this connection a nice little controversy between the *New York Herald* and the *Ledger*. J. C. to McCulloch, Feb. 6, 1872, and to Baron Gerolt, Feb. 17, 1872, lb.; copy of cables of Feb. 4, 12, and 13, in H. F. to J. C., May 1, 1874.

8. Cable of Feb. 4, 1872, as cited above.

9. J. C. to H. C., Feb. 6, 1872, and to Smith, Mar. 1, 1872, lb.; P. C. to J. C., Jan. 30, 1872; J. C., Jr., to J. C., Jan. 9, 1872; P. C. to J. C., Jan. 31 and Feb. 1, 1872.

10. *New York Tribune*, Oct. 22, 1873.

11. 42nd Cong., 2nd Sess. (1871–72), *Cong. Globe*, p. 975; J. C. to H. C., Feb. 14, 1872; Johnston to J. C., Feb. 26, 1872; J. C. to Smith, Feb. 26, 1872, lb. Nettleton wrote to J. C. (June 7, 1872) that the report of the Com. on Pacific Railroads adopted by the House was written by Samuel Wilkeson.

12. J. C. to G. W. Nesmith, to H. Wilson, and to W. S. Pierson, Feb. 24, 1872, lb.

13. J. C. to Wilson, Feb. 24 and Mar. 1, 1872, and to Pierson, Feb. 24, 1872, lb.

14. J. C. to P. C., Feb. 8, 1872, to McCulloch, Feb. 9, 1872, to Roberts, Mar. 1, 1872, to T. L. Foster, Mar. 1, 1872, and to J. P. Henderson, Jan. 5, 1872, lb.; P. C. to J. C., Feb. 9, 1872.

15. J. C. to Barney, Mar. 16, 20, and 23, 1872, N. P. Papers; J. C. to Smith, Mar. 23, 1872, lb.

16. One of the originals was loaned to the author by Mr. G. C. Clark, 61 Wall Street, New York.

17. J. C. to Barney and to Smith, Apr. 25, 1872, to H. C., May 4, 1872, to H. F., July 2, 1872, and to Nettleton, Aug. 3 and 5, 1872, lb.; P. C. to J. C., July 8, 1872; G. T. to J. C., June 1, 1872.

18. J. C. to F. H. Clark, Aug. 4, 1871, lb.

19. J. C. wrote to Clark, Aug. 6 and 12, 1872, lb., stating that there had to be either agreement with the "wheat ring" or warfare. Also, *Report of the Lake Superior & Mississippi Railroad Company*, 1872, p. 17, and 1873, p. 11.

20. J. C. to H. F., Apr. 26, 1871, lb.

21. *Book of Reference, N. P. Railroad*, pp. 96–97, exec. com.; C. C. Gilman to J. C., Jan. 5 and Aug. 22, 1872.

22. Clark to J. C., Oct. 14, 1871.

23. H. F. to J. C., Mar. 18, 1872.

24. J. C. (White, sec.) to Smith, Dec. 28, 1871; P. C. to J. C., July 25, 1872; *Book of Reference, N. P. Railroad*, p. 86, meeting of board, Jan. 11, 1872; *Report, L. S. & M. Railroad*, 1872, pp. 11–13.

25. Clark to J. C., Jan. 20, 1871; J. C. to Clark, Aug. 28 and 31, 1871, lb.

26. J. C. to H. C., Nov. 28, 1871 (lb.), Jan. 8, 22, 23, 30, 31, and Mar. 4, 19, 20, and 21, 1872; J. C. to Smith, Mar. 1, 1872, to Fairchild, Dec. 29, 1871, and to Gilman, Jan. 25, 1872, lb.; H. C. to J. C., Jan. 19, 1872; Lucius Fairchild to J. C., June 20, 1870, and Jan. 7, 1872.

27. J. C. to H. C., Mar. 20, 1872, to Smith, Feb. 20, 1872, and to Windom, Mar. 20, 1872, lb., and copy of letter of J. C. to Fairchild, Dec. 20, 1871; *Book of Reference, N. P. Railroad*, pp. 77 and 79.

28. J. C. to H. C., Mar. 8 and 19, 1872.

29. Nettleton to J. C., Aug. 11, 1871; J. C. to Ogden, Nov. 20, 1871, and to Smith, Nov. 25, 1871, lb.

30. J. C. to Russell, Aug. 17, 1872.

31. J. C. to Banning, Nov. 18, 1871, to Smith, Nov. 25, 1871, and Apr. 5, 1872, to Nettleton, Aug. 15, 1872, to Canfield, Aug. 15, 1872, lb.; *Book of Reference, N. P. Railroad*, p. 102, meeting of directors, Feb. 13, 1873.

32. J. C. to Canfield, Apr. 18 and 20, 1871, and Aug. 12, 1872; J. C. to Felton, Sept. 30, 1871; Wilkeson's manuscript report of meeting of board of L. S. & P. S. Co. for Nov. 14–16, 1871; J. C. to Banning, Jan. 3, 1872; circular of Western Land Assoc., Jan. 25, 1872; J. C. to J. K. Moorhead, Aug. 15, 1872; P. C. to J. C., Sept. 10, 1872.

33. Canfield of Vermont was president and Wilkeson was secretary. The office was at 120 Broadway, New York. J. C. to Canfield, Aug. 4, Dec. 22 and 27, 1871, and Sept. 12, 1872, lb., and to P. C., Dec. 14, 1871; Henry Blood to J. C., Aug. 2, 1872.

34. H. F. to J. C., June 6, 1870 (including resolution of land company). J. C. to Canfield, Sept. 12, 1872. I have no definite information about the price paid to the N. P., but a manuscript report of a meeting of the board of directors of the N. P. of Oct. 10–12, 1871, in CP, contains an order to the effect that bonds be sold to the L. S. & P. S. Co. at not less than full market value. The land company, however, had the advantage of knowing before other buyers did where stations would be located.

35. *Book of Reference, N. P. Railroad*, p. 75, meeting of board, May 10, 1871; Poor's *Manual of Railroads*, 1872–73, p. 577.

36. J. C. to Smith, Sept. 21, 1871, and Feb. 28, 1872; J. C. to A. H. Barney, Nov. 22, 1871, and April 17, 1872; J. C. to H. F., Apr. 17 and 19, 1872, lb.; J. C. to Garland, Sept. 19, 1872.

37. Gov. Archibald to Taylor, Jan. 3, 1871; Taylor to Becker, June 30

and July 10, 1872, Taylor Papers, Minn. Hist. Soc.; H. C. to J. C., Apr. 6, 1871.

38. J. C. to Puleston, Sept. 23, 1871, to Fahnestock, Jan. 16, 1872, lb.; Innis, *A History of the Canadian Pacific Railway*, p. 80.

39. *Ibid.*, pp. 80–83; L. Edgerton to J. C., Dec. 18, 1872, and May 8 and June 7, 1873.

40. J. C. to H. F., Jan. 16, 1872, lb.

41. *Ibid.*, copy of letter of J. C. to Smith, Jan. 31, 1872.

42. J. C. to Puleston, Apr. 11, 1872, lb.

43. J. B. Hedges, *Henry Villard and the Railways of the Northwest* (New Haven, 1930), p. 54.

44. J. C. to Puleston, Apr. 11, 1872, lb.; H. F. to J. C., Mar. 30, 1872.

45. See Hedges, *Henry Villard and the Railways of the Northwest*, chap. III.

46. J. C. to H. F., Apr. 8, 1872, lb.

47. J. C. to Smith, Mar. 23 and Apr. 5, 1872, to H. C., Jr., Mar. 23, 1872, to Barney, Apr. 27, 1872, and to H. F., Apr. 3, 1872, lb.; H. F. to J. C., Mar. 30, 1872; *Book of Reference, N. P. Railroad*, p. 87, meeting of directors, Feb. 13, 1872, and p. 91, exec. com., Apr. 2, 1872.

48. J. C. to H. F., Apr. 5, 1872, to Smith, Apr. 5, 1872, to H. C., Apr. 8, 1872, to Puleston, Apr. 11, 1872, and to Barney, Apr. 29, 1872; F. T. Dodge to J. C., Apr. 13, 1872.

49. J. C. to Barney, Mar. 8, 1872, N. P. Papers.   50. *Ibid.*

51. J. C. to Smith, Apr. 25, 1872, and to Barney, Apr. 25 and Sept. 19, 1872, lb.; G. T. to J. C., June 1, 1872; P. C. to J. C., Sept. 11, 1872; J. C., Jr., to J. C., July 30 and Aug. 20, 1872; *Book of Reference, N. P. Railroad*, p. 95.

52. Barney to J. C., Sept. 16, 1872.   53. W. M. to J. C., Oct. 1, 1872.

54. J. C. to Barney, Mar. 16, 1872, N. P. Papers; Barney to J. C., Mar. 13, 1872.

55. Barney to Smith, July 22, 1872, N. P. Papers.

56. *Ibid.*, Aug. 2, 1872.

57. Becker to Taylor, Feb. 3, 1871, Taylor Papers, Minn. Hist. Soc.

58. Roberts to J. C., June 3, 1872.

59. *Book of Reference, N. P. Railroad, passim.*

60. There are copies of the original reports (which were filed with the Department of the Interior, Washington) in the N. P. Papers.

61. H. F., with postscript by P. C., to J. C., Mar. 11, 1872.

62. H. F. to J. C., Mar. 13, 1872.

63. To Barney, Puleston, H. F., Smith, and McCulloch, Mar. 12, 1872, lb.

64. Memorandum, Apr. 6, 1872.

65. *Com. and Fin. Chron.*, vol. xiv (1872), pp. 446, 477, 509.

66. Wire of Garland to J. C., May 9, 1872.

67. H. F. to J. C., June 8, 1872.

68. According to the report of the N. P. for 1872, that was about the amount of bonds then outstanding.

69. J. C. to P. C. and Garland, Sept. 20, 1872, and to Barney, Sept. 12, 1872, lb.

CHAPTER XIX

1. H. F. to J. C., Sept. 7 and 14, 1872.

2. *Ibid.*, June 22 and Sept. 7 and 14, 1872.

3. P. C. to J. C., Sept. 18, 1872; Garland to J. C., Sept. 18, 1872.

4. *Ibid.*

5. Thus interpreted by the *Com. and Fin. Chron.*, vol. xv (1872), pp. 373, 406.

6. P. C. to J. C., Oct. 2, 1872; J. C. to H. C., Sept. 23 and Oct. 21, 1872, and to J. B. Semple, Oct. 19, 1872, lb.

7. J. C. to H. C., Sept. 18, 1872; P. C. to J. C., Oct. 2, 1872.

8. H. F. to J. C., Oct. 1, 1872; W. M. to J. C., Oct. 1 and 3, 1872.

9. J. C. to H. F., Sept. 23, 1872.

10. J. C. to Puleston, Sept. 18, and Puleston to J. C., Oct. 19, 1872.

11. McCulloch to J. C., Oct. 21, 1872.

12. J. C. to P. C. and Garland, Sept. 18, 1872.

13. J. C. to Barney, Sept. 12, 19, 1872; P. C. to J. C., Sept. 18, 26, 1872; Barney to J. C., Sept. 20, 1872.

14. J. C. to Johnston Bros., Nov. 18, 29, and Dec. 2, 1872, lb.

15. J. C. to H. F., Oct. 26, 1872.

16. P. C. to J. C., Oct. 15, 16, and J. C. to H. C., Oct. 21, 1872.

17. *Book of Reference, N. P. Railroad*, p. 80.   18. *Ibid.*, pp. 80, 88.

19. *Ibid.*, p. 88; J. C. to H. F., Mar. 8, 1872.

20. *Book of Reference, N. P. Railroad*, p. 89.

21. J. C. to Smith, May 24, 1872.

22. *Book of Reference, N. P. Railroad*, p. 94.

23. *Ibid.*, p. 95; J. C. to Nettleton, Aug. 2, 1872.

24. *Book of Reference, N. P. Railroad*, p. 95; Nettleton to J. C., May 27, 1872.

25. Smalley, *History of the N. P. Railroad*, pp. 190–193; Cass to J. C., Dec. 2, 1872.

26. J. C. to Cass, Dec. 3, 1872, lb.   27. Billings to J. C., Nov. 1, 1872.

28. *Book of Reference, N. P. Railroad*, pp. 96–100.

29. J. C. to H. C., Apr. 5, 1872.

30. *Ibid.*, Dec. 18, 1872; and to McCulloch, Sept. 2, 1872, lb.

31. Henry H. Brigham to J. C., Dec. 2, 1872, CH.

32. W. E. Chandler to J. C., Sept. 19, 1872; E. D. Morgan to J. C., Oct. 30, 1872; H. F. to J. C., Oct. 31, 1872; Leonard Myers to J. C., Aug. 19,

1872; copy of letter of J. C. to R. C. Parsons, Sept. 14, 1872; J. C. to H. C., Apr. 27 and 29 and Sept. 14, 1872, to H. F., April 24 and Nov. 4, 1872, lb.

33. H. C. to J. C., Sept. 17 and 30, 1872.

34. H. F. to J. C., Oct. 26, 1872; P. C. to J. C., Oct. 28, 1872.

35. H. F. to J. C., Oct. 29, 1872; H. R. Waddington to J. C., Oct. 31, 1872; Lunt, Preston & Kean, Oct. 19, 1872; Puleston to J. C., Nov. 7, 1872; P. C. to J. C., Oct. 18 and 19, 1872.

36. *Ibid.*, Oct. 28, 1872; H. F. to J. C., Nov. 30, 1872.

37. *Ibid.*, Dec. 12, 1872.

38. H. F. to J. C., Dec. 9, 13, and 26, 1872.

39. J. C. & Co., N. Y., to J. C. & Co., Phila., Jan. 3, 1873.

40. *In the Matter of . . . Jay Cooke & Co., Bankrupts*, "Statement of the Bankrupts as to Causes of Insolvency," pp. 22–23; J. C. & Co., N. Y., to J. C. & Co., Phila., Jan. 21, 1873; H. F. to J. C., Jan. 3, 1873.

41. *Ibid.*   42. H. F. to J. C., Jan. 10 and 20, 1873.

43. Copy of cable to London, H. F. to J. C., Jan. 20, 1873.

44. J. C. to H. C., Jan. 11, 1873.

45. Patterson was quoted in full by the *Ledger*, Jan. 21, 1873.

46. J. C. to H. C., Jan. 22, 1873; *Ledger*, Jan. 21, 1873.

47. H. F. to J. C., Jan. 22, 1873.

48. J. C. to H. C., Jan. 21, 1873; H. C. to J. C., Jan. 22, 1873. In the same letter Jay Cooke instructed his brother to tell President Grant that he had returned a $15,000 note to his brother. It was to be charged to the syndicate.

49. Copy, H. C. to P. C. and Garland, Jan. 23, 1873.

50. Copy of agreement, Jan. 23, 1873, signed by Boutwell, J. C. & Co., J. Pierpont Morgan, and L. P. Morton, in CH.

51. *New York Times* quoted by *Com. and Fin. Chron.*, vol. xvi (1873), p. 181.

52. *Ibid.*   53. Garland to J. C., Feb. 5, 1873.

54. McCulloch to J. C., Feb. 6, 1873.

55. Oberholtzer, *op. cit.*, vol. ii, pp. 368–369.

56. H. F. to J. C., Feb. 7, 1873.

57. Oberholtzer, *op. cit.*, vol. ii, p. 372; *Com. and Fin. Chron.*, vol. xvi, p. 206.

58. Vol. xvi. p. 206.

59. Puleston to J. C., Feb. 6, 1873; J. C. to H. C., Feb. 18, 1873.

60. McCulloch to J. C., Feb. 6, 1873; J. C. to H. C., Feb. 8, 1873; H. F. to J. C., Feb. 24, 1873.

61. The operations are explained in Sec. of the Treas., *Report on the Finances*, 1874–75, pp. ix–x; 1875–76, pp. xi–xii; 1876–77, pp. xi–xii; 1877–78, pp. viii–ix.

62. *Book of Reference, N. P. Railroad*, p. 101.

63. J. C. to H. C., Feb. 14, 1873.

64. 42nd Cong., 3rd Sess. (1872–73), *Crédit Mobilier Report.*

65. Tenney to J. C., Mar. 27, 1873; J. C. to H. F., Mar. 28, 1873; H. C. to J. C., Apr. 2, 1873.

66. Vol. xvi, p. 445.

67. J. C. to H. C., Feb. 21, 1873.

68. Persons, Tuttle, and Frickey, "Business and Financial Conditions following the Civil War, in the United States," *Review of Econ. Stat.*, Supplement, 1920, pp. 41, 43, and 47; *Com. and Fin. Chron.*, vol. xvi (Mar. 15, 1873), p. 340.

69. Vol. xvi, p. 19.

70. J. C. to Cass, Mar. 1, 1873; J. V. Painter to J. C., Mar. 18, 1873; Lunt, Preston, Kean to J. C., Mar. 14 and 26, 1873; J. C. to Ainsworth, Mar. 14, 1872, lb.; W. M. to J. C., Mar. 26, 1872; J. C. to Brady, Jan. 25, 1873, and to W. M., Feb. 3, 1873, lb.; also memoranda, Apr. 5 and 24 and May 16, in CP.

71. J. C. to Cattell, June 5, 1873.

72. Report of the N. P. Railroad for year ending June 30, 1873, filed with the Department of Interior, Washington, D. C.

73. J. C. to Cattell, June 5, 1873.

74. *Book of Reference, N. P. Railroad*, p. 107; Chancellor Bismarck was invited to visit the Northern Pacific country (J. C. to Baron Gerolt, Feb. 7, 1873, lb.).

75. Report of the N. P., 1873, Department of Interior.

76. J. C. to Cattell, May 5, 1873, lb.

77. Townsend of the Cincinnati *Commercial*, quoted by Oberholtzer, *op. cit.*, vol. ii, pp. 339–340.

78. I have used in this connection an excellent manuscript thesis in the Library of Minnesota University: Harold F. Peterson, "Railroads and the Settlement of Minnesota, 1862–1880," pp. 38–47, 53–58, 63, and 71–85.

79. *Book of Reference, N. P. Railroad*, pp. 108–109.

80. There are many signed printed agreements in CH.

81. J. C. to H. C., Apr. 19, 1873.

82. J. C. to Cattell, May 5, 1873, and to Puleston, May 5, 1873, lb.

83. Johnston Bros. to J. C., Apr. 14, 1873.

84. J. C. to Johnston Bros., May 23, 1873, lb.

85. H. F. to J. C., May 26, 1873.

86. J. C. to Cattell, May 5 and June 5, 1873, lb.

87. J. C. to Charlemagne Towers, May 21, 1873, and to Brewster, Sweet & Co., May 21, 1873, lb.

88. According to individual signed agreements in CH.

89. *Red River Gazette*, Sept. 25, 1873.

90. J. C. to H. F., July 1, 1873.

91. J. C. to Cattell, May 5, 1873.   92. These statements are in CH.

93. Cass to J. C., Mar. 3, 1873, President's Letters, N. P. Papers; J. C.

to P. C., Feb. 18, 1873, to H. R. James, May 23, 1873, to Wm. McKnight, May 26, 1873; *Book of Reference, N. P. Railroad*, p. 115.

94. *Ibid.*, p. 109; Cass to E. D. Litchfield, June 13 and July 12, 1873, President's Letters, N. P. Papers; Poor's *Manual of Railroads*, 1874–75, pp. 671–672.

95. Persons, Tuttle, and Frickey, *op. cit.*, pp. 29, 31, and 33.

96. *Com. and Fin. Chron.*, vol. xvii (1873), p. 69; U. S. Treas., *Monthly Reports on the Commerce and Navigation of the United States*, 1874, p. 105.

97. Persons, Tuttle, and Frickey, *op. cit.*, pp. 41 and 43; *Com. and Fin. Chron.*, vol. xvii, pp. 150 and 275.

98. *Ibid.*, pp. 275 and 308; Persons, Tuttle, and Frickey, *op. cit.*, p. 47; O. M. W. Sprague, *History of Crises under the National Banking System* (Washington, 1910), pp. 34–35.

99. *Com. and Fin. Chron.*, vol. xvii, pp. 250, 268; Fowler, *Inside Life in Wall Street*, p. 578.

100. *New York Tribune*, Sept. 19, 1873.

101. *Com. and Fin. Chron.*, vol. xvii, p. 341.

102. Poor's *Manual of Railroads*, 1868–69, p. 24, and 1874–75, p. lv.

103. Samuel Benner, *Prophecies of Future Ups and Downs in Prices*.

104. Garland to J. C., Feb. 6, 1864.

105. 43rd Cong., 1st Sess. (1873–74), *Reports of Committees*, no. 300, pp. 1–7.

106. *Com. and Fin. Chron.*, vol. xvii, p. 214.

107. *New York Tribune*, Sept. 19, 1873.

108. Statement of H. F., *In the Matter of . . . Jay Cooke & Co., Bankrupts*, "Statement of the Bankrupts as to Causes of Insolvency," p. 157; Garland to J. C., Feb. 6, 1874; *New York Tribune*, Sept. 19, 1873.

109. *Ibid.*   110. *Ibid.*

111. The *Com. and Fin. Chron.* and newspapers, especially the *New York Tribune* and *Times*, gave detailed news on the progress of the panic.

112. Clews was more deeply involved in southern State bonds.

113. So he announced at the closing on Sept. 18, as reported in newspapers.

CHAPTER XX

1. An Associated Press dispatch of Sept. 27, 1873, CH.

2. Explained in statement in CH sent out to creditors for their approval and returned with their signatures.

3. H. C. to J. C., Nov. 13 and 20, 1873.

4. P. C. to J. C., Nov. 14, 19, and 24, 1873.

5. There is a great deal of correspondence on this matter between J. C. and H. C., Dec., 1873, and early 1874, in CP.

6. *In the Matter of . . . Jay Cooke & Co., Bankrupts*, "Synopsis of the Assets," pp. 3–17.

7. *Ibid.*, "Statement of the Bankrupts as to Causes of Insolvency," pp. 120–121; Circuit Court of the United States, Southern District of New York, Edwin M. Lewis, Trustee in Bankruptcy of the Estate of the Late Copartnership Firm of Jay Cooke & Co. *vs.* Harris C. Fahnestock and Margaret A. Fahnestock, *Bill of Complaint* (New York, 1875).

8. Oberholtzer, *op. cit.*, vol. ii, p. 532.

9. Clipping from *Enquirer*, dated June 27, pictorial scrapbook, CP.

10. McCulloch to J. C., Nov. 10, 1873.

11. F. H. Evans to J. C., Jan. 13, 1874.

12. *In the Matter of . . . Jay Cooke & Co., Bankrupts*, "Report of the Trustee in Bankruptcy," pp. 56–59; "First National Bank of Washington," 43rd Cong., 1st Sess. (1873–74), *House Reports*, no. 300; *Report of the Comptroller of the Currency*, 1876, p. clviii.

13. Smalley, *History of the Northern Pacific Railroad*, pp. 204–237.

14. *Ibid.*, pp. 232–234.

15. Hedges, *Henry Villard and the Railways of the Northwest*, pp. 56–111.

16. *Ibid.*, pp. 109, 143; Smalley, *op. cit.*, pp. 263–273; *Report of the Northern Pacific Railroad*, 1883, p. 7.

17. J. G. Pyle, *The Life of James J. Hill* (Garden City, 1926).

18. As told by Mr. Barney.

19. Interview with Mary E. Cooke, Pitt Cooke's daughter, Dec., 1931, and letter of Nov. 28, 1932.

20. *Dict. of Amer. Biog.*

21. Oberholtzer, *op. cit.*, vol. ii, p. 537.

22. *Dict. of Amer. Biog.*   23. *Ibid.*

24. *Who's Who in Finance*, 1927; *New York Times*, May 3, 1931.

25. *Pujo Committee Reports*, vol. ii, pp. 1479–1713, 1751.

26. P. C. to J. C., Feb. 24, 1874.

27. According to Harvey E. Fisk, who knows Wall Street from the 1870's.

28. *Ibid.*

29. For information on Fahnestock I have relied chiefly on his son, William Fahnestock, and the *New York Times*, June 5, 1914.

30. The above information on the early years of Chas. D. Barney & Co. was obtained from conversation with Mr. Barney.

31. Jay Cooke's Memoirs.

32. Sargent to J. C., Feb. 26, 1874; McCulloch to J. C., Apr. 20, 1874.

33. This idea appeared frequently in newspaper articles reporting interviews with Jay Cooke. An example is the Cincinnati *Enquirer*, June 28, 1890.

34. There is an agreement between Edgerton and Cooke in CH, dated Sept. 16, 1878, for a negotiation with the owners of the claim to the mine for the organization of a company. Edgerton died before the negotiation was completed.

35. Jay Cooke's Memoirs.

36. Mr. Charles D. Barney has the original certificate of discharge from bankruptcy.

37. W. A. Hooker, *The Horn Silver Mine* (New York, 1879), pp. 3–4.

38. *Ibid.*, p. 3.

39. *Report of the Horn Silver Mining Company*, 1881, p. 5.

40. *Ibid.*, p. 4; *United States Annual Mining Review and Stock Ledger*, 1879, p. 112.

41. *Ibid.*

42. Full details on the transaction covering one-half of the stock is given in Jay Cooke's letter book for Aug., 1879, to Feb., 1888, in letters under dates Jan. 5 to Jan. 16, 1880, including one of Jan. 9, 1880, to Franklyn and Brown from Campbell, Cullen & Co. and Jay Cooke. These letters are in CH.

43. *Ibid.*, J. C. to Edward King, Jan. 16, and J. C. to Franklyn and Brown, Jan. 9, 1880.

44. J. M. Butler (Jay Cooke's son-in-law and assistant) to "Dear Harry," Jan. 24, 1880, and Jos. Brown, Feb. 7, 1880, Jay Cooke's lb., CH.

45. The lb. in CH for 1879–80 contains many letters on Jay Cooke's mining interests. There are also in CH many reports on different mines.

46. List of stockholders and their holdings in J. M. Butler to W. H. Stevenson, June 27, 1887, Jay Cooke's lb., 1879–88, CH.

47. Conversation with Mr. Barney.

48. Gibraltar Records.

49. Oberholtzer, *op. cit.*, vol. ii, chap. xx; conversation with Mr. Barney.

INDEX

INDEX